MW01089484

CONTENTS

FOREWORD

AS YOU PICK UP THIS VERY SPECIAL TEXT, BE PREPARED to walk away with a substantially heightened appreciation for the tremendous faith, courage and sacrifice early members of the Church of Jesus Christ of Latter-Day Saints exhibited in their quest to be fully faithful in the service of their Lord Jesus Christ and God in Heaven.

Author Susan Billings Mitchell has compiled one of the most comprehensive collections of historical information and documentation ever compiled relating to the life of Titus Billings and those he loved, served, sacrificed for, suffered with and so much more.

The death of children, numerous cases of unfair treatment by government leaders, repeated mob attacks, extreme weather conditions, sickness, physical injury, starvation, long periods of separation from loved ones, and Indian attacks are just a few of the challenges these good people endured to be counted worthy to stand with those who were willing to go and do whatever their God would have them do.

Contained herein is a thoroughly documented and inspiring account of some of the most tried and proven beings ever to walk the earth, as we know it.

Lewis K. Billings

PREFACE

Grandma (Lydia Workman Billings, wife of Claude Duval Billings) kept her genealogy papers stacked in working piles on the dining table. I remember summer visits when she would take me with her to the big Genealogical Library in Salt Lake City. One time she wrote five names on a slip of paper, and showing me how to find indexes, gave me a stack of books to examine. If I found any of these names in any of those books, I was to tell her at once. I searched with eagerness hoping to help her important work. After a silent, child's prayer I located one of the names. How excited she was for me! I don't know if the find was really significant at all, but right then I decided that genealogy work was fun.

Back home, during "Show and Tell Time" at school, I informed the class that my Grandpa was in the Bible. (Wonder what my teacher thought.) There is a Titus in the Bible, but my Great-Great Grandpa Titus Billings, is also named in the Doctrine and Covenants (section 63, verse 39).

Over the years, my parents (Evan and Elda Mae Billings) have excitedly collected information about Grandpa Titus. His name seems to pop up everywhere in Church History. Several organizations asked Dad to write a book about this good man. As family historian, the duty was delegated to me. How honored I am for the privilege. I pray that this work is accurate, inspiring to others, and pleasing to Grandpa.

Tiny miracles along the way have influenced my motivation and led me to believe that Grandpa Titus wants his testimony preserved and his story shared. After careful, prayerful study I feel a familiar likeness between my father and great-great-grandfather. Both were extremely hard working, even in later years. Titus was in charge of the Nauvoo Legion cannon and fired it for celebrations and parades in Nauvoo and in Manti. Evan was volunteer chairman of Provo City's Fourth of July Freedom Festival fireworks for numerous years. His early morning blasts kicked off that celebration at 6:00 a.m. Titus was in the Battle of Crooked River. Evan was in World War II. Both were builders of homes and successful growers of gardens. Both, again in my opinion, were strictly obedient, stalwart and loyal. I am so very thankful for their examples and love them both.

When my folks were ready to marry, the Salt Lake Temple was closed for cleaning, so they went to the Manti Temple instead. At the time they were completely unaware of an ancestor founding that valley.

In 1979, they identified the exact location of Grandpa's stewardship property in Independence, Missouri. A "For Sale" sign posted by the railroad on part of that land quickly changed their lives. My parents purchased the available portion where they built a beautiful home with a pioneer guestroom and discovered many tidbits of grandpa's history to share in this book. While researching I was privileged to stay in the "Titus Billings guestroom" several times, searching and sorting leads about Grandpa. Eating and sleeping seemed only to get in the way. I had special feelings about doing a sacred work in such a sacred place.

When my husband moved us back to Utah, I was excited to spend time at the Family History Library. How my little grandma would have loved this new one! One day while gleaning information from a rare document found in the archives of the Salt Lake City, Utah LDS Historical Department, I couldn't help overhearing a young man who approached the table beside me. To the gentleman seated there he asked about the School of the Prophets. "If he were in the School of the Prophets I would know it," the older man answered.

Well, that statement demanded my attention because I was trying to find greater verification that Titus had attended the School of the Prophets. It was closing time. I gathered my papers but could not leave. When the gentleman stood I could not be restrained, but excused myself saying, "I couldn't help overhearing you say you would know if someone had attended the School of Prophets. We are trying to ascertain if our grandfather really attended it."

"Who is your grandfather?"

"Titus Billings."

"Oh yes, Titus Billings was there. Come with me." We stepped out of the glass walled room and he entered an office beside it. I tried to read the name on the door to see who he was, but the door was already open. Without looking, he pulled a book from a wall of bookshelves and turned to a paragraph about Titus Billings. The page was familiar to me, in fact it was a reference on my list, but the book was out of print! I had been trying to locate it.

"To whom am I speaking?" I asked.

"I'm Lyndon Cook," he answered humbly.

"You are the author of this book!" I exclaimed. "I have been trying to find a copy of it."

We talked a few minutes. He had the page photocopied and even autographed it for me. I explained my endeavor and he stated that there was a need for a book about this good man, but cautioned me that it would take five years to do it well. In truth for me, it has been a lifetime project.

Titus' daughter, Eunice, wrote: "My father always kept a record, but in moving around, it became destroyed" (Snow7). As many times as he had to "run for his life" it's no wonder that such a treasured record was lost.

I believe true stories from the past inspire the noble youth of today. Grandpa Titus Billings was a good, quiet, obedient, hard-working man who loved the Lord and His gospel. He did not set out to be a hero. Surely, he was not flawless, but he was stalwart. With faith he endured to the end. May we ever follow in his footsteps.

Susan Billings Mitchell

Author addendum #1:

Back in 1999 I thought this project was complete and ready for press, except for the fact that it didn't do justice to the life and significance of Mary Ann Tuttle Billings. This was bothersome to me, and my mother (Elda Mae Lewis Billings) told me that the reason I was supposed to write this history was to take proper care of my dear grandmother. Needless to say, I started over and included the Edward Tuttle family (Ed being one year older than Titus).

Still, that was not enough. The story of Titus Billings cannot be told without including the story of Isaac Morley, neither can the story of Isaac be complete and proper without including Titus. These two brothers-in-law shared their lives and love of the gospel from Kirtland to Manti, spanning the entire spread of early Church history. Thus, this work is an effort to weave together the stories of these three stalwart pioneer families.

Author addendum #2:

STOP THE PRESSES! After 30 years of research we have made a most amazing discovery and in the nick of time . . . even the very week we are scheduled to print this book. Whatever could be so important, you ask? Brace yourself, this is BIG and wonderful and such a shock. All records available to us showed that Titus and Diantha's second son, Thomas, died at birth. Are you sitting down? Ready? Well believe it or not, he lived! Thomas Addington Billings (not to be confused with his son, Thomas Addison Billings) lived to age 84. He and his wife, Caroline Moreland/Morlan of Shasta California raised 13 children! What does this mean? We are blessed with another big, healthy branch on our family tree! I am so excited; have burnt the all-night oil searching information. His descendent, Sharon Walker Charlesworth Allgood, is our connecton and living proof! I can hardly wait to meet other cousin-friends.

What to do? I have tried so hard to keep this work accurate. After studying, pondering and praying I have decided to keep our press agreement and print the story as it is written. As yet, I have been unable to find true tidbits to share about Thomas and do not wish to fabricate such. Please know that we now know he was privileged to live a full life and father a precious big family. May we all come to know each other and love each other as we remember and honor the memory of goodly parents who love us, each and every one.

OHIO: A TIME OF DISCOVERY

Beginning about 1815 – Located between Kirtland and Mentor

CHAPTER 1

Diantha opposed the idea from the beginning. Why should she and her family leave Montague, the township they loved, and travel hundreds of miles to settle in an undeveloped territory they had never seen? Diantha witnessed the way her brother's letters enticed her father. At first he showed only a hint of interest which she and her mother dismissed at once. Neither of them had set foot outside of Massachusetts and neither of them intended to do so, ever. Then why did she find herself and everything she owned covered with dust on this bouncy wagon?

Why? Diantha thought to herself. *Why? Because Isaac Morley is the most persuasive, persistent creature on earth! He will never give up when he believes he is right about something. Father became infatuated with the invitation to move to "the plushest place on earth" before I realized what was happening.* The thought was exasperating to her, but there was more. *As always, Mother willingly gave up the fight and abandoned me to follow along in agreement with Father.*

Diantha disliked change and the thought of moving away from the beautiful land of apple blossoms to a . . . to anywhere was most distasteful to her.

Yes, Isaac Morley was her hero, always had been. He was nine years old when she was born and as her oldest brother he had forever protected, entertained, and often teased her. Many were the songs they had harmonized and the games they had played together. No one could ask for a better brother, but now this brother was renowned. Why, he was one of the first to clear timbers in Northern Ohio, and he (so his letters claimed) introduced agriculture into the Western Reserve. Many folks were migrating there. It was a chance of a lifetime. She had heard it all. So what? Let the others enjoy it. But oh no, she was just an insignificant girl who had no say in the matter, none at all.

Diantha brushed dust off the dulcimer case she held in her lap. Her plan was to play and sing along the way, but she was in no mood for singing and trail dust would only harm her treasured instrument.

"How 'you doing back here?" Thomas shouted as he rode up beside the wagon. He was the brother just older than she, a very good one too, now that he was an adult. Diantha could not help noticing how different he was from Isaac.

"How much farther is this place?" Diantha asked with irritation.

Thomas picked up on her annoyance and could not hide the smirk it caused to cover his face. He knew she was ready to end this journey before it began. Her attitude had been easy for anyone to detect. Now he witnessed her ongoing frustration and could not pass up the opportunity to provoke her.

"Oh dear sister, we have just begun. It will take days and days and days before we attain our destination."

Diantha stood. Balancing the dulcimer with one hand she attempted to whip the irritating Thomas with an apron tie in her other hand. He kicked his horse and lunged forward as she tumbled back into the wagon, landing on top of Alfred who in turn bumped into Louisa. *So much for adulthood*, she thought as she retrieved the music case and made apology to her younger siblings.

"Is it really going to take all those days to get there?" Alfred asked.

"No," Diantha assured him as she brushed dust from his curly red hair. "Father said we should find Isaac before sunset tomorrow. " Alfred leaned against her. Sliding the black music case to safety beside a soft quilt, she made room on her lap for the tired lad to rest his head.

"It will be good to see Lucy again, won't it?" Diantha said to her sister.

"I can't wait to meet little Philena," Louisa added. "How old is she now?"

"Can you believe our little niece is already two," Diantha answered.

"It will be fun living beside them, won't it?"

"Yes," Diantha admitted. She did adore her sister-in-law. Lucy Gunn Morley was as lovely and as capable as anyone she had ever known. *The last time I saw Lucy was at her wedding.* Again Diantha was daydreaming, remembering. *Isaac was so excited when he came back to fetch her for his bride. He had homesteaded a spot in that "plush place" and built a cozy cabin for his Lucy.*

Deep thinking was Diantha's way of ignoring boredom. *Oh, I do love weddings. Someday I will have a glorious wedding too and drape myself in the elegant lace Grandmother Marsh fashioned with*

4

her skillful hands. Mother promised. She was wed in it and I shall be also . . . if I can find a good man out there in that rugged territory. I feel like we left civilization behind us many miles ago.

Isaac's last letter informed us that Lucy is again in a motherly way. This will be number two. Hope it's another girl. I do wish we would get there. Travel is such a waste of time. I am an adventurous person. I like to do things, many things, but I do not like change. And if this is how it is, I definitely don't like moving.

Diantha's only hope was for Isaac's spot to be so beautiful and inviting she would never need to relocate again in her life!

Historical Background

"Thomas Morley moved his family to Ohio July 6, 1815" (Esplin, 2) OR according to another account the Thomas E. Morley family "moved to Kirtland, Ohio in 1829" (MorleyRH, Appendix B). [The first date seems to agree better with other happenings.] The four youngest children (of nine) came with them. (Bennion, 1).

"Isaac Morley married Lucy Gunn June 20, 1812 at Montague and took her to his property" (Bennion, 1) in the "so-called Western Reserve" where he was one of the first to "cut down the woods and introduce agriculture in northern Ohio" (Jensen1, 235).

When Grandpa Titus lived in Ohio only the upper north-east corner was settled. This was called the Western Reserve. It consisted of eight counties. Grandpa lived in Geauga County.

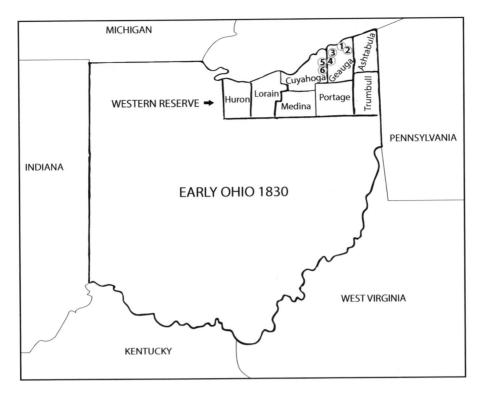

EARLY OHIO 1830

① **Kirtland**: Grandpa Titus lived on the outskirts of Kirtland and though he was part owner, the place was called the Morley Farm.

② **Mentor**: Grandpa Titus attended Sidney Rigdon's Campbellite Church in Mentor, Ohio until the true gospel found him.

③ **Fairport**: Migrating saints first landed at Fairport Harbor (15 miles from Kirtland). Many of them became Grandpa's neighbors at the Morley Farm.

④ **Painesville**: Edward Partridge fed a company of migrating saints (about 80 souls) in his home the night of their arrival. He was called to be the first bishop of the church. Later, in Far West, Missouri, Grandpa Titus was called to serve as second counselor.

⑤ **Mayfield**: Five families joined the Common Stock Effort of Isaac Morley, Titus Billings and Lyman Wight. This religious effort seemed to have prepared them for the Lord's Law of Consecration.

⑥ **Orange**: Grandpa Titus was ordained the first deacon of the church at a conference hosted by the Orange Branch, October 1831.

6

CHAPTER 2

Titus Billings leaned forward, as much to hide his blushing face as to reach for another hand-shaved shingle. His long legs straddled the cabin roof as he worked. He heard every word Isaac Morley was saying from the ground below, although he tried not to show it.

"A thin fellow like you needs a wife who can cook." Titus could hear a grin in Isaac's voice. It continued, "Doesn't hurt none that she's a pretty lass. Turns nineteen in August, you know. Good-look'n, excellent cook, knows how to read . . . what more could you ask for?"

Titus dropped his head and turned away, trying to avoid another wave of embarrassment.

"Not to mention," Isaac added, "Diantha sings like a Meadow Lark."

Young Titus Billings was a singer too and seemed able to play any musical instrument he touched. Back home they called him, "Mr. Music" more often than not. With powerful, rhythmic strikes he inserted the next nail. Any sister of Isaac Morley would have to be special, but he was far from being a "Lady's Man" and very nervous about meeting her. "Better speed-up if we're gonna have this cabin done 'fore they get here," he said.

"Reckon so." Morley agreed. "Should arrive any day now." He leaned a log against the remodeled cabin and wiped his forehead. "I figure it's about six-hundred miles between here and Montague. What a place. Did I ever tell you about my Grandfather Ebenezer building the very first cabin near Taylor's hill?"

Oh yes, Titus had heard that story and was certain he was about to hear it again. He too originated in Massachusetts, same county even. His beautiful hometown, Greenfield, was just northward, up the Connecticut River.

"1726 it was," Morley went on, "That's when they called the place Hunting Hill Township."

"Pretty place," Titus said. Thoughts of home rushed him. His father was an Ebenezer too and his mother, Ester Joyce Billings, claimed that she had been named after a queen in the Bible. Their eleven children, though descendants of Scottish and Irish royalty and English nobility, had for the most part, grown up in an old, log fortress salvaged from the Indian Massacres of 1675. Titus, child number eight, shared a tight bond with Samuel, a brother two years older. He smiled to himself remembering. *We spent hours digging old bullets out of those logs. I wonder if Sam saved any of them.*

"I can still smell the apple blossoms," Morley continued.

Titus jumped down to stretch his long frame and breathe in the fresh country air. His hazel-green eyes gazed over the soft, rolling hillside of plush forest growth. Here lumber was abundant, land was fertile and miles and miles of it stretched out, yet unclaimed.

"Well, this is a mighty fine spot too. Couldn't find more shades of green if you tried," Titus said. "Guess that's why so many folks are comin' out here. Wish mine were. You're lucky yours is on the way." Isaac didn't seem to hear him.

"You should have seen it when I first got here. Hardly a spot had been cleared." Isaac Morley stood with hands on his hips and expanded his chest. Titus sensed another story was on its way.

"Yep, 'brought my bride to this very spot in 1812.'"

"How long were you here before the War broke out?"

"Congress declared war with the British two days before our wedding." Morley shook his head. "Don't know how Lucy did it. We were married in June. I hauled her out here to the middle of nowhere and left her alone in a tiny cabin when I marched off with the Ohio Militia in August." Shaking his head again, he continued. "She stayed by herself in these wild woods, not knowing for certain if I would ever return. What a woman!"

"What a woman indeed," Titus echoed as thoughts of leaving a dainty new bride abandoned in a forest prison overwhelmed him. Lucy enjoyed telling her story too. He knew all about her fears of chimney smoke signaling a savage or British soldier. She worried about meeting up with beasts of the wild at the berry patch. Worst of all, she feared falling prey to rattlesnakes. Nonetheless, Isaac's wife had faith in him and she too loved their little spot in the Western Reserve. *She is a woman worth more than her weight in gold. I'll not marry 'til I find me a woman like that,* he vowed in silence.

"But I did return, sooner than I should have," Isaac said more to himself than to Titus, remembering his miserable journey home when two fellow soldiers dragged him from the battlefield with chills and fever. "I was too ill to walk."

"You were too ill to do anything when I got here," said Titus, climbing back up to the roof with a fresh bundle of shingles. "I had come seeking my fortune . . .

"And you hooked up with me," Isaac finished.

Ohio's thicket had to be grubbed out. Vines wrapped themselves around tree trunks and brush filled in all other spaces. It was heavy work, much too heavy for a sick man. With Isaac's bedside tutelage, Titus went after the green culprits using the wide-blade of a hoe-like pick to carve out more farmland until it was one-half a mile long and one-fourth a mile wide. After seeding an orchard he started on a grove of maple trees.

"Do you know how much we appreciate you, Titus?"

"Heck, I'm just glad you got well," Titus said, staring at the ground.

"I know." Isaac chuckled. "You were tired of doing my work."

"Heck no, I was sick of you smelling like mustard plaster!" They both laughed.

"Yoo-hoo," Lucy called from the doorway of her new, framed house.

Together the two had purchased more land after the war. Lucy's home was built on the new property and they were enlarging the old cabin for Thomas and Editha Morley who were relocating with four of their nine children.

"Supper is getting cold!"

Titus looked up as Isaac challenged him.

"Last one's a monkey's —"

Long-legged Titus was halfway there. Lucy Gunn Morley's cooking skills were not to be ignored.

After evening chores Titus approached the table with pen and paper in hand.

"Mind if I use your candle?" he asked.

"What's ours is yours," Isaac said.

"Thanks," Titus said marveling at the deep brotherly bond he felt for this man.

"Another letter?" Lucy asked.

"Yes, figure I might as well keep trying until they say no."

"If you can't persuade them, no one ever will," Isaac said. Lifting his flute from the mantel he commenced to play short, military songs from his fifer days during the War of 1812.

Titus began to write. The letter was one of many he penned to his family describing what he called "a desirable destination" and inviting them to join other migrating families from Massachusetts and Connecticut.

"I love you," he wrote, "and long to share with you this grandest spot on earth."

Two sisters, Emily and Salome, answered his letters with interest, but his father never wrote back.

Historical Background

Little is known about the parents of Titus Billings or his early upbringing. The family did live for a time in an old, log fortress known for enduring the Indian Massacres of 1675 to 1677. Samuel's history mentions "digging bullets out of the logs as a youngster" (BillingsV; BillingsV1,1).

Somehow life brought Titus Billings to Kirtland Township as one of its earliest settlers. "Peter French moved over from Mentor, and John Parris, Isaac Morley and Titus Billings came soon after" (LakeCo., 22). "Isaac Morley and Titus Billings built their cabin on the farm of the late Hercules Carrel" (Crary, 6). "He [Isaac Morley] served his country in the war with Great Britain in 1812-15, and also held the position of captain in the Ohio militia. In June, 1812 he married Lucy Gunn in Massachusetts" (Jenson1,Vol. I, 236).

"Scarcely had they [Isaac and Lucy] become settled when Isaac was called to serve his country in the War of 1812" (MorleyRH, 2). "Another source of perhaps greater danger to us than the British were [was] the rattlesnakes, which were very numerous and required great cautiousness and watchfulness to avoid them and kill them when found" (Crary, 7).

"Isaac Morley served as a Fifer in the Ohio Militia under Captain Clark Parker, and Generals Wadsworth and Perkins, in the War of 1812, serving from 22 August until 2 October 1812, and again 1 December 1812 until 27 February 1813, marching to Huron after the surrender of British General Hull" (Boren, 25). [Isaac Morley] "was a flutist in the military band during the War of 1812" (Jenson1).

Author's Note: Mustard Plaster was a good remedy for respiratory complaints. A piece of fabric was spread with lard (or shortening) and sprinkled with mustard powder and other spices (or a paste was made with spices and a little water). The cloth, folded to incase spices, was laid on the patient's chest so the strong aroma could be inhaled. Frequent checking was necessary to prevent burning.

CHAPTER 3

Milk sloshed in two buckets as Titus teetered them toward the house. The full pails Lucy ordered for cheese making were ready and full to the brim. Trying not to spill the prized cream, Titus moved at a slow pace, keeping his eyes down until he reached the doorway. That's when he spotted it: trail dust. Someone was coming.

"Company approaching," he announced.

Lucy rushed out with excitement, drying hands on her apron. "Cheese making will have to wait," she shouted back. Isaac followed, but not Titus. He preferred lingering behind with the two-year-old, Philena Morley.

"Want more syrup?" he asked the child as he let the gooey substance drizzle onto another flapjack. Titus savored its fragrance and licked his fingers. Warm maple syrup enlarged his longings for home more than any other thing. It made him conjure up memories of his mother who served it, of his siblings who had harvested the sap with him, and of his father who topped nearly everything he ate with a generous smearing of the sticky delight.

From the open window Titus heard jovial commotion and looked out as a hefty driver slowed his team. A youngster with blazing red hair leaped from an overstuffed wagon before it could stop. *Must be the one they call Alfred,* he thought. As the lad spun around, a face full of freckles flashed in the sunlight. *Yup, that has to be Alfred.* Another brother pulled up on horse-back, blocking view of the females. Titus stretched his neck trying to count bonnets. One was worn by a motherly figure and there were at least two others.

Philena jumped up for a better look too, knocking her milk cup to the floor.

"Ma, maaa," she cried. Titus bounced the child on his knee while he tried to sponge up the mess.

"Don't let your grandparents hear you crying over spilt milk," he said, boosting her onto his shoulders as he started outside.

Thomas Morley was a big man with a powerful handshake. *No one would want to displease someone of his stature,* Titus thought.

"I hear that you helped my son ready a cabin for us." Titus ducked his head with a slight nod while still balancing Philena. Isaac slapped him on the back.

"Titus is my right arm, Pa." The older Morley seemed impressed.

"First things first," Lucy insisted. "Let's all go inside for breakfast."

"Then Philena and her tall friend can show *everyone* around," Isaac teased.

Just as Titus started to unseat his little passenger, she gripped his thick hair with both hands and came down pulling. He flinched, then flung her in his arms and spun around until she giggled, thinking little about it until he noticed that a *certain someone* was watching him.

"Hello there. I am Diantha," Miss Morley announced, batting her beautiful eye lashes in his direction.

Titus lowered the child with gentleness. "This must be your Auntie," he said to Philena.

"And who might you be?" Diantha asked.

Titus cleared his throat. "Oh, I'm just a farmhand," he said.

"Don't let him fool you," Isaac cut in. "He's the hardest working fellow in all the Ohio. 'Couldn't get along without him."

"I still don't know your name," Diantha persisted.

His countenance reddened, eyes lowered, and thumbs awkwardly hung on his pockets, "Billings, Titus Billings," he managed.

*   *   *

Like his father, Isaac Morley was a wheelwright and a cooper as well as a farmer. Every trip to town, Titus returned with more orders for wooden tubs and barrels.

"Guess the word is out," he said.

"What word is that?" Isaac asked.

"The word is craftsmanship. First quality Morley craftsmanship." He pulled a handful of paper slips from his pocket. "Just look at all these orders. Top quality is in great demand."

"Guess we better start building that cooper shop," Thomas Morley said to Isaac.

"Of course we will need you to help us build it, Titus." Isaac said. Titus laughed. He knew who would do all of the building, and

12

it was fine with him.

The new shop was up and filled with fine cooperwares in only a few weeks. Outside on the porch Titus worked on a piece of wood with such keen concentration he did not notice when Diantha arrived.

"What is the mighty builder up to now?" she asked him, seating herself nearby.

"A shop needs a shingle, you know, a sign" he said without looking up at her.

"Oh, I see. 'Morley's Coop' . . . Very nice," she said.

"Well, it isn't finished yet," he said with a touch of pretended annoyance. Diantha watched for a while. He couldn't be disturbed; just kept working.

At length she left, soon to return with two tall glasses. "How about a cool drink of well water?"

"Glad to know your water is well." Her mystified expression caused him to shrug and continue, "Glad it's not sick water." The joke was weak, but she loved it.

Titus closed his blade and accepted her offering. Diantha had embellished the drink with mint leaves! He smiled at her and sipped while she talked.

When the sign was ready Diantha offered to steady it while Titus wired it into place. Before he climbed down, she was off to fetch her family. Isaac stepped out first with pleasure written all over his face.

"Morley's Cooper Shop," he read. "Guess that makes us official."

The older Morley approved the sign by saying, "Makes me feel like a successful man."

"You do wonderful work," Diantha said.

To young Titus her response was the most important.

"Someday we will teach you our trade," Thomas Morley promised, but there never seemed to be time for that day to come. Titus picked up all the slack around the farm while "The Morley Father and Son Business" filled orders establishing a keen reputation all over the valley.

*   *   *

Lucy grew heavy with child and was ordered to complete bed rest after threatening a loss. Diantha moved in to take over household concerns.

"I can't help noticing, Diantha, how that Billings boy watches you when he thinks no one is looking. Seems to enjoy your cooking better than mine too." Lucy's statement caught her off guard. Not knowing what to say, Diantha said nothing.

Being off her feet must have given Lucy lots of time for thought and observation. She ventured more: "Have you noticed how he can do anything?" Diantha was impressed with that Billings boy too, though she tried somewhat to hide it. "Why, he raises the flax for our linen and the sheep for our wool. He produces maple syrup, and molasses. He even extracted our honey from the bees."

Diantha smiled. With that knowledge she would enjoy the honey even more. Still she tried not to respond. Propping pillows, she made a table on Lucy's lap. "You must eat to keep up your strength for the sake of that little one."

"Oh Diantha, what a godsend you are. I couldn't get along without you any more than Isaac could survive without Titus. Diantha felt a warm sensation cross her cheek as she relished the comparison.

After dinner Titus helped out with the dishes. Often he assisted. He was a great help with Philena too.

"You certainly know how to cook," he mustered the courage to say. Diantha smiled at him. For a moment he thought he would drown in the deep blue of her eyes while at the same time her heart shouted in secret for joy because he had noticed and praised her at last.

"You love children, don't you?" she asked.

Titus felt a burning on the back of his neck. A nod was the best he could do.

"That is good," she went on. "Children seem to love you too." *Children are perceptive to gentle hearts,* she thought to herself. "I know Philena loves you," Diantha said. Her next thought came from an undisclosed spot deep in her heart and was by deliberate design left unspoken.

Historical Background

"Thomas E. Morley was a wheelwright" (MorleyRH, Appendix B). "Uncle Isaac Morley's Cooper Shop . . . full of cooper and wooden ware . . . made to sell" (Snow 3, 1).

CHAPTER 4

Titus loaded the wagon with empty containers and hitched a horse to it. Other days he walked to the peppermint field growing north of Morley's farm, but today he would harvest the plant leaves mowed down yesterday, and haul them back. Diantha offered to come along. Titus tried to bridle a smile when he saw her coming with a picnic basket over her arm. She looked beautiful in blue and, like always, wore a crisp white apron. Her golden-brown hair hung in long braids.

"Don't know if your apron will still be white when we come back," he warned her. She smoothed the folds in front of it.

"I'll take my chances," she said.

"Gathering leaves is only the beginning of this project," he explained as they rode along.

"So what do you do with them, the mint leaves, I mean?"

"We dry some to make healing tea. That's easy. It's extracting oil from the other leaves that's a tedious process, to say the least."

"Oh, but it is such a wonderful thing. Don't you just love the smell of peppermint? Not to mention the taste of it," she said.

"It's more than just taste and fragrance. Peppermint is a valuable medicine," he declared.

"I know. Mother used peppermint leaves to cool Alfred's sunburn."

"My mother would put a drop of peppermint oil in the corner of a handkerchief and have me hold it to my nose, whenever I had a cold," Titus said.

"Did it help?"

"Helped me breathe."

"How clever. I'll have to remember that trick for when I am a mother."

"Let me tell you another one," he added. "If you soak rags in peppermint oil the strong fragrance will stop ants or rats from coming into a building."

"You don't say?"

"Works for cats too."

"Now that I think of it, Grandma Morley made some kind of ointment with peppermint in it. Ever heard of that?"

"Oh yes," Titus said. The young girl who shared his wagon seat had a way of pulling words out of him like no one else he had ever met. "You mix the crushed leaves with lard or oil or you can use beeswax. Makes a great salve for itching. Pa rubs peppermint oil into sore joints too. Helps his arthritis."

"Titus, are you studying to be a doctor?"

"No. Not me." He laughed. "Not real big on schooling."

"You certainly know a huge amount of important things," she said with admiration.

Though he tried to brush it off, the comment did make him sit taller.

"Well, here we are," he said pulling back on the reins. The wagon came to a stop on the edge of a spacious dark green and fragrant field.

"It's so large and beautiful," she said. "And it smells wonderful."

"If you like peppermint," Titus said as he jumped down and rushed around to assist her.

"I have never before seen so much peppermint in one place," she marveled.

"Got our work cut out for us, that's for sure," he said unloading baskets. "Let's get started. Do you want to use the pitch fork?"

"Never used one of those before."

"Makes it faster."

"Bet my hands are as fast as your old pitch fork."

"We will see about that," he laughed. The contest was on. Each was determined to fill more baskets than the other as they raced down one row and onto the next. Their gorgeous morning turned into a scorching day. Titus wanted to wipe the sweat beads off of his face, but she might take the lead if he paused at all. He glanced at her, as the high noon sun seemed to crown her head like a halo. Her smooth cheeks were smudged with traces of green and her lips were dry, yet smiling.

"Need a drink?" he asked.

"Only if you do."

"I vote we take a break, before we break ourselves."

"I'll stop when you do."

"Let's be fair about it," he said. "Stop on the count of three. One—" She joined him, "two, three." Together they raised their arms into the air, and then raced for the water.

16

Titus lifted the canvas and started stacking cargo onto the wagon bed. Diantha began to gather her baskets.

"Seems to me we are evenly matched," Diantha said comparing both harvests.

"The day is not over," Titus said. "You'll tire soon and I will take the lead."

"Not without a little nourishment you won't. How about some lunch?"

"Sounds good to me." Titus carried the picnic basket. Together they spread another canvas under a large shade tree. Titus watched as Diantha arranged the food.

"May I butter your biscuit?" she asked.

"Please do," he replied, leaning back against the tree trunk to examine every move she made. She buttered his biscuit and carved a generous chunk of cheese to go with it.

"Do you prefer your apples whole or sliced?" she asked.

"Not fussy," he said. "Apples are good no matter how you serve them."

"I agree, but my favorite is to slice them and remove the core."

"If you are talking favorites, mine would be apple pie," he said.

"I will have to remember that," she said with a soft, feminine giggle. "You will just have to settle for carrot cake today."

"That's my other favorite," he said, eating twice as much as she did in the same amount of time. Convinced that he was satisfied she gathered up the picnic leftovers and tucked them back into her basket.

"I love it out here," she observed. "'So peaceful and beautiful; one of God's best masterpieces, don't you think?" He said nothing, just listened as the sweetness of her voice and the rapture of her soul penetrated his heart. *She loves this land too,* he thought. *That is good, very good.*

The afternoon was blistery hot, but neither peppermint picker seemed to notice. Time raced them as they raced each other, until reason beckoned them to halt and head for home. Titus loaded the wagon with, at her insistence, his yield on the left and hers on the right.

"The only fair thing is to let Isaac be the judge," she said. Somehow that embarrassed him.

17

"All right, you win," he conceded. "After all, it was your first day."

"I don't know." She climbed onto the wagon and measured each pair of tubs, side by side. "If you shake this one a little to help it settle –"

"Oh sure, shake mine down and puff yours up," Titus said. She laughed. He laughed too. "Now jump down here. We need to start back." He held out his arms and she slid gracefully into them. "Thanks for your help Diantha." She looked into his eyes with a powerful tenderness.

"Any time," she whispered, then quickly, slipping out of his grasp she hurried to the other side of the wagon. Together they pulled a canvas over their precious load, tied it down, and started for home. Side by side they rode in silence, both overwhelmed by new thoughts in their heads and new feelings in their hearts, struggling to find appropriate words to speak.

"You were right," Diantha said at last.

"How's that?" Titus asked with breathlessness.

"Just look at this. I am going home with a green apron."

They both laughed.

"And that's not all, I have ruined my hands."

Titus sat rigid with concern. *Had he worked her too hard? After all she was a delicate –*

"Would you look at this," she went on, holding out both hands. "Now I have green fingernails to match my green apron."

Prompted by relief, Titus Billings did something that surprised him as much as it did Diantha. He placed both reins in one hand and with the other reached over, took one of her hands and pulled it close to him.

"I don't mind green fingernails on lovely hands like these," he said. Her hand was softer than anything he could remember touching in all of his twenty-three years. Pulling it to his lips he kissed it with reverence. Then Titus Billings held the feminine hand of Miss Diantha Morley by his side until the homestead came into view.

Historical Background

"From a peppermint plant which grew on the hills north of their home, he was able to mow it, distill the oil taken from the plant and sell the product" (MorleyRH, 5-6).

18

CHAPTER 5

A certain young man asked me to give you this box," Thomas Morley told his daughter.

"Thank you, Pa." Diantha took the small, wooden box and started off.

"Aren't you going to see what is inside?"

"Oh that. I think I know what it is and what it is for," she said turning to face her father. A bright pink nose separated her blue eyes. "Perhaps you would like to see?"

Strong, pleasant fragrance filled the air as Diantha lifted the lid, exposing dark green leaves of peppermint. A brief note rested on top.

"For your sunburn. Hope these help. Sorry, T.B." was all it said.

Diantha avoided visitors for a few days until her sunburned faced healed. Peppermint leaves from Titus were cool and comforting. She was embarrassed to have been so caught up in gathering plants that she had paid no mind to her unused bonnet. Maybe, if the truth were known, she did not want to hide her face with it that day. She and Titus Billings seemed to work well together. *It has been three days since I spoke with him,* she thought. *I must make myself available or he may get the wrong idea.* She was helping Lucy when Isaac walked in.

"Do you need anything from town?" he asked his wife. A tall somebody was with him.

"Hello, Titus."

"Hi, Diantha."

"How is the extraction process coming?"

"Not bad. Taking the first batch of mint oil to Whitney's Store right now," Titus said. "Is there anything you need me to pick up for you?"

"Oh yes, I need buttons for my new blouse. Could you pick out five small ones?" She saw bewilderment in his eyes, so offered more detailed guidelines.

"Don't get four holes. Try to get some with only two-holes . . . Or even better, get shank ones, if they have them. Elizabeth Ann said they're expecting a new shipment from Europe any day now. I hope it's there."

He stared at her, but said nothing.

She continued, "You know, I think pastel ones would be pretty, and don't you like the ones with little designs on them?" Her eyes widened with excitement. "Maybe you could find some with tiny, painted flowers."

His look was perplexed. Perhaps picking out buttons was not one of his virtues.

Philena came to the rescue waving "bye-bye" with both hands.

"Guess she wants to go too. Maybe she can pick out your buttons," Titus suggested.

"I'll get her bonnet," Diantha said. She returned with two bonnets. "May I go along?"

To that his smile seemed to communicate not only relief, but also pleasure.

*   *   *

Lucy's sacrifice and Diantha's service were soon rewarded with the birth of a healthy baby girl born October 4, 1815.

"Our daughter should be named after her mother," Isaac said.

"No, this baby wants to be named after her Aunt. Without Diantha I could never have survived the last few months, Isaac. We have to name her Diantha," Lucy insisted.

Isaac held the newborn in front of him and began to speak as if the child could answer him. "We will let you decide on your own name," he said. "You look like a little Lucy to me. Diantha is a deserving name too. You would do well to walk in the footsteps of either one. What do you think? Do you wish to be called Lucy?" The baby opened then closed one eye. "Or would you like to be named after your Aunt Diantha?" Again she opened and closed the same eye. "Well, what will it be? Lucy or Diantha?" The baby girl opened both eyes at once. "Oh, I see," her father said. "You like both names. Lucy Diantha it is. We shall call you by both." True to his word, they did.

Historical Background

Actual names are used in this account (unless otherwise stated.) "The girls from oldest to youngest were Philena; Lucy Diantha, being named after her mother [and aunt] . . ." (MorleyRH, 6-7).

Author's Note about hand-painted buttons: News from the Kansas City Enterprise, September 6, 1856: "The Steamer Arabia, bound for Council Bluffs, struck a snag about a mile below Parkville last night and sunk to the boiler deck. Boat and cargo total loss." (Hawley, 17). The Steamboat Arabia sunk in a hazardous, crooked neck section of the Missouri River (west of Highway 291, on the way to Liberty, Missouri). The old channel once looped up to Liberty and back, crossing where the highway now runs. It was re-routed in 1952, but the old bridge located about one-fourth mile south of the original channel crossing is still used by the railroad (BillingsEA, 4).

After colliding with a large walnut tree unseen below water, the Arabia started to sink. Passengers were rowed to safety. Expecting to reclaim their belongings in daylight, they sought shelter for the night. By sunrise the steamship had disappeared, sinking quickly as river mud burped out the air and sealed the "Great White Arabia" and her "frontier merchandise" in a grave forty-five feet underground.

In a remarkable three year endeavor, David Hawley, his family and a few supportive friends raised the sleeping ship and her treasures from a Kansas cornfield and invited the public to view the hundred and thirty two year old relics in their new Arabia Steamboat Museum, located at 400 Grand Avenue in Kansas City, Missouri. (Hawley, 50). While examining the extraordinary museum collection, this author was intrigued with the abundant supply and variety of hand-painted buttons being shipped to 1830 frontier stores.

CHAPTER 6

"Isn't it exciting?" Diantha spoke to Titus. "I mean, my parents hosting the organization of a new church, right here in Kirtland. You must come." He said nothing. "You will, won't you?"

"Isaac and I plan to sit in on the meeting, but you and your folks need to understand our commitment to that new pastor in Mentor," Titus said. Diantha knew the two had investigated the church a few miles up the road from their farm. "Sidney Rigdon preaches an impressive sermon and maintains a large congregation," he added.

"Oh, I think it is a good idea to examine all of them. I mean, well, religion is an important thing, don't you agree?"

"Yes I do. Very important."

"Then you will come?"

He nodded.

"Promise?"

"Yes, I promise."

"Good. Now I have to help mother ready the place. See you tomorrow." She hurried off to the log home he had helped construct for her family.

*　　　*　　　*

"Reverend Treat and I have agreed to share the officiating of these Sabbath meetings. We will meet in various homes," Reverend Humphrey said.

"We will ever be grateful to Thomas and Editha Morley for holding this starter meeting here in their home," Reverend Treat added. "Thank you."

"You are welcome to come here again, any time," Thomas said.

"Much obliged. I am certain we will."

*　　　*　　　*

"So, what did you think about the meeting last night?" Diantha asked.

"I don't know. It was adequate, I guess, but I felt better

23

informed and more challenged to do good in Mentor's meeting the week before. You should come to hear Pastor Rigdon for yourself. Then maybe you will understand."

"I don't think father will allow that. Not now, at least."

"Well Di, I mean Diantha." She could tell he was embarrassed. "I'm sorry. That just came out."

"No problem, Titus." She laughed. "You may call me that if you like. No one else has ever, but I think I like it." *I think I would like anything he calls me.*

"Well, aaa, Di, I haven't talked to Isaac about it yet, but I plan to attend both congregations for a few weeks before I make my decision."

"Sounds wise to me. Will you tell me about the other meeting? I am interested, but father will forbid me to go. Of that I am certain."

On the next Sabbath, Isaac introduced his wife to Sidney Rigdon and the Campbellite congregation. She could hardly wait to share her impressions with her young sister-in-law.

"Diantha, I have never listened to a more eloquent speaker," Lucy said. "I cannot imagine affiliating with any other congregation when I find such fulfillment in his words."

Concern washed over Diantha's face. "But Pa," she said. "He is adamant about his congregation and demands loyalty from the family."

"Isaac is of sound mind and sensitive to such matters. I believe he will follow his own convictions, whatever the cost."

"Titus speaks the same way," Diantha said. "I hate to see religion divide us. Such things should unite families, not break them apart."

Diantha worried, fussed and tip-toed around her father for weeks.

"I don't know what to do," she confided to Titus at last.

"I know what you mean," he said. "Sometimes I wish God would declare himself to us. I would do anything if I knew He willed it of me."

"It's not that easy, is it?"

"Certainly not. But that doesn't mean we should stop looking for answers." He paused. What he felt to say was not free of consequence for either of them. Because he felt it strongly he said it anyway. "Diantha, you need to find out for yourself."

"I know," she said. "Will you take me to Mentor next

Sunday?"

Thomas Morley was a religious figure in the community, respected by many, strong in his beliefs and strictly devoted to them. His faithful, supportive wife stood always by his side. His oldest son, however, did not.

"You disappoint me, Isaac," he said with stern harshness in his voice.

"What does it matter which religion we profess?" Editha stated in an effort to soften callused words she feared were dividing her family. Thomas glared at his wife with an alarming look she had never seen before. Seldom would she venture to speak of such things ever again. Diantha, on the other hand, accepted the moment as an invitation to express her desire for unrestricted opportunity in her quest for truth.

"I think we should find out for ourselves, Father," she said.

"All of you are welcome to come," Isaac started. "Once you listen –"

That was enough. Thomas Morley slammed his fist onto the table and knocked over a chair, as he stood straight up with tension furrowing his face and brutal hostility marking his words.

"Choose for your selves," he said. "Forsake the teachings of your parents. Go the ways of the world if you will, but don't cry out for my help when the devil claims your souls into his everlasting fire of brimstone!"

Diantha packed her belongings and moved back into her brother's cabin. The next Sunday, with weather as dark and stormy as her mood, she dressed for church. *Today I will meet this Sidney Rigdon for myself,* she thought.

Lucy and Isaac tried to cheer the ride to Mentor, but failed in their attempt. The sky seemed as bleak as the future for all of them. Titus shared Diantha's pensive mood and rode beside her in silence, watching a chilling wind chase snowflakes to the ground. Diantha looked ready to cry.

"Would you like my handkerchief?" he asked.

"Do you mind?"

He rolled slightly sideways to free his coat and reached into his pocket.

"Here you are," he said. Leaning closer, so his mouth was near her ear, he whispered, "If you like, we could put a drop of peppermint oil in the corner so you could breathe better." It worked. She smiled. He placed his arm around her shoulder. She did not withdraw.

Sidney Rigdon was a very fine speaker. Lucy's word "eloquent" was an accurate description. Before his sermon was complete Diantha understood her brother's allegiance and respected him all the more because of it. Titus Billings had made a good choice. Her decision would be the same.

Snowfall was stacking up as they left the small, wooden church. The air was raw and the drive home was colder by far, but not to Diantha Morley. Renewed warmth in her heart caused her face to glow again.

"Things will work out," she said with a voice only Titus could hear. Returning his hanky still folded she whispered, "Here Titus. Save this for me until I really need it."

"I will," he promised, tucking it back into his pocket.

*   *   *

Titus Billings staked out a spot and cleared land near Isaac's home on their joint property near Mentor, Ohio. At the far end he planted fruit trees. In between milking cows and all of the other chores he did for Isaac, Titus felled horse-chestnut trees to build a cabin. It was fully framed when Miss Morley came to visit.

"So, where will you put the fireplace?" she asked.

"I plan to have two of them. One on this outside wall, in the main room . . ." he took her hand and pulled her to the opposite side of the structure, "and one on this outside wall, in the bedroom."

"Very nice, Titus. It will be a lovely house." She freed her hand, walked around and stopped by an opening in the back wall. "Is this the back door?"

"Yes, and we will have a root cellar down here."

We? She heard him say it, but pretended not to notice.

"A vegetable garden will be back there." He pointed to a spacious clearing.

"We could plant herbs and flowers along this side."

"Where will you plant peppermint? Surely you will want a few clusters near the house."

"We could have them right outside the back door. If you like we could run them as a border all across the back."

"Titus!" Diantha gasped. She had hoped, even believed someday, but he had never . . .

26

"Oh Di, " He felt a wild pounding in his chest and the sensation of being trapped in a gigantic bubble where treading water with all his might was necessary just to stay afloat. He had to do it. He had to say what he felt in his heart. This was the place. Surely it was the time.

"I could never be happy here alone," he said.

She was speechless. Maybe she did not share his feelings and his hopes and dreams. Without her those dreams were useless.

"Diantha, can't you see? I am building this house for you, if you will have it."

Her eyelids closed for a moment as if to hold back emotions welling up behind them. Then she opened her eyes, her beautiful, blue eyes and aimed them to meet his hazel-green ones straight on. She reached out both hands and he took them.

"If I accept the house, do I get you too?" she asked.

"If you will have me?" He wrapped his arms around her and held her so tightly she thought she would break.

"I will," she said. "I will."

Historical Background

"At the house of Thomas Morley, in 1818, was organized the first religious society in Kirtland" (LakeCo.1). "The Presbyterian Church (now Congregational) was organized about 1818 at the house of Thomas Morley, and consisted of twelve members, namely: Levi Smith, David Holbrook, Thomas Morley, Russell Hawkins, and their wives, Mrs. John Morse, Mrs. Christopher Crary, Mrs. A.C. Russell, and Mrs. I N. Skinner. The Revs Treat and Humphrey officiated. Meetings were held at private houses and in the school building until 1822, when a log church was built on the site of the present Congregational church. This was burned and a commodious frame church was built on the east side of the road. The new building was hit by a cyclone in 1842" (Crary, 20).

Isaac Morley and Titus Billings were members of Sidney Rigdon's congregation in Mentor, Ohio (Davis, 90).

CHAPTER 7

Sidney Rigdon's deep voice capped the ceremony with words Diantha Morley had waited to hear: "I now pronounce you husband and wife."

Thomas Morley stood tall and, in spite of religious differences with his daughter, every pound he owned seemed to burst with pride on this her wedding day. At his elbow the bride's mother, his own bride of twenty-eight-years dabbed watery eyes with a wilted handkerchief. Their daughter beamed with joy, though she had not been able to concentrate much on what seemed to her a lengthy sermon.

"You may now kiss the bride."

Titus Billings turned and with awkward gentleness lifted the delicate heirloom lace to unveil the face of an angel. His kiss was quick yet tender. This tall, thin, handsome, bridegroom was not a public person by any means, so Diantha was pleased he had even made an attempt to kiss her in the open. She would tease him later. In private she knew he could, and certainly would, do better. She felt his strong arm wrap around her waist.

"I love you," she whispered.

His squeeze tightened, communicating without words in a way she heard loud and clear. This quiet man who won her heart now shared with her his name. Yes, Diantha Morley would be known as Mrs. Titus Billings. She was going to like that very much.

"Congratulations, you two." Isaac Morley stretched his arms around both newlyweds. "Well, do I get to kiss the bride?"

Engulfed with gratitude Diantha hugged the brother to whom she owed so much. She smiled at the thought that he, her hero, had picked and primed a sweetheart for her arrival to this plush place two years ago. Yes, he was a good brother to have around and his persuasiveness had proven to be her blessing. She was jubilant also that her husband's parents had arrived the day before. Titus was sure they would fall in love with the place and hoped they would soon relocate here as well.

"Come on, Diantha, let's have cake!" Alfred said in an eager, twelve-year-old voice.

"Trust you to think of your stomach," she said to her youngest brother with a laugh.

Lucy handed a knife to Diantha and together the new couple carved the first piece out of their wedding cake. Grandma Marsh had done the honors. Her carrot cake was tasty, as usual, but Diantha was too excited to notice. This beautiful Sunday, two days after St. Valentine's Day, would forever more be known as her Wedding Day.

"Let's have some music," Ebenezer Billings said tuning the violin he had played for most of his sixty-seven years. His wife, Ester Joyce Billings, eight years younger than he, was rather short in stature. Standing next to her towering husband, she appeared to be even shorter. Nonetheless, she was pleased to be present for her son's wedding and to examine for the first time, the property he was so excited about. It was no secret Titus wanted them for neighbors. She could handle the idea as long as she had family members nearby. No use getting her hopes up about it though. Ester knew her husband well and he was as stubborn as the valley was beautiful. Ebenezer stood to fiddle a toe-tapper and dancing began.

Diantha pulled her groom to his feet and pushed him toward the music.

"Excuse me, Madam, but you see, I am a married man!" he said.

Diantha laughed.

Musically, the new couple was a perfect match. Agility and a keen sense of rhythm made the groom a champion on the dance floor, although he would never admit it.

Diantha's wedding lace floated through the air as Titus spun her around. Editha Marsh Morley wore the same veil on her wedding day many years before and came to rescue it. The bobbin lace, sometimes called pillow lace because threads were worked upon a pillow, took hours of work to produce only an inch, but what a remarkable inch it was. As a young girl, Diantha loved watching her grandma's swift fingers pass bobbins one over another forming the lavish trim. Diantha's attempts to learn the art had increased her respect for its value. This long, hand-woven piece was a family treasure. Editha folded it with care knowing there would be other days and other granddaughters with occasion to use the lace too.

The wedding supper was a joyful feast for many family members and friends. As usual, Isaac Morley did not miss an opportunity for match-making.

"Miss Billings," he said. "Let me introduce you to my good friend and fellow homesteader-neighbor, John Wells." Pulling John by the arm, he went on. "This is Salome Billings, John. I dare say, if she works anything like her brother, Titus, she'll be a good catch for some lucky man."

Though both of them blushed at the moment, they kept company for the rest of the evening. The groom was too busy to notice, but his mother did. Before long, they too would "tie the knot" and Titus would have a sister – blood kin -- living in Kirtland, Ohio, at last.

"Are you as happy as you look?" the groom asked his radiant bride.

"I have never been happier!" she said. "And how about you?"

"When you are happy I am happy," he said.

"I love you," she whispered in his ear.

"I love you the most," he said.

Music still played and torches glimmered as womenfolk packed up left-over food. Certain they had greeted and thanked each guest, the newlyweds slipped away into the night.

*   *   *

"Good Morning," Reverend Rigdon said, "and how are the Sweethearts of my congregation today?" Titus' face flushed more than Diantha's did. Then, with a gesture that would become his customary routine for this new couple, Rigdon cupped his hands around both of theirs and added, "You can be sure, my friends, that yours was a partnership made in heaven."

Titus had no doubts he and Diantha were right for each other, still he enjoyed hearing it from the mouth of such a respectable leader.

"We would be pleased to have you sing a duet in our services next week," Sidney Rigdon added. Titus was shy at speaking, but he seemed to enjoy singing invitations when shared with his wife. Folks teased that she could get him to do anything. Diantha hoped it would be the excuse she needed to persuade her parents to attend. The next day she approached them.

"How did it go with your parents today?" Titus asked when he came into the house. Diantha stood at the table, chopping veg-

31

etables. She said nothing.

"Smells good in here," he said hanging his hat. "What's for supper?" Stepping close behind his wife and wrapping his arms around her waist, Titus kissed her cheek.

"Hey now," he said. "Are these onions too strong for my wife, or do I taste real tears?"

"Oh Titus, whatever are we going to do?" She fell into his arms and cried until his shirt was wet. He held her and waited until she was ready to explain.

"It's Pa," she said. Somehow that was no surprise. "Mother wanted to come, but he –"

"Your father is a good man. Extremely set in his ways, but a good-hearted man. We will have to give him a little time, that's all."

"We will have to give him a great deal of time," she corrected. Titus kissed her again, then washed his hands and finished chopping the onions.

Historical Background

Titus (age 24) married Diantha (age 21) on Sunday, February 16, 1817 (Billings/Shaw/Hale, 4; Black, 576; Bennion1); Esplin1; Cook, 102; Pyne, 1; Tulliedge, 429). Eight of their nine children were born in Ohio: Samuel Dwight, 1818; Thomas, 1819; Ebenezer, 1820; Emily and Martha (twins who died at birth), 1822 (or 1819); Alfred Nelson, 1825; George Pierce, 1827; and Eunice, January 3, 1830 (Bennion1; Esplin1). Titus Junior was born in Clay County, Missouri in 1834 (Bennion1).

Titus and Diantha were married in 1817. Sidney Rigdon converted Isaac and Titus in 1828. Although they were members of his congregation and very dear friends, he could not have performed their marriage ceremony according to these dates. We choose to leave our story as though he did, in spite of this more recent discovery. "The Morley [Isaac] family was baptized Campbellites by Sidney Rigdon in 1828" (MorleyRH, 6). Another account suggests that they were "members of the Reformed Baptist congregation" (Gappmayer, 2). Although the Billings family was blessed with abundant musical abilities, Ebenezer's violin playing is just a guess.

"John [Wells] bought land in Kirtland, as early as 1811, but the date of Salome's arrival and settlement in Kirtland is uncertain. Salome married John Wells and they were parents of five children" (Lisonbee, 1). There are two spellings for the name of Titus' sister: Salome (Billings V1; Lisonbee, 7) or Salomi (Sorber).

Titus and Diantha may have moved to Ontario, Wayne, New York, shortly after they were married. If so, their first five children would have been born there (Family Group; IGI printout; Lisonbee, 1). However, Billings Family Group Sheets show that the first eight children were born in Ohio.

Chapter 8

Diantha finished tuning her dulcimer and went outside to gather crops for dinner. She and Lucy, her closest neighbor, grew vegetable gardens side by side. Several times a week the two couples shared a meal and Bible study together. Tonight was the Billings' turn and Diantha's instrument was ready for some musical harmonizing as well. She snipped spinach leaves and pulled long carrots from the fertile ground. *These will be perfect,* she thought with gratitude.

The young wife shielded her eyes and stretched her neck until she spotted her husband laboring in Isaac's field. Titus took over most all of the farming chores these days. Isaac's cooper business was thriving. To his dismay, the father-son partnership was not.

Infant cries from the cabin beckoned inside. She, a new mother, had presented Titus with a son of his own, a healthy, handsome lad they chose to call Samuel Dwight Billings. The same year, 1818, Philena and Lucy Diantha Morley were blessed with a new little sister, Edith Ann.

*   *   *

The next year, Titus was elated about expanding his family again, until the good news turned troubled when Diantha took ill. Lucy kept little Samuel at her home most of the day.

"Our son's first birthday will be here and I am too preoccupied with health concerns to help him celebrate," Diantha complained.

"Sammy is too young to realize it anyway," Titus said. "Next year we can celebrate both birthdays." His words appeased her will to get out of bed. Diantha would have to pay a price for a healthy baby. The prize would be worth the wait.

Before snows melted, however, and during the dark, wee hours of morning, Diantha Morley Billings felt excruciating pain. Breathing was difficult. In spite of the chilling air she oozed with perspiration. Panicked and helpless, her desperate husband rushed next door for Isaac and Lucy. Isaac ran for Mother Morley, and then left on horseback to fetch a doctor. Lucy assisted as best she could.

Titus paced and pondered and tried to pray.

There was no way to save the baby. Samuel Dwight would have had a brother, but such was not to be. Lucy cleaned the infant's body and wrapped him tightly. Titus knelt beside the bed and tried to comfort his grieving wife. On such a scene her parents opened the door.

"I don't want to see him!" Diantha insisted. "I can never hold him. I can never love him. I never want to see that baby."

Editha Morley rushed to her daughter's side. "Now, now," she tried to comfort. "You are my baby, Diantha. Mother is here. It will be all right."

But it was not all right. Everything was wrong. Why? Why did this happen? What could she do about it? It was all so final. Thomas Morley was a big, sturdy man who had been at odds with his daughter over religious beliefs for some time, yet seeing her sorrow melted his heart and sent tears that evidenced it gushing down his cheeks. He embraced his son-in-law and together they wept.

Sleeping was impossible. Titus searched his soul for answers and understanding. He needed peace so he could give comfort. He needed direction himself. Life had too many uncertainties. He wanted to be a believer, but what was there to believe? Somehow he would have to pick up the pieces and move onward. For Diantha's sake, he had to be strong.

"I still think we should name our son Thomas, after your father" he announced. "I cannot tell you now, Diantha, but I know there are some answers to all of this. There has to be a reason for your suffering and for this tiny, perfect body to be already stilled. I do not know how, but I will find the answers for you, I promise."

Quieted by pure exhaustion, Diantha looked into her husband's eyes and accepted his promise in silence. With reverence he kissed her.

"I am going outside to dig a little grave for our Thomas. Do you want me to carry you out when it is ready?"

A slight nod showed she was willing. Oh yes, Mrs. Titus Billings would go forth and she would carry on. His woman was made of good stuff. How he loved her.

Historical Background

"Titus and Isaac bought property adjacent to one another. Some of the property has both of their names on the deed" (CoombsLS). "Thomas, their [Titus and Diantha] second son, was born in 1819, and died as an infant" (Billings Family Group Sheet). Perhaps he was named after his grandfather, Thomas Morley.

[As explained in Addendum #2 of this book, right before going to press, we discovered that Thomas did in fact LIVE. His middle name is Addington, not to be confused with his son Thomas Addison Billings].

CHAPTER 9

Two-year-old Samuel bumped up and down in the back of his father's wagon. They had been to the lake again. Sammy loved to go along. He loved to go anywhere with his father, but a trip to Lake Erie was a favorite, especially in wintertime when one could walk out on the frozen water.

Titus cut huge blocks of ice and wrapped them for the long ride. These would be used to chill root cellars. He cut several for Newell K. Whitney's store, as well, and swung by there on the way home.

"You're a good man," Newell said, as they unloaded the last ice brick. "Now, how about a candy stick for little Sammy?"

Titus was ready to hurry home, but the offer had already brightened Sammy's eyes. There was no denying them. Instead, he plucked the well-bundled cherub from the wagon bed and stepped inside.

Choosing one candy stick from a jar that holds every color and flavor available is a difficult decision. While Mrs. Whitney humored Sammy, Titus took a look around. He had no intention of buying anything, but Diantha was on his mind. She was heavy with child again. They were happy about it, but he could not free himself of worried concern. The loss of little Thomas still burned within him.

"Sammy, listen to this," Mrs. Whitney said as she opened the flowered lid of a tiny porcelain box. Music began to play. Sammy clapped his hands with delight. Titus found it impressive too and wished to buy it for Diantha. He considered doing just that, until frugality won out. Hardly ever did he buy anything without her input, and she always consulted with him. It was a good thing they had going. Still, once in a while a surprise would be fun. Titus put a hand in his pocket to jingle the loose change. Not much. Things were tight right now. Let's face it. Things were always tight. Oh well, maybe some other time . . .

As the homestead came into view, Titus smiled. Trees hugged his little cabin and smoke from its chimney sketched doodle marks onto the sky. It was a peaceful place, this place he called home. Maybe his pockets were empty, but his heart was full. He had a good wife and he had a good life. Yes indeed, he was a fortunate man.

Titus turned the team and pulled them up behind Morley's house where he opened the cellar to shimmy ice into its new resting place. Lucy must have heard him because she came out running.

"Have you been home yet, Titus?" she called.

"Nope. On my way now."

"Oh Titus, you better hurry," she said.

"What's wrong? Is it Diantha?"

"Yes, yes, I mean no, it's not the baby, but . . ."

Titus was already running. He hollered back to Lucy: "Get Sammy, will ya?!"

He found Diantha stretched out on the bed with a wet, folded cloth on her forehead; her face streaked and splotched where tears had left puddle marks.

"Diantha, Diantha!" He knelt beside her. "What is it? Are you all right?"

"Oh Titus," only one hand reached up for him. "I'm so sorry." She started to cry.

"What is it? What happened to you?"

Then he saw it. Her right arm was charred with a deep, open burn.

"Diantha . . ."

"I spilled your dinner, Titus, all of it. I'm so sorry."

"Dinner doesn't matter. You do." He bent down and kissed her.

A wagon was heard, pulling up to the house. Titus rushed out.

"Thanks Lucy," he said. She helped Sammy down as Titus broke a corner off a chunk of ice. Wrapping the icy pieces in a wet cloth he carefully laid it across the burned arm. Again he knelt by her side.

"Don't worry about supper," Lucy said. "We have plenty for tonight. I'll go fetch some."

Titus kissed his sweetheart again. "I thought it was the baby, "he said.

That made her smile, "Thank goodness, not."

"I should have gotten that box."

"What's that?" she asked.

"Oh, nothing."

"Come on now," she teased. "I thought we agreed to keep

40

no secrets from each other."

"Not a secret," he said. "Should have been a surprise."

"Tell me. What surprise?"

"I saw a pretty, little music box in Whitney's Store. Wanted you to have it, but didn't think we could spare the money."

"Oh Titus," she said, "What a sweetheart."

"I didn't buy it. Guess I'm a cheapskate, not a sweetheart."

"You're my sweetheart," she said. "It's the thought that makes me happy."

He found no comfort in the thought.

"Anyway, you should not be buying gifts for a wife who throws your supper away." With her good hand she reached for his. "You are my music box, Titus."

Everyone knew Titus Billings had a pleasant singing voice and a way with musical instruments. How she wished he owned a violin or horn, but her favorite of all was the way he whistled a tune. He could add trills that sounded like birds singing. She loved to hear him whistle and could often tell where he was or how he felt by the sound of his melody.

Diantha pulled his fist to her lips and kissed it. "Now," she said, opening his thumb and fingers, "You be my music box and whistle that tune."

Gently he stroked her hair and started. She smiled.

"Beethoven's Für Elise" she said, closing her eyes with enjoyment.

*   *   *

Titus paced back and forth, up and down, and all around the cabin. Lucy and Mother Morley had been on duty for hours. Why did it take so long? Why did it have to be so difficult? He knew better than to think such things, but–

"Waaaaaaa, waaaaaaaaaaaa!" burst from the cabin.

The living cry of a newborn baby was sweet music to his ears.

"Congratulations!" Isaac said, slapping him on the back.

It seemed like forever before Lucy opened the door.

"It's a boy," she said. "You can come in now."

Diantha was propped up with pillows and a tiny, new son rested on her good arm. It would be difficult to manage for a time;

until the burned arm healed, but she was alive and so was her baby. Often fire or childbirth claimed the life of a frontier woman. Titus felt lucky. His Diantha had been spared from both.

"May I hold him?" he asked.

"Of course, Papa," she said. "Here, meet your new little Ebenezer."

Titus wrapped his big hands around the tiny body and pulled him close.

"Can't wait until Grandpa meets his little name sake," he said.

"Do you think he will be pleased?" she asked.

"Without doubt," he answered.

"Are you pleased?" she asked him.

"Without doubt!" he replied.

Historical Background

"Joseph's other activities included visiting many of the lakes of the region. Among these visits was a trip to Lake Erie where Joseph went to fish and to visit friends in April 1834" (Holzapfel/Cottle, 43). Author's Note: This reference validates the likelihood that Titus too could travel to Lake Erie.

"Ebenezer was born in 1820. He left Nauvoo, Illinois on the Mississippi River in 1847 and was never heard from again" (Bennion1). Perhaps he was named after his grandfather, Ebenezer Billings.

CHAPTER 10

"Titus, what is it?" Diantha could always tell when something was wrong. This time her husband's agitation would have signaled anyone. His face matched the white letter he held.

"It's Ma," he said. "She's badly ill. It says even if I come at once I might not make it in time."

"Oh no! Not Mother Billings." After a startled pause she continued. "You must go, Titus. They will need your help."

"I know, but how will you manage? Winter's not a good time to leave."

"I worry more about you traveling alone in snowstorms," she said.

"My bride is as brave as Isaac's bride was," he said and kissed her. She understood the compliment, but waited for him to embellish it. With a grin, he did. "I can see it now, my courageous little wife defending our spot in the wilderness while I march off to war."

Diantha shook her head. "Not good," she said.

"Nothing would scare you off."

"Only wild beasts and savages."

"No, no. You would charm them with your cooking and calm them with your song. Before my return you would have them schooled in proper etiquette and trained to do household chores." By now his long arms were wrapped around her waist. He boosted her off the floor and spun her around.

"Titus, put me down." Instead of stopping he swung her again. She held on for dear life, hoping their dance would not upset the room.

"The first job is to tame my soldier," she said. With her feet again on the ground she relished his embrace. "I'll miss you, Titus. How soon must you leave?"

"I'd like to get an early start in the morning," he said. She agreed and started packing. He went out to arrange for the animals.

The early December air was fully winterized when Titus left, alone, on horseback. Diantha watched until he was out of sight. Then she threw herself into the routine of daily chores. Her secret plan to knit caps and socks for Christmas would occupy her time

43

during his absence.

"Well, well," she said out loud while inventorying her wool supply, "Looks like we need to make a trip to the mill, Sammy." The child looked up. "Want to go bye-bye where Papa took the sheep skins for carding?" Sammy starred in wonderment. "Your pa shears so many sheep that we take the wool to a place where machines roll out the weeds and seeds and imperfections." Speaking more to herself than the child she went on, "Glad I don't have to waste my time doing all of that. After they smooth it into rolls it is ready to use." Her audience had waddled off.

"Come on, Boys. Let's go bye-bye."

"Bye-bye," Sammy said.

Tucking her baby and toddler into the wagon bed, Diantha drove to her mother's cabin.

"We're headed for the mill to pick up our wool," she said. "Probably stop at Whitney's Store too. Would you like to come along?"

"I'm in the middle of molding butter," her mother said.

"Oh, let me help. Then you can come."

They churned the butter, rinsing and squeezing it several times to work out all the liquid. Otherwise the product would turn sour. Because Mother Morley sold the excess butter, it was molded with an identifying shape imprinted on the top. For her mold the head of a cow had been carved into a flat piece of wood and placed in the bottom of a four-sided wooden box. When soft butter was pressed inside and leveled off at the top, the box would hold exactly one-pound. These bricks of butter were chilled, then dumped out, wrapped and sold.

Each farm put its own symbol on top of the butter, so buyers could identify the ones they liked. Diantha enjoyed helping her mother and the little boys seemed to enjoy playing at their feet. Soon all were in the wagon and ready to go.

"With your husband so long out of town, it will be easier for you to knit a gift without him knowing. Why don't you make him a nice sweater this year?"

"Oh mother, I would love to, but you know how I knit," Diantha confessed.

"You will never learn any younger." Editha Morley, a fine knitter, had turned out many beautiful sweaters. Diantha wore her share of them, over the years, but never took the time to master the skill for herself.

"Will you help me?" she asked.

"Of course, I will." Editha smiled and cocked her head with an all-knowing look. "Then you will have to visit me more often," she teased, her eyes twinkling.

Whitney-Gilbert's Mercantile, the busy hub of Kirtland, was a favorite gathering spot. Today was no exception. A crowd buzzed over the arrival of new fabric and notions. Editha Morley purchased yardage from Europe.

Unable to shop for several weeks, what with the new baby and all, Diantha enjoyed looking around. Though curious about a particular item, she had no intentions to buy. Probably sold, she thought, holding Ebenezer close and raising onto her toes for a better look. The object was nowhere in sight. On her way out she noticed a glass case of delicate items and spotted a flower topped porcelain box inside. If that is a music box I wonder what tune it plays?

Editha's arms were overloaded with purchases and with Sammy. Preoccupied, Diantha refrained from assisting and followed her to the wagon. Once all passengers were situated Diantha started for the driver's seat. A strong pull tugged at her curiosity. *With empty hands it would take barely a moment. I really want to know.*

"I forgot something, Mother," she said turning back. "I'll just be a moment. You don't mind, do you?"

Inside the store she reached for the tiny box and raised its lid. Music began. Sure enough, the tune was Beethoven's "Für Elise".

She returned it with silent longing.

"What was that all about?" Mother asked.

"Just something I needed to check out for Titus," she said.

Historical Background

Many wool growers took their pelts to a mill for carding so machinery could be used to roll out the weeds and seeds and imperfections (McNeil).

CHAPTER 11

Old Man Winter smothered Northern Ohio with heavy snowfall, causing Diantha to worry about conditions her husband would meet on his return from Massachusetts. Isaac split wood for her daily. She ventured out as little as possible. Each evening, soon as the boys were bedded down, she would slide her wheel close to the fire and started spinning. Small pieces of wool were pulled and stretched, then with slow steadiness, fed into the wheel pumped by her foot. Little by little, the soft wool turned into yarn, keeping her hands busy, but not her mind. *I miss you, Titus. If only your parents had moved here when you invited them. How I long to talk with your mother again, your sweet, sweet . . .*

Hours of spinning produced enough yarn for knitting.

"What color shall I make it?" Diantha asked her mother.

"We are in the wrong season for dying wool. All your color producing plants are buried in snow." Diantha looked at the off-white, almost gray fibers.

"Just make it natural," Editha suggested.

"Are you sure it will look right?"

"Should be fine. He'll love it because you made it."

Diantha's plan was to start casting her yarn onto knitting needles as soon as the little boys were bedded down for the night. She lit a candle and stirred the fire for better lighting. In the corner her wooden tub was brimming with yarn balls, each prepared with love. Caps and mittens would be easy enough, but a sweater? How in the world could she accomplish so much? Would it be good enough? Doubts seemed to bounce around the room. Loneliness set in as well. Diantha, weary from work and from worry, missed her precious partner more than ever. Leaving knitting needles on the table she reached for her dulcimer. *Tomorrow my hands will knit, but tonight my heart needs to sing.* Into the night she sang like an angel . . . songs of love and of hope, only the angels could hear.

*   *   *

Sunshine sparkled on the crusty snow where flurries ceased three days before, leaving a beautiful icy scene in the cold. Using a pick and a shovel, Diantha labored to dig out the cellar door so she could retrieve apples, carrots, potatoes and turnips for Christmas. She sliced the tops off her good-sized turnips and dug out their centers. Sammy enjoyed the turnip meat and ate the pieces as quickly as they dropped. Tapered homemade candles, secured with melted wax in turnip holders, were hung on each wall, to be lit on Christmas Eve. *I do hope Titus gets to see them*, she thought.

Strong molasses fragranced the air as Sammy helped his mother make Christmas cookies during Ebenezer's nap. They rolled out the spicy dough, cut into squares and sprinkled it with sugar. Diantha held her hand in a built-in oven at the side of the fireplace and started to count.

". . .ten, eleven, twelve, thirteen, fourteen," she could hold it no longer, proof of 400 degree heat; a good temperature for bread, but a bit too hot for cookies. Stirring the fire she separated some of the coals to allow a brief cooling until the temperature felt right and the first tray of cookies began to bake for the Christmas Eve party at Isaac's house.

Still no word from Titus. She knew now he could not get home in time for the holiday and that was fine. Really, it was fine. The boys were so young they hardly understood the celebration. She would hold off lighting the holiday candles until he came home. They could pretend it was Christmas then. Oh, how she missed him.

*   *   *

"Reverend Rigdon, Phoebe, how nice of you to come," Lucy said.

"Wouldn't miss this," Rigdon answered. "We've heard about parties at the Morley's house."

A large crowd gathered early in the evening and celebrated deep into the night. Everyone came -- well, everyone except Titus. Sammy slept in the corner for a long time before Diantha decided to leave. Isaac carried him home because her arms were filled with the baby.

Christmas Day arrived and disappeared again, leaving Diantha's sewing basket stuffed with little brown paper wrapped packages. Determined to wait for her husband's return, she refused to open them. The boys needed new warm caps, though. If he didn't

48

make it home by New Year's Eve she might have to change her mind.

*   *   *

A lone traveler encouraged his weary horse to keep trotting. He should have stopped for the night, but was near enough to home that he chose to keep going. The ground was snow-covered with leftovers of an old storm. Tied to his horse was a sleigh made of sticks he had lashed together and because the load was heavy it left deep marks in the ground. A few hours before he had used the gun his father had given to him.

"Anyone traveling through Massachusetts' bear country should take a gun," his father had insisted. "I want you to have this anyway. You'll use it more now than I will."

Titus breathed in freezing air and rewrapped the scarf around his neck. Thoughts of loved ones by the home-fire seemed to warm him. How deeply he missed his wife and ached for ruining her Christmas. Other feelings bubbled within him too. The bitter fact that he would never see his mother again was difficult to accept. Then, there was the propitious excitement he had bumped into while crossing New York. The state was building a canal that would connect the Hudson River with Lake Erie by an ingenious man-made lock system. What a boon to transportation.

The load he dragged slowed his ride. *Will be worth it, though. Perhaps I'll need it for a peace offering.* He smiled to himself. How could any man pass up a five-point buck standing in front of him, staring him down? Titus was certain that Diantha would welcome good, fresh meat.

No one was home when he got there.

"Today is Sunday," he said to himself. "Everyone will be in Mentor for church."

After caring for his horse and hanging the venison Titus had time to clean up, but weariness coaxed him to stoke the fire and lay down for a moment of sleep.

"Look Isaac!" Diantha shouted when she saw strong puffs of smoke coming from her chimney. She had ridden to church with her brother's family and she knew, she just knew, that her husband was home.

Titus was asleep by the fire.

"Quiet boys. Let's not wake up your pa." As she tip-toed

near to give him a silent kiss, Sammy lunged and landed on top of his father, squealing with joy for all he was worth! The would-be sleeping man rolled and wrestled with his sons. He had missed them too.

"Tell me about your trip, Titus. Did you talk to her before ..?"

"Ma passed on the twenty-first," he explained. "Got there two days before. Hadn't been coherent for weeks. Pa took me right to her bedside and told her that I was there. Diantha, she opened her eyes and spoke to me. She said, 'Oh, it's my son.' That's the only thing she said the whole time. Those were her last words."

"Then she knew you, Titus. I'm glad you went."

"We buried her there in Greenfield. I tried to bring Pa back with me, but he'll never come now. He wants to stay where she is."

"Guess you can't blame him for that," Diantha whispered.

Historical Background

Ester Joyce Billings, Titus' mother, died at age sixty-two on 21 December 1820 in Greenfield, Massachusetts (BillingsV, 1; Sorber Family Group Sheet;). See picture of her tombstone in Appendix A.

CHAPTER 12

"These will be perfect for Thomas's third birthday," Diantha said as Sammy and Ebenezer helped her arrange bouquets of colorful leaves on top of the beloved little grave site. Three tiny cousins had joined Thomas on the hilltop. Last year Lucy Morley suffered two stillborn births: one a son, the other a daughter. Then only weeks ago, Calista Morley's two-year-old body was also lowered into the ground. Diantha removed wilted flowers from the sacred spot and arranged fresh fallen leaves in their stead. Awkward again with child, she lowered herself to the ground and started singing a lullaby while she rocked back and forth.

Dry leaves fell around her as a chilly breeze started up. She knew it was time to take the boys inside, but the difficulty of leaving baby bodies in such a resting place pulled her back. Sometimes she just liked to talk out loud, pretending little Thomas could hear and understand. Then she tried to visualize what he would look like by now. Calista, too had left a deep ache in her broken heart. Diantha shook the leaves from her apron and used it to bury her face. Then she wept.

"Did you take a tumble, Mommy?" Sammy asked.

"No, no," Diantha tried to gather herself.

"Where does it hurt, Mommy?"

"I'm not hurt, Sammy," she said as she pulled the concerned child into what was left of her lap. "Not really. I'm just sad in my heart."

"Why, Mommy? Why are you crying?"

"Sometimes I just miss Baby Thomas," she said.

"I'll be your baby," Sammy said. By now Ebbie was on top of her too.

"Yes, you are good babies," Diantha said as she cuddled both boys. "And soon we'll have a new baby, won't we?"

"Do you miss Calista too?" Sammy asked.

"Oh yes, I do miss her, and I miss Grandma Billings. I guess we have many loved ones in Heaven now."

"Don't cry, Mommy." Sammy stood up. "I think that Grandma Billings will tend Baby Thomas for us."

"Of course she will." Diantha welcomed the thought.

"You make me happy, Sam. Now be a helper and pull me up, will you please?"

*   *   *

Titus had gone into the hills early that morning and would be gone all day. Diantha felt fine and self-sufficient when he left, but now she was doubtful. Something had gone wrong. She just knew it. That pain, that terrible, rotten, piercing pain was back. She struggled to catch each breath and found difficulty in every movement. Samuel was playing on the floor with his brother. *I can't alarm the little boys. Oh, I must lie down, just for a moment -- then I'll get help.*

"Sammy, what are you doing out here without a jacket?" Lucy asked.

"Mommy won't get up," he said.

"Is something wrong?"

"Mommy won't talk to me!" He started to cry.

Entering as she knocked, Lucy found the cabin darkened and little Ebenezer asleep on the rug. His cheeks looked tear-stained, like he had cried himself to sleep.

"Diantha? Di . . ." The startled neighbor found her sister-in-law draped over the side of the bed, more kneeling than not, as though she had tried to lie on it, but couldn't get there.

"Oh no! Oh no! This can't be happening!"

Muttering to herself as if it would help, she strained to rally the lifeless form and using the fullness of her short stature, Lucy Morley pulled Diantha onto the bed. With a cool, wet cloth she sponged beads of sweat from the burning forehead and beckoned a response. Diantha groaned. She could not talk. Then gasping, she grabbed her swollen womb and cried. By now Ebenezer was awake and crying. Lucy felt like crying too. Snatching Ebenezer in her arms she raced home with Samuel following.

"Philena, watch these boys and Editha. Lucy Diantha, run for your father. Aunt Diantha is having her baby!"

Seven-year-old Philena shooed the children into the house where she gave Editha and the cousins a biscuit. Lucy Diantha ran at top speed to the field. Lucy rushed back to Diantha's bedside with a hopeful prayer beating in her heart and pounding in her head.

52

The night was long and horrible. Titus had returned tired, weary, and unprepared for the tragic trauma that filled his log cabin home. Diantha hung on the edge of life with frantic women trying to save her . . . and the baby? There was not one baby, but two! Diantha was having twins. They were twin daughters. Beautiful twin daughters. Beautiful, healthy looking daughters. But both of them were born dead! If Diantha did survive, how would she ever cope with such a loss? Titus was beside himself. There was nothing he could do. He could not help his wife. He could not save his babies. The women wanted him out of the way. He left the house in great despair.

Wildly his long legs took him. Faster and faster he sped. It did not matter where he went. He just ran. He ran hard and he ran fast. It was cold, but he didn't care. Not at all. Not anymore. He ran through the farmyard and into the forest. Thicker foliage made it harder to run. Deeper darkness made it harder to see. A chilly breeze had long ago turned into a cold wind that iced his tears and numbed his senses. Toes and fingers were numb now as well. He stumbled again and again. Then he stumbled and did not get back up. By now anger had turned to hurt. Exhausted, he laid in the branches and bushes where he pleaded between deep sobs, "If there is a God in Heaven, where are you?"

*　　　*　　　*

From high above him, the sound of birds chirped Titus to consciousness. He felt the warmth of Old Man Sunshine on his face and found himself flat on his back looking straight into heaven, when his eyes opened. He heard no voice. No other living soul was in sight. Nonetheless, he, a humble farmer, felt the strong awareness of a powerful presence. Maybe God was up there smiling down upon him. It was impossible to explain, but he felt certain everything would work out like it should. He had lost three precious babies, but he still had his wife . . . his wife! Reality jerked him to his feet. What had happened to Diantha? How could he have deserted her at a time like this? He had not meant to do that. Was she really alive? How could he have slept so long?

Diantha, Diantha, he said to himself. *Please, please be well.*

Titus was lost. Surely he could find his way, but it would take some doing and time, too much time, he feared.

"Oh please let me find her alive! She's just got to be alive.

Please give me another chance, God. I'll comfort her," he promised out loud. "Somehow I'll find a way to be strong for her. I love her. I really love her. I can't go on without her. Oh please, I need Diantha!"

* * *

"We had one girl's name picked out, but not two," Titus said.

Diantha had wanted a daughter named Emily since her first pregnancy. Every time that name was ready, but every time the baby had been a boy. Now she had two girls and only one name.

"What would you like to call the other one, dear?"

Titus was ready to put names on the little crosses, like he had for Thomas. Diantha looked into his sad eyes and knew his heart, too, was broken. He had given her such alarm the night he disappeared. No one could tell her where he was. When he didn't come home at all, she was beside herself. Such behavior was not like him, causing her to suspect the worst. Perhaps the intense fear of losing him helped to appease the pain of losing infant twins. At least he was here now. With him life would go on.

"What about Martha?" she asked, thinking of Grandma Marsh's beautiful bobbin lace. Her husband smiled as thoughts of Martha Marsh's carrot cake filled his mind.

"Sounds good to me," he agreed. Martha it will be. Emily and Martha were buried in tiny graves beside their brother.

* * *

Devoted minister, Sidney Rigdon, was pleased to see the Titus Billings family back in church. He knew of their tragedy. The husband had been extremely thankful to find his wife among the living. The wife had worried beyond measure that her husband was in harm. When at last they reunited, each felt need to comfort the other and both felt as if they had been given another chance. "Yes," Rigdon smiled as they entered. Then he whispered, "Yours is a partnership formed in Heaven."

"I'll be going away for a time," Titus told the preacher after church one spring day. "Heading for New York to help out with that canal."

54

"Really," Rigdon said with surprise. "They've been working on that for a long time, haven't they?"

"Sure have. They started planning it ten years before I was born," Titus laughed. Rigdon laughed too. "Just opened a section between Rome and Utica when I was passing through two years ago. Incredible project. I'd like to help them finish it up." He paused. "Not to mention that I could use some earnings right now."

"You'll be a good man for the job," Rigdon said. He admired the reputation Titus Billings had earned for being one of the best carpenters and stonemasons in the valley, as well as a farmer.

"We'll keep an eye on that family for you."

All too soon for Diantha, her husband was packed and ready to leave for the distant job. She had no idea when he would be able to return.

"I love you, Diantha," he said.

"Oh, Titus, I wish—"

"I know, dear, it's going to be all right," he hugged her. "I promise, no matter what, I will be home for Christmas this year. Don't know how much winter work they can do anyway."

With that, she smiled. He kissed her and was gone.

Canal digging is hard work, but it produces a paycheck and makes good muscles. Titus was intrigued with the idea of a man-made connection between waterways and loved having a part in it. What a difference it would make for everyone. Weeks flew by, but true to his promise, Diantha's husband took time off to be home for Christmas.

"Sure disappointed Whitney can't get any more of those music boxes," Titus said to his wife. "Sold 'em all before our anniversary last year and didn't get any more in time for Christmas."

"Oh, I love this carpet bag, Titus. Probably get more use out of it anyway." She squeezed him. "But you can be my music box. Whistle for me, please," she begged.

"Should have bought that when I had the chance."

"I'd rather have you any day." She poured herself into his strong, safe arms. "Be my music box, Titus." How could he resist?

Historical Background

Twin daughters, Emily and Martha, died at birth in Ohio. Conflicting Family Group Sheets show the dates of birth as 1822 or 1819. To this writer, 1822 fits better because Thomas was born in 1819. Both records agree on the year of his birth (Bennion1; Esplin1). Martha Marsh was Editha Marsh Morley's mother, thus Diantha's grandmother though dates given on IGI records make it uncertain how much interaction they could have had. "Martha" the baby twin being a namesake is only a guess.

Lucy Morley delivered two stillborn babies in 1821, names unknown. Also, a daughter Calista died when she was two years old. To us the cause of her death is unknown. Isaac and Lucy used the name Calista again when their next daughter was born on 28 November 1823, calling her Cordelia Calista (Morley Family Group Records).

CHAPTER 13

January 1825

My Dear Diantha,

Got back safely and miss you already. Hope that you are happy and that the boys are behaving. So glad Alfred is going to work the farm for me this spring. That little brother of yours grew up fast, didn't he? It's good he did. His planting for me this year will really help out. Mr. Cain said he was pleased that I got back earlier. He expects to finish the entire canal by fall. Hope he's right. Its hard work, but I feel like I'm really doing something worthwhile. At least it makes me sleep well at night. I'm tired now. Going to bed early.
I love you. Titus

February 1825

Dear Husband,

Happy Anniversary! Can you believe that we have been married for eight years? Where does the time go? I have good news, Titus. Are you sitting down? If not, you'd better. I waited to be sure. Now there's no doubt. What would you think about being a father again? How about next August? Well, will that do for an anniversary surprise? Wish I could see your face now.
I send my love, Diantha

March 1825

Dearest Darling Diantha,

What an anniversary present! I'm so pleased. Do you need me to come home? How are you feeling now? Is anyone helping you? Have you picked out any names? What if it is a girl this time? We used your girl name. Better choose another. Oh, Diantha, I'm really happy, but please take care of yourself. When we finish this job I think I'll stick to farming so I don't have to leave you ever again. I don't like being away, especially now. Please look out for yourself until I can come back. I'm going to write a note at the bottom for the boys. Will you read it to them? I love you, Di. More than pen can put onto paper. Stay well. God bless you, my love.
Forever yours, Titus

P.S. to Sammy: Dear Son, I miss you. Thanks for being the man around the house right now. I'm glad that you are seven years old and big enough to help out. Take good care of your mother. She is in a special way and will need your help. Eb looks up to you. Be his hero. I love you. Thanks for doing a man's work. Love, Dad

P.S.S. to Ebenezer: Dear Son, Five years ago you came as a baby into our home. How we love you. Now your mother is getting ready to have another baby. I'm glad that you are grown up and can help out. I need you to look after her for me. Will you? Thanks, son. I love you, Dad

April 1825

Dearest Di,

How's my favorite Sweetheart? Are you taking care of yourself for me? Wish I could be there to help you. Did Alfred get the crop in yet? Thank him for me. You know, I was thinking that you might want to name our baby after him, well, if it's a boy. He's been a good brother to us. Of course, they all have, but it seems kinda timely right now. Let me know what you think. Do you have any girl ideas yet? We are making good progress on the canal. It's forty feet wide at the surface and we taper it to a twenty-eight-foot width at the bottom. It is only four feet deep. When we're done it will stretch for three-hundred and sixty-three miles. Can you believe it? Hope you get to see it someday. Hope I get to see you soon.
Truest love, Titus
P.S. TAKE CARE OF YOURSELF, Di.

May 1825

Dear Titus,

I miss you terribly. Do you know what I wish for most? That you could hold me in your strong arms and whistle a music box tune to our soon-to-be baby and me. How I love you. Well, let me get serious. Things are good on the farm. Alfred has worked his heart out. Says he appreciates you and all you do more than he did before. I like your idea about naming the baby after him, if it's a boy. Kinda hope we have a girl, though. I want a daughter who can wear my wedding lace some day. (Ha) Have you come up with a girl's name yet? Thought about "Lucy" . . . so many Lucys, though. I don't know. Keep thinking. I will be glad when that Erie Canal is a done deal. I'm glad you are helping mankind and learning so much, but I miss you. Until?????? I remain yours completely.
Love, Your Di

58

Diantha Darling,

Your time is getting closer. Are you doing well? Has she or he kicked yet? Did you tell Alfred that we were thinking about using his name? How's the crop looking? Seems like it's been so long. Good they keep us busy here or I'd go crazy worrying about you. Are you sure you're okay? Do I need to come home early? How are the boys? and Isaac's family? and your folks? I miss them all. Give my regards to all of them and to Rigdon's congregation. Will be glad to get home. Already I'm counting the days. My love is even deeper than before.
Remember me, Titus

July 1825

Dear Titus,

Good news. You will never guess who is here. Your sister, Eunice, came to visit with her family. She had no idea that you were away. Thinks it's wonderful that you are helping build such a great thing for America. When she discovered my delicate condition, she insisted on staying to help until the baby comes. What a blessing, especially now that Lucy and I are expecting at the same time. These cousins will be like twins. I am doing well, but can tell that it is getting close. Trying to be careful for the sake of our child. I will be so thankful when this is done. I can't wait to see you, Darling. Please be careful and hurry home when you can. I remain forever in love with you,
Diantha

August 1825

Dearly Beloved Diantha,

I have bad news. Mr. Cain says that there is no way he can let a foreman leave the job right now. He might have to get another foreman, for all I care. Only, we've worked so hard. Our crew has done as much, if not more, than any other on the project. We all want to get it done. Course, we want it done right. The real problem, I think, is that we are already short-handed on skilled workers and the big guys want it done before winter. State funding will run out by then too. Talk is they are going to collect a toll charge to help defray the cost of maintenance. At any rate, I feel like I am caught in the middle. Don't know what to do. Cain promised a big bonus if I stay until it's done. What do you want me to do? I was glad to hear that Eunice is there. Thank her for me. Have you found a girl's name yet? Better hurry.

*What do you think of using Eunice? Let me know. I love you dearly,
don't forget that. T.*

August 23, 1825

*Congratulations, Papa. YOU HAVE ANOTHER SON. Diantha
says he is to be named Alfred Nelson. He is well and so is the mother.
She's a trooper, Titus. You did marry well. Hope you get home soon.
I will probably be gone when you do. We plan to leave any day, but I
won't leave until Diantha is a little stronger. Take care of yourself and
know that you are missed.
Lovingly, Your sister,
Eunice
P.S. Diantha wants to add a note:
Oh, Darling. He's here. He's healthy. I'm fine and happy, but so
tired. I miss you. I love you. Diantha
Oh yes, Lucy had a baby girl: Theresa Arathusa Morley*

October 1825

*Dearest Diantha,
What can I say? My heart isn't in this project any more, only
because it left months ago to be with you. It pains me that I have not
yet held our son. So thankful that both he and you are doing well.
Don't let him grow up until I get back. It will be soon. All eighty-two
locks are complete and operating. A canal boat called the "Seneca
Chief" is scheduled for a maiden run on the twenty-sixth of this month.
It leaves from Buffalo and will follow our waterway clear to New York
City. Cain invited me to the celebration when it arrives. Should be the
first week in November. They are going all out. Sounds like it will be
elaborate. The best part will be when they dump a barrel of Lake Erie
water into the Atlantic Ocean. I'm happy for them and so glad to see
the end of this job. Told Cain the celebration for me was waiting in
Ohio. He agreed. He's a good man. My last check and a good bonus
will be ready tomorrow. I'm headed home first thing the next morning.
Until then . . . I love you the most! If I have my way, I will never be apart
from you again.
With all my heart,
Your Titus*

Historical Background

We have no indication that Titus worked on or used the Erie Canal. Plans for such a waterway were first discussed in 1783, exactly ten years before he was born. Construction began July 1817 and continued until October 1825, two months after Alfred Nelson Billings was born. When Titus' mother died, in 1820, he could have run into the project if, indeed, he was able to cross over New York in a return to Massachusetts, where she was buried. At any rate, we believe that Grandpa Titus was a hard worker and we know that later he dug canals in Utah. Perhaps he helped dig trenches to drain the swamp at Nauvoo as well.

"Many years later, Alonzo Billings, the youngest child and only son of Titus and Mary Ann, wanted to farm a ranch in south-central Utah, near Loa. He dug a trench until it was deep enough to draw water from the Fremont River. He continued digging a channel with the necessary downgrade for proper water level to keep a steady flow with him around the hill and all the way down to his crops" (BillingsEA, 2).

Later, "Alonzo was foreman at the construction of Milford Dam for Delta, Utah. Strong horse teams pulling big scraper-boards about 3 or 4 feet wide and shaped like dustpans, crossed through the stream to dump dirt and rocks in strategic places. When the flow was slowed near the end of the project, employees with big, strong horses were fearful of getting bogged in the mud. Alonzo's seventeen-year-old son, Claude D. Billings volunteered "Molly and Madge" his miss-matched team (one big horse and one little horse) to finish the job closing the flow and damming the Sevier River" (BillingsEA; BillingsGO). The same Alonzo Billings was a member of the Board of Directors for "water users of Fish Lake and Fremont River. He represented the Fremont legal precinct along with F. Archie Young in 1889" (Russell M).

These letters are historical fiction. Mr. Cain is imaginary.

CHAPTER 14

Titus Billings returned from working on the Erie Canal with a new toy, well, a new musical instrument, purchased to fill long, lonely evenings. He must have found lots of time to practise, or maybe it was just his inborn talent again. At any rate, he was a marvelous harmonica player when he got home.

"Play Yankee Doodle," Sammy pleaded. Titus did. The same request came again and again and again.

"This mouth-organ needs rest," he said at last.

"So do your sons," said their mother.

Titus wrestled and rolled with them, then scooted all three off to bed.

"I love your new talent, "she told him, "but don't let it keep you from whistling too."

"Whatever," was all he said.

"It is a good year for flax," Isaac Morley said. Titus agreed. "Good year for sheep too." They had sheared an abundant supply of wool.

"Well, it is a good thing," Titus said. "I gotta wife who loves to spin and weave and stitch." Isaac laughed.

"Seems I remember telling you my little sister could sew and cook and do everything." Diantha was living proof. She made all of the family clothing and hired out for several jobs as well, including knitting, now that she had conquered the skill.

That was not all. Diantha Billings was again in a motherly way. Now Titus enjoyed his sons, all three of them, and taught them to work according to their ages. He could be happy with many more, but Diantha, he knew, wanted a daughter. She needed a daughter. Often she would threaten to sew dainty lace and bows onto garments for his boys to wear. Oh, he knew she was teasing, of course. Truth is, he wished for a daughter too.

*   *   *

"Are you going to the picnic?" Mother Morley asked.

"Wouldn't miss it," Diantha said.

"Wasn't sure if you'd be up to it. Pretty warm out, these

63

days."

July has a way of being warm, that's true, but it would take a great deal more than that to keep the Billings family away from a Fourth of July celebration. After all, Titus was judging the greased pig wrestling contest.

"So we're meeting at the usual place, on the east branch of the Chagrin River, right?" Diantha inquired.

"That's right, where Stoneybrook runs into it. See you there," her mother replied.

Titus and the two older boys pulled their wagon up to Morley's door. They would take the older children for an early start. The women, both heavy with child, would follow with picnic baskets and the two-year-olds, Alfred and Theresa, in Lucy's wagon.

Philena, already a teenager, looked charming in her lemon yellow dress. Twelve-year-old Lucy Diantha climbed in beside her. Editha, who was nine (same as her cousin Sammy), and Isaac's Cordelia, the four-year-old, wore large white bows in their hair. Isaac came last with his arms full of tiny red, white, and blue flags. As always, he was in charge of the program.

The day was beautiful, the weather cooperated, and the food was tasty. Everyone, it seemed, from Kirtland and all of Mentor was present. Perhaps that is the reason they met at the river between both towns.

Contests were held for all ages. Relay races, tug-of-wars, nail-hammering, log sawing, pie eating, pole climbing, stick pulling, and all other events were celebrated with a variety of prizes. As always, the greased pig wrestling was the climax.

Titus was on duty when his son came to watch. Sammy, too young to take part, loved the squealing creatures and laughed at the muddy contestants. In the thick of it, Titus managed to keep himself quite clean, until one of the pigs got out of hand, knocking its victim to the ground and sending the poor soul's eyeglasses flying.

"I can't see without those!" he shouted.

Pigs are dangerous animals. They will eat anything, and anybody, within reach. In an effort to reclaim the rebellious pig and to rescue man and glasses from its approaching jaws, Titus Billings took a tumble and landed flat on his back. In the mud, underneath the squirming armful, he was completely unaware of an object escaping his pocket. Sammy noticed. Before anyone could stop him, the youngster was in the pen too.

"Pa, pa!" he shouted.

"Get back, son, get back!"

"But you dropped–"

Sammy dove for a shiny object partially embedded in the mud while the sightless contestant patted the ground in hopes of retrieving his spectacles and Titus, well, he tried to get up. Unbalanced by pig poundage under one arm, he desperately reached out the other as a helping hand to his son. Again he slipped. Losing grip and balance he fell all the way to the ground, this time landing face down in oozing mud.

The crowd was breathless. Samuel crawled back to the log fence and three volunteers cornered the pig. At length Brother Billings arose with slow, sober movement. Standing in silence he placed the muddy specs onto his muddy face. Relieved onlookers exploded with laughter -- loud, hearty, enduring laughter.

"There will never be another contest like that one," someone shouted.

"Not in my lifetime," Titus replied. Then he spoke to Sammy. "Are you all right, son?"

"I saved it, Pa!" Sammy held up a mud-covered harmonica. "It would have been lost forever if I hadn't saved it."

"Good job, boy. Good job." Titus patted his oldest son on the back. It was a muddy hand on a muddy back. They joined in laughter with the crowd and returned the mud-caked spectacles to a grateful owner.

"We better take a dip in the river before your ma sees us, don't ya think?" Titus said. Sammy liked the sound of that. Together they walked into the Chagrin River, clothes and all, because their clothes were as muddy as they were.

When Diantha next saw her husband and son, they were trying to drip themselves dry. Numerous informants had delivered every detail to her, time and again. She laughed so hard she began fearing her baby might come early. However, *he* did not. George Pierce Billings was born on the twenty-fifth day of the month in a quiet, normal delivery. His parents were so relieved and happy; they didn't seem to mind at all that he was not a girl.

Historical Background

George Pierce Billings was born July, 25, 1827 on the "Morley Farm" between Mentor, Ohio and Kirtland, Ohio (Bennion 1; Esplin 1).

CHAPTER 15

Diantha opened the wooden chest and worked her hand down to the bottom of it. From there she retrieved a brown package. Without looking, she knew exactly what it contained. Eight years ago, when twin daughters were born dead, she had purposely stuck it there, under everything else, in a spiteful effort to push it out of her life. Now, at last, things were different. She wanted to see it again.

Carefully she unfolded the wrapping. The delicate wedding lace, still flawless, had not yellowed in the least. Tradition could be satisfied after all. Diantha looked with fondness at the tiny baby girl sleeping in a home-made cradle. *Titus was right*, she smiled to herself. He believed carving flowers on a cradle would guarantee a daughter this time. It was difficult to say who was most delighted, the father or the mother. At any rate, the Billings Family was blessed with a healthy baby on the third day of January 1830, a daughter at last!

Little Eunice would grow up fast, far too fast. Of that, Diantha was certain. Still she took pleasure in the thought that someday her little princess would drape Grandma Morley's lace over her head, as brides had done for two generations before. This treasured veil, she vowed, must be guarded for that wedding day.

A knock at the door interrupted her dream. Titus responded. With care she returned the treasure to its chest, only this time at the very top. Masculine voices beckoned to her curiosity. Titus spoke to a stranger. Isaac was there too.

"Invite them in, dear," she instructed.

Lyman Wight was a long, lanky fellow. His hair was dark, yet he grew a light beard. Seemingly good-natured and spiritually attuned, he had come with excitement about a proposal for Mr. Morley and Mr. Billings.

"Just like in the Bible," she heard him saying, "We would have all things in common. Think how advantageous that would be."

Titus reached for the family Bible and turning to the second chapter of Acts he read aloud verses, 44 and 45: "And all that believed were together, and had all things in common; and sold their possessions and goods, and parted them to all men, as every man had need."

Neither Titus nor Isaac had met Mr. Wight before. Somehow he had heard about them. Isaac was impressed with the new idea. Titus could not see any reason why it would not work. The more they talked, the more agreeable they seemed to be. Before their guest left he had been invited to move his family into Morley's house on a permanent basis.

*   *   *

After church sermon on Sunday, Titus, with his brother-in-law, waited outside the Mentor chapel until its crowd thinned and its preacher was available for serious talk.

"We're planning to start a common stock community up at the farm," Isaac said.

Sidney Rigdon was pleased with the news. Although he embraced and preached these concepts from the New Testament, the local congregation of Mentor would not accept such ideas or proposals. Now his friends were willing to give this lifestyle a try at the Morley Farm. Excitement seemed to keep the three men warm in spite of the winter chill. The same was not so for their wives and children huddled under quilts in waiting wagons. At length, Samuel was dispatched to summon his father.

"Wight is moving his family in with us the first of February. When we get a few more families we will be holding our own church services at the Farm," Isaac said. "We still want you to visit."

Rigdon agreed to do so and offered his blessing upon them.

"We welcome your preaching any time you can come," Isaac said.

"Truly we do," Titus added with a strong handshake.

As springtime blossomed, so did the community farm. Eight other families joined the organization and moved into small homes built on the Morley-Billings property, two miles outside of Kirtland, Ohio. As promised, church services were held at the farm each Sabbath. Reverent Sidney Rigdon did visit, often.

"I feel a great peace and union in this set-up," Lyman Wight preached. "I have begun to feel as if the millennium is close at hand."

Up and down the valley the group became known as

"The Family." With such rapid growth, a larger meeting place was needed. Many gatherings were held outside, when weather permitted. Soon the common law families had enough children to justify a schoolhouse, too. Such were his thoughts as Titus walked with Isaac to the top of the hill beside their homestead.

"What about this spot?" Titus asked.

Isaac took in the view and smiled as he nodded his head. "Fine choice," he said. "This is a proper place for our school. Let's build it right here in the trees."

Twelve-year-old Sam and ten-year-old Ebenezer were very good workers. Both were excited about building a schoolhouse. Five-year-old Alfred always tagged along, certain his father could do nothing without him.

"You stay in the wagon and keep a lookout, son. When you see a tree start to fall, shout out a warning like this: TIMBER!" Titus said. "Now, you must be in the wagon at all times so you'll have a better view. Keep an eye on all of these trees too. Can you do that?"

"Yes Pa, I can do it," young Alfred said with courageous confidence.

Titus walked deep into the trees until no possible chance existed for his precious wagon load to be in danger of falling timber. He felled several at a time before calling the older boys to help remove branches with their hatchets. Alfred still had wagon detail. He had to count and guard all the tree trunks as they were loaded up. The best part, for him, was the wagon ride up the hill to deliver new logs.

Many days were spent working the trees into lumber and laying them out to dry. When at last the timbers were ready for raising the new schoolhouse everyone gathered to help and to feast and to celebrate.

The hilltop building was tightly framed with fourteen-foot walls on all four sides. To Diantha it was impressive from its lofty setting. She was proud of her husband and her hard working offspring who mirrored their father at nearly every turn.

Historical Background

Titus Billings is listed on the 1830 Population Census of Ohio (Harter, 266). Eunice was a newborn babe when the Restored Church was organized, April 6,

1830 (Bennion1; Esplin1; D&C 20:1). "The Titus Billings Family were members of a congregation led by the gifted and highly acclaimed orator, Sidney, Rigdon of Mentor, Ohio, and they lived out of town about two miles from his home" (Davis, 67).

Lyman Wight records in his journal about forming a group to live as a "common stock family" on the Morley Farm. About the origin of this agreement he writes: "I now began to look at the doctrine of the Apostles pretty closely, especially that part contained in the second chapter of the Acts of the Apostles, where they had all things common. In consideration of this doctrine I went to Kirtland, almost 20 miles, to see Br. Isaac Morley and Br. Titus Billings. After some conversation on the subject we entered into a covenant to make our interests one as anciently. I, in conformity to this covenant, moved the next February [1830] to Kirtland into the house with Br. Morley. We commenced our labors together in great peace and union; we were soon joined by eight other families. Our labors were united both in farming and mechanism, all of which was prosecuted with great vigor. We truly began to feel as if the Millennium was close at hand" (Andrus, 96; Cook, 82-23; Davis, 67; Davis1, 89; Prusha, 40; Smith1, 153).

"As Reformed Baptists of the Western Reserve compared their interpretations of the New Testament with views espoused by Alexander Campbell and other restorationist preachers, some concluded that those restorationists were teaching incorrect doctrines. In an attempt to restore New Testament Christianity more fully, Isaac Morley persuaded some of Sidney Rigdon's followers to create a communitarian system, with all things held in common. Thus, about five families, including those of Lyman Wight, and Titus Billings, pooled their property and established an order called the "Family" or the "Big Family." A few families living in Mayfield organized a similar society. While Sidney Rigdon apparently approved this action, Alexander Campbell denounced the system" (Backman, 35).

White House

Lush trees still adorn the Morley Farm property.
Of course the house is a more recent addition.

(Courtesy S. B. Mitchell, 2002.)

Mailbox

Morley's Farm was located on the
road between Kirtland and Mentor.

(Courtesy S.B. Mitchell, 2002.)

CHAPTER 16

With exquisite penmanship he signed the birth certificate and dated it June 5, 1830. Edward Tuttle's wife always said he should have been a scribe or an artist because of his gifted hand, but he was a baker and that suited him fine. Catherine Vanever Geyer Tuttle smiled up at him.

"Did you spell it correctly this time?" she teased. The new baby would be known as Mary Ann Tuttle. Eighteen months before, such a name had been chosen, but Edward had written Martha Ann instead. Now little Martha Ann and her older sister, eight-year-old Caroline, had a new baby sister. Maybe that would offset their having four older, rugged brothers: Edward Wells [thirteen], Joseph Wells [twelve], Thomas Wells [ten] and Henry Withington [four].

Edward Tuttle, son of Joseph and Elizabeth Pratt Tuttle, was a short, balding man who owned and operated Tuttle's Bakery Shop, starting each day long before busy Boston saw the sunlight. Being a baker in 1830 was not an easy task. Ed milled his own grain and stoked wood fires in stone ovens, both indoors and outdoors. He found delight in his work and his roly-poly shadow evidenced that he enjoyed the taste of what he baked.

Mrs. Tuttle was a learned woman and a slender one, in spite of the bakery. Her parents, George and Mary Lockland Geyer, were of Puritan descent. Sabbath Day adherence and Bible reading were strong priorities in their home. As a child Catherine had learned how to read from the pages of the old family Bible. Now an avid reader, she constantly searched for new material. A large trunk housed her collection of precious books. All books were precious to her. Edward had promised to build her a bookcase on the south wall, but she wondered when he would ever find the time.

The boys made deliveries for their father every day. Business was good. Fortunately the bakery was not far from their home. Before the new baby came Catherine found herself spending more time working in the bakery than working in the house. Now, only a few months after giving birth, she needed to go back.

"Caroline, keep an eye on the baby. I am going to help your pa at the bakery."

Catherine intended to take Little Henry with her. He was

born with a twisted leg and walked with a stick. For some reason, he did not want to go with her this time.

"I'm leaving now," Catherine said. "You will need to look out for Henry too."

She started down the street and almost reached "Tuttle's Bakery" when she heard screaming behind her. Catherine turned to see Caroline running from the house and into the street. Something was wrong, but she could not understand the shrill, screeching of her hysterical daughter. Rushing back she grabbed the youngster by the shoulders and demanded an answer. "What is wrong? Caroline! Caroline, what is wrong?"

"The baby . . ." was all she heard. It was enough. Catherine rushed inside. Henry was sprawled on the cabin floor, sobbing. The bassinet was tipped on its side and empty. Where was the baby? Where was tiny Mary Ann? Catherine pulled up the quilt. Only the corner gave way. A calm, innocent baby lay caught between its layers.

"Look, Henry," Catherine said. It was obvious that Henry had upset the baby's bed, probably while climbing up to see her. He and his sister feared the worst, but the baby was fine.

"Look at this, Henry," Catherine said again. "Do you see?"

By now Caroline was standing above her mother. Henry still sat on the floor. Gently Catherine lifted her baby and patted the thick quilt still positioned on the floor.

"Angels have helped us," she said. "Look how carefully they pulled this quilt out to land first and cushion our baby's fall." Before up-righting the baby bed Catherine Tuttle knelt with her young children and prayed a thank you to their God.

Historical Background

Mary Ann Tuttle [to become Titus' second wife] was born in 1830 (BillingsEA4, 1; BillingsGO; Black,85;) in Boston, Massachusetts, to Edward [1 July 1792] and Catherine Geyer [13 August 1796]Tuttle (DavisH). Her June 5th birthday made her six months younger than Titus and Diantha's daughter, Eunice.

Edward and Catherine's children (and birth dates) are as follows: Edward Wells, 23 February 1817; Joseph Wells, 23 July 1818; Thomas Wells, 19 April 1820; Caroline Elizabeth, 17 November 1822; Henry Withington, 12 November 1826; Martha Ann, 8 June 1828; Mary Ann, 5 June 1830; John Wells, 1 Mar 1832; and Samuel Wells, 17 August 1834 (Davis, H., Family Group Sheet). Edward was a baker by trade. His older sons remained in Massachusetts.

CHAPTER 17

By the time autumn colors adorned the Morley Farm in 1830 its Big Family Organization had grown in number and recognition. Five more families living seven miles up the Chagrin River wanted to join. Because they already owned good farms and good mills Father Morley appointed Lyman Wight to move into Mayfield and open a new branch of "The Kirtland Family Community." Lyman's wagons were loaded and his family was ready to start out when four well-dressed men walked up the dirt road to the Morley Farm.

"We are representatives of the Lord, Jesus Christ," they announced. Lyman was eager to get on his way, but Isaac thought Common Family Members should examine any message professed to be from Deity. Titus agreed with a curious interest.

A meeting was called and everyone living on the Morley Farm was asked to attend. Makeshift benches were produced quickly by overlapping boards across the top of Morley's barrels. A similar meeting, they learned, had been held the previous night for an overflowing crowd at the little white church in Mentor where Reverend Rigdon still preached.

"Rigdon and I go way back," the first messenger remarked. "Years ago we promised to share with each other, if either of us ever found pure truth. We have come from the East to tell you about a true church and this newly published book which explains our beliefs."

The fact that Sidney Rigdon endorsed these men, was now reading the new book, and had allowed them to preach to his congregation, gave the common-law farmers a ripe incentive to hear the message. The meeting began.

Mr. Pratt was a clean-cut man. His fine facial features were accented with dark, piercing eyes. His hair was thick and curly, where he had hair. Much of it was disappearing from the front and sides. He stood with dignity and spoke with authority and conviction. Onlookers were spellbound.

The story was simple, yet almost unbelievable. He spoke of angels from heaven appearing to a young boy. He declared that there was a God. The same young boy had seen him, even God the Father, in person. He had also seen Jesus Christ. They were two distinct, separate personages.

Titus listened intently. At first he felt somewhat amused, but then Parley Parker Pratt testified: "These things are the living truth. I know that a young soon-to-be prophet found the Living God as he prayed in a sacred grove of trees in New York State."

An old familiar feeling rekindled itself in the heart of Titus Billings. He recognized it as the same peaceful feeling that had wrapped around him in the forest several years before.

The next speaker was thin faced, well-groomed, and good looking too. His speech was eloquent. He seemed to be confident and well educated. Listeners were attentive to his message for he also spoke with strong conviction. The man, by the name of Oliver Cowdery, held up the new book.

"This book is called *The Book of Mormon*. I had the honor of assisting with its transcription. I cannot overemphasize the fact that I did not help write this book. It was written thousands of years ago by ancient prophets living on these lands we call the Americas. They engraved their words on sheets of gold, to preserve them for future generations. These golden pages of true history were hidden in a stone box buried in a hillside in New York. No one knew of them and no one could have found them because an angel of God kept watch over them."

Titus heard Diantha breathe deeply. His own mind was spinning. This Cowdery man was so intense. He even went on to call the angel by name.

"On earth this angel had lived the life of a man named Moroni. He was the last person to record on the sacred plates. Moroni was a sole survivor. All of his people were destroyed in battle. God spared his life so he could finish and hide the record. He spent forty lonely years in hiding while he abridged and organized histories to be read by generations yet to come."

Forty years? What sort of man would live alone, in danger every day, as the sole survivor of his tribe, to work on a book for people he would never know? Writing? Abridging? Hiding? . . . For forty lonely years? If any man could care that much about such a book, I would be interested in reading it, Titus thought to himself.

"Now is the time. The Lord has chosen our generation to restore all things," the man continued. "Moroni returned to earth and showed young Joseph Smith where to find the record. He gave detailed instructions of how and when the plates should be removed from their hiding place and translated into our language."

Again Mr. Cowdery held up the book. "In this book you will find light and truth from above. God lives. He loves His children who dwell upon this earth. He still wants to communicate with us, like He did in times of old. You, each of you, are literal offspring of this living, loving God. He wants you to read this book and find truth for yourself."

For some time the speaker went on, explaining how a young boy named Joseph Smith had been searching for answers about God. While he was reading in the *Bible* one day, a verse of scripture jumped out at him and pricked his heart. It was James 1:5 that states, "If any of you lack wisdom, let him ask of God . . ." So with faith, the fourteen-year-old lad secretly entered a grove of trees by his home and knelt in prayer to ask of God.

Now really, to see angels and claim that a *boy* actually saw *God* and His son, *Jesus*, standing above the ground? That was heavy stuff. It was a great deal to believe; and yet, Titus Billings did believe it, every word. He wanted to believe it. He felt good inside when he believed it. This was the answer, his answer, for he too had been searching. He too had prayed. Deep in his heart he felt a powerful peace that expanded throughout his being. A soft hand slipped into his. Turning slightly, he could see Diantha. Her face was glowing. Her beautiful blue eyes were mirrored in tears. She felt it too! They had no idea what God would have them do; but whatever it was, they would do it for Him, together, with joyful hearts.

Historical Background

Parley P. Pratt, Oliver Cowdery, Peter Whitmer, and Ziba Peterson left in October by foot. Near Buffalo, New York, they placed two copies of the Book of Mormon with members of the Cattaraugus tribe who treated them well, but had difficulty understanding their words. Two hundred miles later they had the honor of meeting and presenting a Book of Mormon to the famed orator, Sidney Rigdon. He was already prejudiced with a Bible and would not debate them, but did agree to read the new book. He also consented to a request that they preach to his Campbellite congregation (AndersonLF, 49; Widtsoe, 136).

According to Heber C. Kimball: "These missionaries left in the fall of 1830. On the way they stopped at Kirtland, Ohio, and the neighboring villages. There they preached the newly restored gospel with astonishing results . . . [to] hundreds of settlers who were seekers after truth. Alexander Campbell and his flock were there. Some of these, Lyman Wight, Isaac Morley, and Titus Billings, belonged to a group which attempted to have all things in common. There also Parley P. Pratt presented to Sidney Rigdon, his old friend and teacher, a copy of the Book of Mormon" (Widtsoe, 136).

"The preaching appointment, was published from house to house and a large and respectable congregation assembled. Oliver Cowdery and Parley P. Pratt severally addressed the meeting. At the conclusion Elder Rigdon arose and stated to the congregation that the information they had that evening received, was of an extraordinary character, and certainly demanded their most serious consideration: and as the apostle [Paul]advised his brethren "to prove all things, and hold fast that which is good," so he would exhort his brethren to do like-wise, and give the matter a careful investigation; and not turn against it, without being fully convinced of its being an imposition, lest they should, possibly, resist the truth"(Davis, 63/89).

"About two miles from Rigdon's home a group of members of his church, viz., Lyman Wight, Isaac Morley, and Titus Billings, had 'all things common,' and the missionaries went to present the gospel to them" (Davis, 90). "Ultimately there were about one hundred people in all in Morley's family" (Prusha, 40).

"Go Into the Wilderness"

Parley P. Pratt, Ziba Peterson, Oliver Cowdery and Peter Whitmer carried the Word of God to Ohio.

(Courtesy Robert T. Barrett.)

CHAPTER 18

Limited copies of the precious new book were shared back and forth. Visitors thronged to the vicinity. Four elders -- men of God -- Parley P. Pratt, Oliver Cowdery, Peter Whitmer and Ziba Peterson, preached the restored gospel to Mentor and Kirtland residents, and to those living between the two townships on Morley's Farm. For seven wonderful weeks nothing else was thought of or discussed. It was a time of discovery and rejoicing. Answers avalanched from heaven, for God had spoken again. There was so much to hear and so much to learn.

"Parley, my friend, you have found truth indeed and delivered it to me," Sidney Rigdon admitted after becoming convinced that his ordination and baptism must be invalid because he now realized he had "no authority to minister the ordinances of God. I thank you and stand ready now to be baptized by immersion, according to our Lord, at the authority of your hand."

All four missionaries and Rigdon's entire congregation, probably all of Mentor Township, followed him to the river's edge where Ohio's first baptism was to take place. Many "would-be" saints were ready to covenant with the Lord in the waters of baptism. Sidney and his wife were baptized November 8, 1830 by Oliver Cowdery.

Again, after a meeting in Isaac Morley's home on November 15, 1830, families and friends clustered along the riverbank where Stoneybrook meets up with the Chagrin. Fervent praises were sung at the water's edge and another baptism ceremony began, this time for residents of the Morley Farm and Kirtland, Ohio. Diantha, like others, stood with dry towels and ready quilts draped over her arm. Titus cuddled little Eunice until her twelve-year-old cousin, Editha Ann, begged to hold her. The boys watched and wiggled nearby.

Parley P. Pratt and Isaac Morley stepped into the water. The river was cold, but a warm spirit seemed to wrap itself around both of them. Elder Pratt raised his arm to the square and offered an exact and proper prayer. Isaac was immersed and came up beaming.

Titus Billings reached a helping hand to his newly baptized

brother-in-law as he started into the water himself. A second time Elder Pratt preformed the saving ordinance. Tall Titus bent his knees and went down easy, then came up out of the cold river water with a burning assurance of the truth and rightness of his new baptism. Reaching out to his wife, he guarded her steps and led her through the water to that same Elder Pratt. Diantha Morley Billings also felt a penetrating joy that numbed any awareness of November's chill, even while standing in icy water.

One after another, eager persons stepped forward to be cleansed and become members of God's church on earth. Lucy Morley and her three oldest daughters (Philena, seventeen; Lucy Diantha, fifteen; and Editha Ann, twelve) were also baptized. Samuel Billings (age twelve) and his ten-year-old brother, Ebenezer, followed them. Children had to be at least eight years of age to be accountable for baptism.

Hugs were shared. Tears were plentiful. Sunlight lingered as long as possible setting itself in blending colors across the sky until it finally gave in to the darkness of night. Families started for home, but Titus stood staring. He could not yet pull away. *If only I could hold onto this feeling and carry it with me wherever I go,* he wished.

Diantha had been too excited with anticipation to sleep the night before. Tonight she was filled with joy beyond measure. Though she needed it, sleep was far from her. She lay quietly, hoping not to awaken her tired husband, but her mind was too jubilant to rest.

"Do you feel clean?" a voice asked her.

He wasn't asleep. Shaking from her own thoughts, she tried to focus on what her husband was saying.

"Do you feel clean?" he repeated.

"Oh yes, my darling. I feel clean all over, and so happy. Do you?"

His long arm reached out for her.

"We have been baptized now by immersion, and by authority from God himself."

Gently she rested her head on his chest. She felt safe in his arms. There she could fall asleep.

"Thank you," she whispered.

Historical Background

"At length Mr. Rigdon and many others become convinced that they had no authority to minister the ordinances of God; and that they had not been legally baptized and ordained. They, therefore, came forward and were baptized by us, and received the gift of the Holy Ghost by the laying on of hands, and prayer in the name of Jesus Christ" (Pratt, 47).

"On November 1830, Isaac Morley was baptized and confirmed a member of the Mormon Church by Parley P. Pratt" (BorenKR&LL, 26). "On November 30, 1830 Parley P. Pratt baptized Isaac Morley, his wife, and all the children, except three who were not yet eight years old" (MorleyCO,2).

"Titus Billings became the 2nd member of the Church in Kirtland/was the second person baptized in Kirtland, Ohio" (Billings/Shaw/Hale, 5; Brewster, 45; Flake 509; Hale, 7; Heslop; Jensen1, 242; Ludlow, 337; McCune, 19; Pyne, 2). "Diantha was the first woman baptized there" (Madsen, 199; WhitneyEA). "Samuel and Ebenezer Billings received proxy baptisms in the Manti Temple on 9 July 1889" (Bennion1).

Thomas' work was done 28 June 1949 in the Manti Temple (Allgood, Sharon).

"Titus Billings was baptized November 15, 1830" (BillingsGO, 1; Black, 577; Black2, 23; Cannon/Cook 249; Cook 102; Davis, 444; Heslop; Holzapfel/Cottle/ Stoddard, 144; RLDS Archive, 242; Deseret News; Tullidge, 429; by Parley P. Pratt; Jensen1, 242).

"By the middle of November 1830, many of Sidney Rigdon's followers in Kirtland were convinced that the gospel of Christ had been restored to the earth, and all of the approximately fifty members of the communal society, including Isaac Morley, Titus Billings, Lyman Wight, their wives, and many of their children, had been baptized. Within a few weeks Newel K. Whitney and Frederick G. Williams also joined the Church" (Backman, 1).

Before leaving the vicinity missionaries recorded, "In two or three weeks from our arrival in the neighborhood with the news, we had baptized one-hundred and twenty-seven souls, and this number soon increased to one thousand" (Pratt, 48).

"Within a week others had followed and Pratt reported the baptizing of 127 people in the East Branch of the Chagrin River" (Prusha, 40). "Other Kirtlanders who converted to the new faith were Luke and Lyman Johnson; Newell K. Whitney, owner of the local store; Orson Hyde, an orphan who clerked in

Whitney's store; Frederick G. Williams, who had recently come to Kirtland to practice botanical medicine; and Titus Billings" (Prusha, 41).

"All seventeen souls living as a 'common stock family' on Isaac Morley's farm were brought into the Restored Church" (MorleyRH, 9-10).

Red House

Morley and Billings were baptized where the Sunnybrook meets the Chagrin River, behind the Warren Parrish home (pictured) in Kirtland, Ohio.

(Courtesy S. B. Mitchell, 2002.)

Baptism Spot

The water level was low when these pictures were taken,
nearly 200 years later.

(Courtesy S. B. Mitchell, 2002.)

Historic Kirtland Ohio

This map shows the changes made when the LDS Kirtland Visitors' Center was re-dedicated. Please note how two places (Whitmer Road and Smith Road) have been disconnected from State Road 306, making it more convenient and safe to cross over from the Visitor's Center to the Whitney Store. Also, please locate where the Stoney Brook runs into the East Branch of the Chagrin River, now believed to be the spot where early baptisms took place. Used by permission. (Courtesy Intellectual Reserve.)

Old Kirtland Visitor Center

For many years a large framed photograph of Titus Billings hung on the wall of the Old Kirtland Visitor Center and tour guides would state that he was the second person baptized in Kirtland. Always someone would ask who was first. The answer was uncertain. I grew up hearing that he, my great-great grandfather, was the second person baptized in Kirtland, Ohio on November 15, 1830. After much research and prayerfully preparing this book as requested by my father, Evan A. Billings (pictured) I find it easy to believe that Isaac Morley was first and Titus followed, as was their way in everything they did.

(Courtesy S. B. Mitchell, 2002.)

83

Chapter 19

Like a forest fire, the news of a Golden Bible spread to little towns along the Western Reserve. Within many souls, it left a burning of faith that could not be denied. Others ran from it with fear or blazing hatred.

Every member of Morley's "Big Family" community was quick to join the newly restored church. "They brought the *Book of Mormon* to bear upon us," Lyman Wight said, "and the whole common stock family was baptized."

Father Morley, as Isaac was now called more often than not, welcomed a large gathering into his home. Diantha shook her head as she entered. He knew it meant that their father was not willing to come. Sister Rollins and her children arrived early also. The young widow and her pre-teen daughter, Mary Elizabeth, had been baptized soon after they moved into Kirtland, but her son, James Henry, was still investigating. Before the meeting started, young Mary Elizabeth approached Kirtland's presiding elder.

"Father Morley," she said. "May I take your Golden Bible home and read it while you have the meeting?" Thinking that she probably wanted only to look at real gold, he held the sacred book in front of her and opened its pages.

"You may look at it child, but see, it isn't gold. My copy is just a printed book. Only the original was made of gold and the Angel Moroni took those plates back."

"Oh, I know all of that," Mary said. "But I want to read what it says inside. I want to find the truth for myself."

Morley was taken back by the sincere intent of one so young. She gazed at the book with reverence and communicated her overwhelming desire to read from its pages.

Only a few copies were available. Father Morley hesitated. This special copy had been sent to him from the Prophet Joseph. *Not the sort of thing you'd give to a child,* he thought to himself. Then he looked into her pleading eyes. There was no doubt. This twelve-year-old was hungry for the gospel. How could he stand in her way?

"Child," he said, "If you will bring the book back before breakfast tomorrow morning, you may take it."

Mary Elizabeth was elated. Her mother and brother

stayed for the meeting, but she ran home to the Whitney-Gilbert Mercantile where she lived with Algernon Sidney Gilbert and his wife, her mother's sister.

Never did that door open faster nor bang louder.

"Uncle Sidney! Uncle Sidney!" she shouted. "Here is the Golden Bible!"

At once they started reading aloud, taking turns until late into the night. At the first sign of daylight Mary's eyes were in the book again. She memorized the first verse before returning the treasured volume as she had promised.

"I guess you did not read much in it," Father Morley said when he saw her. Mary showed him the place where they had ended. Then she recited, word for word, the first verse in the *Book of Mormon*. "I can't even do that," he laughed. Accurately she walked him through the story of Nephi. Father Morley was impressed. Recovering from the surprise of it all, he hugged her with tenderness and said, "Child, take this book home and finish it. I can wait."

In less than two months one hundred and twenty-seven souls took upon themselves the name of Christ. The new church in this part of God's vineyard was now larger in membership than in New York State where it had been restored.

Because none of the new members had, as yet, been instructed in the duties and expectations of their new commitment, Sidney Rigdon and Edward Partridge journeyed to Fayette, New York, seeking instruction from the Prophet. Others met together often in the hilltop schoolhouse at Morley's Farm.

With such increase of knowledge came strong feelings and deep questions. Titus and Diantha enjoyed discussing the new concepts and reasoning them together. There was so much to feast upon. Most teachings were comfortable, but sometimes there was confusion. Several new members claimed "manifestations." Some could see angels. Others had received letters that floated down from heaven. These unnatural distortions were distasteful to Titus and to his wife, who sat together in a religious meeting when a man named "Black Pete" jumped up from his seat shouting: "I am a revelator. I was a revelator in the life before this world was." When he started reciting wild ideas, a few onlookers joined in.

"Look," he said. "Do you see it?"

Titus looked into the direction that he pointed and saw nothing. An uneasy feeling was building inside him.

"It's a revelation being carried by a black angel." He started for the door. "Come, we must catch it!"

Black Pete ran down the road with an excited group behind him. They followed him to the edge of the Chagrin River. Titus could not believe his eyes when he saw Pete run right off a twenty-five-foot cliff! He fell through the top of a tree, which slowed his descent, and landed in the river. Titus helped with the rescue. The "inspired" runner ended up with only scrapes and scratches, however, the plunge seemed to cool his pride a bit.

*   *   *

Having received a revelation for church members to gather in Kirtland, Ohio the Prophet Joseph Smith and his attractive wife, Emma, returned with Rigdon and Partridge.

The Smith couple stayed in town a few weeks with the Newell K. Whitney family. Whitney's partner, A.S. Gilbert, had a young niece that Joseph wanted to meet. He had heard about the Rollins child who had persuaded Father Morley to share his rare gift copy of the new *Book of Mormon*. Mary Elizabeth was introduced to the Prophet. For a long moment he looked deeply into her eyes then he placed hands on her head and offered a blessing.

"You keep this *Book of Mormon*," he said. "You have earned it. I'll get another for Father Morley."

Historical Background

"In the true sense of the word, this 'common stock' order of things was not the same system as described in scripture. Nevertheless, when Joseph Smith received the 'law of consecration and stewardship' from the Lord, he had only to direct the 'family' living on the Morley farm into the appropriate patterns. Here the stage was already prepared for the principles revealed through the Prophet Joseph Smith" (MorleyRH, 9-10).

" …many signs and wonders [were] seen in the heavens above and in the earth beneath in the region of Kirtland, both by saints and stranger. A pillar of light was seen every evening for more than a month hovering over the place here we did our baptizing" (Lambert, 78).

"There was an attempt in Kirtland, a society that had undertaken to have a community of property; it has sometimes been denominated the Morley Family, as there were a number of them located on a farm owned by Captain Isaac Morley. There persons had been baptized, but had not yet been instructed in relation to their duties. A false spirit entered into them, developing their singular, extravagant and wild ideas. They had a meeting at the farm and among them was a Negro known generally as Black Pete, who became a revelator. Others also manifested wonderful developments; they could see angels, and letters would come down from heaven, they said, and they would be put through wonderful unnatural distortions. Finally on one occasion, Black Pete got sight of one of those revelations carried by a black angel, he started after it, and ran off a steep wash bank twenty-five feet high, passed through a tree top into the Chagrin River beneath. He came out with a few scratches, and his ardor somewhat cooled" (MorleyRH 13; YoungB, 4).

"Twelve-year-old Mary Elizabeth Rollins borrowed Isaac Morley's new Book of Mormon" (Black 2, 53).

"When she first glimpsed the book, an overwhelming desire came over her to read it. Gathering her courage, she asked if she could take the book home and read it while Brother Morley attended a missionary meeting that evening" (JohnsonS, 47). "She begged so earnestly that he gave it to her on condition that she have it back before breakfast the next morning" (AndersonLF, 49). "Uncle and Aunt were Methodists, so when I got into the house, I exclaimed, 'Oh, Uncle, I have got the 'Golden Bible.' Well, there was consternation in the house for a few moments, and I was severely reprimanded for being so presumptuous as to ask such a favor, when Brother Morley had not read it himself. However, we all took turns reading in it until very late in the night" (Backman/Cowan, 37).

"The new church in the West had now a larger membership than in the state of New York" (Davis, 64; Esplin, 2).

CHAPTER 20

Sitting again on make-shift benches at the little school-house, a small gathering of adults listened to a prophet's voice. By now, most church members lived on the seventy-six acres of Morley's Farm located northeast of the Kirtland Flats. The Prophet's first matter of business in Kirtland was to instruct and caution this Common Stock Family.

"You good people are trying to live the Word of God as best you know it," Joseph said. "But I have deep concern. Beware, for there are false spirits and strange notions among you."

After praising their good intentions and marveling at the preparations they had made on their own initiative, Joseph Smith Jr. announced that the Lord was ready to teach them His order of things.

"Truly he is a prophet of God," Titus whispered to Diantha when the young prophet sat down. "He knows without flaw what is going on."

Hand in hand they started for home after the meeting ended. Titus' head was swirling with new truths and astonishment for the wonderful ways of the Lord. Diantha was excited to share the latest news she had heard from the women, sisters rather, as they were now called in the restored church.

"I adored Sister Emma from the moment I met her," Diantha said, "but you will not believe what happened when Elizabeth Ann [Whitney] first met her." Not convinced that her husband was listening and knowing she had one of the best stories ever, Diantha squeezed his hand demanding his full attention before wasting her voice.

"Titus, did you hear what happened when Joseph Smith entered Gilbert and Whitney Mercantile for the first time?"

"What was that?"

"Well, Elizabeth Ann said that an unfamiliar sleigh stopped deliberately in front of their store. This young man she had never seen before came bursting in like he knew the place. He walked right up to her husband, stuck out his hand like he was greeting an old friend and said,   'Newell K. Whitney! Thou art the man!'"

"He knew his name?"

"Yes, he knew everything. Newell answered, 'You have the

advantage of me. I could not call you by name, as you have me.' Then, get this. The stranger said that he was Joseph Smith, the prophet!"

"Bet that was a thrill."

"Titus, that's not all. He went on to say, 'You have prayed me here. Now what do you want of me?' Libby Ann said that they had been praying . . . praying hard for truth and understanding to know what was right and how to live."

"Talk about an answer."

"Can you imagine?"

"But Joseph Smith is not your ordinary stranger, Diantha," Titus interrupted. "He is a prophet of God!"

"I know," Diantha said. "I know."

The family practice was abandoned at Morley Farm. Joseph Smith taught the new saints about the Lord's Holy Spirit and how to discern between it and the evil one who tries to deceive. At an important meeting, February 4, 1831, additional leadership was called and ordained.

"It shall not be given unto any one to go forth to preach [the] gospel, or to build up [the] church," the Prophet taught by revelation, "except he be ordained by someone who has authority, and it is known to the church that he has authority and has been regularly ordained by the heads of the church."

The prophet showed how the principles of the gospel, even the fulness thereof, are found in the Bible and the Book of Mormon. He spoke about covenants and commandments and a Holy Comforter. Titus Billings was edified by the prophet's words. Slipping a piece of note paper from under the cover of his Book of Mormon copy he wrote word for word what he heard. "If thou lovest me thou shalt serve me and keep all my commandments." Once folded, the paper was tucked into his shirt pocket, close to his heart.

As the meeting ended, Titus walked up to Edward Partridge. They were the same age -- well, Partridge was a year and a half older, but that was close enough -- and very good friends.

"Congratulations, Bishop" Titus said.

"Thank you, Billings," Edward said as a humble handshake changed into a heartfelt hug. Through his prophet, God had called this good man to do a mighty work. Revelation Joseph had shared still rang in Titus' ears. The Lord had referred to Edward Partridge as a man of pure heart like Nathan of old, in whom there was no guile.

"The Lord has chosen well," Titus said.

"Thank goodness he gave me good helpers," Edward said. Titus agreed.

"You all have my vote," he said. Moving through the crowd he sought out his brother-in-law, Isaac Morley, and another friend, John Corrill, who had just been sustained as counselors to the first bishop, even the presiding bishop of the restored church. Now God's church had its own leaders in Kirtland.

Titus helped Isaac build a new room onto his house for the Prophet and Sister Emmy, as Diantha liked to call her. Because the Whitney home was in the heart of Kirtland, and Smiths were staying in a room above the busy store, Joseph would be in a better situation for his work of translating the Bible in this quiet spot outside city limits. Emma was heavy with child when they moved in, the first part of March,

Isaac's excitement knew no match. What a joy to have a true prophet living in the walls of your home where he could instruct you and your whole family at the dinner table every day.

"Titus, you and Diantha are always invited to join us. You know that, right?" Isaac asked.

"Thanks for the honor."

The Billings were present as often as possible. One such evening Philena Morley asked the Prophet Joseph to help her carry a large trunk to another room. He was always quick to be helpful and jumped up saying, "Yes, I will, with all my heart and part of my muscles." Everyone laughed. *This young man is so down to earth and filled with good humor,* Titus thought to himself, *and yet, he is a living prophet of the Living God.*

An important and sacred law was revealed to the Prophet on February 9, 1831 instructing all saints living on the seventy-six acres of Morley Farm to covenant and begin living the Lord's law of consecration.

"You will be embracing the law of the church," Joseph Smith explained. "It is a holy law, given with specific guidelines. Consecration of property must be done with covenant and deed that cannot be broken. Remember all of the poor and needy. Care for them until no poor remain.

"Under such covenant all belongings should be laid before

the bishop and his counselors or two other appointed priesthood leaders. Each man becomes a steward over that which is consecrated back to him according to the needs and wants of his family. All excess will be kept in the storehouse for future use as needed to support church leaders, help new saints as they arrive, and to build up the kingdom of God on earth. No one should be idle.

"On your own, you people have prepared yourselves," Joseph reminded the congregation. "Now the Lord can use you to build His kingdom again on earth." Those words bore deeply into the heart of Brother Billings. That was exactly what he wanted to do.

Historical Background

"During 1835, the Saints gathered for weekly meetings held on Tuesday evenings and Sunday mornings and afternoons in the schoolhouse on the flats" (Holzapfel/Cottle, 58).

"In December 1830, Sidney Rigdon and Edward Partridge went to Fayette to meet the Prophet Joseph Smith, and to inquire of the Lord regarding the work He had for them to do. Both brethren were given blessings and callings by the Lord and while there, the Prophet and his wife, Emma, decided to return to Kirtland with them. [They] left Fayette, New York the end of January 1831, and arrived in Kirtland, Ohio about the first of February" (MorleyRH, 14; Smith1, 2-3).

". . . [A] sleigh containing four persons drove through the streets of Kirtland and drew up at the door of Gilbert and Whitney's mercantile establishment . . . One of the men, a young and stalwart personage, alighted, and, springing up the steps, walked into the store and to where the junior partner was standing. 'Newell K. Whitney! Thou art the man!' he exclaimed, extending his hand cordially, as if to an old and familiar acquaintance. 'You have the advantage of me,' replied the one addressed, as he mechanically took the proffered hand, a half amused, half mystified look overspreading his countenance. 'I could not call you by name, as you have me.' 'I am Joseph, the Prophet,' said the stranger. 'You have prayed me here; now what do you want of me?' Mr. Whitney was astonished, but no less delighted. As soon as his surprise would permit [he] conducted the party across the street to his house on the corner, and introduced them to his wife. She shared fully his surprise and ecstasy" (MorleyRH, 15; Sjodahl, 215).

When the Prophet Joseph and Emma, first came to Kirtland they stayed several weeks in the home of Newel K. Whitney while Isaac Morley built a room onto his house for them. "The farm house was large enough to accommodate the needs of both families until Spring. Isaac fed the Smiths at this own table while the Prophet enlightened him on some of the deeper doctrines of the Kingdom" (Esplin, 3; MorleyRH, 16).

Revelations are quoted come from Doctrine and Covenants, Section 42.

When the Prophet Joseph came to Kirtland "he found a church consisting of nearly one hundred members, who were, in general, good brethren" (Romig, 191). Most of these lived in homes on Isaac Morley's farm of seventy-six acres on the north half of Lot 6, which was located to the northeast of the Kirtland Flats.

"An 1827 Geauga County, Ohio tax duplicate shows that Morley paid tax on a frame house in the northeast part of Lot 6, house and land valued at $250. See Elizabeth G. Hitchcock, The Historical Society Quarterly, Lake County, Ohio, February 1979, 18:2-3, copy in Kirtland Ohio Subject Folder, RLDS Library-Archives" (Romig, 192).

Joseph and Emma first stayed several weeks in the home of Newel K. Whitney while Isaac Morley built a room onto his house for them. When Philena Morley asked for help the Prophet Joseph answered, "Yes, I will, with all my heart and part of my muscles" (AndersonKR2; Friend, July 1989, 48).

CHAPTER 21

Diantha walked briskly. A chill filled the morning air in spite of all the early signs of springtime. The temperature was not her concern, nor the cause of her gloomy mood. She was distraught to say the least. After all of these years there was no explanation for it. She could not begin to understand. It didn't make any sense at all. No, she would never understand it.

"Stubborn!" she said out loud. "Just plain, insensitive stubbornness."

Diantha spotted a rock in her path and kicked it as hard as she could. The walk was long from her parent's house in Kirtland to her residence on the Morley Farm. "It even bears his name, but no! He will not live there, not with all those Mormons!"

Diantha cringed at the thought, remembering the disgusting day he packed up and moved away. They had been over it again and again. If the persuasive, persistent Isaac could not influence their stubborn father what made her think that somehow, sometime she would persuade him to reconsider? She didn't really care if he lived on the Farm or not. Her desire was to share the message of the true gospel with him. Oh no, he wouldn't listen to anything. He would not give the Church or the Prophet the slightest chance. Now she knew it, he would never change his mind or his stubborn position. Their morning encounter had proven pointless. Diantha left her parents' home with her father raging. Titus planned to pick her up later. No, she could not wait there and would be home long before he started out. She had better things to do than listen to her father verbally smear everything she held dear and sacred.

By the time she reached the uphill of Chillicothe Road her fury had faded and her feet all but failed her. Diantha sat by the side of the road and wiped tears with the edge of her skirt. Then she prayed for her stubborn father and for her mother who would love to be a Mormon if circumstances differed.

With courage she pulled herself up and started again at a much slower pace. Although she felt exhausted, the physical exertion had soothed her soul. Diantha looked up the road and counted about twenty little frame homes built or being built on Morley Farmland. Sister Emmy and the Prophet were still living with Isaac's family. Soon they would be moving into a white-washed little framed house of their own.

Three weeks before, Joseph Smith Senior, the prophet's father, had been introduced and welcomed at church. His wife was on her way to join him when tragedy struck. While traveling to Ohio with a branch of saints from New York, the ship sank into the icy waters of Lake Erie. Local newspapers reported the loss of all passengers. Diantha wished she could have met Sister Smith, the mother of a prophet. She was heartbroken for Father Smith and all of his family. Her father was stubborn, but he was alive.

Diantha stretched her neck trying from a distance to identify the house Titus had built for her. With ease she spotted the maple trees he planted years ago, now referred to as Morley's Grove. How she enjoyed working the sap season with Titus. She loved being with him, doing things with him. Gratitude swelled in her heart as she realized how blessed she was to have such a husband, one who was willing to worship with her, one who embraced the gospel as tightly as she did, and one who loved her with all his heart. No matter what, she could count on his love. As she walked she pondered, *My Titus is a noble man of meekness.* Never before had she noticed it, but now the fact seemed crystal clear: Everything her husband touched bore the Morley name. It was the Morley Farm, the Morley Grove, the Morley family. He played a big part in all of it, even owned a share of the property, but never once demanded recognition. He loved her brother like his own. Titus Billings was not a glory seeker. He just wanted to help, and help he did. Also, he was humble and teachable. How she loved him.

Diantha decided to stop at Lucy's and peek in on Sister Emmy's new twins before going home. She had been called to help April 30th when the Smith twins were born. She and Lucy had worked with little Thaddeus and Louisa for three hours but could not save either one of them. Julia Murdock had delivered twins the same day, but in her case it was the mother who died. John didn't know how to care for two babies himself. He brought them to Emma wishing she would raise them as her own. He requested that she and the prophet adopt them when they were only nine days old.

Diantha found Sister Emmy, a beautiful woman with dark curls enhancing the fairness of her face, rocking Little Joseph. She who had given up two babies within hours of their birth now sat holding another's child as lovingly as if he were her own. No won-

96

der the Prophet loved her.

"How are you today, Diantha?"

"I've seen happier days," Diantha answered. She could see a concerned look cross Emma's face and offered a quick explanation before the question was asked. "I visited my father this morning," she said with sadness. "He still refuses us and our new found religion, as he calls it. I don't know how to get through to him."

Emma Smith reached out for Diantha's hand. "I am so sorry," she said.

Just then another baby cried out from her cradle. "Could I pick up the other half?" Diantha asked.

"Oh yes, that would be most helpful," Emma said. "I feel like I don't have enough arms sometimes."

"I am so happy our daughters are the same age," Diantha said as she lifted Little Julia and wrapped her snuggly in a small quilt.

"Yes, now they will both grow up with good playmates."

Lucy walked in carrying her youngest. Isaac Junior was already two years old.

"The church is growing by way of little people," Emma said with a laugh.

"Mother Smith is here," Lucy said.

Mother Smith? How could that be? She was drowned! She and a large group of Saints had met their demise in Lake Erie . . . just days ago . . . Diantha was puzzled.

A tiny woman entered the room with a well-worn, wrinkled, but smiling face.

"Hello. I'm Lucy Smith," she said. "I am the grandma here." Her broad smile widened even more. "Now, who would you be, dear?"

"This is Sister Billings, Mother. The one I told you about," Emma said.

"Oh yes, I believe I met your husband this morning. Fine man."

Is this woman really the mother of the prophet? Diantha mused. Her face must have reflected the shock and confusion of her mind. Before she could ask anything -- Mother Smith began to explain.

"You must have read the newspapers. Emma thought I was gone too."

"Can you imagine our joy when Mother Smith and the

saints arrived yesterday?" Emma asked.

Diantha was swirling with joy and confusion and wonderment. "Is it really true?"

"Touch me and see for yourself," Mother Smith teased. "Yes, it's really so. Sit for a spell and I'll tell you of our little miracle."

Little? It must have been a big miracle. Diantha's time was far spent, but nothing could be more pressing at that very moment than the testimony she was about to hear. Isaac's Lucy pulled up chairs for both her guests and faced them towards Emma's rocker.

"With eighty souls we started out on a flatboat down the Erie Canal." Mother Smith turned to look at Diantha. "I understand Brother Billings helped build that canal. You'll have to thank him for me."

Sister Billings smiled and nodded.

Lucy Smith went on, "Not long after we embarked I discovered that fifty of our passengers, twenty adults and thirty children, were destitute for food. They had converted all belongings into clothing for the trip believing that fluent saints would assist them with necessities of food and travel. Their expectations were disappointed. So, it seems, this burden fell upon my shoulders."

The other sisters shook their heads with concern. "How did you ever do it?"

"A stranger by the name of Esquire Chamberlain came up to me when we first boarded the boat and offered seventeen dollars for our cause before he left. Such a gift proved helpful. I knew the Lord was with us. He would provide." Mother Smith directed her attention to her listeners as she said, "We must hold to our faith at all times, sisters, and in all circumstances." Then she continued her story, "I became concerned when many of our group began to complain and murmur instead of singing and praying. I told them that they were acting like the children of Israel!"

Diantha imagined a scolding by this strong-willed, unwavering woman. She was extremely short in stature, physically, but her spirit must have been as tall and strong as that of her prophet son.

Mother Smith continued, "Can you believe that some of them were afraid to publicly claim membership in the church? A few of the brethren even told us to cease our prayers and deny our Mormonism or we would be mobbed before morning."

"What did you do?"

"I told them, 'Mob it is then, [for] we shall attend to prayer

98

before sunset, mob or no mob!' Then I sent Brother Humphry and Brother Page to search among the boatmen for a Captain Blake."

"Captain Blake? How did you know him?"

"He had captained a boat belonging to my brother, General Mack, and purchased that boat after my brother died. I believed that he would still be commanding it."

"Did they find him?"

"Yes, but the boat was fully loaded with freight and passengers. All he could offer was deck passage. There was no other possible solution, so we accepted. Just as we loaded our goods and ourselves onto the deck, it started to rain."

Weighty sighs escaped the listeners.

"That's when dispositions got as stormy as the weather. Many of the children were ill, and their mothers were exhausted. Again they murmured and demanded shelter, since the boat would not sail until morning. After Brother Page returned unsuccessful in his attempt to find lodging, I set out to make overnight housing arrangements for the women and children. This, the Lord helped me to do.

"When we returned to the boat the next morning, Captain Blake asked us to remain on deck and be ready to sail at first opportunity. About that time his crewman returned with alarming news that harbor ice measured twenty feet. He believed it would be at least two weeks before we could pull out. At that point, my son, William, came for me to settle a ruckus that had broken out among the saints. I'm sorry to say that our good people were grumbling, murmuring, debating, and some of the young ladies were even flirting with passing gentlemen.

"I stepped into the midst of them and called out: 'Brethren and sisters, we call ourselves saints and profess to have come out of the world for the purpose of serving God at the expense of all earthly things; and will you at the very onset, subject the cause of Christ to ridicule by your own unwise and improper conduct? You profess to put your trust in God. Then how can you feel to murmur and complain as you do? Here are my sisters pining for their rocking chairs, and brethren from whom I expected firmness and energy, declaring that they positively believe they shall starve to death before they get to the end of their journey. And why it is so? Have any of you lacked? Have not I set food before you every day, and made you, who have not provided for yourselves, as welcome as my own children? Where is your faith? Where is your confidence in God? Can you not realize that all things were made by him, and that he rules over the works of his own hands? And suppose that all the Saints here should lift their hearts in prayer to God, that the way be opened before us. How easy it would be for him to cause the ice to break away, so that in a moment we could be on our journey!"

The room was silent.

"From the shore I heard a man shout, 'Is the Book of Mormon true?' I bore strong testimony of it so all could hear. Then, again I turned to our people and said, 'Now brethren and sisters, if you will, all of you, raise your desires to heaven that the ice may be broken up and we be set at liberty. As sure as the Lord lives, it will be done!'

"At that instant a noise exploded like thunder and our captain shouted, 'Every man to his post.' A narrow passageway opened in the ice. Buckets from the waterwheel were torn off as our boat passed through it. The terrible commotion of all the scraping and crashing and shouting must have frightened onlookers from the shore as they watched the ice close immediately behind us. Our friends from Colesville couldn't even get through."

She paused. No one spoke or stirred even the slightest.

"Of course we prayed our thanks to the living God," she continued. "The captain's mate broke in before we dismissed. 'Mrs. Smith,' he said, 'do have your children stop praying or we will all go to the devil together; we cannot keep a single man on his post!' They were all taken up with our praying. We closed the meeting. "It wasn't over though. There was much sea sickness. Captain Blake and his crew treated me with the utmost respect and kindness, especially when the captain learned that I was the sister of General Mack. We parted with tears at Fairport.

"Our people were even more distraught when we landed. They believed we could go no further and wanted to give up. Fortunately, that is when Joseph and Samuel found us. We spent the night at Brother, I mean Bishop, Partridge's home in Painsville and made our way to Kirtland yesterday."

Diantha was not only pleased, but honored also to be one of the first who met this remarkable, woman of God.

"Have you seen our new home?" Mother Smith asked. "The kind saints are building us a cottage next door to Emma on the Morley Farm."

"Diantha is a Morley too," Emma explained.

The prophet's mother turned and asked, "You are? How?"

"Isaac is my brother," she answered.

"We hope to move in before the month is over," Emma said. "Won't it be wonderful? I can hardly believe that Joseph and I will have a home of our own, at last!"

"And what a joy for you to live next door to Mother Smith," said Diantha.

"Yes, yes, I feel so blessed to have a spot I can clean and fix the way I like -- where my husband can work on the revisions of the Bible in his own home. I could be happy forever in a tiny house on the Morley Farm."

Historical Background

"Lucy Mack Smith, the prophet's mother, led "eighty souls" to Kirtland, Ohio. "The first part of the journey was made on a flat boat on the Erie Canal to Buffalo" (Backman/Cowan,48; SmithLM, 195).

When the Prophet's parents moved into Kirtland they too stayed first with the Morleys. "Joseph Smith, Sr. was living with his son, Joseph, in the Morley home when he joyously reunited with his wife" (MorleyRH, 17; Smith1, 260).

Saints had received word that Mother Smith's boat sunk in icy waters before she could share her ice miracle with saints in Kirtland (SmithLM,195-208). Lucy Smith recalls, "The first house that I entered was Brother Morley's. Here I met my beloved husband and great was our joy in the reunion of our family. We remained two weeks at Brother Morley's, then removed our family to a farm which had been purchased by Joseph for the Church" (Esplin, 3; SmithLM, 209). This "farm" in all probability has reference to the house the saints built for Joseph to continue his revision of the Bible. There was land adjacent to this house, for Lucy Smith continues, "On this farm my family were all established with this arrangement, that we were to receive our support; but all over and above this was to be used for the comfort of strangers or brethren who were traveling through this place" (MorleyRH, 19; SmithLM, 209).

May 8, 1831, the nine-day-old twins of John and Julia Murdock were brought to the Morley farm and given to the Prophet's wife, Emma. She had given birth to twins, a boy and girl, on April 30, 1831, the same day the Murdock children were born. Her own twins lived only three hours. "She took the Murdock babies, their mother having died following childbirth, in the fond hope that they would fill the void in her life occasioned by the loss of her own" (JonesG, 56; MorleyRH, 17; Smith1, 260; SmithLM, 208).

"The names of Joseph and Julia Murdock Smith are found written in the family Bible. Names are also recorded there for her twins, Thaddeus and Louisa" (JonesG, 56). "The Joseph and Emma Smith Family Bible is in possession of Buddy Youngreen of Orem, Utah" (JonesG, 76). [Note: Brent Ashworth of Provo, Utah is the current owner of the Joseph and Emma Smith Family Bible. He purchased it in December 2010. It makes the first and only reference to their 7th son, Thomas, who was born and died in Nauvoo in 1842.]

"The Murdock twins were also a boy and girl named Joseph S. and Julia. At least four members of the Smith Family resided in the Morley home during the first two weeks of May 1831; namely the Prophet, his wife, and parents" (MorleyRH, 17).

Diantha Billings was set apart as a mid-wife by the Prophet Joseph Smith. The call probably came at a later date. She was medically inclined and did "sewing and doctoring" for the Prophet's family in Nauvoo. Perhaps she helped with the twins too. "I [Eunice] played with the Prophet's adopted daughter, Julia" (Snow3, 6).

While the Prophet was living in the Newell K. Whitney home, he received a revelation (February 4, 1831) which suggested that he move to a place where he could live in peace and translate. "Since the Whitney home was in the busiest section of Kirtland and the Morley farm was beyond the city limits, Joseph decided to move to the farm where more privacy could be enjoyed for the purpose of translating the Bible. The Saints were commanded to build a house for their Prophet; and, therefore, his residence with the Morley family was only a temporary arrangement. There was extra property and timber on the Morley farm. Brother Morley's land holdings became an important factor in fulfillment of this revelation: 'And again, it is meet that my servant Joseph Smith, Jun., should have a house built, in which to live and translate'" (D&C 41:7; MorleyRH, 18).

While other Saints helped to build the structure, Isaac Morley donated the property, timber and other materials. This small frame house was similar to the larger house on the farm. It was completed in the spring of 1831, and the Prophet intermittently lived in it until 1837. "From 1831 until 1832, most of the Saints gathering in Kirtland settled on the Isaac Morley Farm. Twenty houses, mostly small, were built along the bottom of this hill, including one for the prophet Joseph Smith. He only lived in his home four months, then moved to Hiram, Ohio to the John Johnson Farm. "The Fourth of June came and we all met in a little string of buildings under the hill near Isaac Morleys in Kirtland, Genoya County, Ohio"(Hancock,47).

"Kirtland Saints Land and Tax Records" show "Titus Billings" paid taxes on eight acres: "21 January 21, 1832 and 26 March 1832" (Backman1).

CHAPTER 22

Investigators, as they were sometimes called, were welcome at all Mormon meetings, so no one was surprised when John Johnson and his wife attended one evening. Ezra Booth, a Methodist minister, also attended. The meeting was held in Joseph and Emma's new home.

"We are often called Mormons," Mother Lucy Smith explained, "because that is what the world calls us, but the only name we acknowledge is Latter-Day Saints." She was seated beside Mrs. Johnson. As the evening wore on, a question about supernatural gifts arose. Such things were mentioned at the time of the apostles in the New Testament. During the discussion someone blurted out, "Here is Mrs. Johnson with a lame arm; has God given any power to men now on the earth to cure her?"

After the subject had changed to something else, the young prophet crossed the room where he took Mrs. Johnson by the hand and blessed her rheumatic arm.

"Woman, in the name of Jesus Christ I command thee to be whole." So saying, he left the room. Immediately she lifted her arm with ease. It was pain free! Such healing was a miracle, and that miracle lasted. She was able to go about her chores and her laundry without pain or difficulty as before. Like many others, the Johnson family eagerly joined the newly restored church. So did the Methodist minister.

*   *   *

The little schoolhouse was packed and overflowing, not only with eager conference goers, but also with the spirit of prophecy. This conference was the first held in Kirtland, and number four for the church. The light and love of truth seemed to burn brighter in the hearts of this people than sunshine at noon in Ohio's bright June sky.

After addressing the congregation, the Prophet Joseph Smith announced that the Lord was ready for a number of elders to journey westward, two by two, preaching the "Good News Gospel." Those called would be ordained to the High Priesthood and assemble again when they reached Jackson County Missouri.

103

"Brethren, please stand when your name is called." He began reading the list.

Titus placed a hand on his heart, feeling the folded piece of paper he carried in his Sunday shirt pocket. He knew what was written there without taking a look and he was determined to do it, what-ever the Lord required. He and Diantha had discussed the pos-sibility of a mission call. They did love the Lord. They would serve Him at all cost and try always to keep His commandments. Diantha slipped a hand in his arm and seemed to hold her breath.

The list went on. "Ezra Booth to be a companion to Isaac Morley." Diantha gasped. Now Titus was breathless. The list continued to its end. It was true. Father Morley would be leaving. This brother, friend, and champion whom Titus had shadowed for so long, with whom he had shared everything, on whom he leaned and . . . How could they let him go? How in the world could they ever let him go?

Hour after hour their minds could think of nothing else. Titus and Diantha spent all afternoon with the Morleys and many other concerned visitors who were in and out.

"Don't know how we'll manage without you," Titus said when at last the two couples were alone. Huge father-like arms hugged him tightly. Then, Isaac Morley held his brother-in-law by the shoulders and looked with courage into his eyes. "You are in charge now, Brother." Titus started to weaken and question and pull away, but Isaac held him fast. "I'm going on the Lord's errand," he said, "and you will be serving Him here. Take good care of the Farm and all of the families on it, for me. This is a special part of His vineyard too, you know."

The hour was late and the night was dark when they said their good-byes.

"Let's take a walk," Titus suggested, as he reached for Diantha's hand. They started up the hillside with cricket music playing in the background of their thoughts. The world should have seemed turned upside-down with all the changes. He should have been overwhelmed by it all, and yet, there was a stronger feeling of peace in his soul than he had felt the day before.

"You know it is right, don't you?" he said.

"Yes, dear," she answered.

"Hope I can do it," he said.

"You won't be alone," she said.

"Thanks, Diantha."

"Don't thank me, Titus. It's the Lord that will help you."

He didn't reply. In silence he petitioned the Almighty. Meekly he committed himself. Thy will be done. Thy will be done.

They circled the schoolhouse and started back down the hill as a horse and buggy turned into their lane. Titus recognized the lantern design and knew at once that it belonged to his brother-in-law, John Wells. He and Salomi lived on the other side of the flats and had two little girls by now. They had not joined the new church, as yet. Titus hoped they would soon. He hurried to meet them.

John jumped down and assisted Salomi. She was beaming with joy.

"Titus, Diantha!" she shouted. You'll never guess. Look who's here . . . and they are moving to Kirtland!"

Samuel Billings, that beloved brother only two years older than Titus, who had been so close to him in days gone by, stretched his lengthy legs to the ground as the two encompassed each other. Samuel had known difficult times. Already he had buried two wives and was now the only parent of his two little girls. Titus lifted Lucy (8 years) and Olive (six) from the buggy and carried them into the house. He needed Sam. How perfect for him to settle now at the Farm.

Needless to say, the Morley Farm was buzzing with excitement all week. Before he left, just seven months after his baptism, Isaac announced in public that care of his farm and everything thereon would rest in the hands of his brother-in-law and loyal friend, Titus Billings.

Fifteen pairs of newly called missionaries left for Missouri. Each pair followed a different route, ready to share the good news of the gospel along the way. Isaac left with his companion, that former Methodist Priest, Ezra Booth. Isaac was forty-five-years-old when he left Kirtland on June 15, 1831. Except for river ferry rides, he and Booth walked all the way. They made good time and were present in Independence for the "Land of Zion Dedication" August 2, 1831.

Samuel settled on the flats and took a job as miller at the Kirtland Flour Mill. He did not seem to be fond of the new religious ideas that his brother embraced and wanted nothing to do with them or the Farm situation. All else was good. They remained congenial and respectful of each other, but paths seemed to be going in opposite ways.

When the Prophet returned from a trip to Missouri, he stopped by Lucy Morley's home before returning to this own. He had a mes-sage from Isaac.

"Your husband is well and sends word that he would like you and the children to join him. He has occupied and cleared land in Kaw Township, near Independence. Already he is building a cabin for you."

"Sounds like my Isaac," Lucy said with a smile and shake of her head.

"It's a peaceful little spot," Joseph went on. "That man of yours knows how to find good places. Bishop Partridge is sending for his family, too. Perhaps you and Lydia could travel together."

Historical Background

"The miraculous healing of Sister Johnson took place in a meeting at the Smith home. "Here is Mrs. Johnson with a lame arm; has God given any power to men now on the earth to cure her?" A few moments later, when the conversation had turned in another direction, Smith rose, and walking across the room, taking Mrs. Johnson by the hand said in a most solemn manner: 'Woman, in the name of the Lord Jesus Christ I command thee to be whole' and immediately left the room" (JonesG, 59).

The "Mormon" quote from Mother Smith actually took place as she journeyed to Kirtland. While seeking shelter for sick women and children who traveled with her, she spoke to: a cheerful old lady, near seventy years of age . . . "What be you? she said. "Be you Baptists?" I told her that we were "Mormons." "Mormons!" ejaculated she, in a quick, good-natured tone. "What be they? I never heard of them before." "I told you that we were 'Mormons,'" I replied, "because that is what the world calls us, but the only name we acknowledge is Latter-Day Saints" (SmithLM, 201).

At the Fourth Conference of the Church, first one held in Kirtland, June 1831, "the spirit of prophecy was abundantly manifest and . . . a number of elders were called to take their journey through the western country going two by two, preaching the Gospel." They would assemble again in Jackson County, Missouri. Isaac's name was called. He was to serve such a mission with Ezra Booth as his companion. "In 1831, he was called to go to Jackson County, Missouri to find a location for the Mormon people to settle" (Cox, 1).

"In June, 1831, he was also appointed by revelation to travel to Missouri in company with Ezra Booth, preaching by the way" (Jenson1, 236). [Unfortunately, Elder Booth soon apostatized and wrote letters that were published in the Ohio Star and later in an anti-Mormon book called Mormonism Unveiled. (Rowley, 31; Wikipedia.)]

"Four days after his ordination in the High Priesthood, this forty-five-year-old gentleman received a divine call to leave his farm and family and travel to Missouri" (MorleyRH, 24). "He left Titus in charge of all things on the farm" (Esplin, 4; MorleyRH, 30).

Samuel Billings [brother to Titus] was born in 1791 in Deerfield, Massachusetts. As a young man he went to Virginia and learned to weave carpets. There he also met and fell in love with Maria Polsley. They were married April 3, 1823. Three years and two daughters later, she died (in 1829 - cause unknown). It is believed he and the girls returned to Massachusetts. There he again fell in love and married Charlotte Childs on September 20, 1830. She died one year later. (Cause unknown.) He moved to Ohio in 1831. He was befriended by a lovely schoolteacher, Mary Russell, and married her October 16, 1832. They parented six children. Three of their babies died at birth (Lisonbee, 7). "In 1832 Samuel Billings, twice a widower, came to Kirtland with his two little girls, Lucy and Olive, eight and six years of age, to visit his sister" (BillingsV2, 2).

Titus had three siblings living in Kirtland, Emily, Salome and Samuel, but none of them ever embraced the Gospel. Samuel became so disenchanted with the "Mormons" that he moved to Gates Mill to get away from them. He returned to Kirtland in 1858, after the saints relocated (Lisonbee, 1).

CHAPTER 23

Only a few months after moving onto the Morley Farm, into their first home, Joseph Smith, the Prophet, received a revelation that troubled him greatly.

How could he tell his wife about this one? She had been through so much sorrow and pain. Things were better now and she was happy at last. He could not bear to break her happiness, but was afraid that such news was sure to do so. It would trouble his friends, too. How could he ever tell them? Oh, why did it have to be so? Why here and why now?

Being a prophet is never easy. Things have to be done whether you want to do them or not. This assignment was one of those things. He had been to the Lord again and again. Instructions were clear. He would tell Emma tonight and the Kirtland saints tomorrow.

*   *   *

Joseph stopped his wagon in front of the Billings home. Out in the field, he saw Titus and his older boys working. Many times he had walked out there to speak with Brother Billings, but this time he wanted Diantha present as well.

"Show us how fast six-year-old legs can run," Alfred's mother coached him. The small lad ran with all his might to fetch his father. He was on an errand for a prophet of the Lord and that very prophet was watching him run. Young Alfred Nelson gave it his all.

With hospitable grace, Diantha placed two pieces of apple pie onto the table. She had coaxed Brother Joseph into eating one because she knew Titus would welcome a piece of his favorite dessert and he should not eat alone. Her guest was nearly ready for a second taste, but refused it when her farmer stumbled in and rinsed his hands.

"Titus, the Lord has spoken to us again by revelation," he started.

"Would you like me to step out?" Diantha offered.

"No, Diantha. You are part of this."

She looked first at the prophet, and then turned to her husband who appeared to be as puzzled and curious as she was. For many weeks the humble leader had been instructing his people about Zion. Titus pulled out a chair and his wife too was seated at the table.

"I teach the saints as the Lord teaches me. The Lord is ready for us to take action." He paused.

Titus tried to help, "What kind of action?"

"We have been commanded to purchase lands in Missouri upon which to build Zion."

Titus Billings was a hard-working man who provided sufficiently for his family's needs. Year after year they got along well, but never with any to spare. If money was what the prophet needed, he would give all he had, but it could not amount to anything. He did not know how they could be much help at all.

The Prophet looked solicitous and leaned onto the table before he continued, "Brother Billings, these are the Lord's exact words." He paused with a piercing prophetic gaze as if to reemphasize he was speaking for the Almighty God, not just for himself, a man.

"Wherefore, let my disciples in Kirtland arrange their temporal concerns, who dwell upon this farm."

This farm? Isaac's farm? Titus' mind was swirling, reaching, trying to grasp what he was hearing.

"Let my servant Titus Billings. . ."

That hit him bulls-eye! *Exact words? The Lord's words? To me?*

" . . . who has the care thereof, dispose of the land, . . ."

DISPOSE? Diantha's mind was racing too. Her brother Isaac loved this land. It was his place since the very beginning. He had entrusted it in good faith to them. He planned to return.

" . . . that he [Titus] may be prepared in the coming spring to take his journey up unto the land of Zion, with those that dwell upon the face thereof, excepting those whom I shall reserve unto myself, that shall not go until I shall command them."

Brother Billings never touched his pie. For a moment he stared into the face of the young prophet who sat across from him. This uneducated fellow who owned very little of what the world considered to be of value and who was a full twelve years younger than himself, was now requesting, in the name of the Lord, that Titus Billings give up, not only everything that he owned, but also much that was not even his to give. Many other families would be affected as well. Even Joseph and Emma would lose their new home, the only home they had ever owned. The instruction did not make sense. It made no sense at all.

Titus searched his soul. He loved this humble, hard-working, unselfish leader called Joseph, the Prophet, but that was not enough. Perhaps that was why the whole thing was so incredible.

He and Joseph counseled at great length. Question after question arose.

The assignment sounded impossible, but the words, "My servant Titus Billings" kept ringing in his ears. Each time they did he felt that burning feeling that he loved. Joseph had taught them all how to recognize instructions from the Lord. This counsel was definitely from the Lord. At length he reached for Diantha's hand. Her eyes met his with wonderment, but with his touch she felt warmth penetrate her soul. From her that same feeling returned again to him. The Lord was working with them, of that Titus had no doubt. He turned to the young prophet and spoke.

"I can't explain any of this, but I know it is right. We will sell the farm, all seventy-six blessed acres, and every cent will go to purchase land for our Lord in Missouri."

Historical Background

A direct command to Titus Billings and the Kirtland Saints: "Wherefore, let my disciples in Kirtland arrange their temporal concerns, who dwell upon this farm" (D&C 63:38). "[Upon this farm] Refers, probably, to the Morley farm. Isaac Morley accompanied the Colesville Saints to Jackson County and arrived there in the latter part of 1831" (Sjodahl, 382).

"Titus Billings was to dispose of property over which he had responsibility" (Barrett1, 197; Cook, 98; Times and Seasons3, 466-467). "Let my servant Titus Billings, who has the care thereof, dispose of the land, that he may be prepared in the coming spring to take his journey up unto the land of Zion, with those that dwell upon the face thereof, excepting those whom I shall reserve unto myself, that shall not go until I shall command them. And let all the moneys which can be spared, it mattereth not unto me whether it be little or much, be sent up unto the land of Zion, unto them whom I have appointed to receive" (D&C 63:38-40).

While seeking direction from the Lord, early in August of 1831, Joseph Smith writes: "In these infant days of the Church, there was a great anxiety to obtain the word of the Lord upon every subject that in any way concerned our salvation; and as the land of Zion was now the most important temporal object in view, I inquired of the Lord for further information upon the gathering of the Saints, and the purchase of the land, and other matters" (D&C 1, 114).

CHAPTER 24

At every opportunity the Prophet Joseph Smith preached the Lord's warning to Saints who would be dwellers in Zion. "You must be called by those in authority," he taught. "Then you must prepare adequately to go. Let it be known, the Lord has made it very clear, that saints must go there with pure hearts and unselfish desires.

"We are commanded to purchase lands on which to build Zion, but the Lord's Zion cannot be purchased with blood," he went on. "We must not go in haste, lest there be confusion. Let every saint take righteousness as his staff and faithfulness as his girdle. We lift a warning voice unto the inhabitants of the earth and declare both by word and by flight that desolation shall come upon the wicked."

*   *   *

"Look at this, Diantha." Titus unfolded a piece of paper. "What do you have?"

"This is our recommend to migrate to Zion."

Diantha studied the paper. It was signed: "Edward Partridge, Bishop of the Church in Ohio."

"This move is a calling from the Lord," Titus said. How well she knew that! It certainly was not her idea. "We and any other migrating saints must carry one of these official recommends signed by the bishop or by three of the elders. Confusion and pestilence will follow if we do not obey."

Titus Billings was supplied a list of names of persons and families who would follow him from Kirtland, Ohio to Zion in Independence, Missouri. When springtime came these families would relocate permanently and there build up the Kingdom of God.

Often, prayer meetings were held in the homes of members. One was scheduled at the Billings' home on the day Thomas and Editha Morley visited in an effort to rescue their daughter from the new beliefs she embraced. They were invited to stay for the meeting, but refused. Neither of them could appreciate a religion responsible for uprooting their posterity. Isaac's family prepared to follow him to the frontier's edge and now Diantha was ready to march off with her husband and children to the same rough waste-land they called "Zion" both in the name of religion. Thomas could not understand how his son-in-law could sell a farm that belonged to another, especially while the true owner was away on so-called religious business. He was also troubled about the six little graves that would be sold and forsaken.

"I know how much you dislike change and moving," her mother said. "How can you go along with all of this?"

"It's not my will that matters, Mother. Titus and I are obeying the Lord."

"I suppose God talks to that husband of yours," her father interrupted.

"Yes, through his prophet."

Thomas Morley was not listening. He never listened to her any more. "I suppose Isaac talks to God and angels too."

Diantha was silent.

"Does your God tell you and your brother to abandon those little graves on the hillside? Does your God teach you to dishonor your parents? Since when does God command a man to sell someone else's property and take all the money on a wild goose chase?"

Thomas' face reddened with anger. Diantha was glad Titus and members were already inside. She hoped they could not hear. Her mother's face was wet with tears as Diantha tried to kiss her goodbye. Never in her wildest dreams did she ever expect to walk a path contrary to her parents. She latched the gate behind them realizing without doubt that the road they traveled was now divided. *The journey of life is taking us in different directions. Will it ever reconnect?*

Diantha returned from bidding her parents farewell as the Prophet asked her to lead an opening song. Suppressing the pain in her heart, she breathed deeply to expand her beautiful singing voice and began. Others joined in song of praise.

The prayer was long and pleading. As was always the case, the Prophet Joseph inspired those present with truth and testimony. If only her parents had stayed and listened. How could she leave them and her buried babies behind? The thought had tormented her for days and fought her sleep at night. But now, in this reverent little meeting of saints, she felt peace smother turmoil, like water putting out a fire. Then a most happy and holy feeling wrapped itself around her as if squeezing out all doubt, confusion, and even the hurt she had known. This was truth from heaven. The

Lord, through His servant, had spoken to her husband. Titus was willing to listen and obey. At all cost, she was willing too.

*   *   *

Brother Billings returned from priesthood meetings with brighter excitement and renewed hope. Diantha loved to see it in him. He was eager to share new instruction and inspiration with her. Tonight, however, was an obvious exception. His heart was heavy and concern was written all over his face. She fetched a dipper of water and bid him sit down.

"What is it, Dear?" There was no answer. "Is something wrong?"

"Joseph had another revelation," was all he said.

"Was your name in this one?" she asked.

"No, but Isaac's was."

"Is that bad?"

"I think it is, for me?"

"How so?"

"The revelation was about forgiveness. Sounds like Isaac and his companion had some problems with the church." Titus reached up for his wife's hands and pulled her to a standing position between his knees. "Diantha, Ezra Booth has apostatized!"

How could anyone misplace the sureness of truth and the burning of light from the gospel of Jesus Christ like that? Diantha panicked.

"What about Isaac? He didn't, he couldn't have . . ."

"No, no. Isaac is strong. The Lord rebuked them both, but Isaac stayed true. He retained his membership. The Lord revealed his forgiveness of Isaac and named him as a servant still."

Diantha was relieved. "Then, it's all right now," she said.

"I still don't know his feelings for me. Maybe my doings are part of his problem. Oh Di, I hope he will forgive me for selling his farm!"

"You didn't sell it. The Lord did. You only did as you were commanded. Isaac will see through all of that." Her words were welcomed, but still he ached. She wrapped her arms around his head and pulled it to her.

"I see through all of that myself," she said. Then, with firm placement of her hands on his shoulders she pushed backward until he looked into her eyes. "I could not allow you to do any less,"

115

she added. "I love you, Brother Titus Billings, servant of our Lord!"

Historical Background

The Saints were commanded "to assemble themselves together unto the land of Zion, not in haste, lest there should be confusion, which bringeth pestilence" (D&C 63:24). "The Saints, in their exodus, should also be prepared, but righteousness must be their 'staff,' and faithfulness their 'girdle.' No one should go to Zion unless so equipped" (D&C 63:37; Exodus 12:11; Sjodahl, 381).

Titus may have felt deep concern when Joseph Smith received a revelation about forgiveness, September 11, 1831, that mentioned the missionary companionship Ezra Booth and Isaac Morley by name (D&C 64:15-16).

CHAPTER 25

"Titus Billings" was the first name called by the Prophet at an important conference held October 25, 1831, in Orange, Ohio. He along with John Burk and Serenes Burnett were ordained to the Priesthood of God as the first deacons of the Restored Church.

Diantha was thrilled with her husband's assignment. She spent most of the next week helping Lucy pack for the Missouri trip. While Titus pulled up carrots that had been left in the ground she filled a tin with baked biscuits. Soon two courageous women, Lucy Morley and Lydia Partridge, gathered a dozen excited children around two over-loaded wagons for prayer before setting out.

"We'll miss you," Diantha said.

"You'll be coming soon." Lucy hugged her. "The world will be back to springtime before you know it."

"Be careful," Titus said. "I do wish a man was going with you."

"We'll be fine," Lucy said, beaming up at him. "Thanks for caring."

It was a fact the only male members of this company were two-and-a-half-year-old Isaac Morley, Jr. and two-year-old Clisbee Partridge. Each family had five daughters. The Morley girls were: Philena (18), Lucy Diantha (16), Editha Ann (13), Cordelia (8), and Theresa Arathusa (5). The Partridge sisters were: Eliza Maria (11), Harriet Pamela (9), Emily Dew (7), Caroline Ely (4), and young Lydia (1).

Titus reviewed again the hundred mile route they would follow on land before meeting up with the Ohio River where they would travel most of the way on steamboat. Both sisters seemed well informed and righteously confident. With broad smiles they started out.

"We'll see you in Zion!" they waved.

Titus stood with his arm around Diantha's waist until the feminine excursion was out of sight. "We'd best get busy," he said.

*   *   *

Before the year of 1831 ended, Titus had a buyer for the

two parcels of land that he owned and one for all of the Morley Farm. Ownership would be taken in the spring when Billings and designated families planned to leave. That was when they were commanded to head out for Zion.

"Brother Billings," Joseph said as he offered a strong hand-shake. "How is the Lord's new deacon today?"

Titus ducked his head, but did so smiling. "Fine," he said. "Things are falling into place. Guess that means it is the Lord's will."

"Indeed it is, my good man," the prophet said, extending his hand to the stranger who stood with Titus.

"Let me introduce you to Mr. Cain. He was my boss on the Erie job," Titus explained. They shook hands.

"Calvin, this is our prophet."

"Not many workers out there like this one." Cain said as he slapped Titus on the back. "Best foreman I ever had."

Joseph questioned with his eyes, but said nothing. Titus went on. "Wants me to help with Ohio's branch of the Erie Canal." Joseph knew Titus had helped build the New York canal. Still he said nothing. His prophetic eyes penetrated those of the new deacon while he waited for Titus to continue.

"They're digging all the way from Cleveland to Portsmouth. That will give Ohio an important north - south route," Titus said.

"Give a man a good paycheck, too," Calvin Cain added. "I can't believe this man just turned me down. Says he's committed to a new cause now. Bet it doesn't pay better than my offer."

A grin broadened across Titus' face and a new twinkle seemed to spark in his eye as he answered, "Maybe not in this life."

Cain shook his head and excused himself. He started off with parting words, "You know how to find me if you change your mind. Sure could use a good foreman like you."

Titus sighed and faced his prophet who seemed to radiate a powerful feeling of divine approval. Though he greatly delighted in this feeling of holy validation he felt a bit uncomfortable being its sole recipient in such a public place. Joseph must have sensed this for he said nothing.

"Did you find a place to take your family?" Billings asked.

"Yes, Elder Rigdon and I are moving our families to the John Johnson home in Hiram. It will be a good place to finish the New Testament revisions, yet keep me close to church headquarters here."

Most other farm residents had received calls to Zion and

were packing to move out.

"I will miss this place," Joseph said. "The Lord must like it here because He has blessed it in sacred ways." Titus understood and remained silent. He had heard the prophet refer to the Morley Farm as his second Sacred Grove because of other visitations there. Yes, he would miss Ohio too.

In front of the entire congregation, Thursday, March 10, 1832, with the Prophet Joseph Smith presiding, Elder Thomas B. Marsh laid his hands on the head of Titus Billings and ordained him an elder in the Church of Jesus Christ of Latter-day Saints, authorizing him to lead a chosen group of saints on a thousand-mile trek to Missouri. Fourteen days later, on the eve of his thirty-ninth birthday, Titus gave the order. Wagon wheels started rolling and the journey to Zion began.

Historical Background

Before the first anniversary of his baptism, "Titus was ordained as one of the first three Deacons of the Holy Priesthood, October 1831" (Black, 575; Cook, 102). He, Serenes Burnett and John Burk are recorded as "the first deacons ordained in the Restored Church" (Cannon/Cook, 19; Hartly, 6; Journal History2, 3). "At a second conference in Orange [Ohio] on October 25, 1831 additional high priests were ordained" (AndersonKR, 146).

Titus Billings was listed as one of "a number of influential men and saints in Kirtland to whom the Prophet Joseph was personally devoted" (Roberts, 283).

Minutes of General Conference held in the Town of Orange, Cuyahoga, Ohio October 25, 1831, showed Titus in attendance as a deacon (Cannon/Cook, 19). That same meeting, as Brother Frederick G. Williams inquired about the somewhat destitute condition of Sister March and her family, Titus is recorded as reporting that "he was surprised that the case of Sister Marsh should be brought to this Conference, as she and her family were provided for as well as her brethren around her" (Cannon/Cook, 23; Journal History1, 4).

"In the fall of 1831, Sister Morley and the children prepared to leave Kirtland, Ohio, to make their way to Missouri (MorleyRH, 34). "Lucy and the children did not travel alone . . .Bishop Partridge's wife and children made arrangement to travel with them" (MorleyRH, 35).

"Thirteen revelations (Sections of the Doctrine and Covenants: 45, 46, 47, 48, 49, 50, 52, 53, 54, 55, 56, 63, 64) were received here [on the Morley Farm in Kirtland,

Ohio] (Knowles, 6). The Prophet and Emma lived in Isaac Morley's home for six months. Heavenly visitation occurred at the Morley Farm (Knowles).

Migrating Saints were to bring a recommend from the bishop in Ohio or from three elders. They were also advised not to proceed to Zion without being told by one of the bishops that preparations had been made for them. Failure to observe this caution [W.W. Phelps wrote in the Star] would produce pestilence and cause confusion" (CES, 111).

Elder Thomas B. Marsh ordained Titus to the office of an elder on Thursday, March 10, 1832 (Black, 575; Cook, 102; Reorganized, 242).

"Kirtland land and tax records dated 21 January and also 26 March of 1832 show that Titus owned 2 parcels of land, 8 acres each in the 1-027 tract. One was taxed $30.00 and the other $75.00" (Backman, 133; Billings/Shaw/Hale, 6; Kirtland Saints Land and Tax Records). So, Titus "sold his farm by revelation in 1831" (Cook, 99; Deseret News obit) and began preparations to move "to Zion."

After sufficient preparation, Titus led a band of Saints going up to "Zion" in the Spring of 1832. "On 10 March 1832 Billings was 'authorized to take the leave of the Kirtland Church whilst traveling to the land of Zion'" (Cook, 144: Hyrum Smith Journal). "We started from that place March the 24" (Johnson1, 139).

CHAPTER 26

"Oh Joseph, thank God you are home." Emma, fatigued from sleepless nights with sick babies, fell into her husband's arms. "It's a measles epidemic. Everyone in Hiram is sick. Maybe all of Ohio too."

"Both of the babies?

"Yes, both of them, and all of the little Rigdons."

"Come, let's get you some rest," he reassured her. With tenderness Joseph tucked his wife into bed and took feverish crying Little Joseph into the other room to prevent awaking his sleeping sister.

Smiths and the Rigdons had found temporary housing at the John Johnson farm. The young father/prophet was himself weary from travel. He and Brother Rigdon, whose family slept in the log cabin across the street, had just returned from a strenuous trip. Joseph settled onto the sofa with his exhausted little namesake resting on his chest. A much needed deep sleep overtook him when right before midnight boisterous bullies burst into the house screaming threats to Mormon leaders Joe Smith and Syd Rigdon. They, reeking of sweat and alcohol stench, overpowered the sleeping prophet, dragged him outside and began to beat him. A violent attempt to force poison down his throat chipped off a tooth, scraped his face and bruised his neck, yet he swallowed not a drop of it.

Rigdon was next to be dragged into the night. Harsh winds fanned the tar-melting fire as well as the two bare bodies. Joseph, drenched with the black, suffocating goop, was smeared with smelly feathers. Rigdon was tied to a horse and dragged behind it while more tar was heated. He too was plastered in black, smothered with feathers and left to die.

Brother John Johnson suffered a broken collarbone during the attack as he tried to defend his prophet. David Whitmer was called in to administer priesthood blessings. John recovered instantly.

Emma, aided by despairing sisters, labored to undo the work of evils thrust upon innocent victims. Tears splashed and mixed with the tar as they peeled it off the raw, bleeding flesh. Joseph kept his eyes closed during those tedious hours. One could see his pain, but none would ever hear it. Sidney was delirious. Sister Rigdon was certain her husband suffered severe brain damage. She feared he would never be the same.

At dawning of day Emma could not pull herself away from the lifeless form of her precious baby boy who died in the night from exposure. Sleep deprived and heartbroken she refused to attend church services the next morning. Julia and the Rigdon children were still ill anyway. Joseph dressed. His tired body was scraped, bruised and aching. His face was swollen and the hair on his head had been thinned from the tar-removing process. The abused families could still be in danger. Emma had many concerns, but Joseph intended to keep his Sabbath morning preaching appointment at Hiram. God's prophet walked to the meeting with faith.

His sermon was profound. Joseph recognized mob participants in the congregation. To their astonishment his entire being was filled with love and compassion for each one of them. With power from the Holy Ghost he spoke of that love and taught about God's love, about forgiveness and about righteous duty. None in attendance, not even those who may have questioned his position the night before, could now deny the facts. Joseph Smith, Jr. was a chosen prophet of the living God. Following the service, three individuals were baptized.

In a touching graveside service, Little Joseph was called by his prophet-father the first martyr of the restored church. He was buried that afternoon. Elder Rigdon and his family were escorted to Kirtland where friends awaited to care for them. Joseph sent his family to Kirtland friends too. Nothing could stop him from taking an important, pre-planned trip. Early the next morning he was ready and started out on the first day of April, as scheduled.

The usual route from Kirtland to Independence was 1,000 miles. Travelers would go by land across Ohio from Kirtland to Dayton, then drop down to the Ohio River and ride it to the Mississippi where they traveled upstream to St. Louis, Missouri. From there the Missouri River could be taken to Independence. The purpose of this trip, however, required a different route to Independence. They were scheduled to pick up printing paper at Wheeling, West Virginia and hoped the detour would confuse mob efforts.

George Pitkin escorted Newel K. Whitney, Peter Whitmer, Jesse Gauze, and the prophet in his wagon. In order to avoid Kirtland mobs, they dared not return to fetch Sidney Rigdon, but rather sent him a secret message to meet them at Warren, Ohio. The next day they traveled all the way to Wellsville, Ohio, a little town on the banks of the Ohio River. Here they could have gone on by steamer, but Brother Pitkin had business in Stubenville, so he took them along by wagon the next day.

"Thanks, George. You are a good man." Joseph shook his hand. "Are you at all worried about returning alone?"

Brother Pitkin assured him that he would do fine and started back with an empty wagon.

At dawn the five boarded a steam packet (regularly scheduled passenger and cargo boat) and spent the day floating down the mighty Ohio. River travel was by far the best way to get around. One was fortunate when his path followed a river. Before dinner time they arrived at the first important stop, Wheeling, West Virginia. William W. Phelps had printing presses ready to run in Zion, but his letter stated that he had no paper for printing. Word must have gotten out that this was the prime purpose of their trip because angry men shouted threats to them when they carried paper bundles out of the warehouse.

Paper and passengers boarded a steamer called "Trenton." Tickets allowed for night lodging although they did not sail until morning. Someone did not want them to sail at all. Twice in the night they were awakened by frightening fires. The next morning the entire width of the steamship was charred. Even the cabin was damaged. By some miracle the precious paper had been spared.

"I don't understand it," the captain complained. "Why would anybody do a thing like that?"

After careful examination, his crew assured him that they could still sail. "Gotta get this cargo delivered, even if my ship is black. I'm sure we can make it to Louisville, and that would be a better place to make repairs anyway."

Though most passengers refused to travel on a damaged vessel, Smith and his companions were willing. When they reached Cincinnati, Ohio, they docked for an hour. By the time they sailed to Louisville, Kentucky, it seemed their enemy had turned away.

In the meantime, Titus Billings and his party of relocating saints traveled down the Ohio River by steamer. At one point, while their steam packet called the "Charleston" docked at Louisville, Kentucky, to take on new passengers, Diantha heard her husband calling.

"Send the boys up, Di, quick. The Prophet is here with a

load of heavy paper going to Zion!" Eager to help, they loaded crates and crates of paper onto the "Charleston."

For Titus and his companions on the "Charleston" the long winding ride under the bottom of Indiana and around the tip of Illinois where it caught the Mississippi was most memorable and enjoyable -- with the Prophet in their midst.

Diantha was anxious for news about Emma. So much had happened in such a short time that it was hard to believe. Little Joseph martyred! The Prophet and Sidney brutally abused, even tarred and feathered! How could anyone . . .? The sight of her prophet's injuries enraged Diantha's soul. Titus was alarmed when he spoke to Sidney, his friend and exemplar, who did not respond in his usual eloquent manner.

They parted at St. Louis where Joseph rented a stagecoach to race needed paper across the state by land, setting a record by traveling from Kirtland to Independence in only twenty-three days!

The Billings band of saints continued down the slow wandering waterway. Titus studied the variety of timber types as the steamer steadily strutted up the great Missouri River. He was a builder, relocating not only his family, but also a cluster of Mormon farmers and their families. They would need good lumber. He spotted soft and hard maple along the river bottoms. Tall oak trees, hickory, box elder and cottonwood were abundant. A multitude of fruit and nut trees were mingled in everywhere. This beautiful countryside, rich in materials needed to build the Lord's Zion, was ready and waiting for them.

Brother Billings tipped his head back and for a moment closed his eyes as sunlight kissed his face. *This too is a sacred place*, he thought. *Thanks, Dear Lord, for such a good home. It will be an honor to help build up Zion.*

Historical Background

Joseph Smith's family found retreat in the Johnson home at Hiram, Ohio. Sidney Rigdon also moved his family there temporarily. Joseph may have been sleeping on a trundle bed in the entrance hallway when mobsters dragged him from the Johnson home. Rigdons were bedded down in a little log cabin across the street when the same mob pulled Sidney from his bed (Perkins: Ensign, Jan. 1979, 39). David Whitmer was asked to administer to John Johnson when his collarbone was broken by the mobsters who tarred and feathered Prophet Joseph and Sidney Rigdon (Perkins, 34; Star).

"In March the Smith twins and all the little Rigdons developed measles" (Davis, 118). Joseph was sleeping on the sofa in the living room or possibly a cot in the entry hallway (Perkins, 39) when about midnight [March 24, 1832] he was carried away by a terrifying mob who beat, then tarred and feathered him and Sidney Rigdon. "Little Joseph, recuperating from the measles, suffered exposure" and died of the incident (AndersonLF, 51).

"The mobbing took place on Saturday night. The Prophet had an appointment to preach at Hiram on Sunday morning, and all bruised and scarified as he was, he appeared before the congregation, held the appointed service; and in the afternoon administered baptism to three converts" (Roberts, 282). "Earlier, when the Prophet was tarred and feathered in Hiram, Ohio, John Johnson had gone to the Prophet's defense, and during the attack his collarbone was broken. David [Whitmer] was asked to administer to him, and he was instantly healed" (Perkins, 40).

Because the planned trip to Missouri was necessary, both the Smith and the Rigdon families were sent to be with friends in Kirtland. Even Sidney Rigdon was taken there in an extremely ill and delirious condition. Although still bruised and lacerated, Joseph left Hiram, Ohio, in Brother George Pitkin's wagon on April 1st, accompanied by Newel K. Whitney, Peter Whitmer and Jesse Gauze. To avoid Kirtland mobs, they planned to meet Elder Rigdon in Warren, Ohio (He left that same morning from Chardon, Ohio). "Proceeding onward, we arrived at Wellsville the next day, and the day following at Steubenville, where we left the wagon" (Smith1, 266). Instead of the usual route to Cincinnati, they traveled to Steubenville, Ohio then by steam packet to Wheeling, West Virginia so that they could obtain paper for the press in Independence. "Indeed this was one of the primary purposes of the westward trip; W.W. Phelps had written that the new printing press was all set up, and they were ready to go ahead with the printing as soon as paper could be brought from the east" (Davis, 119).

Paper and passengers were loaded onto the steamer "Trenton" which suffered mob fires twice during the night "burning the whole width of the boat through into the cabin" (Smith1, 266). Surprisingly the next morning, damage did not prevent sailing to Cincinnati where some of the mobsters gave up. Then it was on to Louisville, Kentucky the same day.

There it was necessary to change steamers. While loading the "precious paper" onto the "Charleston," Joseph's company was greeted by Titus Billings and the Kirtland Saints on their journey to Zion. Together they traveled the long winding Ohio River to St. Louis, Missouri. "On account of so many delays, Joseph Smith felt it imperative to make the journey in shorter time than usual, and leaving the party at St. Louis, took the stage for Independence, carrying as cargo his load of paper. He records with satisfaction that he made the trip by the 24th of April! Only twenty-three days from Kirtland!" (Davis, 199; Journal History3).

"At Louisville we were joined by Elder Titus Billings, who was journeying with a company of Saints from Kirtland to Zion, and we took passage on the steamer Charleston for St. Louis where we parted from Brother Billings and company and by stage arrived at Independence, Missouri, on the 24 of April, having traveled a distance of about 300 miles from St. Louis" (Ludlow, 337; Nibley, 147; SmithJF, 85; Smith1, 266; Times and Seasons3, V4).

The number of saints Titus Billings led from Kirtland, Ohio to Independence, Missouri in the spring of 1832 is unknown. "In Jackson County the population of Saints grew rapidly. Between 300 and 400 arrived in the spring of 1832, and by the end of the year there were over 800 members in Missouri" (Brown/Cannon/Jackson, 34).

MISSOURI: A TIME OF TESTING

March 1832: Independence, Jackson County, Missouri

November 13, 1833: Clay County, Missouri

September 1836: Far West, Caldwell County, Missouri

CHAPTER 27

"Next stop, Independence Landing, Jackson County, Missouri" the captain announced as his steamship glided toward shore.

Titus pulled at his sweaty collar. Humidity pressed heavily upon him. *It's only the month of May,* he thought to himself, *yet what will this place be like in the heat of summer?*

Oh, but the greenery was magnificent! Lush land stretched as far as the eye could see. Grassy hills, shrubbery, and tree leaves blending together a landscape of the infinite shades of green he loved. Brilliant flowers blossomed here and there for accent. "He was right," Titus said aloud. Diantha heard him.

"Who was right . . . about what?" she asked.

"Oh," Titus said, returning to his senses. "The Prophet Joseph."

"The prophet is always right," Diantha assured him in jest. "But right about what?"

"Well, it's sacred," he said. Diantha perked up.

"When Joseph called me to lead certain saints to Missouri and purchase lands here, he told me it was the place where the Garden of Eden had been."

Now Diantha was sober. "You mean Adam's Garden of Eden?"

Titus nodded. "We've come to a sacred place to do a sacred work," he said softly.

Without doubt, the place was inviting. Titus squeezed his wife then stretching his neck to see over dense treetops outlining the river's edge, he asked for directions.

"Just follow that road straight into town," he was told.

Independence Township, the furthermost frontier settlement of western America, had existed only four years, yet it proved already to be a hub for river trading. Mormon passengers began to unload. Titus and his "big" boys, Samuel fourteen and Ebenezer twelve, helped the others off first. Diantha knew that they would. She positioned two-year-old Eunice and five-year-old George on a grassy spot and assigned seven-year-old Alfred to look after them. Then she started unloading her own things. Titus was shaking hands with the steamer's captain when an empty wagon approached the ramp.

"Uncle Isaac, Uncle Isaac," Georgie shouted on the run. Alfred grabbed his baby sister and stumbled to the wagon too. Isaac Morley raised the adorable girl over his head and lowered her with a tender squeeze. Eunice was the only niece he really knew. His other siblings lived far away and did not seem to care for his new religious ways. Diantha was the only other member of his family to join the true church. He was pleased to welcome them at last.

"Brother Billings," he shouted with exaggeration.

Titus looked up at the sound of that deep, wonderful voice he loved, hoping his brother-in-law still loved him. So much had happened since Isaac's mission call. Titus, as commanded, had sold Isaac's farm. For a time he worried if Isaac would forgive him for that. Thomas Morley certainly could not. The stubborn father-in-law refused to look beyond what he referred to as the abandonment of family farm and cemetery, to consider any spiritual justification for it. Leaving her parents so forsaken had all but broken Diantha's tender heart.

"Welcome, Little Brother," Isaac teased as his huge arms caught Titus by the neck. Titus was definitely the taller man, but he would have tolerated any title while in the comfort of "Father Morley's" friendly embrace.

"I feared we might not be on talking terms these days," Titus ventured.

"How so?" came quick reply.

"'Feared a land owner might dislike a guy who sells property when he's not looking."

"Ya, how 'bout that." He smiled. "I confess some wonderment about the issue. The Lord worked me over good, though. Think it was His way of teaching me humility and priorities. Don't know if I would have been as trusting and obedient about it as you were. At any rate, I know now that it was right before our God and that pretty much takes care of it, don't you think?"

Of course there was agreement. Diantha witnessed the dialogue with great jubilation. How she loved these two men, both heroes in her life. Both of them, she thought to herself, on the way to becoming true saints of the Lord.

Sam and Ebe continued helping their father assist others. Diantha and her three youngsters were loaded into the wagon and it started off. Isaac had come to lead them all to Mormon purchased land where they would build new homes.

"We are building more than a church," he told his sister. "We are building the Kingdom of God."

When they arrived at their new location, Diantha was thrilled to see Lucy Morley and Lydia Partridge again. After hugs she helped her little ones climb down.

"How was the trip?" Lucy asked.

"Fine, very fine. We journeyed all the way from Louisville [Kentucky] to St. Louis [Missouri] with the Prophet on our steamer!" Diantha continued, "You are looking well. I see that you made it safely too." An unexplainable look passed between Sister Morley and Sister Partridge.

"Safely, yes," Lydia said.

"What happened?" It was obvious that they had a story to tell.

"We did fine for the first hundred miles," Lucy began.

Diantha remembered Titus instructing them to travel the first hundred miles by land, the same route the Billings' group had taken, then to follow the Ohio River on steamboat. It had worked for their group. "What happened then?" she asked.

"Insufficient water. When we reached the river it couldn't float a boat."

"What did you do?"

"First, we rented a cabin and waited for rain."

"Waited a whole week" Lydia added.

"It was a long week," Lucy said. "No storm came and there was no way we could keep going by wagon. We finally decided to take a keel boat."

"A keel boat?" Diantha was amazed. "How could you go so far up the river on a keel boat?"

"We had no other choice," Lucy stated. "A steamboat could never have made it up the dry channel so we loaded onto a flat bottom. Shortly after we started a storm hit. Turned out to be a bad one."

Lydia slowly shook her head. "The wind and the rain and the darkness made it impossible to see anything."

Diantha pictured the sight of two drenched mother hens bent over a dozen crowded, shivering little chicks. "It must have been miserable," she said.

"Everything was wet."

"The boat was leaking."

"We rammed into a sand bar and were stuck. I don't know

why, but we were not allowed to light the lanterns."

"Probably couldn't have lit them. Anyway, that made things worse. Isaac Jr. was so cold and frightened that he would not let anyone else hold him. He sat on my lap until daylight." Lucy paused. "Come inside. You must get out of this sun."

Once they were settled, Diantha helped Lucy peel potatoes.

"So, finish your story. Did that storm let up at daybreak?" she asked.

"Yes, thank goodness. Three sailors swam to shore where they found long logs to pry the keelboat off of the sandbar. We floated down the river until about noon when we spotted a steamboat."

"The storm made us miserable," Lydia said, "but it did make the river run again."

"We gladly changed over to the steamboat," Lucy said.

"You poor things. What a trip!" Diantha said.

"Oh, but that's not all," Lucy added. "We had a hundred miles left to go when we hit river ice! By then it was late November and the river was freezing."

Diantha tipped her head back and almost laughed. "I can't believe it!"

"Believe it or not," Lucy said, "we stopped at the nearest landing and rented another little house while we looked for land passage. Finally we found and hired a man with a span of mules who agreed to take us in his teamster wagon."

"Oh, good . . ." Diantha sighed.

"Not so good," said Lydia. "That wagon had a huge Pennsylvania box with the cover drawn so tightly we could not see out at all. It was nauseating for me to bounce up and down in that airtight darkness, hour after hour, day after day; let alone our, poor, bored-to-tears children."

"None of us will forget that trip, will we?" Lucy smirked as groans resounded from the background. "Isaac was a true hero the day he rescued us on the path and transported us to our castle in Kaw Township."

"And now, here we are in Independence, living in cabins on the edge of the temple lot," Lydia smiled.

So it was. The Colesville Branch first settled in Kaw Township, about twelve miles west of Independence, on the other side of Big Blue River. Isaac built his first Missouri home at that settlement. He had exciting news updates to tell Titus as they walked to

Bishop Partridge's home after dinner.

"Symbolic of the twelve tribes of Israel, twelve of us, including Joseph Smith laid the first log for a school house in Zion at Kaw Township [August 3, 1831]. Elder Sidney Rigdon dedicated and consecrated the land for the gathering of saints with a beautiful prayer. The next day we dedicated the temple site in Independence. The Spirit was there, Titus."

A strong, sweet spirit filled the air as Isaac spoke.

"Then the Colesville Branch met at Brother Joshua Lewis' home for the first church conference in Zion."

Titus marveled at the things he heard, and marveled perhaps even more as he considered himself an honored participant of this Zion effort. Isaac spilled out more words before Titus had chance to find any.

"You haven't met Brother Lewis yet, but you'll like him. Good man. Many good men have been called to the work."

Ever so many good things were happening so quickly.

"It's an honor to live in such a time," Isaac concluded.

Titus nodded. "Yes, I know," he said.

Historical Background

Jackson County, Missouri in the 1830's was on the extreme western frontier of the then existing United States. The Billings party "arrived in Jackson County Missouri in May" (Johnson1, 139). This region was still largely unsettled, with the county seat in a new town called Independence (Romig/Siebert, 298)."The Prophet Joseph Smith was exuberant about the prospects for the area. He taught that Jackson County, Missouri, was the location of the Garden of Eden" (CES, 106).

A historical marker is placed at Wayne City Landing, formerly Independence Landing, where River Road runs into the Missouri River. "This was a major landing for river travel and marks the spot where the migrating Billings Party arrived" (BillingsEA5)

"Independence was only four years old and lacked many amenities, but the incoming Mormons -- primarily from New York and Ohio -- worked industriously to realize their goal of an earthly paradise. They built homes, started a school, operated a ferry, farmed, opened stores and churches, and published two newspapers, one directed toward members and the other toward secular society. The Mormons brought with them a deep-seated evangelistic belief in their religious and social philosophy. However, some were overzealous in their attempts to share the good news with their new neighbors, to claim this land as their inheritance, and to expostulate against the evils of slavery. This gave birth to a feeling among some of the older settlers that both Independence and Jackson County would be far better off without the Mormons" (Foester, 14).

Isaac Morley was present when the temple site was dedicated in Independence, Missouri and was one of twelve men who placed the first log "as a foundation in Zion" in Kaw Township, August 1831 (Curtis, 16; Esplin, 4; MorleyRH, 26).

"The Titus Billings family and the Isaac Morley family were exceedingly close and united in their efforts" (Bennion, 2). Isaac, was seven years older than Titus. He was the only other member of Diantha's family to ever join the Church. "His home was always open to persons interested in the Restored Gospel. Many meetings and parties were held there" (MorleyRH).

Bishop Edward Partridge, who was "the man that God had appointed in a legal way, agreeably to the law given to organize and regulate the church, and all the affairs of the same" (Geddes, 53) "purchased the 63 43/160 acres [approximately 63.25 acres] west of town that encompassed the temple site" (Jackson County, Missouri Land Records, Book B, 1; Romig/Siebert, 292).

"There were about three acres set apart for the temple lot . . . and the rest of it was for the purpose of settling saints on it, for the homes of saints ultimately, and they concluded to buy more lands than that, and settle homeless saints on it" (Romig/Siebert, 293).

"Beyond the sixty-three acres, Partridge acquired an additional fifty-five acres of land in section 3 from Flournoy, on February 28, 1832. Jackson County Land Records, Book B, 129. Several members such as Titus Billings and Calvin Beebe received inheritances on this land" (Romig/Siebert1, 120).

Partridge built his own home, as well as an adjacent schoolhouse that also served as a meetinghouse in bad weather, on a portion of this larger tract. John Corrill, counselor to the bishop, lived on the temple tract [as did Isaac Morley, the other counselor (according to Ron Romig interview 1999)] and Partridge may have begun establishing other members on portions of this acreage as well. Titus Billings' inheritance was part of eighty acres Partridge had purchased. This allotment was west of the acreage surrounding the temple site. This land presently contains the sanitarium [Independence Regional Health Center at 1515 West Truman Road] and land south of it (BillingsEA4; Romig/Siebert, 293).

A Historical Marker

Wayne City Landing, formerly Independence Landing, where River Road runs into the Missouri River was a major landing for river travel and marks the spot where the migrating Billings Party arrived (BillingsEA5).

(Courtesy Anne B. Untch, 2014.)

Historical Trailhead and Overlook

"Wayne City Landing was a busy river port in the 1830 period. When the Saints were driven from Jackson County they crossed the Missouri River at that point" (Billings,EA3).

(Courtesy Anne B. Untch, 2014.)

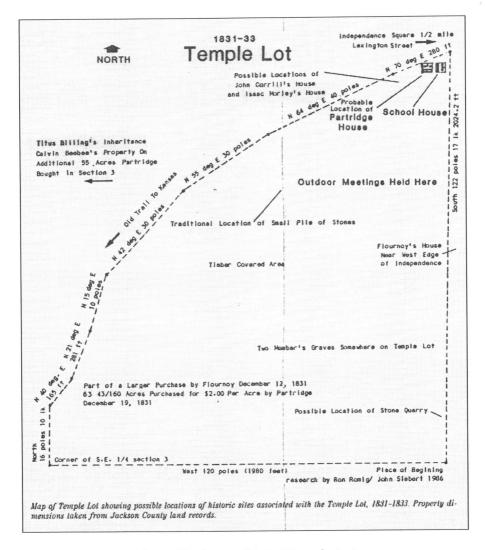

Map of Temple Lot showing possible locations of historic sites associated with the Temple Lot, 1831-1833. Property dimensions taken from Jackson County land records.

Map of Independence Temple Lot

The probable location of Bishop Edward Partridge's home and the school also used for a meeting house beside it are here shown as well as the possible home locations of Counselors Isaac Morley and John Corrill. An arrow shows the Titus Billings and Calvin Beebee properties are off the map, to the west.

(Courtesy Ronald E. Romig and John Siebert. From Place of Beginning, 1986.)

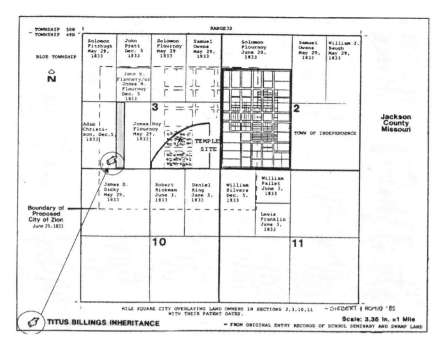

Billings Inheritance

The 27 ½ acres deeded to Titus Billings are outlined on this Independence, Missouri map.

(Courtesy Ronald E. Romig and John Siebert. From Original Entry Records of School Seminary and Swamp Land, 1985.)

CHAPTER 28

With delight Bishop Edward Partridge showed Brother Titus Billings a sketch for a wonderful new township mapped out around the temple site. As yet, Independence Township was very small and spread out in a rectangular fashion.

"We plan to build our Zion, well, the Lord's Zion," Partridge corrected himself, "in all this area west of town."

Titus studied the bishop's drawing and rejoiced in knowing funds from the Morley Farm had helped to purchase property in the heart of the planned settlement.

"We bought this land at a dollar-and-a-quarter per acre. Bought sixty-three acres west of the existing town and another fifty-five acres over there."

Titus was impressed. All purchases for the church were done in the name of Bishop Partridge. John Corrill surveyed three acres for the temple lot first. Just north and off to the east of it, he plotted three homesteads. These were for the families of the bishopric, Partridge, Morley, and Corrill. The Partridge portion was a larger tract so a schoolhouse could be built adjacent to his home. On bad weather days this would be used as a meetinghouse as well. Other assignments were ready to be consecrated and deeded. Brother Billings made an appointment with the bishop for the next day and retired to his wagon.

Before dark Titus and Diantha Billings listed and totaled all their belongings to be worth $316.52. The next morning, along with their only horse, two wagons, two cows and two calves (valued at $147.00), the Mormon couple also consecrated to the church: two beds, bedding, and extra clothing (worth $73.25); farming utensils (totaling $41.00) and various articles of furniture (worth $55.27). This was everything they owned. Willingly Titus Billings signed his name to the deed, legally binding him and his family to a new establishment of the United Order in Jackson County, Missouri.

"Brother and Sister Billings, lawfully releasing your right to this property fulfills a threefold purpose." The bishop went on to explain how building Zion, the New Jerusalem, purchasing land in Jackson County, Missouri, and relieving needs of the poor, secures one a land stewardship and the lease of certain personal property from the church.

Bishop Edward Partridge then signed a document releasing twenty-seven and one-half acres west of the temple lot into the stewardship of the Titus Billings Family. They would have to pay yearly taxes on the property. The land could be improved and farmed as they saw fit.

Certain that he was on Billings acreage, Titus spaded the dark, rich soil. Deeper and deeper he dug. Still, the earth was black and fertile. As it filtered through his callused hands, he detected traces of sand and clay. The area would be productive. This was good land. He could hardly wait to plant it.

The sacred allotment was a long strip of land that ran parallel to the temple ground property. Trees cradled a lane that turned off of Lexington Road and led to the center of his new homestead.

"What do you think, Diantha?"

"I love it, Titus. I really love it."

"Thought we could build our cabin right here at the end of the lane and a barn over yonder," he said as he pointed.

"I feel so blessed, Titus. We will be living in the very heart of Zion."

"We will indeed." Titus stood behind his sweetheart with his arms wrapped around her and together they lingered in the holy place with reverent silence."

Billings put his boys to work at once, building a home, raising a barn, and clearing land for farming. While plowing and planting, he wondered what the future would hold. More saints immigrated daily. Fortunately, he had planted extra crops, for soon it would be too late in the season for the newcomers to plant at all. Hopefully, with everyone working for the new Order, there would be enough to sustain life. The hay crop would be sufficient for his animals, but not many others. Somehow they needed to find more feed.

The thirty-nine-year-old farmer arched his back to remove some kinks and then wiped his forehead dry. Frontier territory was covered with untouched, wild grass. For a moment he just stood there gazing at the beautiful fields that rolled on and on over the hills. This was a wonderful place to be. Titus felt gratitude for such a stewardship. God had blessed him greatly.

Just then a breeze rustled the prairie grasses and made them wave like an ocean. There was so much of it out there. The grass was tall and tanned and ready to harvest, if one wanted to harvest wild grass. Why not?

After church a shy, country farmer approached his bishop with boldness. Diantha knew his plan. He was out of his mind to ask such a thing, but she was proud of him and turned to hide the grin on her face.

"Well?"

"Well what?"

"Well, how did it go?"

He kept a straight face until it worried her. As their buggy turned onto "Billings Lane" he burst out with the biggest, most mischievous, chessy-cat grin she had ever seen.

"Got' cha," he chided.

"You asked for it," she retaliated. Ask for it he had. Titus Billings had volunteered to build the biggest pile of hay ever stacked in America. This he would do with wonderful, free of charge, prairie grass.

"So, where will you build this masterpiece of yours?"

"On the Governor's land!"

"What? Where is that, in Jefferson City?"

"Nope. Right in the middle of little ole' Independence so folks can get at it."

"What makes you think the Governor of Missouri is going to let you stack prairie grass for Mormon cattle on his property?"

"Partridge has rented it already. Said he knew he should, but he didn't know why."

Diantha couldn't hide her delight.

"You're quite a man!" she sighed. That made him smile with a timid look in his eyes that she adored.

"So who is going to help you with this grandiose project of yours?"

"You, I guess." She shook her head. "And the boys. It will be good for them."

The Billings teenagers were only fifteen and thirteen years old. There was no question that they already knew how to work. A summer of stacking wild hay would build muscles for sure.

Historical Background

Titus settled his family "on 34 Acres of Land within a half a mile of Independence" (Johnson1, 139); a township referred to by the Saints as Zion. "The land being only one dollar and a quarter per acre, the Saints, though generally poor, were enabled, many of them, to make very extensive purchases" (Snow6, 146).

Bishop Edward Partridge "purchased the 63 43/160 [approximately 63.25 acres] acres west of town that encompassed the temple site" (Jackson County, Missouri Land Records, Book B, 1; Romig/Siebert, 292).

"Not in Zion, but in Thompson, a settlement a little way out of Kirtland, Ohio, the experiment of the United Order was first tried by the Prophet" (Evans, 242). The Colesville Branch of sixty members moved to Thompson in 1831. Edward Partridge, the first bishop, was given the Lord's plan of the United Order by Prophet Joseph Smith and instructed to implement it in Thompson. Results of this effort are unknown. When these members of the Order moved to Zion and became part of the twelve hundred Saints in Jackson County, Missouri, the Order was again put into place under the direction of Bishop Partridge.

"One deed (or lease) executed by Titus Billings and Edward Partridge (that consecrated all property to the church) and another executed by Edward Partridge and Titus Billings (that secured his stewardship) inform us about the legal transactions incident to the establishment of the Order" (Evans, 242). In the first, Billings deeded over:

Sundry articles of furniture..............	$ 55.27
2 beds, bedding, extra clothing........	$ 73.25
Farming utensils................................	$ 41.00
1 horse, 2 wagons, 2 cows, 2 calves..	$ 147.00
Totaling…...	$ 316.52
All for the purpose of	1) purchasing land in Jackson County, Missouri 2) building up New Jerusalem, even Zion 3) relieving wants of the poor and needy.

Titus "consecrated his property to Bishop Partridge. His 27-acre inheritance lies northwest of the Temple Lot" (Consecration Form, 26-30; MO Land Claims, Ms 2703, f3; Romig2, 13).

This document "is said to have been found among the papers of Bishop Partridge. It was a 'lease-lend' document. Under this instrument the Church leased to Titus Billings a certain amount of real estate and loaned him a certain amount of personal property" (Arrington/Fox/May, 372-3; Backman, 55; Huff, 14; Smith1, 365-367). "Titus agreed to do this of his own free will and accord, having first paid all just debts. He had agreed to release all rights to the consecrated property and also to bind himself and family to pay taxes yearly on the stewardship. Such were the terms on accepting membership in the Order. He was portioned twenty-seven and one-half acres" (Geddes, 49) near the Temple Lot in Independence, Missouri.

"The first of the following deed-forms was used in consecrating property to the Church; the second, in securing the stewardships to those entering into the law of consecration and stewardship, sometimes called the Order of Enoch, because it was the law under which the Patriarch Enoch and his people lived" (Smith1, 365; Sperry, 172). "Titus Billings, one of the early church leaders who gathered to Independence, executed this deed to Bishop Edward Partridge" (Howard, 252).

"This was an answer to the economic needs of families, still allowing for the individuality of family groups. Each had a different kind of home, different kind of furniture, different tools or equipment to suit the different needs. All of this was: gauged according to the size of the family or actual need, yet every man had enough to eat, enough clothes to wear, and a house to live in and every man was required to turn into the Community Chest whatever he produced above what he needed, whether it was much or little whether it was the Bishop or the most insignificant member. The law was uniformly enforced in the Order" (Evans, 243).

"The project is said to have failed for two reasons: 1) expulsion of the entire Mormon Community from the county, and 2) reluctancy of many rich or more "well-to-do" to put their all into a public fund and to give up all surplus earnings. This law was not practiced in new locations" (Evans, 243).

"On the subject of the Titus Billings deed, the very fact that only one has been found when thousands of deeds must have been executed may tend to show that there were no special Church-created property documents, and that normal land documents were used. Some original research on this point would be most useful (Huff 14).

President J. Reuben Clark, Jr., has stated flatly concerning the single deed of Titus Billings, often mentioned as an example of communal transactions, that "this instrument is not in accordance with the principle laid down in the revelations touching upon the United Order.' A possible explanation for the existence of this deed follows: Titus Billings was baptized in Kirtland in 1830, probably indicating that he had been a resident there for a time, and probably had some useful knowledge of the area. That might have made him a good candidate for being a real estate agent. Titus Billings is first mentioned in conjunction with the administration of real estate in Kirtland in the 1831 revelation directing him to travel to Missouri" (D&C 63:38-40).

"We may fairly assume that since Titus Billings had the care of the farm on which many lived, and the land was held in a single title, it is likely that most of those people were there on either a free guest or rental or lease basis, the lease basis being more likely since some might expect to remain for an extended time. If leases were used in Kirtland and administered by Billings, it is quite possible that upon his move to Missouri he might propose a similar system for use there, especially since he would be dealing with the same group of people whom he dealt with on the farm in Kirtland. As counselor to Bishop Partridge, he was charged with similar real estate responsibilities in the new location. It would be tempting to use a lease system in Missouri because it would avoid the administrative burdens of getting land deeds for everyone, and would be a way of enforcing the counsel that individuals should not sell their land to nonmember -- what they did not own they could not sell. It would also make it easier to expel people who may have occupied land under false pretenses or who later left the Church. If made, this lease proposal was not accepted, and according to Joseph Smith's instructions, deeds were given in most cases. In some cases, lands were signed over to mobbers at gunpoint, showing that the mobbers assumed that the 'mormons' held title to their property and could transfer it to others" (Huff, 144-142) [Note: Billings was not called as a counselor to Bishop Partridge until much later when the saints moved to Far West.]

"The law of consecration is actually the first of three stewardship systems reflected in the Doctrine and Covenants. Following the Jackson County, Missouri attempt at practicing the law of consecration, or Celestial Law, there was a period of relaxed application as a result of the church's exile in Clay County, Missouri. After that, a modified version of the law of consecration was officially introduced by Joseph Smith, Jr., at Far West in 1838. At this point elements of tithing were incorporated into the stewardship structure. In 1841, during the Nauvoo period, Joseph suspended the practice of consecration in favor of the law of tithing" (Arrington, 38; Romig, 192).

Titus Billings did erect a long, gigantic stack of prairie hay on property rented by Bishop Edward Partridge from Governor L.W. Boggs. He wrote: "knowing many of my Brethren was a comeing (sic) to this County & not haveing (sic) a chance for raiseing (sic) a crop that season I thought best to cut a quantity of hay which ammounted (sic) to 24 tons Weight which was hauled 6 miles & was worth 5 Dollars per ton" (Johnson1, 139).

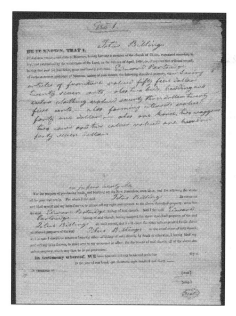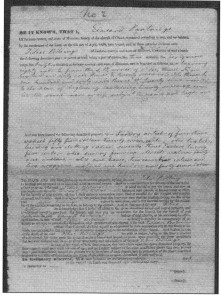

Deed of Stewardship
See full-sized documents in Appendix A.
(Courtesy LDS Church Historical Department.)

The Titus Billings stewardship property in Independence, Missouri: Northern boundary: Truman Road. Southern boundary: Winner Road (turns into Lexington Road). Eastern boundary: From Truman Road follow Woodland Street behind the hospital until it jogs at 1501 West Maple, continues to 1501 Short Street and down to Winner Road. Western boundary: Forest Avenue.

Billings Lane in Independence, Missouri: "Turn off Lexington Road, travel parallel between Walnut Road and Short Street, and enter center of Billings Stewardship Property, where we believe the homestead cabin was built" (Billing-sEA1,2).

Haystack Plaque

This ceramic tile plaque featuring Titus Billings and his gigantic volunteer haystack (Henry Inouye, artist) was presented by the Missouri Mormon Frontier Foundation to my mother, Elda Mae Lewis Billings.

(Courtesy S.B. Mitchell, 2013.)

Evan A. and Elda Mae Billings pictured in photo.

In Recognition of Elda Mae Billings for her contribution to local Independence and Jackson County, Missouri, Latter-day Saint history through service to her church, community, the LDS Family History Center, and the MMFF.

MISSOURI MORMON FRONTIER FOUNDATION

CHAPTER 29

"A School of the Prophets? Here in Missouri?" Titus Billings was honored by the invitation. The Prophet Joseph taught a selected group of brethren in Kirtland, Ohio. Now, Elder Parley P. Pratt was called to start a branch of the school in Missouri.

"Yes, Brother Billings, you have been chosen," Elder Pratt said.

Elder Billings sat in council on numerous occasions. He could be trusted with confidences. He loved to watch the prophets and apostles in action. God's ways were orderly and they inspired him. Titus supported the work and deemed it an honor to witness the restoration of God's will on earth. His heart broke when others criticized or fell away.

"We'll meet in the timbers come July."

Titus knew the spot, a wilderness area near Pratt's Blue Ridge home, only about 12 miles from the Billings homestead. As of yet, Titus had no idea he would be experiencing the gift of tongues and prophecy.

An autumn chill diluted the brilliant sunshine as Elder Billings and his family started home from church. Their massive haystack gleamed like a pile of gold. No one could miss it. Other members heard of the project's purpose and their Mormon community buzzed about it being a service of love.

"T'aint done yet," he told them. "Lots more grass out there and we got many weeks before it snows!"

Teaming for the folks of Jackson County was a good, honest way for Titus to earn a living. Though word of mouth advertising landed more jobs than he wanted, none were ever turned down. He went out of his way to please every client.

Titus unloaded a large shipment and stacked it neatly onto the deck. The cargo would go out with the next steamer. Usually he loaded the goods onto a boat, but this time instructions were different. His empty wagon backed away from Wayne's Landing and started up River Road. Titus noticed a newcomer walking alone. He stopped to offer a ride. Chapman Duncan was a young man, about twenty years, who had a most interesting story to tell. They talked all the way home. Titus took him in to meet Diantha.

"I had been seriously ill with consumption so my father sent me to South America for my health. We were traveling down the Ohio River when I got so sick that I went to bed during the day. I know that I wasn't asleep, but I heard a man speak to me. It was more in my mind that he spoke."

"Did that frighten you?"

"No, it was very peaceful. My first impression was that the Lord or his angel had a message for me. I remember the message exactly. 'Thou shalt prosecute thy journey no further south than the mouth of the Ohio River. If you do you will die."

Samuel Billings commented out loud, "That would scare me, I think." The visitor continued.

"I was pondering this when, not more than five minutes later there was more." He paused.

"Go on. Please tell us. What more?"

"This time the voice in my mind said, 'If thou wilt go to the western border of the state of Missouri to the place of gathering of my people thou shalt live!'"

"So what did you do?"

"Well, I didn't dare to go any further south. Instead I turned my course toward St. Louis and ended up here."

As he listened, Brother Billings experienced that same good feeling he had come to know as validation from the Holy Spirit. This young guest was speaking truth.

"Welcome to Independence," he said. "Let us teach you about Zion."

For the next five weeks Chapman Duncan was tutored by loving Saints. His study of the Book of Mormon was intense. He prayed over each page. Church meetings inspired him. He had a great deal to learn.

"So you think you're ready to join up with us?" Brother Billings asked.

"Yes Sir, I have no doubts. That is exactly what I want to do."

"Then I would be honored to perform this ordinance. Thank you for asking."

Sunday, after services, a sizable crowd followed Chapman Duncan to Bush Creek and stopped at a spot three miles west of Independence. There, with priesthood authority and much rejoicing, Titus Billings baptized his young friend. Immediately afterward the bishopric pronounced a confirmation of the gift of the Holy Ghost upon him.

Duncan moved into Isaac Morley's home and spent the rest

of the winter working for him. The next spring he raised a crop on the temple lot for Morley.

Uncle Isaac, called "Father Morley" by the saints who loved him, welcomed with open arms anyone interested in the restored gospel. His home, a favorite gathering spot, soon became a frequent target for disgruntled outsiders as well [1833]. The shatter of glass and loud thud of a stone hitting the headboard jolted Chapman Duncan from a deep sleep.

"It's a miracle you weren't injured," Lucy said as she gathered up the glass filled bedding.

"Yes," Duncan agreed. Broken glass could have blinded him! "Can't believe it didn't cut me all up."

"The Lord sends His angels to help us," Father Morley said.

"Those mobsters are keeping his angels busy these days," Duncan said.

Together they replaced the window.

"Father, why do people do such things? Why don't they like us?" At the dinner table Isaac tried to help his children understand.

"The Book of Mormon tells us that there will be opposition in all things," Morley said.

"I think the devil is angry that the truth of God is in this land," Duncan added.

Isaac nodded his agreement and went on. "This is a southern state and most of its citizens believe in slavery. We, as saints, do not. I think that makes us a threat to their way of thinking, to their way of life."

Terrified screams startled the sleeping Morley household again in the night when Cordelia and Theresa, sleeping together in a bed under the window, awoke to a crashing downpour of shattered glass falling on their bed, their pillows, even their faces.

"Another stone-bomb!" Isaac said as he lifted a two-pound-rock from off their bed and marched straightway out of the house. He would have reckoned with these troublemakers, but the cowards ran off.

Tension was building. Disgruntled citizens felt threatened by the fast-growing Mormon population in their midst and wanted something done about them. God-fearing, hard-working, Mormon do-gooders, were not quiet about their beliefs and aspirations. They had big plans to take over everything and turn it into what they called "Zion." They did not believe in slavery and would have too many votes against it. Certain Missourians felt the need to take law matters into their own hands.

Historical Background

"Behold, I say unto you, concerning the school in Zion, I the Lord am well pleased that there should be a school in Zion; and also with my servant, Parley P. Pratt, for he abideth in me; and inasmuch as he continueth to abide in me he shall continue to preside over the school in the land of Zion until I shall give unto him other commandments . . ." (Pratt, 94).

The first School of the Prophets met March 18, 1833, "in an eleven-by-fourteen-foot room over Joseph's kitchen, in a house attached to Bishop Whitney's store. Joseph was designated to preside over the school in Kirtland" (Brigham Young, Journal of Discourses 12 (1869) 158; Romig/Siebert1, 103).

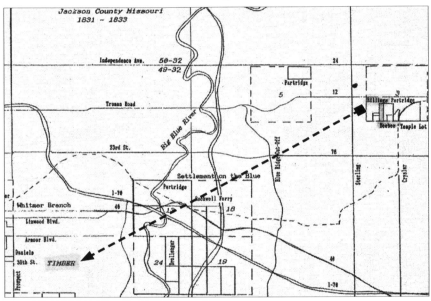

School of the Prophets in Missouri

Parley P. Pratt was authorized to start a branch of the School of the Prophets in the Timbers of Jackson County. Titus Billings walked to these meetings from his home, pictured on the upper right-hand corner.

*(Courtesy Ronald E. Romig, 1990.
From Church and Member Lands Jackson County Missouri, 1831-1833.)*

As a counterpart to the School of the Prophets, a School of Elders was organized in Missouri, which was presided over by Parley P. Pratt. In July 1833, from Independence, John Whitmer wrote of the activities of this school, "God is pouring out his Spirit upon his people so that most all on last Thursday at the school received the gift of tongues and spake and prophesied" (Cook, 188; Romig3; Romig/Siebert1, 103).

For a short time Parley P. Pratt taught a 'School of Elders' in an area of wilderness by his home in Blue Ridge. It is believed that Titus may have attended that school, about 12 miles from his home. [See area labeled TIMBER on map of Church and Member Lands of Jackson County Missouri 1831-1833 by Ron Romig] (Romig5). He probably attended the Kirtland School of Prophets on his return there.

"Following the early efforts of the School of the Prophets in 1833, the School of the Elders met during the next two winters, when the men were not so busy with farming or missionary assignments. It convened in a thirty-by-thirty-eight-foot room on the main floor of the printing building just west of the temple. The purpose was to prepare the men who were about to go forth as missionaries or to serve in other church callings. The curriculum included English grammar, writing, philosophy, government, literature, geography, and ancient as well as modern history. Theology, however, received the major emphasis" (CES, 160-161).

As an elder, Saturday, May 26, 1832, Titus was called to sit in council on a case concerning "our Brother Oliver" (Cannon/Cook, 49). At a conference held in Brother Algernon Sidney Gilbert's home in Independence, Jackson County, Missouri, a "transgression committed in Ohio in the fall of 1830, was resolved and forgiven. High Priests attending were: Edward Partridge, John Corrill, Isaac Morley, Wm. W. Phelps, Algernon Sidney Gilbert and Jesse Gauge. Elders present were: Titus Billings and Calvin Bebee" (Journal History4, May 26, 1832).

Again as an elder it is recorded on July 3, 1832, that he [Titus Billings] "sat in council concerning a regulating revelation received earlier in Hiram, Ohio" (Cannon/Cook, 51; Journal History5).

Chapman Duncan joined the Church at age twenty "in the county of Jackson, state of Missouri, in December" (Duncan, 1). He had been ill with consumption and left his father's home in New Hampshire to go to South America for his health. While traveling on the Ohio River he had become so ill that he had gone to bed during the day. He was not asleep, but it seemed that a man spoke to him:

"I heard no audible voice: it was a quiet peaceable yet sure impression. In fact I knew that the Lord or an angel spoke to me. This is the message he bore to me: 'Thou shalt prosecute thy journey no farther south than the mouth of the Ohio river. If you do you shall die.' I looked to see the personage. I saw none. I began to meditate upon what I had heard and the feeling that pervaded my person, and while thinking I cannot say whether it was five minutes or more, the spirit again spake and said further, 'If thou wilt go to the place of gathering of my people thou shalt live.' The force of the message rested so heavily upon me that

I dared not go farther south and turned my course for St. Louis, Missouri . . . I think I arrived in Independence the last of November, found the Saints enjoying themselves tolerably well. After [conversion] listening to the doctrine of Christ and getting somewhat acquainted with the new-made friends (for they took me in), I joined the Church I think the last of December, baptized by Elder Titus Billings on the Sabbath Day" (Duncan, 1).

A second record states: "The following sentence was spoken to me in an audible voice. I was not asleep. 'If you proceed your journey you contemplate, you will surely die, but if you will go to the western border of the state Missouri by the border of the Lamanites you shall live there and you shall find my Church.' I looked around to see who spoke to me. An audible voice answered, 'The Holy Ghost.' The confirmation I experienced of the fact that it was the Holy Ghost, I cannot here describe, only that it was I felt a perfect assurance of the spirit of God which affected my whole system. I had not fear or doubt of the heavenly message . . . In December I was baptized in Brush Creek, three miles west of Independence of Titus Billings, confirmed by the bishopric (Duncan1, 5). Chapman Duncan lived with "Father Morley" that winter and "raised a crop on the temple lot for him, and in all things gave thanks" (Duncan, 2).

"Because of his influence among the saints, mobsters targeted the Morley home" (Morley). An enraged mob shouted threats and threw "stones into the window at Father Morley's, into the room where we slept" (Duncan, 2). "The first demonstration of mob violence that I know of was in the evening after we had gone to bed. A stone was thrown into the window. It hit the bed on the bed-stead very near my head" (Anderson1, 52).

One evening after the Morley family was again sleeping: a rock weighing two pounds was hurled through the bedroom window shattering the glass and filling the room like the impact of a bomb. The bed in which Cordelia and Therissa [daughters] were sleeping was situated under the window, and as a result pieces of glass covered the bed, some of it landing on the faces of the girls. Father Morley was awakened by the shatter of glass which was followed by the hysterical crying of his daughters. Fearlessly, upon seeing what had happened, he ran out into the dooryard to contend with the troublemakers, but they fled before him" (Morley, 49)

CHAPTER 30

"Congratulations, Bishop. It's a boy!" Diantha announced on June 25, 1833. "You can go in now." The Partridge household buzzed with joy and excitement over its seventh child. Lydia was thankful her son had arrived before his father had to kiss her good-bye. Bishop Partridge had many duties that called him away, but he knew Sister Billings would take good care of his wife and new-born while he was gone.

The next time he saw them, his tiny son was three weeks older.

"Edward, I'm glad to see you home again," Diantha said. He smiled and nodded.

"At last he's home to stay," Lydia said with weary voice.

"Well, that's a comfort. You'll probably sleep better tonight," Diantha teased. She started for home, relieved that little Edward Jr. was well and the mother was starting to be. Tonight she would probably sleep better herself.

A few hours later a committee of thirteen Jackson County citizens approached Mormon leaders demanding that printing of Mormon publications cease and that all Mormon families move out of the county at once.

Bishop Partridge made a reasonable request. "Give us three months to consider these things and work out a plan."

"You got fifteen minutes!" someone shouted. "And that's all!"

Leading citizens of Jackson County, including Missouri's Governor, Lilburn W. Boggs, and 400 to 500 others, had met earlier that afternoon, Saturday, July 20, 1833, at the Independence Court-house. There a "secret constitution" was read. Then the angry group drafted a "bitter ultimatum" against the Mormons. Tempers flared. A civilized people turned into a hateful mob, determined to destroy the Mormon printing presses and expel every living Mormon from the county.

Not long after dark, a terrified messenger summoned Titus.

"Come quick, Brother B. The devil is trying to burn down our town!"

Titus left with boots barely on his feet. For speed he took the wagon, rushing to the fire with all his might. He was too late. He could save nothing. Presses that printed the Mormon newspapers, "The Morning and Evening Star" had been dumped into the Missouri River and the type scattered to the four winds. Papers, books, furniture, walls, everything had been burned. Brother Phelps' home was destroyed.

Angry souls were gathered at the Square. Titus wanted to punch them all. As he started toward them, the crowd was dispersing. Still he strutted forth. When he glimpsed a wounded soul on the ground he broke into a run.

"Too late Mormon, go home."

Brother Billings ignored their threats. Someone was hurt. Those simple cowards had tarred and feathered a boy! Charles Allen was only twenty-seven years old, a new convert from Pennsylvania. He had not been here long enough to hurt anyone. How could they . . .?

"Help me get this boy out of here!" Titus shouted.

That was not all. Monsters were still bent over something else. *Not another body*, he hoped. Indignation filled his whole being.

"GET OUT OF HERE!" he screamed.

The mob was satisfied with itself and peeled off, some wearing faces of shame because their victim had suffered it so patiently. Billings rushed to the human heap they left behind. No, no, no! It was the Bishop, his beloved friend! No kinder man ever lived. How could anyone find fault with this man? Why would they hurt a bishop of God?

With help, Titus loaded the wounded ones into his wagon and hurried them to shelter. Sister Partridge stood rigid with shock. She needed Diantha. Titus' wife had a way with helping hurt people. He left at once to fetch her.

Lamps burned all night as Diantha and a group of caring sisters labored frantically to save the suffocating skin. Tar and pearl-ash containing flesh-eating acid had to be removed from head to foot. No matter how painful it was, the sickening job had to be done. Titus did what he could. Mostly he watched and guarded. The night would never be forgotten. For the rest of her life, Diantha Billings would cry every time she remembered its tragedy.

Only three days later, a mob of five hundred seized Bishop Partridge, Isaac Morley, John Corrill, John Whitmer, W. W. Phelps and A. S. Gilbert. At the point of bayonets they were marched to the Jackson County Jail.

Helpless saints watched with appalling fear.

"Why do they carry red flags?" Ebenezer asked his father.

Billings knew red flags meant that the mobs wanted to spill Mormon blood, but how does one explain that to an innocent child. The horrible, sickening yells were something no one should ever have to hear.

The six prisoners offered their lives for the safety of the saints, but to no avail. An instant sentence without trial and without any promise to terrified families demanded all prisoners be sentenced to die in three days. A last request the night before execution allowed only thirty minutes for saying goodbye. Two guards escorted each prisoner to his home. The Billings family was grieving with the Morley household when Isaac arrived.

Father Morley called his loved ones to pray with him and to eat together one last time. As was his way, he invited the guards to join them. The younger guard accepted politely. The other spoke crude words and refused the kind offer with disgust.

"America is intended to be a land of freedom," Morley proclaimed. "It is not lawful to persecute the saints of God." He continued to testify to the truth of his words. His courageous declarations caused the more sensitive keeper to weep. Such weakness made the other guard livid. Jumping to his feet, he shouted at the children.

"Look upon your father for the last time, for tomorrow you shall have none!"

Thirty minutes is inadequate to cover all the heart would have spoken. When they pulled him from the arms of his wife, Isaac asked that the family remain in the house. They wanted to follow as long as they could, but instead he admonished them to use all their strength to call upon God. He was gone. Falling to her knees, Lucy Morley asked Titus to lead the family in prayer.

All through the night the Morley house was filled with prayer. No one slept. Each took turn petitioning the Lord over and over in earnest prayer.

At dawning of day, when the hour of execution had come, a huge, seething mob gathered at the prison. Too many wild men had differing ideas of what should be done with their prisoners and argued incessantly.

"Hang 'em. They deserve hang'n."

"Shoot 'em and get it over!"

"No, they should be tarred and feathered and burned to death!"

Fighting broke out. It was not long before guards forgot their charges and joined in with punches. Prisoners watched as an unseen power opened the jail door. Whereas the mob had not honored their part of the bargain, so to speak, by refusing to allow saints to live in peace, and whereas the Lord, it seemed, had opened the way for them, the innocent prisoners felt obliged to leave. All six of them walked through the door, passed the bickering mob and returned uninjured to their various homes.

Sobs broke the silence as the bereaved Morley household awaited confirmation of their patriarch's doom. They expected a messenger to come, but instead were astonished when the victim himself stepped into the doorway.

"We have no time to lose," he warned them. "The enemy could show any moment."

With haste they packed him a change of clothes in a kerchief, tied to a hooked stick and again he was gone.

Alone, Isaac Morley journeyed through the forest about five miles before a voice admonished him, "Go back to your family. If they perish, you perish with them."

Obediently he started for home. After a four-hour absence, his family and close friends, still confused and shaken, were again startled when he reappeared. Nearby, in a massive cornfield, grew an enormous tree. Loved ones of Isaac Morley followed him to the spot where they took refuge from the mob.

Historical Background

"On Saturday, 20 July, four or five hundred disgruntled citizens met at the Independence Courthouse" (CES, 132). These leading citizens of Jackson County, including Missouri's Lieutenant Governor Lilburn W. Boggs, read a "secret constitution" and "drafted a bitter ultimatum" against the Mormons. "The meeting quickly turned into a mob that decided to destroy the printing office and the press" (CES, 133) and "that members be required to move from the county" (Romig/Siebert, 295).

"The mob commenced greater hostilities, finally whipped some of the brethren and tarred Bishop Partridge. I, Chapman Duncan, saw them about to commence as I was brought into the ring for that purpose, but I escaped unhurt. They tarred Charles Allen also" (Duncan, 2). "Charles Allen, a twenty-seven-year-old convert from Pennsylvania was also taken to the public square" (CES, 133). So, on 20 July 1833, while sitting with his frail wife, three mobsters burst in on them and forced Edward out of his Zion house into the bedlam of the street . . . they rushed upon Edward Partridge and Charles Allen and dragged them to the public square

156

where a murderous mob of five hundred stood ominously armed with rifles, dirks, pistols, clubs, and whips. Their spokesman demanded that Edward and Charles either renounce their faith in the Book of Mormon or leave the country. Edward quickly responded: 'If I must suffere [sic] for my religion, it is no more than others have done before me. I am not conscious of having injured anyone in the county and therefore will not consent to leave it. I have done nothing to offend anyone. If you abuse me, you injure an innocent man.'

" 'Call upon your God to deliver you!' they yelled. When neither would give in to their demands, the mobsters . . . brought their buckets and daubed Edward and Charles from head to foot in a mixture of tar and pearl-ash which contained a flesh-eating acid. Then they threw a quantity of feathers over the sticky tar. The two men bore this cruel abuse with such restraint and dignity that the crowd stopped their taunting and grew still. The sky was darkening; and as evening descended, the two brethren silently left the ugly scene" (Faust, 74).

"The beloved Bishop Edward Partridge was disrobed by the mob and given a coat of hot tar and feathers" (Morley, 41). "Edward Partridge and Charles Allen were tarred and feathered on the county courthouse lawn" (Romig/Siebert, 295). "Partridge was forced from his home and tarred and feathered on the public Square" (Curtis/Romig, 11).

Sister Partridge "had, three weeks before, been delivered of a baby boy and was still very weak" (AndersonLF, 52). Diantha was one of a few other women who helped the wives care for their tarred husbands. They worked hours into the night trying to clean off the suffocating skin. Forever afterward Diantha would weep when the incident was mentioned. "She could never forget the terrible condition of their damaged heads and hair" (Hale, 1; Snow3, 1).

"Early in July 1833, Jackson citizens met to determine action against what they called fanatical Mormons. Missourians were from the south and as nearly all the Later-Day Saints were from the northern and eastern states they feared the Mormons would take away their political power. The question of slavery was becoming quite keen and they wished the state to be controlled by slaveholders, but that which engendered their hatred was the fact that the Mormons believe in revelation by heavenly messengers who had appeared to their leader" (Esplin, 4).

"It was then determined that 'No more such persons would be allowed into the county and all now residing would be forced to move 'in a reasonable time.' Their first committee spread the word to startled saints. Immediately a second committee was sent out to determine the response. A committee of thirteen came to Edward Partridge, A.S. Gilbert, John Corrill, Isaac Morley, John Whitmer and W.W. Phelps, and demanded that we should immediately stop the publication of the Evening and Morning Star, and close printing in Jackson County; and that we as Elders of said Church, should agree to move out of the county forthwith. We asked for three months for consideration. They would not grant it, but said fifteen minutes was the longest, and refused to hear any reason" (Smith1, 411). Church leaders could not answer for the saints on such notice so "the type in the printing office was ruined and the two-story brick building leveled" (MorleyRH, 41). "I [Chapman Duncan] saw them throw down the printing office after throwing the type and press out of the window. Directly the mob gathered to drive [out] the Saints" (Duncan, 2).

On July 23, 1833, a group of five hundred men seized Isaac and five other Church leaders: John Whitmer, Edward Partridge, John Corrill, W.W. Phelps and A.S. Gilbert. They were marched to jail at the point of bayonets. The mob "flew a red flag which indicated they wanted to spill Mormon blood, and their horrid yells were sickening to the tenderhearted Saints" (Esplin, 5; Smith1, 412).

Titus "was there during the troubles of Jackson and when Bishop Partridge and Father Morley were put in prison he was present" (Deseret News obit).

"When offering their lives as ransom if 'the inhumane cruelties' would desist the six prisoners were immediately sentenced to die in three days. As a last request each was allowed thirty minutes to bid farewell to his family" (MorleyRH, 43). "Father Morley asked permission to see his family once more" (Cox1,2). Two guards accompanied each elder to his home. As Father Morley called his family around him to pray and eat together for the last time, he invited the two guards to join them. One accepted and joined in but the other guard was rude and refused to cooperate. Father Morley said America was intended to be a land of freedom, and that it was not lawful to persecute the Saints of God. He also proclaimed the word of the Almighty God unto the two which caused the more friendly guard to weep, but made the other so angry that he said to the children, "Look upon your father for the last time for tomorrow morning you shall have none" (MorleyRH, 43).

That night, after the prisoners had been marched back to jail, Isaac's family gathered in the Morley home and prayed together all night. When the hour of execution arrived, the guards argued and some unseen power opened the door, giving the prisoners freedom to leave. "The mob had not honored their half of the bargain, to let the Saints live in peace; therefore, Morley and the others felt the Lord desired they should escape, and they did" (MorleyRH, 44).

CHAPTER 31

Life went on for the Zion-seeking saints, but it was never the same. Peace became a gift most rare. Diantha was surprised to see her husband bump down the lane with an empty wagon so early in the day. Only last night he had fussed about all the loads he had to haul before he could get back to building the community haystack. This was the pile's second year. He and the boys vowed to make it the world's biggest this time. *Big talker*, she thought to herself. Truth was he always did what he said he would. She ran out to meet him.
"Is anything wrong?"
"Nope."
"Are you okay?"
"Yep."
"Is it the mob?"
Titus shook his head, but didn't say more until he had dipped a drink of cold water and dumped another dipper of the cool liquid onto his head. The silver dipper hung on a nail over the sink, awaiting its master who routinely used it when he came into the house. Titus sat down and slapped the seat of an empty chair. His wondering wife assumed it was her cue. She sat beside him.
"Got something on my mind," he admitted. Titus Billings was a man of few words. If he had something to say, she was ready to hear it.
"Remember the day they stuck Isaac in jail and nearly killed him?" Remember? How could she ever forget? "D'you remember what day of the month that was?" Diantha calculated quickly.
"July 23rd, I think it was a Tuesday."
"Right, do you know what else happened on that very day?" She did not, but certainly wanted to know. Word had come from Kirtland that saints had laid a cornerstone for a temple. At last they would be building a House to the Lord. Presently the church had two centers: one here in Independence, Missouri and the other still in Kirtland, Ohio. She knew all of that. What was so important that he had stopped everything to tell her?
"Diantha, can't you see a pattern?" He had lost her completely. "It seems to me that when the Lord does something wonderful the Devil has to do something horrible in an effort to offset

159

it."

Well, that was food for thought. Her mind was still trying to process this concept when her husband suddenly had to get back to his work.

Challenges increased daily. The Lord was really trying to do great things, she determined, because everywhere one looked an evil hand was stirring up trouble for the saints.

Satan is wasting his time, she thought. *We will never give up.*

During hot summer months, the Billings boys helped their father haul twenty-four tons of prairie hay, six miles into town. They were working at the haystack when their mother's buggy pulled to a stop. She carried a long letter, mailed to her, that made no sense at all. She hoped Titus could figure it out.

The letter, addressed to Mrs. Billings, was dated October 1, 1833 and sent from Elder Frederick G. Williams. Hastily Elder Billings jumped down from the wagon.

"Did you read it?" he asked.

"Not really," she started, "Didn't make much sense. I . . ."

"Good," he stopped her. "This is really important." He put his arm around her and started walking back to the buggy, almost as though he was trying to shelter their conversation. "I would have told you, but I didn't think it would be so soon."

Diantha was confused, but wise enough to play along. She said nothing as her husband escorted her to the passenger seat and stepped up to drive the buggy. He called out instructions for his boys to keep working. "I'll be right back," he told them.

The Independence saints had enemies lurking all around them. Some suspected that anti-Mormons were intercepting church mail. The Brethren had discussed secretly using a woman's name for correspondence.

"I suggested your name and they all agreed you would be perfect," he explained at length.

"Thanks for telling me." She tried to sound sarcastic, but in reality she was honored that her husband and the brethren had chosen to trust her. Now she would be watching. Together they left to deliver the letter.

*   *   *

Diantha picked small branches of red, orange and yellow leaves to decorate the mantel. How she loved this time of year when Missouri hills blazed with October colors. Supper smelled good as she stirred it. Her men would be hungry tonight. Over the last several weeks her young sons had worked as hard as any man. She was proud of them and of their father whose giant haystack was by far the "biggest in all the world." Of that she was certain. More important to her than its size was its unselfish purpose. *Who else but Titus would have thought to harvest prairie grass?* she thought, *and donate every blade of it to the Lord and His cause of Zion.*

Titus looked extra tired and seemed bothered by cross words he had overheard on the street. Strangers were saying things they should never say about the prophet. Why didn't people just leave them alone? Never before could Diantha remember her husband leaving hay in the wagon all night, but tonight he intended to do so. They would start out extra early tomorrow and drop it off. After praying, he fell to sleep in no time.

Part of the joy in working hard is being able to sleep well. Another part is the feeling of satisfaction that goes with one's accomplishment. Titus had earned great satisfaction with his generous, volunteer effort. He had done a good thing for a good reason. Tomorrow he planned to run a couple more loads before winter storms buried the prairie crop.

Billings always woke early. This morning was no exception. Even eight-year-old Alfred was dressed earlier than usual and pleaded for a chance to help. With fondness his father tossed him onto the loaded hay, and the foursome started down the lane. If ever a sight was worthy of memory the view of her beloved and sons embarking on the Lord's errand that morning, was one Diantha wished to treasure forever.

Brisk air whipped a trace of smoke around their heads. Titus sat tall and held his breath. Something was wrong, very wrong. They rode on. The smoky stench grew stronger. Soon stinging eyes began to water and noses filled up with unbreatheable air. Elder Billings continued a slow and steady pace as an unsettled feeling of alarm seemed to crawl up his back and wrap around his neck. The boys were silent with puzzlement and fear.

Before their wagon cleared the last bend, they saw the impossible. It was unbelievable. How could anyone be so cruel? There, before them, in a hallowed spot, remained only a long, black strip of smoldering ground, where the mighty haystack should have been!

The Lord's haystack had disappeared in the night. Some-time between sundown and dawn it had been torched and burnt to the ground. *How could any living soul ... and why? ... why would they?* The height of his accomplishment's satisfaction was now matched by the depth of his anguish. He could not speak. Three of his sons watched their father with horror. A few gathering saints were silent too. Nothing could be done. There was nothing to say.

Tall, tired Titus stepped down from his wagon. He still had this one load they did not take away. Slowly he shuffled closer to the place where the world's largest haystack should have been standing. There he smoothed a spot with his tattered boot, knelt on the ground and started to pray. "Dear God, please accept this as our sacrifice to Thee."

Historical Background

In an effort to outwit the enemy suspected of intercepting Church correspon-dence, Elder Frederick G. Williams sent a letter addressed to "Mrs. Billings", October 10, 1833 (Smith1, 417; Times and Seasons V6, 864).

Fire was set to the giant haystack that Titus had stored for incoming saints on property rented by Bishop Partridge from Governor Boggs. That October, between sundown and dark it was burnt to ashes. (A year later James Allen told Titus that a man named "Franklin" had started the fire. Allen had been asked to help, but had not. Franklin thought the haystack belonged to Bishop Partridge and threatened to drive out all the Mormons (Johnson1, 139).

Ron Romig, RLDS Church Archivist, stresses that Titus Billings gathered prairie hay to build the gigantic, 24 ton haystack. All community property was listed un-der the name of Bishop Partridge. The haystack was located on a piece of ground rented from Governor Boggs for church use. It was prepared for the good of all saints, by Titus, in the Bishop's name (Interview with Romig, April 26, 1999).

[Titus Billings] "cut a quantity of hay which ammounted (sic) to 24 tons weight .. . this was set on fire and burnt to ashes between sundown & dark this was in Oct" (Billings,T).

A letter dated June 25, 1833, had been sent from Kirtland to Brother W.W. Phelps and the Brethren in Zion. Concerning bishops it recommended that Isaac Morley and John Corrill be ordained the second and third bishops in Zion allowing Bish-op Partridge to "choose as counselors in their place, Brother Parley P. Pratt and Brother Titus Billings, ordaining Brother Billings to the High Priesthood" (Clark, 11; Faust, 73; Journal History6; MorleyRH, 40; Smith1, 363; Times & Seasons4, 800). Before these instructions could be carried out, persecution of Mormons grew commonplace in Jackson County. Saints suffered untold hardships (Black2, 24).

CHAPTER 32

Mormon persecution burst out like a widespread epidemic during November 1833. Most church leaders were away when angered citizens forced Isaac Morley, A.S. Gilbert, William McLellin and John Corrill to again appear at the Jackson County courtroom.

"These men are a dangerous threat to our community!" The speaker was tightly buttoned into an almost too small, dark suit. He motioned toward the innocent, gentle-looking Mormon representatives then continued by shaking a finger at those in the jury box.

"We must free our communities of these fiends and their devilish ways!"

Titus Billings looked across the room, into the pensive face of his brother-in-law. Isaac's blue eyes were filled with tears, hurt, and pity, but one could find no hate or even a trace of malice in them. How could anyone accuse such a gentle soul with fiendish intent and devilish ways? He and the others volunteered themselves as ransom for their brethren. With pure hearts they were willing to die for the prophet of God! *How can that be devilish?* Titus shouted in his mind!

Ruthless threats and harsh arguments crowded the stuffy log building. Not only were the Mormon victims sentenced to incarceration in the Jackson County Jail, but because of their so-called cruel natures and wicked plans these dangerous men also required strongest security. They would be detained in the underground dungeon.

Outside, all Mormons were forced to surrender their guns to Missouri Militia. Ironically at gunpoint, Titus leaned his rifle - a prized gift from his father - with the others against a huge tree stump that stood in the courthouse yard. The gigantic tree, with a twelve-foot diameter trunk, had been chopped down, leaving a spacious stand for stacking confiscated firearms. Billings stepped back allowing others access to the old tree. He looked upward imagining how tall it must have stood and how broad its branches must have stretched. The seasoned farmer knew that a tree's root system is as extensive underground as its branches are above. It would take great doing to remove the mighty old stump. One would never get all the roots out. Surely that was why it had been left.

They can chop us down Titus thought to himself, *but they will never get Mormon roots out of Independence.*

Isaac and his companions were marched to a sixteen-foot square log prison. Its only access was an outside stairway that led to the upper room. The new, extremely dangerous Mormon prisoners were led to the lowest level of the Jackson County Jail.

Diantha tied some biscuits, a little venison jerky and some dried fruit into a cloth and gave it to Titus.

"How can you guard the prophet without a weapon?" she asked. Titus shook his head. *A gun would be nice,* he thought. Anger once suppressed, began again to gnaw at him. *They have no right to treat fellow citizens like this. What happened to our freedoms here in America?* He did not trust them for protection and now he had no means to protect his family, nor his prophet. *I can't even hunt for table meat, he thought.* This is wrong. All of it is wrong. But maybe his biggest bother was losing the gift his father had given him. *Will I ever see that dear man again?*

Titus closed his eyes and drew in as much air as his lungs could hold. He rotated his shoulders to release tension. He had every right to be angry, or did he? *The new gospel teaches that no one should allow himself to become angry. The Savior would not do so. If I want eternal life with God and with loved ones . . . well, I just have to be bigger than all of that.* Titus turned to his worrying sweetheart. She was reason enough for him to choose right. He reached out for her. "The Lord will provide," he said, as he hugged her goodbye and left with other men to help protect their prophet on a necessary trip.

During dark, wee hours of the night, Diantha and others awoke to a loud ruckus. Isaac Morley couldn't stop them because he was behind bars, so mobsters set his cooper shop on fire. Skillfully made barrels, tubs, and churns burst into devouring flames. Fine, ready to sell, cooper ware was completely destroyed. The loss was incalculable and senseless.

Then, as if to top it off, wild fiendish creatures bounced around like demons cursing and swearing and threatening more of the same to any Mormon still in Independence the next night!

Morley's shop was a short distance from the Billings farm. Diantha and the children saw it burn to the ground. Titus was gone. Isaac was in jail. What could she do?

Evil threats of the night were renewed by wicked shouts in

daylight.

"Evacuate Jackson County now or be burned out of it!"

Frightened, Diantha counseled with several other sisters in the same perplexing situation. For the safety of their families they had to stand on their own and take action at once. They decided to take their smallest children and hide out in old man Beebe's cabin.

Brother Beebe lived alone, back in the trees, on the edge of the settlement. He was too old for guard duty. They hoped he would welcome and hide them. To attract less attention it was agreed that each mother should take her own children and brave the mile distance separately. The plan was to leave as soon as it was dark enough to hide them.

The house was cold, but Diantha feared chimney smoke from a fire might betray them. There was no time for supper anyway. With sadness she took a final look, wondering what could be saved. It was getting dark. They had to escape. Quickly she opened the wooden chest. Still on the very top, rested the brown wrapper from which she pulled out the wedding lace and tied it to her waist.

Then the worried mother and three frightened children, ages four, six, and eight years, knelt for what would probably be the last time in their beloved little cabin. Her prayer was intense, "Please protect the boys already in hiding!" She prayed for courage, safety, and guidance for all of the saints. Then bravely she lit a lantern and hid it under her apron.

"All right little soldiers. Stand tall and take a deep breath." For her own good she demonstrated. "Now, let us be off."

Going down the lane or along the highway would be unsafe. The frightened foursome would have to blaze a path through the forest. Growth was thick and untamed. Branches flipped faces and scratched arms. Prickly briers snagged their clothes. Children clung tightly to their mother's skirt as they stumbled on together. With abundant caution Diantha maneuvered her brood from behind one tree to another, hiding in each shadow. The journey was taking so long that she feared getting lost, or going in the wrong direction because of the darkness. *If only Titus were here!*

Finally she spotted and recognized the crossroads, a main intersection. They would have to leave the shelter of trees to cross it. This called for another deep breath and silent prayer.

"Please help us . . ."

Carefully she stepped into the clearing and waddled on like

165

a mother duck with a trio of scared ducklings under her feathers. Just as they started onto the road a man jumped out from behind a tree, flashing a sword in front of her face! Diantha jumped back screaming before the man could make himself known.

"Sister Billings, is that you?" Brother Morgan Gardner rushed to help her. "I am so sorry. I thought you were . . ."

A friendly face was never more welcome. He had been left to guard the crossroads.

"Guess I thought you were too," she said.

"Hurry," he warned. Riders have been up and down this road all night. Taking her elbow, the kind gentleman hurried her across. He was back in hiding before she could thank him.

Beebe's cabin was already overwhelmed with frightened women and children by the time Diantha arrived. Youngsters were bedded down on the hard, cold floor, few with quilts or coverings. Little arms were bleeding from scratches and tummies were hungry. Not a soul was allowed to talk or even cry.

Mothers took turns, two at a time, dressing up in Brother Beebe's clothing and standing guard over the others. Because of his homebound health condition Brother Beebe's gun, not yet claimed by the militia, was available for the patrol. Sister Billings pulled guard duty with a young woman who was very much with child, for the first time. By now Diantha was certain that she was expecting too, but she had not been able to tell her husband and would tell no one else until he knew. Oh how she ached for him. *Please keep him safe*, she prayed.

Diantha was ready, but her partner struggled to get all her thick, long hair into a hat.

"Here, let me help you."

With the old man's handkerchief she tied up the hair and stuffed it under the brim.

"That will do. If the mobbers get close enough to see your hair it won't matter anyway."

Packing the heavy gun over one shoulder, she tried to walk like a man up and down the dooryard. Their two-hour shift seemed to last forever. Both were well worn when at last their turn was finished.

Back in lady's clothes Diantha tried to sleep for a moment. Rest would be needed to get through the morrow. She was all but there when, deep in the night, a gunshot exploded. Hearts pounded as mothers clutched children trying to silence them. Some held their breath. Others tried to peek out of windows.

Soon crying was heard from outside. It was one of the women.

Lydia Partridge opened the door. Two sisters entered. "It's okay," they whispered. "Don't worry. Everyone is safe."

"But we heard a gunshot."

Movement of Brother Beebe's old, white horse had startled the weary, inexperienced gun handler as she desperately tried to protect the others.

"I shot him," she said. "I shot an innocent horse." Relief filled the crowded cabin. "I'm sorry, Brother Beebe. I'm so sorry," she cried.

Diantha made her way to the sobbing sister and cradled her like a baby. "It will be all right," she comforted. No one seemed able to sleep for the rest of the night.

Historical Background

"Isaac Morley and five others stepped forward and offered themselves as a ransom for their brethren" (Jenson1, 236). "Mormon leaders appeared in the [Jackson County] courtroom in November 1833. Upon surrender to the Militia, Mormons stacked their guns around a twelve-foot diameter tree stump in the courthouse yard" (Jenson, 7; Curtis/Romig, 10). "Nov. 5: Col. Thos. Pitcher, commanding the mob militia, in Jackson County, demanded that the Saints should give up their arms, which order was reluctantly complied with. During the following night and the next day the mob forced the Saints from their homes at the point of the bayonet" (Jensen, 7).

"An outside stairway to the upper room was the only way to enter Jackson County's 1827 sixteen foot square jail built of hewn logs. Leading Mormons, A.S. Gilbert, Wm. McLellin, John Corrill and Isaac Morley, were incarcerated in the lower level, [dungeon] in November 1933." (Curtis/Romig, 10).

"I was also imprisoned in Jackson County falsely [sic] for twelve hours and shot at by a mob in 1833" (Morley, I).

Fear gripped the Billings family late one night as Uncle Isaac's cooper shop burst into flames. "It was full of cooper ware: barrels, tubs, churns and numerous other articles he had made to sell. The mob set it on fire and stood around and cursed and swore and yelled like demons from hell at the time it was burning. I [Eunice Billings] can remember how frightened I was and how light it was from the flames" (Hale, 1; Snow, 1; Snow3, 1).

"Our house was threatened to be burned and my father was at that time guarding the prophet and my mother took three of her youngest, I [Eunice Billings Warner Snow] among the number, to Calvin Beebe's house" (Snow1,1). Lillian

Billings Brady, a granddaughter of Titus and Mary Ann Tuttle Billings, said in an interview at her Fairview, Utah home, 1995: "My grandfather [Titus Billings] was a bodyguard to the Prophet Joseph Smith" (Brady, 1).

Morley's shop was "out a short distance from the house" (Snow, 1). "Our house was threatened to be burned, and my father was at that time guarding the prophet" (Snow8, 1). Troubled Diantha did not know what to do. She counseled with 15-20 other sisters. All concluded to take their smallest children to the home of an old man, Brother Beebe, who lived alone. Hoping to attract less attention it was decided that each mother should take her own children and brave the dark nearly mile-long journey separately. "Hiding a lantern under her apron, Diantha stumbled with three small, terrified children" (Billings/Shaw/Hale, 27) clinging to her skirts.

"I [Eunice] was the youngest [four years old, Alfred would have been eight and George six]. None of us had had a bite of supper. We went through fields of briers and all kinds of stubble that scratched our arms and legs" (Snow, 1-2). "My mother, fearing to take the highway dragged us as speedily as possible through the brush and over the stones" (Snow8, 1).

In order to cross the main road they had to step out of the trees into a clearing at one point where four roads crossed. At that moment a man jumped out from behind a giant tree "and flashed a bright sword in front of her face" (Hale, 1; Pyne, 4; Snow3, 1). Diantha jumped back screaming before the man could make himself known as Brother Morgan Gardner, left to guard the crossroads.

Brother Bebee's cabin was overwhelmed with frightened women and children. Youngsters were bedded on the hard, cold floor, most without quilts. "I remember well how my limbs were scratched and how they bled when I was put to bed and not allowed to cry or make a loud noise" (Snow, 1). Mothers took turns, two at a time, dressing up in the old gentleman's clothing to stand guard. In two hour shifts "they walked the dooryard, each with a gun over the shoulder" (Snow8, 1). "Deep into the night a gunshot exploded. Movement of old man's white horse had startled the weary and inexperienced guard as she desperately tried to protect the others" (Bennett, 554; Hale, 2).

[Note: Isaac Beebe, known as Father Beebe, was from New York. He moved his family to Jackson County, Missouri, in 1833 (Cannon/Cook, 248). An 1831-33 Temple Lot Map (made by Ron Romig and John Siebert, 1986) shows Titus Billings and Calvin Beebe having inheritance of property on an additional 55 acres of land that Bishop Partridge bought according to the RLDS D&C section 3. The cabin referred to could have been on that property. Father Beebe is described by Titus' daughter as being elderly and living alone. Isaac could have lived in a cabin on property in his son's name. His date of death is listed as 1834; no month is given. Place of death is Jackson County, Missouri. Saints were driven out of the county in November 1833. Calvin Beebe "was whipped and beaten while prisoner and his father was killed" (Romig, "Members" RLDS Archives).

Chapman Duncan, schoolteacher, reports staying in Calvin Beebe's cabin while suffering from "fever and ague" in 1834 (Duncan, 3). (That must have been in Clay County.) Calvin Beebe, also Bebee and BeeBee, was born in Paris, New York, 1 July 1800. He served in the Far West High Council. (Cannon/Cook, 248). He died in 1868 (Ancestral File).

CHAPTER 33

Zion is on fire! Alarming reports from Independence reached the Prophet and his body guards who were hours away from helping their families. Saints were literally being burned out of their homes. Titus left the moment he heard it.

To his dismay the report had been sound. Dozens of homes, stores, barns and fields were charred like his haystack. Destruction was devastating, but where were the families?

Fifteen to twenty husbands could not find their sweethearts or their children.

Fearing the worst, Titus rushed down "Billings Lane" only to find his homestead, his sacred stewardship, smoldering. The home he built and the barn he raised were burned to the ground. Four acres of golden, ready to harvest wheat were disintegrated. The twenty-seven and one-half beautiful acres he loved and labored to magnify lay before him scarred and ugly. In desperation he searched for his family.

Sam and Ebenezer, heard his call and came running. A look of fear smeared their faces. Hugging their father they described their hiding and how they had watched all the fires from start to finish. They saw everything happen, but could not do anything to stop it.

"Where's your ma and the babies?" panicked their father. Words tumbled from both mouths like they were reading a fictitious tale – a story that should not be true. The female plan to meet at Brother Beebe's cabin was their only clue as the worried trio sped off in the only possession Titus Billings had left, his wagon.

Brother Beebe was alone at the cabin. He had difficulty speaking. "I tried to help them," he said. "There were so many of them. I was as frightened as they were."

Brother Gardner found the dead horse in the yard. "It's been shot in the belly. Poor thing must have had a terrible time."

"We all had a terrible time," Beebe said.

Titus sent Samuel to fetch fresh water. "We need to get out of here," he said.

"You go. I'll slow you too much. You must hurry and find them. They need your help more than I do."

"I'll be back," Titus promised.

*   *   *

Over and back, again and again, the ferryboat transported passengers and sometimes, meager supplies, to the far side of the Missouri River. Forced evacuation of the Mormon settlement over-worked local ferry men. Hundreds and thousands of misplaced people stretched in every direction. Many were detached from their families. Confusion abounded -- also were fear and fatigue.

November chills did not make for good timing. Folks on the river's north side sought safety in Clay County. South of the river belonged to Jackson County where Mormons of all ages were forbidden. A multitude of evacuees waited for turns on the ferry. Many were displaced without funds for the fare. Such was mostly the case of an unsheltered group of women with young children, who had literally run for their lives, many from burning homes.

"Whatever are we going to do?"

"I do not know," Diantha answered, "but the Lord will pro-vide, somehow."

*   *   *

Billings had seen some big crowds on the dock at Indepen-dence Landing, but never before was the confusion anything like this. Chaos was rampant. Finding a particular person would be im-possible. Nonetheless, he had to find them. Slowly he drove down the riverbank. Both boys stood up in the wagon for better view.

Anguished faces and crying children lined the river. Titus ached for every person he passed. He wanted to stop again and again to offer some kind of aid or encouragement, but first he needed to find his family. He stopped his wagon at the extreme east end of the encampment, if it could be called that, then turned around to go back. As he straightened the horses an idea came into his mind. Titus Billings began whistling a hymn. It was the one William W. Phelps had revised and published in "The Evening and Morning Star" newspaper last year. Diantha loved it. He always whistled it. If by chance, Diantha could hear, she would recognize him.

"Boys, help me whistle 'Redeemer of Israel,'" he said. "Let's make your mother hear us, even if she can't see us." They made the attempt, but the volume was too weak. "Let's try singing it," Titus said.

In his strongest bass voice and with the accompaniment of two younger singers, Brother Titus Billings began: "Redeemer of Israel, our only delight, on whom for a blessing we call . . ."

As his wagon rolled by, others looked up. Some even smiled. Then the miracle began. New voices joined in. "Our shadow by day and our pillar by night, our king our deliverer, our all!" More people joined in as the wagon passed them. "How long we have wandered as strangers in sin, and cried in the desert for thee! Our foes have rejoiced when our sorrows they've seen, but Israel will shortly be free."

The further he went the bigger grew his echo. Saints of the Lord were singing along the riverbank, in spite of their plight. Rain started falling, but that only made them sing all the louder. "Fear not, and be just, for the kingdom is ours. The hour of redemption is near."

"Keep looking, boys. They've got to be here."

"Restore, my dear Savior, the light of thy face; thy soul-cheering comfort impart; and let the sweet longing for thy holy place bring hope to my desolate heart."

Again and again they repeated all six verses. "He looks! And ten thousands of angels rejoice, and myriads wait for his word; He speaks! And eternity, filled with his voice, re-echoes the praise of the Lord."

Singing from behind them died down. They had only gone half way. Maybe singing was not such a good idea after all.

"Try a new song," someone shouted. Titus stopped singing. Heavy rainfall gave too much competition. The wagon kept rolling and the tired boys kept watch. They heard shouting a time or two, but it was too weak to decipher. Then a new burst of singing started up. It sounded like angels. They must have been female angels because he could hear no bass harmony.

"We know he is coming to gather his sheep and lead them to Zion in love . . ." Titus recognized one of the voices. It could be no other. He started singing again, "For why in the valley of death should they weep . . ."

"Hey, Brother Billings, over here, over here!" He had found her at last.

Historical Background

"Titus' home, barn, four acres of wheat, and all improvements were destroyed by fire" (Johnson, 139).

By November 7, numerous Saints took refuge along the Missouri River Banks. "The ferry was constantly employed; and when night again closed upon us the cottonwood bottom had much the appearance of a camp meeting. Hundreds of people were seen in every direction, some in tents and some in the open air around their fires, while the rain descended in torrents. Husbands were inquiring for their wives, wives for the husbands; parents for children, and children for parents. Some had the good fortune to escape with their families, household goods, and some provisions; while others knew not the fate of their friends, and had lost all their goods. The scene was indescribable" (Pratt, 102).

"William W. Phelps was editor of the 'Evening and Morning Star,' a newspaper in Jackson County, Missouri, when "Redeemer of Israel," was first published in that newspaper in 1832. It was published three years later in Emma Smith's hymnal" (Davidson, 35).

CHAPTER 34

Night rain left mud on the riverbank, adding one more problem to inconvenience the troubled saints. The Billings family was at last intact, now they needed to cross the river. Titus had only a few coins in his pocket, not nearly enough. However, one of the ferrymen owed him for a freight job. If he could spot the right raft, he might negotiate a possible trade with its driver.

The wait was extensive. Lines seemed unending. Paying customers were allowed to crowd ahead of them. In her delicate condition Diantha was grateful for the luxury of a wagon seat. She longed to discuss the upcoming event with her husband, but the opportunity had not arrived. Speaking about it now would only increase his burden. Titus was out and about helping folks here and there anyway. *He will never sit still when he sees someone in need.*

The sky was getting too dark for ferrying.

"This will be the last crossing today," shouted a harsh, tired sounding voice. "Billings. Get your wagon up here."

As his family floated across the mighty Missouri River, Titus studied its northern bank, searching a vacant spot in the swarming mass of dislodged victims. Populace spread in every direction. Tents poked out here and there. Folks huddled around open fires. Some used wagons for houses. Whoever would have thought the cottonwood bottoms would be used in this way.

At last he found a hillside spot, and built a quick lean-to shelter. Rain interfered non-stop. "It shows that God is crying too," Diantha said. At least they had shelter for the moment.

"I will return and build you a cabin out of the cottonwoods," Titus promised early the next morning, "but many families remain in danger. I have one of the few good wagons left. Gotta lend a helping hand."

When the next raft dropped its homeless passengers, Billings and his wagon caught a ride back to the Jackson County side of the river.

Sam wanted to go, but his dad told him, "Your charge is to look after things here. Gather more wood and keep a small fire going. All wagon space is needed for the others anyway."

A miserable week of being "misplaced Mormons" took its toll on everyone. Brother Billings and his precious wagon evacuated a multitude of saints. Around the clock its wheels dug ruts into River Road between Independence Township and Independence Landing. Late into the night of November 13, 1833 mob violence peaked. Mormon folks had to be out of Jackson County before dawn. Titus searched for the elderly and the poor who were left behind.

"Come on," he coaxed. "Every Mormon has to be out of Independence tonight! I'll get you to the river bottoms. We'll cross over tomorrow."

It was well after midnight when he made a final sweep through the deserted, damaged town. Piercing the darkness, he stared one last time at the place of holy inheritance where his beloved farm had been. *If only,* he thought. Then, pulling the reins of a tired, miss-matched team, he halted at the edge of the forbidden township.

Brother Beebe's cabin was dark and deathly silent. "Wake up, Brother B. We gotta go!" he shouted. There was no answer, not a sign of life. *Good,* Titus thought. *Someone must've gotten him out. Guess that 'bout wraps it . . .*

"Ouch!" he stumbled. "Oh no, Brother B, Brother B. What have they done to you?" By now his eyes had adjusted to starlight filtering through the open door. The sight was not worth seeing. It was not one to be remembered, but Titus Billings would never be able to forget it.

This good, helpless man had suffered a brutal beating, perhaps because he had aided desperate mothers and children. His hand-carved crutch had been snapped in half and thrown on top of his lifeless body. Titus carried the remains of his kind, beaten friend outside and dug a shallow grave. On his knees he prayed, then covered Brother Beebe for a heavenly sleep. Danger lurked around him. He could feel it. There was nothing of value left for him here. In moments, he was gone, never to return.

*   *   *

Across the Mighty Missouri River the Titus Billings family suffered with the rest of the saints. His wife had good news, but waited for a happy and private time to tell him. Sleep was nonexistent anymore. There were no beds and seldom any bedtimes, even for children. The whole ordeal was a big nightmare. When would it end?

"Are you sleeping, Mother?" Diantha felt six-year-old George crawl up beside her.

"No son, I'm awake."

"Where is God? Why doesn't He help us?"

The question was innocent. It came from a hurting heart. She hugged her youngest son with tender reassurance. Still, he started to cry.

"God is there," she answered. "I know He loves us, it's just --"

A brilliant star shot across the sky with a bright, glowing tail lingering behind it. Never had she seen anything so amazing.

"Look, George, look up into the sky."

Another star erupted; then another. Suddenly the darkness boomed with vivid animation. Constellations exploded and danced like fireworks. The sights and the sounds were enough to awaken every sleeping soul on earth. Indeed, they did, even the tiny ones.

Diantha gathered her children close and together they gaped at the spectacular display.

"I wonder where your father is now."

"Do you think he can see it?" George asked.

"Of course he can," Alfred answered with haste.

"Even if he is still across the river?"

"Everyone can see this!"

"Even the Prophet?"

"I'm sure of it."

"Even Jesus?"

"Who do you think is making it?" Al asked.

"Praise God. The Lord is merciful to us," their mother said. "Can't you see, He is validating our cause."

"'Bet he is scaring off our enemies too," Alfred added with a confident hope.

The bursts of light silhouetted numberless spectators huddled together along the river bottoms. It did not slow nor stop. Hour after hour it adorned the sky.

"God lives!" Diantha whispered.

"I know, mother, I know."

Historical Background

The River separated Clay County from Jackson County. As long as they were on the Clay side, Mormons should have been safe. Cottonwood trees were cut down to build small cabins. Late into the night, November 13, 1833, Titus was "engaged in helping Saints evacuate their homes in Independence" (Bennion, 2; Jensen, 7; Jensen1, 242). Few could have been sleeping that terrible night of suffering in Zion. Titus' own son, six-year-old George, was outdoors about 2:00 a.m. when the heavens themselves burst open. He ran into the house shouting for his mother to come quickly as "the stars were falling from heaven!" (Hale, 1; Snow3,1).

[Note: If they had evacuated November 7 and 8 (Jensen, 7) and their home had been burned to the ground (Johnson1, 140) how could George have come out of the house during the night of November 13th? Eunice was only three years old. She records remembering the event through the reminding of her brother George, three years older. I know they witnessed the spectacular event, but believe they did so from the river's edge.]

"I can remember when I was four years old of hearing my older brother [George Pierce] exclaiming about the stars falling from heaven, and my mother saying, "Praise God, the Lord is merciful to us'" (Snow8, 1). "I then dressed myself and went out doors and saw the falling of the stars, which so encouraged the Saints and frightened their enemies" (Lambert, 85).

"I [Joseph Smith, Jr.] arose and to my great joy beheld the stars fall from heaven like a shower of hailstones, a literal fulfillment of the word of God, as recorded in the Holy Scriptures, and a sign that the coming of Christ is close at hand" (Hale, 14; Smith1, 439).

For hours the skies celebrated with fireworks that frightened the enemies of the 1200 Saints huddled on the cold banks of the Missouri River. "Thousands of bright meteors were shooting through space in every direction, with long trains of light following in their course" (Roberts, 347). "In Zion, all heaven seemed enwrapped in splendid fireworks . . . and resembled large drops of rain in sunshine . . . The appearance was beautiful, grand, and sublime beyond description; and it seemed as if the artillery and fireworks of eternity were set in motion to enchant and entertain the Saints, and terrify and awe the sinners of the earth" (Smith1, 439, 440; Times and Seasons V6, 898).

The appearance of these signs was witnessed by many in differing parts of the country. "During the fall of 1833 occurred a natural phenomenon of a most wonderful character. This was on the night of the 13th of November. It was what is known as the 'meteoric shower,' or the 'falling of the stars.' It was witnessed with amazement and astonishment throughout the entire limits of the United States" (Pratt,110).

"Thousands of meteors were shooting through space in every direction, with long trains of light following in their course. This lasted for several hours, and was only closed by the dawn of the rising sun" (Pratt, 110). "Every heart was filled with joy at this majestic display of signs and wonders, showing the near approach of the coming of the Son of God" (Flake, 510). "A grand meteoric shower took place, which cheered the banished Saints and frightened their enemies" (Jensen, 7). [Note: Parley P. Pratt records the event occurred at 2:00 a.m.; Joseph Smith observed it at 4:00 a.m.] From twelve hundred to fifteen hundred church members were expelled from Jackson County, in 1833. "The records of the Church state there were ten branches of the church in Jackson County" (Jensen2, 1).

"The damage done to the property of the Mormons by the mob in the county of Jackson . . . as near as they can ascertain, would amount to the sum of $175,000.00. The number of Mormons thus driven from the county of Jackson amounted to about 1200 souls" (Billings/Shaw/Hale, 13; Flake, 509; Millennial Star17, 435).

Another report lists Titus Billings as head of one household that was "driven out of Jackson County Missouri, by the mob in 1833" (Jensen2, 1), "212 men, 166 women and 505 children" were counted (Jensen2, 1).

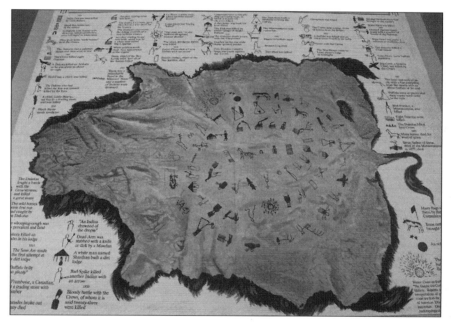

Winter Count Plaque

A Native American skin drawing depicts a life story. Drawings begin on the outside circle and work around and around recording highlights of a person's life until it ends with the center drawing. We viewed one at a funeral and were amazed with its accuracy.

(Courtesy S.B. Mitchell, 2008.)

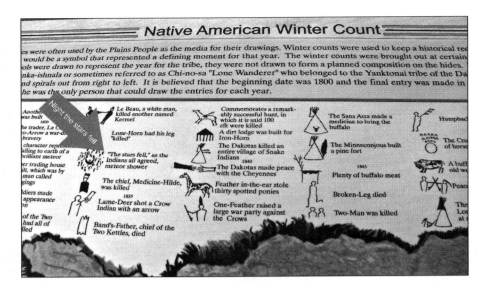

Native American Winter Count

es were often used by the Plains People as the media for their drawings. Winter counts were used to keep a historical rec
would be a symbol that represented a defining moment for that year. The winter counts were brought out at certain
ols were drawn to represent the year for the tribe, they were not drawn to form a planned composition on the hides.
nka-ishnala or sometimes referred to as Chi-no-sa "Lone Wanderer" who belonged to the Yanktonai tribe of the Da
nd spirals out from right to left. It is believed that the beginning date was 1800 and the final entry was made in
he was the only person that could draw the entries for each year.

Translation of Winter Count

Here the drawn symbols are translated. Please note how the drawing verifies the night "The stars fell" in November 1833. Native Americans witnessed the event and recorded it in this way. Photos are of a monument/placque at a public park in Nebraska. Sorry, I can't remember exactly where we were. Guess I was too excited about the find.

(Courtesy S.B. Mitchell, 2008.)

CHAPTER 35

I *can rest my bones in this miserable spot no longer!* Diantha said to herself.

The ground was crusted with sleet and her feet were bleeding, but she was more concerned about the feet and well being of her children. Titus, humped beside her, seemed to be asleep, though she knew he had not been that way very long. With careful movement as not to awaken him, she slid herself away and straightened. It was cold. How she longed to wear more layers of clothing. Clothing? Food? Dishes? Books? Bedding? On her person hung the only possessions she had left. The lace? Diantha pulled up the ends of the wedding lace tied around her waist and tried to shake mud from them. The sight of her wilted treasure made her eyes want to cry though no tears were left in them. *Someday I will renew you,* she whispered, *but for now I must protect you.* Quickly she stuffed the lace ends under her skirt and pulled her waistband up over the belted part. *Who cares if I look chubby? At least it is safe.*

Diantha stirred the fire. *Where will we find dry kindling?* she wondered. Just then Titus arose. She had nothing to feed him.

"I'll take the boys to scavenge some limbs and build you a lean-to. Have the youngsters look for fire wood," he said.

Elder Isaac Morley was released from jail and stood ready for whatever the Lord had in store. Another mission call delighted him, this time to his beloved Massachusetts. Nonetheless, his big heart nearly broke when it came time to leave his family in a make-shift settlement on the river bottoms of Clay County. The place was unhealthy. His own health was weakened from days of dark prison confinement and little nourishment. Nonetheless, his life had been spared and again he was called to serve the cause and to build up Zion.

"The Lord has a work for me to do," he announced to his family. "Like Nephi of old, I must go and I must do it. He will provide the way." Elder Morley turned to his brother-in-law friend. "Titus," he said, "I am entrusting all that I own into your care." This time there was not much by way of possession. "All I have is my

181

family. Please take care of them."

Obediently he started to leave with his assigned companion, Bishop Edward Partridge. Then, turning back as with an afterthought, he called out, "Titus, try not to sell them."

The next day Billings and his young friend, Chapman Duncan, found an abandoned stable over the hillside. This they cleaned out and repaired, best they could. By nightfall, Duncan and the two families settled inside it.

Titus made arrangements to rent a small farm. Deep into the winter, before he had a chance to build her a Clay County home, Diantha gave birth to a new son. He was a Godsend. His dark curly hairline pointed to a "V," a widow's peak as folks called it, in the center of his forehead just like his father's did.

"What will you name this little boy?" inquired Lucy, who, with limited resources had been Diantha's only help. Having her near was a blessing, though Lucy was quite sickly these days.

"Titus Junior, of course." Diantha went on, "Why he looks just like his father!"

The name pleased his namesake. Titus, Jr. it was. Diantha was concerned about her husband though. He was ill too, but he could not rest. There was so much to do. Day in and day out he labored to plant crops. Corn was in and potatoes were started. He finished early one day, because of fever, and found Diantha crying. Kneeling by the makeshift bed, he kissed her.

"What is it, my Dear?"

"Oh Titus, do you realize that our baby was allowed to be born in a stable too?"

*   *   *

"Chills and Fever" [now known as Malaria] took its toll on river bottom victims, including Lucy Morley and her children. Of the Billings Family, only the new baby escaped the disease. No one was well enough to care for the others. Even a drink of water was unattainable.

The Prophet Joseph Smith led a company of men referred to as Zion's Camp, from Kirtland to aid the suffering saints driven from Independence. These would-be soldiers hoped for a redress of wrongs that would reinstate ownership to homes in Missouri. Camped between two branches of the Fishing River they were miraculously saved from an army mob of eight hundred men, when a violent and unexpected storm displayed the hand of God and made crossing impossible for the enemy. Then Cholera broke out and many suffered.

Joseph S. Allen was a convert from Ohio who survived Zion's Camp. Upon meeting lovely Lucy Diantha, Isaac's daughter who was named after her mother and aunt, he managed to relocate the Morleys onto a better farm where he worked the remainder of Isaac's fifteen-month mission. This blessed answer came just in time, because Titus' health took a turn for the worse. He and Diantha were deathly ill. The children suffered too.

Malaria's unrelenting chills shake a body nonstop, until one seems ready to fall apart. Then, without fail, a blistering fever returns, shocking the system to the opposite extreme. During this episode a patient is too ill to eat or move. After three days the symptoms lapse for three or four hours. The starving victim eats one hearty meal, then only small amounts until the next sick day when violent shivering returns. In and out of consciousness the Billings family suffered a full six months, until an angel of mercy in the form of Lydia Partridge came to call.

"Diantha, I haven't seen you in ages," Lydia said. Her friend was unable to reply.

The entire Billings family suffered diverse effects from the terrible disease and had become too weak to recover. Lydia rescued the crying baby and held him close.

"I think he is hungry," she said.

Diantha opened sad eyes and tried to speak. She was no longer able to nurse her baby and feared he would die of starvation. Severity of the illness left each of them dangerously run down and on the verge of not caring.

"Save your strength, Diantha. Don't try to speak. I can see what needs to be done."

Lydia bundled Baby Titus to take him home with her promising to find another mother who could nurse him until Diantha was well. Her bishop husband was on a mission, but she knew who to report to and took action the moment she left. Each member of the Billings family was placed in a different, caring home until the fever and chills could be cured. In spite of it all Titus still harvested a crop of corn for bread.

Historical Background

"The saints who fled, took refuge in the neighboring counties, mostly in Clay County which received them with some degree of kindness" (Times and Seasons4 V6, 898).

"Leaving a lovely garden and thirty bushels of sweet potatoes buried in a pit" Morley's crossed the Missouri River into Clay County "and camped on the River Bottoms" (Esplin, 6). "This was a very unhealthy location and the family took down with malaria fever. Isaac was called to accompany Bishop Partridge on a mission to his native state, Massachusetts. He went leaving his family in this condition, trusting in the Lord for their welfare" (Esplin, 6). "We [Morleys] went to Clay County, Missouri and settled on a piece of low, swampy land. Soon his[Isaac's] family was taken down with chills and fever; all the family was sick with not well ones enough to take care of those that were sick. In this condition Father Morley was called on a mission to the Eastern States" (Cox1, 1).

Titus Jr. was born in Clay County, Missouri during the year of 1834. The month of his birth is unknown (Family Group Sheets).

The next day (Flake, 509) Titus moved his and Isaac's families into Clay County, Missouri. "I [Chapman Duncan] crossed the river with Brother Morley's family and obtained an old stable which we repaired and cleansed out where his family and Titus Billings remained most of the winter" (Duncan, 2).

Titus rented a small farm and planted most of the land in corn and potatoes. There he took ill with chills and fever. (Probably Malaria: Billings/Shaw/Hale, 13; Esplin, 6; Pyne, 4). Every third day he would suffer shaking "hard enough to shake himself into pieces" (Snow3, 1). Soon five in the Billings family were very sick; at times so weak they could not even bring themselves nor each other a drink of needed water. Diantha had to wean her seventh month old baby boy, Titus Jr., because of the illness.

Off and on the fever would break for three or four hours leaving the patient nearly starved. "We would then eat a hearty meal and then we would eat but little until our next sick day came" (Bennett, 554; Snow3, 1). For six months they suffered, then church brethren realized their condition and placed each in a different home for care until the chills and fever were cured. There were "so many of our People that we had to settle in places that was [sic] sickly and my Family was all taken sick & were not able to help ourselves and lost one year" (Johnson, 140). "My baby brother [Titus Jr.] was taken to Bishop Partridge's home to be taken care of on account of sickness" (Snow8, 1).

"During the period when my father was not suffering with the chills, which occurred every third day, he succeeded in raising a crop of corn for bread" (Snow8, 1).

While Titus was so ill, a young convert from Ohio who had marched with Zion's Camp by the name of Joseph Stewart Allen "came to the assistance of the

Morley Family" (Esplin, 6). "He relocated them and helped Sister Morley with the farm while her husband was on a fifteen-month mission" (Esplin, 6; MorleyRH, 60).

CHAPTER 36

Lucy Diantha Morley awoke early with excitement on the second day of September 1835, the day she would forever change her name. Although her father's mission had a full month left to go, Uncle Titus had promised to "give her away" and the Prophet Joseph was ready to perform the ceremony. She was elated.

Outside her groom-to-be, Joseph Stewart Allen, paced in front of the cabin.

"Good Morning, Joseph" greeted Diantha Billings as she carried a mysterious bundle into the Morley home.

"Oh, Auntie, it's beautiful."

"Just what we need," Lucy agreed. She and Diantha draped the revived wedding lace into place with graceful perfection.

"Now a piece of Grandma Morley is with us, even if she can't be." Enough said. A radiant bride hugged both namesakes.

More trouble was brewing, even in Clay County. Often disgruntled, former members of the church, made frightening threats and phony claims against loyal, obedient members. Holding public meetings was unwise in these circumstances. Instead, Priesthood Brethren visited the scattered saints and encouraged them to remain faithful.

When the prophet visited Missouri with Zion's Camp in 1834, he called certain families to return to Kirtland. Elders were chosen to receive temple blessings. They should return to Ohio and help build the house of the Lord. Titus was delighted to be chosen for that sacred assignment.

Diantha wanted her parents to meet Titus Junior. How she hoped their hearts would change. Titus was eager to see his siblings again too. Emily still lived there. Salomi may have moved, because his letter came back unopened. Samuel had grown very bitter toward the church and moved out of Kirtland for that reason. Titus hoped to find him and maybe win him back. What a strength this good brother could be for the cause of Zion. They made preparations for their return.

Diantha's parents offered a warm welcome and arranged beds for all eight of them. Thomas and Editha Morley enjoyed their grandchildren, but were not pleased with the temple building project. Their son-in-law worked on it full-time without any thought of payment. The Billings boys helped their grandfather with farming, and then worked on the temple as well.

Diantha was engaged with other sisters, in spinning and knitting clothing for temple workers. She was willing to weave carpets or stitch draperies. Saints were giving all they had to these efforts. Diantha hoped that the spirit of such a righteous work would soften her parents' attitude toward the church she loved. Her mother, who started attending weekly choir practice with the saints, seemed to be responding.

Titus was determined to locate his kin. Each day he gave his all to the temple project, but a rainstorm halted the work early, one afternoon, so he decided to call on Emily. Rain was pouring heavily when he returned.

"You are soaked through and through," Diantha scolded. She removed his hat and poured a stream of water off the brim. He did not flinch. "Let's get that wet coat off of you."

He did not respond. She did all the unfastening. That's when she realized his cheeks were drenched with more than rain-drops. His face was dripping with teardrops too.

"Titus! Whatever is wrong?" Diantha knew Samuel Billings was antagonistic to Mormonism. She expected some heartache from him, but surely Titus did too. This seemed bigger, deeper than expected. "What happened, Titus," she asked again.

The news, when finally he shared it, caused her amazement and agony as well. She could not believe it. How could it be? She stumbled to a chair and sat to catch her breath.

Salomi had not moved. She died.

"Exactly one year and twelve days after we left Ohio," Titus calculated. Emily didn't know why my letter came back."

Diantha was speechless.

"Salomi's husband, John, still lives on the old property. He remarried a year later. Brace yourself Diantha."

"What?"

"John married Emily."

"Your sister?"

"Yes, my other sister."

"Oh, that's wonderful."

"Wonderful if they'd told me."

"Well, she had a lot going on just then, I guess."

"Yes, I can understand that, but Pa died too, and they didn't let me know!"

"Your father? When?"

"On his birthday, May 8, 1832. Only two months after we left . . ." Titus dropped to his knees. "Pa died the day we reached Independence! Diantha, that was three years ago. Why didn't they let me know?"

Though Diantha tried to find an explanation, she too was baffled. Titus loved his father and his sister; both deaths pained him. Nevertheless, his relationship with each of them was pure to the grave. Not the case with Sam. Opposing religious beliefs now divided their minds and tarnished their hearts. Disengagement with his brother bothered Titus most.

"They want nothing to do with me? Didn't even tell me that Pa died," Titus lamented. His fingers pried into the deep creases of his forehead as he sat holding his head in his hands. More than anything, Titus wanted to close the gap he felt between himself and his brother. Why couldn't he and the others understand the joy of testimony that Titus and Diantha had found? For now the two of them would have to lean on each other.

"Remember Mary Russell?"

"The school teacher?"

"Yes, Samuel married her. They moved to Gates Mill."

"That is good news."

"They moved there because we Mormons invaded Kirtland. He hates Mormons. So now he hates us." They both sat in silence for several long moments.

"I love him, Diantha. He's my brother and I love him."

"Of course you do."

"Next chance I get, I'm looking him up. I would do anything for Samuel."

The colonial-styled Mormon temple grew daily until it reached inside dimensions of fifty-five feet by sixty-five feet and measured two stories high, with additional classrooms in the attic. By the end of the year 1835 meetings were held in the parts that were finished.

"Diantha, I want you to turn these in for your temple." Diantha looked up. Editha Morley was holding something wrapped in a dark cloth. She sat down beside her daughter and began to open the mysterious bundle. Diantha gasped as she saw its content sparkle in the light of day.

"Oh Mother, are you certain you can do this?" Editha smiled

as Diantha's excitement tumbled out. "What will father say? Does he know about this? Will he allow it?"

"Your father is very stubborn, but he is a good man."

"Oh, I know, I know, but right now he's so . . ."

"Maybe we won't bother him with this little detail right now."

Diantha ran her long, thin fingers through the colorful pile of gleaming jewels.

"I heard the talk of your church 'sisters' at choir practice and I know how much you wanted to contribute to the cause." She spoke quickly. "Well, you can't give something you don't have, but, if I give you these you will have something to contribute," Editha took a breath. "I do say, that was a mouth full."

Both of them laughed joyfully and the daughter hugged her mother with heartfelt gratitude.

"Come with me, Mother. Let's run them over right now."

"No, I think I'll stay here. You go. Go quickly, before I change my mind." There was a teasing twinkle in her eye. "I wouldn't care to watch the crushing process anyway."

"I'll never forget this, Mother. Every time we look at God's temple we'll know that part of the shine is because of you."

"Off with you, now."

Running with childlike excitement Diantha rushed to the temple site where workers were grinding glass jewels into mortar and plaster for finishing effects on the outer walls. What a pleasure to contribute, but Diantha's joy sparkled more than all the jewels in the world because now she knew her unbelieving mother believed!

Historical Background

When Joseph Stewart Allen returned from the march of Zion's Camp" he came to the assistance of the Morley Family" (Esplin, 6). During this time he fell in love with Isaac's second daughter who was named Lucy Diantha (after her mother and her aunt). The two were married September 2, 1835, by Prophet Joseph, just one month before her father returned (Esplin, 6; MorleyRH, 60).

In 1834 the High Council in Zion assembled in Clay County appointed Edward Partridge, Isaac and others to "visit the scattered saints in their afflicted condition and encourage them to remain faithful and true and ready to receive any instruction that the Lord might direct for their benefit. It was not considered wise for the elders to hold public meetings in that region" (Esplin,6).

Ebenezer Billings (father of Titus) died 8 May 1832 in Greenfield, Franklin Massachusetts and was buried near his wife's grave (Ester Joyce Billing) on 11 May 1832 (Billings Family Group Sheet). See picture of his tombstone in Appendix A.

Salome Billings Wells died 12 March 1833 in Kirtland, Geauga, Ohio. A year later her sister, Emily Billings, married her husband, John Wells 10 May 1834 (Billings Family Group Sheet). All three are buried in Kirtland, Ohio. See picture of their tombstone in Appendix A.

"On Monday, June 23, 1834, a council of High Priests met according to revelation and chose some of the first elders to receive their blessings in the Kirtland Temple" (Esplin, 6). "Though accompanied by marvelous spiritual experiences, the ordinances as administered in the Kirtland Temple were not as complete as they would be in later times. Speaking in 1853 at the cornerstone-laying ceremonies for the Salt Lake Temple, President Brigham Young declared that in Kirtland the 'First Elders' received only a 'portion of their first endowments or we might say more clearly, some of the first or introductory, or initiatory ordinances, preparatory to an endowment" (Cowen, 10).

"In February 1835, certain brethren were called to return to Kirtland and help complete the Temple. Titus and Diantha returned to Kirtland where they worked and sacrificed to help build the Kirtland Temple" (Billings/Shaw/Hale, 14; Pyne, 2).

"One apparently apocryphal story was that women furnished their finest glass and crockery to be mixed with the stucco for the outside walls. And when it was finished, the temple did sparkle when the sun shone on it" (AndersonKR, 163). "When the wall of the temple was finished, [Artemus Millet] sent men and boys to the different towns and places to gather old crockery and glass to put in the cement which [he] had invented" (AndersonKR, 163; Millet, 93-95).

[Author's Note: During one of our visits to the Kirtland Ohio Historical Site the then Mission President Donald Brewer told us that Karl R. Anderson claims the saints did not crush dishes and jewels for the temple finish work. Diantha's contribution here is only fiction.]

CHAPTER 37

Wrapped in the beauty of springtime, Kirtland, Ohio welcomed guests from everywhere to witness the dedication of her gleaming new temple on the Lord's Sabbath, March 27, 1836. Though the second floor was not complete, nine hundred to one thousand saints crowded into the House of the Lord. Even so, many remained outside the walls. Temple windows were opened in hopes outsiders could hear and a schoolhouse near the temple was filled with saints for another meeting. A repeat of the entire service was scheduled for Thursday, March 31 for those who still could not attend. Because Titus and Diantha (and their daughter, Eunice) were singing in the choir, they would be allowed to attend both sessions.

Choir members were divided into four groups and positioned in each corner of the new building. Diantha tingled with the Spirit as she sang: "Ere Long the Veil Will Rend and Twain" and "O Happy Souls, Who Pray Where God Appoints to Hear." Heaven was close, so very close. She could feel it. Titus felt it too. Sacrificing saints had prepared a holy place for the Lord. To this sacred ground, He was no stranger. Miraculous events were seen by some and felt by all.

Sidney Rigdon spoke eloquently for two and one-half hours. There were more songs: "This Earth Was Once a Garden Place," also known as "Adam-ondi-Ahman," and "How Pleased and Blessed Was I."The Prophet Joseph Smith read a revealed dedicatory prayer. The congregation joined the choir to sing a rousing hymn written for the occasion by W.W. Phelps: "The Spirit of God Like a Fire is Burning."

Diantha kept eyeing a young sister seated nearby who held a six-week-old baby on her lap. Infants in arms were restricted from the dedicatory service. Outside, while waiting in the crowd, she and Titus had overheard the young mother, when she rushed up to Patriarch Joseph Smith Sr. with great concern. Unaware of the restriction, she had walked a long distance with the baby in her arms, so she could witness the dedication. Now she had no one to care for the child. In desperation she appealed to Father Smith. With his compassionate heart he promised the faithful sister that her son would not disturb the sacred meeting. Sister Billings did not mean to stare, but the child appeared so angelic. He did not make a sound during the talks or the songs or the prayers. The dedication lasted for seven hours. At last, when time came for the Hosanna Shout, he, the tiny babe, joined in with the adults, speaking the sacred words perfectly. Diantha nudged her husband. He, too, was in awe.

*   *   *

"Well, there she is," Heber C. Kimball said with pride as he stretched his neck to view the beautiful, holy building. "Three years and $60,000.00 later . . . who would have believed?" He paused thoughtfully and patted Titus Billings on the back. "I thought it was impossible" he went on.

Titus shook his head. He was thinking the same things Heber was saying and added, "Not just because of our poverty, but like Rigdon said in there, we wet these walls with our tears while praying for God to stay the hands of ruthless spoilers who vowed that these walls would never be reared. I feared we would fall short."

Heber was elated. "Proves nothing is impossible for the Lord," he said.

Billings was elated too, but also tired, worried, and aching in heart. His friend was sensitive.

"Something troubling you?"

"We're packing up and heading out as soon as we can," Titus stated.

Billings had been right. Whenever the Lord did something wonderful there would be opposition from the evil one. He had seen it before. It was here again. Diantha's parents were upset with Mormonism. Well, they were *more* than upset. At least, "*he*" was more than upset. Diantha's father had raged before the first session and forbidden her mother's attendance, in spite of the fact that she had trained with Diantha to sing in the choir. He was angry and they needed to get out of his way.

"We're going back to Missouri. There's work to do in Clay County."

"Guess there's work to do everywhere," Heber agreed. "God's speed, Brother."

Billings raised his eyes again to the top of the temple, for one more look. He was grateful they had come. To him it was a sacred privilege. Now he had to leave, but would do so with miracles ringing in his ears, for many had witnessed visions in the holy temple of the Lord Jesus Christ. The Savior stood on the pulpit's breastwork, accepting their efforts and allowing His name to rest upon them and the holy structure. Prophets of old, even Moses, Elias and Elijah, returned specific keys for the restoration of the Lord's work. Oh the gospel was true. Titus knew it was true. If only others could understand. He would call on his brother one more time before they left.

Thomas Morley had started a church of his own in Kirtland. He wanted his talented son-in-law to help with construction of a new chapel for it. "We need you here, Titus. Forget all that Joe Smith talk and that Zion thing that obsesses you. Come be one with us."

Oh, to be united in faith and hope with this good man was a wish of his peacemaking heart, but Titus Billings knew the place of truth was only with the Lord and Savior Jesus Christ. The true church was His church. Things had to be done His way, no matter what was required. Titus would sacrifice anything and everything for the Lord. Diantha was weeping as they pulled away for the last time.

It was pre-planned. Titus and Diantha would stop at Gates Mill to search for Sam and Mary, before they left Ohio. Warm, cheery weather was doing its part. Bringing the children to see their cousins might soften the blow. At least, Titus hoped that would be the case.

Samuel raised a crop of broomcorn and happened to be lacing brooms on his porch when their wagon pulled up. "Well, well. Would you look at this?" With a louder voice he shouted, "Mary, come out here and see what the dog drug in." She and happy cousins appeared in an instant. "So, what brings you out here, Little Brother?"

"You do," Titus said. Samuel did not answer. "Diantha thinks she needs a good broom. Came to buy one from the best."

Samuel kept his fingers lacing. He did not look up again. "Take your pick," he said. A row of tightly laced brooms leaned against the cabin wall. Titus stepped up to examine them while Diantha and Mary went inside, chatting like schoolgirls.

Titus seemed silent. He was praying. Samuel spoke the next word. "You still hooked on Mormonism?"

"Yes I am, Sam."

"Ya mean you really buy into that Joe Smith stuff?"

"He is a true prophet of God, Samuel." There was a long, awkward pause. Titus picked up one of the brooms. "This looks like a good one," he said.

"It's a good one to sweep away Mormons," Samuel said.

"That's me, Sam. I am a Mormon."

"So be it."

Conflicting emotions spun wildly, swelling the gap between two brothers like a violent tornado sent to destroy them. Both hearts were pounding and aching. They wanted to be united, but were not. Samuel was closed mouth. Titus was not sure what to say. At length, he ventured, "I love you Samuel."

"Love you too," Sam replied.

"Still glad we named our oldest after you."

"Glad we named our son Titus."

"Sorry he died, Sam."

"Sorry too." Samuel Billings hardened with pain. His brother's namesake had died in infancy. Now that self same brother was being ripped out of his life and torn out of his heart. He hated what he felt, but put his feelings into words anyway, "You go your way, brother, and I'll go mine!"

Titus had agonizing feelings too. "Hope we meet again in Heaven," he said.

"If there is one."

"There is, dear brother. There is."

The two shook hands, as if good sportsmanship required it. Then both broke down and hugged each other heartily.

"We've raised a holy house to the Lord, Samuel. Why don't you come back to Kirtland?"

"I'll go back to Kirtland only after you holy believers remove far from it."

"Guess I best be going."

"Guess you best."

Titus Billings walked to his wagon where Diantha and the children were waiting. Samuel tossed a broom to him. "Take this," he said. "You'll need it." The wagon drove out of sight. Neither brother looked back.

The Billings family was not alone. Several other Mormon families, returning from the temple dedication, were traveling in the same direction. One of those families captured the attention of young Samuel, or at least their lovely daughter did. Martha Anderson was not a stranger. Though she was born in Virginia, her family had lived in Kirtland for as long as she could remember. Samuel knew her before, from when he lived in Kirtland, but she had changed like a beautiful butterfly. Her father, Theodore M. Anderson, was in the lumbering business and was relocating to St. Louis, Missouri. He could use a strong arm and a dependable worker. Well aware of the Billings' reputation he offered the job to Samuel. There would be good pay and opportunity for growth.

Sam agreed to remain in St. Louis when the steamer docked there. Diantha would not hear of it. Titus could see the longing and better understood his son's reasoning. "He is eighteen, now. This needs to be his decision."

While Diantha struggled with all of her sorrows, Ebenezer made friends with the steamer's captain and enjoyed assisting crew members throughout the voyage. River travel had always intrigued him. He claimed, even as a youngster, that it would be his life some day. To him that day had come at last.

Captain Daniel P. Miller offered the lad a real job. "Stay on," he said, "and work your way up and down the Great Mississippi."

Well, that was more than Ebenezer Billings could refuse. What a wonderful life! His for the taking. Only a fool would pass the offer by.

"No, Titus, no! He's only sixteen. He's still a baby. I need him. We can't let him go."

Brother Billings choked up. His father-heart was aching too, but sometimes such things must be allowed. With tenderness he cradled a sobbing wife inside his strong arms.

"We're losing too much, all at once," she whimpered. She was right, of course, but could not control the fate of her children any more than she could control the denial of her parents. Life was hard, so very, very hard.

Historical Background

The Kirtland Temple took "three years to complete, and was to cost the Saints, in material and labor, $60,000" (BerrettWE,125).

"Hundreds of Latter-day Saints attended the dedicatory services of the temple, coming from surrounding branches and also traveling on foot and horseback from Missouri" (BerrettWE, 126-7). "Isaac Morley was one who walked from Missouri to attend the Kirtland Temple dedication" (MorleyRH, 32). "It was the greatest gathering of members of the Church in one place up to this time" (Morley CO,8).

Billings was present at the dedication Sunday, March 27, 1836. "Diantha, who possessed a beautiful voice, sang at the dedication services" (Billings/Shaw/Hale, 14; Pyne 2).

"Titus was one of the Elders who received his blessings in the Kirtland Temple, and he had the privilege of attending the School of Prophets" (Billings/Shaw/Hale, 14; Pyne, 2).

Hundreds of Latter-day Saints came to Kirtland anticipating the great blessings the Lord had promised to bestow upon them. Following the [closing] prayer, the choir sang the hymn "The Spirit of God." It had been written especially for the dedication by W.W. Phelps . . . "The congregation concluded the seven-hour service by standing and rendering the sacred Hosanna Shout: 'Hosanna, hosanna, hosanna to God and the Lamb, amen, amen, amen and amen,' repeated three times." Eliza R. Snow said the shout was given "with such power as seemed almost sufficient to raise the roof from the building" (CES, 165-166). "When the congregation shouted hosanna, that babe joined in the shout. As marvelous as

The Kirtland Temple

(Courtesy S.B. Mitchell, 2008.)

that incident may appear to many, it is not more so than other occurrences on the occasion where the Spirit of the Lord worked wonders beyond the comprehension of fallen man" (McConkie, 141).

Several keys were restored to Joseph Smith and Oliver Cowdery on April 3, 1836, in this holy temple. The occasion for such a spiritual experience was that of a Sabbath Day Meeting. "The Lord's supper was distributed to the Church, having been administered to by the First Presidency and passed by the Twelve Apostles. After the sacrament ordinance, Joseph Smith and Oliver Cowdery retired to the pulpit, the veils being dropped, and bowed themselves in silent but solemn prayer. After rising from prayer, several visions were opened to them.

Jesus the Christ first appeared to them, standing upon the breastwork of the pulpit from which place He said: "Let the hearts of your brethren rejoice, and let the hearts of all my people rejoice, who have, with their might, built this house to my name . . .Yea, the hearts of thousands and tens of thousands shall greatly rejoice in consequence of the blessings which shall be poured out, and the endowment with which my servants have been endowed in this house. And the fame of this house shall spread to foreign lands; and this is the beginning of the blessing which shall be poured out upon the heads of my people" (D&C 110:6, 9-10). Next, "Moses appeared, he being followed by Elias, and Elijah who, in that order, restored the essential keys of their dispensations, that additional blessings might be poured out upon the heads of the faithful believers in Christ" (BerrettWE, 126-129; D&C 110:5, 7, 11, 12-16; MorleyRH, 33). "Many mentioned hearing heavenly singing and others witnessed visions and appearances of heavenly beings. Eliza R. Snow testified that a babe in arms participated in the Hosanna Shout" (AndersonKR, 182).

"Here he [Samuel Billings, brother to Titus] made brooms for the farmers all around" (Billings V1,2).

A Billings Family Group sheet show Samuel Billings (son of Titus) "died in St. Louis, Missouri leaving three children." No date is given. No wife's name is given. However, a 1850 census lists "Martha A." and an 1860 census shows "Martha" as his wife. [Note: We do NOT know Martha's father's name. Theodore M. Anderson is a fictitious name.]

Ebenezer (Titus' son) did work on the river. Captain Daniel P. Miller is a fictitious name.

CHAPTER 38

"Well, there you have it," Titus Billings said to his wife. The minute the Lord does something wonderful . . . "He didn't finish his statement. He didn't need to finish it. Diantha Morley Billings knew full well his meaning. Emotions of her heart and hopes of her soul soared toward heaven one minute and came crashing down to the ground the next. Oh yes, the Lord had done something marvelous and wonderful. She and Titus had helped finish a House of the Lord in Kirtland, Ohio. Together they had witnessed the dedication of its sacred walls and felt holy presence within them. Such was the wonderful part, from the Lord. In the midst of it all, however, Titus pointed out how Satan opposes every good thing.

While many of the saints were laboring on the Temple a dark prejudice was brewing in Clay County. Clay County? Yes, those Clay County residents who were so understanding and welcoming seemed now to be alarmed, defensive and embittered.

"They want us gone," Titus said.

"But why?" asked Diantha. "They were friendly and neighborly when we left. We told them we were coming back."

Titus shook his head and tied his neck tie. Diantha adjusted it for him. He was ready.

"Will you be long?" she asked.

"As long as it takes" he said, already aware of a resolution requesting *all* Mormons to leave the county. Zion's Camp had not succeeded in helping Missouri saints reclaim their Jackson County homes. A heartless declaration was drawn up by Clay County residents during a public meeting.

Diantha turned to answer a knock at the door. It was Isaac, her brother as expected.

"Ready to go?" he asked.

"Ready as possible," Titus answered.

"I am proud of you both," Diantha said, "My two favorite men off to settle our affairs here in friendly Clay County."

"Wish they were still our friends," Isaac said to his sister.

"What happened?" she asked.

"Satan doesn't want us here," Titus said. "He doesn't want us to succeed anywhere."

"That is a fact," Isaac agreed. He continued, "I think they are afraid of a civil war."

"A civil war? Here in Clay County?" Diantha was appalled.

"Heard talk of it. We Mormons are increasing in numbers, you know, and our religious lifestyle seems to worry them."

"Worry them? They should learn the truth and join us!" Diantha meant it.

"We oppose slavery. Most of them depend on slaves."

"And we are friendly with the Indian Tribes on the Frontier. That riles a lot of people," Titus added.

"Don't be late for your meeting," Diantha warned. "What are you going to do anyway?"

"Tonight the full resolution will be read to us. After much prayer and pondering we will formulate our reply," Isaac said. The task was daunting and each of them knew it to be so.

Mormon brethren living in Clay County met together Friday, July 1, 1836. The meeting began with prayer. W.W. Phelps was appointed chairman with John Corrill acting as secretary for the project. The upsetting resolution from Clay County citizens was read aloud. In their discussion the truth of a statement that Mormons came to Clay County to make temporary homes was acknowledged, but they had expected the officials of the state to assist them in regaining the property from which they had been driven. They were trying to live in peace!

A respectable committee of twelve was selected to work with W.W. Phelps and John Corrill. Issac Morley, Titus Billings, Edward Partridge, Lyman Wight, Thomas B. Marsh, Elias Higby, Calvin Bebee, Isaac Hitchcock, Isaac Higby, Samuel Bent, James Emmett, and R. Evans departed from the meeting in time returning with the following written document: Reply to Clay County Citizens' Resolution to Remove All Mormons:

Preamble and Resolution

Resolved, that we (the "Mormons," so called) are grateful for the kindness which has been shown to us by the citizens of Clay county since we have resided with them; and being desirous for peace, and wishing to do good rather than the ill-will of mankind, we will use all honorable means to allay the excitement, and so far as we can, remove any foundation for jealousies against us as a people . . .

We believe it just to preach the gospel to the nations of

the earth, and warn the righteous to save themselves from the corruption of the world: but we do not believe it right to interfere with bond servants, nor preach the Gospel to them, nor meddle with nor influence them in the least to cause them to be dissatisfied with their situation in this life; thereby jeopardizing the lives of men. Such interference we believe to be unlawful and unjust, and dangerous to the peace of every government allowing human beings to be held in servitude.

We deny holding any communications with the Indians; and mean to hold ourselves ready to defend our country against their barbarous ravages, as any other people. We believe that all men are bound to sustain and uphold the respective governments in which they reside, while protected in their inherent and inalienable rights by the laws of such governments; and that sedition and rebellion are unbecoming every citizen thus protected, and should be punished accordingly.

First. Resolved: For the sake of friendship, and to be in a covenant of peace with us, notwithstanding the necessary loss of property, and expense we incur in moving, we comply with the requisitions of their resolutions in leaving Clay county, as explained by the preamble accompanying the same; and that we will use our exertions to have the Church do the same; and that we will also exert ourselves to stop the tide of emigration of our people to this county.

Second. Resolved: That we accept the friendly offer verbally tendered to us by the committee yesterday, to assist us in selecting a location, and removing to it.

Third. Resolved. Unanimous that this meeting accept and adopt the above preamble and resolutions which are here presented by the committee.

Fourth. Resolved. That T. [Thomas] B. Marsh, L. [Lyman] Wight and S. [Samuel] Bent be a committee to carry these proceedings to the meeting of citizens of Clay, to be held tomorrow at Liberty.   [signed]   W.W. Phelps, Chairman   John Corrill, Secretary

Diantha mulled over the Mormon dilemma in bed while she waited for her husband's return. He would be weary. The hour was late; his meeting must have been intense. She worried. So much was at stake.

My life, my future? I have no control over my life in the now or in the future. Her thoughts were raging. *Where are my boys?* Now her mind cried out in agony. *Ebe! Sam! They will have no idea where to find me if they want to!* "Oh God, what am I supposed to do?" The fact that she said it out loud startled her. Memories she wanted to forget raced through her mind rekindling the fear and the heartache. The fires, the tar, the screams, the hunger, the pain, were they all in the past or would there be more? *How can there be more? I can't do more.* A burst of rage engulfed her entire soul. She flipped back the covers and leaped out of bed.

"Get out of here," she demanded. "Get, get, get. You are not wanted here." Spinning in her nightgown she kicked a forceful foot into the air. "Out, out, out!" Swishing the skirt of her gown she shooed toward the door and opened it. "Off with you." Again she kicked into the air with a bare foot and slammed the door shut. With a powerful gesture she bolted her back to the door and reached out with both arms as if to keep someone from entering. Her rigid body matched her resolute mind. "I will not let the Stinky One control me! Get behind me Satan!" Negative thoughts and feelings dissipated at once. The fury she felt dissolved like butter in a heated cooking pot. Her entire body collapsed onto the dirt floor and she wept.

"Mother, why are you crying?"

Diantha looked up and called out to her angel. "Oh Eunice. I didn't mean to wake you up. Come," she beaconed. The small girl sank into her mother's arms and waited in silence as sobs subsided and her mother's heart slowed its beat. This patient child needed an explanation, an example. Diantha wanted her only daughter to be stalwart and valiant for the cause of Zion. Was this a test, an opportunity for her to teach of testimony in the Lord Jesus Christ and His Atonement?

"My Angel," she said caressing the child's curls and kissing both cheeks. "Mother was sad, very sad. Have you ever felt sad?"

"I'm sad when you are sad, Mommy."

"Do you know who can help us both to be happy again?" Their eyes met in sacred seriousness. Diantha's daughter nodded her head.

"I think Jesus can," she said.

"Of course He can. Shall we ask Him to help us now?" Together they knelt on a rag rug and an angel mother pleaded with Heavenly Father to bless her angel daughter and all of the saints no matter where they lived, no matter where they were forced to move. She prayed with humble faith, even the faith of a child. As she closed the prayer in her Savior's holy name she felt His peace come upon her. His Atonement was a bestowal of pure hope. "My cup runneth over," she whispered.

Historical Background

"Elder Morley with others left Kirtland on April 9, 1836 to return to Missouri, having been in Kirtland a year" (Esplin, 7). Zion's Camp "was not successful in helping reinstate the Missouri Saints to their homes in Jackson County" (Esplin, 7).

Titus Billings was present when the resolution was read to Mormon Elders. The brethren in Clay County met to "formulate their reply. They acknowledged the truth of the statement that they came to Clay County to make temporary homes, but they had expected the officials of the state to assist them in obtaining their property from which they had been driven. Their property had been legally obtained through purchase, they had tried to live in peace with their neighbors and had not molested any living soul" (SmithJF, 85).

"At a respectable meeting of the elders of the church of Latter-day Saints, held in Clay county, Mo. on Friday, July 1, 1836" (Messenger) "W.W. Phelps was appointed chairman with John Corrill secretary and a committee of twelve: Titus Billings, Isaac Morley, Edward Partridge, Lyman Wight, Thomas B. Marsh, Elias Higby, Calvin Bebee, Isaac Hitchcock, Isaac Higby, Samuel Bent, James Emmett and R. Evans, were assigned to study that resolution and write a response" (Berrett/Burton, 273-274; Journal History7; messenger; Roberts, 88).

CHAPTER 39

Titus' plan was to build a nicer cabin for Diantha when they returned from the Kirtland Temple dedication. He had purchased land for it, but felt compelled to plant crop before starting construction. Sam's hand woven broom stood in the corner of the old cabin. Sometimes they used it to sweep the dirt, but Titus envisioned a wooden floor and hoped for one before the treasured broom wore out. Diantha worried if the object was a painful reminder of sorrow between two brothers, heartache that refused to be swept away. At first she suspected those memories to be the cause of a deep scowl on her husband's face. He was anxious for some reason, even agitated. The more she observed him the more confused and concerned she became.

After supper he couldn't sit still. He paced back and forth while she tried to knit until it nearly drove her wild.

"Titus, what is it?"

"What's what?"

"What is bothering you?"

"Nothing."

"Would you like to talk about it?"

"No."

"Would you like to read to me while I knit?"

"No."

"Are you ill?"

"No."

"Have I done something wrong?"

"No. No, nothing you've done."

Diantha emptied her hands and intercepted his pacing. She put her arms around his neck and peered into his eyes.

After all she's been through, she still has the most beautiful eyes in the world, his mind told him.

"I thought we didn't keep secrets from each other," she said. He said nothing. "Let's go for a walk." She tossed a shawl over her shoulders and took his arm.

Outside the sun was beginning to set. It gilded the sky in stunning colors with the promise of springtime. His mouth was still, but her mind was spinning. At last she spun one of her thoughts into words.

207

"We've been very blessed, Titus." He grunted a sound making no attempt to speak. She did not halt. "We've traveled down some painful paths, but we've never traveled alone."

They walked a distance in silence. She had no idea where his mind was, but hers was full of gratitude. She decided not to pry. Unrest in the county made them cautious. They turned back.

"I have bad news," he said at last. She listened to hear more, aching for him as he struggled to get it out. "I know you hate it, Di." He paused. It was a long pause and she tried to wait. He needed help so she prodded.

"What do I hate?" she asked. He stopped walking.

"Diantha, we have to move again!" Was that it? Was that why he suffered? Because they had to move? Again? Before she could question him, he spoke.

"We have agreed to give up all our land and move away from Clay County. We are going to Caldwell County where we will have no neighbors."

"I know," she said.

"You know? How could you know?"

"I didn't know about Caldwell, but I knew we were leaving. The Lord is taking us away, Titus."

"You're good with that?" Her response caught him off guard.

"We're not wanted here. Why should we stay?" They lingered at the cabin door. "It doesn't matter where we live, Titus. The thing that really matters is the way we live."

He enfolded her in his arms as she offered a precious afterthought.

"What a blessing we are still alive and together."

*   *   *

"How far are we going?" Alfred asked his Father. To him it seemed like they had been traveling a mighty long time already. The freckles that danced all over his face matched the rusty curls on his head and gave his mother a longing for her brother, his namesake. From her seat in the wagon bed beside George, Eunice and Titus Jr. Diantha watched the lad and his father drive the team.

Who would have thought the day would come when she looked forward to moving out of the country to settle in the wilderness of its outskirts? By now civilization was far behind them. She was going to set up house in a county with zero population.

They would probably sleep in the wagon until Titus could raise a cabin. As yet the place had no schools, no churches, and no shops.

Diantha looked at the bundles around her. She was taking very little. Very little is all she had left. *There will be no place to purchase anything when we arrive,* she thought to herself. It was like she was starting all over again.

The absence of Sam and Ebenezer pained her more than the loss of possessions. Diantha closed her eyes and pictured two cute little boys singing in the wagon bed as she accompanied them on her prized dulcimer. *If only,* she dreamed. *The boys had moved on to their own lives. The dulcimer? Was it stolen? Was it burned with the cabin? She would never know.*

Diantha smoothed a place in her lap for Titus Jr. to rest his head. She began to hum a tune as peaceful feelings calmed her soul. Any sacrifice on her part had been for the Lord. Her fingers stroked her son's four-year-old head. His hair was dark and curly, like his father's. How she loved this little boy. She loved all of her children and would do anything for their good. *Sacrifice? My sacrifice is nothing,* Diantha thought. *"Heavenly Father sacrificed his Son!"*

Historical Background

As Mormon misery built up in Clay County, "we all gave up our land and agreed to go to Caldwell County. We were to be let alone there so we were glad to do so" (Carter3, 254).

CHAPTER 40

Missouri Mormons made another exit from established communities and distanced themselves far away on unclaimed government issued land. Under the leadership of W. W. Phelps and John Whitmer the relocating congregation labored to build a new town designed after the inspired layout of their prophet's "City of Zion" proposed for Independence in Jackson County, Missouri. A large "Public Square" in the center of town was made up of four squares, each containing four acres, and each reserved for a specific religious, public or governmental building. A new Temple or "House of the Lord" would be raised on one of them.

Bishop Partridge and his two counselors, Isaac Morley and John Corrill worked with Phelps and Whitmer in supervising layout and determining proper prices for each piece of land. Isaac Morley cleared a spot and started building a cabin not far from the Square. Titus cleared ground two lots down, beside Edward Partridge and Hyrum Smith. He helped construct a log schoolhouse they would also use as a courthouse, for public meetings and for worship. How he missed his two older hard working sons. In no time all of the wide square-cornered streets were busy. Business thrived. The large "little town" buzzed with industrious residents who left their former homes with an agreement for Clay County citizens to purchase them, yet never collected a cent due.

Titus was working with a committee of brethren to build a high log fence around the new town when Isaac's wagon drove up and stopped.

"There you are! We've been all over looking for you." Isaac called out.

We've? Billings wondered as he shaded his forehead and tried to see through the searing sun. Diantha was in the wagon with others.

"Titus, Titus," she shouted with excitement. "Look who is here." A tall, young man jumped off the wagon and ran to his father.

"Samuel! Samuel! How did you find us?"

"God knows all things," Samuel said, "so we asked him. Come meet my Martha Ann."

*   *   *

"Far West?" Diantha said with surprise and wonderment. "Interesting name."

"Tells it like it is," Titus said. The County of Caldwell was created to compensate misplaced Missouri Mormons. Only one town exists in that county and it had been named, "Far West" by its occupants.

"We surely are far out here in the West," Alfred said.

"'Bout as far as you can go." Titus laughed. He kissed his wife. "Grab that wooden box, Alfred, and let's be off."

The two crossed over John Clementon's property to the next lot where Samuel was building a cabin for Martha Ann. Because timber was so plentiful most homes in the new settlement were log cabins. Families built inside the walled township as the Prophet advised them. Farmland was cleared outside those walls. Water wells were dug from sixteen inches to three feet in diameter and walled with stone. Titus and Sam fenced one hundred and twenty acres of good farm land and planted it together. With another hundred dollars Titus bought twenty acres of timberland.

Farming was good. Families were happy. Far West expanded constantly. In this remote place of unclaimed, undeveloped, unwanted frontier land, Mormon converts found everything they needed. After all, the only thing they wished for was to be left alone to live their religion in peace. They had come a long way for the privilege, but soon outsiders started to move in as well. No problem. New comers would embrace the truth once they learned of it, right? For some this was not the case. Certain non-member grocery retailers started marketing spirituous liquors as well.

"High Council Meeting was interesting last night," Isaac said. Titus and Diantha were all ears so he went on. "John [Corrill], Calvin [Bebee], and I were assigned to open up a mercantile establishment."

"Really?" Diantha said. "Why?"

"Well, you can't be a member in good standing if you purchase groceries at a place selling forbidden strong drinks!"

The Lord's "Word of Wisdom" had been revealed through his prophet in Ohio after Titus led a group of saints to Missouri; yet he knew all about it. "Makes good sense," he said.

Isaac sighed." So Titus, I have come to see if you could give us a hand with erecting a shop right away."

Titus grinned.

"It is rather urgent, you see."

Diantha caught her husband's grin and produced her own. *Good ole Isaac,* she thought. *He still leans on my Titus.* She had no doubt her faithful husband would begin at once. Of course, she was right.

Soon the new shop was up and doing business when Church leaders unanimously voted to begin building a temple as means would permit. Bishop Partridge was appointed treasurer of the project with Isaac Morley as secretary. They were to collect donations for the holy endeavor.

With his flat blade mattock and digging spade, Brother Billings started on foot for the temple lot. Alfred and George wanted to go.

"This time it is for the fathers," he told them.

Diantha noticed their longing. Usually their father wanted their help.

"This is a rather sacred occasion," she said. "It's a job for priesthood holders." The eager boys still looked betrayed. "Come help me pack a picnic. Later you can deliver it to your father."

In only one morning, more than five hundred men excavated an area one-hundred-twenty feet long and eighty feet wide. They lovingly dug the five-foot deep hole with hand tools, and hauled the dirt away with handbarrows. Brother Billings walked home with dust and sweat and jubilation all over him. Diantha could not believe excavation for the Grand Temple could be completed in half a day.

She baked her best cake for the celebration after a cornerstone laying ceremony on July 4, 1838. Saints would raise another House to the Lord.

Brother Billings escorted his wife and four unmarried children to seats on the second row where he readied them for an unforgettable Far West Conference. He glanced over his shoulder, smiling at Sam and Martha already seated three rows back. Uncle Isaac was called to serve as a Branch Patriarch. It was announced that he would still remain first counselor to Bishop Partridge. John Corrill who had been elected as State Representative from Caldwell County was released as the second counselor. Titus Billings was proposed as the new second counselor and sustained without a dissenting vote. His children were pleased and his wife was delighted with the new appointment, perhaps even more than he.

Brother Billings returned from one of his meetings shaking his head. "It never fails," he told his wife. "The Lord does something good. The devil . . ."

"What now?"

"We finally have a safe place to live our lives here in Far West."

"Yes. I am so happy here, Titus."

"Well, apostasy and mobocracy are raging in Kirtland!"

"No. Not by the Temple."

"It's bad, Di."

"Is that why the Prophet left Kirtland?"

"Probably, and Kirtland Camp is coming?"

"Kirtland Camp? What's that?"

"They say 515 souls are coming. They travel together and pitch their tents along the way. Should arrive tomorrow."

"How exciting."

"I'm going out with Isaac and others to meet them and escort them into the city. They will camp on the Square until we can situate them in good homes."

"By the Temple Lot. Wonderful."

"That's not all. Isaac is roasting a beef for them."

"They are sure to be hungry."

"He wants all the trimmings ready when they arrive. Wanna help?"

"You know I do." Diantha handed her husband a large pot. "Fetch some potatoes from the cellar, please, and lots of carrots."

Life in Far West was desirable and many good saints found refuge in its logged walls. Their moment of peace, however, was brief. All too soon little troubles started creeping in and little troubles always grow into big ones. Diantha's first sadness came when Sam and Martha Ann announced they were leaving.

"We're going back to St. Louis," Sam said.

"He wants to work as a painter for my father," Martha Ann said.

"The offer is too good to pass up," Sam said looking with concern at his mother's face where sorrow was already evident. More persecution was in the air and his young wife wanted no part of it. He hated to leave his parents again, but the job offer was a good one.

Diantha could see in their eyes it was no use trying to dissuade them. Their decision was firm before they mentioned it. All too soon they were packed and departed.

"Be thankful they came for a little while," Titus tried to comfort. Diantha was grateful and rejoiced in the tender mercy that they had found them when they did. Perhaps another such time would come again. After all, *one can always hope*, Di thought to herself.

It was such a joy to have the Prophet Joseph in their midst again.

"Titus, we need to practice . . . today . . . now!" Her husband rolled his eyes, but Sister Billings was serious. "When you accept an assignment from the Prophet you are answering to the Lord. And, anytime we do something for the Lord we must do our best."

Titus smiled to himself. His lady owned the highest standard of excellence his forty-four years of living had ever bumped into and she lived by that standard, always. He was very proud of the fact and supposed she realized his appreciation for it. At this moment he suspected her verbiage was more geared to teaching their children than to beckoning him.

"Come Eunice. Your father is ready to rehearse with us," she announced. His assumption was accurate.

Diantha had taught the gifted seven-year-old to harmonize the alto part and she did it very well. The Prophet Joseph requested they sing "Redeemer of Israel, Our Only Delight." For Titus Billings just hearing its title opened flood gates of memory and sent them rushing throughout his being. How he loved "our King our Deliv'rer, our All!"

"The meeting is only a day away," his wife continued. Turning to her husband she added, "Titus, I think Eunice is ready to do a solo part." The child's eyes lighted up. "What do you think about her taking verse four by herself?" The proud father was in total agreement. In such a manner they practiced.

The Prophet (and other leaders, for that matter) routinely called upon Titus and his wife to sing hymns in church meetings. For young Eunice, however, it was a new experience, but she was very willing. About half way through the service the trio stood to harmonize. Diantha felt an outpouring of the Holy Spirit and squeezed her husband's hand. Eunice stood in perfect posture and with a clear, unhesitating voice began her solo: "As children of Zion, Good tidings for us. The tokens already appear." She noticed the Prophet's eyes. They were upon her. "Fear not, and be just, for the kingdom is ours. The hour of redemption is near."

Her tiny solo was a highlight of the meeting. Everyone loved the new voice, but none more than the Prophet Joseph whose eyes focused upon the young performer all the time she was singing. He was delighted and told her so when he shook her hand.

"Too bad Brother Phelps isn't here," he said. "When he gets back in town we'll have to tell him that you made his song even more beautiful." A toothless grin appeared on Eunice's excited face. Then the Prophet of God blessed her. "My little sister," he said, "you shall be able to sing songs of Zion for as long as you desire."

"I think the Prophet likes music," Eunice said on the walk home.

"Yes." Diantha was beaming as much as her child. "He loves music and he loves children," she said.

"May we sing our way home?" the child asked.

"Of course we can. You start us." And so she did.

Historical Background

"Towards the end of 1836, Caldwell County was created specifically for Mormon settlement to recompense Mormon losses in Jackson County. Shortly after the creation of Caldwell County, Far West was made the county seat." (Wikipedia, the free encyclopedia).

In his own words, and spelling, Titus wrote: "In the Spring of 1837 we then moved to Caldwell County, there I entered 120 Acres of land fenced & broke 15 Acres built me a house which cost me one hundred Dollars besides another piece of land I bought containing 20 Acres of timber land which cost one hundred Dollars I also bought a village Lot which cost forty Dollars all which I have ben [sic] driven from together with my farming tools household furniture Provisions" (Johnson, 140).

[Note: This redress account states that the Billings Family moved to Caldwell County in the Spring of 1837. Land records show Titus purchased land there in the Fall of 1836.]

"The Saints built as though they were going to be there permanently and a cornerstone for a temple was laid" (Esplin, 7).

Titus Billings purchased acreage in Caldwell County at Far West. Early Land Records show that he purchased from the government the following property:

- September 5, 1836, record # 2425, description: 12 E ½ of NW 1/4 of sec. 28

- February 13, 1837, record # 2042, description: 11 NE 1/4 of SW 1/4 of sec. 12

- February 13, 1837, record # 2404, description: 12 E ½ of NE 1/4 of sec. 24
  (Johnson1, 12).

"At this meeting [June 11, 1837] an assignment was given Isaac Morley, John Corrill and Calvin Beebe to open a mercantile establishment to compete with certain individuals, not of the Church, who were retailing groceries and spiritu-ous liquors. The committee held that no Latter-day saint could support any establishment that sold spirituous liquors and still be considered a member of the Church in good standing" (Brigham Young Journal History, June 11, 1837; MorleyRH,54).

Bishop Edward Partridge was nominated to still act as bishop and was unani-mously chosen, who then nominated Isaac Morley and Titus Billings for his coun-selors, who were unanimously chosen. Elder Isaac Morley was then unanimously appointed patriarch of this branch of the church (Elders, 2; Journal History9; MorleyRH, 63; Smith2, 524).

 Bishop Edward Partridge chose Elder Titus Billings (age 44) as his second coun-selor in the Presiding Bishopric on August 1, 1837 (Cannon/Cook, 117, 249; Flake, 510; Jensen1, 242; Journal History 8,1; Ludlow, 337; Mortimer, 77, 78; Smith2, 504). That day he was ordained to the office of a High Priest with Bishop Edward Partridge and Isaac Morley officiating (Brewster, 45; Black, 575; Cannon/Cook, 249; Cook,102).

Titus Billings served as second counselor with his brother-in-law, Isaac Morley, the first counselor, until Bishop Partridge died in 1840 (Esplin, 6). [Note: Titus Billings made it into the Work and the Glory Series when Gerald Lund used him as number eighty-two of eighty-five high priests receiving calls in Nauvoo (Lund, 179).]

A meeting of Church Authorities at the schoolhouse in Far West on August 5, 1837, also shows him in attendance (Cannon/Cook, 118). "August 5, 1837 [Isaac Morley] named one of the five wise men to handle the sale of lots in Far West." Minutes of a Conference at Far West, Missouri, November 7, 1837, show the general assembly "again unanimously supporting the same Presiding Bishopric" (Cannon/Cook, 124; MorleyRH,64; WhitneyOF, 183). "At a general assembly of the church held November 7, 1837 he [Isaac Morley] was chosen Patriarch of Far West, and ordained to that office under the hands of Joseph Smith, Sidney Rigdon and Hyrum Smith" (Jenson1,235). "Ordained a patriarch by the Prophet Joseph Smith" (Esshom, 1044).

During a meeting, February 5, 1838, to transact business concerning an accusa-tion against two of the brethren for "using the monies which were loaned to the Church," Titus Billings is quoted as saying that he "could not vote until they had a hearing in the common council" (Berrett/Burton, 257,258; Cannon/Cook, 139; Elders1; Journal History10; Smith3, 5).

This was a conference held at Far West, then the headquarters of the Church in that region. The Priesthood was reorganized and the Church set in order, in the same manner as had been done in Kirtland. Hyrum Smith was sustained, in lieu of Frederick G. Williams, as one of the three First Presidents, in which office he had before been acting. Elder Boynton and the two Elders Johnson were rein-stated in the Quorum of the Twelve, though later they again fell away. Bishops Edward Partridge, Isaac Morley and Titus Billings were retained in office; while President William W. Phelps and John Whitmer were severed from the Church. The former afterwards returned (WhitneyOF, 183).

Titus and Diantha "were called upon" to sing "Redeemer of Israel" at a meeting held in a Far West home. Eunice was 7 years old and they let her solo a part. "Joseph watched me all the time we were singing. Joseph certainly loved sing-ing and he also loved children" (Bennett, 555; Hale, 2; Pyne, 4). Diantha taught Eunice to sing the alto part, even at a very young age. Prophet Joseph seemed impressed with this and would have Eunice sing to him every opportunity. "While just a small child the Prophet took me on this lap every time I went to his home and had me sing for him" (Snow4, 4). "Redeemer of Israel" was written by William W. Phelps (Davidson,35).

Another meeting at the schoolhouse in Far West was held February 24, 1838. Bishop Edward Partridge and Brother Titus Billings were present (Cannon/Cook, 142).

During three industrious years of peace, the Saints attended Church meetings, studied scriptures, practiced the Word of Wisdom, baptized their children when old enough, registered land with government offices and paid money, made their own clothing, etc. "and began to live as we supposed the Saints would live" (Carter3, 254: words of Drusilla Hendricks).

Kirtland Camp arrived at Far West on Tuesday, October 2, 1838 (MorleyRH, 68).

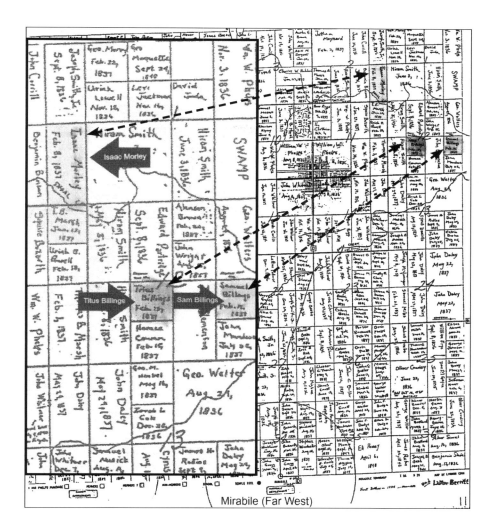

Mirabile (Far West)

Billings Property in Far West

Map of Mirabile Township, formerly Far West, Caldwell County, Missouri.
Billings and Morley properties are highlighted in map insert.

This Mirabile map validates Far West property assignments to Isaac Morley, Titus
Billings and Sam Billings. Titus' lot bordered Partridge and H. Smith. [Note about
Sam: This map shows he owned a spot in Far West, but scant records show he
married Martha Ann Webster sometime about 1849 or 1850 – later than Far
West. He died in St. Louis, Mo 1879 at age 52. We have plugged him into the
story as best we could.]

CHAPTER 41

"Far West," a magnet for attracting searching souls, began with 1500 saints, 150 homes, 6 stores and 1 school, but soon exploded to a population of 4,900 Mormons living on the legally purchased land they worked with their might to improve. They were "far" away "west" of other statesmen. No one else wanted the spot. At last they could be left alone!

Yet two problems lurked around them. First, because Mormons were an industrious, hard working people (and hard work produces success), skeptical outsiders feared the Mormon county would soon become the richest in the state of Missouri. Second, and probably more heartbreaking, was the fact that conspiring traitors were within their midst and had turned against the Prophet and his brother, Hyrum, who were jailed again, this time in Liberty -- for things they did not do. Even Oliver Cowdery, David Whitmer and Martin Harris, great leaders who had witnessed the actual golden plates of the Book of Mormon and had seen an angel of God, fell away and left the fold. These were dear friends. Oliver Cowdery, as a missionary, had carried the truth to Titus in Ohio. His close friends, W. W. Phelps and John Whitmer, had also left the church. How his heart ached for their souls and longed for their association.

Persecutors, looking for any excuse to cause trouble for the Mormons, sometimes resorted to creating their own excuses. If force would not work, maybe blame would. Some accusers emptied their own log cabins and torched them to the ground so they could report loss to authorities. These and other crimes were charged to innocent and often unsuspecting Mormons. Lies and rumors spread anger and created fear in the hearts of Far West residents who lived in constant peril.

Priesthood brethren rotated guard duty. All of them were alert day and night. Every man agreed to converge at once on horseback at the Square whenever a trumpet blast or three taps on a bass drum signaled alarm. Then it happened. Titus was just coming on guard duty the night of Election Day [August 1838] when he heard the news.

"We got Mormon trouble in Daviess County!" someone shouted.

"What kind of trouble now?"

"Sam Brown got beat up in Gallatin – pretty bad."

"Samuel Brown is a gentle soul. Who'd want to beat him?"

"Somebody who don't want us Mormons voting."

"Must have been that Peniston candidate. He knows Mormons wouldn't vote for him."

"It was Richard Weldon?" another voice pitched in.

"Oh, yes." He was known as the town bully and notorious for his opposition to Mormonism. "He'd help William Peniston or anybody opposed to us."

"It was a set-up. He started a fist fight and lots of mobbers jumped in on it, so of course some Mormons did too."

"Of course."

"We won, but it backfired. Now everybody's after us."

Everybody seemed to include the state militia. Captain Samuel Bogart, also a Methodist minister, led an assemblage of armed soldiers to demand evacuation of Mormon homes scattered on the outskirts of Far West. Early in the afternoon Brother Thoret Parsons viewed their coming from his cabin window. He stepped outside in hopes of sparing his frightened family.

"Be out of here by 10 o'clock tomorrow morning!"

"But how can I?"

"Not my problem, but I'm warnin' ya. Gilliam is bringin' more men from Platte and Clinton Counties as we speak. They will camp near Far West tonight. You Mormons ain't got a chance."

"Please, our women and children. Give us time to . . ."

"Don't bother 'bout going to Far West for help neither." He laughed and raised his gun. "We're givin' that place all hell before the noon sun hits tomorrow"

Cheers went up from a mobbish army. Bogart led them to the ford on Crooked River and gave orders to set up camp for the night. "Tomorrow will be a big day!" he said.

But today is not over yet, Bogart realized. *I will send a detachment out to Pinkham's cabin. He's in a lone spot out there and we havn't threatened him yet.* "Give it to 'em good," he shouted as troops moved out.

Brother Parsons sent word to Far West. He and his family tried to load belongings into their only wagon, but they didn't know where to go or what to do.

Bogart's detachment returned with bounty beyond his expectation. Not only had they left terrified women with cruel threats in place of stolen food, firearms and four horses, but also they dragged back three men. Bogart had prisoners!

News that Nathan Pinkham, William Seeley and Addison Greene would be killed before daybreak reached Far West at a very late hour. A bugle call and three booming drum beats sounded at midnight. The double signal was alarming.

"This is supposed to be a free country," Titus mumbled as he pulled a stiff new boot onto his foot. "I'm glad we're finally going to do something about it."

Diantha knew her husband was right, but the midnight call sent chills of fright and uncertainty racing through her. She had not been asleep when it sounded. Sleeping was difficult these days. One never knew where the enemy was or how it would react. Oft times it was difficult to know who was an enemy and who was not. Her husband was true and brave and always willing to stand for the cause of Zion. He loved the Lord's Prophet and defended the faith. She was proud of him. She too tried to be strong, but the grip of fear from this summons of militia to battle at midnight almost smothered her.

"Titus," she gasped. "Your new boots have not been sized yet!"

It was true. They had been issued that very afternoon, but his old shoes were so tattered and worn that he had already burned them. Leather boots made in early frontier days were shaped exactly the same for each foot. The new buyer was supposed to pull them on and wet them down. Then he would walk in them until they dried. Thus, the shoes or boots would take on the shape of his foot and be sized left or right from then on. But, Titus Billings had no time to size his new boots and was now being called to battle in the middle of the night.

"They will be fine," he assured her. "I'll probably get them wet anyway and they'll be sized when I get home."

The farmer-soldier reached for his new gun.

"Keep me in your prayers," he teased, giving a last, one-armed hug to his sweetheart.

"I love you," she whispered. "You are always in my prayers!"

His blood-shot eyes focused on her as though he wanted always to remember the way she looked. Tears fell in abundance, but she tried to smile between them. Long, soft curls fell down her back. She stood, looking beautiful in her old nightgown and shivering with sobs.

No one was asleep. Alfred and George were up and dressed, with their mother too preoccupied to notice.

"I'm ready to go."

"Me too."

"No, you men must stay to guard the women and the house," Titus said.

They had heard that before. This time they wanted to go.

"You'll need a drummer boy, Pa. I could do it," Alfred offered. After all, he was thirteen years old and a fine musician.

It was no use. Billings was a man of his word. When he said "no," he meant it.

Fondly he bent down to kiss each wide-eyed son and embrace with tenderness his only daughter. Then, turning again to his beloved Diantha, he said something she would never forget. "Gotta go earn ya for Eternity!" With another kiss he was gone.

Sounds of shuffled footsteps and shouts and animal noises peaked at the hasty gathering. Diantha watched from a window as her priesthood holder mounted his horse to join them. The boys ran behind to see and hear what they could, still hopeful to join, but not expectant.

Diantha was curious and concerned too. She saw other women outside and grabbed her shawl. "Watch the baby, Eunice. I'll be right back."

George counted at least seventy-five men on horseback at the public square in Far West that night. Alfred spotted Apostle-General David W. Patten in the center of them. Patten waved a sword into the air and shouted strong statements about life and liberty and the Lord's work. Already he held the title of "Captain Fear Not." The boys had heard their father quote him many times. Diantha was pleased to hear his words firsthand. They were positive, fearless, mighty, and powerful. He was a good, righteous leader. She took comfort knowing he would be in charge.

"We must trust the Lord for victory!" he shouted. "I would rather die than exist in a country which allows such unjust conditions."

Men were cheering. Women were crying. Children peeked out from everywhere with wonderment in their eyes. To Diantha, the moment felt like a big event. Maybe this would be a turning point at last. She hoped it would. With all her heart she hoped it would.

Historical Background

The Billings and Morley families had become quite comfortably situated again and there were many happy homes in Caldwell County, but it did not last long. There were enemies both within and without the church. The mobs began to carry out their old threats. Cordelia Morley wrote: "We did not know what to do; there was no place to go, nothing but trouble and vexation all the time. There were traitors in our midst that were conspiring against the saints" (Esplin, 7).

"I was always very much affected by the Spirit which he [Prophet Joseph Smith] manifested. At first I did not know what it was, but my mother told me it was the power which Joseph possessed" (Snow8, 4)."It was but a very short time after that meeting that Joseph was taken by a mob and put in prison for something they could not prove against him. Hyrum Smith also was taken at this time" (Hale, 2; Pyne, 4).

Tension rose as some mobsters even set their own homes on fire in order to blame and punish innocent Mormons. "The mob, seeing that they could not succeed by force, now resorted to strategem [sic]; and after removing their property out of their houses, which were nothing but log cabins, they fired them, and then reported to the authorities of the state that the 'Mormons' were burning and destroying all before them (Smith3, 164). Crimes of the mob were charged to the saints. These and their associates were the ones who fired their own houses and then fled the country crying "fire and murder" (Smith3, 165).

Then, August 6, 1838, "trouble began over the election" in Gallatin, Daviess County (Morley, 69). Husbands "had to stand guard for [the next] three months, as the mob would gather on the outside settlements. The brethren had to be ready and on hand at the sounding of a bass drum. Three taps on the drum and my husband would be on his horse in a moment, be it night or day, while I and my children were left to weep, for that is what we did at such times" (Carter3, 154: words of Drusilla Hendricks).

Captain Samuel Bogart of the state militia [also a Methodist Reverend (Jensen3, 164)] and about forty (Allen2 caption) or seventy-five (Jensen4, 164) soldiers rode up to Brother Thoret Parson's home on Wednesday, October 24, 1838 "at the head of the east branch of Log Creek and ordered him to leave by ten o'clock the next morning; Bogart saying that he expected to 'give Far West hell,' before noon of the following day" (Roberts, 474). It was also reported that a Neil Gilliam had gathered men from Platte and Clinton counties (west of Clay and Caldwell counties) "to march against the 'Mormons'; who would camp within six miles of Far West that night" (Roberts, 474).

Bogart took his camp to Crooked River. They "were committing depredations on Log Creek" (Jensen3, 164). "The same day a detachment of Bogart's men entered the house of a brother Pinkham, took three men prisoners, also took four horses,

225

some firearms and food, and warned Pinkham to leave the state at once or they would 'have his d---d old scalp.'" (Roberts, 475).

These reports were brought into Far West about midnight; and Judge Elias Higbee, "first judge in Caldwell county, and the highest civil authority therein, and the officer in whom the state law vested the right to call upon the militia to enforce the law immediately called upon Colonel George M. Hinkle to raise a company of militia to disperse the mob and rescue the prisoners" (Roberts, 475).

A trumpet call [or a drum beat (CES, 200)] sounded at midnight and about seventy-five Mormon volunteers gathered at the public square on horseback (Allen; Billings/Shaw/Hale, 16; Carter3, 255; Jensen, 12; Jensen3, 164, 616; Roberts1, 169-71). "The trumpet sounded and the brethren assembled on the public square in Far West about midnight" (Jensen3, 615). " . . . they had taken three of the Brethren prisoners and intended to kill them that night the trumpet was sounded and men com [sic] together and prepared for to march . . ." (Johnson1, 707-words of Charles C. Rich).

Titus arrived in new shoes. He had no others to wear (Snow3, 2).

CHAPTER 42

The Mormon Prophet was not in Far West to hear the midnight alarm. Judge Elias Higbee, as First Judge and highest civil authority in Caldwell County, was vested by state law as the only officer who could call up militia to enforce the law. When he heard of plans to murder three innocent Mormons at sunrise, he sent for Colonel George M. Hinkle, instructing him to raise a company of militia at once, disperse the mob and rescue the Mormon prisoners. General Patten took the lead, hoping to surprise and scatter the enemy.

About twelve miles south, down the main road, soldiers dismounted and left their horses protected near a ford of the winding Crooked River. On foot, they searched for the hidden camp.

Divided into three companies, the men spread out for a full sweep down the hillside. Billings, assigned to David Patten's Company, followed the road route. James Durphy's Company started through the fields, and Charles C. Rich led his company down the east side of the fields. The march was unsuccessful, so they regrouped and fanned out again.

Approaching the ridge within a mile of the militia camp the Mormon posse was ordered to halt by Bogart's picket guard, John Lockhart. During a brief exchange of words, Lockhart heard a snap and fired wildly, thinking someone was going to shoot him. Young Patrick O'Bannion was hit and fell to the ground. The shouts and gunshot alerted Bogart's men who ran from their tents to positions along the riverbank.

Mormon troops lined the top of a small hill only eighty yards above the river. Captain Patten ordered a charge and started down the hill on a fast trot. Billings followed. He was running between the Captain and James Hendricks. About fifty yards from the enemy camp they formed a line, but the mob was forming one on the riverbank, below their tents. It was too dark to see much when looking downhill toward the west. At the dawning of the day, their opponents, however, had the distinct advantage of an uphill view toward the east. God's sunshine seemed to be aiding the enemy by exposing Mormon soldiers as silhouettes. Thus, Patten's men became moving targets. Bogart's mob fired broadside at them. Several saints fell. Commanding a return of fire, Captain Patten gave the watchword, "God and Liberty!" and ordered another charge. Obeying his command, the two parties came into contact with their swords.

Bullets flew everywhere. Billings heard an extra loud shot. *Must have been close!* He thought he saw General Patton fall. Another nearby blast downed Hendricks on the other side of him. Captain Billings whirled around with such force he slammed himself into a tree trunk and there he prayed, "Oh God, help us! What would Ye have us do?"

Before he could get to Hendricks he heard a voice ask, "Which side ya on?" The trees were still in darkness so he couldn't see who spoke, but he heard Hendrick's voice give answer: the watchword, "God and Liberty!"

Hearing another voice he turned to see Charles C. Rich on his knees anointing Patton who took a ball in the bowel and fell in a helpless heap just north of the river crossing.

Not the General! Our Fearless Leader! An apostle of God!

Rich was second in command. He raised his sword and ordered another charge. The enemy was on the run, crossing the river and trying to flee thinking (perhaps with divine help) the number of Mormon troops was greater than it really was. Only one of Bogart's soldiers, Moses Rowland, was killed. Six were wounded.

Titus stumbled to find Hendricks in the darkness. He could see dark splotches on Hendricks clothes, blood on his chin, and by squinting into a glimmer of light he could see a bleeding hole in his neck! Titus pulled a handkerchief from his pocket and tied it around his friend's neck. Blood saturated it in an instant. He fumbled in Hendrick's pocket for another kerchief and tied it as tight as he could.

"Don't leave me, brother," Hendricks said.

Titus knelt at his head and placing hands with the greatest of care he called upon the Almighty. "Bless this thy servant," he pleaded. "Help us know what to do. God let us get him to help and to his family --" He gasped a quick breath, "--alive! Lord please let him live! If that be in keeping with thy plan for us." He sealed the heart-rendered plea with his Savior's name.

"You're in the Lord's hands now, James. You'll be all right."

Titus stood. *Now what? I need help to move this man.*

Several soldiers had gathered around General Patton. As Titus started towards them he stumbled over another human heap. It groaned and he bent down to examine.

"No!" he cried. He didn't mean to say it out loud, it just came out. Tears came out too. Tears he couldn't control for the sad events he couldn't control. *Why? Why an innocent lad?* It was the drummer boy! His Alfred had wanted the job! The poor boy took a ball in his leg, but he was alive. Billings had no hanky so he tore his shirt and tightened it with all his might to stop the bleeding. Fatigue, pain, and fear were forgotten. He lifted the lad and held him tight.

"You'll be all right," he promised.

With his load Captain Billings started uphill into the daylight. Again he mused, *if only the sun hadn't betrayed us, we'd be heroes instead of sitting ducks!*

Two wagons waited at hilltop. He unloaded young Arthur Milliken into the corner of the first and tried to whisper comforting words to the wounded boy.

"We're taking these to Widow Metcalf's cabin," the driver said. Upon seeing Brother Billings he added, "Diantha will meet us there to help nurse the wounded."

"Good," Titus nodded. "I'm going back down to double check. Meet you there when I'm sure we got 'em all."

Bogart's men left everything, including the prisoners. One of them, Brother Seeley, had been shot but still lived. An abandoned wagon was loaded with injured men. One man had a musket ball in his shoulder. Another suffered one in the hip. Still, another was shot through the thigh and one through the arms. One brother had his arm broken by a sword.

Messengers rushed ahead to Far West to summon help. The bumpy wagon aggravated injury with each jolt. Patten was hurt so badly they carried him by stretcher to lessen the abuse. Still, the stress was too great and he pleaded to be left by the wayside.

"Stephen Winchester's cabin is three miles before Far West. Let's stop there," someone suggested.

"Widow Metcalf's cabin is closer. We're taking the general and most seriously wounded to her place."

Only three beds were available. Patten was placed on one of them. Hip wounded Brother Hodge and already paralyzed Brother Hendricks were laid onto the others. Young Brother O'Bannion was groaning on the floor when Diantha arrived with Drusilla Hendricks.

Ann Patten was already at her husband's side. "Don't weep, Ann. I have kept the faith. My work is done," he told her.

Only three feet away, Drusilla found James. He could speak, but that was all. She tried to make him move his feet but he could not. She went to work rubbing and steaming and trying to warm his lifeless body. There seemed to be no circulation in it. Diantha left to find another bed for O'Bannion.

The Prophet Joseph, his brother, Hyrum, and Lyman Wight had been out of town when the trouble broke out. News reached them on the trail while returning. They rushed to the cabin of wounded men. The crowded room reeked with stench and was smeared with blood everywhere.

Diantha and others with doctoring skills were laboring with wives in the care of their dear ones. She heard Elder Patten's strained voice call out again for Ann.

"Whatever you do else, do not deny the faith!" he told her. Though spoken at his weakest moment, these last words to his wife were by no means lacking strength. He pronounced them with dignified power and fervent commitment that left his unquestionable testimony ringing in her ears and the ears of all present.

Then he reached for the Prophet and beseeched brethren in the cabin to release him from their faith and let him go, "as he wished to be with Christ, which is far better." He died in peace and quiet.

It was nearly dark when Hendricks was loaded onto a bed in Brother Winchester's wagon and driven back to Far West. Patrick O'Bannion was taken to Sidney Rigdon's home where he died the next night.

Titus helped deliver the other wounded to their homes. When he tried to make an accounting, one man was still missing. Brother Gideon Carter had not returned. With Brother Hosea Stout sharing the wagon seat and Brother Charles C. Rich riding on horseback beside them, Brother Billings and his team returned to the battle site.

Gideon Carter must have died suddenly from a head wound that defaced him beyond recognition. Mistaken as enemy, he had been left behind. Now a sorrowful trio wrapped their friend and returned him for burial.

Trouble in Far West had only begun. October's last week was overloaded with fear, pain, confusion, unrest, false accusations, rumors, exaggerations, lies, and fury. Members had nowhere to go. Women and children did not know what to do.

Titus returned home at last. His feet were sore from wearing new boots to battle, but he was too fatigued to take them off. For five sleepless nights, the tight boots remained on his now miserable feet. Begging Diantha to remove them and wash his feet, he closed his weary eyes. "Wake me in two hours," he said. "I must have a little nap!" He slept only one hour before someone started pounding on the cabin door.

"Brother Billings, Brother Billings!" It was Brother Hosea Stout.

Before Diantha could quiet him, Titus was awake.

"Run for you life. They're coming for you!"

Soldiers or mobsters or both were out to get every man who fought at Crooked River. Charles C. Rich had been warned by the Holy Spirit that they should flee or be dead before sunrise. Hyrum told him to take all such brethren he could find and leave immediately.

"We depart in two hours!" Hosea said.

Diantha scraped her flour bin to make as many quick biscuits as she could. Titus forced his poor feet back into the new, battle-scarred boots. At least they had been washed and rubbed by loving hands. All too soon Brother Smoot, another escaping soldier, was at the door. He and Titus left together about midnight to join up with thirty-some-odd others.

Diantha gathered her frightened children around her. Just as they knelt to pray for protection, a mobbish gang burst into the cabin.

"Where is he? Where ya hiding 'em. He's a dead man now!"

At least he was gone. Silently she prayed for his safety, then submitted to a ruthless, mobocratic search.

Historical Background

David W. Patten, one of the Twelve Apostles, was known as "Captain Fear Not" among his military comrades. "In combating the attacks of the mobocrats he made the remark that he would rather die than to witness such a condition in his country" (Jensen3, 164). "Captain Patten wore a conspicuous white blanket overcoat that night as he led his men into battle" (LeSueur, 138-142).

"D.W. Patten took the first Division of the Company and kept on the road. Charles C. Rich took the Second Division and went Round on the east side to Fields Farm. James Durfee to [took] the third Division and went through the field" (Johnson1, 707).

"Pickett guard, John Lockhart, fires on army [at ridge on Main Road] mortally wounding Patrick O'Bannion. (Approximately 5:45 am, October 25, 1838.)" (Allen map.)

"It was just at dawning of light in the East when they were marching quietly along the road, and near the top of the hill which descends to the river that the report of a gun was heard. Young Patrick O'Banion reeled out of the ranks and fell mortally wounded. Thus the work of death commenced. Captain Patten ordered a charge and rushed down the hill on a fast trot, and when within about fifty yards of the camp they formed a line. The mob formed a line under the bank of the river below their tents. It was yet so dark that little could be seen by looking to the West, while the mob, looking towards the dawning light, could see Patten and his men. They fired broadside, and three or four of the brethren fell. Captain Patten ordered the fire returned, which was instantly obeyed, to great disadvantage in the darkness which yet continued. The fire was repeated by the mob, and returned by Captain Patten's company, who gave the watch-word, "God and Liberty." Captain Patten then ordered a charge, which was instantly obeyed. The parties immediately came in contact with their swords and the mob was soon put to flight, crossing the river at the ford and at such places as they could get a chance. In the pursuit, one of the mob fled from behind a tree, wheeled, and shot Captain Patten, who instantly fell mortally wounded having received a large ball in his bowels" (Allen, 2; SmithJF, 3:153).

[Titus] "was in Crooked River Battle, standing by Apostle Patten when he fell" (Tullidge, 429). [Titus was standing between Brother James Hindricks and Brother David Patten when both were shot.] "Bullets were flying all around him [Titus], but he had no fear until he saw Brother Patten fall. Then he stepped behind a large tree" (Snow3, 2). Hosea Stout "was the first man to approach Apostle Patten" (Jensen1, vol.3: 30, 531) after he was wounded. Charles C. Rich, second in command, "laid down his sword and administered the ordinance of the laying on of hands for the healing of the sick of his dying comrade; then arose and led the charge upon the enemy" (Jensen1, vol. 1:102, 103; Roberts1, 484, 485).

"The number of the saints seemed to be multiplied by divine power, and the enemy thinking the number was greater that it really was, fled leaving their horses and equipment behind" (Snow8, 1). "The brethren freed the three prisoners. One of them was also wounded" (CES, 200).

Brother Hindricks was wounded in the neck (Jensen1, 403; Johnson1, 231). David Patten and two others suffered bowel injuries. Musket balls were also found in four other men: "one in the shoulder, one in the hips, one through the thighs, one in the arms" (Smith8, 154)". Still another man had his arm broken by a sword. Arthur Milliken, the drummer boy, "was shot through both legs and above the knee" (Davis, 719). Defaced and dead from head wounds Brother Gideon Carter could not even be identified. He was left at first as enemy, but later reclaimed and buried (CES, 200; Jensen1, vol.1: 615).

"Elder Patten was carried to the home of Stephen Winchester near Far West" (CES, 200; Smith8, 154). The seriously injured were moved to Goose Creek where their wives, Prophet Joseph Smith, Hyrum Smith and Lyman Wight (who had not been in battle) joined them (Johnson1, 707-8).

In Widow Metcalf's cabin, there were three beds in the room where my husband [James Hendricks] lay: he in one, Brother David Patten in one and Brother Hodge in the other. Brother Hodge was the one shot in the hip. Brother O'banyon was on the floor begging for a bed and some of the sisters ran and got him one. My husband was shot in the neck where it cut off all feeling of the body. He was dead from his neck down.

One of the brethren [possibly Titus Billings] told me how he fell, for he was close to him. After he had fallen, one of the brethren asked him which side he was on (for it was not yet light enough to see) and all the answer he made was the watchword "God and Liberty." On hearing this it melted me to tears and I felt better. Then I was told how many of the brethren were wounded and who they were and was shown the weapons used and they bore blood from hilt to point. It makes me chill to think of it (Carter 20, 257: quoting Drusilla Hendricks).

In his dying moments at the cabin, Elder Patten spoke to his beloved wife, "Whatever you do else, do not deny the faith!" Then, aware that brethren were exercising faith in his recovery, Elder Patten requested that they "let him go, as he wished to be with Christ, which was far better." Moments before he died he prayed aloud, "Father, I ask thee in the name of Jesus Christ that thou wouldst release my spirit and receive it unto thyself." Then to those in the room, "Brethren, you have held me by your faith, but do give me up and let me go. I beseech you." He died without a groan (Bitton). Patrick O'Banion died soon after (Bitton, Smith8, 154). "Nine others were wounded" (Roberts, 475).

"The mobbers were dislodged and the men kept as prisoners were rescued; the posse then returned to Far West with their dead and wounded" (Jenson3, 164).

"Of the casualties in Bogart's forces the most reliable account fixes the number as one killed, Moses Rowland, and six wounded" (Roberts,475). "Sometimes when the prisoners [Joseph and Hyrum] were visited by their enemies, many of whom were very angry with the Prophet, especially, and would accuse him of killing a son, a brother or some relative of theirs at what was called the Battle of Crooked River. 'This look[s] very strange to me,' says Alexander McRae, one of the Prophet's fellow prisoners, 'that so many should claim a son or a brother killed there, when they reported only one man [was] killed'" (Roberts1, 521).

View of Crooked River
(Courtesy Evan A. Billings, 1998.)

Crooked River Battlefield in Modern Day
(Courtesy sbmitchell, 2002.)

Elder Billings (Evan A.) gave guided tours to LDS missionaries as they finished their Independence Missouri Missions. He obtained permission to include a visit to the Crooked River Battlefield.

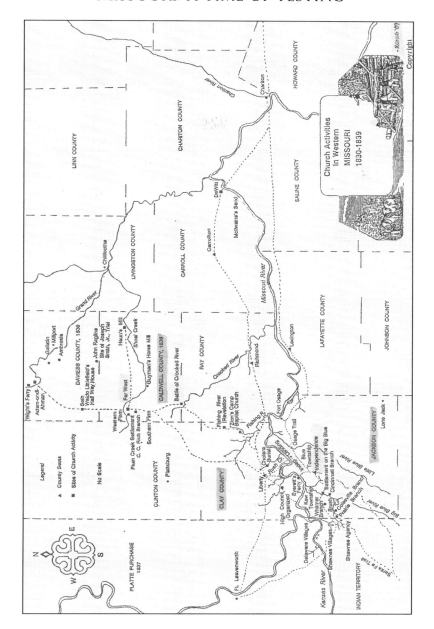

Western Missouri Map

Jackson, Clay and Caldwell counties are highlighted on this map. Please note Independence and Independence Landing, Far West and the location of the Crooked River Battle. Bogart's soldiers camped on the river banks near the county border.

(Courtesy Ronald E. Romig, 1987. From Church Activities in Western Missouri 1830-1839.)

CHAPTER 43

Dark clouds threatened the morning sky as Diantha walked to the cemetery. I hope the new gravesites can be closed before the downpour, she thought. A heavy sadness and cold fear hovered all around as she hurried along. Before the first funeral began rainy weather dampened attendees, but not the spirit surrounding them. The Prophet Joseph Smith preached an inspiring sermon to all and dedicated the life of Apostle David W. Patten unto the living God whom he had loved and served.

"Here lies a man who has done just as he said he would -- he has laid down his life for his friends and the cause of Zion." General Patten, Patrick O'Bannion and Gideon Carter were given military honors and laid to rest in a holy place at Far West, Missouri.

By early afternoon, a vast army of over two thousand men surrounded the town. Far West citizens did not know if soldiers had come to protect or to destroy them. They deserved and hoped for governmental assistance. Word of an Extermination Order signed three days before [October 27, 1838] had not yet reached the saints. In Jefferson City, Missouri's state capitol, Governor Lilburn W. Boggs (elected two years earlier) officially signed into law an order for extermination of all Mormons --"who must be treated as enemies."

General Samuel D. Lucas brought the terrible news to church leaders. Two thousand more men were expected the next day. They were acting with direct orders from the state's leading executive officer. Mormons had no choice but to leave immediately.

Terrible news of a brutal extermination at Haun's Mill reached Far West as well. Nineteen defenseless men and boys had been butchered by a senseless mob. Saints had to flee; all of them, at once!

Father Morley with Joseph Smith Senior and several other priesthood holders called on Drusilla Hendricks.

"We've come to help," Isaac said.

"Bless you. I sold what I could including our land to purchase a yoke of cattle. My wagon is ready, but I don't know how to get James into it," Sister Hendricks said.

Father Smith anointed and Father Morley administered

to the suffering soldier whose neck wound had paralyzed him. With effort they stood him on his feet and maneuvered him to the wagon bed.

*   *   *

Resorting to trickery, Colonel Hinkle betrayed church leaders and turned them over as prisoners to General Lucas. Joseph Smith, Sidney Rigdon, Lyman Wight, Parley P. Pratt, and George W. Robinson were forced to lie on cold ground in a terrible rainstorm. All through the night they were subjected to mocking, shrieking, blaspheming, and illegal sentencing to execution by pitiless fiends. Terrorized saints in Far West heard the ruckus and feared their prophet had been killed in the night.

The next morning Mormon troops were marched out of Far West. Part of Hinkle's agreement was that Mormon Militia would be forced to surrender all guns and ammunition. These did not belong to the state. They were private property. Nonetheless, about six-hundred-fifty guns were grounded, leaving no means of protection for already threatened families.

Pretending to search for more arms, a fiendish mob under the guise of Missouri Militia, was turned loose on the city. Wildly, they vandalized, ransacked, plundered, robbed, whipped, destroyed, exposed, raped and defiled.

Then men -- many men, forty, fifty, eighty men, were rounded up and taken as prisoners. Diantha's brother, Isaac, was one of these. When he asked to see his family. The request was granted, and two guards escorted him at gunpoint to his home.

"I am a prisoner now and must go to prison," the brave man told them. Lucy handed him an Indian blanket with a rope tied to one end. He gave quick instructions and kissed her. Then he kissed each sobbing child and his sister, Diantha.

"Be brave now, all of you, and trust in the Lord." With that, he was gone.

Armed mobsters riding horses herded the prisoners on foot through the mud as if they were a pack of hogs on their way to slaughter. Fifty miles later the weary, but innocent men were locked up in the Richmond Jail.

*   *   *

Saints were evacuating as quickly as possible. The air was thick with fear, confusion, and the sound of suffering. So many priesthood brethren had been captured and many more had fled for their lives.

Diantha hid herself behind a bush and prayed. "I'm not a midwife, Lord, but no one else is available. Please help me!" She, knowing firsthand about the pain and heartache of loss could not leave her friend unattended. In circumstances like this, with death all around, starting a new life seemed almost futile. Nonetheless, it was God's will. To Diantha that was all that mattered.

"Eliza Ann is bedridden and heavy with child," she told her sister-in-law, Lucy.

"But Diantha, you can't go back . . . you'll be killed!"

"I will be on the Lord's errand, Lucy. He will help me." Diantha swallowed hard. "I need your help too," she pleaded.

"Of course, but how?" Lucy asked.

"Please, keep my children with you and keep going."

"I will, but I don't know where we will end up. Oh Diantha, are you certain that you should chance it?"

"I must. Brother Snow is gone too. I can't leave her alone."

Both sisters were crying. Lucy nodded.

"I'll find you," Diantha said.

Again Lucy nodded.

Quickly she kissed her sons and only daughter. Then she flashed them a courageous smile and turned on the run.

Nine-year-old Eunice watched until her devoted mother was out of sight.

"Come now," Aunt Lucy said. "We must do our duty too."

Diantha raced to the Snow cabin. No one else was available to assist. As she expected, Brother James Chauncy Snow was away and all others had evacuated or were evacuating. Eliza was grateful, but terrified to see Diantha come.

"You can't stay here. They'll kill you!" she cried.

"The Lord's will be done," is all she said. It was all she could say. She would do her part. He would take care of the rest.

What should have been a joyful and glorious moment, even the birth of her first child, was to Eliza Ann a nightmare. She pleaded with her loyal friend, but Diantha would not leave until little Sarah Jane was safely delivered.

"Now go! Thank you, thank you, but go!"

"You carry the baby and I will carry you," Diantha instructed as she whipped the patched quilt to the foot of the bed.

"No, Diantha. You must go yourself. If you carry me, none of us will make"

"I can't leave you like this."

"You must. Please."

Diantha reached out to touch the soft bundle resting on Ann's arm as she bent down to kiss her friend on the forehead. Truth lumped in her throat. She would give her life trying to save them both, if only she could.

"Go now!" Ann demanded. You've done all you can for us. The Lord will do the rest."

A sudden feeling of concern for her children pounded in Diantha's heart. With tender aching she tucked the beautiful baby girl into her mother's arms and kissed them both.

"I love you," she cried. "I will get help!"

Though her body and her feet seemed driven by a power other than her own, it was too late. She heard them, a whole band of them on horseback. They stampeded around the tiny, cabin and with ugly, hateful shouts began to dismount. She turned to see several men charge into the humble cabin, their boot heels hammering the wooden floor. What could she do? Diantha dropped to the ground and screamed a silent prayer, *"Oh God. Help Ann. Please don't let her suffer!"*

In her mind Diantha could see it all. Angry men with weapons, at least eight, maybe more, circled around the bed of a newborn and its helpless mother. How unfair. Ann had no chance at all to escape. Why would a loving Lord bring new life into a world where it had no possible chance for survival? Diantha knew. She knew of the Lord's plan allowing His spirit children a place to receive mortal bodies. She knew mortality was only a temporary resting place. *Death is not the end*, she reasoned. *Heaven would welcome the two innocent spirits back with joy and celebration. Please God, don't let it take long.*

Eliza Ann Carter Snow looked up. Eight pairs of hateful eyes peered at her and the newborn child. She had done nothing wrong. She was not afraid. She looked up at the group's leader, the tall one closest to the bed. The man tried to muffle his voice. "How old is the baby?"

He was unsuccessful. Eliza Ann recognized him.

"How old do you think, John F. Boynton?"

She knew this man. He was the missionary who had taught her the Gospel, then apostatized and was excommunicated just a year ago! Flat on her back in bed, weakened from childbirth and holding onto that precious bundle with all of her might, Eliza used the only weapon she had. Fearlessly she shamed him with her tongue.

Diantha heard everything from outside. She heard Boynton's voice give orders.

"This woman and her child are to be left untouched," he said.

Diantha started to pray a thank you, but the angry voice went on.

"No one else will be spared!"

The command triggered shouts and stomping feet as boisterous men lunged like animals out of the cabin. Eliza Ann started praying for her friend. There had not been time for her to get away.

Diantha lay motionless. Her chin was frozen with fright to the ground. She could not breathe, but felt like her throbbing heart was as loud as an army drum. Her wide eyes counted eight demons as they left the cabin and pounced onto their horses making so much noise she hoped they would not hear her run. If only they would not see her. She had to try. Diantha ran. With the Lord's help, she ran to find and save her own.

Historical Background

"Although the company of 'Caldwell Militia' had legally set out to protect their own, news of the fight on Crooked River against Captain Bogart's Patrol flashed wild reports and all the Gentiles in the northern part of the county abandoned their homes and fled southward near Richmond and elsewhere for safety" (Roberts, 475). "Claims were that three hundred Mormons had supposedly attacked Bogart's fifty men, killing many and taking prisoners they were sure to murder. Reports that Mormons planned to burn the township of Richmond sent women and children running for their lives" (Roberts 476).

Such rumors, exaggerations and lies fanned flames of fear and furry that led to an actual Extermination Order against all Mormons only three days after the battle.

The Extermination Order (BoggsLW) was signed the same day [October 27, 1838] that "Brother Patton was buried at Far West" (Smith9, 138). "It was a cunning piece of diabolism which prompted the mob of Davis County to set fire to their own log cabins, destroy some of their own property and then charge the

241

crimes to the saints" (Roberts1, 84). "And, as if it were not enough, parties set fire to their own houses, or that of their neighbors, and then laid it to the Saints" (Pratt, 156).

"About the middle of January, Father Joseph Smith, Sr. and Father [Isaac] Morley, with five of six others came and anointed and administrated to my husband [James Hendricks]" (Godfrey/Derr, 93; Holzapfel/Cottle, 178).

[Again I, Isaac Morley was] "imprisoned in Richmond Ray County 20 days and have never had an accusation found against me in the State [Missouri]. This was in 1838" (Morleyl).

Diantha helped Eliza Ann Carter Snow, wife of James Chauncy Snow, deliver a baby October 30, 1838 under mob orders for Mormon evacuation. The child survived and was named Sarah Jane Snow (LDSARF). "He left her unharmed, but no others" (Bennett1, 20; Billings/Shaw/Hale, 15). The Lord saved Diantha.

GOVERNOR BOGGS' EXTERMINATING ORDER

Headquarters Militia, City of Jefferson
October 27, 1838

Sir: Since the order of the morning to you, directing you to cause four hundred mounted men to be raised within your division, I have received by Amos Rees, Esq., and Wiley C. Williams Esq., one of my aids, information of the most appalling character, which changes the whole face of things, and places the Mormons in the attitude of open and avowed defiance of the laws, and of having made open war upon the people of this state. Your orders are, therefore, to hasten your operations and endeavor to reach Richmond, in Ray County with all possible speed. The Mormons must be treated as enemies and must be exterminated or driven from the state, if necessary for the public good. Their outrages are beyond all description. If you can increase your force, you are authorized to do so, to any extent you may think necessary. I have just issued orders to Major-General Wallock, of Marion County, to raise 500 men, and to march them to the northern part of Daviess and there to unite with General Doniphan, of Clay, who has been ordered with 500 men to proceed to the same point for the purpose of intercepting the retreat of the Mormons to the North. They have been directed to communicate with you by express; and you can also communicate with them if you find it necessary. Instead therefore, of proceeding as at first directed, to reinstate the citizens of Daviess in their homes, you will proceed immediately to Richmond, and there operate against the Mormons. Brigadier - General Parks, of Ray has been ordered to have 400 men of the brigade in readiness to join you at Richmond. The whole force will be placed under your command.

L.W. Boggs

Governor and Commander -in -Chief

CHRISTOPHER S. BOND
GOVERNOR

EXECUTIVE ORDER

WHEREAS, on October 27, 1838, the Governor of the State of Missouri, Lilburn W. Boggs, issued an order calling for the extermination or expulsion of Mormons from the State of Missouri; and

WHEREAS, Governor Boggs' order clearly contravened the rights to life, liberty, property and religious freedom as guaranteed by the Constitution of the United States, as well as the Constitution of the State of Missouri; and

WHEREAS, in this Bicentennial year as we reflect on our nation's heritage, the exercise of religious freedom is without question one of the basic tenets of our free democratic republic;

NOW, THEREFORE, I, CHRISTOPHER S. BOND, Governor of the State of Missouri, by virtue of the authority vested in me by the Constitution and the laws of the State of Missouri, do hereby order as follows:

Expressing on behalf of all Missourians our deep regret for the injustice and undue suffering which was caused by this 1838 order, I hereby rescind Executive Order Number 44 dated October 27, 1838, issued by Governor Lilburn W. Boggs.

IN WITNESS WHEREOF: I have hereunto set my hand and caused to be affixed the great seal of the State of Missouri in the City of Jefferson on this 25th day of June, 1976.

GOVERNOR

ATTEST

SECRETARY OF STATE

A Report and a Challenge

President Spencer W. Kimball

Since our last conference we have had a delightful message from Christopher S. Bond, Governor of the state of Missouri, who advised us that he has rescinded the 138-year-old Executive Order of Governor Lilburn W. Boggs calling for the extermination or expulsion of the Mormons from the state of Missouri. Governor Bond, present Missouri governor, writes:

"Expressing on behalf of all Missourians our deep regret for the injustice and undue suffering which was caused by this 1838 order, I hereby rescind Executive Order No. 44 dated October 27, 1838, issued by Governor Lilburn W. Boggs."

To Governor Bond and the people of Missouri, we extend our deep appreciation for this reversal and for the present friendly associations between the membership of The Church of Jesus Christ of Latter-day Saints and the people of Missouri as it is now in effect.

In Missouri now we have five stakes in fifty-one communities, with approximately 15,000 members of the Church, who, we are confident, are law-abiding citizens of that state of Missouri. Thank you, Governor Bond.

Ensign, November 1976, page 4

ILLINOIS: A TIME OF SACRIFICE

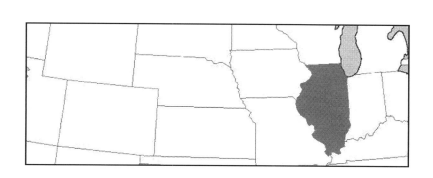

Today God may require all that we have, yet tomorrow He will
return abundantly all that He hath.

November 1838: Quincy, Adams, Illinois

March 1839: Lima, Adams, Illinois

Yelrome, Hancock, Illinois

Nauvoo, Hancock, Illinois

CHAPTER 44

Titus Billings pulled a large, tin pan from the open fire and cut the morning cake equally into four-inch squares. Its taste displeased him; but without a trace of salt, it was the best he could do. The one-inch high servings were passed to grateful and hungry men.

With only fifty pounds of unsifted corn meal, Billings did his best to feed the weary soldiers. They had fled in the night, most of them with threadbare thin coats. It was cold, and they were hungry. Another corn cake would be served after they camped at evening and one again the next morning. It was all they had.

These desperate but remarkable refugees somehow managed to cross the Grand River and camped at Hickey Creek. Two men were sent down the road ten miles into a township called Diamond for a few supplies. Huddled around a campfire, the twenty-six determined to organize themselves.

"We need a leader," someone shouted. Then a different voice was heard.

"Wish Patten was with us." They all wished that. No one hushed them, but a solemn moment passed in silence. Each survivor of the Crooked River Battle pictured a memory of the scrimmage. Everything happened so fast. Nonetheless, their brief encounter had claimed three precious lives, wounded seven others, and caused survivors to run for their lives.

At length, another voice broke the silence. Billings thought it was Hosea Stout, but he could not be certain.

"I nominate Elder Rich to be our captain."

Rich had been second in command. Titus saw him drop to Patten's side and bless him with the priesthood, a sight he would remember always. When he started to second the motion, others were already voicing agreement. Charles C. Rich was officially appointed their new leader.

The next day forced them on to Big Creek. A different, small group was sent into town. On the third day, they had traveled all the way to Sugar Creek. Each day different men were sent into town for provisions. Today they came back without goods. Instead they carried bad news.

"General Cook sent a cavalry of sixty troops to hunt us

down," the first man reported.

With alarm his partner added, "They have overtaken Diamond Township. Said they'd take us all, dead or alive!"

Food was scarce now. Fervent prayers were not.

A cold unbearable blizzard blanketed the soldier refugees all through the night, yet each man seemed to have unexplainable inner warmth that sustained him. Somehow the animals survived as well.

Sleep is a good refuge, Titus thought to himself. Too bad it doesn't last longer. He rallied well before sunrise to get a corn cake on the fire. A stone oven would bake more evenly. No one complained though; all were grateful for the nourishment and willing to let him do the baking. Titus liked to keep busy. Idleness never had a place in his life.

November's wild wind blew at their backs as though she was trying to push them out across the Iowa wilderness. Everything was well covered with snow, making it difficult to navigate. Still, the innocent soldiers marched on day after day, plowing through freezing temperatures with no sight of relief. Cornmeal ran out after seven days. Hunger enlarged their empty stomachs. Twice daily they tried to gather weeds and grasses from under the snow for their horses to eat. Now nothing was left to feed the animals, and not even a trace of food was left for the men.

Billings opened his pocketknife and forced its point into the bark of a slippery elm tree. His weary body had been leaning against the old tree as his mind repeatedly and inwardly protested starvation. By now he was certain of his ability to eat anything. He continued to cut.

"Leaving your initials in the tree?" Colonel Rich was teasing, but they could not leave any evidence behind. In fact, the miserable storm conditions had proven a Godsend to hide their footsteps as quickly as they were made in the snow.

"Ever chewed on tree bark?" Titus demonstrated with a piece between his teeth. "Better than noth'n and gives yar jaw something to work on." All the men took samples. For the next three days tree bark was all they had to eat.

The Crooked River veterans tried to melt snow for their thirst and for their horses to drink. A white settlement on the Des Moines River bank, spotted the next evening, was their first glimpse of civilization in two and a half weeks. The enemy had lost them. With grateful hearts, humble men prayed and shared testimonies around a campfire.

"The Lord has spared our lives," Elder Rich declared. "I feel certain that we are now free of pursuit. The purpose of our northern route was to mislead militia. Now, I think we can turn southward and seek out help to sustain us."

A vote was unanimous. At dawn they would start a journey that paralleled the Mississippi River until they could find a good place to cross it.

"We must exercise our faith," he went on, "Trust the Lord to lead us into a community that will befriend us."

"Twenty-six destitute men could be an overwhelming sight," Elder Smoot cautioned. "We must divide up to go out two by two. T'will give us a better chance to find help."

Pairs were chosen at the campfire. Titus Billings and Lorenzo Dow Young were teamed together. Each twosome would be on their own when they reached a settlement.

Next day the meek Mormon travelers crossed the mighty Mississippi River. By late afternoon, they split into partnerships and filtered through a quiet community called Quincy, Illinois. Lorenzo's trousers were worn out to the point of indecency.

"Wait here," Titus told him. "I'll get you a change before you go public." With a teasing smirk he added, "I wouldn't want to get kicked out of town on account of an indecent partner."

Billings started toward a nearby farmhouse. He approached a man about Lorenzo's size who stretched his neck to look at the bushes where Titus pointed at his waiting friend. Then both of them disappeared into a cabin. Not long afterward, Titus returned with a pair of well-patched pants and two crusts of bread.

It was a good fit. If anything, the pants were loose, but then he had not eaten in a long time. Together the two men knelt on the ground where they prayed with gratitude for direction and aid. Both stomachs were growling as they approached another farmhouse.

Dinner time aromas of real food tantalized their frozen nostrils. A plump, aproned figure invited them in to wash up. She added two table settings and seated them promptly. Her hard working farmer husband and his spellbound offspring listened in amazement to tales of Mormon treatment and religious beliefs. A look of pity mixed with curiosity, radiated from both the man and his wife. Titus was careful not to eat too much all at once. The food was wonderful, but their bodies needed time to re-adjust. Mrs.

Talbot was impressed with his controlled wisdom and insisted that they spend the night. She left the room to fetch fresh bedding.

"Believe it or not, these boots were new when I put them on," Titus said. They had not been off his feet since fleeing Far West.

"Looks like they' been through a war," Lorenzo said with a slight grin. The fact was almost funny. Titus smirked at it, but his weary feet were so sore that it was impossible to pull them out. The boots were literally frozen to his miserable feet. They refused to come off. Mrs. Talbot heard a ruckus and came to assist. She and the children steadied their victim as George Talbot and Lorenzo Young pulled the left boot with full might. It broke loose tearing skin tissue with it. The right foot was no different. Flesh peeled off his feet just as a pair of socks should do. Pain was intense, blood oozed everywhere. Walking was now impossible.

"Well, that's a fine state," Sarah Talbot told her husband. "This man is bedridden for sure. Titus heard her muttering and fussing, but his pain was so great he could not reply.

"You will have to lie still until you grow back a new pair of feet!" she insisted.

"You're in good hands," her husband added. "Sarah's a good nurse."

Oh yes, Titus felt grateful; yet he longed for the care and comfort of his personal nurse, Diantha. Wonderment of her where-abouts concerned him. There was nothing at all he could do to help her, nor himself, for that matter. Communication had been impossible too. *God bless her,* he prayed.

"There be plenty of little ones here to keep you enter-tained," the good man went on. "Do ye have family?"

"Yes," Brother Billings slurred the answer. Total exhaustion made it impossible to speak. Time for talk would come later. For now he just had to sleep.

*   *   *

Winter was lonesome, long and cold for bedridden Titus Billings. His gratitude was beyond expression for the kind care he received around the clock. Yet, for such an industrious worker the chore of lying in bed for three months while flesh grew back onto both feet was pure torture. Perhaps the worry of his family abandoned in Far West troubled him most. Reports brought horror stories of evacuation and extermination of Mormons from all of Missouri. Such stories, however, seemed to fuel warm flames in the hearts of God-fearing, brotherly-loving residents of Quincy, Illinois. Every displaced Mormon soldier had been taken into a home and cared for as needed. So sincere and plentiful were the prayers of thanksgiving that abundant blessings from Heaven should fall upon the considerate township forever.

All the time his feet were not available, his hands never stopped working. The Talbot children kept him supplied with sticks to lash into shelves and other functional items and wood to whittle into useful shapes.

New, young friends were constantly visiting his bedside in hopes that he, who they called the "Mormon Whistle Maker," would whittle their willow sticks into whistles like he had done for all the Talbot children.

Elder Billings spent time doing missionary work, too. He preached to anyone who would come and listen. It was a season of study for him when at last Brother Young obtained a copy of the Book of Mormon for his use. The Talbot Family gathered around his bed and listened to him read from its pages almost every evening. He was certain that they would accept the Gospel. They lived saintly lives, and he loved them dearly.

"You'd make good Mormons," he often chided; but they never did, to his knowledge, embrace the true Gospel.

Word was that W. W. Phelps had apostatized from the Church and was no longer to be trusted. Because he was Postmaster at Far West, Titus wrote under the name of Skinner to prevent betrayal. His letters were addressed to a special lady he would call Diane Skinner. He waited and waited. There was no reply. Titus was filled with worry, but there seemed to be nothing he could do. His feet were useless. His heart was broken.

"Got that letter ready?" J.D. Young asked. He knew of a wagon leaving for Far West. The driver promised to look for Diantha.

"Here it is," Titus said. "Thanks."

Ten days later Mrs. Talbot burst into the cabin with loud excitement.

"Mr. B., Mr. B." That is what she chose to call him. He had explained the "Brother and Sister" thing; but she had not taken to it, not yet at least. "Would you happen to know a Titus Skinner?" Her smile was nearly wider than her face. "Here's a post from a Mrs.

Diane Skinner. I wonder who that might be?"

Just the sight of her handwriting hastened his heart to a drum beat loud enough for dancing, if one's feet were not still too raw to touch the floor.

She is alive! Her letter was short:

Dear Titus,

We are so happy to hear from you at last. YOU ARE ALIVE! My heart has been pained these many days as I've worried the worst in your behalf. Thank you for the welcome letter to let us know where and how you are.

So sorry about your poor, frozen feet. You must take care of them, Titus. Please thank those good people for me. I will come to you as soon as I can. I know not when or how, but I will find a way. Isaac was in jail again. He is out.

I love you, Titus Billings. I always have loved you and I always will. We will be reunited again soon.

Forever and ever,

Your Di

Titus kept the tiny composition under his pillow to re-read again and again. *Praise be to God. He is with us yet!*

"I have more good medicine for you, Mr. B.," kind Mrs. Talbot said three weeks later. She waved another letter in her hand. "I think your Mrs. knows how to cheer my patient." Then she grinned until her cheek dimples deepened. "Oh, I beg your pardon, Sir, looks like there has been a mistake. This is not addressed to you. I better send it back. It belongs to Mr. Skinner."

She turned her back to him and started out of the room.

"Would you like me to get out of this bed and run you down?" he asked.

"You wouldn't dare!" she exclaimed.

He sat up and flung the patchwork quilt to one side of the bed.

"Not yet," she scolded. "Don't you dare undo all my hard work on your miserable feet!"

Titus returned to his pillow.

"Here is your medicine, "she said handing over the letter. "And don't you get out of that bed until I give you the word." Pleased with herself, she strutted out of the room so he could enjoy the letter.

My Dearest Titus,

Brother Slade has offered to help us move to Illinois. Plans are to come early next spring. By then your feet should be healed. We will be together again. . .

Titus Billings could hardly wait for snow to melt away leaving blossoms in its place and skin between his toes.

Historical Background

Fleeing brethren (Crooked River Soldiers) crossed the Grand River two miles above Diamond that first wintry day of November. A few men went into "Diamond" for provisions. The remainder journeyed on up "Hicky Creek" about ten miles where they stopped to camp and organize themselves. Elder Rich was appointed Captain. Twenty-six men were present. On the second day they traveled to Big Creek and sent for more provisions. The third day they moved to Sugar Creek where they learned that Diamond had been "taken" and that "forces" were in pursuit of them. The fourth day they set out through the wilderness for Iowa. "It snowed heavily that night" (Johnson1, 708), perhaps to hide footprints. After seven days all food was gone so "they tried to survive on bark from slippery elm trees" (Snow3, 2). "We had but little to eat and [our] horses nothing only what they could gather from under the snow" (Johnson1, 709: Words of Charles C. Rich).

"When we started there were twenty men, who were to subsist on fifty pounds of unsifted corn meal during a journey of 350 miles. There was a large tin dish to bake it in. Morning and evening a cake was baked, without salt, before the fire, and a piece was dealt out to each man about an inch thick and four inches square. For three days there was no food at all!" (YoungLD).

"General Cook learned of our departure and sent a troop of sixty cavalry in pursuit; it was only a few miles behind on our trail, and their orders were to bring us back dead or alive. That night the snow commenced falling and appeared to come down in sheets instead of flakes. In the morning it was about a foot and a half deep. The company felt the hand of the Lord was delivering them from their pursuit. We started on, the wind began to blow, drifting the snow so that our tracks were completely covered soon after they were made" (YoungLD).

"Hunted, frozen, hungry and fatigued they trudged eleven and a half days" (Charles C. Rich account) or "fifteen days" (Lorenzo Dow Young account) before finding white settlements on the Demoines River. "We crossed the Mississippi at Quincy where we found friends and was [were] kindly received" (Johnson1, 709). "On this trip men and animals appeared to have a wonderful power of enduring cold, hunger and fatigue" (Billings/Shaw/Hale, 18; YoungLD).

At one home Titus obtained a pair of pants for his companion, Brother Lorenzo D. Young (Billings/Shaw/Hale, 18). Billings was a partner to Young (YoungLD). Abraham Smoot was present (Hale, Snow3).

"It was six days before Diantha had any word from him" (Hale, 3). Then it was just "a slip of paper posted somewhere on the road" (Snow8, 3) instructing her to again write under a false name as W.W. Phelps, Far West postmaster at the time, would have betrayed the brethren had they let him know from whom they were getting letters. "He took the name of Titus Skinner, and she was to be Diantha Skinner so they could correspond. Eventually the men stopped at Lima, Illinois, about forty miles from Quincy, Illinois. Titus was laid up for three months with his frozen feet" (Hale, 3).

"For Titus Billings, his escape from mobocracy in Missouri was plagued with starvation and frostbite. For three days and nights he had only slippery elm bark for food. His feet were frozen so badly the flesh came off in pieces" (Billings/Shaw/Hale; Black3, 3).

"Father was laid up for three months with his frozen feet" (Snow3, 4). A kind family in Illinois took him in and cared for him. Oh, how we wish we knew that family's name. This author would love to find and thank their descendants. The Talbot name is not authentic.

CHAPTER 45

Morning sun poked bright rays through the cabin window and across the colorful bed quilts. Titus had been awake for what seemed like hours. This would be a big day, and he was excited for it. Already he had been out of bed and walking again in stocking feet. It felt good to do that at last. Today the plan was to try boots once more. By next week he hoped to be raising a log cabin for his family. If only he could finish building before they arrived. So much time had been lost. Nonetheless, he had been blessed, even nursed back to good health. Forever he would praise the Lord and remember the kindnesses of his new friends in Quincy.

Sarah Talbot insisted on cleaning his feet one last time. Gently she rubbed them with oil and slipped them into clean socks.

"Take this extra pair with you so you'll have a change," she bossed him. "You must keep your feet clean!"

Just then someone knocked on the cabin door. "It's Hosea Stout come with a wagon for Titus," Mr. Talbot shouted to his wife.

"So soon?" she said.

So soon? Not to Titus, a man who lost three months of his life lying in bed. Billings was ready to move on and itched for a spot to homestead. Stout had a job offer lined up for him too.

"How can I ever repay you?" Titus asked George Talbot as they shook hands. "You and your wife have been so kind to me." His arms encompassed both of them and squeezed until appreciation was undoubted. "I will never forget you," he said. Sarah Talbot used her apron hem to catch tears.

"Now you take care of yourself," she scolded.

The man had nothing in the world to give this kind and generous family. His story and example of faith had inspired them, and they assured him that they sought no payment. With reverence Titus handed his copy of the Book of Mormon to a tearing Mrs. Talbot. He hoped the letter of testimony and gratitude tucked between its pages would find a place in their hearts.

*   *   *

Titus Billings cleared and fenced a small acreage in Adams

County about twenty-five miles north of Quincy, Illinois. His mind and body were well rested, thanks to his feet; and his desire to work had been suppressed for so long, that it seemed to explode the moment it was let loose. By himself, in record time, he raised a one-room log home for his family.

It seemed like forever since they had been together in their cozy cabin at Far West. Why? Why when things were going so well, when they had a temple to build, and when they were trying to obey with exactness . . .? Oh, so many questions, so many problems. No, he would not go there now, not again. His mind had pondered it before, over and over, from a bed prison where his heart had told him to let it go. He was alive. They were alive. The Lord was alive! No doubt, God was mindful of it all. He would guide them. He would instruct, and only He should.

That's right, Titus told himself, *I will trust my God and seek only to do His will.*

Lima Lake was huge and beautiful. Titus calculated its rough dimensions while trying his hand at fishing . . . more than five miles long and at least four miles wide.

Wish I had my old gun now, he thought. *Every duck in existence knows about this place.* Millions of wild ducks and wild geese tormented his hunger. Someone was prepared. He heard gunshots nearby, then voices. Fishing was no good, so he pulled up to leave.

"Hello there." Two strangers had spotted him. Titus was more friendly than shy. As he approached the old timers, he could tell they were brothers.

"Hi, I'm William and this is Grayson. We're the Orr Brothers from Lima Township." They shook hands.

The other one spoke. "New here, aren't you?"

Titus filled them in briefly.

"So you built a log home up north, near the county line? Good sod up there. We run the Orr Mill over on White Oak Branch," Grayson said.

"Built the first brick house in Adams County," Bill boasted. "It's over there near the center of section twenty-five, second north and ninth west. Come see it sometime."

Titus perked up. He liked brick buildings. "Someday I'll have brick too," he vowed.

"Well," Grayson explained, "It's easy to do when you own a brick kiln. Got one over there, near the mill." Titus was very interested. "Thanks for the invitation," he said. "I will check it out." The brothers loaded him with birds to pluck for dinner.

"Let us know when you are ready to build with bricks," William said in parting.

"Oh, by the way," Grayson turned back around, "Welcome to Lima."

Long, long days seemed to torture Titus Billings. He was a lonesome and homesick man. *Any day now*, he said to himself. "Any day." He said it out loud, then shook his head with wonderment. "Now I am talking to myself. What's next?"

Only a few miles away, another Titus Billings grew anxious. "Aren't we there yet?" Titus Junior asked. Because he asked the question so many times no one else paid him any mind. "I want to see my Pa again," he added.

Brother Benjamin Slade's wagon was followed by a rig his son drove. Diantha Billings had a bundle of belongings in each of them. For twenty-one cold, snowy nights she and her children had slept in tents as they crossed the backwoods from Caldwell County in search of their father. Brother Slade had made the trip before and knowing where Titus homesteaded he had promised to deliver them. "It won't be long now," he said, "Should get there tonight."

"Maybe we should sing some more," Eunice said. She loved to sing and her voice was strong, even after singing most of the day.

Titus sat alone in the cabin. Tired from hard labor, he dozed off before dark only to awake to the sound of approaching wagons. *Probably another false alarm, so I won't get up any hopes,* he thought. Just the same, it seemed wise to light the lantern.

"Pa, Pa, are you in there?" A young voice was calling. It sounded like Alfred.

"Better knock, Boy," someone said. "Make certain it's the right place." Titus flung the door open. It was Alfred Nelson. It was all of them. They had arrived. Yes, it was the right place, a place that would never be the same. Pa was bombarded with hugs and kisses, and tears of joy from his family, and handshakes from good friends.

Brother Slade, who had a predetermined destination to meet his family in town, was ready to move on after unloading Diantha's things. They spread out quilts for everyone. No tents tonight! Sleep would be welcomed.

"You did it again," Diantha said. Her husband looked up. "You built us a fine nest," she continued.

"This quick, log-job is only temporary," he said. "Soon I will make you the home you deserve." He was thinking of bricks. She smiled at him and they stepped outside to gaze at the stars.

"So this is Quincy," Diantha said.

"No, Lima. Lima, Illinois," Titus corrected. It mattered not. The only place in the world she wanted to be was in his arms! And here she was, at last.

Historical Background

"Possibly the earliest industry in Lima Township was the Orr Mill, located on White Oak Branch, and operated by William and Grayson Orr sometime in the 1830's" (Genosky, 119).

"The next spring, 1839, Diantha and the children left Far West to meet Titus in Quincy" (Bennion, 2; Hale 3; Pyne, 4). "Benjamin Slade took my mother and her children to Quincy, Illinois, where we met my father" (Snow 83). "He found safety in Lima, Illinois, where his family joined him in 1839" (Black1, 25).

Welcome to Quincy

Early settlers of Quincy befriended displaced Mormons.

(Courtesy S.B. Mitchell, 2002.)

Welcome to Lima

Titus Billings built a home in Lima, Illinois and served as
Lima Branch President in that location.

(Courtesy S.B. Mitchell, 2002.)

CHAPTER 46

"You've got to be kidding," Titus said. "You've been here all this time?"

"Got here in February," Isaac said. "Sure was cold and miserable. Did a quick fix on that deserted building." He pointed to the remains of an abandoned log structure where his family had battled a tough winter. "I replaced the floor and windows and doors best I could," he said. New logs were stacked beside the house. "Building a better one now."

"I can't believe that we landed so near each other and didn't even know it," Titus said. It was true. Billings property bordered the Adams County line. Morley took out a claim on land to the immediate north in Hancock County. Again they were neighbors, so to speak, back to back, although in different counties.

"Let me give you a hand with that thing and get it done," Titus offered.

"I can't seem to get along without you, can I?"

"No need to," Titus said with a grin. "That's what brothers are for."

The area was thick timbered, even more so along creeks. Lima was an important center for trade and exchange. Its farms produced quality corn, wheat, oats, soybeans, and fruit in abundance. Titus had chosen a good place. He helped Morley finish the house, and they planted vegetable gardens.

"I hope we never have another winter like that one," Lucy told Diantha. "All we had to eat were the sweet potatoes we brought from Missouri. Clothes were so sparse we had to take turns layering on enough to go out for firewood,"

Diantha's lot had been no better. "I'm just thankful we survived," she said. "And thank the Lord, we are neighbors again." The two shared a joyful hug.

Many other displaced Mormons began to move in. The Cox Family landed next door. Prayer meetings were held two or three times each week in a nearby grove. Diantha was seated on a makeshift log bench at one such meeting when someone called her name.

"Sister Billings, Sister Billings. I am so happy to see you again."

"Elizabeth?" She gasped. "Elizabeth Ann Whitney, one of our nearest and dearest friends from Kirtland, how wonderful . . ." They embraced.

The Whitneys never made it to Far West. "Missouri was our destination," Elizabeth explained, "but so much trouble had broken out by the time we neared the place that we passed it by and spent last winter in Quincy. Now we are here and ready to start anew."

"Have you found a spot yet?"

"No. We just arrived, but Newell is eager to get a crop into the ground."

"Oh Elizabeth, there is a perfect piece right next to us. Coxes are on one side. You could be on the other, again."

"I would love that, Diantha. We enjoyed having you for neighbors before."

"We must find the men and tell them."

Such a plan was already in the making by the time they found their men. The location was meant to be. The Billings, Morley, Cox, and Whitney families would again be together like in those good Ohio days of the past.

"Look at all this open country. We could build a wonderful township here." Isaac Morley was daydreaming out loud. His dream was one that seemed to be coming true. As homeless saints drifted in, Brother Morley and Brother Billings helped them choose a nearby spot to homestead. Good families in a good place would make for a good life. Morley was excited. It was like the Kirtland Farm situation was returning to him. This time he wanted to call it "Morley Settlement."

"Ya know," Titus inserted, "there are a lot of new places these days that name themselves by spelling the founder's name backwards."

"Oh, yeah?"

"I guess yours would have to be Yelrom." The idea was intriguing. "Don't know if mine would work very well . . . S-g-n-i-l-l-i-b. Nope, I don't think so."

Both of them laughed. Titus concluded, "Guess we'd better stick to Yelrom."

Just then Diantha arrived. "What are you two up to now?" she quizzed them. "And, what is a Yelrom anyway?" Between sips of cool, fresh water delivered to them with love, they explained their conversation. She seemed pleased with all of it and soon

264

started back to the cabin. After a few steps she paused, turned around and shouted a correction to them.

"I really think your new name needs a silent "e" at the end. It would look and sound better, don't you agree?" As a matter of fact, they both did agree. "Yelrome" was better, more like a place, an important place.

"Thanks Diantha," Isaac told his younger sister, "we appreciate your silent 'e'." With that she grinned, batted her eyelashes, and almost skipped back to her female chores. She had a way with finishing touches. There was no doubt about that.

Before long Yelrome (still sometimes called Morley's Settlement) was a thriving community where many good families gathered to make their homes. Industrious settlers raised cabins and planted vegetable gardens. The community was well laid out and trimmed abundantly with flowers. Yelrome citizens were a happy people. They had an inner appreciation for peaceful surroundings that seemed to be far and above the ordinary. All of them had sacrificed in the past and put great energy into rebuilding better lives as well as better homes.

Diantha propped the cabin door open, not just for fresh air, but also to free up her hands. With her head in the fireplace, she did not hear anyone enter as she scraped ashes for dumping. *This is a job to do when you are alone. No,* she thought, t*his is a job for the boys. I will remember that next time.* A throat cleared from behind her. Startled, she spun around, fanning gray powder in the process.

"Oh, it's you," she said. The back of her hand swiped from cheek to chin in an effort to clean her face, leaving instead, a dark, black line. Her husband said nothing. He stood there grinning at her, but said not a word.

"I thought you were in town," she said.

"I was."

"I didn't know you were back," she said.

"I am."

Titus Billings wore the most mischievous look his wife had ever seen. There had to be more behind his grin than just her untimely situation.

"All right," she said. "Let's have it. What's so funny?"

He mimicked a serious profile. "Nothing is funny," he said.

Keeping his smile down was impossible; it popped up again every time he tried. She pretended not to notice and went back to her work. "So, what did you learn in town?" He wanted her to ask that.

"I now know the reason why we have to live in Lima and not in Yelrome." That made no sense. She must not have heard it correctly.

"Come again?"

He repeated the same, word for word.

Still confused, she ventured, "Why?"

"Why what?" he asked.

"Why is it necessary for us to live in Lima and not in Yelrome?" *They're nearly one and the same anyway,* she thought. "I was a Yelrome spelled backwards myself, you know."

"Oh, because of Dr. Joseph Orr."

"Who?"

"Dr. Joseph Orr and his Peruvian friend."

Diantha stopped. She wiped her hands on the backside of her splotchy apron and seated herself on a straight-backed wooden chair. This was going to take all the concentration she could muster. Looking into his eyes she pleaded again. "What does all of this mean?"

"What's that?"

"Who is Dr. Orr?"

"He was one of the founders of our fair town. Built the first store in 1833."

Oh, that was a bad year. She remembered the persecutions of 1833. Maybe they should have been here then, rather than there. No, that was not what she wanted to know.

"You said Peruvian. Do mean a person from Peru?"

"That's correct." He seemed to enjoy how hard she worked to dig it out of him.

This better be good, she thought.

"What does a person from Peru have to do with a doctor building the first store in this little town of Lima, Illinois?"

"I thought you'd never ask," he said. She moaned. He continued. "They say Dr. Orr named our little settlement." He paused. She waited. He went on. "He chose the name of Lima as a compliment to a Peruvian visitor who claimed that nowhere outside the capitol of his homeland, even Lima, Peru, had he seen more beautiful women than those he met here in Adams County."

Diantha threw her head back and groaned. "Now I've heard it all," she said.

266

He picked her up in his arms. "Now I have it all," he said, "the most beautiful woman in the county, and I have her swept off her feet."

She grabbed his shoulders as they twirled, black fingerprints dotting his tan shirt. "Brother Billings, you are crazy. I think you need eyeglasses." The black streak smudged his face when he kissed her. "Now we're both beautiful," she laughed. Gently he plopped into the chair. She landed in his lap.

"I'm a lucky guy," he confessed. Then, with reverent soberness he added, "I love you Diantha."

Historical Background

The Morleys left Far West February 6, 1839 and after camping out twenty-one nights arrived at Quincy, Illinois. Father Morley pitched his tent in the back woods. It was very cold weather and the snow began to fall. "They had but little to eat and very few clothes to wear," (Esplin, 8), in fact, they took turns "layering clothing to go out for firewood" (MorleyRH, 76).

"Early in March 1839, when Isaac Morley and Titus Billings first made plans to settle Yelrome, only one partial building was standing in the vicinity" (MorleyRH,75). "Other refugees moved into the area settled by Morley and Billings" (MorleyRH, 77). "That summer Titus built a log room in Lima, Illinois for his family" (Bennion, 2; Hale, 3). Isaac bought the shell of a log house built nearby for a claim. "It had no doors, windows or floor but Isaac bought it and fixed it the best he could and moved his family into it" (Esplin, 8).

Soon "they built a small community near Lima, Adams County, Illinois, which became known as the Morley Settlement or Morley Town", named after Titus' brother-in-law, Isaac Morley. It was also referred to as "Yelrome" which is Morley spelled backwards with an "e" added. "The name may have originated from a Mormon penchant to spell words backwards" (Black/Hartley, 29). It was located two and one-half miles north east into the south end of Hancock County (Esplin, 8). "By October 1840 they listed 424 members living there" (Billings/Shaw/Hale2, 3; Black/Hartley, 29).

"Extremely cold weather accompanied by heavy snows prevailed during the spring of 1839" (MorleyRH, 76).

According to Elizabeth Ann Smith Whitney: "From there we went up the river to Quincy, Illinois, where several families of the Saints who had been driven from Missouri were living: among these was the family of Titus Billings, one of our nearest neighbors in Kirtland; his wife was the first woman baptized in Kirtland, and is still living" [1878] (Madsen, 199; WhitneyEA, 13).

"The Doctor [Joseph Orr] is also said to have named the settlement Lima, in compliment to a Peruvian visitor" (Wilcox, 633). "Lima Township has been known for its agricultural production since early settlement. The climate is ideal for production of corn, soybeans and wheat" (Genosky,720). "Lima is the center of a rich district productive of corn, wheat, oats and fruit" (Wilcox, 633).

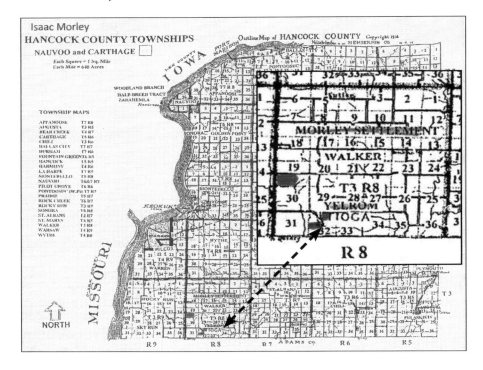

Isaac Morley Property at Yelrome/Morley Settlement

Please note Yelrom (no silent e) and Tioga at the bottom of map.
Billings had already settled across the county line in Lima, Adams County, Illinois.
Courtesy Historic Nauvoo Land and Records Research Center.

Morley's Settlement

Another tender mercy! Edward Durfee's family erected a beautiful marker telling the story, proving the spot, and identifying the location where their ancestor was killed when disgruntled mobbers burned out the settlement. (Courtesy S.B. Mitchell, 2002.)

Years later (in 2014) my neighbor, Carolyn Patton from Carthage, Illinois, showed me an article from the "Hancock County Historical Society Newsletter" about Morley Town AKA Yelrome. I was excited to see the exact dimentions. "The plat for Morley town was recorded on 24 April 1844. Total acreage for the entire town was 48.60 and each lot was 198' X 198'. There were four streets measuring 66' wide and a Main Street which was 82 1/2' wide. Two of the streets lay north-south and three were east-west streets. There were a total of four stores, including a barrel shop [Isaac Morley's shop] and a chair-making shop.

"The duration of this Mormon town was short lived and the events leading to its demise are interesting to say the least. During this period of time, there was unrest and disorder in Nauvoo which resulted in much stealing and depredation of property. In September of 1845, the Anti-Mormons held a meeting at the school house in Green Plains, a settlement west of Morley Town. This meeting was fired upon by persons hiding in the bushes. The Anti-Mormon group assumed it was the Mormons and they took the law into their own hands by decidint to expel the Mormons personally. They started at the southermost village, Morley Town, and gave warning. The first night they burnt two houses and continued nightly for an entire week to set other homes and buildings on fire until Morley town was in ashes. Approximately 125 houses were burned, along with other Mormon homes in the Bear Creek and Green Plains area.

"It was then Governor Ford sent a detachment of volunteers in order to render residents of Hancock County peaceable. Governor Ford then entered into a written agreement with authorities of the Mormon Church in Nauvoo that stated all Mormons would leave the state in the Spring of 1846. By the winter of 1847, the Mormons had left the township and the state, beginning their exodus to Salt Lake City, Utah.

"In the Spring of 1855 the present town of Tioga was laid out, just north and slightly east of where Morley Town had once stood. Today there is [a] marker on the south edge of Tioga where Morley's Settlement once stood" (HancockCO, 9).

(Courtesy Cynthia Huffman. 2013)

Miracle at Hancock County

Dad and I inquired at the Hancock Historical Society about the location of Yelrome. The receptionist had no clue, but a volunteer, Don Parker, overheard and said he had read something on it. "Where?" I asked him. "Yes, where?" the receptionist echoed on her way out to lunch. Don started pulling out possible books for me to examine: a statement here, a paragraph there . . . not much, but real, documented facts. I asked if he could make copies for me. When we had everything we could find he turned with a strange look and ques-tioned me. "How long can you stay here?" Well, my father was waiting in the car. I needed to go as soon as possible. He said, "You need to know something. This copy machine has been out-of-order for two weeks, yet it copied everything you handed to me!"

Welcome to Tioga

Although Don knew no location for Yelrome he thought he remembered it might have been somewhere near a township now called Tioga. We decided to pass by on our way out.
(Courtesy S.B. Mitchell, 2002.)

Wishing for Yelrome

Dad turned when we saw the Tioga sign. We drove to a dead end. I asked if I could get out a take a photo of a large field we saw at the end of the lane. The day was beautiful. How we wished to find Yelrome. We had come as far as we could. This picture would have to do. I turned around to get back in the car and noticed a nice marker: "Morley's Settlement." We were there, on the very spot!

(Courtesy S.B. Mitchell, 2002.)

(Courtesy S.B. Mitchell, 2002.)

CHAPTER 47

Growth was nonstop in the happy, new development called Yelrome. Bishop Edward Partridge and his two counselors, Isaac and Titus, had religious jurisdiction over the place and all the surrounding area. If only their Prophet could get out of jail. This time he was confined in Liberty, Missouri.

The faithful bishop penned a letter to him including local information.

"For the present, Brother Morley and Brother Billings have settled in a place they call Yelrome -- Morley spelled backwards -- twenty to twenty-five miles north of here, Quincy, Illinois."

The Prophet wrote back.

"One of the first things I wish to do when released from here is to visit the fine saints in this new place called Yelrome."

Isaac and twenty-three other prisoners had been released from the Richmond Jail last November by Judge Austin A. King. He, a circuit judge, had come to Far West for an earlier trial, and dismissed the Mormon defendants in Richmond because he said, "There was no evidence against them." The Prophet and several others had remained until April when embarrassed civic leaders allowed them to escape. Isaac's committee of nine had already sent eight pages to the Missouri Senate and House of Representatives declaring mistreatment of 15,000 Mormons who had been driven from comfortable homes and lost property totaling two million dollars. It had been ignored. So, when the bishop read the newest request from the jailed Prophet, Isaac shook his head.

"We are instructed to write grievance affidavits of our recent persecutions, sufferings and losses. These statements against the State of Missouri are to be notarized and collected by a committee to be submitted to the United States government for redress. 'Please be accurate, complete, and legally authentic'" he quoted.

"I hope it helps," Isaac said to Titus on the walk home.

"This time we're going all the way to the US government, not just to the State of Missouri. Might make a difference."

"Guess it is worth a try."

"Yes, if the Prophet says so we better do it."

Titus Billings sat at the wooden table with pen in hand. Writing was not his virtue, but obedience was. "I don't know where to start," he said. Diantha dried her hands and came to sit beside him. She knew the Prophet had asked all the brethren to write letters of redress. The task was not pleasurable, but it needed to be done. Together they wrote (and spelled) these exact words:

"A Brief a count of the suffering and loss of property of myself and Family by the people of upper Missouri—In the Spring of 1832 I started with my Family together with many others for the purpose of finding a permanent home together with other Settlers of that State—we moved from Kirtland Ohio we started from that place March the 24 & arrived in Jackson Co. Mo. in May & settled on 34 Acres of Land within a half a mile of Independence I built a house & Barn which cost 200 Dollars & got my liveing [sic] mostly by teaming for the People of the County and always had a good understanding amongs them but in the Summer and fall of 1832 & knowing that many of my Bretheren was a comeing to this County & not haveing a chance for raiseing a crop that season I thought best to cut a quantity of hay which ammounted to 24 tons Weight which was hauled 6 miles & was worth 5 Dollars per ton this hay was put into a large stack very long & put upon a farm belonging to Gov Boogs rented by Bishop Partrige and the Inhabitants of that place supposed the hay to belong to Bishop Partridge him this was set on fire and burnt to ashes between sundown & dark this was in Oct it was a year afterwards before I found out the Person that set it on fire there was a man by the name of James Allen asked me if I suspected who set it on fire I told him not he said he knew he was presant when it was done a man by the name of Franklin told him he was a going to commence driveing the Mormons that Evening & would commence by burning Partriges Haystack & wanted him to go & assist him this he said he would be gratified too when called upon and when called upon failed to appear and the act was thrown upon me which was 30 Dollars the next was driveing me from Jackson Co and burning my house and Barn & destoying my improvements with four Acres of Wheet we was driven from that Co in Nov. 1833—we went into Clay Co & there being so many of our People that we [had] to settle in places that was sickly my Family was all taken sick & were not able to help ourselves and lost one year. after liveing 3 seasons in Clay Co we were then compelled to leave that Co in the Spring of 1837—we then moved to Caldwell Co, there I entered 120—Acres of land fenced & broke 15

Acres built me a house which cost me one hundred Dollars besides another piece of land I bought containing 20 Acres of timber land which cost one hundred Dollars I also bought a village Lot which cost forty Dollars all which I have ben driven from together with my farming tools household furniture Provisions &c, &c,—and now driven from the State of Missouri with my Family amidts the blasts of a cold and chilling winter and that too by an unmer[ci]full mob after liveing in Missouri 7 years and never have had a writ served upon me not broken the law in one instance and now I say that these things have come upon me us on acount of the religion which we profess takeing all these things into consideration the loss of my Property cannot be less than two thousand Dollar. May the 23 1839 Titus Billings."

"Are you ready to go?"

"Yes, let's get it over with."

The ink was barely dry on Isaac's petition which read:
"Illinois Quincy May 28 1839

A bill of Damage against the state of Missouri in concic-quence [sic] of the Goviners Exterminating order. First for moving into the state. For Damage in Jackson county. Being Driven from the same and for loss of propperty in 1833. For being driven from Clay County to Caldwell Loss of propprty and time. Being thrown out of [?], for loss of property in Caldwell Co. and being driven from the state time and expenses: 2,000.00. I was also imprisoned in Jackson County falsly twelve Hours and Shot at By a mob in 1833, imprisoned in Richmond Ray County 20 Days and have never had an acusition found against me in the State this was in 1838. I Cer-tify the a bove a count to Be Just and true a cording to the Best of my knowledge. $2,800. ~Isaac Morley."

Together their grievances were sworn in before C. M. Woods who notarized them in Adams County, Illinois that day in May 1839. Next they registered with Thomas Bullock who added their names and the totals lost to his list. When ready the collection was submitted. (Nothing ever came of it, but they tried.)

Although Diantha's brother and husband were both serv-ing as counselors to the Presiding Bishop of the Church each of them held local assignments as well. Isaac still served as Patriarch and Titus became acting President of the Lima Branch. Both were very busy, but seemed happy to be in the service of their God. She was proud of them.

*   *   *

Titus was conducting a prayer meeting in the grove when a young, tall, whisker-faced gent showed up and stood in the back. President Billings could hardly contain himself.

"We would like to insert a special testimony here," he said.

Diantha looked at him with suspicion smeared all over her face. She could tell when her husband was up to something.

"If he will do us the honor, we will be privileged to hear a few words from a newcomer. Truly we hope he has come to stay. Brothers and Sisters, we would like to hear from Ebenezer Billings, my son."

With wide eyes, Diantha turned to see for herself. It was true! He was here. Ebenezer was really here. She wanted to hug him right now, even in public, but Titus Junior had already wrapped himself around his brother's long legs and would not pull away until they reached the front. His words were brief and heart-felt. He still loved the Lord who authored miracles for the good of mankind. Finding the saints in this new community, finding his family alive after all the terrible things he had heard, being here now, being alive himself; all of it was a kind miracle from a loving Heavenly Father. He was glad to be with his loved ones again. Diantha went home a very happy mother.

Historical Background

"A letter written by Bishop Edward Partridge to Joseph Smith, who was at that time confined in the Liberty Jail, [states that] Brother Morley and Brother Billings settled twenty to twenty-five miles north of this place [Quincey, Illinois] for the present" (Journal History11; MorleyRH, 73). "The town was called Yelrom (Morley spelled backwards" (Cox, 2). "Upon the final expulsion of the Saints from Missouri, he [Isaac Morley] located in Illinois, near Lima, Hancock county; the settlement made by him and others was named Yelrome" (Jenson1). "The town was called Yelrom – Morley spelled backwards" (Cox1, 2).

Since the members of the Church were so greatly scattered after fleeing from Missouri, Bishop Partridge thought the location settled by Morley and Billings was only temporary. "It later proved to be an important settlement during the entire time the Church headquarters remain[ed] in Nauvoo, Illinois" (MorleyRH, 73).

Ebenezer, the third son (twin daughters died at birth), is listed with his parents, Titus and Diantha, as early residents of Nauvoo. Eunice and Titus Jr. are also listed residing in this settlement (Platt).

"Titus Billings was appointed to succeed John Corrill as a counselor to Bishop Partridge. [John] was excommunicated from the Church at a conference held in Quincy, Ill., March 17, 1839" (Jenson, 241).

[Note: According to this reference Billings was called as second counselor in 1839 at Quincy. Other references back up 1837 in Far West: "Bishop Edward Partridge chose Elder Titus Billings (age 44) as his second counselor in the Presiding Bishopric on August 1, 1837" (Cannon/Cook, 117, 249; Flake, 510; Jensen1, 242; Journal History8,1; Ludlow, 337; Mortimer, 77, 78; Smith2, 504). "That day he was ordained to the office of a High Priest with Bishop Edward Partridge and Isaac Morley officiating" (Brewster, 45; Black, 575; Cannon/Cook, 249; Cook,102). He served with his brother-in-law, Isaac Morley, as second counselor until Bishop Partridge died in 1840 (Esplin, 6).]

"Titus was called to serve as Branch President of Lima, located only three miles south of Yelrome" (Black, 25; Black/Hartley, 29).

Billings is named on a list "of brethren who presented claims against the State of Missouri for losses of property, etc. alphabetically arranged . . . Billings, Titus 2000.00" (Journal History12).

Redress petitions written May 23, 1839 are included in exactness of words and spelling by Isaac Morley and Titus Billings (Johnson1, 501 and 139; BillingsT; MorleyI). While the Prophet Joseph Smith was held in the Liberty Jail he instructed the persecuted saints of Missouri to "collect and publish an account of their sufferings" and petition a redress from the government (D&C 123:1-6).

Isaac Morley Grievance Letter

A Missouri Claims letter as requested by President Joseph Smith. 23 May 1839.
(Courtesy LDS Historical Department.)

See full-sized original document in Appendix B.

Titus Billings Grievance Letter

A Missouri Claims letter as requested by President Joseph Smith. 23 May 1839.
(Courtesy LDS Historical Department.)

See full-sized original document in Appendix A.

CHAPTER 48

"Parties and dances have become the trademark of Yelrome," Elizabeth Ann said with a smile.

Diantha had to agree. "Sure keeps the boys busy."

The Billings Boys and the Whitney Brothers hired out as musicians, not only in town, but in many surrounding areas as well. Demand was heavy. It was a good job for them.

"I don't know about your house, but that income has been a blessing to ours."

Diantha agreed again.

"Hi, Ma," a young voice interrupted. "Can I go fishing?"

"Titus Junior, why aren't you in school?"

"Cordelia let us out early."

"Miss Morley to you, young man."

"Oh Ma, she's my cousin."

"She's your school teacher, too. You must show proper respect to her." Cordelia Morley, now sixteen, taught the younger children at Yelrome's schoolhouse.

"Yes Ma'am, but can I go fishing with the guys?"

"Excuse me, son. Where are your manners? I was talking with Sister Whitney."

"I be begging your pardon, ma'am." He removed his hat. "How de do?" Sister Whitney nodded; but before she could say anything, T. Jr. was back to business with his mother. "I gotta hurry, Mom. We're all meeting at I.J.'s, right now."

"So Isaac Junior is taking you?" She excused herself. "Nice talking to you, Elizabeth. I better look into this."

Building his cooper shop adjoining the family home proved a real blessing for Isaac. Soon he was training and employing a dozen others to help craft barrels that were sold in Quincy. The large room became a favorite meeting place of young adults as well. Evening classes for older students were held there regularly. Other nights the young men rearranged Father Morley's cooper ware to ready the popular spot for dancing, games, or spelling bees. When winter came, families gathered inside to share stories and jokes while they cracked the walnuts and butternuts and hickory nuts collected earlier from the forest. The Mormon way of life was a wonderful -- when they were allowed to live it. Here, at last, it seemed possible. Numbers grew almost daily.

Not all activities in the new community were pleasant, however. At a conference held in Quincy on March 17, 1839, many hearts were saddened with the excommunication of Elder John Corrill. Billings took the incident extra hard. Corrill was a great leader -- his predecessor in a way, because he was second coun- selor before Titus. He was also a very dear friend. Now all ties were severed by bitterness. John had testified against his former friends and fellow priesthood associates at a bitter trial of church leaders in Richmond, Missouri. For a considerable time, his conduct had been unbecoming to a representative of the Lord. He refused to yield his judgment to priesthood proposals, to church leadership, or even to the voice of the Lord when given through His appointed prophet. John pulled away.

"We will miss him," Titus said.

At last the Prophet Joseph Smith and a few companion prisoners were able to escape from Liberty Jail. They made their way to the Quincy area at the end of April [1839]. True to his word, Joseph visited the new settlement at Yelrome in southern Hancock County.

Soon the Church purchased property on the north end of Hancock County. This land was an undesirable, swampy place, referred to as Commerce, Illinois; but it came at a good price. With their Prophet's vision, the saints went to work draining and groom- ing their land, located at the bend of the Mississippi River. The work was, of course, tedious and germ-infested. Many who worked and settled the river bottoms became deathly ill, unaware that malaria-carrying mosquitoes were their constant and dangerous enemy. Still, the work went on with dedication.

Joseph and Emma moved into a log cabin in the new area on May 10, 1839. Many of the saints were without homes and camped out in the Prophet's yard or any other spot they could find. Sickness spread. Dozens died from the unhealthy conditions. The summer was filled with suffering. On July 22, 1839 the Prophet arose from his own sick bed to go forth, blessing and healing a multitude of needy.

More land was surveyed and purchased in August. Lima's branch president and his wife spent most of their time aiding the ill and building up the new communities in Lima/Yelrome and the tamed swamp renamed "Nauvoo the Beautiful."

Early one morning, Diantha sent ten-year-old Eunice to pick a bouquet of flowers for Bishop Partridge. Severe illness made it necessary to delegate more and more to his counselors. The two feminine well-wishers set out in the wagon.

Approaching the Partridge home, they spotted Lydia at the clothesline. "How is the Bishop today?" Diantha inquired.

"About the same," sighed his weary wife. "He just can't get over it. The pleurisy is so bad in his side that he hasn't been able to get out of bed yet."

Diantha remembered back to that terrible day in Independence when he had been so wrongly tortured with tar and feathers. To her, he never seemed able to recover. Tears welled up in her eyes as she recalled hours of scraping his skin and trying to comb tar out of his hair and off of his scalp. The dear man had been so patient through it all. He was patient now. For more than a week he had been bedridden. Why did he have to be so sick? Diantha reached down to pull a shirt from Lydia's basket. After a good shake to flip out wrinkles, she handed it to her friend.

"I don't know what to do, Diantha."

"Do about what?"

"Well, all day he wants me to sit beside the bed and hold his hand and talk to him."

"Sounds like a noble request to me."

"But there is so much that I need to do. How can I just sit there?"

"Funny thing," said Diantha, "I came over here to free you up a bit. Let me finish hanging these for you. After Eunice helps me deliver these flowers to the bishop, we want to take the children home with us. We will return them with dinner tonight."

"Oh, Diantha . . ."

"Now Lydia, you need to spend the afternoon with that good man of yours. You want to don't you?"

"Of course," she smiled. "Diantha, you are an angel of mercy!"

Diantha's thoughts were a flood of more vivid memories from the past. With reverence she tried to express them.

"I recall an angel of mercy who nursed my baby and saved my life!"

The two embraced in true friendship. Both of them finished

filling the clothesline and went inside.

Perhaps it was the white pillow that made his face look so chalky and pale. Excessive weight loss was obvious. To Diantha, he appeared to be mere skeleton. There was no doubt Bishop Edward Partridge was a very sick man.

"So how about it? Are we making good progress in here?" she asked reaching to shake his hand.

"Trying to," he answered. His lips smiled, but they were sore and cracked. His mouth was dry and his voice was hoarse. Seeing him this way broke Diantha's heart.

"Eunice has some posies to cheer you, Bishop."

"That should do the job." He spoke to the child, "Do they come with a smile?"

Indeed they did. She grinned from ear to ear.

"I'll fetch water for these," Lydia said as she took the flowers. With a sniff she added, "They smell lovely, dear. Thank you."

"Yes, Eunice, thank you for thinking of me."

"We always think of you," Diantha said.

"We pray for you too," said the child. That put a light in his face, but his tired eyes closed. His head made a weak nod.

"Thank you, thank you. I need all the prayers I can get," he whispered.

Historical Background

"We remained in Quincy during the winter, and passed the time rather pleasantly; my eldest son was fond of music, and so were the Billings' boys, and they used to go out together to play for parties, and thus rendered some assistance in obtaining a living, for we had left our means in Kirtland" (WhitneyEA, 13).

As soon as warmer weather approached, land was cleared and vegetable gardens were planted. The Billings, Morley, Cox and Whiting Families worked together harvesting gardens, wild fruits (berries and plumbs) and nuts (walnuts, butternuts and hickory nuts). "During the next winter many long evenings were enjoyed in cracking nuts and telling jokes" (MorleyRH,76).

Isaac built a small schoolhouse in Morley Settlement where his sixteen-year-old daughter, Cordelia, taught school to the younger children. In the evening she attended school for "older" students at her father's cooper shop. This time Morley, a cooper by trade, built his shop adjoining the home. It became a popular place of recreation for the young folk. "They would gather in the evening, clear out the barrels, buckets, tubs, churns and rubbish to make merriment in dancing, playing games and having spelling matches. They had five years of peace and prosperity which was a gleam of sunshine they long remembered" (Esplin,

8). "Isaac employed twelve men in Yelrome to make barrels to sell in Quincy" (Black/Hartley, 29).

John Corrill became a member of the Missouri legislature and published a fifty-page booklet against the Mormons, exposing their doctrine and discipline and his reasons for leaving "their" church. This effort produced even greater heartache for the saints (Jensen1, 241).

The Prophet Joseph Smith escaped from Liberty Jail and after tremendous hardship arrived in Quincy, Illinois, on April 22, 1839. The Church then purchased an area of swampy ground called Commerce, located at the bend of the Mississippi River, and started to develop the City of Nauvoo. The governor of Illinois and the general citizens passed the famous Nauvoo Charter, which was such a blessing to the Church. "This act gave them authority of almost a 'city state'. They could have a university and their own legion. The city council had powers to levy and collect taxes, regulate common schools, and to borrow money on the credit of the city, and much more" (Billings/Shaw/Hale2, 3; Roberts4, 239-249).

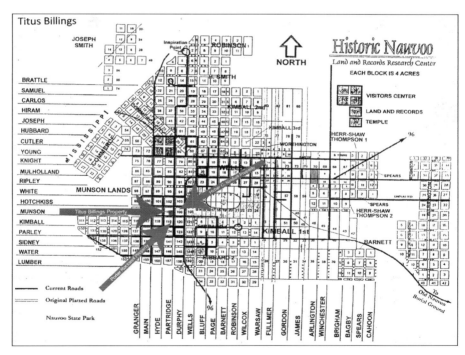

Titus Billings Property in Nauvoo

Billings purchased a city lot at the corner of Munson and Partridge.
Heber C. and Vilate Kimball lived straight across the street (East)
and Orrin Porter Rockwell lived directly south. Good neighborhood.
(Courtesy Historic Nauvoo Land and Records Research Center.)
See larger map in Appendix A.

Original Document of Titus Billings Property Bill of Sale.

Hancock County property to Titus Billings 1840.
(Courtesy L. Tom Perry Special Collections, Harold B. Lee Library, Brigham Young University, Provo, Utah.)

See Appendix A.

CHAPTER 49

At the first opportunity, Billings purchased a piece of Nauvoo on February 6, 1840. "You'll love it, Diantha. It's a corner lot. You and Vilate [Kimball] will be neighbors again." That pleased her. "Porter Rockwell bought the other corner across the street. We'll be in good company," he said. Diantha agreed.

For a long time, Titus had planned to buy bricks from the Orr Brothers when he built his next home. Nauvoo saints, however, were very independent. They produced most things for themselves, bricks included. Thanks to his Lima friends, Titus was primed in the art of making bricks and he went on to become a brick and stone mason.

In one year, two hundred and fifty Mormon homes were constructed in Nauvoo. These were made of logs, wood frames, or bricks. Billings started his at the corner where Munson Street crossed Partridge Street. Earlier he bought and planted a large acreage of farmland outside Nauvoo city limits.

The Prophet asked to see Brother and Sister Billings after Prayer Meeting on Sunday. Eunice waited with them. Titus Jr. was out and about, of course, but Eunice shadowed her mother everywhere. The special calling was for Diantha to serve not only as a mid-wife in Zion, but also for her to do doctoring among the saints. Joseph Smith laid his hands upon her head and pronounced an eloquent blessing of sensitivity and wisdom in lending comfort and care to those who suffered the ailments and sorrows of this world. The Lord would bestow gifts upon her that would bless the lives of many others. She would be instrumental in the safe entry of countless new spirits into this world. Diantha was overcome by the awe-inspiring honor. Then, to her amazement, the Prophet of God laid his hands upon the head of young Eunice and pronounced that she too would receive these same gifts and blessings.

They walked in silence most of the way home. Titus was first to speak. "Sounds like you two have a great work to do," he said. Diantha's heart and mind still pondered all she had been offered. It felt too sacred for her to talk about. Eunice was quiet too. She held tightly to her mother's hand.

*   *   *

Deep sorrow struck on May 27, 1840. Diantha dropped everything when Lydia sent word. She and Eunice ran all the way. Nothing on earth could have saved their beloved bishop. He suffered for the cause of Zion, suffering ever since that dreadful day of persecution at Independence Square. Edward Partridge was only forty-six years when he passed away. After a touching funeral service, his body joined with other saints in the Nauvoo Cemetery. Diantha's love and deepest care went to her now widowed friend and their children.

Sister Billings was trying to offer comfort when she felt gentle arms wrap around her own shoulders. With angelic softness Sister Emmy whispered good news into her ear. "I think I will be needing your help soon." Gracefully, she pulled the ends of her black shawl together and rested both arms onto her expectant middle. Tears of mourning still filled her eyes. Her smile was dignified and reverent. "I will be there," Diantha said. "Send for me at any hour."

Tiny Don Carlos Smith was born soon afterward. Emma was overjoyed that her baby was healthy. At the same time she was saddened that her father-in-law was not. Titus took Diantha to call upon their dear patriarch friend with Eunice tagging along, as usual. Father Smith was very close to passing; it was obvious. All too soon, September 14, 1840, they returned for his funeral.

"I will never forget how peaceful and heavenly he looks," Diantha said on the way home.

"Another great builder of the Kingdom is laid to rest," Titus said.

*   *   *

"Brother Billings, will you do it?" Mr. William Huntington had asked for the hand of Mrs. Lydia Partridge in marriage. She wanted Titus Billings to perform the ceremony. This he did on September 27, 1840.

Even though she was excited about the move to Nauvoo and happy the home was ready to move into, Diantha was so ill she could hardly stand up. Titus tied on the last load as Eunice swept out the cabin and climbed onto the wagon with the broom. Diantha watched. Her mind was spinning, though she was too ill to speak. She wondered about another broom, Samuel's broom from Kirtland. It would have been a keepsake from Titus' brother, if they could have kept it. Was it burnt with the house? Was anything salvaged first? She did not know. She would never know. Oh well, they were off to new and better . . . if she could survive this miserable condition.

Recovery did not come with speed or with ease. Diantha was down for days and days. "I don't understand it. I am supposed to be a help to the sick and I can't get well myself," she said of her bewildering situation. During the epidemic last summer she had nursed victim after victim with never a trace of illness herself. All winter she was fine. Now, when it was springtime and moving time, she was deathly sick.

"Maybe it is to give you insight," her husband said.

"Insight?"

"Yes, and compassion. It will help you know what your patient is feeling."

"Oh, I see," she said. "Well, I think I have had enough insight and compassion by now."

He laughed at her. "I hope the Lord soon agrees."

Eunice tried to keep up with household duties as well as nurse her ailing mother. She was young and inexperienced. Mother was too ill to give instructions. Vilate Kimball, their nearest and dearest neighbor, became an angel of mercy who checked on them daily and delivered a tray of dainties for Diantha to eat. This nourishment, loving care, and tutelage for Eunice made all the difference. Diantha improved. Still, she was bedridden for three months and started wondering if better days would ever come.

Diantha heard voices at the front door. It sounded like Titus was instructing someone to wait while he primed his wife. Whatever could he be up to now?

"How are you feeling?"

"About the same."

"I wish you were well enough to meet our new neighbors."

"I will be," she said.

"But you are not now?"

What is the big deal? Why is he pressing me so?

"This little family is buying a lot three blocks down Partridge Street."

"Good." She tipped her head back and closed her eyes.

"I thought you might want to see them, since we knew them in Kirtland . . ."

"Who are they, Titus?"

"Looks to me like she will be needing the help of a midwife soon. Hope you are well in time to help out."

"There are other capable midwives, you know."

"I just thought you would be upset if you were not the first to see this baby. I know I can hardly wait to meet it." Now she was curious. This was strange conduct and unusual talk from a man she knew inside and out.

"What is it, Titus? Who is it?"

"Don't worry, dear. I'll tell them they will have to –"

"SAMUEL!" Eunice could be heard for miles around.

"I can't wait out there any longer, Pa. Where is my . . ."

Diantha could not believe her eyes. "Samuel Dwight Billings! Oh, Samuel, come here. Let me get a better look at you."

"Hi, Ma. Sorry you're ill. Do you remember Martha?

"Of course I do. Hello, Martha. Looks like she is taking good care of you."

"This year we're gonna make you and pa grandparents."

"So I see. That's wonderful, Sam." Diantha turned to face her husband. "And nothing will keep this Grandma away from delivering that baby. Nothing!" she said.

Samuel and Martha built a small log home down Partridge Street, on the block between Parley and Sidney. Joy had no words. Both of her wandering sons were at home in Nauvoo. The place was more beautiful than ever.

"I love living here. I love the Lord," she told her husband after their sweetheart prayer. As usual, they were holding hands to pray. He let go to raise his arm and slid it around her. With tenderness he cupped her hand with his other. "Do you love me, too?" he asked.

"Of course I –"she started, but he cut her off with a kiss. They always kissed after prayer, while still on their knees. The Savior, even Jesus Christ, was an important part of their marriage relationship. They were like the three sides of a triangle, as the prophet had explained it. The Lord was the high point of that triangle and they would spend their lives trying to get closer to each other by getting closer to Him. They had felt Him near during many hard times. Now they felt Him with them in this moment of great joy.

Soon Titus was a grandpa. Samuel named the healthy baby boy Titus M.

Historical Background

"His father [Titus Billings] was a stonecutter, stone mason, carpenter, and even though a small boy during the time of their migrations with the church from Kirtland to Nauvoo, Illinois, George assisted his father in every way he could in the erection of the Mormon temples in these cities" (Carter, 575).

"While in Nauvoo, Diantha was set apart by Prophet Joseph for a special calling in Obstetrics as a midwife. This she practiced for many years, never losing a mother in birth" (Hale, 3; Snow3.) "Mrs. Billings was ordained and set apart by the prophet Joseph to be a nurse, in which calling she has ever since been very skillful" (Tullidge, 430). At the time she was ordained as Midwife, Joseph also turned to young Eunice and laying hands on her head, said, "I ordain you to follow in your Mother's footsteps." Eunice also spent many years bringing "thousands of babies into this world" (Snow, 4).

"Sister Billings moved to Nauvoo about the same time as the Prophet Joseph Smith, and while there was blessed and set apart to administer to the sick and act in the capacity of nurse, in which calling she has been skillful and reliable, until her health rendered it impossible" (Women's Expo- obituary).

Bishop Edward Partridge died May 27, 1840. Titus was his second counselor until then. Isaac Morley had been the first counselor.

"I went with my mother to visit the Prophet's father, Joseph Sr. when he was on his deathbed. He looked so peaceful and heavenly that I have never forgotten his appearance" (Snow8, 3).

Elder Titus Billings performed the marriage of John Tippets to Caroline Pew on September 25, 1840. On September 27, 1840 he performed the ceremony for William Huntington and Lydia Partridge (Times and SeasonsV1, 191).

"The next move we made was to Nauvoo, on the east side of the Mississippi River, in a bend of the river." When the Saints first settled there it was called "Commerce" (Hale, 3,9). "Titus bought land in Nauvoo on the sixth day of February in 1840" (WhitneyNK, 3).

"We reached Nauvoo in 1841. The Prophet's house was located on the flats near the Mississippi River, while our house was situated in the northeast part of the city, close to Brother Heber C. Kimball's home" (Snow8, 3).

Diantha was very sick their first three months in Nauvoo. Eunice, her daughter, tried to take care of her and the household. Sister Vilate Kimball delivered food and "dainties" and nursed Diantha back to good health. Eunice writes, "No doubt she saved her life since she had no one but myself to do for her, and I was so very young and inexperienced at the time" (Snow4, 3). (Note: Later, Eunice names one of Titus' granddaughters after the kind Sister Vilate; (Bennett, 553).)

"At first there was much sickness in Nauvoo. Many people died from exposure they had endured before arriving. Nearly every family had some sickness. Joseph went from house to house and from tent to tent healing the sick. He certainly did perform great miracles at that time. When Joseph Smith felt his strength giving way, he sent Brother Wilford Woodruff with his silk handkerchief. Joseph blessed it and sent the handkerchief to heal the sick. He told Brother Woodruff that as long as he held the handkerchief he should have the gift of healing. I have heard that Brother Woodruff had the handkerchief when he died" (Hale, 10; Smith4, 5).

Titus "served as president of the branch in Lima, Illinois, until 1845" (Cannon/ Cook, 249). [Must have served part of that time while living in Nauvoo.]

Nauvoo Property Records list Titus Billings owning Lot # 107 in Nauvoo City. The same list also shows Samuel Billings owning Lot # 141 (NauvooPR).

1840 Census of Hancock Township Illinois lists Sam Dwight Billings as a male between 20 to 30 years and married. 1850 Census of Missouri shows Samuel D. as a painter with Martha A. Billings his wife. She was born in Virginia. 1860 census of Illinois show 3 inhabitants in town living in dwelling #70 - a Sam 43 years old, painter vocation, owning $100.00 personal estate. Wife (unnamed) 29 years. Also lists: William 8 yrs., Lucy 6 yrs., James 2 yrs., George 3 yrs. all born in MO. Also residing there a James Ellis 19 yrs. born in IL.

Ebenezer, the third son (fifth child), is listed with his parents, Titus and Diantha, as early residents of Nauvoo. Eunice and Titus Jr. are also listed (Platt).

Titus Billings' home was "just about five block from theirs [the Smith home]" (Bennett,558). "Diantha Billings did sewing and doctoring for the Prophet's family" (Snow, 2). She [Eunice Billings] was in their home a great deal. "Mother was as intimate with Sister Emmy as anyone could be with another" (Bennett, 558).

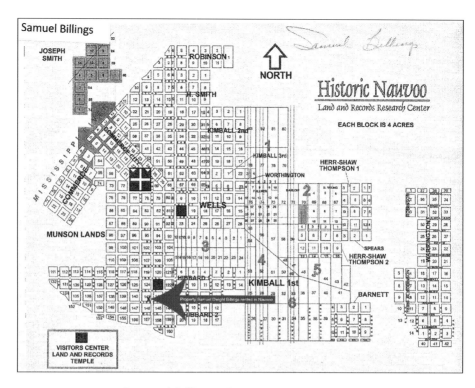

Samuel Billings Property in Nauvoo.

Home at Partridge and Sidney Street.
(Courtesy Historic Nauvoo Land and Records Research Center.)

See Appendix A.

CHAPTER 50

"We will build a new temple here in Nauvoo," Prophet Smith announced at October Conference. Excitement buzzed throughout the crowd.

"Oh, Titus. Congratulations, dear!" The new high councilor managed a humble thanks and was quick to change the subject.
"Good meeting, wasn't it?"
"Titus, tell me again please, what is the meaning of Nauvoo?"
"It's Hebrew. The Prophet says it is a word signifying a beautiful situation or place with a feeling of rest," he explained.
Diantha liked the sound of it and the fact that every time she spoke it she was speaking Hebrew. "Nauvoo the Beautiful - such a perfect name for this holy spot." She focused her view on the mighty Mississippi River which wrapped around the new community like a huge hug. Draining miserable swamp land had made the place most desirable, even beautiful. For the Saints their journey had been long and difficult. Diantha was now delighted. *Thank you, Lord, for bringing us to this blessed home, at last.*

Father Morley was never more excited. At a second October Conference held in Yelrome, on October 22, 1840 (two weeks after the first in Nauvoo), a new stake was formed.
"Isaac Morley has been called to serve as President of this new Lima Stake. All in favor of this transaction please raise your hands." Often the Prophet preached to the congregation in the Lima - Yelrome area. This time he sent three apostles -- Brigham Young, John Taylor, and Willard Richards -- to organize the new stake and give instruction.
Additional meetings were held at President Morley's home for the next two days. Saturday evening, between conference sessions, a special meeting was called for the brethren. "Priesthood holders of this new Lima Stake: I hereby pledge that we tithe our time and our property for the building of the Nauvoo Temple. All in favor?" Affirmative response was loud and clear. No one opposed it.

*   *   *

"Here is something you may want to read," Titus said as he handed a copy of the newspaper to his wife. She already knew that a bill had been passed to incorporate the city of Nauvoo. John C. Bennett had pushed a charter through the legislature in a record twenty-one days. Now the Nauvoo Neighbor Newsletter featured him as the new Mayor of the new city.

"Thank you," she said. Only then did she notice a humble, almost embarrassed look on his face.

"Oh Titus, the New Legion . . ." Her husband had attended the organizational meeting of the Nauvoo Legion last Thursday morning [February 4, 1841] where six companies were established. He was made captain of the sixth. It was called the Silver Greys for men over forty-five years. He was forty-eight.

Diantha found a news article detailing the formation and function of the new Mormon Regiment. He had not mentioned it so she read aloud.

"'Smith, Joseph -- elected Lieutenant-General, Bennett, John C. -- organizer and Major General . . .'" Hurrying through a long list of names she found the one she wanted. "'Billings, Titus – Captain: 1st Cohort, 1st Battalion, 1st Regiment.' Wow, Honey." By now she had an audience of children who wanted to see their Father's name in print. She read on. "Here you are again. 'Billings, Titus –Brevet Major.' What does that mean?"

"Nothing really," he said.

"Well, it means a lot to me." Relinquishing the paper to eager sons, she flung her arms around his neck. "You will look handsome in a uniform," she said.
"Whatever," he replied.

The Nauvoo Legion and the University of Nauvoo were established about the same time. Brother Billings, who sang in the Choir of the Stake of Zion in the City of Nauvoo, was called to be a warden in the Department of Music. He was quizzed about his new assignment at the family dinner table.

"So, Pa," George asked, "what does a warden do?"

"First of all, I sit on a board for the music department."

"Watch out for slivers," Titus Junior said. "They hurt pretty bad, if you don't get them out." Little Titus knew first-hand about festered slivers. His brothers laughed. His seriousness probably made them laugh even more.

"Your father sits on a board of men, not a board of wood," Diantha said for clarification. Her words conjured more hilarity.

"Which men do you sit on, Pa?" Alfred asked. Even Titus Junior started laughing.

Eunice was the first to sober up. She loved music and hoped to attend classes at the university some day. At present she, with her brothers and her best friend, Julia Smith, attended a school taught by Eliza Roxy Snow.

"I thought wardens were guards," she said. "Do you take turns guarding the music school?"

"Yeah, that's what I thought too," George said.

Titus ventured with care. "Our 'board' regulates music in this city. My specific assignment is to oversee the quality and use of music in our 3rd Ward. Brother Hills is the Professor of the 'Board.' Brother Wilber, Brother Goddard, and Brother Pack represent their wards." Then, turning to his talented wife, he continued; "We are to prohibit the flat sound of the notes and adopt the broad sound."

"Good," she said.

"Yes, at the meeting the Prophet Joseph said he was opposed to anything flat."

She smiled and started dishing up dumplings.

The Nauvoo Legion dramatically influenced life in Nauvoo. Fifteen hundred men enlisted within six months after the charter went into effect. Billings Boys were among the first.

"Ready?" Sam asked.

"Been ready since day break," Ebenezer answered.

"Well then."

"Today's the day." Together they walked down Main Street to the spot where they had read and re-read the Cavalry poster multitudinous times: "All who are willing to join a company of Cavalry and uniform themselves according to Law written six months will please subscribe their names hereto."

"What you waiting for boys?" Porter Rockwell asked, with a grin.

"Nothing neighbor," said Ebe. "Let me borrow that pen." He bent down to sign his name in bold letters with a May 1st date. Sam followed. That evening more companies were organized. Captain Titus Billings was made lieutenant colonel under Colonel Charles C. Rich.

Alfred Nelson Billings barely met the age fourteen requirement; and, at length, persuaded his parents that he too should join. Samuel Dwight, the Billings' married son, was appointed official drummer of the legion.

Families scraped to fund uniforms. Diantha hired out to do sewing and continued such services long after earning outfits for the men in her life. Sister Emmy and Sister Lucy Smith became her best customers. Titus was home when Diantha returned from a fitting for Sister Emmy. "I'm glad you're here," she said.

"Happy to please," he said. Somehow his jovial spirit did not seem to match her mood. With heaviness she dumped herself into a chair. "What's wrong, Di?"

"I am confused," she admitted. Leaning forward, she aimed her eyes into his and asked, "What can you tell me about plural marriage?"

"Oh that," he said swallowing with effort. Shaking his head he continued, "I really don't understand it. In fact, I really can't tell you much at all."

"Bishop Noble sealed Louisa Beaman to Joseph Smith last spring." He did know about that. "Sister Emmy always has guests in her home, so another doesn't really matter; but, well, I just don't understand it. Titus said nothing. "I am concerned for Sister Emmy." Tears she had refused were no longer hers to control. They spilled all over her husband, as he held her in his arms. Her heart was pure; she wanted to do right, but she did not understand. He did not understand.

"I know only one thing, Diantha. Whatever the Lord commands is right. Let's kneel down and ask Him about it."

A prayer at mid-day was not uncommon. The prophet taught by example that saints should pray three times a day like Daniel of old . Sacred music was conducive to the spirit as well. They prayed hand in hand and sang together.

"A man must be commanded by the Lord to take another wife, Di. That's one thing we will never have to worry about."

*   *   *

Huge amounts of time were required for drills and marches. Nauvoo residents were entertained by frequent parades. These troops were the city's hope for security. It was a united effort. Soon all citizens were required to attend every parade and muster. Absentees could be fined up to $25.00 per miss.

Somehow John C. Bennett, quartermaster general of the state of Illinois, arranged for two hundred and fifty fire arms and three cannons for the Mormon militia use. These included rifles. State militia still only used muskets. Titus Billings was designated captain of one cannon and kept it in his charge. His wife and daughter spent hours helping him make the needed cartridges. They were finishing a batch one evening when Sam's wagon pulled up with an excited load returning from Boys' Corp practice drills. These youngsters imitated their fathers and believed their group, which had grown to be five hundred strong in no time, was as important as the grownup detachments. Sam, Ebe and the Whitney brothers assisted the boys. Ebe stood in the wagon holding a new banner as George Pierce and Titus Junior jumped down.

"Pa, Ma, look at our flag!" Titus Junior shouted.

"We got a banner with our new slogan on it," George said. The boys were elated. Stretching out the poster took four of them, George and Titus Junior, Isaac Junior, and Joseph Smith III.

"Look at this," George said.

Eunice read it aloud: "Our fathers we respect; our mothers we protect." Everyone cheered.

"Was the Prophet there tonight?" Brother Billings asked.

"Oh yes," Sam answered. "He plans most, if not all, of our drills and parades. I think he enjoys the Boys' Corp as much as the boys do."

A glorious, fully outfitted army of fifteen hundred soldiers posed at attention on the morning of April 6, 1841. When the Lieutenant-General Prophet arrived at 9:30 a.m., the ladies of Nauvoo presented him with a beautiful, silk, American flag. Proudly he passed the lines in review and paraded them to the temple grounds. At noon, Elder Sidney Rigdon addressed the congregation. Then, for the third time in latter-days Church leaders laid temple cornerstones, beginning with the southeast corner as done in ancient order. A marvelous General Conference followed.

Historical Background

"The name of our city [Nauvoo] is of Hebrew origin, and signifies a beautiful situation or place, carrying with it, also, the idea of rest; and it is truly descriptive of the delightful location" (Smith4, 133).

Counselors were released when Bishop Partridge died. "Titus Billings was a member of the High Council" (Billings/Shaw/Hale, 19). "A stake organization embracing the Saints in Lima and vicinity was effected October 22, 1840 and Isaac Morley was made President" (Bennion, 2; Pyne, 4).

"A Stake Conference held at Father Morley's, October 23 and 24, 1841 was attended by three apostles: Brigham Young, John Taylor, and Willard Richards" (MorleyRH, 81). "President Morley called all the brethren together for a special (Saturday evening) meeting between sessions. It was decided that, the Priesthood of Lima Stake should forthwith be more active in forwarding the construction on the House of the Lord in Nauvoo. "This body of Priesthood signified by their uplifted hands that they would willingly give a tenth of their time and property to complete the Nauvoo Temple" (MorleyRH, 82).

"The Choir of Singers presented a petition to the Board of Regents of the University, at their last sitting, for the appointment of a 'Professor and Wardens in the Department of Music in the University of the City of Nauvoo,' to constitute a board for the regulation of Music in this city, which was adopted, and the following persons appointed: to wit: GUSTAVUS HILLS, Professor. Wardens: B.S. WILBER, 1st Ward, STEPHEN H. GODDARD, 2nd Ward, TITUS BILLINGS, 3rd Ward, JOHN PACK, 4th Ward. The Chancellor, General Bennett, recommended the Regents to instruct the board composed of the Professor and Wardens, aforesaid, to prohibit the <flat> sound of the notes, and adopt the <broad>; whereupon General Joseph Smith, observed 'I move the instruction, for I was always opposed to any thing <flat>.' The motion prevailed" (Times&SeasonsV3,653).

Titus was appointed to be a warden in the Department of Music in the University of the City of Nauvoo, 1842. He was the representative from the Third Ward, serving with B.S. Wilber, First Ward; Stephen H. Goddard, Second Ward and John Pack, Fourth Ward (Berrett/Burton, 232; Times and Seasons2).

"Titus Billings was a Captain in the Nauvoo Legion" (Cook, 102; WhitneyNK, 1) and "was present at the meeting that organized it, Thursday, February 4, 1841. Six companies were formed" (Smith4, 295). He is first on a "List of Names for Field Artillery" (WhitneyNK, 2) and again as Captain on a list of "Returns of Field Artillery" with notation that "The Company above consists of 52 rank and file liable to do duty" (WhitneyNK, 3). Newel K. Whitney's Poll Book records Titus Billings voting for Stephen Goddard in an election of the First Company, First Battalion held in Nauvoo on March 19, 1841.

On Saturday, May 1, 1841, the first Regiment, first cohort, of the Nauvoo Legion, consisting of four companies, was organized. Captain Titus Billings was given the rank of Lieutenant Colonel. On Saturday, September 4th, Titus replaced Charles C. Rich as Colonel in the Legion. General Rich replaced Don Carlos Smith, the prophet's brother, who died as a result of persecution (Billings/Shaw/Hale, 20; Journal History15; Journal History16, Journal History17; Journal History18; 1 May 1841; Smith4, 393-399).

"Although enlistment was open to all Hancock Co. citizens between the ages of 14-45, and it was a branch of the state militia, the Mormon Legion had its own internal government independent of state interference and its members were exempt from all other military duty" (Smith4, 297-307).

"The Nauvoo Neighbor once advertised wedding cakes ranging in price, from $1-25." [Note: The first issue of "The Nauvoo Neighbor Newspaper," published with the "Times and Seasons," John Taylor, editor, came out May 3, 1843. Unaware of this date, author used the newspaper to announce creation of the Nauvoo Legion February 4, 1841. Some say the "Nauvoo Neighbor" was a continuation of "The Wasp." (Jensen,563)]

Military Records of the Nauvoo Legion May 1, 1840: "All who are willing to join a company of Cavalry and uniform themselves according to Law written six months will please subscribe their names hereto" (WhitneyNK).

"Minutes of the Meeting which Organized the Nauvoo Legion . . . on Thursday at 10 o'clock a.m., the 4th day of February, 1841: present–John C. Bennett, quartermaster-general of the state of Illinois; Lieutenant-Colonel Don Carlos Smith; Captains Charles C. Rich, Wilson Law, Albert P. Rockwood, William Law, Titus Billings, Stephen Markham; first lieutenants, Francis M. Higbee, John T. Barnett, John D. Parker, Benjamin S. Wilber, Amos Davis; second lieutenants, Chancy L. Higbee, Nelson Higgins, David H. Redfield, Hosea Stout, Stephen Winchester, Thomas Rich; third lieutenants, John C. Annis, and Alexander Badlam" (Smith4, 295). "As a Colonel he also served in the Sixth regiment of the Silver Greys" (Black, 25).

"Billings, Titus: Captain – March 9, 1841, Brevet Major–March 9, 1841, Lieutenant Colonel–May 1, 1841, Colonel–September 4, 1841" (NLMembers, 2). "My father for many years was captain of the cannon when the legion was on parade, and many a time my mother and I made cartridges for him" (Hale, 4). Father "kept the cannon in his charge" (Bennett, 556; Hale, 4; Snow, 4).

"Saturday, 4 [September 1841]–Colonel Charles C. Rich was elected brigadier-general of the second cohort, to fill the vacancy of General Don Carlos Smith, deceased, and Lieutenant-Colonel Titus Billings was elected colonel in the place of Colonel Rich, promoted, and Major John Scott was elected lieutenant-colonel in his place, and Captain Hosea Stout was elected major in his place" (Smith4, 414).

Titus and Diantha's oldest son, "Samuel Dwight, was a member of the Nauvoo Legion Band. It is believed that he was the first drummer" (Nauvoo, 5). "Samuel Billings listed as a flute player in the Nauvoo Legion Band, March 8th" (WhitneyNK). "George was taught by his father [Titus] to play the violin and every instrument in the band" (BillingsLB, 1).

"The citizens of Nauvoo, when this temple was begun, was (sic) most of them who had been driven from Missouri and stripped of all they then possessed. Most of the Saints paid tithing but the best of the property was of necessity taken to buy nails, glass, paints, and such things as our labor would not produce. We would rather live poor and keep the commandments of God in building a temple than to live better and be rejected with our dead" (Shurtliff, 1).

"I saw the Prophet lay the cornerstone of the Nauvoo Temple" (Snow, 3). The

Billings family "saw the Prophet lay the cornerstone of the Nauvoo Temple" (Hale, 3). "The Nauvoo Temple site was dedicated and the cornerstone laid April 6, 1841" (MorleyRH, 99). Living near the temple spot Titus worked on its construction every possible moment (Bennett, 555; Snow, 4; Snow8, 4). Young George "went with his father who was a stone cutter, mason and carpenter. He did errands to help with building the Temple" (BillingsLB, 1).

See additional Nauvoo Legion Military Records in Appendix.

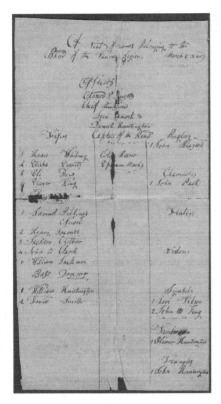

The Nauvoo Legion Band

List of Band Members shows Samuel Billings playing the flute. (Courtesy L. Tom Perry Special Collections, Harold B. Lee Library, Brigham Young University, Provo, Utah.)

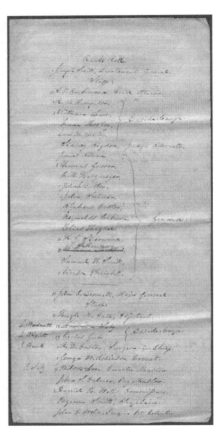

Nauvoo Legion Rank Roll

Isaac Morley (Courtesy L. Tom Perry Special Collections, Harold B. Lee Library, Brigham Young University, Provo, Utah.)

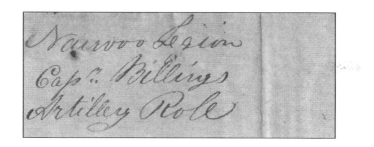

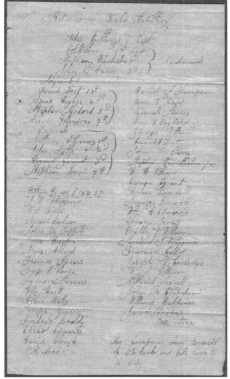

Nauvoo Field Artillery Roll

Titus Billings, Captain (listed on top)
(Courtesy L. Tom Perry Special Collections, Harold B. Lee Library, Brigham Young University, Provo, Utah.)

Nauvoo Election

Titus Billings voted
for Stephen Goddard.
(Courtesy L. Tom Perry Special Collections, Harold B. Lee Library, Brigham Young University, Provo, Utah.)

CHAPTER 51

"**W**atch out! Here it comes." A powerful pitch from a prophet put the ball back in the schoolyard. Children cheered at the sight of their beloved leader jumping the fence and joining the game. Eliza R. Snow shook her head from the doorway of her classroom. The small school house built on the bank of the Mississippi River where she taught thirty students was close to the Smith homestead. *He would play with the children every day, if he could,* Eliza mused, standing with patience to extend recess time for his sake.

"No school tomorrow because of the big grand opening." Children cheered.

Eunice and her friends stood near the front of a long line waiting for the doors of Joseph Smith's Red Brick Store to open for business for the first time. [Jan 5, 1842] All were eager to spend their hard-earned pennies.

Near the river's edge, at the heart of the Nauvoo business district, the new shop was packed with dry goods, its shelves and drawers filled to overflowing with every needful thing. The open, upper level was a ready place for meetings of all kinds. Bishop Newell K. Whitney issued tithing receipts from his office on the first floor. Extra supplies were stockpiled in the loft and in the cellar.

No one seemed to notice a chill in the air. Eunice held onto her nephew. "I'll watch him," she told her sister-in-law, Martha. "He wants to choose his own treat."

"You spoil him, Auntie," Martha said. Titus M. (often called "Tiny Titus" because Titus Jr. was called "Little Titus" though he preferred T.J., and the Grandpa, though thin, was now called "Big Titus") enjoyed all the fuss and pampering.

The colorful store was packed with happy people.

"It's like a huge party in here," Diantha said as she and Martha helped Sister Emma Smith select buttons for her new riding outfit. "Oh yes, shiny gold is a perfect accent for that dark fabric," Diantha said. Martha agreed. Sister Emmy, as Diantha called her, bought some Scotch plaid for a skirt too and sent it home with Diantha for stitching.

"Where's your horse, Charlie?" Titus asked the Prophet. "Did you get a new horse?"

Joseph nodded. "Yes, Brother Billings, meet my new horse, Joe Duncan."

"Joe Duncan?" Titus knew that name. Mr. Duncan was the Whig Party's candidate for governor and had embarked on a strong anti-Mormon campaign promising that he would personally "run Joe Smith and the Mormons out of town" if elected. Billings did not know what to say. Joseph seemed to enjoy his stupor for a moment.

"You see," he said, "it pleases me, to ride him out of town any time I feel like it." Both of them laughed. Nauvoo citizens were more supportive of a candidate for the Democratic Party, Mr. Ford.

*   *   *

"Eunice, do you get to spend the night with me tonight?"

"Yes Julia. Brought my things to school in this bag."

"Just wait 'til you see what's at our house!" Julia Smith seemed extra excited. Her eyes were big, almost mischievous. "Promise you won't be scared."

"Scared? Julia, how can I promise that?"

Julia giggled. "Just wait," she said.

Dinner at the Nauvoo Mansion was always a delight. Sister Emmy served dignitaries and important guests around the clock. Eunice loved to be there and Julia invited her to come often.

They helped with kitchen chores and listened to conversation around the fireplace. Soon Julia wanted her friend to herself.

"Excuse us please. I think we will get ready for bed now."

"Rather early, isn't it?" her mother wondered.

"We need lots of time for talking."

"I'm sure you do. Run along then."

"What's all the mystery?" Eunice asked when they were upstairs alone.

"It's down in the reception room."

"What? What's down there?"

"Oh Eunice, you won't believe it. Father has real live mummies in the house!"

"Julia, mummies are dead bodies . . . they can't be alive."

"No, but I mean they are real. You want to see them, don't you?"

"Not sure about that."

"You'll probably never have another chance."

"Probably not." Eunice was still uncertain if she wanted any part of this.

"Come on. Let's get into our night clothes and then we'll venture down."

It wasn't forbidden to take a look, but doing it privately in night clothes after dark gave such atmosphere to the experience. More than anything, Eunice did not want to be seen in her bed gown. "Where are your brothers?" she asked.

"Joseph Jr. sleeps on the other side. Alexander and David are probably out somewhere." J.J. was the object of her concern. Eunice didn't have too much to do with the older boys, but she was very much aware of quiet, studious Joseph Junior.

"Eunice, there are three of them."

"Yes, I know you have three brothers." Eunice was a bit confused.

"No. There are three mummies."

"Really?"

"Yes, two are men and one is a woman!"

"Where did they come from?'

"Egypt, of course."

"Why are they here?"

"A man wants father to sell them. Father is translating papyri that were buried in a pyramid tomb with them. Isn't this exciting?"

"Yes." Eunice had to agree. "It is of great interest for me to view them, although it gives me a strange feeling of awe to do so."

*   *   *

Regular parades increased in length as the Nauvoo Legion expanded its numbers. Both the Mormon city and its military ranks had been blessed by rapid growth. This Fourth of July celebration and parade promised to be the grandest of all. Captain Billings and his boys woke the town with an early morning cannon salute.

"Come on, Eunice. You look beautiful," T. J. said. He danced around a moment and soon started complaining again. "Do I have to wait for her, Ma?"

Diantha finished loading a picnic basket and covered it over with a white cloth. "Tuck your shirt in, and you may go," she said. He was out the door before she could blink.

307

Nauvoo was bursting with American patriotism. Every street was trimmed with banners and flags. Even the sky overhead was a royal blue as pleasant crowds lined up for the big parade.

"Diantha, where is that boy of yours?" her brother asked. Isaac Morley stood there with his arms full of tiny flags. She could not help laughing when she saw him. "You never forget, do you?" she said.

"What's the Fourth of July if you can't share a flag," he replied. "Now where is that boy? He's supposed to be helping me hand out the flags."

T.J. Billings met up with David Smith and other Boys' Corps members who perched themselves on the bowery platform for a perfect view of the mighty marching Legionnaires. General Joseph Smith and his wife, on horseback, led two thousand troops down the streets of Nauvoo. Wearing his full military suit: a black coat and white pants sporting a red stripe down the outside seam, a red plume in his cap, a red sash across his chest, and a shiny sword at his side, the handsome Prophet-General thrilled an eager crowd as he waved to them from the back of his favorite horse, "Charlie" a massive, black steed. Sister Emmy wore the new riding habit trimmed with the shiny gold buttons. A black plume accented her cap. She rode gracefully with her long, black skirt draped over "Joe Duncan." Her dark features and the prophet's fair ones made a striking impression, as Nauvoo's first couple passed by a good twelve thousand spectators. Passengers from three steamers looked on as well.

Historical Background

The Billings children attended school taught by Eliza Roxy Snow "in a small room that was built on the bank of the Mississippi River close by where Joseph then lived. There were about thirty children who went to school in that small room" (Hales, 10; Snow8, 3).

"The Prophet's sons: Joseph, Alexander and David attended the same school also. I remember Joseph, Jr.. He was a quiet, studious boy. I have a slight recollection of David and Alexander. He [the Prophet Joseph Smith] was a great hand to play ball with the school boys and he pleased the children always" (Bennett, 557). "I [Eunice] attended the school at Nauvoo which Eliza R. Snow taught, in company with his children. I was at their home almost every day" (Snow2).

Eunice was one year older than the Smith's adopted daughter, Julia. They were playmates. "She being a great friend of mine caused me to be at Joseph's house more than I should have been" (Hale, 10). "She was a constant friend of mine and for that reason, I often visited the prophet's home, eating there and spending many nights at a time with the adopted daughter." She did not know that she was adopted until someone told her. Emma had tried to keep that a secret. "It nearly broke her heart. After awhile she appeared not to be very much affected" (Snow8, 3).

"Information taken from a Day Book kept in the [Red Brick] store (now housed in the Masonic Library in Cedar Rapids, Iowa) gives the following examples of items bought and sold during that [Nauvoo] period --Scotch plaid bought by Emma Smith" (SmithJSHC).

In one of Smith's reception rooms "there were three mummies: two men and one woman. It was of great interest to us to view them, although they gave me a very strange feeling of awe at times" (Snow8, 4). [These may have been from the "exhibit of four Egyptian mummies and papyri" brought to Kirtland in July 1835 by Michael Chandler. "Within days they were purchased by Church members and given to Joseph Smith, who immediately began to translate the ancient writings. He soon discovered they contained the writings of patriarchs Abraham and Joseph of Egypt." Several of these documents are found in the Pearl of Great Price. (Bagley/Slaughter, 8)]

"Some of the most impressive moments of my life were when I saw the Nauvoo Legion on parade with the prophet, then General Joseph Smith, with his wife, Emma Hale Smith, on horseback at the head of the troops" (Hale, 4). His favorite riding horse was named Charlie, a big black steed (Bennett, 556; Hale, 4; Snow, 1,4; Snow3, 3; Snow4, slides G-60 and G-71). Emma rode a horse called "Joe Duncan" (Gardner, 1; Young). "Hiram [Hyrum] Smith rode on the right side of General Smith and his wife, Emma, on the left. Emma wore a long, black riding skirt. She was a fine horseback rider" (Hale, 10). "I remember in particular the general parade day. Joseph rode at the head of the Nauvoo Legion, Sister Emmy at his side"(Bennett, 557). Emma rode a horse called "Joe Duncan" (Gardner, 1; Young).

"Mother was as intimate with Sister Emmy as anyone could be with another" (Bennett, 558). "Sister Emmy and Sister Lucy Smith became her best customers" [Eunice speaking of her mother' sewing skills].

Father "kept the cannon in his charge" (Bennett, 556; Hale, 4; Snow, 4).

LIEUTENANT-GENERAL JOSEPH SMITH.
FIRST COMMANDER OF THE NAUVOO LEGION.

Leading the Nauvoo Legion Parade: Lieutenant-General Joseph Smith

"I remember in particular the general parade day. Joseph rode at the head of the Nauvoo Legion, Sister Emmy at his side' (Bennett, 557).

(Courtesy Intellectual Reserve.)

CHAPTER 52

"Sister Billings." Sarah Kimball was calling to her and stepped with haste to be at her side. "I need your help, Diantha," she said, pausing to catch her breath.

"Who is ill?" By now Diantha's gift for healing was common knowledge in Nauvoo.

"Oh, I don't need your doctoring skills today. Rather, I need your sewing skills to help us stitch shirts for the temple workers."

"Just finished a red one for Titus. Working with all that stone takes its toll on fabric."

"Yes it does. We believe we can assist the temple construction work by supplying warm shirts to the workers."

"What a beautiful idea, Sarah. How can I help?"

"I have purchased plenty of dark colored yardage and Miss Cook has completed several shirts already, but it is far too much for one seamstress."

"Indeed."

"I am hoping to expand our efforts by recruiting others with sewing skills."

"You can count on me," Diantha committed.

"Good. Let us gather in my parlor tomorrow afternoon to plot our strategy."

"I will be there."

"Please, will you help spread the word to other sewing neighbors."

"Of course, I will be most happy to do so."

Diantha, who loved to sew, was delighted with the thought. *Such a worthy project.* Her step quickened. *In this way I will really be helping with construction of the Lord's House!*

Excitement buzzed from Kimball's parlor early in the afternoon. Skilled females discussed their temple sewing project and soon found themselves in conversation about forming an organization of their own. In keeping with popular trends of the day, Eliza R. Snow, their children's school teacher, was selected to write up a constitution and by-laws they could submit to the Prophet.

"This constitution and these by-laws are the best I have ever seen," he said. "But, my dear sisters, this is not what you want.

311

Your offering is acceptable to the Lord. He has something better for you than a written constitution."

"We are meeting upstairs in the Red Brick Store," Diantha told her husband.

"Sounds official then."

"Official indeed. Come along, Eunice. We don't want to be late for the first meeting." Diantha was excited.

"Eunice is going with you?"

"Certainly. She may be too young to join the Society, but she will learn a great deal just observing."

"Is that what you want to do?" Her father knew the answer before he asked the question, but it seemed like the thing to say.

"Indeed it is, Father. I plan to be present for every meeting!" [Without fail, she was true to her word.]

Eunice wrote on her tablet: "March 17, 1842, today Nauvoo Ladies organize themselves into a society. They are strictly parliamentary in their proceedings." Several other young daughters also accompanied their mothers. Eighteen charter members with charity in their hearts and sincere desire to relieve suffering and sorrow from the earth chose to call themselves the "Female Relief Society of Nauvoo." Prophet Joseph Smith and two apostles, John Taylor and Willard Richards, acting with divine authority, sanctioned the event. Emma Hale Smith was appointed president. Sisters were challenged to: "Encourage the brethren to do good works in looking to the wants of the poor, searching after objects of charity, and in administering to their wants."

Twelve years prior the Prophet had received a revelation from the Lord for his wife, calling her "an elect lady" and instructing her (when properly ordained) to "expound the scriptures, teach and exhort the church as prompted by the Holy Spirit, be a scribe for her husband, compile a collection of hymns, be faithful and victorious, comfort her husband, keep her covenants, write and learn, lay aside the things of the world, be meek, be humble, keep the commandments and murmur not." After reading the entire blessing to the newly organized society Joseph Smith declared, "This revelation is the Lord's instruction to each and every member of the female community." Diantha glanced behind her to make certain Eunice was recording every important point.

"Today prophecy is fulfilled." Joseph blessed the organization and "turned the key" in behalf of the sisters. "You are organized under the priesthood after a pattern of the priesthood. The church was never perfectly organized until the women were organized."

Sister Emmy stood and addressed the group with new energy: "We are going to do something extraordinary," she told them.

John Taylor gave closing remarks. "[My] heart rejoices [when I see] the most distinguished characters stepping forth in such a cause, which is calculated to bring into exercise every virtue and give scope to the benevolent feelings of the female heart. [I also rejoice] to see this institution organized according to the law of heaven – according to a revelation previously given to Mrs. Smith appointing her to this important calling . . . to see all things moving forward in such a glorious manner. [I pray] the blessings of God and the peace of heaven may rest on this institution henceforth."

Eunice and her mother stood with a small feminine choir and sang: "Come Let Us Rejoice in the Day of Salvation" before their first meeting closed with a prayer of gratitude to a kind, loving, everlasting God.

Historical Background

"The women sewed clothing by hand as sewing machines were not available. The clothing was not fancy, but the greater concern was that it be warm" (MorleyRH, 77). "The color of material purchased for men's shirts was often red" (MorleyRH, 78).

"Being accustomed to attend all meetings with my mother, I was present at meetings of the first Relief Society in the Church in Nauvoo, and when my Mother was called as a teacher with Sister Markham as a companion. I was not old enough to be a member of the organization" (Snow, 3).

"Diantha attended the first Relief Society Meeting in Nauvoo, March 17, 1842, when Emma Hale Smith was set apart as first president. Eunice attended also but she was not old enough to be a member" (Snow, 4).

"On March 17, 1842, Emma Smith became the first president of the Relief Society." She chose Sarah M. Cleveland and Elizabeth Ann Whitney as counselors. (Tanner, 13)"And thou shalt be ordained under his hand to expound scriptures, and to exhort the church, according as it shall be given thee by my Spirit" (D&C,3). "We had the privilege of being present at their organization, and were much pleased with their modus operandi, and the good order that prevailed. They are strictly parliamentary in their proceedings" (Smith4, 568).

"A choir then echoed Elder Taylor's remarks, singing "Come let us rejoice in the day of salvation" (NauvooRS, 14).

"At the conclusion of the revelation, the Lord declared that what He had said to Emma was not for her alone but was His voice unto all" (D&C3, Tanner, 14).

CHAPTER 53

"Early Mission"
(Courtesy Robert T. Barrett.)

"A mission to Massachusetts and Vermont . . . Elder Luman Shurtliff companion . . . Leave as soon as prepared." Brother Titus Billings was elated. Many calls had been extended to younger elders; but today, August 22, 1842, at a special conference in Nauvoo, the Lord had chosen him. Elder Titus Billings was going on a mission, an errand for the Lord!

Necessities were scarce in Nauvoo. Sickness and death knocked at every door. It was a difficult time to leave a family behind. Elder Billings did have the luxury of leaving older, hardworking sons at home.

"Shurtliff has a young family," he told them. "I hope you boys will keep an eye on their place too."

"Ya, sure."

"Okay, Pop."

"What can we do?"

"See to it that they have firewood all winter." It was agreed. Elder Shurtliff sold one cow so he could buy hay to leave for the other cow.

"When are you going?" Isaac asked his two friends.

"Soon as I get a coat to wear," Shurtliff said. Brother Abbott stepped up, removed his coat, and offered it. "Try this on for size." It fit perfectly and was in excellent condition.

"It's yours," he said.

"Guess we'll be leaving right away," Shurtliff said.

"Good," Billings said. He was ready. Turning to Isaac he added, "Keep that temple coming."

"Don't know how we can without you," Isaac said with a grin, "but we will try."

The Billings family knelt around the room for an early morning prayer. Titus raised his head, but remained on his knees until he looked directly into the eyes of each child. "I feel it a great honor to know you," he said. "I love you all very much." Next, he stood to face his wife, "I leave you in good hands, Mother. These faithful children will see to your needs."

"I know they will." Diantha started to cry. "It's hard to say goodbye, "she said.

"At least we part for a happy reason this time." They all followed him to the wagon and waved until he was out of sight.

Elder Billings drove to the other homes and witnessed the farewell of each family. Elder Noah Packard, Elder Daniel Allen and his own companion, Elder Luman Shurtliff, each left families crying and smiling and waving goodbye. Elder Shurtliff's heartache seemed too heavy to bear. He looked back from eighty rods out, and wept at the sight of his wife, Eunice, and their children still waving farewell. "They have no breakfast," he whispered. "I am leaving them with no food in the house. "Pray for them," Elder Billings said. Elder Shurtliff bowed his head and dedicated his family to the Lord. A feeling of peace replaced worrying with rejoicing.

The new missionaries journeyed eastward. After a few days Elder Packard became ill and was confined to the wagon so others had to walk. When they reached Camden Township on the Wabash River he determined to remain in the area and teach on Sundays until he was well.

Before leaving town a tall, dignified man approached the humble servants.

"You are Mormon elders aren't you?"

"Yes, we are. I am Elder Billings and this is Elder Shurtliff."

"Well, I am Colonel Shelby. Both my wife and I are medical

doctors. We have one of your kind in our home and he is very sick. He keeps asking to see some of his 'brethren.' You must come and not leave until his is better or buried."

Once inside Elder Shurtliff recognized the other missionary who looked near death, yet rejoiced to see them. He requested a priesthood blessing at their hand. The Shelbys watched it all. By morning the patient's improvement was obvious. Mrs. Shelby was impressed and not ashamed to show it.

"You must go to our daughter and heal her too," she pleaded. "It's three hours by horseback. Our son will take you tomorrow." But her son could not get away until late in the afternoon. The journey was not one of ease with river water high and rising fast. When they crossed over the Wabash River it was more than half as high as their horses. Soaked legs and shoes dripped themselves dry from the stirrups. At length they found the sick daughter and administered to her. Nightfall was very dark when they started back.

The young man and his horses were accustomed to the river, but the missionaries were not. Both of them dreaded the Wabash and worried about it all the way back. Sure enough, its waters were elevated even more and the darkness made swimming impossible because they could see nothing on the opposite shore. It was difficult to spot their leader and keep up with him.

"Stick to your horse and let him come as he has a mind to," the son instructed. They had no other option. Elder Shurtliff pulled himself up on the saddle, closed his eyes and prayed as his horse plunged into the deep waters. Elder Billings followed behind him hugging his mount with all of his might.

"Wasn't certain I was going to make it across," Titus confessed after his horse scrambled up the muddy river bank.

"I doubted too," Luman said.

"Just proves, when on the Lord's mission He never lets you down."

Three wet horsemen rode in silence the rest of the way. They were thankful to Shelbys for dry beds to rest their weary bodies. Come morning the sick elder was up and walking about the house. The other elders prepared to leave. Without trying they heard Mrs. Shelby's loud voice as she spoke to her husband. "I know we are skilled doctors, but there is no use in our doctoring any more. The Mormons can cure two men to our one!" She turned around and saw her guests standing with carpet bags in hand.

"And where do you think you are going?" she asked.

"We are on the Lord's errand, Ma'am. We need to share His word with others."

"Well, you can't leave now. Your work isn't done here." Neither elder answered so she continued. "After all, I'm not baptized yet!"

"Are you ready to be baptized?"

"Yes, I am. Will you baptize me?"

"Oh, certainly," Elder Shurtliff said. "That's our business."

Of course they stayed. Next day Colonel Shelby drove around to the front door and everyone climbed into his wagon. When they reached the swollen Wabash it had more than enough water for baptizing and they located a perfect spot. Mrs. Shelby followed Elder Shurtliff into the flow where he performed the sacred ordinance. Colonel Shelby stood on the bank staring into the water. He spoke not a word. Everyone was silent, until at length Elder Shurtliff asked, "Would you like to be baptized too?" Still he spoke not a word. No one spoke. All stood quietly on the river bank until the Colonel started toward the wagon. Everyone followed.

Soon the missionaries said their good byes to their newest member and her uncommitted spouse and journeyed to Kirtland, Ohio where Elder Allen was to remain and where Brother Billings had relatives and friends to call upon.

"Looks real good, Sam," Titus said. "Nice farm. You have done well."

After the Mormons evacuated Kirtland, Samuel moved back into town. He bought an abandoned Mormon home and moved it onto his South Kirtland property. He also turned an old schoolhouse into a broom factory to use up the broom corn he grew himself. Titus was impressed.

"You're very industrious, my brother. Goes to show, hard work pays off."

"Oh, I work hard enough, but there's little money in brooms. The very best sell for 3 shillings, and the others for 25 cents."

Wish I could get one to Diantha, Titus thought to himself.

"By the time I purchase handles and twine it's not very profitable."

"Keeps you out of trouble."

"Guess it does. What brings you here?" Sam asked.

"Good news. I've come to share good news from God for

all of His children." The older brother was unimpressed. He tried again, "Let me teach you God's plan for happiness."

"I don't acknowledge any Mormon missionaries, not even you, Little Brother. If you have come to 'save my soul,' you have come to waste your time."

Thomas Morley was even more disagreeable when Titus left the house, his mother-in-law was in tears. Emily took him to visit Salomi's grave. She had married her sister's widowed husband, John Wells. Emily was receptive enough, but he was not.

It pained Elder Billings to see the abandoned temple in disrepair. This township he loved was no longer a place he cared to be. *Diantha must never come back*, he thought. *It would break her heart.*

Titus stopped to pray and to ponder at a quiet spot on the hillside of what used to be called Morley's Farm. He spent time at three little grave speaking to Thomas, Emily and Martha, as if each occupant was sitting in front of him alert and attentive. "This gospel is true, my little ones. By now, you probably know that better than I do. We are building a temple in Nauvoo. Soon your mother and I will be endowed from on High. Then we can be sealed together forever and you will be ours again, for all eternity. This is God's plan. It is a beautiful plan for happiness made possible by our Lord and Savior, Jesus Christ, who atoned for us all." The humble father prayed again. Then, pulling himself away from the sacred spot he left with his companion, knowing full well in his heart that he would never walk this pathway again.

Historical Background

"Brother Titus Billings and Daniel Allen and myself agreed to fit up a horse and wagon and go together. For some reason, Brother Abbott did not go. Brother Billings was my partner and Brother Allen was going to Kirtland" (Shurtliff, 1).

"I [L.A. Shurtliff], left Nauvoo on the nineteenth of September last, in company with Elders T. Billings, N. Packard and D. Allen, without money 'purse or script,' and with the intention of spending the winter in holding forth the principles of our religion in New England. Accordingly we journeyed east to the east line of this State, where we found some brethren, baptized by myself two years before, and the prospect of others embracing the truth, led us to hold two meetings, when it was thought wisdom that brother Packard should tarry to preach to them" (Times and Seasons3, V4).

Elder Noah Packard writes: "When I was called upon by the Twelve Apostles to take another mission to the east, I got ready and started on the 19th day of September in company with Luman Shurtliff, Titus Billings and Brother Allen. I was taken sick near the Wabash River in Vermilion County, Illinois, where I tarried until November 24th when I had so received my health that I started on east alone; my companions having gone on at the commencement of my sickness" (Packard, 1).

"We continued our journey to Kirtland, Ohio. There we left Brother Allen. Brother Billings and myself [Brother Shurtliff] pursued our journey alone" (Times and Seasons3, V4).

"On the 26th [September 1842] we came to Camden. Here we held a meeting and held a council about Brother Packard. He was a little better so we left him here to preach on Sundays and to work on the book he was writing. We thought this as suitable as any place for him to stop. He consented and we left him. We went back and came to Colonel Shelby's [home]. On going in, behold, there lay one of my neighbors called to go the same time I was. He started first and came there sick and was much rejoiced to see us. We administered to him and then was [sic] sent to go three miles and administer to a daughter of Colonel Shelby's" (Shurtliff, L).

"October 1 [1842] we made ready to take our leave when Mrs. Shelby said she could not think of our leaving and she was not baptized and asked me if I would baptize her. 'Oh, certainly,' I said, 'that is my business.' When I had baptized her we all stood silent some time. Mr. Shelby stood looking at the baptismal water. At length I broke the silence and asked him if he wanted to be baptized. He seemed deep in thought or overwhelmed with grief and spoke not a word. After some time he turned and prepared his team and we rode to his house. We gave them our parting hand, and continued our journey. He lived on a few years; disease took hold of him and soon laid him low. He then sent out to find an elder to baptize him but found none and he died out of the Church. Truly, delays are dangerous" (Shurtliff, L).

"On the 23rd of October [1842] we took the road to Rochester and traveled on as fast as we could. On the 26th we reached our destination. It was now late in the season and the roads were muddy, the days short and the weather was getting cold. We thought it better to get on a canal boat and work our passage and travel 40 miles in 24 hours and get our board and lodging, than walk 25 miles and beg for our food and lodging and there was no chance for preaching or doing much good in either case. Accordingly, we went to the boats in Rochester but could find no one that would take us so we started praying the Lord would open up the way for us. We had walked but a few miles when we came to the canal and looking, we saw a boat coming toward us. While waiting on the bridge, Brother Billings said he would drive the boat half the way if he could have his board and ride the other half of the time. When the boat came under the bridge, Brother Billings asked if they wanted to take a couple of passengers to work for their passage. The boatman said he would take one if he would drive half of the time but they had no use for the other man. At that Brother Billings jumped on and I following, not knowing how I would pay as I had but 70 cents and Brother Billings nothing" (Shurtliff, 3).

While Titus drove ship the Captain and Elder Shurtliff restored damaged barrels of flour being shipped to Albany. This effort saved the Captain's contract and reputation.

"When the captain saw us making preparations to go he said we must stay until morning and get our breakfasts and then we could go. We consented and in the morning when about to leave, I asked the captain what his demands were upon me. He said, "Nothing." If I was willing to call it even, he was and so we parted in friendship, the Lord having opened the way for us" (Shurtliff).

CHAPTER 54

The late October air sent chills up his back and caused Titus to tighten the scarf around his neck. *Sweet Diantha,* he thought pulling one end across his face and inhaling the memory of her who had knit it for him. "You warm enough?" he asked his companion.

"I am, thanks to Elder Abbott." Titus patted the faithful servant on the back and together they took passage on a boat headed for New York.

"You're right, Brother B, it will be better to ride the water than to walk in all this mud."

"Don't like the looks of that sky," Billings said. Elder Shurtliff looked up to where gathering clouds had intensified and appeared to be near bursting. "Glad we won't be walking in another storm," he said.

The two, crammed with seven others in an eight-foot space, soon felt the fury of a violent storm as their tormented craft was tossed to and fro. Elder Billings became deathly ill and struggled in agony for hours as the storm raged on and on all through the night.

Next morning the Mormon missionaries set out by foot on the road to Rochester. Season changes made travel even more difficult. Days grew shorter, the air was colder and the ground was muddy, always muddy. Three days later, they arrived. Readily the two accepted an invitation to breakfast from an acquaintance of Elder Billings.

"Still working for your God, are you?" Mr. Cain said. "You know I'd take you on in a minute. Got a big contract opening up next spring. I'd like you to foreman that crew, Titus."

The conversation was respectful both ways, but Cain was no more interested in the Golden Book and God's Plan of Happiness than Billings was ready to work for him again.

"Let me know if you change your mind about the job," Mr. Cain said.

"Let me know when you are ready to embrace light and truth," Elder Billings said.

With a handshake, they parted.

"Maybe we should take a canal boat and go the forty miles

in twenty-four hours with food and lodging," Elder Billings said.

"Sounds good to me . . . but I'm surprised you would be ready for it after your last episode."

Billings had not forgotten that miserable voyage by any means, but the Lord's work must come first. "If we keep walking, it will take much longer and we still have to beg for food and lodging. Not much chance for preaching either way."

"How will we pay for it?" Elder Shurtliff asked, rummaging seventy-cents from his pockets. Elder Billings had no money left, not even a penny.

"Have to find one that lets us work for our passage." The search began. Many boats were docked at Rochester, but no one agreed to take them on.

"Let's ask the Lord," Billings said. "We are ready to do Thy will," he prayed. "Please guide us . . ." They commenced walking. After a few miles, they came to the canal and started across its bridge. A boat was coming. "I'm willing to drive half the voyage if he'll let us ride the other half."

As the boat approached the bridge, Billings shouted to its captain, "Will you take a couple of passengers to work for their passage?"

"Can take one if he'll drive half way," the boatman called back. "Have no use for another." Elder Billings jumped from the bridge and landed safely onto the boat. Elder Shurtliff had no other option, so he followed.

While Elder Billings guided the ship, its captain and Elder Shurtliff worked below to restore damaged barrels of flour being shipped to Albany. This effort saved the captain's contract and reputation. The Lord had blessed them all.

"You must stay the night," said the captain. "Get a good breakfast and then be on your way." That sounded wonderful. "Much obliged," said the first. "Much obliged," echoed the second. It was their best night's sleep since Nauvoo.

"So, what demands do you have upon me?" Shurtliff asked the Captain as they readied to depart.

"None," was the answer. "I'm willing to call it even, if you are." They parted friends.

Forty-eight days after leaving Nauvoo, Elder Shurtliff and Elder Billings stopped in Hampshire County, Massachusetts. They had traveled thirteen hundred miles. Their next stop was to call on the home of Horace and Elizabeth Hatch.

"How long since you've seen your sister?" Elder Billings asked.

"Eighteen years. She is a devout Methodist and she despises Mormons." He talked on as they walked. "She is my only sister. Married Horace Hatch. A good man, Horace. Lost his sight in an accident twenty-three years ago."

Elizabeth answered the door and invited them in. It was obvious she did not recognize her brother. "You will stay for dinner, won't you?" The meal was welcomed and cooked to perfection. *She cooks like Ma,* Luman thought, choosing not to reveal himself as yet.

"Come sit by the fire and warm your feet" she offered. Horace was eager and receptive for conversation. When Elizabeth passed by Brother Billings, he pointed to his companion and asked, "Have you seen this gentleman before?"

"No, I think not," she said and continued to the pantry. Upon her return, Elder Billings continued. "I guess you have. He has been here before."

Elizabeth held a candle in front of his face and declared, "I think I do not recall his countenance at all." At that her blind husband responded, "Elizabeth, I believe it is Luman. He sounds like your brother, Luman."

"No," Elizabeth said. "He is not Luman."

"I guess he is," Elder Billings said.

She spun around and Elder Shurtliff spoke at last, "My name is Luman. I am your brother, Elizabeth." Stunned, embarrassed and overjoyed she rushed to him.

"It's been so long," she said. He agreed and embraced his sister.

Early the next morning the Elders left to teach in East Springfield, Caborville, Westfield, West Springfield and Middlefield and on to Boston. Two weeks before Christmas a young man known as J. W. paused to see why a large crowd had gathered at the town square on such a cold day. Straining his neck he spotted two men in the center. One had an armful of books, the other stood on a wooden box of some kind where he spoke out with fervor and enthusiasm. His message gave J.W. a good feeling. It was positive, full of hope and peace. Afterward they offered books containing words from a living God that told of Jesus Christ and paralleled truths in the Bible. For generations the Tuttles had been a religious, Bible-loving family. J.W. was sincerely interested, but he purchased a book even more for the purpose of using it as his mother's Christmas gift.

Alone in the barn, he wanted to sneak a preview of the book before wrapping it, but instantly found himself wrapped up in the book instead. Joseph Wells Tuttle could think of nothing else during the day and read it secretly at night. The account was very interesting, even amazing. It talked of people and places that existed anciently. He could hardly find enough time to read it. The new concepts spilled into his thoughts constantly. Soon, the fact that their son was up to something became apparent. His mystery was exposed on Christmas Day.

His mother, Catherine too was charmed by the book. "They call it a golden Bible, Mother. You should hear them speak of it. They tell how the words were carved into sheets of gold to preserve them forever, and how an angel guarded over them until God was ready to bring it forth."

Edward Tuttle was an honest, hard working man. His Boston bakery kept him busy from dawn until dark, day in and day out. Nonetheless, his son's excitement was contagious.

"I've never read anything like this, Edward." Catherine was as well read as any woman. Her religious up-bringing made her selective as well as sensitive. She carried the treasured volume to the bakery and read aloud to Edward as he worked.

"We need to find those preachers," she said. "I really want to meet them, Edward."

"May be too late by now. Probably just passing through." She knew he was right, but the desire hung in her heart. Tired from a long day, Catherine finished cleaning the bakery and readied to leave when J.W. burst in with loud excitement. He was not alone.

"Ma, Pa, look who I found!"

"Did you finish your deliveries?" Edward asked without looking up.

Catherine looked past her son and eyed the two strangers. "Are you new to Boston" she asked?

"It's them, Ma. The ones with the book!"

Elder Titus Billings and Elder Luman Shurtliff enjoyed hot bread and cookies and pie as they introduced Edward Tuttle and his family not only to the Book of Mormon, but also to the Lord's church restored.

*　　*　　*

Elizabeth was waiting for Luman and Titus to return. She had arranged a visit with her only living uncle, a wealthy man who was staunch Presbyterian. She wanted the privilege of taking her brother to see him.

The old man seemed pleased to meet the Mormon missionaries and had many questions for them. Their humble, ready answers were directed by the Holy Spirit. At length he asked, "Where did you go to school to train for the ministry?"

"Only the school of experience," Shurtliff replied.

"We are taught by the Holy Spirit, even the Holy Ghost," Elder Billings added.

"I know many ministers who have gone to college and studied divinity who do not know the scriptures as well as you two Mormons do," he said.

Elder Shurtliff remained to teach his relatives. Elder Billings took a journey to Vermont.

Deep snowfall made it difficult to travel. Elder Billings returned on March 25, 1842, the day after his birthday and the night before the big storm hit. "I feel a Divine Hand protecting us and helping us with this great work," he wrote to his wife.

"Listen to this." Elder Shurtliff was eager to share his letter from home with his companion. "The Billings boys, who were to get me wood for the watch, got over one boat load," Eunice Shurtliff wrote. Titus was pleased to hear that his sons had come through. Of course, he knew that they would. *They are good boys*, he thought.

On April 3rd the Mormon elders organized a branch of the church at Little River. After two weeks with them, Elder Billings moved on again for Vermont. Elder Shurtliff remained to continue his work with relatives. That night his journal entry read: "I walked a mile with Brother Billings and expected to be separated but two weeks, yet I could not refrain from weeping when I committed the good man to God, in whom we all trusted."

Historical Background

"In forty-eight days from the time we left Nauvoo we stopped in Hampshire county, Massachusetts, a distance of thirteen hundred miles. Here we found, as we expected, ourselves surrounded by men of learning . . . Elder Billings left me to visit his friends" (Times and Seasons3, V4).

"Horace Hatch had been blind for 23 years. He lost his sight in an accident before Luman left home" (Billings/Shaw/Hale, 22).

"We took breakfast with an acquaintance of Brother Billings." Then they called on Elizabeth Hatch, a sister Brother Shurtliff had not seen in 18 years. The two were invited in unrecognized. She was Methodist and did not care for Mormons. After dinner we "seated ourselves before the fire to warm our feet. Conversation was resumed. As my sister was passing, Brother Billings said, referring to me, 'Have you ever seen this gentleman before?' Elizabeth replied, 'I think not,' and passed on into the pantry. As she returned he said, 'I guess you have; he has been here before.' She stepped before me with her candle, looking me full in the face and said, 'I think I do not recollect his countenance at all.' Horace, my brother-in-law, raised his sightless eyes, 'I believe this man is Luman.' Elizabeth said 'This is not Luman.' Brother Billings replied, 'I guess it is.' She shook her head. And Horace repeated, 'It is Luman.' At that, I said that Luman was my name" (Shurtliff, 3).

Later, the two reunited, traveled on to East Springfield, Cabotville, Westfield, West Springfield and Middlefield. A letter from Elder Shurtliff's wife, Eunice [not Titus' daughter, Eunice], stated that: "Brother Billings' boys [Titus' sons] who were to get me wood for the watch, got over one boat load" (Shurtliff, 5).

"We then returned to my sister's and found that she had made arrangements to accompany me to my uncle's home. He was the only living uncle and was very wealthy and a stanch Presbyterian. He seemed very pleased to see us and asked many questions about Mormonism. After he heard our answers he asked where we had gone to school and we replied only the school of "Experience." He said many ministers that have gone to college and study divinity do not know the scriptures as well as you two Mormons" (Billings/Shaw/Hale, 23).

On March 25, again "Brother Billings returned from Vermont. Soon after this the snow fell so deep it was difficult traveling. On the 3rd of April, Brother Billings and I went to Little River and organized a branch of the Church. On the 25th, Brother Billings left me and went again to Vermont. I [Elder Shurtliff] felt lonesome" (Shurtliff, 5).

After two weeks Titus left Shurtliff working with relatives and moved onward to Vermont (according to Shurtliff's journal, his native place - Titus was born in Massachusetts). "I walked a mile with Brother Billings and expected to be separated but two weeks, yet I could not refrain from weeping when I committed the good man to God, in whom we all trusted" (Shurtliff, 4).

No account has been found that states when Titus returned from his mission.

They crossed over a stormy swollen river on horseback by night. October 22, they took passage on a storm-tossed boat headed for New York. Conditions were miserable. Titus was one of seven "deathly sick men" who suffered that night in an eight-foot room on the rocking vessel (Billings/Shaw/Hale, 21).

CHAPTER 55

Rapid and abundant growth made it challenging to keep track of all the new comers flocking into Nauvoo the Beautiful. Indeed, Zion was growing.

"Sister Billings, have you tried the new bakery yet?"

"No, Sister Emmy. I --"

"Oh, you must. The Tuttles are new members just in from Boston."

Tuttles? Boston? New members?

"Titus wrote me they were coming. Are they here already?"

"Just setting up shop. You will love Catherine!"

Emma's words soon proved an understatement. Catherine Tuttle was delightful. She loved everything, could do anything, and was comfortable in every conversation. Her busy baker husband was only a year older than Titus Billings, the missionary who had baptized him. Best of all, her daughter, Mary Ann was the same age as Eunice. In no time they were best bosom buddies.

Problems and persecutions increased. The Prophet Joseph was hunted for false accusations and spent considerable time in hiding. Mormon life seemed to grow more difficult. Diantha was overwhelmed with duties and yet, each day she seemed able to accomplish far more than should be humanly possible. Plans were made for Joseph to find work where he would be safe in the Pineries or in Canada. When Sister Emmy took ill, however, he could not tear himself away from her. Keeping out of sight he pretended to be gone and hoped his enemies would believe he was away.

"Eunice, I need you to deliver these caps to the Smiths. One is for Sister Emmy and one is for Sister Lucy. Tell them I will be down again this evening." Emma's condition always worsened at night. With Joseph in hiding, Diantha tried to be near his ailing wife as much as possible. He would slip in whenever he could.

"May I take a bundle of posies for Sister Emmy?" Eunice asked.

"Of course, dear child. Go pick some of those colorful mums at the side of the house, and I'll have this ready when you return."

Mother Smith answered Emma's door. She was pleased with her new cap; and upon seeing the lovely bouquet, invited Eunice in to deliver it in person. Someone jumped behind the bedroom door as she entered. "Oh thank you dear," Sister Emmy said. "The coast is clear, Joseph. It is Sister Billings' daughter. You may come out." Eunice was surprised to see the Prophet. She knew he was in danger and believed from all she heard that he was far away.

Joseph Smith placed his hands upon her head and said, "God bless you, child. You won't tell where I am, will you?"

"No Sir, I will not," Eunice promised. She ran all the way home so no one could stop her to talk. "I love the Prophet," she said when safe in her mother's arms. "I had a new feeling when he put his hands on my head."

"You were feeling the power of his priesthood from God," she explained.

"Oh," Eunice said. "I knew he was true!"

*   *   *

President Morley closed the Prayer Meeting. Most everyone in Yelrome attended these sacred gatherings held in the Grove two or three times a week. A new law had been introduced to the Saints in Yelrome and many of them lingered to ask for insight from Father Morley.

"I too struggle for understanding," he told the crowd. "We do not know the mind and the will of the Lord in all things. Sometimes we must just trust Him. That is how we show our faith. If we could see the end at the beginning we could not develop faith in Him because we would already know the outcome. In this case we will have great opportunity to walk with faith because we do not as yet have all the answers."

Faces around him exposed a variety of expressions. A few men may have been pleased with the thought of plural marriage or teasingly appeared to seem so, but most, including all females, were devoid of frivolity.

"One thing I do know with certainty," Isaac continued, "is that Joseph Smith Jr. is the Lord's prophet mouth-piece upon this earth and I will follow his instructions in full obedience until the day I die."

He turned to his sweet little Lucy who sat on a tree stump with rigid back, her feet together and hands linked in her lap waiting for him. Isaac reached out to raise her up. Hand in hand they started a silent walk homeward.

After weeks of intense knitting Diantha stuck her needles into an extra ball of yarn and dropped them into her sewing basket for safe keeping. Her newest knit sweater was dry from blocking, so she folded it with care. The matching socks, knit with leftover wool strands, would be a surprise bonus. Now she was ready for delivery.

"Eunice, T.J., time to go."

"Can we stop at the bakery on the way?" Titus Junior asked.

"Perhaps on the way home. We wouldn't want to carry delicate fresh bread all the way down and back, now would we?"

"No." He paused. "Unless we carry it in our tummies."

Tuttle's Bakery smelled extra yummy as they passed by. "Must be using the outdoor ovens," Diantha said. "Run in and see if Mary Ann wants to come. We will keep walking, so be quick and catch us."

No day could be more beautiful, Diantha thought. *The sights, sounds, and smells of this peaceful place restore hope to the heart and peace to the soul. The Lord is very near. All gratitude be unto Him.*

Julia was playing in the front yard.

"Eunice! Mary Ann!" she shouted, running to greet her friends the moment she noticed them. Then, wishing to be polite she added, "Hello T.J." He blushed and nodded. *So much like his father,* Diantha told herself.

"I don't know how you do it so quickly," Sister Emmy said acknowledging her pleasure with the knitting projects. Diantha chuckled a bit. "There was a day," she remembered, "my mother wondered if I'd ever catch onto knitting. I was a married woman when I completed my first real project."

"Oh, what was it?"

"A sweater. It was a Christmas surprise for Titus. I made hats and mittens for the boys too." More to herself she added, "I really should be making him another sweater."

"Excuse me Sisters." It was the Prophet. Diantha had not intended to stay so she shook hands and readied to leave. "Sister Eunice, Brother Titus Junior, may I borrow your mother for a few important moments." The children looked surprised at first, but welcomed any excuse to linger longer. Joseph led his wife and Sister Billings into the back bedroom where they stood beside him

331

as he received a revelation for sacred temple garments. Following precise instructions, Diantha cut out a pattern. "We will need many of these," Joseph said. "Only authorized sisters will be allowed to sew them." She was directed to prepare a chamber where this sacred work would take place.

"When it is ready we will set it apart," he said. "Fabric bolts will be delivered to you when the order arrives."

Diantha pondered the Lord's ways and marveled that this sacred honor had come to her. She was unaware of any sights, sounds or smells on the way home. Her mind and her heart were in a far better place. Somehow all of them passed by the bakery without noticing. Titus will not be getting a sweater from me any time soon, she thought. And this sacred assignment will occupy my loneliness until he gets home.

Historical Background

"They [Edward Tuttle family] were converted to the church in 1842 and moved to Nauvoo from Boston, Massachusetts. Only four of their children moved west with them: Henry, Martha, Mary and John" (Hansen, 1). [Edward and Catherine Tuttle were parents to nine children (Tuttle Family Group Sheet).]

He too was born in Massachusetts and was a year older than Titus. He opened a Bakery in Nauvoo. "Edward's second daughter, Mary Ann Tuttle, was six months younger that Eunice" (CoombsT1, 1). "I came to Nauvoo in June of 1842 with my parents Edward and Catherine V. Tuttle" (GardnerMA, 1). [Author's note: We do NOT know who baptized Edward Tuttle and his family.]

"Prayer meetings, which nearly everyone attended, were conducted regularly two or three times a week in a grove at Yelrome; and the law of plural marriage was introduced to Latter-Day Saints while they were residing in this settlement" (MorleyRH, 81).

"I remember delivering a cap to the Smith home, that mother had made. At the time the prophet was in hiding and had just returned for a change of clothes . . . I ran home as fast as I could so I wouldn't see anyone" (Bennett, 557; MitchellSB; Snow, 4; Snow8, 4). (Note: Zenna Hannah Cluff Peck, granddaughter of Eunice Billings Warner Snow, writes that the "cap" delivered was really two bonnets. One stitched for Emma, the other for Lucy.)

Again another account: Diantha finished sewing a cap for the Smiths and sent Eunice to deliver it. Joseph was in hiding at the time, but had just returned home for a change of clothing. "He called me in and took me on his lap and blessed me and told me not to tell a soul that he was there or that I had seen him. I ran home as fast as I could so I wouldn't see anyone. I would have had my tongue torn out, rather than tell anyone" (Bennett, 557; Snow, 4).

"My mother sometimes did knitting for Emma Hale [Smith] and one time when I took some work home I was ushered directly into Emma's bedroom when some person jumped behind the door. Emma called to him, it being the Prophet, and said, 'Do not be afraid, it is Mrs. Billings' young daughter.' It was time of a raid, and when Joseph appeared from behind the door, he put his hand on my head and remarked, 'God bless you, you won't tell where I am, will you?' I replied, 'No Sir, I will not!' I would have suffered punishment before I would have told where he was" (Snow8, 4).

Titus Billings' home was "just about five blocks from theirs [the Smith home]" (Bennett,558). "Diantha Billings did sewing and doctoring for the Prophet's family" (Snow, 2).

"Mother was as intimate with Sister Emmy as anyone could be with another" (Bennett, 558).

Diantha cut out the first pair of temple garments. "One day the Prophet took her in a room, told her how they had been revealed to him and she cut them out, then she and the Prophet showed them to his wife, [who] said that they needed a collar added because they didn't look finished without one, so a collar was added" (Snow, 4, 5, 6).

"My mother stood by the Prophet when he received the revelation in regard to the garments and many were the bolts of cloth which were cut into garments in our chamber which was set apart for the particular purpose of making garments for the use in the temple, and for the people who had received their endowments" (Snow8, 4).

Also, one account shows: "Church History records a wonderful assignment given to Diantha at this time. She was delegated by the Prophet Joseph to design and embroider the first temple apron, which has been used as a pattern throughout the history of temple endowments" (Snow8, 2).

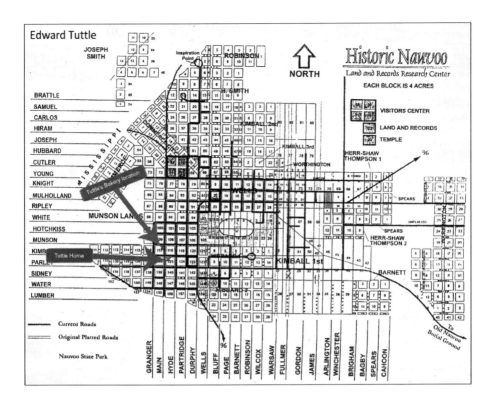

Edward Tuttle Property in Nauvoo.

Rented two lots in town: Bakery at Munson and Main, Home at
Kimball and Main. May have gardened a piece at Sidney and Fullmer.

(Courtesy Historic Nauvoo Land and Records Research Center.)

Chapter 56

John Wells Tuttle raised his hand, "Sister Snow, I won't be able to do any homework tonight."

"Oh, why is that John?"

"I'm helping my dad work on the new temple."

"That is good, John. The Lord is pleased when we help with His work." He beamed proudly. She continued, "The temple will be a house of learning. It is like a sacred school where the Lord is the teacher. For He has said, 'The Glory of God is intelligence or in other words, light and truth. Light and truth forsake that evil one.' It says so in the Book of Commandments. How better may we receive His light and truth than by being able to read His words from the Holy Scriptures? John started slipping down into his chair.

"So John, the Lord would have you practice your reading quickly so you can also work on the temple tonight." Laughter from the remaining twenty-nine students filled the tiny, one-room schoolhouse that sat on the edge of the Mississippi River. "All of you practice your reading tonight. And remember the poetry contest. The deadline is next week."

Eunice hurried with her Saturday morning chores. "I have to meet Mary Ann and go to Julia's house. We are working on our poems for the contest."

"That is well and good, but first we must ready this house. We want things in order when the youth of the church come calling, don't we?"

"Yes, Mama." Eunice started dusting the mantel as her Mother and Titus Jr. took the rugs outside to beat and clean them. It was an honor to host the second gathering of the teenage church members. Eunice was only twelve, but she liked being included. Julia had to wait another year, and Mary Ann needed a few more months. The first such fireside had been at Elder Heber C. Kimball's home last January.

"Sorry I'm so late. Had lots of chores to do," Eunice said when she finally reached the bakery late in the afternoon. "That's fine," Mary Ann said. "I've been busy too. Let me ask if I can go now." Soon she was back with one cookie for each of them and several others wrapped in a cloth. "Those are for later. Let's taste these on the way," she said.

Rhyming as a group was much more fun, but made it tricky to concentrate on the message and purpose of the compilation, as Sister Snow had instructed. The girls were struggling with words under an old shade tree in the Smith yard when the Prophet and Hyrum rode up on their horses.

"How are you lovely ladies today?" Joseph asked. Always, since she was very young, The Prophet Joseph insisted that Eunice sing for him whenever she visited. Years ago, he laid his hands on her head and blessed her with words she would never forget: "My little sister, you will be able to sing the songs of Zion as long as you desire." Now, she was in his home with Julia nearly as much, if not more than he was. She wondered if he would ask her to sing now. Julia explained their project to her father and told him of the difficulty they were having. His gaze visited each pair of eyes. Then he spoke. "Maybe you could sing your poems," he said.

"Yes, yes, let's make them into songs," they agreed.

As always, Diantha had everything in perfect readiness when the young fireside crowd arrived, March 21, 1843. Elder Heber C. Kimball who was a wonderful speaker gave the talk, but Eunice believed they would have had her father speak if he were home from his mission. The group organized themselves into what they called the "Young Gentlemen and Ladies Relief Society of Nauvoo" and voted to meet weekly, starting next Wednesday evening.

"You are welcome to hold your meetings in my schoolroom," Brother Farr offered.

Diantha was relieved. The group was getting too large for her little home, not to mention her concern for young Titus whose illness needed her full attention.

"You really should join the choir," Eunice told Mary Ann. "We will be singing at conference, and they are holding it on the finished, main floor of the temple."

"I don't know. I don't sing wonderfully like you do."

"You'll do just fine." Her friend seemed to require more coaxing. "Really, you have a beautiful voice. You just need to develop it." Eunice was determined. She loved to sing and thought everyone else should enjoy it as well. "Let's get Julia to come too, and you can sit between us." One more last effort seemed in order. "Mary Ann, we are singing for the Lord. He will help you."

* * *

"Thank you, students. This year's poetry contest had more excellent entries than I have ever seen before." Sister Snow presented awards and ribbons on the last day of school. "I hope all of you will continue writing over the summer." She looked at John Tuttle. "Keep reading and helping on the temple, too!"

* * *

"Thanks for the wagon," Isaac said after parking the Billings' rig behind the house where he had found it. "We unloaded 90,000 feet of lumber today." Diantha marveled. He went on, "Sure miss your Titus on days like these." She said nothing, but her heart missed him more than anyone could imagine. "Anyway, let him know the wagon he left behind is helping build the Lord's temple, even if he is not." Morley laughed at his own joke. "When does that man come home?" he asked.

"Returns in two months." The sound of her words warmed her own lonesome heart.

"Well, he may just get back in time to help finish up," her brother said. He turned to leave and mumbled to himself, "Yup. I bet he will."

Diantha fixed her eyes on the nearby construction spot where the hilltop temple would become a beacon to the world beckoning honest seekers to everlasting joy. Her sweetheart would be home soon to take her into the sacred edifice for very sacred purposes . . . when at last it was finished . . . when at last he was home.

No time for distraction. Pressing duties piled high. Emma and others required much nursing for long periods. Brigham Young suffered with scarlet fever and Titus Junior was not well. Joseph Smith came out of hiding last December and was tried in Springfield for shooting Governor Boggs. After reviewing ample proof that the Mormon Prophet was in Illinois, not Missouri, when the shooting took place, Judge Pope acquitted Smith early in January. The next month he was elected Mayor of Nauvoo.

"Ask Julia to let us see the mummies," T.J. said with a cough.

"You cough too much, too loudly to sneak you in anywhere," Eunice said.

"Oh, come on, Sis, you've seen them zillions of times." He coughed again. "We really want to see them before the Prophet sends them away, don't we John?" John Wells Tuttle nodded his head.

"Well, maybe if you feed the chickens and gather the eggs for me, I'll see what I can do."

"It's a deal," he said. "Come on, John." That surprised her. She was only kidding and never believed he would do it. Not so willingly, at least. She would scheme with her friend tomorrow.

That night Titus Junior awoke from his sleep with a blazing fever and stumbled into his mother's room. "Ma, I don't feel well at all," he said. Diantha rallied.

"I'm sick, Ma. I feel real bad." His forehead, the palms of his hands, his entire body were burning with fever. "Alfred, George, wake up! We need some ice chips from the cellar."

"Do you need them tonight?" Alfred said, still half asleep and weary from his labors at the temple site.

"Yes, we need them now. We must break this fever."

T.J. was dipped into the rainwater barrel. His teeth were chattering when Al returned with a block of ice. "That should cool you down, if anything can," he said.

Even though the lad was ten years old and tall and skinny, like his father, Diantha wrapped her son in a thin sheet and rocked him on her lap. Eunice was up and worried about her brother. "Mother, what can we do for his mean cough?" she asked.

"I'm making a plaster for his chest. It will be ready in a few minutes." Oh yes, they could smell the strong poultice ingredients. It was Mother Morley's recipe. "I have seen many coughs burned out with that remedy," she said.

It was daylight before the fever seemed to break.

Titus Junior stayed in bed for several days which in itself, signified the seriousness of his illness. Eunice kept her word. "Julia says the mummies are being displayed in one of the reception rooms. She is sure it will be okay for you to view them when you get well."

"Tell me about them again, Eunice." He looked so pale that

it pained her. She sat beside his bed and told him everything she could think of that might be of interest. "There are three mummies. Two of them were men, well, I guess they still *are* men." That made him laugh. "The other *is* a woman, of course."

"Of course," he repeated.

"Julia says she thinks there were supposed to be four mummies when the church bought them back in Kirtland. We were babies then, so we don't really know. She just tells me what she hears the grownups say." Her brother was smiling with interest, so she went on. "The Prophet translated ancient papers that were rolled up with the mummies. Some of the papers were written by Abraham in the Bible. Some were written by the Joseph who was sold into Egypt." It really was amazing, now that she thought about it.

"Eunice, have you read the Book of Mormon?" asked Titus Junior.

"Yes, most of it ."

"It must be an important book if an angel of God guarded it for hundreds of years . . ." He closed his eyes while he spoke.

Eunice thought about the words he spoke. "You are right," she said. "It is an important book. It changes lives. Would you like me to read to you while you are ill?" She could tell he was tired because he did not open his eyes.

Still he answered her question. "Yes, Eunice. I really would like to have you read to me."

"Go to sleep now, and I'll start reading the Book of Mormon to you tomorrow."

"Thank you." He looked so sick. At that moment she would do anything for him.

Oh that I could take his place so he could run and play and be a tease and do all the things he likes to do, she thought.

"I love you, T.J." she whispered.

Historical Background

"Lorenzo Snow and Eliza R. Snow taught at the school in Lima until January 20, 1844, and left sometime in February of 1844" (Black/Hartley, 29). [She was sealed to the prophet 29 June 1842. He lived in Nauvoo. Eunice Billings remembers attending her school classes in Nauvoo.] The Book of Commandments was later called the Doctrine and Covenants. Reference quoted here by Eliza R. Snow Smith was D&C section 93, verses 36 and 37.

It was the second such meeting, the first having been held "in the latter part of January, 1843" at Elder H.C. Kimball's home. Elder Kimball was speaker at both meetings [again suggesting that Billings was still on this mission]. The "message was so well received by the assembled congregation that it was voted, almost by acclamation, that a similar meeting should be held in the ensuing week. An appointment was accordingly circulated for the next Wednesday evening at Brother Farr's schoolroom, as Elder Billings' house was too small to contain the assemblage" (Journal History14, 28 March 1843; Times and Seasons4, V4, 154-155). This was the beginning of the "Young Gentlemen and Ladies Relief Society of Nauvoo."

CHAPTER 57

Titus Billings Junior was bedridden for many days. His sister spent hours with him. They talked about everything imaginable, and she read to him from the pages of the Book of Mormon. He was young, but started asking very deep questions as they read. Several times Eunice sought help from her mother or brothers to explain and answer his queries. The reading sessions seemed to give him peace. She thrilled with the light and truth of discovery. "Well, we are certainly filling our summer reading requirement," she told him one day.

Julia Smith and her brothers were worried about Titus Junior. They told their Prophet father how the boy wished to view the mummies, but got too ill to get out of bed. "Come with me," he said. Julia, Joseph III, Alexander, and David climbed into the wagon with their father. They drove to the corner of Partridge and Munson. "Wait here," he said.

The long legged Prophet was at Billings' front door in an instant. "I have come to borrow your son," he said. Diantha looked perplexed. "He has an appointment to meet some mummies." Eunice jumped up with glee. She seemed to be the only one with any inkling of what was happening. "With your permission I would like to escort him to the Mansion House for a quick peek. You are welcome to join us if you feel so inclined."

The pale-faced boy beamed like a lighthouse when the Prophet of God picked him up, quilt and all, and carried him out to the wagon. He had not been out of the house for weeks, and now he was going to see mummies from the days of The Pearl of Great Price.

The desired color refused to come back into his face, but Titus Junior was happy and peaceful. Each day his sister continued to read aloud to him. Every day they talked about ancient mummies and long ago happenings. The headaches and nausea increased, he experienced a burning numbness up and down his left side and then in both hands and both feet. Soon his speech slowed and lessened. His consciousness seemed cloudy.

George and Alfred returned in uniform from Legion Meeting. Due to illness their little brother had missed for several weeks.

They removed their hats and found their mother and Eunice at the lad's bedside.

"Well, they did it tonight," George said.

"Did what?" Eunice asked. Diantha was pre-occupied wringing out cold towels for her son's fevered forehead.

"Elected a new colonel to fill Father's vacancy." George sounded disappointed.

"It needed to happen," Diantha said. "With troubles brewing all around us we need every position occupied, don't we?"

"Yeah, and how can Papa do it when he isn't even here?" Alfred added.

"Who did they choose?" Eunice wanted to know.

"Brother John Scott."

"He'll do a fine job." Everyone knew he would.

"I wish Papa was here," T.J. said in a very weak voice of longing.

"Soon," Diantha comforted her youngest son. "It won't be long now. Try to rest, Dear."

Obediently he tried, but rest was impossible. The fever blazed no matter what they did to relieve it. Diantha felt the situation slipping through her fingers. Again she woke her older sons.

"Alfred Nelson: get up quick. Go fetch Elder Kimball to give T.J. a priesthood blessing. George Pierce: Hurry, fetch Elder Whitney at once. Your brother's brain is on fire!"

Eunice wanted to help. She did not know what to do, so she prayed a silent prayer. Then she remembered how the Prophet would ask her parents to sing to him during difficult times. Often they took her with them. She knew many of his favorite songs. Maybe they could comfort her little brother too. Eunice stood in the corner and started to sing with a soft voice. "Fear not, I am with thee; oh, be not dismayed, for I am thy God and will still give thee aid."

She finished "How Firm a Foundation" and was singing "The Spirit of God" when her brothers returned with Elders Heber C. Kimball and Newell K. Whitney.

"Your singing has invited the Lord's Spirit," Elder Kimball said. "Thank you, sweet sister."

They placed kind hands upon the head of her ten year old son as Diantha wept while they prayed. The words were beautiful, peaceful, and final. The suffering lad gasped his last breath before the blessing ended. He was gone! Her child born in a stable had finished his life's mission. Titus Junior was gone!

With reverence George pulled out his violin and started a soft melody, as if playing it represented his missionary father, his teacher of every musical instrument. Come morning Alfred took on the task of finding wood to start preparing a casket. Before noon Uncle Isaac and Aunt Lucy arrived from Yelrome. *If only Titus could be here!* Diantha anguished. His return was nigh, but the stiff little body could not wait. Lucy helped Diantha prepare and roll it in a heavy blanket. Eunice observed it all. Her little brother would never see his father again. She felt the pain of it pierce her heart as if with a sword.

"Titus already knows through the Spirit," Isaac comforted. "Because of our Savior Jesus Christ, all is well enough." The grieving mother believed his words, but was unable as yet to feel them. Her youngest son was tucked into a grave beside the one belonging to beloved Bishop Edward Partridge, in whom there was no guile.

Historical Background

On July 21, 1843 "Lieutenant-Colonel John Scott was elected colonel of the First Regiment Second Cohort, to fill the vacancy of Colonel Titus Billings, resigned" (Journal History18, 21 July 1843; Smith5, 515).

Titus Billings Junior died in Nauvoo on March 14, 1844 and was buried in Lot A (Nauvoo, 3, Nauvoo1).

"Brother Heber C. Kimball and Brother Newel K. Whitney were called to administer to him. While they were so administering to him he died" (Hale 3; Snow, 1, 3).

Titus Billings Junior was ten years old when he died, March 14, 1844, of "inflammation of the brain" at Nauvoo (Cook1, 7; Woods).

Edward Partridge Tombstone

Titus Billings Jr. is buried in the Old Nauvoo Burial Grounds Cemetery. It was impossible to locate his exact burial spot, but we like to believe he is buried close to the beloved bishop with whom his father served.

(Courtesy S.B. Mitchell, 2002.)

CHAPTER 58

Still in bereavement Sister Billings and her children joined other saints for the conference-funeral of a friend, Elder King Follett, whose body was crushed when a tub of rocks fell in on him while digging a well. The Prophet taught a sermon of hope, creation, exaltation, the character of God, and man's relationship with him, all in a way never to be forgotten. His words were comforting to all, especially to a sorrowing mother who longed for her husband's return. With reverence she walked her brood to a fresh grave in the Nauvoo Cemetery where their beloved Titus Junior had been laid to rest only three weeks before. Eunice dropped to her knees on the sacred spot. "Oh T.J., we didn't finish the Book yet," she sobbed. "I wanted to read it to you. Why couldn't you wait?"

Jolted by her daughter's pain, Diantha too dropped to her knees. Two brave Billings boys felt helpless as they stood by and watched their mother and sister embracing and sobbing. At length George ventured to speak.

"Bishop Partridge will take care of T.J., won't he Mother?"

Diantha nodded and dabbed her tears.

Alfred knelt by his mother. "Do you think we should pray again?" he asked.

Again Diantha nodded.

*   *   *

Isaac dipped his pen one last time. He was ready to sign the letter and send it to Church Headquarters. The report pleased him: "Nineteen elders have been ordained and twelve new members have been baptized in Yelrome." His little homestead had grown into a thriving community and was regarded as a "happy place" to live. President Morley was considered a dear friend of the prophet, even though he was a good nineteen years older. Joseph always spent the night with Isaac and Lucy when he visited on church business.

"Now what are you smiling about?" Lucy asked.

"Was I smiling?" Isaac kept his eyes on the sealing wax.

"Grinning is more like it," Lucy corrected.

"Can I help it if I live in the perfect place and share it with

345

the perfect wife?"

Lucy blushed. "I'm not a spring chick," she said, "but I do love your Yelrome."

"Wouldn't you rather move into Nauvoo?" he teased.

"No, I like it here and plan to wear out my days in this very spot."

Her words pleased him.

"Come with me to post this letter."

"But Isaac! I have so much to do before . . ."

"It will wait. Let's go for a stroll." How could she refuse?

*   *   *

Sister Billings was called to be a traveling teacher for the Female Relief Society of Nauvoo. She and her companion, Sister Marcum, were assigned a list of sisters to visit on a regular basis offering comfort and love to each of them. Eunice was too young to be an official member, but she never missed a meeting and enjoyed traveling with her mother and Sister Markham. Early one afternoon Sister Tuttle saw them coming and stepped out of the hot bakery to greet them.

"Welcome, Sisters. I appreciate your visit," she said. "John, fetch some chairs out here for the sisters."

Mary Ann emerged with bucket in hand. "Ma, could Eunice come with me to the well?" Both Catherine and Eunice looked at Diantha who nodded her approval. Eunice grabbed onto the bucket handle too and the girls swung it back and forth as they skipped their way to the well.

"I've been thinking a lot about the Prophet's words in our meeting last week," Sister Markham said. No one else spoke, so she went on. "He said it was our solemn obligation to seek out our own salvation and that we can only live by worshiping God."

"Yes," Diantha added. "I was impressed when he said each of us must do it on our own – no one can do it for anyone else."

Now Catherine was ready to venture into the conversation. "I understood how every man should do so, but when he stipulated that we as sisters need to acquire testimonies of our own . . . well, that eye-opener really inspires me." The others nodded. "Truly it validates my desire to read the Book of Mormon. 'Can't get enough of that book, and now I feel I can justify my time in it. I don't have to feel guilty when I read it."

"Actually, we should feel guilty when we don't read it," Sister Billings said.

"Cultivating a testimony of Jesus Christ and his atonement is an important part of our preparation to enter the Holy Temple, when it is finished. The Book of Mormon teaches of Christ and will help grow testimony more than any other thing I know," Sister Markham added.

Their discussion continued about the House of the Lord, how they could aid its construction and what would take place inside once it was completed.

"I rejoice in the blessings it will give us."

"And the blessings it will allow us to give to those who have gone on before us."

Diantha's voice strained and her mother's heart beat faster. "We must earn a part in the First Resurrection so we shall have our children just as we laid them down in their graves." She was quoting the prophet's words . . . somehow when she spoke them they came alive in her soul and she could hardly await the day she could sit down with Titus Junior and impart her joy!

*   *   *

Isaac Junior rushed into the house waving something in the air.

"Another letter to you from the Prophet, Pa."

Three clerks had been sent from Yelrome to Nauvoo as record keepers for the church. Soon afterward Saints living under Isaac Morley's jurisdiction were invited to supply any "extra cash, food stuffs, hand soap, and oil to keep the lights burning so the clerk's pen might stay in motion." Now another request. President Morley carried the letter to church and read it to his congregation: "The measure you mete shall be measured to you again. If you give liberally to your President in temporal things God will return to you liberally in spiritual and temporal things too."

Again Yelrome saints were generous in supplying the Prophet's house with "two cows, as many loads of wheat as possible, beef, pork, lard, tallow, corn, eggs, poultry and venison." Still they tithed their time to work on the temple; one day in every ten.

*   *   *

Elder Billings and his trusted companion quickened their pace as they neared Nauvoo the Beautiful. Both filled with testimony and the joy of righteous service also carried heavy, even broken hearts.

"I will do anything for you at any time, Brother B," Luman Shurtliff said. Titus embraced the younger man.

"You would give me your last nickel wouldn't you, dear friend?"

"Of course, if I had one." Together the two had pinched pennies for many long months. Now their shared mission was complete.

"Would you like me to walk you to your doorstep?" Luman asked, sympathetic to the sorrowful loss of Elder Billings' youngest son during their absence.

"No, Luman. You hurry on to your family. I'll be fine." He turned to leave, then paused. Looking back he could see his companion had not moved a muscle. "Luman, shall we seal our mission with a last joint prayer?"

Together they knelt behind a cumbersome bush and praised the Lord.

Historical Background

"It was during this conference that the Prophet gave his greatest recorded sermon in honor of Elder King Follett, who was crushed while digging a well" (Barrett, 592).

"To her mother, who had also lost a child to death, Sally testified, 'Oh mother, if we are so happy as to have a part in the first resurrection, we shall have our children just as we laid them down in their graves" (Godfrey,138-9; Tanner,21).

"When[ever] the prophet attended a conference in Yelrome, he stayed in the home of Lucy and Issac" (MorleyRH, 84).

"The letter requested the Saints under President Morley's jurisdiction to supply extra cash" etc. (Young,B3; MorleyRH, 86). "The measure you mete shall be measured to you again" (Jenson6, 509).

Diantha was called and set apart to be a [visiting] teacher with Sister Markham as companion (Bennett, 555).

"We can only live by worshipping our God – all must do it for themselves – none can do it for another" (Tanner,17).

CHAPTER 59

"Ready now? Let's lift on the count of three." Martha Ann Tuttle counted, while she, Mary Ann and John each hefted a table leg and the three siblings dragged the heavy wooden table outside.

"Now, help me get this under the shade of that tree," Martha Ann bossed.

"You and your bright ideas!" John complained.

"Oh, it will be lovely," Mary Ann said. "Wish I had thought of it."

"You get the chairs, John. Come Mary, let's get a cloth and bring out the dishes.

"Why so much fuss? Why don't we just eat inside like always?" John asked.

"Too hot and crowded in there . . ."

Mary Ann interrupted her sister's words. "You know this is a special dinner, John. After all, Elder Billings brought the gospel Truth to us – least we can do is bring dinner to him in a shady spot."

John knew better than to argue with his two older sisters. They were always united, thinking and acting alike. Pa called them his twins. Good smells from mother's cooking pots appeased his mind and enticed him inside for the chairs.

*   *   *

Titus could not wait to return to the work of building the temple. "Well, you are right back where you left off," Isaac said.

"Not exactly. Looks like you did a little bit while I was away."

"Thanks for noticing."

"Yeah, Pa. We' been working hard!" George said.

"I know you have son, and I am very proud of you, Alfred too." Both grinned. "Sure was nice of you to save a piece for me to finish."

"Anytime, Pa," Al said.

Though saints had worked hard to create a peaceful, happy place of rest in Nauvoo, old problems were brewing in the hearts of some outsiders. In nearby Warsaw, the price of flour or a cord of

349

wood was inflated for Mormon purchases. Church leaders counseled Warsaw saints to move into Nauvoo.

Little Charles Spaulding Kimball was the next baby Diantha welcomed to earth. His father, Heber C. Kimball, and the other apostles were serving missions to the East to collect money for the temple. For weeks Diantha carried dainties to Vilate Kimball. "You will wear yourself ragged," Sister Kimball said.

"I remember the day you saved my life by such an endeavor," Diantha said. "I was too ill to care about anything and totally unable to take care of myself, let alone see after my family. Eunice never stops talking about the way Sister Kimball does things." Vilate smiled. Diantha continued. "You influenced her for life and I thank you."

"Eunice is growing into a fine young woman, isn't she?" Vilate said. Then pausing, she took a deep breath. "You know, Diantha, this may sound silly; but I have been lying here thinking . . . maybe I have an appreciation for this law of plural marriage." Diantha was speechless. Heber had been called by God to practice the holy order. It was a great trial for him. It nearly broke his health before he could come to grips with the commandment. Sweet Vilate sensed that something was terribly wrong and prayed to the Lord in his behalf. She learned of it, through the Spirit, before he could bring himself to tell her. Three sisters were sealed to him in the spring of last year. One of them, Sister Sara Peak Noon, entered the room as they spoke. "You see, now I have lots of help when I need it!" She reached up and took Sara's hand.

"Yoo-hoo, Mother, are you in bed like you are supposed to be?" Her married daughter, Helen Kimball Whitney, had come to visit. She carried a letter from her father.

"It is nice to see you, Helen. I will be going now," Diantha said.

"No, Sister Billings, don't leave. Father mentions you in his letter. Here, let me read it to all of you: 'Now, Helen, kiss your dear mother for me, and tell her to kiss the dear little babe for me. I can hardly think of them without weeping. I received the little lock of hair she sent me and carry it in my pocket . . . give my love to Bishop Whitney and family, and to Sarah Noon. Tell her to be of good cheer." Diantha noticed Sara's eyes fill with tears, "and also Brother and Sister Billings and all that inquire of me."

See, he is thinking about all of us."

"How nice," Diantha said. "Please give him our love when you write back." Again she started to go.

"Take care of yourself, Diantha. You have so much to do and your husband has been home only a short time." Diantha had never seen nor expected a mischievous simper from such a benevolent soul. However, she caught a slight glimpse of one as her beloved friend and exemplar chided, "Maybe he needs to take another wife." Quickly she sobered. "How are you keeping up with the garment production?"

"We are right on schedule, I think. The Lord always helps us when we try to do his work."

"He does, indeed."

Historical Background

A letter written by Heber C. Kimball to his daughter, Helen Kimball Whitney, on July 19, 1843, suggests that Titus was home. "Now, Helen, kiss your dear mother for me, and tell her to kiss the dear little babe for me. I can hardly think of them without weeping. I received the little lock of hair she sent me and carry it in my pocket . . . give my love to Bishop Whitney and family, and to Sarah Noon. Tell her to be of good cheer, and also Brother and Sister Billings, and all that inquire for me" (Kimball, 2).

CHAPTER 60

"Why do you look so perplexed?" Diantha asked her husband.

"I'm just considering a prophecy from Joseph. Not sure I understand it." He tried to expound what he had heard. "Says that saints would continue to suffer much affliction and would be driven to the Rocky Mountains."

"I cannot imagine ever leaving this wonderful place," Diantha said.

"That's not the part that concerns me most. Joseph said many would apostatize or be put to death by persecutors or lose their lives from exposure or disease. Some of us will live to build other settlements and cities, becoming a mighty people in the midst of the Rocky Mountains."

Perhaps Diantha should have been bothered by his words, but she felt so close to the Lord that she knew all things would work out. With tenderness she kissed him and whispered, "His will be done."

"A five-hundred dollar reward! Do you see that?" George Pierce Billings asked his brother as he read the new notice posted by Porter Rockwell.

"Yeah, I see it. Too bad we don't have "sufficient proof" for any of those trouble makers," his brother Alfred Nelson Billings said.

"Sure hope it puts an end to all of this wickedness," Titus Billings said.

His sons knew about the phony money circulating around the city and of all the hypocritical robberies. This was the prophet's way of cleaning it up. Several excommunications resulted (most of them members in name only), but the painstaking effort to clean his beloved Nauvoo also put his life in greater peril.

"Is your man home, Sister Billings?" It was their neighbor, Porter Rockwell.

"Yes, please come in and I will fetch him," Diantha said.

"No Ma'am, I'll just wait out here."

"Porter, what is it?" Knowing his colleague was a busy,

rough and tough chap who never made courtesy calls, Titus felt an urgent fretfulness from the visit.

"Need some help!" Rockwell was acclaimed as the Prophet's chief bodyguard.

"Of course, what can I do?"

"Things ain't very sweet these days. Gotta guard Smith's place 'round the clock." Billings already knew the prophet's life was in danger. Everyone knew of the evil threats that bombarded him non-stop.

"Need you and your boys to take shifts with us."

"You can count on us," Titus said.

"Sure can," Al added.

"Sure can," George echoed.

Diantha and Eunice heard it all from the cabin doorway. After Porter crossed the road she addressed her husband.

"Why can't they leave us alone?" she demanded. "The poor Prophet, Sister Emmy . . . why can't they have peace anywhere anytime?" Titus put his arm around her in an effort to comfort.

"He's doing the Lord's work, Diantha, and you know who doesn't like that."

Billings stopped his wagon in front of Morley's Cooper Shop and found Isaac busy as ever inside. "How are things in Yelrome?" he asked.

"Yelrome is fine. Our people are united and industrious," Isaac reported.

"Just like their leader," Titus added.

"If only the world outside would leave us alone."

"That's why I'm here, Isaac. Tension is growing all around us. We're worried about you being alone out here."

"I'm hardly alone. Yelrome is a thriving community, if you haven't noticed."

"Yes, we know it is. But word is that mob threats are building up again. We might need to pull our two settlements together."

"Last week Brigham Young and Wilford Woodruff were here for our stake conference. Twenty-six elders volunteered for missionary service. This Sunday we organized a quorum of high priests. Guess how many?"

"I have no idea."

"Thirty-one enrolled."

"Very impressive, but I'm sure the evil one knows it too."

"We can't coward just because of unrighteous opposition."

"No, never. But all the same, you be safe." The two embraced. Titus loaded his wagon and departed with goods for Nauvoo. After dark a group of unexpected visitors surprised Morley at his home. Recognizing most of them as former members, he stepped outside to talk.

"Joe Smith is a fallen prophet!" someone shouted.

"You got three choices, Morley," someone else shouted.

"Wait a minute," another voice piped in. "Whereas Joseph Smith and seventeen other men have broken the law and order of society, you Mormons need to arrest them. Use your influence, Morley. Arm your congregation and march with us to Nauvoo."

"I hear only one choice," Isaac said. "You offered three."

Another voice shouted, "You can surrender all arms and remain neutral in Yelrome. Or you can move all the Mormon families out of here and into Nauvoo with the rest of them."

"You have until eight o'clock Monday morning to decide."

Isaac Morley walked back into the house and started writing a letter to President Joseph Smith: "Sir, believing it my duty to inform you of the proceedings of a wicked clan against the Saints in this place, I improve this opportunity." He penned every detail, including exact names of the visitors. "We have made up our minds that we shall not comply with any of these proposals, but stand in our own defense. We have no signature from the Government, or any official officer, to accept of such wicked proposals -- I have thought it my duty to inform you of the proceedings here. This from your humble servant, Isaac Morley."

The letter and its reply were delivered by Joseph S. Allen (Isaac's son-in-law).

"To Colonel Isaac Morley: Sir, In reply to yours of this date, you will take a special notice of the movements of the mob party that is stirring up strife and endeavoring to excite [incite]rebellion to the government and destroy the Saints, and cause all the troops of said Legion in your vicinity to be in readiness to act at a moment's warning: and if the mob shall fall upon the Saints by force of arms, defend them at every hazard unless prudence dictate the retreat of the troops to Nauvoo, in which case the mob will not disturb your women and children; and if the mob moves towards Nauvoo, either come before them or in their rear and be ready to cooperate with the main body of the Legion. Instruct the compa-

nies to keep cool, and let all things be done decently and in order. Give information by affidavit before the magistrate and special messengers to the Governor of what has occurred, and every illegal proceeding that shall be had on the subject, without delay. Also notify me of the same, and demand instruction and protection from the Governor.
Joseph Smith - Lieutenant General Nauvoo Legion"

*   *   *

"Pa's com'n and he ain't got good news," George said. He had been on day watch at the Mansion House with his father. Diantha rushed out to meet her husband at the gate. His look was sad, stressed and even more somber than before.

"Eunice, fetch your father a dip of water," she instructed as she reached down to remove his boots."

"No, Dear," he stopped her.

"But Titus, you're tired. You need a nap."

"Not now. Can't miss council meeting." He sipped the drink and was gone before she could ask any questions. Diantha busied herself making some corn bread to please him when he returned.

"George, what was all that about bad news?" she asked.

"Oh Ma, our enemies put out a newspaper and it is saying bad things about us. Pa read the first issue and he was really upset."

"Do you know if that's what the council meeting is about tonight?"

"Yeah. It is."

"I'd like to see a copy. Do you know where to get one?"

"No I don't Ma."

Alfred interrupted, "Don't think Pa would want you to read it, Ma."

The hour was late when Titus returned. Diantha was awake and alert, still darning socks by the fire when he arrived.

"You look worried," she said.

"I am worried," he admitted.

Diantha put down her mending and offered her full attention to the matter.

"We voted to destroy the "Nauvoo Expositor.""

"What is that?"

"A newspaper determined to slay the prophet and extin-

356

guish the Church."

She thought so. "Where did it come from?"

"Our enemies set up shop right here in Nauvoo. They have circulated the first – and it better be their last issue. Tomorrow the Council will demand the City Marshall demolish their press and shut down their office."

"Sounds like it's all under control," she tried to comfort.

"I fear it will just get worse . . . and worse . . . and worse."

She cut the corn bread and dobbed butter on it. At first he didn't seem in the mood to eat it, but at length he did.

Historical Background

". . . which caused Joseph Smith to announce that he would give five hundred dollars as a reward to anyone who brought sufficient proofs against [scoundrels] to enable him to put an end to their wickedness" (JonesD,73).

"They often attacked him cruelly, and threatened his life, so that he had to have a guard around his house at night" (JonesD, 73).

"Twelve days before Joseph and Hyrum were martyred in Carthage, Illinois, the Saints in Yelrome experienced renewed persecution from the mob. Several men called upon Elder Morley at his home and gave him a choice between three alternatives." Actual letters are here quoted. (MorleyRH, 88-90; YoungB1, June 15, 1844).

"Isaac Morley informed the Prophet that representatives of the mob had given the Saints at his settlement until Monday to join them or give up their arms" (Barrett, 597).

"June 7, 1844, the Nauvoo City Council had declared the Nauvoo Expositor, a newspaper dedicated by these enemies to the destruction of Joseph Smith and the Church of Jesus Christ, a nuisance, and had ordered the city marshal to pie the type and destroy the office contents" (Widtsoe,317).

CHAPTER 61

Edward Tuttle walked his family to the Grove just east of the temple lot where Saints gathered for Sunday meetings. He was delighted to see the prophet there. Mary Ann, his daughter, was delighted to see Eunice Billings and Julia Smith there. The three friends sat on the grass together. Martha Ann, and Caroline, his older daughters, were much more dignified. They sat beside their mother.

"What a beautiful day this is," Diantha commented to Catherine as she and Titus positioned themselves on the other side.

"Tis a lovely day," Catherine agreed.

Just then Joseph Smith stood to face the congregation.

"My dear Brothers and Sisters, with soberness I ask you this day if you choose to sit and hear the discourse I wish to deliver or would you rather now return to the safety of your homes?"

Titus jumped to his feet. Edward and others joined him with voices merging together.

"We will tarry! We will tarry!"

The Prophet smiled and silenced the crowd to thank them. "You are some of the grandest people to walk this earth . . . and Nauvoo the Beautiful, our Lord's chosen city, is one of the finest anywhere on earth." He continued to deliver a sermon that would never be forgotten, not by Titus, not by Edward, not by anyone else who listened to it. Even the young ones would remember it always.

*   *   *

"Joe Smith is opposed to freedom of the press!"

What a barefaced lie, and yet it was proclaimed throughout the countryside to a people who deemed such news as a serious crime. Disgruntled opponents, still fuming at the loss of their printing press determined even more to rid the earth of this church and its so-called prophet. Yes, the mayor of Nauvoo, as directed by city council, had issued the order. Nauvoo's chief sheriff and forty policemen removed the printing press from its "Nauvoo Expositor" office and demolished it in the street.

"Thanks for taking the night watch for me," Brother Rock-well said.

"Sure," Titus said. "Brother Tuttle will be standing in too. Didn't bring the boys this time."

"Glad you didn't. Best they don't hear the disgusting threats that bellow through the night air around Smith's home."

"Sorry the Smith children have to hear them."

"Yeah." Porter Rockwell was tough and fearless, but in his own way, no one could have loved the Prophet more than he did. "Ain't decent. Ain't justified," he mumbled to himself.

"What's that?" Titus asked.

"Oh, it just ain't right the way those scoundrels abuse the Prophet!"

The new guards nodded in agreement.

"Be alert. You never know what they will do." He started off.

"Guess we ought to situate ourselves on opposite sides of the house. Do you agree?"

"Sounds wise to me."

"Think you can stay awake?" Billings said with a yawn.

"Think so."

"Maybe we should have a prayer together."

"Oh yes. That would be good."

Titus asked the newer convert to be voice of the prayer. Edward Tuttle prayed with a pure, humble heart.

"Thanks Ed. Now we'll be guarded as we guard."

The two concealed themselves in shadows on either side of the house. Moonlight made it easy to see. All was calm and quiet. Billings leaned on his gun and must have fallen asleep because he didn't hear them come.

The mob was large, wild and on horseback. He stood in the shadow trying to get his bearings and trying to count heads of the crowd. Talk about fowl, abusive language. Their threats were dark and evil. It sickened him that any human being could stoop so low, but worst of all was the way they addressed Joseph. Titus stood calculating his next move, but before he could take it Smith's door opened and Joseph stepped outside.

"Brethren, Brethren," he beckoned. With gentleness he tried to reason. "Come now, leave all evil behind you," he urged them.

"You broke the law, Joe Smith."

"You don't believe in freedom of the press."

"You burned down our office."

Titus was confused by the accusations. Yes, the printing press was destroyed, but there was no fire. He and Edward moved toward the Prophet, one on each side, with their guns on the mob. Horses trampled the grassy yard, and one incompetent rider let his horse flatten a section of the new white fence. All the ruthless threats made it difficult to hear commotion up the street. Joseph tried again and again to reason, but he never threatened back.

Edward, the jolly, kind baker, found himself too terrified to shoot a man. How could two guns save the Prophet from so many? Again he prayed; this time in his heart. *"Oh God, help us know what to do."*

More horses thundered down the street. *We are already out numbered. We haven't a chance,* Titus thought. Still the young Prophet was tranquil. In all earnest he was trying to save souls!

A large steed jumped the fence and halted between Joseph and the mob.

"You men should be arrested!" It was Porter and he was furious.

"On what grounds, Mister?" a smart aleck asked.

"For destroying your own property and blaming the innocent."

"Like you can prove that."

"Yes we can. Caught your men in the act . . . and they have been arrested."

"Stupid fools," the leader said more to himself. "Can't they do anything right?"

"What they did was really wrong and what you are doing is wrong too. GET OUT of here. Don't you ever come back or we will press charges!"

Slowly the mob dispersed. Rockwell's posse gathered around the Prophet.

"Never so glad to see you," Titus admitted.

"Just hope this puts an end to it all," Porter said, though in his heart he knew it would not.

Historical Background

"Julia Smith was a constant companion of mine" (Snow8,3). Both Eunice Billings (3 January) and Mary Ann Tuttle (5 June) were born in 1830.

"He [Joseph] asked them whether they would sit in a ring and hear a discourse he wished to deliver to them or whether they would return to their homes" (Cox,13).

"The "Nauvoo Expositor," a paper established by apostates, created considerable trouble for the Mormons. Its destruction marked the beginning of mobbery in Nauvoo, June 10, 1844" (Hale, 4; Smith6, 432-550; Snow, 4).

"This made the organized enemies of Joseph more furious, and set fire to their purposes. Despite all this, he did not threaten back, but reasoned gently against them, urging them to leave their evil ways" (JonesD, 73).

"They were caught in their trickery that night, that is the ones of the faction left there for the purpose trying to set fire to the building themselves. . . their deceit came to light through the police finding the fire in time and extinguishing it before it managed to burn the office, and others" (JonesD, 74).

Chapter 62

"Please Father, everyone is going."

Edward Tuttle slid another batch of bread into the big brick oven without acknowledging his daughter's request.

"The Prophet and all Legion members will be there in uniform!" Mary Ann said with excitement. Her father said nothing. "Eunice says Brother Billings will be on the stand, holding the flag," his daughter persisted. "Oh please, Father. Eunice is leaving right now!"

"Well, run along and catch her," Edward said. He turned around to discover three other sets of beautiful eyes staring him down. One pair belonged to Catherine. "You want to go too?" he asked.

"Oh yes, Edward. All of us should go."

"Well, I can't leave the oven now." Edward Tuttle was a softy, especially where his wife was concerned. "Go ahead and I will follow," he said.

Catherine and her daughters needed no persuasion. They hurried down the street and found themselves on the outskirts of a large crowd of Saints.

"I wonder where the boys are," Martha Ann said.

"You can be sure they are in the thick of it all," Catherine said. Of course she was right, but her youngest daughter was in the thick of it even more. Eunice navigated her friends to the corner of the bowery where her mother waited.

Captain Titus Billings stood on the platform holding the American flag. Hyrum stood beside him. Lieutenant General Joseph Smith Junior stepped forward to address the Nauvoo Legion and the citizens of Nauvoo.

Soldiers stood at attention. Some of their leaders were on horseback. People were everywhere: men in hats, ladies in bonnets, babies in arms, so many people, and yet the crowd hushed as the Prophet began to speak.

"The enemy will not be satisfied with shedding my blood, but will thirst for the blood of every man whose heart burns with testimony of the fulness of the gospel," he warned them. "I am innocent of the charges against me."

He is so young and wholesome and holy. How could anyone

doubt his goodness? Catherine thought to herself. She and every other resident of Nauvoo knew full well of a dark effort to make an example of him by cutting him down. She strained to hear every word he spoke.

"I challenge you to stand by me to the death in sustaining your liberties and privileges."

The crowd roared their agreement.

"It is well," he said. "If you had not done it, I would have gone out there (pointing to the west) and would have raised up a mightier people." Joseph drew his sword and pointed it toward heaven. "I call God and angels to witness that I have unsheathed my sword with a firm and unalterable determination that this people shall have their legal rights, and be protected from mob violence, or my blood shall be spilt upon the ground like water, and my body consigned to the silent tomb. While I live, I will never tamely submit to the dominion of cursed mobocracy. I would welcome death rather than submit to this oppression.

"I do not regard my own life. I am ready to be offered a sacrifice for this people; for what can our enemies do? Only kill the body, and their power is then at an end. Stand firm, my friends; never flinch. Do not seek to save your lives, for he that is afraid to die for the truth, will lose eternal life. Hold out to the end, and we shall be resurrected and become like gods, and reign in celestial kingdoms, principalities, and eternal dominions, while this cursed mob will sink to hell.

"God has tried you. You are a good people; therefore I love you with all my heart. Greater love hath no man than that he should lay down his life for his friends. You have stood by me in the hour of trouble, and I am willing to sacrifice my life for your preservation. I go like a lamb to the slaughter."

Catherine's heart and head were full to bursting as she made her way home.

"Oh, Edward. Did you hear it?"

"I did indeed," he said, slicing a golden loaf of new bread.

Catherine took a crust and sat down with it. Together their tongues conversed what their eyes had just beheld and what their ears had just heard.

Historical Background

They were determined to make a public example of Joseph Smith by cutting

364

him down" (Barrett, 587).

"My father was by Joseph when he made his last speech. He was on the stand with Joseph Smith--I think he held the flag--during the last speech Joseph made in Nauvoo when he said he was going like a lamb to the slaughter. I [Eunice] was also there" (Bennett, 558) referring to "the great shadow which seemed even then to hover over his life and foreshadow his impending doom" (Snow4, 3). "I was at the meeting when the Prophet told the Saints he was going like a lamb to the slaughter, and I remember it distinctly" (Snow2). "I go like a lamb to the slaughter" (D&C 135:4; Gibbons, 20, 23, 24; Millennial Star, XXIV, 333).

Last Public Address of Lieutenant-General Joseph Smith Jr.

Drawing by John Hafen.

(Courtesy Billings Family.)

I grew up loving this picture because they said Great-Grandpa Titus Billings is depicted in it. Many believed he is sitting because of the widow's peak on the forehead (like Titus) and others insisted he was standing by Hyrum Smith, holding the flag. Then, while deep in research for this book we found a statement written by his daughter, Eunice stating: "My father was with Joseph when he

365

made his last speech. He was on the stand with Joseph Smith – I think he held the flag – during the last speech Joseph made in Nauvoo; when he said he was going like a lamb to the slaughter. I was there also." Later, when I interviewed my great aunt, Lillian Billings Brady, she said: "According to my father (Alonzo Billings) my grandfather (Titus Billings) is standing backside in the painting." She also stated: "Titus Billings was a body guard for the prophet."

"Joseph Smith raised the sword. Titus Billings, his bodyguard and father of Emily Billings Stringham was holding the flag," (Russell, 2).

Words spoken by Joseph Smith at his last public address are quoted in this chapter (Barrett, 598-599).

Words of Lieutenant-General Joseph Smith Jr. delivered 23 June 1844: "I wish to render you thanks as soldiers under my command and as your General. You have done faithfully your duty in guarding this beautiful city, and in preserving the lives of all the people as well as mine in a special manner. I have seen you on duty without shoes or comfortable clothing and if I had the means to buy, or if I could obtain those necessary things for you I would gladly do it. However I cannot mortgage any of my property to get even one dollar. But I will say this: You will forever be named the Nauvoo Legion and I have had the honor of being your General. You shall be called the first Elders of the Church and your mission will be to the nations of the earth. You will gather many people into the vastness of the Rocky Mountains, which will be the center for the gathering of our people, and you will be faithful because you have been true. There will be many that come in under your ministry, but because of their much learning they will seek for high positions and seek to raise themselves in eminence above you. But you soldiers of the Nauvoo Legion will walk in low places unnoticed: and you will know all that transpires in their midst. And those that are your friends will be my friend[s] and this I will promise to you my brethren of the Legion, that I will come again to lead you forth. But now I will go to prepare a place for you so that where I am you shall be with me. I thank you for your service and duty done. You are now dismissed to take care of your wives, children and homes."

CHAPTER 63

"Seven thousand armed men are ready to launch attack on Nauvoo!"

News spread through the city like wildfire, even though a lawless mob had cut off all mail services making it difficult for Joseph to request protection, explain false accusations, or send word to the apostles who were out campaigning for his presidential election. He feared for his brother's life and pled with Hyrum to take his family to Cincinnati on the next steamboat.

"I can't leave you!" Hyrum said, walking away to perform a marriage ceremony for Lovina, his daughter, to wed Lorin Walker that night.

Orders came from the Governor for the two Smith boys to face charges made against them in Carthage, Illinois. Neither of them had slept in two nights, but they had to leave Nauvoo by 6:00 am to meet the Governor's deadline. They started out early with a promise of safety and a fair trial for crimes they did not commit. A multitude gathered at the Mansion House, hoping to dissuade them. Emma wept at the prophet's side, and his sons clung desperately to his clothing. His mother pleaded with him, "My son, my son, can you leave me without promising to return? Some forty times I have seen you dragged from me, but never before without saying you would return. What say you now, my son?"

Joseph knew the "trial" was a plot to destroy him. He lifted his hands to silence the crowd. "If I do not go there, the result will be the destruction of this city and its inhabitants; and I cannot think of my dear brothers and sisters, and their children, suffering the Missouri scenes again in Nauvoo; no, your brother Joseph prefers to die for his brothers and sisters, for I am ready to die for them. My work is finished; the Lord has listened to my prayers, and has promised me that I should have rest from such cruelties before long, so then do not prevent me with your tears from going to bliss."

Tears washed over everyone anyway. For several weeks rainy skies had made it seemed like the heavens were crying upon them too. This day June skies were pleasant, but the people were not.

At a slow pace Joseph rode his horse up the street, soaking

in everything he loved about Nauvoo. Hyrum, who seemed dazed with sadness, rode beside him.

Diantha and Eunice were standing in the yard when the solemn procession passed by their home. Hyrum kept his face down. Joseph looked directly at Sister Billings, bowed his head, and tipped his hat to her. *He is a living Prophet. All will be well,* she thought to herself as she strained to watch until he was out of sight.

A few hours later Titus rushed into the house.

"George! Alfred! Come help me put the cannon in our wagon."

"No! Titus what is it?"

"We've been ordered to surrender all arms to the state militia!"

"We can't, Pa," Alfred interrupted.

"No choice, son. A company of mounted militia stopped us on the way to Carthage with an order from Governor Ford demanding all state arms from the Nauvoo Legion. The Prophet came back to help us do it. For our safety we must turn over everything we have."

"Safety? What good is a Legion with no weapons?" George asked.

"I know, but we must obey. Come, give me a hand."

Eunice stood by her mother watching as her brothers loaded the cannon assigned to her father into the wagon. "Well, they're not getting the cartridges I made!" she said with spunk.

*   *   *

Personal threats from a mob committee were delivered to Saints residing in Yelrome. Under oath Father Morley wrote a declaration before acting Justice of the Peace, Aaron Johnson, reporting that the saints had been "compelled to leave their homes in Yelrome and flee to Nauvoo for protection. We are afraid to stay on account of the mob threatening to utterly exterminate us!"

Because they did not comply to mobocratic wishes, Morley and his neighbors suffered horrid persecution. They gathered proof that Illinois mobs were supported (and sometime driven) by Missouri mobs, but the Governor and even the President of the United States did not answer earnest pleas for help.

$$* \qquad * \qquad *$$

Joseph borrowed a map of the West from John Fremont and told Legion members, "Now I will show you the travels of this people." Tracing a course across Iowa, he pointed to a spot and said, "Here you will come to the Great Salt Lake Valley."

Someone nearby asked, "Where will you be at the time?"

"I shall never go there," he answered.

All arms were collected by six o'clock p.m. and Joseph's party started again for Carthage.

"Boys," he said to the few remaining, "take care of yourselves. I am going like a lamb to the slaughter, but I am calm as a summer's morning. I have a conscience void of offense toward God and toward all men. If they take my life I shall die an innocent man, and my blood shall cry from the ground for vengeance, and it shall be said of me 'He was murdered in cold blood!'"

Joseph looked longingly at his farm as they passed it on the road to Carthage. He turned around repeatedly to look again. Someone made a remark about needless delays and the lateness of the hour.

"If you had such a farm and knew that you would never see it again, would you not want to take a good look at it for the last time?" he asked.

They arrived in Carthage just before midnight.

Historical Background

"All mails were cut off from Nauvoo by the mob" (Barrett, 599).

"Within a few days he was boasting that they had seven thousand armed men ready to attack on Nauvoo!" (JonesD,75).

"On Thursday, June 20 1844, Joseph urged his brother Hyrum to take his family on the next steamboat and to go Cincinnati. But Hyrum replied, 'Joseph, I can't leave you'" (Barrett,599). "Hyrum performed the marriage ceremony of his daughter Lovina to Lorin Walker" (CES 276). "To keep the governor's deadline they would have to leave very early --a 6:00 a.m. departure at the latest" (Madsen,118).

"On the last day which he spent in Nauvoo, he passed our house with his brother, Hyrum, both riding" (Snow8, 6).

"When the Prophet Joseph and his brother Hyrum were taken to Carthage, it was a time of great anxiety for the Saints" (Gardner,1).

369

"It had rained for weeks, but this morning was sunny and beautiful" (CES, 277).

"At about ten o'clock the group arrived at a farm four miles west of Carthage, where they met a company of sixty mounted Illinois militia. Captain Dunn presented an order from Governor Ford for all the state arms in possession of the Nauvoo Legion to be surrendered" (CES, 277).

CHAPTER 64

Never ever could she remember a longer day in her life! Diantha didn't like the quiet eeriness in the air, especially after dogs -- every dog in Nauvoo it seemed -- had howled all night long. Maybe I'm just tired from a sleepless night. She tried to sew, but lacked motivation or concentration, so she fell to her knees and prayed for the Prophet and for Hyrum and for all of the saints and for all of Nauvoo. Still on her knees she heard Titus calling from the road. Before she could go to him, he exploded into the room.

"The Prophet is dead! Hyrum is dead! They have been murdered in cold blood!"

"How can it be possible?" Diantha said. "Will the Lord allow anything like that?"

She reeled from the shock of it and fainted. Titus and Eunice worked to revive her.

A thick heaviness seemed as a blanket over all of the saints, making it difficult to think and impossible to function. Diantha rallied, but she needed answers. She counseled with her husband, who turned to the scriptures. Together they cited numerous, significant examples of other prophets throughout the history of time who had been required to seal their testimonies with their blood.

"The God of Israel has taken His Prophet home unto his rest" Titus said.

"I must go to Emma." Diantha said. "She will need my help."

"Take the horse," Titus said. "You have no time or strength to walk." He boosted his wife sidesaddle and hoisted his daughter behind her.

"Pray for me to be helpful," she pleaded.

"I will, dear. Let the Lord guide you."

*   *   *

Sleep evaded the Mansion House all night as well. Weeping and grieving continued nonstop. The way Joseph left without reassuring his mother had caused her great alarm. Emma was certain the Lord would protect her prophet husband as always. Still there was a sharp pain in the pit of her and she could not relieve it. Even the skies were dark and miserable when the letter came. It, signed by Brother Willard Richards and Brother John Taylor, was dated "Carthage Jail, 8:05 o'clock p.m., June 27th 1844" and it read:

"Joseph and Hyrum are dead. Taylor wounded, not very badly. [He added that part for the sake of his family.] I am well. Our guard was forced, as we believe, by a band of Missourians from 100-200. The job was done in an instant, and the party fled towards Nauvoo instantly. This is as I believe it. The citizens here are afraid of the Mormons attacking them. I promised them not!"

*   *   *

Diantha tied her horse and was standing in the open doorway when a messenger approached.

"I have a letter for Sister Smith," he announced.

"Thank you kind sir. I will give it to her."

Diantha found Sister Emmy in anguish.

"This letter just came – to you from Carthage."

"Oh Sister Billings, I can't do another letter. Will you please open it for a me?"

With care and shaking fingers Diantha opened the letter and began to read:

"The Governor has just arrived; says all things shall be inquired into, and all right measures taken. I say to all the citizens of Nauvoo, my brethren, be still and know that God reigns. Don't rush out of the city – don't rush to Carthage – stay at home, and be prepared for an attack from Missouri mobbers. The Governor will render every assistance possible. The people of the county are greatly excited, and fear the Mormons will come and take vengeance. I have pledged my word that Mormons will stay at home .. . and no violence will be their part . . ."

"It's signed by Willard Richards, John Taylor, and Samuel H. Smith."

"Samuel!" Sister Lucy gasped. "Then Sam is in Carthage. He is alive!"

Word was out. The martyred bodies were coming home to Nauvoo in hay wagons. Thousands of saints lined up and down Main Street awaiting their arrival. Edward's bakery was open, but not for business. Outside his family waited with other grieving onlookers stepping inside for occasional relief from the sun.

"Here they come," someone shouted. The swollen crowd grew silent. People holding hands lined both sides of the street. Heads were bowed in solemn reverence. Slow trotting horse hooves and weary wagon wheels passed by each block. Could it be true that a prophet and a patriarch, so alive yesterday, were now dead in wooden boxes on those wagons?

Mourners strained to see branches piled on top of each coffin. This was alarming to some, at least to Henry Tuttle who could see the wooden boxes beneath them.

"Father, why are they buried with tree parts when they already have boxes to hide them?"

"I'm sure the branches are to shade the caskets from the sun, "Edward said.

Willard Richards, Samuel Smith and eight guards delivered the sacred bodies to the Mansion House where they were prepared for burial. A family viewing was held at eventide. Eunice followed behind her mother who supported Sister Emmy by the arm in an effort to help her stand. Slowly they slipped down the hallway and passed through the large doors. The sight of the prophet and his patriarch brother stretched out before weeping wives now widowed, sobbing sons and daughters and suffering siblings was more horrifying than any fourteen-year-old eyes should ever behold. Eunice wanted to comfort her dear friend, Julia, but for a moment her body was numb to any command her brain sent to it. Just then Sister Lucy Mack Smith entered the room for the first time. The tiny woman fell to her knees and clasping her hands together cried out, "Oh God, why were my noble sons permitted to be martyred?" Through her own tears, Eunice witnessed this frail woman manage herself with unmatched dignity and pray out aloud, "Thy will, not mine, O Lord, be done."

The agonizing grief was more than Sister Emmy could endure. Her oldest son approached the first coffin to kiss his father. Pressing his cheek next to the lifeless one, he cried, "Oh, my father! My father!" Diantha summoned help to literally carry Sister Emmy back to her room.

A few hours later, Lucy called Diantha into her bedroom where Samuel Smith was curled up on her bed. He had jumped on a horse that dreadful day, and ridden with haste to the Carthage Jail where his brothers had been taken. An armed mob with faces

painted black, red and yellow had done their evil deed of shooting innocent men before he arrived. Joseph the Prophet had fallen
from an upper window to a spot near the well. Samuel was too late
to help; or was he? As a burly, boasting mobster stepped forward
to harm the prophet's dead body a bolt of lightning struck near
the well. Hearing Samuel's horse someone shouted, "They are
coming." The murderers fled in panic. A few of them, however,
realized that he was alone and when they discovered him to be of
the Smith family they tried to shoot him too. Samuel took a serious wound in the side and was chased at top speed for hours. He
returned to help load his brothers' caskets into different wagons.
Each was covered with bushes to shelter them from the heat of
the sun. Samuel and Brother Willard Richards drove the Prophet's
wagon. Mr. Hamilton (whom Brother Richards had convinced not
to leave town like most of the confused community) drove the
Patriarch's wagon.

Now Samuel's fatigue and the shock of such dreadful
happenings had drained him of all strength. He could not sit up.
"I think I am going to be really sick," he said. Diantha grabbed a
silver pot and placed it beside him. "Use this if you need it," she
said, then she went to work at once trying to prevent infection and
fever.

Two brothers; together in life, and now together in death,
were laid out in the Nauvoo Mansion House the next day, June
29, 1844. Black velvet covered each coffin. A square plate of glass
covered and protected their faces. Eunice sat quietly in the corner watching blood drip from their wounds into tubs underneath
them.

From 8:00 in the morning until 5:00 in the evening a constant stream of reverent onlookers entered through the west door
and left out of the north. All day Mother Smith paced the floor
wringing her hands and crying to the Lord for the strength and the
courage to endure her sorrow. A multitude of weeping friends filed
past the martyred remains paying their final respects.

Fearful of enemy threats to mutilate the blessed bodies,
family members exchanged them for sand bags and continued
with a public funeral sermon by Elder W. W. Phelps followed by a
public burial. The actual bodies were buried in secret under the
Nauvoo House where it was under construction.

Sorrowing saints congregated in the grove Sunday morning. Elder Sidney Rigdon presented his claim as successor to the

prophet. Brigham Young, Acting President of the Twelve Apostles, arrived from his mission in time for the afternoon session. He stood to speak.

"Our prophet is dead, but he left behind the keys of the kingdom," he said.

"Mother," Eunice whispered, "Brigham Young's voice sounds like he's really Joseph Smith!

"The same power and authority have been conferred upon each of the Twelve Apostles," he continued.

Martha Ann spoke softly to her sister, "Mary Ann, do you see what I think I see? Most onlookers witnessed it. The humble speaker took on the actual appearance of the Prophet Joseph Smith.

"This Church will not be left without a leader and a guide."

The mantel had fallen upon Brigham Young rather than Sidney Rigdon. President Young spoke with power even to the convincing of the Saints of his calling and assuring them that they had nothing to fear, as all would yet be well if they would hearken to the word of God and the counsel of His servants and keep His commandments.

It was impossible for Samuel to recover. Only thirty-three days behind his brothers, he also entered into the glory of God. "He is a martyr too, you know, " Titus told his sobbing mother.

"Now Father Smith has five of our six sons on his side of the veil," Lucy said. Only William was among the living. He was on a mission back East.

Historical Background

"My son, my son," she [Lucy Smith] said, "can you leave me without promising to return?" (Gibbons, 22).

"My father came home and told mother that the Prophet and his brother had been murdered, whereupon my mother exclaimed, 'How can it be possible? Will the Lord allow anything like that?' And immediately she sank back in her chair and fainted" (Snow3, 5).

"When the bodies were brought into the city, thousands of the Saints were gathered on Main Street to witness the sad and mournful arrival of our martyred Prophet and Patriarch"(Gardner, 1). "The evening the Prophet Joseph and Hyrum were brought home from Carthage I will never forget, everybody stood out in the street holding hands and bowed their heads in solm [sic] reverence, everyone was so filled with sorrow it seemed their hearts would break. I felt like the world was coming to an end" (Robinson).

"The bodies were brought into Nauvoo the morning after the murder and placed in the Nauvoo mansion to be viewed by hundreds of people. The Latter-Day Saints in the city were full of melancholy, and sadness prevailed over the place. Tears were shed on every hand, and deep mourning shrouded the city" (Snow 5).

"The bodies of Joseph and Hyrum were taken to Joseph's mansion and were exhibited to all who wished to see them" (Cox,14).

[Diantha (who did doctoring for the Smiths) and then fourteen years old Eunice, were with Emma and her Mother-in-law, Lucy, when the two bodies were brought to the house.] "I shall never forget the impression made upon me when the Prophet's Mother saw the bodies of her dead sons. Falling on her knees and clasping her hands she cried out, 'O God why were my noble sons permitted to be martyred?' Then controlling herself with a mighty effort, she said, 'Thy will, not mine, O Lord, be done'" (Snow4, text to slide G-71).

"My mother and I went to the Mansion House and saw them both after they were laid out. I DO KNOW THAT HE WAS AN INSPIRED PROPHET OF THE LIVING GOD. I am leaving this testimony to my children and to the world and expect to meet it in the great beyond. [Signed] Eunice Billings Warner Snow" (Snow2).

A multitude of weeping Saints viewed the bodies as they lay in state at the Nauvoo Mansion House next morning. "It can well be imagined the sorrow and darkness that seemed to prevail the whole place" (Gardner, 1).

"I saw the two brothers after they were laid out in the Nauvoo Mansion. The scene I saw then and there I shall never forget as long as I live. The blood dripping from their wounds into the tubs under them. Oh! Their poor aged mother wringing her hands and crying to the Lord to give her the strength and courage to bear her sorrow. That scene I cannot describe. My eyes are blind with tears when I attempt to write about that day, but I will say it was surely a time of mourning with the Saints at Nauvoo at that time" (Hale, 11). [This quote was written by Titus' daughter, Eunice, in her later life. She was eighty years old, 1910, but still the pain burned within her.]

"The bodies were buried in the basement of the Nauvoo House, which was under construction. The next fall Emma had them relocated to the south side of the homestead. A grandson, Frederick M. Smith, son of Joseph Smith III, reinterred the graves closer to the homestead, January of 1928, placing Emma on Joseph's right and Hyrum on his left" (Smith11).

"Emma was carried back to her room . . .Her oldest son approached the corpse and dropped to his knees, and laying his cheek against his father's and kissing him, exclaimed, "Oh, my father!" (SmithLM, 324-325).

"Soon after this, Samuel said, 'Mother, I have had a dreadful distress in my side ever since I was chased by the mob, and I think I have received some injury which is going to make me sick" (SmithLM, 325).

Martha Ann Tuttle wrote in her journal: "I well remember the Sunday morning when sorrowing Saints were gathered together in the little grove where they were accustomed to meet. Sidney Rigdon presented his claim as successor to the Prophet Joseph making quite an impression upon the people, but Brigham Young, President of the Apostles, had just arrived in Nauvoo from his mission in time to attend the afternoon meeting and in a voice not unlike the Prophet he told the people that all though the Prophet was dead, Joseph had left behind the keys of the Kingdom and had conferred the same power and authority that he himself possessed, upon the Twelve Apostles and the Church would not be left without a leader and a guide. Truly the mantle of Joseph had fallen upon Brigham and he spoke with power even to the convincing of the Saints assuring them that they had nothing to fear, as all would yet be well if they would harken to the word of God and the counsel of his servants and keep his command-ments" (Gardner, 2).

[Note: Martha Ann Tuttle wrote in large letters: BRIGHAM YOUNG AS OUR LEADER OF THE CHURCH and began numbering the pages of her journal with "1" again. Her entry is significant to this history because she is the sister of Titus' future second wife, Mary Ann Tuttle.]

"Brigham Young stood up and spoke with the power and voice of Joseph. He surely had the Prophet Joseph's mantle on him. There seemed to be no doubt of Brigham Young being the one to lead the Saints at that time" [Testimony of Eunice Billings] (Hale, 11).

"The meeting was in the bowery. Then President Brigham Young began to speak. I jumped up to look and see if it was not Brother Joseph for surely it was his voice and gestures. Every Latter-day Saint could easily see upon whom the priesthood descended, for Brigham Young held the keys" (Testimony of Drusilla Dorris Hendricks: Carter3, V20: 263).

CHAPTER 65

"I can't believe it," Diantha said. "They are supposed to appear in court on charges of killing Joseph and Hyrum!

"They are," her husband agreed.

"They have been proven guilty of deliberate murder!"

"They have."

"And you stand there telling me they have been released on bail?"

"For less than twenty pounds!"

"That's wrong, Titus!"

"Very wrong. And the worst part is all of those unsettled rioters are ready to follow their lead again."

His words were validated in no time.

"The mob will hide stolen goods in Yelrome, then get a search warrant and bring authorities out so they can accuse us of stealing the items they have planted," stated Isaac Morley.

Titus was appalled at the words his brother-in-law spoke. "I can't believe anyone would stoop so low. Have you reported this to the brethren?"

"Yes, President Young thinks we should move into Nauvoo," Isaac said with a worrisome weariness in his voice.

"Maybe you should," Titus said, perceptive of President Morley's love for the beautiful, friendly little settlement that bore his name (well, his name spelled backwards). Yelrome and other small Mormon communities in the vicinity were threatened at every turn. Now, more than ever, saints wanted to be endowed with the eternal blessings that come to man, only from the House of the Lord. Every tenth day Isaac drove a crew of good workers in from Yelrome, sometimes even more often. Titus worked on the temple several days a week.

"You know," he added. If you move into Nauvoo we'll get this temple done faster." Isaac smiled. Titus spoke with seriousness. "I really hope you do, soon."

Edward Tuttle belonged to one of the ten Seventies Quorums organized and active in Nauvoo. Diantha was visiting Catherine when he came home from a Seventies meeting. Tall excite-

379

ment radiated from his short frame.

"We are building a place of our own," he said. The ladies did not understand what he meant, but that did not stop him. "With donated land, donated labor, and donated materials, how could we lose?"

"Lose what?" Catherine asked.

"Not lose, gain. We are building a Seventies Hall."

"Oh."

"Wonderful." The women did not know one was needed.

"It will be a two-story, brick building. We will use it as a preparatory school for new missionaries." Edward's excited pleasure delighted his wife. "Guess where we're building it?"

"I have no idea. Where?" Catherine said raising her shoulders and shaking her head.

"On the corner of Parley and Bain."

"Beside the Blacksmith Shop?"

"Yes!"

"Why, that's just around the corner from us."

"It certainly is." The man was energized and the ladies relished his pleasure.

"I will spread the news to Titus" Diantha said.

"Thanks. We will probably allow him to donate labor." Edward laughed.

"You probably will." Diantha laughed back.

Edward devoted every available moment to working on the new Hall. Titus made time to help out, but continued his dedicated focus on the temple effort.

"Did you hear what happened to our charter?" Edward asked.

"Afraid so. It's illegal by law, you know." Titus said.

"I wondered about that. Seems wrong the senate could up and abolish it like that."

"They can't, but they did. If the truth were known, I think we have some mob-leading enemies sitting on the senate."

"Wouldn't surprise me. Don't Mormons have enemies everywhere?"

"Why are you wearing your uniform?" Eunice asked her brother. "Pa said the whole Legion was dissolved when they repealed our Nauvoo Charter."

380

"Yes, it was. All legal protection was dissolved as well," George Pierce said. "That means we can't use our police force."

"Legally they don't exist anymore," Alfred Nelson said as he walked into the conversation, also wearing his Nauvoo Legion uniform. "Our community has been forced to surrender all arms," he added.

"What are we going to do?" asked their mother.

"Major-General Charles C. Rich is calling us together as a priesthood military organization."

"Priesthood military organization?" Eunice echoed. "That sounds impressive."

"Yes, it does," Diantha agreed.

"Brother Young asked every man from sixteen to a hundred to enlist. We're meeting tonight to see what we can do." Both soldiers kissed their mother and started for the door.

"You do look handsome in your uniforms," she told them.

Ward bishops called and set apart deacons to patrol city streets and stand guard around the temple, protecting it and its workers. Henry Tuttle's bishop selected him to serve in the "Whistling Brigade."

"What is that?" Sister Tuttle asked him. "We walk around the city, you know, just wearing plain clothes, but we keep our eyes open for strangers and any suspicious character. When we find one like that, we get as close as we can and start whistling and whittling with our knives flipping close to the intruder and his face, until it scares him out of town."

"Now I've heard everything," she said.

"It works, Ma." Henry seemed to stand taller since joining the brigade and walked like one with authority even though a lame leg still followed him.

Historical Background

"... although Thomas Sharp and others were proven guilty of 'deliberate murder,' yet they were released on bail of less than twenty pounds!" (JonesD, 94). "Murderers of the Prophet Joseph and Hyrum were given bail at $1,000 each, but when [some of the wealthiest] Brethren from Nauvoo posted bail in Carthage for Mormon sympathizer Sheriff Minor Deming $10,000 were required" (Smith7, 439).

"For a short time after June 27, 1844, when the martyrdom occurred, the persecution in Nauvoo ceased, partly because the mobsters felt they had succeeded in overthrowing the Church by killing its prophet. By early 1845, however the mob leaders heard reports of the progress on the Nauvoo Temple, could see that the Saints were united and therefore, recognized that the Church had not been destroyed" (MorleyRH, 92).

"Members of the mob secretly hid stolen goods in the vicinity of Morley's Settlement and then, having obtained a search warrant, returned to accuse several of the elders living there with theft" (MorleyRH, 93).

It was illegal by law, but the Senate abolished the Nauvoo City Charter anyway. Later it was proven that "some members of the Senate were leaders of the mob" (JonesD, 94).

"In Nauvoo Brigham Young asked every man from the ages of sixteen to one hundred to be enlisted into companies under General Rich for the protection of the Saints" (BarrettIJ, 642).

In spite of much sickness and death, "we had to gird our arms at night and guard the temple, our streets, landings and our authorities to keep the enemy from destroying our brethren and our buildings and works and thus break us up or frustrate the work and establishment of this place" (Shurtliff, 1).

"The city was kept relatively free of unwanted characters by an organized group of young men and boys known as the "whistling and whittling brigade" (CES, 300; Moody).

CHAPTER 66

By December the Seventies' Hall was ready for a dedication. A five-day Seventies Conference began the day after Christmas. President Brigham Young officially dedicated the building, and a dedication service was repeated each day of the conference to accommodate as many as possible. Both the Nauvoo Band and the Nauvoo Choir performed. Several speakers gave inspiring talks. Seventy Edward Tuttle was one of them. For a quiet baker, such was a huge undertaking. Catherine was delighted with him and his wonderful sermon. (She knew better than anyone else how long and hard he had worked on it.) Refreshments were served to the many attendees making it a Christmas jubilee to be remembered.

"Fruits, nuts and desserts of every kind for each family – wow, you seventies really know how do to things," Titus said. Edward grinned. Eating was one of his priorities.

*   *   *

New converts continued to come, and Nauvoo continued to grow. Thousands of members were in attendance when President Brigham Young stood to conduct his first General Conference (April 1845).

"It is proposed that our beautiful city, Nauvoo, be re-named."

Backs stiffened and faces scowled in wonderment as "why do that" questions popped up in many minds. The new Prophet continued with his new proposal.

"All those in favor of calling Nauvoo the 'City of Joseph' please show by the raise of hands."

Excited sighs rush through the crowd. No hand rose higher than Brother Titus Billings' did. The vote was unanimous.

Everyone knew President Young was hunted by the mob. All of the brethren were in constant peril. Nonetheless, the new prophet continued with boldness.

"Springtime is here already. We covenanted to labor on the temple until it was finished; but we have not done it. Let us plow and sow and build. One plowshare will do more to drive off the mob than two guns! If the brethren will go to work now, there will be no lack of provisions. It will be made up to you in your crops," he promised.

What more could you ask than that? Titus thought to himself with a silent pledge to double his temple time.

Their leader went on: "A select group of high priests will now be called to go abroad in all the congressional districts of the United States to preside over the branches of the church," he announced.

Titus Billings pressed a hand over his shirt pocket to feel the old folded note resting inside. He carried the reminder everywhere, especially to general church meetings where mission assignments were called out from the pulpit.

"It is not the Lord's design that these go and tarry six months, then return. Rather they are to go with their families and build a permanent settlement."

Diantha felt her heart come to a halt for a moment. Titus was a high priest. It would mean leaving her home by the temple.

"These good families will tarry in their new places until the temple is built. Then they will come back to get their endowments, afterward returning to their families to build up stakes as large as this one."

The list of names began. Titus Billings was called. He pulled the note from his pocket; and without taking a look, handed it to his wife. She was well aware of his pre-pledged commitment. They would go.

Even though church leaders found it necessary to go into hiding they met with the saints early on the morn of May 24th (1845) to lay the temple capstone. Samuel D. Billings played drum in William Pitt's Nauvoo Brass Band which formed a circle near the southeast corner and began to play. Mortar was spread by William Player and the last stone was positioned so President Young could step on it, and then tap it secure with a heavy wooden hammer. The band played "Capstone March" (written for the occasion by Brother Pitt) and President Young spoke.

"The last stone is now laid upon the temple and I pray the Almighty in the name of Jesus to defend us in this place and sustain us until the temple is finished and we have all got our endowments."

Everyone cheered the "Hosanna Shout." Standing on the new capstone on top of the temple wall, Brother John Kay sang

"The Capstone Song" by W.W. Phelps.

*   *   *

"I wish Isaac would give up Yelrome and move into Nauvoo for safety," a worried Titus told his wife. Word was that barns and property were being burned to ashes. After what happened to his haystack and homestead in Independence Titus harbored an unsettling apprehensiveness. He knew nothing of the letter dispatched to the outlying areas of Bear Creek, Green Plains, as well as Yelrome.

"Bring your families and your grain into Nauvoo."

The letter suggested Saints sell out and gather in for safety. Soon news came that homes were being burned without warning. Women and children who were sick in their beds were dragged into the fields and left there. Belongings and animals were taken at will.

On September 11th Billings and Tuttle left Nauvoo with a group of other men and wagons to haul Yelromites to safety. "Look at that smoke. I hope we are not too late. " Something was burning. "Look, there is another one."

"Hurry men, Morley Town is on fire!"

Isaac's wagon was loaded with furniture when they pulled up. He and all of his family stood weeping in the yard. His house, his cooper shop, his granary, everything was on fire. Titus jumped out. "Is everyone accounted for?"

"Yes, I think so," said Lucy. Titus counted the children for himself. "Thank goodness for that," he said.

"We were coming," Isaac said. His sad eyes made him look a hundred years older. "They accosted me and demanded that I order my family into the dooryard at once. Then they proceeded to stuff our house with straw and lit it. You can see the rest." Titus shook his head.

"Come on, Brother. Let us get you out of here."

Edward offered to steer Morley's wagon. Isaac climbed up with Titus, and the others crawled into the back. "The place was so beautiful and peaceful and thriving. "30,000 bushels of corn up in smoke! How could fellow countrymen . . ."

For ten days Sheriff Backenstos pleaded for help from the state militia. They refused to assist. By the time he discovered that militiamen were the culprits, they had burned more than two hundred homes, taken many lives, and caused much destruction and loss.

The Sheriff summoned Nauvoo's militia and led them to battle. Many rioters fled across the Mississippi River and into Missouri. Sheriff Backenstos himself sought safety with the saints. Peace was restored for a short time, but troublemakers were set on doing a thorough job. Mormons signed a treaty to leave Nauvoo the next spring. Morley found a house to rent until then.

"Good morning, Mr. Secretary," Titus said to Isaac. Now that you are one of the secretaries to the collector of revenues we expect to see lots of revenue for the temple project. Maybe we'll be able to get it done faster."

"I hear mission calls for high priests to settle in new areas and build up the church abroad have been cancelled," Isaac said.

"Titus, does that mean you?" Diantha asked.

"Yes, all missions are cancelled," he said with disappointment, carrying some sheets of paper and black ink to the table.

"What are you up to now?" Diantha asked with keen curiosity.

"Think I will write a letter to Ester and William in Springfield. Ought to let someone in my family know where I am." His older sister was the only one he knew who still lived in Massachusetts, and probably the only one who was the least bit respectful of his religious beliefs. Springfield was way south of their hometown, Greenfield, but he had made that journey once while on his mission. "Don't think she was fired up about the Book of Mormon I gave her. At least she was gracious."

"I wonder if she ever read it."

"Doubt it. Said she would, sometime."

"You never know."

"Think she'd write us if she found the light."

"Your letter is a good idea."

"At least she will know we are going West; whatever, wherever that means." Neither of them had a clue. Nonetheless, the Lord was taking them there. Nothing else really mattered.

Titus penned two-and-a-half pages of his feelings and testimony.

"Would you like to add a note, Diantha?"

"Yes, I believe I would." She sat down and filled the remaining page.

Ebenezer stuck his hands into his pockets and kicked at the ground.

"You're certain that is what you want to do?" his father asked.

"It is, Pa. It's where I belong."

"You better go tell your Ma." Titus said.

"Yes," Ebenezer paused. "Maybe you better come with me."

"Maybe you better take an arm load of squash and pump-kins with you."

"Think I need a peace offering?"

"You never know."

They both walked into the house bearing plants from the garden. Diantha sat in her rocking chair with the sound of knitting needles clicking at a steady pace.

"What is all this?" she asked. The two men looked at each other. "Something to keep you busy," Titus said.

"What are you knitting, Mother?"

"Funny you ask. These are to be socks for you, Ebenezer. Aren't you due for a pair?"

"I am always due for socks," he laughed, remembering the holey pair he wore on his feet.

"How soon will those socks be finished?" Titus asked.

"They are almost -- why do you ask?"

"He might be needing them soon," Titus said.

Diantha looked bemused. "How's that?" she asked.

"Better ask Ebenezer," Titus said.

She turned to her son, "What is it, Ebe?"

"I am leaving, Ma. Going up the Mississippi."

Historical Background

"The remembrance of this glorious jubilee [Dedication of the Seventies Hall] will never be erased from the minds of those who were participants. Each family was provided with fruits, nuts, and every dessert that the heart could wish. Well might it be said that the Saints enjoyed a 'feast of fat things'" (Lee, Dec 1844).

"Early in September Isaac Morley was selected first counselor of the Nauvoo Stake" (MorleyRH, 98).

During Conference 8 October 1844: "President Brigham Young then appeared and proceeded to select men from the High Priest's Quorum to go abroad in all the congressional districts of the United States, to preside over the branches of the Church as follows: . . . Titus Billings . . ." (Journal History19).

"Titus served as President of the Lima Branch until the house burning that drove them into Nauvoo" (Cannon/Cook, 249). [Note: Titus served his mission in 1842. Many accounts of the Billings Family while living in Nauvoo, make it likely that they moved there before the 1845 burnings. Eunice recorded that they moved to Nauvoo before 1844.]

"Brigham Young renamed Nauvoo 'The City of Joseph,' a name approved by the Saints at the April general conference" (CES, 300).

"President Young counseled the Saints to plow, sow, and build. One plowshare, he said, would do more to drive off the mob than two guns" (BarrettIJ, 637).

"Sensing the need for the Saints to emigrate, President Brigham Young inspired his people with a renewed desire to hasten the completion of the temple. On May 24, 1845, the temple capstone was laid and the upper two stories completed" (MorleyRH, 99).

"Prophet Young was hunted by the mob and had to keep guard at all times. Under his direction, Saints continued work on the Temple up at the Square" (Gardner, 2).

"On September 11, 1845, eight homes were burned to the ground" (Smith7, 44). "The Twelve met in council; it was agreed to dispatch a messenger to the Lima Branch and counsel the brethren to propose to sell their property to the mob and bring their families and grain here" (Smith7, 440). "In the fall of 1845, they [Morleys]were driven by the mob from their homes and their settlement burned. They sought refuge in Nauvoo" (Snow8,5; Billings/Shaw/Hale,5). [Note: This validates author's belief that Titus Billings moved his family into Nauvoo long before Isaac Morley did. (Quote is by Eunice, Titus' daughter.)

"Under the leadership of Col. Williams about 800 or 900 gathered . . . burning barns and the Saints' property . . . burning houses over the heads of some women and children who were ill in their beds at the time, without giving them any warning, but dragging them to the fields and leaving them there. They plundered houses of anything they wanted, driving animals with them. . . . militia refused to turn out at the request of the sheriff [Backenstos] to disperse the scoundrels until he realized that the militia had caused a loss of many thousands of dollars and had taken many precious lives as well" (JonesD, 94).

"The labor and toil of years was ruthlessly destroyed; houses and haystacks were burned, cattle taken possession of and driven away. Helpless old people, women and children robbed of shelter and the necessities of life. Oh! The inhumanity of our countrymen, for they left ruin and desolation where had been happy, prosperous homes" (Esplin, 8).

"While in the process of loading the family furniture into wagons, Father Morley

388

was accosted by mobsters and told to order his family into the dooryard. Straw was then taken inside, stuffed into the corners of the house and lit on fire. The Morley house, the cooper shop and granary were completely destroyed by the fire" (Morley, 93).

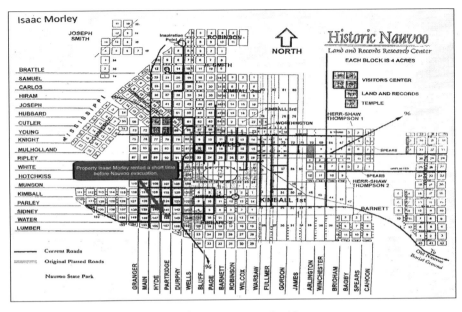

Isaac Morley Property in Nauvoo.

Morleys came to Nauvoo much later, after Yelrome was burned out. They lived at Partridge and Sidney Street. Perhaps they took Samuel's place.

(Courtesy Historic Nauvoo Land and Records Research Center.)

"Father Morley rented a house in Nauvoo, 25 miles north of Yelrome, and moved his family there with the body of the saints; He was called to be "the collector of revenues for the erection of the temple" (Esplin, 8). "Isaac Morley was sealed by Brigham Young to four other wives: Hanna Sibley, Nancy Back, Eleanor Mills, and Harriet Cox in Nauvoo" (Cox, 21; Cox1,2; Morley 104, 111).

The following are exact excerpts (and spelling) from a Nauvoo letter written on October 27, 1845 to Ester and William Pynchon in Springfield, Mass. [Ester is Titus' oldest sister. He visited her during his mission.] Titus Billings wrote one-and-one-half pages. Diantha Morley Billings finished a half page (BillingsT&D).

[by Titus] "Dear brother and sister and all inquiring friends. I seat myself at my table at this time to write a few lines that you may know we are alive and that we are enjoying tolerable health at present. We have ben called to part with our youngest child since I saw you. Titus, he was ten year old when he died.

I do not know what will be of interest to you the most for news although I will venture to write something of the news of the day and the scenes that are transacted in Illinoice although my heart sickens at the thought and if I should attempt to give you a history of the persecution of the Latter-day Saints in this place it would take more that a rime [ream] of paper to do it justice, suffice it to say many have sealed their testimony with their blood. Joseph Smith and Hyrum Smith and others. Joseph Smith has been a man of affliction ever since he was called of God to go and take the plates from the earth he has ben taken with writs thirty times and all on account of his religion for there never was an action sustained against him for I have ben acquainted with him since the fall of 1830. His life and time has been for the good of mankind and so has his brother Hyrum that while they gave themselves up and the Governor and people had promised to protect them they rushed into the jail and murdered the two Smiths and left for dead John Taylor on the floor but has since recovered and many of the latter-day saints have ben pursecuted unto death. They have been driven from their homes in Missouri and their bones are bleeching in the Prairies for nothing but their religion. But I know it is very natural for you to ask why all this [?], why all this persecution, why do not the other [?] of the day have the trouble that the Latter-ay Saints do[?] I can answer the question - just for a moment go back and look at the Apostolic church at Jerusalem and see what they had to pass through.

"We have a beautiful city here. The census was taken this fall. There are eleven thousand inhabitants in this city, 15,000 in the county in other countys and in all about 30,000 are expecting to remove in the spring in a body for California, Oregon, or some other good place. I often think of my relations in Mass. with gratitude for they were kind to me there and I know that many of them would have ben glad to have me anything but a Mormon, although that is a nickname given to us. And I sincerely believe that we shall be the means of saving many of our friends when the judgement of God are spread abroad over the Earth. The times here are good. Crops of all kinds are first rate. Wheat 40 cents. Corn 12 ct.

"I expect to send this by Mr. Shurtliff of Russell. I expect you will be troubled to read this letter I write so seldom. I shall leave a space for Diantha. And shall close by bidding you adieu. This from your brother T. Billings."

[by Diantha] "William and Ester Pynchion, as Titus has left a little space for me I will [?] it although he has written the news, yet I will testify to the truth of what he has written, yet it may appear like an idle story, but it is the truth of heaven and you will sooner or later have to acknowledge it and you cannot say in a coming day we have not warn[ed] you of these things. We have got to leave our homes to a distant land we know not where. We have just got plesantly situated. We have a farm, house and good well of water and other conviences so as to make life plesant, but it is not more than the Sts. [saints] has to suffer anciently and I hope we shall bear it patiently. I must draw to a close hoping you may never regrert truth whereas it is made plain to you. From you friend and sister, Diantha Billings."

[Note: In 1998 a Robert F. Lucas advertised a Mormon Nauvoo Letter written in 1845 by Titus and Diantha Billings over the Internet. He was asking $4,500.00 for the letter addressed to William and Ester Pynchon of Springfield, Massachusetts.

Later efforts to reach him were unsuccessful. Today, June 20, 2003, contact was made with his widow. He became seriously ill and she auctioned his business of antique books and letters to pay for medication. She has no idea what happened to the letter.

Years later my brother, Lewis K. Billings, viewed the letter mentioned on display by a keeper of sacred records, Brent Ashworth of Provo, Utah and was allowed to photograph it. A copy of the 1845 hand-written treasure is now preserved in the LDS Church History Library, Salt Lake City, Utah.]

Original 1845 Mormon Nauvoo Letters

Written by Titus and Diantha (Morley) Billings before leaving Nauvoo
to Ester Billings Pynchon (Titus' sister).

(Courtesy Intellectual Reserve. LDS Church History Library.)
See Appendix for complete documents.

So, Grandpa Titus did not get his brick house in Nauvoo. Diantha's letter states that they lived in a "framed" house. Anyway, "he was a stone mason" (Carter).

Ebenezer Billings, about twenty-six years of age, "left Nauvoo on the Mississippi River and was never heard of again" (Bennion1).

CHAPTER 67

Diantha awoke early from a short night's rest with worry and wonderment in her heart. *How are we supposed to complete the temple and do all our ordinances and build wagons and pack everything and disappear from our beloved homes in an instant? It is not fair!* She must have spoken her thoughts out loud because her husband responded to them.

"What's not fair, Di?"

"Oh Titus, I didn't mean for you to hear me complain." She was embarrassed a bit, but her concerns were his as well. The would-be travelers were right on schedule until persecutors dishonored their springtime arrangement and demanded Nauvoo become Mormonless NOW . . . in the dead of winter!

"How will our sons ever find us if they try?" Diantha asked her husband.

"How will we all get our ordinances done before we have to leave the temple?" Titus worried back.

"So much to do and they are pushing us out sooner than agreed. It's not fair, Titus!"

"Nothing is fair when it comes to Mormon treatment" Titus admitted with disgust. Then, as if pulling up faith from deep within his soul he added: "Remember though, nothing is impossible to our God!"

Together they walked to prayer meeting.

*   *   *

Elder Isaac Morley, first counselor to Nauvoo Stake President John Smith, quickened his pace. An urgent excitement warmed his soul to the point he was unaware of November's chill. He and other selected church leaders stepped into the temple structure and started climbing to the attic story which was finished and ready for sacred use. Rooms would be dedicated and used as completed. About noon the brethren sang together: "Come All Ye Saints of Zion." President Young dedicated both the finished portion of the temple and the lives of the people to God. Afterward John Taylor sang "A Poor Wayfaring Many of Grief" – his last song for Prophet Joseph sung in the Carthage Jail. Heber C. Kimball prayed "that the Lord would hear and answer the prayers of his servant Brigham, and break off the yoke of our enemies . . . " Holy ordinances were prepared.

"We must accelerate our preparations to go West." President Young announced with firmness. "Follow this approved list of essentials for each family. Only the required food, clothing and necessities should be prepared. Sale or exchange your valuables for horses and cattle.

"We, the First Presidency and the Council of the Twelve Apostles have dedicated the attic floor of the temple so ordinance work can begin."

Excited gasps rushed through the congregation. Brother Billings put his arm around Sister Billings and whispered something in her ear. She closed her eyes and gave a concurring nod. They would be endowed by God and sealed to each other for this life and the next. What else really mattered? Their obedient hearts were empowered by the grace of God and they would serve Him no matter how, no matter where. They, like many other couples, left more devout than they came.

Fifteen minutes after doors opened on the second day Lucy and Isaac Morley entered to be endowed. President Brigham Young and Elder Heber C. Kimball officiated ordinances until 3:00 a.m. the next morning. After a little breakfast, they returned to administer many more. Other apostles were trained in the work.

Titus and Diantha entered with the second company on the third day, December 13, 1845. "I cannot tell you how wonderful it was," Diantha said. "Now I feel like I could do anything the Lord requires."

"I am so happy for you," Catherine told her.

"When do you go, Catherine?"

"Our appointment is scheduled for January 3rd. I can hardly wait."

"Mother, you will not believe this . . ." Mary Ann Tuttle had never interrupted anyone before, but she burst into the room with an excitement she could not contain. "Guess when Eunice is getting her endowments?" Before anyone could respond she blurted: "January 3rd."

"Wonderful. The same day your father and I --."

"Oh, but Mother, that will be her sixteenth birthday. Can you think of a better gift?"

Temple ordinance work took first priority and was performed in shifts around the clock, halting only when clothing needed to be laundered. Over a thousand endowments were completed by the end of the December. January 22, 1846 Isaac was sealed also to Hannah Blakeslee Finch, Abigail Leonora Snow, Harriet Lucinda Cox, Hanna Sibley, Nancy Anne Back, Eleanor Mills, and Betsy B. Pinkham before President Brigham Young announced that the Nauvoo Temple would soon be closed. Diantha was sealed to Titus on January 3, 1846. George Pierce Billings was endowed January 21st.

Two hundred and ninety five worthy persons thronged the holy house February 3, 1846 seeking sacred ordinances. Joseph Lamoni, Hannah's son was sealed to her and Isaac that busy day. Five-hundred and twelve showed up the next morning; and another six hundred ordinances were completed the following day. Saints were receiving the glory and intelligence of the Almighty God. He was arming them with his divine power. Angels were in place to look over them and their righteous efforts. Blessings, promises, and privileges of the celestial kingdom were in their grasp! By sharing the knowledge of truth to all the world they would come forth in the first resurrection as saviors on Mt. Zion. The Lord was with them and his words would be fulfilled.

Nauvoo homes turned into workshops as families prepared themselves for a long journey westward. Often green timber was boiled in salt water or dried in kilns to hasten its preparation for use. Saints made wheel spokes, rims and wagon boxes.

"No better wagons were ever constructed," Isaac boasted.

"Plenty cold out there," Titus said entering the house at the same time Eunice walked into the room.

"Mother, will you fix my bow? Oh Father, how do I look?"

"Mighty fine," he said. Someone knocked at the door.

"Good evening, girls" Diantha said. "You certainly do look lovely tonight."

"Thank you, Sister Billings," said Martha Ann.

"Thank you," said Mary Ann.

"Are you bringing Mother to the last big dance?" Eunice asked her Father.

She referred to the farewell Nauvoo dance being held in the spacious hall of the temple. Sacred canvases had been removed. The Billings and Whitney Brother's Band was scheduled to furnish the dance music, so her brothers needed to leave early.

"There is room for a hundred dancers. You better come."

"We leave tomorrow," Titus said.

"Orson Whitney and I are leading the promenade," Eunice said with excitement.

"That would be worth seeing," Diantha said.

"Father, he likes me."

"Everyone likes you."

"I mean really, he likes me, Pa. I think he will ask me to marry him soon."

"He is too young," her father insisted. "You should agree to being sealed to Elder Heber C. Kimball like your cousin [Therissa Morley]."

"Oh Father. He is too old."

"He is a wonderful man."

"I know he is, very wonderful, but he is old enough to be my father.

"Older than your father," George piped into the conversation. Martha Ann smiled at him.

"I still say Whitney is too young."

Alfred walked in with an armload of musical instruments. "Better get these over there. Come on George, let's go." The girls left with them.

"I think it is wonderful teenagers can be happy and have good fun even in these trying times," Diantha said. "Maybe we should go over for a while, Titus. The boys are playing, our daughter is promenading, and we won't be in the City of Joseph much longer."

"That's the problem. We must prepare to leave."

"Please." He went to wash up and put on a clean shirt.

Historical Background

"President Young opened the services of the day with [a] dedication prayer presenting the temple thus far completed as a monument of the Saints liberality [sic], fidelity and faith. Concluding – 'Lord we dedicate this house and ourselves unto thee'" (Knight, 103).

"It was not long before it was so far finished that they could begin giving endowments. The work in the Temple was pushed through in a short time" (Hale, 11).

On Sunday, November 30, 1845, Brigham Young and the Council of the Twelve

Apostles dedicated the attic story of the temple for temple work. The endowment was given to more than 17,000 Saints before the Church had to abandon the temple. At times ordinance work was done continuously for 24 hours a day. They would only stop to wash and clean the temple clothes (Smith7, 560-567).

"Rooms in the temple were dedicated as they were completed so that ordinance work could begin as early as possible" (CES, 302). "The attic rooms were dedicated by President Brigham Young on Sunday, November, 30, 1845. Seven of the apostles including Heber C. Kimball, Willard Richards, Parley P. Pratt, John Taylor, Orson Hyde, George A. Smith and Amasa Lyman were present on this occasion" (MorleyRH, 101).

"Complete listing of Isaac Morley Family: Lucy Gunn, mother of seven children: Philena, Lucy Diantha, Editha Ann, Calista, Cordelia, Theresa Arathusa, and Isaac Junior; Hannah Blakeslee Finch mother of three children: Joseph Lamoni, Simeon Thomas, and Mary Leonora; and wives with no children: Abigail Leonora Snow, Harriet Lucinda Cox, Hanna Sibley, Nancy Anne Back, Eleanor Mills and Betsy B. Pinkham" (MorleyRH, Appx. D).

Isaac and Lucy Gunn Morley received their endowments in the second session held in the Nauvoo Temple (December 1845). Abigail Leonora Snow and Hannah Blakeslee Finch were also sealed to Isaac on January 14, 1846. A week later, January 22, 1846, four more wives, Hanna Sibley, Nancy Back, Eleanor Mills, and Harriet Cox, were sealed to him. Betsy B. Pinkham was also sealed to Isaac on January 27, 1846.

In a short period of time a great amount of temple work was completed in the Nauvoo Temple. Sessions were held through the night. "Those 5,000 endowments gave power to the Church to cross the plains" (Blaine Yorgason quote from Heritage Stake Self-Reliance Fair, September 14, 1996). "The House of the Lord was thronged all day, the anxiety being so great to receive [the endowment]" (Smith7).

Isaac and Lucy Morley were endowed December 11, 1845.

Diantha and Titus were endowed December 13, 1845.

Edward and Catherine Tuttle were endowed January 3, 1846.

"Isaac Morley's youngest daughter, Therissa, was sealed to Heber C. Kimball eight days after Cordelia was sealed to the Prophet, on February 3, 1846. [Cordelia married Frederic Walter Cox for time only.] Brother Morley and his wife, Lucy, were adopted and sealed to President Brigham Young's family the day before the Saints were driven from Nauvoo" (MorleyRH, 105).

"The saints for a few weeks from the 10th of December 1845 to the 7th of February 1846 were permitted to enjoy the blessings of the temple before they took up their forced march from Nauvoo" (Esplin, 9).

Titus and Diantha were endowed in the Nauvoo Temple, second company,

December 13, 1845 (Cook 102; NauvooT). [Note: A family group sheet lists the endowment date, for both of them as December 11, 1845 (Bennion1).] Eunice was endowed there on her sixteenth birthday, January 3, 1846 (Hale, 11, 18). She was baptized in the temple font and worked at the temple the last two weeks work was done there.

"Diantha was sealed to Titus in the Nauvoo Temple January 30, 1846" (Cook, 102).

Edward and Catherine Tuttle were endowed in the Nauvoo Temple on January 3, 1846 (NauvooT).

Mary Ann Tuttle was endowed along with her sister, Martha Ann on February 6, 1846 (Archibald, 2; Black, 86).

Saints prepared to leave their beloved city, Nauvoo the Beautiful. "Hasty preparations were made; working night and day to get their outfits, food, clothing and other necessary things ready for the journey" (Esplin, 9). "In each home all work was concentrated on making wagons. Wheel-spokes, rims, everything that was needed was assigned to families to do at night or anytime they had a spare moment. It is recorded that never did a people make better wagons than those produced by the 'Mormons' that winter in Nauvoo" (Billings/Shaw/Hale, 27). "Green timber was prepared for spokes and fellos, some kiln-dried and some boiled in salt and water" (Cottam/Malouf, 8).

Knowing that the temple would be destroyed "they removed all the canvas that last night we stayed there. That left a very large hall. There was room enough for one hundred people to dance at one time. We surely had a fine time" (Hale, 11). Eunice "with Orson Whitney as my partner, led the dance" (Snow, 4). "Before we left Nauvoo, we were sure that Temple would be destroyed after we were gone, so that night before we had a dance in the Temple. Orson Whitney and I led the grand march at the dance" (Hale, 5). "This would have been between 29 December 1845 and 9 January 1846 when Brigham Young stopped all dancing, etc. in the temple" (Hale, 15; Smith7, 557-8).

"About five thousand Saints had the inexpressible joy and gratification to meet for the first time in the House of the Lord in the City of Joseph [Nauvoo]. From the mites and tithing millions had raised up to the glory of God as a temple where the children of the last kingdom could come to gather and praise the Lord" (Knight, 102).

CHAPTER 68

"All who can get out, go!"

Large groups of Mormons were no longer allowed anywhere in the United States. Wild and violent mobs took it upon themselves to enforce outrageous demands. Sensible preparation time was forbidden. "Mormon families must go now!" even in the dead of winter.

"Church leaders are in greatest danger," Edward Tuttle told his wife in a whisper. "I caught wind of their plan to slip out of here first thing in the morning." Catherine wore a serious look on her face, but said nothing. Edward gave her a full-tooth grin as if to ease her troubled heart, then added, "How would you like to help the cause of Zion?"

"Of course, but how?"

"We are bakers, aren't we?"

Her eyes seemed to question him, though her lips did not.

"Well, let's do what bakers do best."

She still looked stupefied. He laughed. "You fetch your daughters and I'll send John to invite Henry. We are going to have the best secret family cracker baking party ever held and it will probably take us all night."

Tuttle's ovens blazed for hours as his family measured, kneaded, rolled, cut, pricked and baked life saving morsels in secret. John welcomed an excuse to stay up late. Mary Ann, though typically quiet most of the night, threw arms around her father's waist when at last he pulled the final batch of crackers from the oven.

"Don't you think, Father, that baking crackers for the brethren is like giving to the Lord?"

Tears renewed Ed's tired, bloodshot eyes.

"Oh yes, my sweet daughter, I do."

Catherine supervised packaging. Generous, cloth-wrapped bundles rested on the table as shades of early sunrise spread over them with reverence. Six members of the Edward Tuttle family gathered them up and started for the river where they would have the honor of delivering their gifts of love to Brigham Young and the other Apostles, even the Lord's anointed servants upon the earth.

Now they will have something to eat as they run for their lives!

*   *   *

Many saints felt a panicked concern after their leaders left Nauvoo. The plan to leave in companies at orderly intervals was abandoned because too many left too fast, wanting to travel with the brethren. Hosea Stout directed the Nauvoo Police to help families move their fully loaded wagons one-at-a-time across the Mississippi River. Charles Shumway was the first to go. A fleet of paddle-wheel-propelled flatbeds, lighters, skiffs, even rafts, crossed again and again at all hours of the day and all hours of the night.

The Titus Billings family waited in line behind Isaac Morley and all of his family, who waited behind the Vincent Shurtliff family for a turn to cross. Sam and Martha lingered with them while a miserable wind whipped around their legs and chilled their bones. They huddled about their wagons as a ferryboat glided them across the icy water. Titus staked a quick shelter for his family on the other side, but Diantha never used it. Midwife duties drove her up and down the riverbank where she helped deliver nine babies in the freezing night.

*   *   *

Smoke continued to puff out of Tuttle's bakery ovens. He was trying to finish his wagon, but lingering populace needed bread to eat. His horse died of distemper, and a barter arrangement for an ox team fell through.

"Maybe we will have to buy one of those stubborn Missouri mules," he told Catherine. "They are supposed to be very strong, sure-footed, and able to pull a steady wagon." She laughed. "Perhaps you should name one 'Joe Duncan.'"

"Fire, Fire. The temple is on fire!" John Wells shouted. Sure enough, at 3:30 in the afternoon of February 9, 1846 an overheated stovepipe that was drying clothing in the upper room, caught the roof on fire. Damage was mostly to the interior. Women carrying water, tried to put out the flames. A ten by six foot section of the north roof was burned. Edward ran to help with the clean up.

At precisely the same moment, trouble began on the river,

too. Thomas Grover's oxen and wagon were loaded onto a flat-boat and ready to move out when "a filthy, wicked man squirted some tobacco juice into the eyes" of one of the animals. Wildly it plunged overboard, breaking the wagon and pulling its yoked partner under water. The boat sunk. Men fought the water to safety, but both beasts were drowned. The broken wagon was pulled from the river. All possessions were damaged, many floating downstream.

Cold snow layered the ground nonstop for days. Then storm clouds changed their gift to chilling rain. Every day it rained without ceasing, deepening the muddy layer of ground where roads should have been. Teams were tied up double for strength to pull wagons free.

"I doubt there has ever been a body of people since the day of Enoch who have done so little complaining under such unpleasant and trying circumstances," President Young stated. His thermometer dropped to twelve degrees below zero on the next morning (February 24, 1846) and soon managed to hit twenty below.

Miraculously, the cold made an ice bridge, more than a mile wide, over the Mississippi River from Nauvoo to Montrose. Charles C. Rich was the first to cross. The frozen path lasted for several days allowing thousands of others to follow.

Historical Background

"Father helped the heads of the Church to get out[.] He baked crackers for them as he was a baker" (Gardner).

". . . plans were shattered by the Saints who panicked and did not want to be left behind after the Twelve had left" (CES 307).

"Crossing the river was superintended by the police, under the direction of Hosea Stout" (Smith7, 582).

"February 4, 1846, The Saints at Nauvoo commenced crossing the Mississippi river for the purpose of moving west. Charles Shumway was the first to cross the river" (Jensen Chronology, 1846).

"On February 4, 1846, Isaac Morley bundled his family into a wagon, crossed the Mississippi River, and started westward with many other members of the Nauvoo Stake" (MorleyRH, 105). "[We] crossed the Missouri River on a ferryboat constructed by skilled craftsmen" (MorleyRH, 110).

"Brigham Young and the Twelve Apostles crossed on February 15" (Cottam/Malouf, 1).

"Church members in large groups could not remain in Illinois or Missouri" (Cox, 13).

"Diantha was on midwife duty all night as nine of the families driven across the river ice welcomed new babies" (Bennion, 2; Cottam/Maloaf,12; Pyne, 2).

"The Titus Billings family left Nauvoo with Vincent Shurtliff, but it was too late to cross the plains that year" (Pyne, 4; Worsley, 1). Winter came upon them before reaching Council Bluffs or Winter Quarters.

"Monday, 9th [February 1846] At the office packing. At 3:30 the temple was seen on fire. Women carrying water" (Clayton Journal,1). "A fire, which broke out in the Nauvoo Temple, was put out before it did much damage" (Jenson Chronology, 1846).

"At the same time the temple roof caught fire, a flatboat began to sink when a filthy wicked man squirted some tobacco juice into the eyes of one of the oxen attached to Thomas Grover's wagon" (Smith7, 582).

"President Young was heard to declare that he doubted if there had ever been a body of people since the day of Enoch who had done so little complaining under such unpleasant and trying circumstances" (Esplin 9).

CROSSING IOWA, NEBRASKA, AND WYOMING: A TIME TO ENDURE

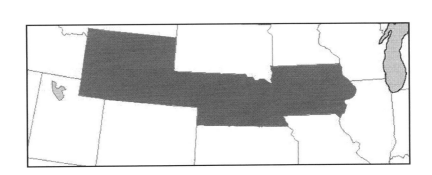

1846 - 1847

IOWA: *Montrose Crossing, Sugar Creek, Locust Creek, Garden Grove, Mt. Pisgah, Miller's Hollow (later Kanesville-Council Bluffs).*

NEBRASKA: *Ponca Settlement, Winter Quarters, Pawnee, Liberty Pole Camp, Chimney Rock, Scott's Bluff.*

WYOMING: *Fort Laramie, Warm Springs, Heber Springs, Independence Rock, Devil's Gate, Three Crossing, Ice Springs Slough, Fort Bridger, Needles.*

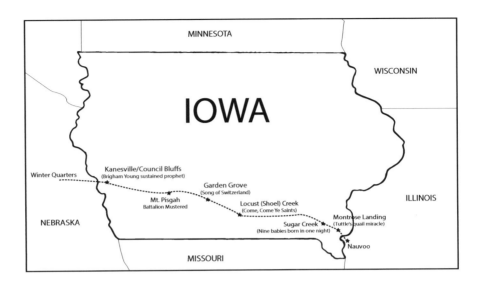

CHAPTER 69

"I wish the brethren to stop running to Nauvoo, hunting, fishing, roasting their shins, idling away their time," President Young said when he arrived at Sugar Creek. Some saints had been at the camp nine miles west of Nauvoo, for two weeks. Young was disappointed with their lack of industry. "Fix nose-baskets for [your] horses and save [your] corn, and fix comfortable places for [your] wives and children to ride, and never borrow without asking leave, and be sure and return what [you] borrowed, lest your brother be vexed with you. All dogs in camp should be killed if the owners [will] not tie them up."

About five hundred wagons and at least three thousand saints were encamped at Sugar Creek by the end of March. Each wagon was heavily loaded with sacks of flour and beans, books, casks of water, clothing, farm implements, rocking chairs, and featherbeds; but only half of them had adequate teams. Because many families were already low on food, the Mormon "share and share alike" principle went into effect at their very first camp.

The weather continued to be uncooperative for travelers. Many of them waited a week for safe conditions to cross the Des Moines River. A few nights later, they camped at Locust Creek.

"Congratulations Elder Clayton," Diantha said one evening in April. His band had just dismissed for the night. "We are so happy to hear of your new arrival. How is the mother?" Sister Clayton was named Diantha as well. She had been too heavy with child to leave Nauvoo; but as company clerk, her husband was required to keep a daily written record of the first company West.

"Our son is well, but Diantha is ill with ague and mumps."

"How dreadfully unfair," Diantha said. "Our prayers will be with you."

"Thank you, Sister Billings. I hope to send for her very soon."

Several friends must have followed Elder Clayton to his wagon because instruments and singing voices resonated for hours after dark.

"I think they are helping him celebrate, "Diantha said to Titus. "Why don't you join them?"

Titus was much too tired. "I'll just listen from here," he said. Sleep claimed him in no time. Diantha rested her body, but could not quiet her mind. She prayed for her sick friend, Diantha Clayton. She prayed for her friend Catherine Tuttle who, to her knowledge, had not yet left Nauvoo either. She prayed for her widowed friend, Emmy Smith, who did not wish to leave Nauvoo. She prayed for her children and parents; the list went on . . .

Music from Brother Clayton's tent continued to fill the night air. One particular melody caught Diantha's attention. She had no idea that the beautiful, unfamiliar song, freshly composed in a new father's wagon, would soon become her favorite. She and other saints would come to remember it as "All is Well."

Diantha was cooking over an open fire at Garden Grove when Titus brought news about the temple. "They are having the private dedication in Nauvoo tomorrow" [April 30, 1846].

"Oh?" Diantha was interested. "Who are they?"

"Wilford Woodruff, Orson Hyde, and twenty other priesthood leaders." Diantha kept stirring the watered stew.

"We have to leave first thing in the morning if you want to attend the public dedication [May 1, 1846]."

"We will be ready," she said with excitement.

"Alfred has agreed to stay and guard the camp."

"Bless him."

At dawn Diantha kissed her son good-bye and left with his

father, George and Eunice to sing at the temple dedication with the choir.

Brother Billings escorted his wife and daughter past the crowded lines waiting for admittance and entered the holy temple without delay. George, with his fine singing voice, was already inside. Choir members had assigned seats for both sessions. Again they were divided into four groups and positioned in each corner of the new temple for effect.

"Don't you feel a powerful unity at this glorious gathering," Diantha whispered. Eunice looked out at the crowd and began to feel nervous about singing for so many. She expressed her concern. "We didn't come to sing for the people, Eunice. We came to sing for the Lord."

Somehow that seemed even more overwhelming to one so young, at least until she spotted her friends. She and Julia Smith sat with Mary Ann Tuttle between them, as they had promised, and sang, "Ho, Ho, for the Temple's Completed, The Lord Hath a Place for His Head." An inspired dedicatory prayer was offered, but the words Eunice heard most clearly were: "Lord, we dedicate this house and ourselves unto thee." The service was glorious.

"I do wish you were coming with us, Sister Emmy."

"Now Sister Billings, you know that Mother Smith and I must remain here where our two Josephs are laid to rest. You go on with your Titus to a wonderful life in the West and we will stay here, where we belong."

Diantha did not know what to say. Sister Emmy corrected the silence between them. "You leave many remembrances in your path, Diantha. I will never forget you and all you have done for me."

"Oh Sister Emmy, it is I who have been blessed." The two sisters embraced with tenderness.

"Diantha, be sure to stop by the house before you go. I have some cookies for Titus."

"Your famous almond cookies?"

"Most certainly," she said with a joyful face.

"We have a marvelous plan," Eunice told her parents following the dedication.

"I don't know about that," her Father said, shaking his head at the two sixteen-year-old schemers.

"Please," she went on. "If it is all right with the Tuttles, please let it be all right with you." After long discussions and deliberate planning, the girls feared they had no hope of persuading their parents to meet with their wishes. Only then did the surprised agreement come. Mary Ann climbed onto the wagon with Eunice. She was going west with them. Her parents would follow soon and join her in camp.

Historical Background

Brigham Young quote at Sugar Creek, "I wish the brethren to stop running to Nauvoo" (Smith7, 585).

William Adriel Benoni Clayton was born in Nauvoo on Wednesday, April 13, 1846. Word reached his father, William Clayton at Locust (also Shoal Creek) on the 15th when he wrote the now famous hymn, "All is Well" or "Come, Come, Ye Saints" (Clayton,19; Cottam/Malouf, 13-14).

Brother and Sister Billings, George and Eunice returned from Garden Grove to sing in the Nauvoo Choir at the dedication. They sang, "Ho, Ho, for the Temple's Completed, The Lord Hath a Place for His Head" at the temple dedication [May1-3, 1846] (Bennett, 558; BillingsLB, 1; Hale, 3; Snow, 4).

"President Young opened the services of the day with [a] dedication prayer presenting the temple thus far completed as a monument of the Saints liberality [sic], fidelity and faith. Concluding - "Lord we dedicate this house and ourselves unto thee" (Knight, 103).

"On account of persecution the temple was privately dedicated on April 30, 1846, but public ceremonies in connection with the dedication were held the following day, May 1, 1846" (Jensen1, 563).

CHAPTER 70

"Word has it that Brother Brigham compared us here at Garden Grove to a hive of bees," Titus announced as he walked his wife to the evening campfire.

"Well, I would say that's a nice compliment. I know I'm proud of my worker bee," Diantha said with a teasing squeeze of his arm.

Titus lifted her hand from his elbow and pulled her closer to him. A grin outlined his teeth in the fading light as he replied, "Think I got all the honey!"

It was true. Garden Grove, situated half way between Nauvoo (144 miles away) and the Missouri River (122 miles the other way), was the ideal spot for an Iowa Territory way-station. Three hundred acres were cleared for a permanent encampment. Under President Young's direction jobs were delegated to three-hundred and fifty-nine men. Most were designated to fashion fencing rails. Ten men started erecting fences. Titus and forty-seven others commenced building houses. A dozen men began digging wells. Ten went to work constructing bridges and the rest cleared land for plowing and planting.

As always, campfire talk was about "the place" where they were going. No one really knew where that was, not even President Young. Everyone did, however, know their new prophet had seen it in vision and they loved hearing him describe it as a most desirable destination.

"It is a wonderful valley so far away from civilization that mobs will never find us," Brother Isaac Morley said.

"And spacious," Titus Billings added. "I heard him say it is large enough to be a gathering place for all of the saints."

Everyone wanted to speculate. Why, even the Prophet Joseph envisioned it and taught of a great work to go forth in the Rocky Mountains. When Swiss saints shared their national anthem as a new theme song for migrating seekers of "the place," Diantha and Titus were quick to learn it. "For the strength of the hills we bless thee, our God, our father's God," was sung nearly every night.

Startling news reached camp before the next day passed.
"The United States is at war with Mexico!"
"Not our problem. We've been expelled from the country."
"No more Mormons to fight with so now they have to pick on the Mexicans."

President Young did not say much about the war, but continued as planned to lead an advanced party onward. His selected group pulled out of Garden Grove the next day.

Parley P. Pratt had gone ahead to secure another location. After many days of searching for a spot with a water supply, he came across a beautiful setting of timber forests and open groves by a branch of the Grand River.
"This place looks like a garden," he said. "It reminds me of the biblical place on the east mountain ridge at the north end of the Dead Sea called, "Mount Pisgah." He chose to call this spot, 172 miles from Nauvoo, by the same name.
The Billings' wagon passed through the new Mt. Pisgah during a wet and muddy season. Persistent rain made everything wet all of the time. The cold air became more unbearable because they could find no dry fuel for a fire. Sometimes they spread branches and limbs on the ground to prevent tents and beds from slipping away in a mudslide.
Titus Billings drove his wagon over a bridge at the same time Hosea Stout started across in the opposite direction.
"Hello there," Billings said when they started to pass.
"Hello, Brother Billings," Stout said. He looked weary and sounded unhappy.
"Are you doing well?" Titus asked.
"No, not the best," was the reply. Both teams stopped.
"What is the trouble?" Titus inquired.
"You won't want to ask that," Hosea said. A line of wagons on their way to the Bluffs now waited behind Titus.
"How can we help you?" he wanted to know.
Brother Stout was overwhelmed with bad luck, the worst of all being the death of his small son, Hosea Junior, but he spoke of other things.
"Got three wagons but no other driver. My daughter drove a one-horse wagon with a borrowed harness for a short distance, but we had to give the harness back. The big bolt broke on our

other wagon, which sits in a bog of mud. We are nearly out of food, and I feel terrible," he said with a hoarse voice and a cough.

"Well Brother, we are at your service." Titus called out to Henry Nebeker who was not a member, but a most generous, kind man. Henry loaned Hosea a chain and went to assist him. Billings led his group to the shelter of a small, welcoming grove that looked out of place on the flat, expansive prairie. They stopped to fix up and clean up, making camp for the Sabbath. Soon Stout and Nebeker caught up with them.

Diantha shared her pot with Mr. Nebeker and the Stout family.

"We should make a song," Eunice said. "We will share and share alike, for we like and like to share . . ." she started singing to Mary Ann as though it were a famous, well-known song and she a trained music teacher. Both girls sang the ditty as they wandered around camp and collected many smiles in the process. Mary Ann missed her family. Eunice tried to keep her friend busy and happy.

Isaac Junior walked along beside the lead oxen with a willow whip to tease and guide the beast forward. "Wonder why I always have to be on your left side," he asked the strong, steady-stepping animal. "The science of oxteamology" his father had called it. "Well, I'm just glad I don't have to pull that overloaded wagon like you do." It was true; there was a simple science behind choosing oxen to pull a ten-foot wagon a long distance. These preferred animals did not require complicated harnesses, they didn't spook easily and they were easy to keep.

"Guess my job is much easier than yours."

"What did you say?" Lucy called form the wagon seat. Arduous toil had weakened her capacity and forced her to ride. Soon their advanced company reached the east bank of the Missouri River.

"Looks like we are stopping here," IJ said as he helped his mother from the wagon.

Isaac was there to check on her in no time.

"They found a good spring of water not far from the river so we've decided to set up another rest camp here." Lucy was relieved.

"You look very warm, Mother." Isaac untied his neckerchief. "IJ, go wet this down for your mother," he said.

The new Iowa rest stop would be named Kanesville in

honor of Thomas L. Kane who befriended the saints at this time of great difficulty. Even later yet, it would be called Council Bluffs and would in time become the Midwest Headquarters of the Church. Here Isaac received a call to preside over an incorporated council of twelve high priests.

Soon a letter of instruction came from President Young: "We would instruct the High Council to . . . advise all those Saints who will tarry here, as well as others who may hereafter arrive this season to use all the means in your power to have all the poor Saints brought from Nauvoo and locate them here for the winter, or at either of the farms back as circumstances and your best judgment may dictate; and further, to oversee and guard the conduct of the Saints and counsel them, that the laws of God and good order are not infringed upon, nor trampled underfoot. It will also be expected that you will assist and counsel the bishops who are appointed to take charge of the families of those who are gone as volunteers in the service of the United States . . . It will also be wisdom and necessary to establish schools for the education of children during the coming winter in this region and we wish you to see that this is done."

*   *   *

The next day black storm clouds darkened the sky and dripped off and on. Roads remained solid, however, and travel was good. Not so the day afterward when heavy storms rained down non-stop. Trekking became impossible. In spite of the harsh conditions the Billings party reached the east bank of the Missouri River by June 14.

A steep, broad-faced cliff along the Iowa side of the River was the spot where renowned trappers-explorers, Lewis and Clark sat in council with the Oto and Winnebago Indians in 1804. Because of this notable event, the place would later be called Council Bluffs. A convenient source of fresh spring water was found near the river. Mormon leaders chose the Bluffs as another important rest camp. Morley was already at the spot. Now Billings had reached it too.

"Pa, Captain Allen is here," George said.

"Who?"

"Captain James Allen of the United States Army."

"Oh no," Diantha said.

412

"He's here? Here at the Bluffs?"

"Yes, with a circular to the Mormons. Said he went to Mount Pisgah and talked to Apostle Woodruff who sent him here to see President Young."

"I wonder what –"

"You are supposed to come for a general council meeting, Pa."

"I hope they are not . . ." Diantha failed to continue, but sent her husband off with worry and wonderment spilling out of her heart. Her concentration strained as she waited and waited for his delayed return.

George Pierce was first to enter and he did so with a puffed chest and rather cocky grin on his face. The fear and guesswork of feminine minds seemed suddenly betrayed by his untroubled manner. Diantha stood speechless, with Eunice and Mary Ann awaiting their cue from the mature Brother Billings. He too entered more relaxed than expected. That was enough.

"So, what is going on?" Diantha asked.

"You are looking at a new soldier," George announced.

"What?" Diantha was baffled.

"That's not funny," Eunice said.

"Not meaning to be funny," George said. "Not when it is the gospel truth."

Diantha turned to her husband. "Are we at war with the United States Army?" she asked.

"No, but the United States is at war with Mexico," Titus said.

"Well, we are no longer citizens of the United States," Eunice said. "They kicked us out, remember? So what does it matter to us?"

"Captain Allen addressed our assembly and requisitioned a battalion of volunteers."

"Volunteers? Mormon volunteers to fight for the country that kicked them out?" Eunice was disgruntled at the suggestion.

"What did the brethren say?" Diantha asked.

"We discussed it and voted to comply," Titus answered.

"Did many volunteer?"

"I did," George spoke up. Diantha shook her head.

"I would have, if I were any younger," Titus said. His quiet manner and humble admission softened all three female hearts. Diantha wrapped her arms around him remembering his service with her brother Isaac in the Silver-Gray Company for older men of the Nauvoo Legion. His spirit was willing. She was grateful he recognized his aging limitations and had courage to accept them.

"These feet might have a hard time walking all the way to Mexico," he added.

"And how do you propose to transport yourself to the Rockies?" Diantha asked. By now she was seated on his lap.

"That's different," he said. "You will need me to drive your wagon." She kissed him and jumped up to serve supper.

Historical Background

"On April 24, 1846, a model city-building organization was established at Garden Grove under the direction of President Young" (MorleyRH, 107).

Thirty miles west of Garden Grove, Parley Parker Pratt found and named another permanent camp Mount Pisgah (Cottam/Malouf,15; Pratt).

While traveling from Council Bluffs to Pisgah, Hosea Stout met up with Titus Billings. June 17, 1846: "When I crossed the bridge I met with Henry Hepker who lent me a chain. He was in company with Br. Titus Billings and they were going on and agreed to help me. June 19, 1846: This morning I went back to the bridge to see what became of Br. Billings and company as I could not find them" (Stout1, 168-169).

"June 21, 1846: We traveled on very steady until about noon and came to a beautiful little grove in the midst of boundless prairie [sic] as it looked. Here we found Br. Billings and those who were with him encamped. They had stopped to wash and fix up and so we overtook them. The prairie which we had last passed was 15 or 20 miles across. Mostly a level good road. We put up here for the day & found Br. Billings and most of those with him very kind and accomodating [sic] and more especially when they found that we were sick and afflicted as we were"(Stout, 168-169).

"Father Morley was called to preside as the head of an incorporated council of twelve high priests" (MorleyRH, 109). "That these high councils had a wide range of duties can be ascertained from the instructions of Isaac Morley when he was installed as president of the high council at Kanesville" (Rich, 89).

"The winter of 1846-47 found approximately 15, 000 Saints and perhaps 30,000 head of livestock scattered across an area of over 500 miles" (Rich, 89).

CHAPTER 71

Although he was one of the first to volunteer as a Mormon Battalion soldier, George Pierce Billings was not listed to be mustered in. Several Apostles addressed the first four companies before their departure. George sat in on the meetings, enjoyed the excitement and learned from the messages, but he could not leave with them a few days later when they started for Fort Leavenworth. Again he was present at noon when the fifth and last company pulled out.

"We'll miss you, George," someone called out.

"Take care of that foot, Brother," shouted another. "Maybe next time."

Yeah, maybe, George thought to himself. He kicked the ground with disgusted disappointment. What a mistake; made his foot start hurting all over again.

"Your bandages are bloody, George," Titus said. He had come along for the well wishing and felt disappointment too, though not as much as did his son. Because of age and accident the Mormon Battalion was leaving them behind.

"Let's get you home so mother can nurse that bleeding wound again." Without deflection the two rejected soldiers started for the cabin.

*   *   *

Not long after Titus Billings drove his family into the Council Bluffs/Kanesville Camp, he received word of more trouble in Nauvoo.

"War? A war in Nauvoo?"

Mary Ann's heart skipped a beat and seemed to freeze up when she overheard the news.

"A father and his young son were killed trying to defend themselves."

"No!" She cried out, "Please not my father! Not my brother!"

"Do you know their names?" Titus asked.

No one seemed to know for sure. Mary Ann worried about her sister and her Mother and her little brother. Eunice heard her crying under the quilt during the night.

"Are you all right?" she asked.

Mary Ann never possessed a large number of words, but tonight she retained a very large number of fears. For hours they whispered about Nauvoo, enumerating all the good memories they could muster. The City of Joseph was such a beautiful and happy settlement. Why couldn't other people see the goodness of the gospel, or at least, leave them alone? Dawning of day was not far away when at last they prayed together and fell asleep.

*   *   *

Bullets were flying everywhere. Edward Tuttle fought more with a prayer than he did with his new weapon. Young Henry leaned on a crutch beside his father and fought the best he could. *If my older boys were here, we'd show you . . .* , Edward thought to himself. He and a few other Mormon remnants were still in Nauvoo only because they could not get out. Some were too ill to travel. Others, like Tuttle, were still trying to sell property and possessions to obtain an ox team and rig for the escape. Many more were latecomers migrating from other lands who wanted only to catch a rest and upgrade their supplies before continuing westward.

How senseless it was. Mormon families were run out before proper preparations could be made; now the same insensible persecutors wanted all stragglers gone as well. Young and old were threatened, the city was attacked, and their holy monument desecrated. Edward looked above him to see the mayor of Quincy watching the battle from the top of the temple.

"We have to get everyone out of here," he said.

"I know we do, Pa, but how?" Henry asked.

Edward gathered his family around him and asked Catherine to petition the Almighty in their behalf. Her pleading words sprung from a wholesome heart like a fountain of fervent faith. Peaceful assurance fell upon each of them with such natural power young Henry opened one eye to see if angels were surrounding his praying mother.

Their big, framed building sold the next day. Edward bought a team of oxen, loaded his wagon, and started for the river where many others, mostly elderly or ill, were trying to cross. Edward let them go first, helping out wherever he could. At noontime he pulled his wagon to the river's edge and waited for the next flatboat. A band of angry mobsters wearing black and red paint on their faces, swarmed down on Edward Tuttle and his wagon-- searching and rummaging, breaking and taking, undoing and leaving undone.

"Here's something we want," one of them shouted as he held up a new rifle.

"I need that to hunt meat for my family," Edward Tuttle exclaimed.

"Not anymore you don't."

"It's his now," a different voice replied.

John Wells looked terrified, and Martha Ann started crying.

"Well, well. What do we have here?" one of them said as he lifted a lock of her golden hair.

Henry Tuttle swung around fighting mad. "Get your paws off of her!" he ordered.

"Now boys, let's not get touchy . . ." one of them started, but Henry held up his fists and threatened, "You touch her and I'll –"

"Oh, please," Catherine begged.

"You wanted us to go, now let us do it." Edward said.

"Come on boys. We got enough." The trouble-makers left with Edward's new gun.

From Montrose Landing, Catherine looked back over the blue water to where a grand and stately building crowned the hilltop. In that holy temple she had been endowed and sealed to her family. *No matter where we go, no matter what happens to us now; as long as we are true to our covenants with the Lord, we will be reunited, not only with each other and our dear Prophet Joseph, but also, even more significantly, with our Savior Jesus Christ, in His peaceful, eternal place of Nauvoo, the beautiful.*

Henry Wirthington Tuttle stood to stretch his good leg. Sunrise was still an hour away, yet he hadn't slept much and could tolerate the hard, damp ground no longer. Since crossing the river, his family and so many others were free of enemy pursuit, but not free from the miserable, wet weather, chaotic confusion, and most of all, the pains of hunger. Henry leaned against the wagon and must have dozed off for a spell. At any rate, he caught a ray of sunshine on his face and hobbled around the wagon bed to embrace the warmth it promised for a new day.

Hundreds of refugees were scattered for two miles up the riverbank. Henry saw a large flock of quail fly into camp and land everywhere. They were all around him. One plump bird came right up to him as if to say, "I'm ready to be your breakfast."

Stunned and sure he was dreaming, Henry whacked two birds with his walking crutch. This dream could not be ignored, but it wasn't a dream! He stooped down and pulled the creatures up by their feet. They were real all right. "Yahoo!" he belted.

"Henry? Is something wrong?" his mother asked from the wagon.

"It'll be a whole lot better when these birds are cooked and ready to eat."

"Eat?" John Wells Tuttle was ready for food. His excitement was echoed throughout the camp as several other flocks delivered themselves to starving saints. John ran after a prize of his own. Edward had them cooked to perfection in no time. He gathered his family around the little fire, and holding hands with reverence, Catherine praised the Lord for sending quail, as sure a miracle to them as manna had been to the ancient Israelites. It was more than just desperately needed food. To humble servants, the miracle was a sacred sign of God's love and never ending mercy.

*   *   *

The Tuttles worked their way westward searching for Mary Ann and the Billings family at every encampment they passed. Council Bluffs was overwhelmed and overcrowded with the religious exiles by the time they arrived. Another new settlement was beginning across the river. Newcomers were encouraged to stop there at Winter Quarters. Edward secured a small hillside property where his family could make a dugout shelter.

"Let's find Mary Ann before we start digging," he said.

"Titus Billings? Oh sure." Everyone seemed to know the man, though no one knew his whereabouts.

"I think he is camped at the Bluffs," someone said at last.

Edward crossed back over the river and drove down the narrow, dirt roads of a congested community. Martha Ann was first to recognize anyone. "Look, there is George Pierce Billings," she said. The young man stood taller with his nineteen-year-old muscles enlarged from heavy labor, making him even more attractive.

418

She was impressed, but careful not to show it.

"Follow me," he said. "Mary Ann will be glad to see you."

"Papa, Papa, you are alive!" Mary Ann sobbed in the safety of her father's arms. She looked up at her tall, crippled brother. "Oh Henry, I was afraid I would never see you again!"

Historical Background

[George Pierce Billings] "was enlisted in the Mormon Battalion, but accidentally got his foot cut so that he could not go" (Jensen4, 72). "The Battalion volunteers marched off to Fort Leavenworth on July 16th and 22nd of 1846" (Jensen, 1846).

[After the first company had gone, a mob came into Nauvoo. Mary Ann's father and brother, Henry, were in the battle. Bullets were flying. Another father and son were killed, but Tuttle survived unharmed. It was June before their oxen and wagon left Nauvoo. While waiting for a flat boat to ferry them across the Mississippi River, Edward Tuttle's family was again attacked by angry mobsters.] "The black and red painted demons searched each wagon and confiscated every gun" (Gardner, 2).

"September 12, 1846 (Saturday) The battle of Nauvoo took place. Wm. Anderson, his son Augustus and Isaac Norris were killed, and others of the defenders were wounded. The mob force, which again was driven back, also sustained considerable loss. September 16, 1846 (Wednesday) The enemy was driven back from Nauvoo the fourth time" (Jenson Chronology).

"We sold our big frame building and all the things that we could and got oxen and wagon and started in June and was camped on the bank of the Mississippi River waiting to be ferried across on a flat boat when the mob came in all painted black & red and searched the wagon and took all guns they could find" (Gardner,2).

"On October 9, food was in especially short supply, when several large flocks of quail flew into camp and landed on the ground and even on the tables. Many were caught, cooked, and eaten by the hungry Saints. To the faithful it was as sign of God's mercy to modern Israel as a similar incident had been to ancient Israel (see Exodus 16:13)" (CES, 318).

"During the following October, when the remnants of the Mormons were leaving Nauvoo and resting on the Iowa shore of the Mississippi River [Montrose Landing]; flocks of exhausted quail began to fall to the ground and were gathered for food" (Cottam/Malouf, 10).

CHAPTER 72

"Brother Billings, Brother Billings . . ." Titus turned around to see who was calling his name.

"Oh, it's you, Brother Stout. How are things?"

"Fine, thanks," Hosea said, then with a grin he added, "much better than when I met your on the bridge, traveling from Mt. Pisgah to Council Bluffs."

Titus remembered him as a man who had been laden down with sickness, poverty, and stress. "Glad to see your luck has changed," he said.

"Indeed it has," Hosea continued, "and my dear brother, if you ever have a need please know that you can call on me."

"Likewise, I'm sure," Titus said.

"So where are you living?" Hosea asked.

"We are still camped at the Bluffs, but I hope to move into a house at Winter Quarters as soon as one opens up."

"Come live in one of my houses for a while," Hosea said.

"You have more than one?" Titus inquired with surprise.

Hosea laughed. "Yes, I put up several log units for the rotation. I'm certain one of them will be available any day."

"Sounds like that's the answer," Titus said, "I thank you."

Hosea's smile was broader than ever before. "No, I thank

you," he said.

Skilled craftsmen constructed a ferryboat to transfer folks across the Missouri River. Titus Billings and his family were among its first passengers. Hosea Stout escorted them to one of his houses in Winter Quarters.

"This is mighty kind of you," Titus said.

"Well, someone needs to live in it; who better than you?"

"Thanks," Titus said.

"No, my thanks to you. I will never forget your kindness to me." Titus ducked his head in humble embarrassment. "Your brotherly love pulled me through." The man spoke with sober earnestness. Then looking up, he smiled at Titus' wife and added: "Not to mention Diantha's cooking."

Titus opened the door of the one-room house and stepped inside. He estimated the walls were about eighteen feet long. The cabin was twelve feet wide.

"At least we'll have a roof overhead, even if it is only a sod one," he said.

Diantha walked across the dirt floor, straight to the chimney and stroked its stone work.

"Looks like a good one, right?"

"Should do fine," Titus said, with gratitude.

For a moment Diantha let herself remember the first home Titus built her; with a stone chimney on each end of it. *No time for longings now*, she thought to herself. *I need to turn this spot into a home, even if it is just temporary.*

*　　　*　　　*

"How soon must you go?" Diantha asked her husband.

Titus bent over to catch his breath before answering. He had run all the way home.

"Immediately," he said. Both of them gathered basic supplies with haste.

"Who else is going?"

"John Clark, Lucien Noble, Newel Knight, Anson Call."

Diantha rolled up a thick quilt as he continued, "A. Russell, John Dalton, George Brimhall, and many more."

"Will you be gone very long?"

"Don't know. Not sure how far they got."

"Do you plan to bring them back?"

"President Young is concerned that they left before being fully outfitted. We are taking supplies to replenish them, but word is they are supposed to return to Winter Quarters." Titus tasted the last biscuit before Diantha could pack it with the others. She smiled at him.

"You be careful," she said.

The relief party started out. Bishop George Miller's company was determined to reach the Rocky Mountains before the others, and had started west without authority or proper provisions. When President Young returned and learned of it, he felt great alarm for their safety. A powerful group of priesthood holders was sent to their rescue.

Many days expired before they returned.

"We caught up with them at Pawnee Village," Titus said, "and not a moment too soon."

Diantha listened as she tugged at his boots until both of them fell.

"Their teams were exhausted, not to mention the people." He shook his head. "It's barren out there; a desert of desolation."

"Then it's a good thing you went."

"Oh yes," he agreed. "And it's a good thing the kind Lord gives us a prophet to take care of us; even when we are foolish."

Winter Quarters exploded with growth. Soon log homes, cave dugouts, or sod houses filled up twenty-two wards. A gristmill was built and put into production and a council hall was raised for meetings. Elder Heber C. Kimball built accommodations for his large family of twenty-five wives and the twelve children who were with him. Isaac Morley's large family found housing in Winter Quarters too. Edward Tuttle's family helped him finish the dugout and move into it. Church leaders prepared and perfected their emigration plans all winter.

"Winter Quarters"

By C.C.A. Christensen (1831-1912)

The Edward Tuttle Family were asked to remain
and build up Winter Quarters.

Both new Mormon settlements (on opposite sides of the river) were in Indian Territory. The Potawatomi Tribe owned the east bank. The Omaha Tribe owned the west.

"I think Chief Pied Riche was quick to connect with us because of polygamy," Isaac said.

"Why? Do you think he is a polygamist?" Titus asked.

"Yes, many Indians are."

"Is he the one they call 'The Clerk'" Titus asked.

"He is. The French named him that because he is well educated."

"What do you know about the Omaha on our side of the river?" Titus knew Isaac had a deep interest in his Lamanite brothers.

"Chief Big Elk is friendly too, but he has difficulty controlling his young bucks. We need to build a stockade around the Quarters to corral our cattle so they don't steal them all."

Titus had heard about missing cattle. "I think they are as hungry as we are," he said.

Mormon leaders also found it necessary to obtain permission from the Oto Indians to camp on the land because they claimed ownership of it as well. The Oto and Omaha tribes often quarreled with each other, but Iowa and Sioux warriors were very hostile to both of them. Bishop Miller's company had tried camping at Pawnee Village two months after the Sioux burned out most of it.

Early in August Brother Newel Knight and Brother John Hay returned with a letter from the Council of the Twelve. "They don't want us to cross the mountains this fall," Titus reported as he walked his wife to camp prayer meeting.

"What are we to do?" Diantha asked.

"Suppose to winter at Pawnee or Grand Island or somewhere nearby. Come springtime the brethren will catch up with us and we can cross over together."

"I like that idea," Diantha said. Her husband agreed. "Where do you think we'll go?" she asked.

"Sounds like we will be going to Grand Island."

The same letter, suggesting names for leadership positions of the winter camp, was read aloud at the meeting: George Miller to serve as president with Newel Knight, Joseph Holbrook, Anson Call, Erastus Bingham, John Maxwell, Thomas Gates, Charles Crismon, Titus Billings, David Lewis, Hyrum Clark, and a Brother Bartholomew to serve as high councilmen; Jacob Houtz as clerk.

"We are to set up and direct this encampment in like manner as other winter camps," Titus said. His family packed and started off with the others in August. They, however, never made it to Grand Island.

Eight chiefs of the Ponca Tribe arrived at Bishop Miller's camp the same day orders came from President Young. A council of saints and Indians was held in an effort to help the Ponca make peace with the Pawnee. The Ponca Nation seemed relieved to find no Pawnee among this white-man group as they had expected.

"You come Ponca village; share hunting grounds," Chief White Eagle said.

"How far away is your village?" Bishop Miller asked.

"Ponca only three sleeps from here. You come make house."

"Well, I don't know . . ."

"Good timber build house."

425

"Oh, I'm sure –"

"Good fuel; cook. Cattle 'much, much pasture. You come. We be friends."

"We be friends," Miller agreed. They shook hands.

The kind invitation led to a journey much further and more difficult than expected when a three day pony ride turned into an eleven day hardship for one hundred and sixty wagons. The undeveloped ground was rocky, and unyielding. Alfred Billings rode horseback beside the wagon his brother drove. George who had charge of a small cannon seemed to attract a lot of attention from Ponca escorts.

"I believe that cannon played a big part in Chief White Eagle's offer," Titus said.

"What do you mean, Pa?"

"Bet they believe it will come in handy when the Sioux decide to attack."

Eunice, already disturbed by Indians, overheard the discussion and was alarmed until her eyes met the dark, fascinated eyes of Ponca prairie children. They questioned and marveled and giggled. For the first time Eunice realized they were as amazed with her as she was with them. She was a "pale-face" with a sunbonnet and wagon home as peculiar to them as their dress and manners and teepee houses were strange to her.

The beautiful Running Water River (now Niobrara) ran through Ponca country, ninety miles away from other settlements and far north of the westward route. Saints set out to build an industrious settlement on a spot where the bank was high above the river. With winter on its way the men went to work at once building a fort structure for shelter. Because they had no time to cure lumber it was erected with green logs. Brother Newell Knight chiseled out a stone for a mill. Ponca warriors left on a winter hunt.

"This is not a time for preaching doctrine," Bishop Miller told his congregation late in autumn (November 30, 1846). "It is a time for every man to get himself over the mountains as best he can."

Diantha felt confusion. When she turned to look at her husband it was obvious, he did not agree. Bishop Miller went on.

"The warmth and union which should prevail in our camp is withering like a tender plant that has sprung up in a refreshing

Mormon Canal by Ponca Camp

This beautiful photo was taken near Niobrara, Nebraska at
a location very close to the Ponca Camp of 1846-47.

(Courtesy Jared Tibbitts, 2004.)
From Joy Tibbitts, 2013, "Poncas and Mormons,
A Friendship Remembered," electronic file, page 1.

shower, but is straight way nipped by the frost of Northern blasts."

Titus made little conversation that night. He seemed to be
deeply preoccupied with concerning thoughts. Diantha struggled
with disappointed feelings of her own. The Lord's Sabbath Day of
rest and rejoicing offered peace to weary hearts. It was the highlight of each week. Today, it seemed, they had been shortchanged.

No Sabbath meetings were held for several weeks.

President Miller was called away in December and left
Brother Billings to act in his stead. After council meeting one night
Brother Knight lingered. Titus could sense deep concern.

"What's on your mind, Brother?"

"Brother Billings, don't you think it would be advisable to

427

appoint a meeting for next Sabbath? It is a commandment binding on us to meet together on that day and to offer up our sacraments unto the most high."

"I've missed that too," Titus said, "but we must follow our leaders."

"I do not feel that we as a council will be justified in neglecting this duty and as we have witnessed the good effect of the Brethren meeting oft to speak one to the other, I feel to take courage. If we knock it will be opened unto us."

"Well stated, Elder Knight. I thank you." The two parted after a heartfelt handshake.

At home, Brother Billings spoke from the doorway, before removing his hat, "I need your help, Mother."

Diantha looked up. "Of course. What is it?" A look of worry covered her face. She sat in silence as he hung his coat and his hat.

"They need your house, Mother."

"It's your house, Titus. You built it." Indeed he had, though ever so quickly, even with green timbers.

"Well, the church would like to borrow it."

"How do you mean?" Thoughts raced through her mind. *Are we moving again?*

"It's high time we worship in meeting on the Sabbath day."

"Oh yes, yes." Longing burst out of her. "You want the meeting here?"

"Yes please, if you do."

"Tomorrow?"

"That's right."

"Wonderful." She jumped up to kiss his cheek, then quickly drew her arms back and stood in a reverent stance. "We would be honored to meet your wishes, 'Brother Acting President'," she said. Instantly she flew into action. "Eunice, did you dust the mantel this morning? George, come quickly. We need you to borrow some chairs." Titus ducked his head trying to hide a grin. He had not given her much time to prepare, but when Diantha Morley Billings went into action anything was possible.

Joyful saints packed into the Billings home where the spirit was warm and messages were inspiring. They renewed sacred covenants with holy emblems.

"It is so good to meet together again."

"Now it feels like the Lord's Day."

"Thank you, Brother Billings."

Titus reached out for Elder Knight. "This is the man we want to thank," he said. "And we will meet again, same time, same place; next week."

Diantha was prompt to visit Sister [Lydia] Knight when she heard the news.

"I've come to meet your new house guest," she said.

A very old Ponca woman, who had hobbled into camp the night before, sat looking forlorn in the corner.

"Your husband was kind to bring her home."

Lydia smiled.

"How do you communicate with her?" Diantha asked.

"We really can't. She speaks French though. Newell said a French interpreter was at the meeting last night. He translated her story for them. Did you hear?"

"Bits and pieces, I think."

"Well, she and her son were on a long journey to visit the Sioux. He even went on a war party with them."

"Interesting. Please go on . . ."

"They stopped to visit some Punahs on the way home. That angered the Sioux so they killed her son."

"How barbaric."

"Yes, they threatened to kill her too, if she did not leave at once. Somehow she journeyed back with no help, only a tiny bundle of skins, and a few slivers of meat. He said she survived on roots dug out of the ground with her knife."

"Talk about determination."

"She was fatigued, nigh unto starvation, but she arrived."

"Poor dear."

"The sad thing is when at last she reached the land of her people they were gone hunting and our Mormon camp was here instead."

"Bless you for taking her in. She is in good hands now. Here are the clothes I promised to bring."

Just then Newell Knight walked in and greeted both ladies; one with a kiss and the other with a handshake. Then he added to the conversation about the poor old woman.

"Her situation was named in our meeting," he said. "Some proposed to build her a house to live by herself. I expressed my belief that she would be better off living with a family as it would be only one step towards civilization."

Both women agreed, though the old woman, not able to understand his words, looked on.

"I will be by with more clothing tomorrow" Diantha promised.

Early the next morning Sister Billings and Mother Shurtliff helped Sister Knight wash and dress the woman. She was cooperative and seemed grateful.

"You can tell these clothes feel strange to her," Diantha said.

"My guess is she has never had anything but skins touch her body," Lydia said.

After meeting the next evening the French interpreter told the brethren that the old woman wanted to visit the Indian burial grounds. Brother Knight and Brother Billings volunteered to go with them. She seemed drawn to the grave of Black Warrior and made signs to the men that he was also her son. Upon spotting his bullet bag hung on the head of his grave she burst into loud mourning and threw herself onto the monument that covered his remains. Great was her anguish. The men waited, unable to comfort. At length she visited another grave, that of Chief Two Bulls who died after the Mormons arrived. Again she burst into agonizing grief.

"The Chief was her brother," the Frenchman said.

Historical Background

"This morning Br. Titus Billings & family moved into one of my houses to live awhile. They were in company with me while journeying from Mt. Pisgah to the Bluffs and were uncommonly kind, benevolent & attentive to me, at this time when I was so much worn out with sickness, poverty and distress" (Stout, 254).

"By the end of 1846, Heber C. Kimball had the largest company prepared for winter . . . at least 25 wives and twelve of his children with him at Winter Quarters" (Kimball1, 10).

"A company headed by Bishop George Miller determined to reach the Rocky Mountains in advance of the general body. They either left without the authority of the leaders of the Church or in the absence of Brigham Young, for soon the president became greatly concerned over the fact that they were only partially outfitted for a long journey, and he determined to organize a party to either bring them back or replenish their supplies" (CarterVol.9, 423).

"The relief party included many of the men well known in Church history. Among them were Father's family [from history of John Haslem Clark], Lucien Noble, Newel Knight, Titus Billings, Anson Call, A.Russell, John Dalton, George Brimhall and many others" (CarterVol.9, 423). "The relief party overtook the Miller Company at Pawnee village in Nebraska. It was a timely arrival, for teams were almost exhausted and the country a barren dessert" (CarterVol.9, 423).

A letter from the Council of the Twelve dated August 7, 1846, suggested that they not cross the mountains this fall and "suggested organization for the camp for the winter, advising as president George Miller; as high councilors Newel Knight, Joseph Holbrook, Anson Call, Erastus Bingham, John Maxwell, Thomas Gates, Charles Crismon, Titus Billings, David Lewis, Hyrum Clark and a Brother Bartholomew; as clerk Jacob Houtz" (Rich, 85).

"August 8th, 1846. Names of Council: George Miller, Newel Knight, Joseph Holbrook, Anson call, Erastus Bingham, John Mikesell, Thomas Gates, Titus Billings, David Lewis, Hyrum Clark, N.W. Bartholomew, Charles Christiansen" (Tibbitts, 99).

"You will do well to organize a council of twelve men to superintend the affairs of the Church with you temporally and spiritually and see that offenders of the law do not go unpunished. We would suggest for your consideration that Geo (sic) Miller preside, assisted by Newel Knight, Joseph Holbrook, Titus Billings, Hiram Clark, Bartholomew, Anson Call, David Lewis, Thomas Gates, Charles Chrisman, Ashael Lathrop, or sufficient of them to constitute the quorum of Twelve" (Journal History21; Tibbitts, 129).

"The whole camp came together agreeable to [the] notice from the twelve and adopted the following as recommended in the letter by Brother Knight to camp: George Miller to be president, Newell Knight, Joseph Holbrook, Anson Call, Erastus Bingham, John Mixwell (Mikesell), Thomas Gates, Charles Christman (Crismon), Titus Billings, David Lewis, Hyrum Clark, (Noah W.) Bartholomew, High Councilsor [sic]. Brother Jacob Houtz act as clerk" (Tibbitts, 130).

President Young sent word for them to "move no further westward that season, but to go into winter encampment on Grand Island: also appointing twelve men, with Bishop Miller as president, to direct the affairs of the camp, as in other camps that were being settled for the winter. About the same time eight chiefs of the Ponca tribe arrived at Miller's camp, and proposed that he move to their villages on the Running Water. This invitation Miller accepted instead of following President Young's instructions to winter at Grand Island, and dragged his company eleven days' drive almost due north from the general course of the western march of the church" (Roberts, 158).

"It was here that White Eagle, an Indian chief, came amongst us and invited us to his villages and hunting grounds, saying it was only four sleeps away, but it took us ten. The village was situated on the Loup Fork of the Platte River, another on Running Water River" (CarterVol.9, 423 John Haslem Clark's journal). "The Ponca chief invited the Saints to winter with them in their country which they said was only 'three sleeps' away; there they would find timber for their houses and fuel and pasture for their cattle" (Rich, 85).

"The trip to Ponca country turned out to be a major mistake, since it put the camp far away from provisions that could be procured no nearer than the settlements in northern Missouri. They built a fort at a settlement they called Ponca on the Running Water River, today the Niobrara River, about three miles from its confluence with the Missouri" (Rich, 85).

"On August 14 the rest of the camp, consisting or over 160 wagons, started for the Ponca country. . . the journey took eleven days" (Rich, 85). "The party comprised sixty-five families with one hundred and fifty wagons" (Tibbitts, 170).

". . . his party had with them a small cannon which much attracted their attention and he thought that this was one reason for their solicitation, since the Sioux always annoyed the Poncas" (Tibbitts, 170). "On the 8th of August, our men that we had sent for the cannon got back, bringing another letter from Brigham Young directing me [George Miller] to stop short where I was" (Tibbitts, 56).

"The Indians were very kind and hospitable to the white men. Many of them had never before seen a pale-face" (Tibbitts, 111).

"27 December 1846, Sunday, Meeting at Brother Billings" (Tibbitts, 154). "8 February 1847, today we had a meeting . . . to reorganize the camp . . . Titus Billings, president; Erastus Bingham and Joseph Holbrook councilors [sic] from Holbrook journal" (Tibbitts, 158). "14 February 1847, Sunday, held meeting at Brother Billings" from Holbrook journal (Tibbitts, 158). "At the Ponca Settlement, the Saints were organized into an immigrating company by Elders Ezra T. Benson and Erastus Snow. Titus Billings was elected president, with Erastus Bingham and Joseph Holbrook as his counselors" (Baugh,1; Journal History20).

The council had met that evening to attend to business after which Brother Knight asked Brother Billings, acting in Brother Miller's absence, if it would be advisable to appoint a meeting for the next Sabbath, "as it is a commandment binding on us to meet together on that day and to offer up our sacraments unto the most high. I did not feel that we as a council would be justified to neglect this duty and as we had witnessed the good effect of the Brethren meeting oft to speak one to the other heretofore I feel to take courage knowing that if we knock it will be opened unto us that if we seek we shall find rest to our souls and the plants that are now drooping will again revive and many of them may yet become very glorious or plants of renown. Therefore I think we would do well to use every exertion that is expedient for the welfare and encouragement of this people. Brother Billings appointed meeting at his house for the next day" (Knight, 104). Records show that the meeting was held and another the next week, December 27, 1846 (Knight, 105).

Newel Knight mentioned Titus Billings in his journal, December 19th and 20th of 1846. There had been no meeting at the camp since November 30th, the Sabbath after President Miller had returned from the Bluffs. "He told the congre-

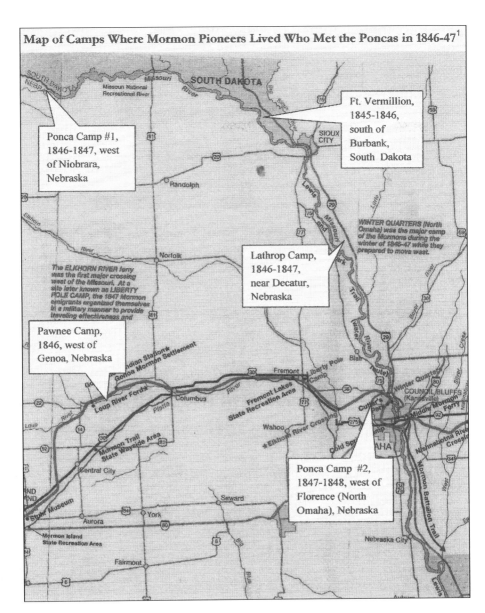

Map of Camps Where Mormon Pioneers Lived Who Met the Poncas in 1846-47[1]

Ft. Vermillion, 1845-1846, south of Burbank, South Dakota

Ponca Camp #1, 1846-1847, west of Niobrara, Nebraska

Lathrop Camp, 1846-1847, near Decatur, Nebraska

Pawnee Camp, 1846, west of Genoa, Nebraska

Ponca Camp #2, 1847-1848, west of Florence (North Omaha), Nebraska

Ponca Camp Map

Scanned section of Mormon Pioneer National Historic Trail Map,
National Park Service, U.S. Government, text labels added by Joy Tibbitts.

(Courtesy Joy Tibbitts, 2004.)
From Joy Tibbitts, 2013, "Poncas and Mormons, A Friendship Remembered,"
electronic file, page 18.

gation it was no time to preach a doctrine new but it was for every man to look out for himself and get over the mountains the best he could...that warmth and union which prevailed in our camp is withering like the tender plant that has sprung up in the refreshing shower but is straight way nipped by the frost of Northern blasts" (Knight, 104). "I do not feel that we as a council will be justified in neglecting this duty and as we have witnessed the good effect of the Brethren meeting oft to speak one to the other, I feel to take courage knowing that if we knock it will be opened unto us, if we seek we shall find rest to our souls, and the plants that are now drooping will again revive. Many of them may yet become glorious plants of renown. Therefore, I think we will do well to use every exertion expedient for the welfare and encouragement of this people" (Knight, 194).

Newell Knight's journal: "Attend prayer meeting at Brother Billings's. [sic] The Spirit of God was with us" (Tibbitts2, 81).

Again from Knight's journal: "Sister Billings, whose compassion is ever towards the needy, had been at my house and seen her [the old Ponca woman] situation she replied that she had felt the necessity of clothing the poor woman and had already obtained one suit for her. The next day Sister Billings and Mother Shurtliff come [sic] with the clothes for the old woman . . .and assist my wife in washing her" (Tibbitts2, 81).

"After meeting we went to the graves of the Black Warrior and the Old Chief who died soon after we came here, to show the old woman where they were buried" (Tibbitts2, 82).

CHAPTER 73

"Fire! Fire! Everything is on fire!"

The music stopped and Christmas dancers stood as if frozen. Titus jumped to his senses and ran to the window where he could see smoke filling the evening sky evidencing the prairie fires all around them.

"Ponca is on fire!" he said.

Back and forth from the river more than two hundred saints passed water in buckets, kettles, anything they could find. Flames ignored their efforts and covered the dry ground like a thundering herd of wild, charging buffalo. Devoted men, women and children fought deep into the darkness of night. High winds enhanced flames all the more. Prairie grasses blazed in every direction. Many fires refused to stop until they burnt themselves out.

Fearing for their lives, families grabbed whatever they could and fled to the river where they spent the rest of the night crouching on a sandbar for survival. Daylight exposed the charred, smoldering fields and smoky skies. The fort, to their surprise, had been saved. Green logs refuse to burn.

"Look," Eunice shouted. "Our cabin is still standing."

Ponca saints gathered at the Billings property to report their losses. Many wagons and five stacks of precious hay had burned. Miles and miles of grazing grasses were lost as well. In panic frightened horses and cattle had charged wildly, destroying fences, wagons, anything in their path. Over-exertion and exposure marked many lives and soon would claim most of them.

"Thank you, George," Diantha said watching him set a fresh pail of river water in the center of the room for cleaning. "Now fetch a green branch and sweep a fresh pathway to the door," she instructed. "Tomorrow is the Sabbath and you heard your father announce that church services will be held again in our home." She and Eunice resumed their chores.

"I don't know, Ma. We're not presentable for company," Eunice said.

"We are no worse off than anyone else." Diantha's words were true. She added to them, "We must do all we can and the Lord will take care of the rest." Eunice had heard that before -- many times. She knew it was so.

The Sabbath meeting was well attended and inspirational. Brother Billings assigned several men to leave for supplies the next morning. Bishop Miller returned to camp Monday afternoon preaching a new agenda that he--not the Twelve Apostles--should be in charge of the Ponca saints. His proposal was overruled.

Food was scarce. Alfred rigged up some traps to catch small animals. All grazing spots were burned. Temperatures dropped so low it was too cold for snowfall. Many animals expired from cold and hunger as a result of the great fire. Families made meals of their carcasses.

Titus returned to his cabin and slumped into a chair.

"You look worried," Diantha said.

"I am worried," he admitted.

"About Bishop Miller?"

"Well, that too, I guess." Diantha flashed him a look of let's have an explanation.

"I'm worried for Elder Knight," he said.

"Newell?"

"Yes, he missed another meeting because of poor health. Can't seem to recover from our fire episode. I'm not sure he is going to pull through, Di."

She had no flour with which to bake dainties. "Tomorrow I'll steep him some broth and we can have a good visit."

Diantha was true to her word. Elder Knight sipped the warm drink and engaged in grateful conversation. Titus' worries also came to pass. Newel Knight died at Ponca before January ended.

The Ponca Camp was reorganized on February 8, 1847. Brother Titus Billings was called, sustained and set apart as President with Erastus Bingham and Joseph Holbrook as counselors. Bishop Miller and his family returned to Winter Quarters with the Apostles on March 23, 1847. Two days later a letter came from Church leaders addressed to the new Branch President.

"Winter Quarters, March 25, 1847
From the Twelve Apostles
To Titus Billings and counselors and the captains and saints in camp at Ponca.

Beloved Brethren: In consideration of the difficulties we have met with, in making a seasonable and necessary fitout for the pioneers, so as to plant a colony on the foot of the mountain and take forward our families, this season: we have determined to leave our families at this place, until we shall have gone over the mountains, and found a location for a stake of Zion, and made the necessary preparation by planting, sowing and building and then take them forward to their place of rest.

Before this reaches you, we shall be on our way, with all the pioneers who are ready to go with us; and the remainder of the brethren at Winter Quarters, will tarry here, raise all the grain they can, and be prepared to winter themselves and stock, and go forward to their destination as fast as their circumstances will permit.

Small families and those who can fit themselves out with 18 months provisions, or from 300 lbs. of breadstuffs per soul, may follow the pioneers, when grass is high enough to sustain their teams this spring. Perchance some buffalo may be secured by them on this side of the mountain; but this is uncertain, and if found, they will be poor at that season, and these animals have left the west side of the mountain so that these who go cannot depend for their living, only on what they carry with them, until they can sow and reap; they cannot depend on the pioneers for their crops are uncertain also.

By your report sent by Elder Benson we understand that you have not provision as a people to fit you for this journey, and it is not wisdom for you to separate into small parties, surrounded as you are, or attempt to plant or sow where you are, as in either case your crops or your persons would be in danger. Therefore, our council [sic] to you is, that you return to this place, or somewhere in this vicinity as speedily as your situation will permit, and retaining your present organization, put in crops sufficient to sustain yourselves, and prepare you to go at a future day.

The season for planting is fast approaching and it is about time for you now to be fencing and clearing for the plough. When you arrive here, if there are those who can fit themselves out, they can go forward with the company this spring.

From your present location, you cannot strike our contemplated route much nearer than at this point, and the time and place of our union would be uncertain, while there are but few of you prepared for the enterprise and those few would be in danger of robberies and destruction on their leaving their camp, and if you all come together, you will be safe on the route, if you watch as well as pray.

We have advised Bro. Daniel Lewis, who has recently arrived, to return immediately to your camp with this epistle, that no time may be lost to you in preparing for your summer crops.

We have very little late news of importance from any quarter. We are determined to be up and doing and plant ourselves and families as speedily as possible at a Stake of Zion, where all the saints may gather and help to open up the way for the coming of the Son of Man, and a united and persevering action of all saints will speedily accomplish a great work, "and if ye are one, then are ye mine," with the Lord.

We have contemplated going by your place to the mountains, but this we cannot do, for this reason, if no other, there are brethren here from the Battalion who will return with us, they will have to follow up the South Fork of the Platte, and we shall have to send men with them. We have looked at your camp and studied how you could go ahead without coming back, but realizing that we are surrounded with enemies on every hand, we think we had better be as compact as possible.

We have no fault to find with you, and we trust you have no fault to find with us; we would be glad if it were otherwise or, that you were on the route. We believe you have acted in good faith, and we are sure we have, and the Lord will bring good out of it.

P.S. Messrs. Grosland and Cardinal, we understand were to have been at Ponca by the first of March. If you see them, tell them of our contemplated route, and destination and they will probably be the best judges of the course, whether to join us on the Platte or at Ft. Laramie. Should they not arrive before you leave, you will seek an opportunity to send them a letter by the Indians or some travelers, and give them the desired information, as you will not have time to go to them.

Bro. Lewis will be able to give you much information concerning the affairs of our camp which you will be glad to hear, but we have not time to write. We feel in our hearts to bless you and we do bless you and say you shall be blessed, if you will be careful and never grieve the spirit of the Lord, but so live as to cherish the whisperings of the small still voice, and it will always guide you right, and you will know your duties and privileges for the fruits of the spirit are intelligence and light and life and salvation, to which you shall all attain through obedience and this is your blessing in the name of Jesus Christ, Amen. For the Council Brigham Young, President Willard Richards, Clerk."

The task was complete within a month after President Young's letter arrived. After loading their wagons and making ready to pull out, when Diantha found her husband kneeling beside Newell Knight's grave. For two months Brother Billings had served as an obedient branch president, trying to undo what had been done. Even nature seemed to oppose his efforts by blazing the land and claiming many lives. The dedicated priesthood leader had conducted graveside services for twenty-three beloved saints. Now he found it difficult to pull away from the little Mormon cemetery and leave it unprotected.

"It pains my heart to leave so many dear friends in this forsaken spot," Diantha said. "I can't help but wonder if we hadn't come so far off the trail . . . if we hadn't had that wicked fire . . . Oh Titus, I cannot bear to lose any others!"

"They dwell in a far better place," Titus whispered. With reverence he stood and took the love-of-his-life by the hand. Deep in the blue of her eyes he sensed the power of eternity. In the House of the Lord with authority from God, she had been promised to him forever.

"It matters not where we live, but how; not where we are buried, but why. We must be true to the faith and keep the covenants we have made with the Everlasting God." He paused for her to absorb his words. "Promise me, Diantha, no matter what comes our way we will stay true to each other, to Christ, and to the cause of Zion." His words were alarming. "Promise me, Diantha. We must keep our covenants with the Everlasting God." She closed her eyes with a slight nod. "Promise me, dear. Together we must be stalwart forever!"

Diantha looked toward heaven and smiled.

"Forever stalwart!" she said.

Billings' wagon was the last to pull out of Ponca and head back to Winter Quarters.

Historical Background

"At evening on Christmas day the people at Ponca sighted the prairies afire about ten or twelve miles . . . the fire swept down upon them like swift horses, and soon more than 200 men and women were carrying water from the river in an attempt to protect their property. That the fort had been built of green logs saved it" (Rich86).

"A line was immediately formed including men, women and children extending from the river to the outside of the fort, with buckets, kettles, and so forth, by which quantities of water were thrown on to the haystacks and sides of the houses most exposed to the flames . . . during this time the wind increased to almost a hurricane" (Tibbitts, 90).

" . . . all rushed down to the river [and] crouched on a sandbar expecting everything to be consumed" (Carter, 423).

"Bishop Miller tried to persuade the camp at Ponca that he, instead the Twelve Apostles, should be their leader. The camp had overruled him, however. On February 8 the camp was reorganized, and Titus Billings became president with Erastus Bingham and Joseph Holbrook as counselors. The next day Bishop Miller returned to the main settlements with the Apostles" (Rich, 87).

"On February 8 the camp was reorganized, and Titus Billings became president with Erastus Bingham and Joseph Holbrook as counselors" (Rich 87).

"Titus Billings was sent as a Branch President to bring the group back to the main camps" (Tibbitts, 75).

Official letter dated 25 March 1847 from Brigham Young in on file at the LDS Church Achieves (Journal History, 13). "They left twenty-three of their number buried at Ponca" (Rich, 887). "Others who died at Ponca, in the years of 1846-47: Mr. Corvall, Mrs. Spicer Crandall, Mrs. Corvall, Mrs. Newel Drake, Lucy Bronson, Mrs. Dame, Ann Boyce, Garduous Noble, Mrs. Rufus Pack, Benjamin F. Mayers" (Tibbitts, 70).

"Being too late to cross the plains, we wintered at Punckaw. Then we went back to Winter Quarters" (Bennett, 558).

"It was so cold that we had no snow of any consequence during the entire winter"[Wilmer Bronson autobiography](Tibbitts, 91).

"Newel Knight died in January as a result of the fires" (Rich, 86).

Ponca Camp in Modern Day

This spot on the hill, beside the Niobrara River is where Titus Billings served as Branch President for two months and where Newell Knight is buried.

(Courtesy S.B. Mitchell, 2008.)

Gravesite of Newell Knight

Beloved friend of President Billings who died from effects of a Ponca prairie fire that started on Christmas Day.

(Courtesy S.B. Mitchell, 2008.)

1846-47 MORMON WINTER CAMP

In 1846, some 65 Mormon families with 150 wagons were headed West along the north shore of the Platte River. Somewhere between present-day Columbus and Genoa, a government agent contacted them to harvest some grain planted by white laborers who had fled in fear of the Pawnee. While they were at work, a courier from Kanesville (now Council Bluffs, Iowa) brought orders for them to stay put. It was too late to reach the Great Salt Lake before winter set in, and prairie fires had devastated much of the country west of Laramie. While the Mormons pondered their situation, a band of Poncas happened along and led the group to the Niobrara Valley, where they set up winter camp. During their stay, millwright Newell Knight chiseled two granite mill burrs, which were intended to grind grain via horsepower. Unfortunately, Knight and 16 others, mostly women and children, died of pneumonia over the winter. The Mormons may have dug the canal below this site to divert the Niobrara River for water power. The island created by this canal was given to the town by the federal government in 1891 and became the site of Niobrara Park. The town deeded the park to the state in 1930.

Niobrara State Park Marker

This marker at the Niobrara State Park depicts the Mormon camp at Ponca.

(Courtesy S.B. Mitchell, 2008.)

CHAPTER 74

Mary Ann sat up from her quilt bed on the dirt floor. Something in the night awoke her. She had to admit that all the talk about Indians spooked her, but this time something was out there. She heard it! Before she could crawl to her father's bed a voice started calling from behind the dugout's quilt door. Edward was up in an instant.

"Brother Stout needs all policemen to come at once," the messenger said.

"What's wrong?" Ed asked.

"Sounds like a band of Iowa attacked the Omaha camped outside of town. It's really bad." Tuttle knew a small, friendly band of the Omaha Tribe was camped outside Winter Quarters. He had visited them once with Brother Morley.

"President Young says we need to help them. 'Know you're not a policeman, but thought you might . . .'"

"Of course," Edward said. Henry too was up and ready to go in an instant. They left.

Sleep for women folk was gone for the night. Martha Ann started and could not stop talking about her wonderful Walter [Gardner]. Listening kept Mary Ann's mind distracted from Indian concerns. Catherine must have heard it all. At length she spoke: "Mary Ann, get dressed. Martha Ann, you stay here with John. Father Morley is probably with the men and I feel a need to check on his wife."

Lucy Gunn Morley had been down with winter fever (typhoid) for many weeks. Catherine suffered "black leg" (scurvy) until a leafy plant of horseradish was discovered at an abandoned fort a few miles north of town. If only it could cure the fever as well. Isaac had gone out with the men, just as Catherine supposed.

Sweet Lucy's pale face was alarming to see. She was very thin. No one had enough food these days. Lucy could hardly lick what was given to her. Catherine noticed her cracked lips and sent Mary Ann to fetch fresh water. She tore a piece from her underskirt to make a wet rag for the burning forehead and another for under her neck. With gentle touches she patted another wet cloth all over Lucy's face. Her friend was too weak to sit up and almost too unconscious to sip a drink. Catherine tore another strip, folded it and saturated it in water. "Put this in your mouth and suck on it," she coaxed. Again and again she re-moistened the cloths. Mary Ann slumped in the corner, sound asleep until the men returned. Father Morley had blood all over him. He was alarmed to see Sister Tuttle, but thankful she had come.

"Did you have to fight?" Catherine asked.

"No, the damage was done when we got there. It was vicious. They attacked in the night shooting up tents and flee-ing back over the river (Missouri) before we arrived. Most Omaha warriors are away on a hunting trip. The invaders must have been watching and planned it that way. All the tortured survivors want to be near President Young, so we moved the wounded into sod huts and the rest are relocating around his cabin."

"I'm worried about Lucy," Catherine said. "If you like, I will call on her tomorrow."

Isaac was grateful. Concern seemed to bleach the life out of him as well.

*   *   *

Sister Tuttle wrapped hot biscuits in a cloth and tucked them into her basket.

"We're leaving now to call on Sister Morley," she told her husband. Martha Ann and Mary Ann bundled up to follow along.

"I wish we could pick wild flowers for her," Mary Ann said.

"Three days after New Year's? Wrong season, Sweetheart," Martha Ann taunted.

"I know. I'm just wishing."

"Wishing? Oh, I'd use all my wishes to see Walter. What if he just happened to come walking down the road any minute now?"

"What would you do if he did?"

"I'd smile and curtsey and introduce him to my beautiful sister," Martha Ann said.

"You are the beautiful one," Mary Ann said.

"Both of you are beautiful. Now, step it up to a more beauti-ful pace," their mother advised.

Lucy Diantha opened the cabin door. She and her sister, Ed-itha Ann, were both married so their presence caught Catherine by surprise. She looked in to see Isaac's new wives of plural marriage

444

huddled around the fireplace, wearing worried looks.

"I know Lucy cannot eat these, but I thought you might enjoy them."

Lucy Diantha started to cry.

"Thank you," Editha Ann said. "Father and I.J. are in there now. We've all said good-bye."

Catherine was caught off guard, "I am so sorry," she said.

*   *   *

Only three months after losing his Lucy, Isaac Morley accompanied Brigham Young and eight pioneer wagons as they ascended the hill west of Winter Quarters and traveled seven miles to a parcel of land ideal for farming. With a stream of pure water and natural pastures it would be easy to fatten cattle in the spot they called: "Summer Quarters." Father Morley was left in charge. As Patriarch he still gave blessings whenever asked, and presided over the Winter Quarters high council, visiting its wards and the branch at Council Bluffs as well.

*   *   *

Henry Tuttle had a difficult time falling asleep after viewing the Omaha massacre. The sight of Chief Big Head's wounds and his squaw's shattered arm seemed to haunt him. When George Billings returned to Winter Quarters, Henry felt he had a friend in whom he could confide at last.

"You better get yourself a cannon," George said after Henry described every gory detail.

"How so?" Henry asked.

"Well, let me tell you my Sioux experience. Early last January six large Indians showing off their war outfits came into the fort at Ponca."

"Really? Dressed for war?"

"There was no doubt. Mountaineers had already alerted us of their threats to massacre all of us at the fort. They claimed our friendship with the Poncas made us their enemies."

"Didn't that alarm you?"

"Sure thing. We believed they were casing us out."

"You mean spying on you?"

"That's what I mean. Anyway, the brethren instructed us set up the old cannon at the square in the center of the fort and load it with blank cartridges." Henry's eyes could open no wider. He sat in silent expectation. "We discharged the cannon and could tell from their astonished reaction that none of them had seen anything like it before."

"Did they leave?"

No. We reloaded and fired five or six more times. It was funny to watch them run for cover with every blast. Think they got the message not to mess with us because we owned a Grandfather of rifles. And know what? They never visited or bothered us again."

Henry was impressed. "Come on, I'll show it to you. Still loaded in my wagon."

Henry hobbled along with his hero as fast as his crippled leg could take him.

"How'd you like to babysit this thing for me?" George asked slapping the cannon barrel.

"You kidd'n?"

"Nope. I'm very serious." George Pierce Billings stretched his six-foot-four-inch frame with pride. His face was beaming with joy. President Brigham Young handpicked members for an initial company to head westward. Soon they would leave to explore the Great Basin region in search of a permanent home for the saints in the Rocky Mountains, as the Prophet Joseph had foretold.

"I leave tomorrow as a scout for President Young."

"Awe, George. You'll be a great scout."

"Thanks pal." George slapped Henry on the back. "You take good care of this cannon for me -- well, for the Lord and His church."

"I know what you mean, but I'm not sure how to do it."

"My pa can tell you. He is on his way back from Ponca. Wish I could see him before we leave, but there isn't time."

"Too bad. Bet your ma would want to see you."

"Yeah, I bet she would. Here, how about you give her this hug for me."

"Sure George. You know I'd do anything for you, but . . ."

He had been caught off guard by the sudden gesture and looked rather embarrassed by the suggestion. George came to his aid.

"Get yourself prepared for a future journey. Right now saints are supposed to build up Winter Quarters. You know, build fences, raise crops, herd animals."

"Yes, I know. My pa's been called to shepherd the cattle."

"Shepherd cattle? Never heard it put that way before."

"Pa is a baker, not a cattleman. He thinks "shepherding" is more Christlike and not so intimidating." Both of them laughed.

"I better go pack up now."

"Can I help you?"

"Sure." They started off. By dawning of the next day Henry stood leaning on his home-made crutch waving farewell to his hero until the initial pioneering wagon train was out of sight.

*   *   *

Lucy Diantha guided her Aunt Di toward the eastern edge of the Mormon graveyard where her mother was laid to rest. Together they found Isaac kneeling in the snow when they arrived. Diantha stepped behind her brother and placed a hand on his drooping shoulder.

"Oh Isaac, I'm so sorry!" She fell to her knees, unaware of the frozen ground, and sobbed out loud. "I didn't get to tell her good-bye," she anguished.

Constant croupy coughing behind her, alerted Diantha to the presence of other grieving hearts. She stood and wrapped her arms around Lucy Diantha who coughed between sobs.

"Aunt Diantha," she cried, "now half of my name is gone!"

"There, there."

"You'll have to be my mother now." Diantha hugged her again, even tighter.

"Your mother's eternal work has been done in the temple," she reminded. "Now her earthly work is done too, but she lives on. She waits for us in a better place, you know."

When Titus taught me that truth at Ponca I had no idea one of the most precious persons in my life was exiting mortality that very moment!

Harsh coughing echoed in triplicate. Three of Lucy Diantha's children were seriously ill.

"We must get your little ones home and doctor their colds," Diantha insisted.

Daily she carried homemade remedies to the little brood. Their weakness was alarming. Not one of them seemed to be responding to her care. Fearing they were undernourished she prepared fresh biscuits and steaming stew for their supper. Isaac was there when she and Eunice arrived. He was holding little Joseph Lorenzo in his arms and crying like a baby.

"He's gone with Lucy!" was all the heartbroken grandfather could say.

Before the month ended a trio of small graves rested beside Grandma Morley's on the hillside at Winter Quarters.

Historical Background

"A company for ten rough Rangers was to be raised to guard the herds from the Omahas. They were to be led by Hosea Stout. The ten men were: Parley P. Pratt, Daniel Russell, John Taylor, David Boss, Daniel Spencer, Alpheus Cutler, Joseph Young, Isaac Morley, George D. Grant and John Neff" (Pratt1, 380).

"On the night of December 9, 1846, the Iowa [tribe] attacked a small band of Omaha [tribesmen] who were camped near Winter Quarters. Big Head, the Omaha second chief, was severely wounded, and a squaw's arm was shattered" (Rich, 90).

"Some time in the fore part of January, 1847, six large Sioux Indians, dressed in their war costume, came into the fort with a view (it was thought) of spying out the strength of our position" (Tibbitts, 91).

"The disease, called 'Black Leg' by the Mormons, is more commonly designated as scurvy. Many deaths resulted from this dread[ed] disease before potatoes could be purchased in Missouri to check the diet deficiency. Horse-radish, a leafy plant which was discovered growing a few miles about Winter Quarters at an abandoned fort, was made part of the diet and proved a great boon to the ill since it was a most excellent antidote for their illness" (MorleyRH, 111).

After suffering two months with Typhoid Fever, Isaac's wife, Lucy Morley died at Winter Quarters on January 3, 1848 (Cox,20; Family Group Sheet) or January 3, 1847 (Morley,111).

"Three of his [Isaac Morley] lovely grandchildren who died from lack of proper food and medical knowledge were buried in graves next to the one occupied by the body of their grandmother. These children belonged to Isaac Morley's daughter, Lucy Diantha and her husband Joseph S. Allen" (MorleyRH, 112). Three children of Lucy Diantha and Joseph Stewart Allen, died of insufficient food and medical care. They were buried beside their grandmother's grave (Cox, 21; Morley 104, 111).

My research shows that three Allen children died near that time period, but not in the same month as the above describes: Joseph Lorenzo Allen b. 25 FEB 1847 d. 17 AUG 1847; Calista Allen b.25 FEB 1845 d. 17 OCT 1846; Cordelia Allen b. 31 JAN 1843 d. 6 NOV 1846 (Family Group Sheets).

"Three months after Lucy's death, April 7, 1848, Isaac led eight wagons about ten miles out of Winter Quarters. After climbing the hill west of the city, the group traveled seven miles on the Ponca Road and camped for the night. On Thursday morning, April 8, 1847, Brigham Young, Father Morley and a few other brethren located a parcel of land with plenty of pasture and natural stables. A small stream of pure water supplied all the moisture necessary to make a farm prosper. In addition to his High Council responsibilities . . . Isaac Morley was put in charge of 'Summer Quarters.' There he remained for a year "to fatten cattle" (MorleyRH, 113).

CHAPTER 75

Elder Titus Billings and Elder Isaac Morley were both called to serve on the High Council at Winter Quarters. Council members were instructed to teach the Prophet's preparedness message: "Saints should spend a year in this place to prepare themselves for the trek and to create a turn-a-round set-up for nurturing others yet to come."

The rotation plan worked straight away for Edward who moved his wife and the four younger children from the dugout into a log house six miles down the road. They planted thick vegetable and flower gardens and worked as a team for the harvest. Henry, in particular, thrived with the project. "You were meant to be a farmer," his father told him.

Edward Tuttle was assigned by President Young to remain at Winter Quarters for a year overseeing the livestock and protecting it from Indians.

"This last 'permanent' encampment between Nauvoo and the Rocky Mountains will become an important stopping place for future travelers. We need to plant it and build it up as a place of relief and replacement for settlers who will follow," the President instructed.

Tuttle helped build a stockade around the settlement and took his turn standing guard. A company of Ten Rough Rangers was raised to guard the herds as well. Parley P. Pratt, Daniel Russell, John Taylor, David Boss, Daniel Spencer, Alpheus Cutler, Joseph Young, Isaac Morley, George D. Grant, and John Neff, were led by Hosea Stout.

"Our Prophet Brigham Young said we must refrain from killing the Indians, but we should not allow them to take advantage, steal our cattle, or overtake the city," Stout reminded his men.

"So you have gone from baker to butcher," Titus teased his friend.

"Either way I help you eat," Edward said grinning. He still did a lot of baking; wedding cakes at Winter Quarters seemed to keep him busy.

"I am so excited for you," Mary Ann said to her sister.

"I know. I can hardly believe its true myself.
!" Martha Ann Tuttle had accepted a proposal of marriage to Walter Elias Gardner. They were married at Winter Quarters on April 28, 1847. Her wedding cake was the most beautiful in all the territory. Her father would not have it any other way.

Henry Tuttle was watering his plants when he heard his brother screaming like a mad man. *A fifteen-year-old boy is too old to carry on like that*, he thought to himself, until John came into view running full force with panic written all over him.

"Ma, Ma! Pa's been hurt!"

Henry ran without his crutch as though he never needed one. Pa needed help. That was all that mattered now. He arrived on the scene the same moment his mother did.

"Oh Edward!" she exclaimed.

Her husband was flat on his back with blood spewing from his abdomen. His insides had been chopped up leaving him in terrible pain. Several men struggled together to restrain a vicious bull.

"He's lucky to be alive," one of them said.

"Let's get him out of this heat," said another.

"I'm sorry, Catherine," her husband said with faint voice.

"Oh, Edward," she said again dropping to her knees beside him. Raising her skirt for a cleaner underside, she wadded it, and pushed it into the wound, pressing firmly to stop the bleeding.

When a wagon appeared, Catherine tore the wad of fabric from her skirt so it could remain in place. Friends hoisted the wounded man into the wagon bed and helped his wife climb in beside him.

"I'll go for Sister Billings," Mary Ann shouted on the run.

They took Brother Tuttle home.

"I'm a midwife, not a doctor," Diantha declared, examining the damage.

"Please help me know what to do until a doctor can came," Catherine pleaded.

Martha Ann was boiling water. With great care the two women proceeded to clean the mutilation.

"Hear you had a fight with a bull," Brother Billings teased. "Next time pick on one your own size." It hurt to move and it hurt to laugh.

"There won't be a next time," Edward protested.

When medical help came at last, not much more was left to be done. "Good thing you cleaned it so well," the doctor said. He did some stitching, lots of wrapping, gave instructions for changing the dressing, and wished his patient the best of luck as he left.

Bedridden for many weeks Catherine guarded her patient around the clock. She took meticulous care of his bandages.

"It's looking better," she said. "I think you'll make it."

In record time, Ed could sit up and walk around a little.

"How about having dinner at the kitchen table?" Catherine suggested at last.

"Sounds good to me," he agreed.

They invited the newlyweds and Catherine cooked her husband's favorite meal. Mary Ann set the table with her mother's best dishes. A glass of Henry's colorful flowers provided the perfect centerpiece.

"This is a special occasion for all of us," Brother Tuttle told his family. I am happy to be on the mend and thank each of you for your help these many long weeks. It goes to show that when families pull together with love, they can accomplish great things. I love you all. Don't ever forget it."

Catherine jumped up and kissed his cheek. "We have a surprise for dessert," she said.

Their little, quick-built house had make-shift cupboards on the wall. Catherine was slicing pie below when the upper cupboard began to pull away. Edward saw it first and leaped up to catch the falling cupboard before it injured his sweetheart. Such exertion reopened his wound and complicated his condition.

He spent more time in bed. The laceration refused to close the second time. For some reason the new tissue seemed unable to connect, and fresh bleeding occurred each day. On top of all that, Ed got sick. Each cough agonized his injury. Soon a high fever troubled him, evidence of infection. During the hush of an August night, Edward Tuttle's gentle spirit slipped out of its aching frame. Catherine found him lifeless the next morning. He was buried on the hill beside a tree at Winter Quarters.

*   *   *

Titus had good connections in St. Joseph, Missouri and agreed to take a job for the winter in an effort to raise sufficient funds for the Rocky Mountain Trek next spring.

453

"We are going back to Illinois," Samuel said one evening when he and Martha came to visit.

"Not Nauvoo, it's too dangerous there," Diantha said.

"No Ma, Centralia, Illinois. Martha got a letter from her parents."

"They like it there," Martha said.

"Her father offered me a job. We think we should go," Sam added.

Titus inquired about the matter. "What kind of job?"

"Painting. I'll be a painter again."

"That's good, honest work. You should do well, son."

"I'm going too," Alfred announced.

Diantha gasped.

"Are you sure son?" Titus asked. "Do you have plans?"

"I want to find work in St. Louis."

"Sam to Illinois. Alfred to Missouri. George to the Rocky Mountains. My husband to St. Joseph." Diantha's heart felt like it was bursting wide open. "Eunice," she cried, "please don't leave me!"

Titus traveled part way with Sam and his wife, then left Alfred Nelson in St. Louis. Being so far away, he missed out on the Solemn Assembly where Brigham Young was officially sustained President of the Church. Diantha sent word to him.

January 1848

Beloved Titus,

We are doing well, but miss you completely. I pray you obtain adequate funding quickly and return to us very soon.

Did you hear of the miracle at the Bluffs a few weeks ago? (Well, I guess they are calling it Miller's Hollow now.) Anyway, as I understand it, the Lord told the brethren, in a meeting at Brother Orson Hyde's home, to reorganize the First Presidency. Brother Henry Miller was asked to build a tabernacle so saints could gather for the occasion. Titus, they say he built it in only 2 1/2 weeks. (Well, he had a little help. About 200 men.) Anyway, the log structure was adequate for 1,000 people. I know. I can hear you now. You would love to have helped them. The important thing is that Brigham Young has been properly sustained as President of the Church. Heber C. Kimball is his first counselor and Willard Richards is the second. Thought you would want to know.

I send you God's speed and all of my love,

Diantha Morley Billings

P.S. Please don't feel bad about missing out on the action. I'll let you build me a tabernacle when we get to wherever it is that we are going.

Henry Tuttle stepped up to the responsibilities of preparing his family to be ready for the big journey. He did not want them to be left behind and knew his father would expect it of him. He and John Wells worked hard for an abundant harvest.

Historical Background

"On Tuesday, April 6, 1847, conference was held at Winter Quarters" (Cottam/ Malouf). "Titus and Isaac were appointed to the High Counsel at Winter Quarters April 16, 1847" (Bennion, 2; Pyne, 3) "Brigham Young encouraged the Saints to remain for a year at Winter Quarters before they moved on. Thus, by rotation, some homes became vacant" (Archibald, 3).

"Father built a dugout and we lived in it all winter until April 28, 1847, when I married Mr. Walter E. Gardner" (Gardner,2). "Martha Ann married Walter Elias Gardner on the 28 April 1847 at Winter Quarters" (Archibald, 13).

Winter Quarters, now known as Florence, Nebraska (a suburb of Omaha) was the last "permanent" encampment between Nauvoo and the Rocky Mountains. "By December it consisted of 538 log houses and 83 sod houses where 3,483 people resided. The 12 feet by 18 feet single-room dwellings had a sod roof and floor. Each had a good stone chimney. The population was divided into twenty-two wards" (Morley, 110).

"Although Chief Big Elk, of the Omaha Nation, wanted friendly relations with them, he could not control all of his warriors. To protect their cattle, the Mormons built a stockade around the settlement" (Morley, 110-111; CES, 320).

"It was here one evening when her husband [Edward Tuttle] was bringing in the Church cattle that he was gored by one of the bulls and died from the effects of the wound. He was buried in Winter Quarters on the 17th of August 1847" (Carter2, 334).

"Edward Tuttle, who extensively looked after livestock, was gored in the abdomen by a vicious bull . . . one of the cupboards started to pull away from the wall. Edward tried to catch it and in doing so, the strain reopened his wound, which was fatal" (Archibald, 3).

"Isaac Morley remained behind to fatten cattle at Summer Quarters" (MorleyRH, 113).

[Titus Billings went] "to Saint Jo and earned means to come to the valley, leaving their son, Alfred Nelson, at St. Louis to come later" (Bennett, 558).

[Titus Billings] "came as far as Council Bluffs, but being too late to cross the plains wintered at Punckaw then went back to Winter Quarters and then to St. Jo and earned means to come to the Valley, leaving their son Alfred Nelson at St. Louis to come later" (Tibbitts, 75).

Henry Miller's crew built a log tabernacle in only two and one-half weeks, at Miller's Hollow on the east side of the Missouri River. The place was renamed "Kanesville" in honor of Col. Thomas L. Kane at a conference held in the tabernacle April 6, 1848. Now it is called Council Bluffs again (Cottam/Malouf 17; Jenson; LSD Hist. Kanesville). "Brigham Young was unanimously sustained as President of the Church, with Heber C. Kimball as his first and Willard Richards as second Counselor" (Jenson).

Billings spent time in St. Joseph, Missouri, and "earned means to come to the valley" (Worsley, 1). His son Alfred Nelson Billings stayed behind in St. Louis "to come later" (Bennett, 558). Samuel Dwight Billings, oldest son, stayed in St. Louis (Bennion1, 1). Titus' third son, Ebenezer, left on the Mississippi River (1847) and was never heard from again (Bennion, 2).

Billings, fourth son, George Pierce Billings, was twenty years old when President Brigham Young asked him to join the first company west as a scout and a teamster (Pyne, 3).

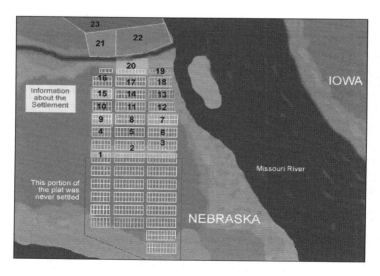

Wards at Winter Quarters

The Edward Tuttle Family belonged to the Winter Quarters 22 Ward.

(Courtesy Winter Quarters Project. BYU http://winterrquarters.byu.edu.)

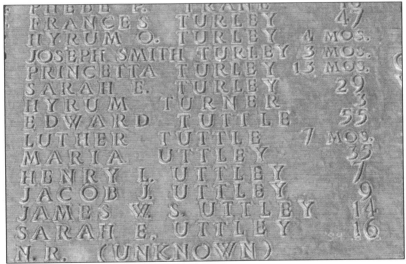

Mormon Pioneer Cemetery at Winter Quarters

Edward Tuttle was 55 years when he died at Winter Quarters, as engraved on monument.

(Courtesy S.B. Mitchell, 2002.)

Omaha Hospital and Winter Quarters Visitor Center- Burial Lot

Discovering Grandpa's Resting Place

Mary Billings Jones was in Nebraska for her daughter's hospitalization. Corinna, the daughter, was allowed to leave for a few hours when we went to see her. We paused a moment at the LDS Visitor's Center for Corinna to rest during the tour and I mentioned that her ancestor was buried somewhere out there on that hill. Our missionary guide picked up on the fact, offered to check the record, and returned with the burial plot map identifying grandpa's gravesite as #200.

(Courtesy S.B. Mitchell, 1994.)

Edward Tuttle's Grave at Winter Quarters

We rushed to the site for pictures. When our photo was developed (no digital cameras back then) we thrilled at the way a sun's ray seemed to point to Edward Tuttle's burial spot. —sbm

(Courtesy S.B. Mitchell, 1994.)

CHAPTER 76

"Where's your Ma?" Titus asked as he walked into his Winter Quarter's cabin after many months of working out-of-state. Eunice jumped up and raced for her father's neck.

"Oh Pa, you're home!"

"Did you miss me?" he teased.

"Did we ever!"

"And Al! Did he get back safely?"

"Yes, Pa. He's out watering the horses."

"Is your mother home?" he asked.

"She went with Sister Tuttle to take flowers to the cemetery."

"Guess I'll go find her."

"I want to come too."

Titus paused outside to pick a few posies. Eunice smiled at him.

"Ma will like those," she said. "But seeing you will be the best."

*　　　*　　　*

George Pierce Billings returned from the Salt Lake Valley with an excitement unmatched and pretty tall tales to tell.

"We arrived in the Valley a day before my twentieth birthday," he boasted.

Eunice, Mary Ann, Henry and John Wells were his best audience as he told how his proudest claim to fame was turning over the first spade of soil in the new land.

"Someone else did the first planting," he laughed. "But I got my shovel into the ground first!"

"Tell us more about Clayton's invention," his father said.

"Oh, you mean the odometer. He and Brother Harman built it."

"Appleton Harmon is a very skilled mechanic," Titus said.

"Yes, well I think it was Orson Pratt's idea in the beginning. Anyway, it worked really well. Poor Brother Clayton was going crazy counting every time the wheel turned."

"How could he do it?" J.W. Tuttle asked.

"How could who do what?"

"How could Brother Clayton, or anyone for that matter, tell when a wagon wheel has spun clear around?"

"Oh that. You see, Brother Clayton tied a red piece of flannel onto the outer edge of one spoke and then he walked beside it counting every time if made a full revolution."

"I would hate to have that job."

"He had measured the circumference of the wheel so he knew the distance of each rotation. All he had to do was count how many times and multiply."

"Yeh, that's all," Titus said.

"When Brother Harmon fitted that little gadget onto the wagon they only had to count miles, not revolutions. It was much better."

Diantha noticed her son's shirt was made of pillow ticking. She had never seen it before.

"My shirt was shredded with wear when we got to the valley, so Sister Kimball sewed me a new one."

"That was kind."

"Yup. All of Elder Kimball's wives are kind." He looked mockingly at his sister. "You could be one of his kind wives, Eunice . . .whenever you are ready, dear sister."

"Not funny - in the least." In fact, it was a sore spot between his sister and her father. "Come on, Mary Ann. We don't have to take this."

George helped his mother pack for their long journey westward. Now that Titus was back from St. Joseph, they would soon be ready to go.

"Hurry," Titus said. "Meeting starts at 10:30."

"We're ready," Diantha answered as she took his elbow and stretched her stride to keep up with his. "Do you know who all will be there?"

"Anybody who wishes to head west this season," Titus answered.

Many folks had such intentions because the meeting stand at Winter Quarters was surrounded with an excited multitude when they arrived (May 1, 1848). President Young gave experienced and timely instructions. The face of George Pierce Billings beamed with an all-knowing glow as he nodded agreement to everything that was said.

"I propose that the companies emigrating west be organized at the Elkhorn River," Brigham Young said. Several brethren were appointed to build a bridge across the Papillion River for future use. "This will shorten the road to the Elkhorn three miles."

A vote was taken. All agreed to meet at the Horn where they would be divided into groups for their trek west.

"According to Elder Clayton's roadometer it is 1,031 miles from here to the Salt Lake Valley," George told his parents as they started for home.

"Sounds like a nice little walk," his father said.

"Nice little walk indeed," Diantha added.

George chuckled. "Best little walk I ever took."

Though saints rolled out of Winter Quarters in different clusters on different days, they all experienced the challenges of springtime mud, upset animals, broken wagon parts and steep, slopes. Nonetheless, all of them arrived safely at the Horn where they were divided into three divisions with a member of the First Presidency leading each one. President Young's group included 1,229 souls in 397 wagons. Isaac Morley was sustained as one of his camp leaders. The Billings, Tuttle and Gardner (Tuttle's married daughter) families were assigned to the second division, led by Elder Heber C. Kimball. Titus Billings was chosen captain of the hundred in the first company.

"I am so happy that we will be traveling together, all the way to the Rockies," Eunice said to her friend, Mary Ann Tuttle.

"Me too. My sister and her husband are going with us."

"Isn't she going to have a baby?"

"Yes, in two months. She will make me an 'Auntie' on the trail." Eunice was happy for her friend, but could not help remembering her nephew's tiny grave left back in Nauvoo, and her younger brother's grave too. *I miss you Titus Junior,* she said in her thoughts.

Church leaders continued to organize the crowd. Saints began ferrying across the river and swimming the cattle. President Isaac Morley, his counselors Titus Billings and William W. Majors, and clerk Thomas Bullock left at sundown (May 31, 1848) to help President Young organize other companies. Zerah Pulsipher was made captain of the hundred, with John Benbow a captain of the first fifty and Daniel Wood captain of the second fifty. As in other camps, they were instructed to use common sense and abide orderly conduct.

"Never abuse the cattle, but take care of them," President Young said. "You have no need to yell or bawl or make noise or be up late at night. Attend to your prayers. Put out fires. Go to bed at 9:00."

Lorenzo Snow was made captain of the hundred at the next camp. Herman Hyde and John Stoker were made captains of the fifty groups. President Morley gave instructions this time: "Brethren, be united or you will smart for it." Ten men were chosen to help build a bridge over the creek. In an effort to separate the cattle and the sheep of one group from the other, one company was sent toward the Platte River and the other to go over the creek. Both would start out the next day.

"Get a good rest tonight," Titus told his family. "We'll be heading out at 7:00 in the morning for a very strenuous journey."

*　　　*　　　*

Mary Ann helped her mother tuck another bundle into the wagon as her new brother-in-law tightened the tarp.

"Thanks for all your help, Walter," she heard her mother say. "Is that everything?"

"Oh, I hope so. Everything we can take." Catherine was thinking of the one thing she would be forced to leave behind, her gentle, beloved baker who slept deep beneath the earth at Winter Quarters.

Travelers left the settlement in small groups, leaving at differing times and taking different routes. The plan was for all to meet up some twenty miles later on the Elkhorn River and re-group.

Men were already building rafts when Gardner found a spot and parked his wagon. He lit a little cooking fire for the women and started off to counsel with the men. Henry followed him.

"How big do you think this one is?" Henry asked, looking across the river as the setting sun started pinking its waters."

"Don't think it's very deep, but it sure is wide," Walter ventured.

Just then Henry spotted George and waved his crutch at him.

"George."

"Well, hello there. How we doing?"

"Good right now," Walter said, "but not so sure when we

have to cross over the river."

"Do you know how wide is it," Henry asked.

"Well, they say it's a hundred and sixty feet at the spot they picked for us to cross. Doesn't look very deep, though. You should have seen it last year."

Henry was not at all excited about crossing rivers. "How so?" he asked.

"It was really deep when we came through here. I helped Brother Sessions find dry timbers and we built a huge raft to get the wagons across, all five-hundred and sixty-six of them. The ten of us did it in two days."

Henry was impressed. So also was his brother-in-law.

"After we cross over tomorrow keep watch for our Liberty Pole," George added.

Now Henry was intrigued.

"Brother Session had us scrape a seventy-five foot cottonwood trunk and we raised it with a white flag on top."

"I'll have to tell Johnny about that. Wonder where he is."

"Look for him while you help me pass the word," George said. "President Young wants everyone at a meeting tonight. 'Need to let them know."

Word got out because everyone gathered.

"We have a thousand miles ahead of us and in order to make those miles as pleasant as possible we will expect every person to observe these rules of conduct."

Brigham Young's Rule of Conduct for Crossing the Plains

1. A bugle will blow each day at 5 a.m. and every man is expected to arise and pray, then attend to his team, get breakfast, and be prepared to travel at 7 a.m.
2. Each man is to walk at the side of his team with his gun loaded and within reach.
3. The camp will halt about noon to rest the animals. People must have their dinner pre-cooked so as not to delay camp by fixing meals.
4. At night the wagons are to be drawn into a circle, and the animals placed inside the circle when possible.
5. The bugle will blow at 8:30 p.m. when every man must return to his wagon and pray, except the night guard. Fires must be out and people in bed by 9 p.m.

6. *The camp will travel in close order, and no man is to get farther than 20 rods away (about 330 feet) without permission from his captain of ten.*

7. *Every man is to help take care of his brother's cattle. No man will be indulged in idleness.*

8. *Every man is to have his rifle and pistol in perfect working order. A piece of leather should be kept over the firing mechanism to protect it from moisture.*

9. *All persons will start together and keep together. A company guard will attend the cannon in the rear and see that nothing is left behind at each stopping place.*

"Pioneers Crossing the Plains of Nebraska"
by C.C.A. Christensen (1831-1912).

Henry nudged George. "Bet you'll get that job," he grinned, almost with envy.

"We are now about twenty miles west of Winter Quarters," Brigham continued. "We will travel another twenty miles until we reach the Platte River, and then we will follow it for the next six-hundred miles.

"Oh," sighed Diantha. "That sounds so far."

"At least we will have water," her husband comforted.

Next day all six hundred and sixty-two souls of Kimball's company were ready for the early start from their Elkhorn River encampment. The first hurdle was to ferry their two hundred and twenty-six wagons, fifty-seven horses, twenty-five mules, seven hundred and thirty-seven oxen, two hundred and eighty-four cows, one hundred and fifty loose cattle, two hundred and forty-three sheep, ninety-six pigs, two hundred and ninety-nine chickens, seventeen cats, fifty-two dogs, three hives of bees, three doves, five ducks, and one squirrel across the Elkhorn River.

Roads on the other side were soft from an earlier storm. At least the air was cool as they pushed forward.

"There it is!" Johnny shouted.

"Sure enough. Just like George said it would be."

Liberty Pole Camp, in the valley of the Main Platte River, was a perfect meeting place. Captains had already been assigned to each group of ten. Now a squad of men was chosen to help the captain of the cannon "make thunder" to frighten off Indians, if need should arise.

After watering the animals, they pressed on because it was too early in the day for stopping. About 3:00 in the afternoon, George, on horseback, rode up beside his parents' wagon.

"There's a good spot just ahead by the Platte River. Going to stop there. We've come fifteen and a quarter miles today!"

Evening encampment fenced animals in a tight circle formation of covered wagons with family tents and cooking fires scattered around the outside perimeter. Necessity and President Young's rules required preparation of not only the evening meal, but the next day's lunch as well. There would be no stopping to do it during the day.

The company grasped the basic routine of pioneer travel without delay. A bugle call at 5:00 a.m. alerted everyone of the new day. After prayers and breakfast, mothers readied children and fathers prepared teams for a 7:00 move out call of "Westward Ho."

Each man walked beside his team keeping a loaded gun within easy reach. A short break at noon allowed the animals to rest and the saints to eat their pre-cooked meals. Obedience was expected and required.

The weather, however, was fickle. Sometimes it was too cold, next it would be too hot, or much too wet, or dreadfully dry.

"Can't find kindling wood anywhere," John Wells complained to his brother.

"Start picking up buffalo chips then," Henry told him.

"Yuck, remember how terrible those smell when they get wet?"

"Better warm and smelly than freezing and fragrant," Henry laughed. "Now get to work, little brother."

Whenever possible the evening camp was laid out near a wood and water supply. Laundry and other domestic chores filled the few remaining hours of daylight. An 8:30 p.m. bugle blow called all to prayers. Fires must be put out and folks of all ages should be in bed by 9:00 p.m., except the men pulling guard duty, who often found it difficult to stay awake after coaxing their oxen all day.

Brother Billings welcomed the Sabbath Day before it was daylight. He was up and turned his cattle out for grazing by 4:00 a.m. (Sunday, June 11, 1848) then began studying for a talk Elder Kimball had assigned him.

At 11:00 a.m. John Wells Tuttle was sent to all the camps ringing the warning bell with an announcement.

"Sabbath Meeting today on the bank of the river," he called again and again.

The weather felt pleasant and the crowd seemed receptive to messages of patience, praying, keeping the Sabbath Day holy, being kind to cattle, refraining from swearing, living with love and order -- as instructed by Brother Harriman, Brother Billings and Brother Kimball.

Another religious meeting was held at 4:00 p.m. in the same location. Brother Jack Pack spoke again of patience and keeping the commandments. Brother Joseph Fielding addressed the blessings of being privileged to help build up the kingdom of God and again Brother Kimball gave sound instruction concerning general principles. Brother Titus Billings dismissed the meeting with prayer.

Historical Background

"[George Pierce Billings] was the driver of one of Heber C. Kimball's teams. Because his clothing was worn out when he reached the valley, Mrs. Kimball made him a shirt out of a striped bed tick and gave him some moccasins" (Carter, 2, 575). He "arrived in Salt Lake valley the day before he was 20 years old" (Jensen4,

72). His name is listed on the "This is the Place Monument" in Salt Lake City. "On his grave stone it says that he turned the first furrow in the Salt Lake Valley" (Pyne, 3).

"The pioneers . . . left Winter Quarters on May 1, 1848, for the Great Salt Lake Valley which was located, according to William Clayton's roadometer, 1,031 miles westward" (MorleyRH, 116). President Young then gave timely instructions to those who were preparing to start for the mountains (Esplin, 10). "Nine rules were laid down for the trip and everyone was expected to be obedient" (Knight/Kimball, 25; Cottam/Malouof, 22).

"Cows and calves were yoked up, two wagons lashed together, and a team barely sufficient to draw one was hitched onto them, and in this manner they rolled out of Winter Quarters some time in May. --finally succeeded in reaching Elk Horn, where the companies were being organized for the plains" (Tullidge, 345-346). "The emigrants were divided into three divisions each division being led by one of the First Presidency: Brigham Young the First Division, Heber C. Kimball the Second Division and Willard Richards, the Third Division. Brigham Young's division had three companies of one hundred, subdivided into fifties and tens. Patriarch Morley with Titus Billings and William W. Major, captains of fifty, as councilors [sic] formed a general presidency over all the companies under Brigham Young" (Brewster, 45; Esplin 10).

"Instructions were given by Father Morley, and ten men picked out to prepare the bridge over the creek," (Journal History22, 31 May 1848).

Thomas Bullock wrote: "After breakfast I crossed my two wagons over the Elkhorn River hearing that the President was numbering the wagons in his corral. I immediately went there to assist and divided his corral into 14 companies of tens. President Young then went to the ferry and President Morley with his counselors and myself commenced the organization of Lorenzo Snow's hundred and Zerah Pulsipher's hundred; we completed the organization of Allen Taylor's and Isaac Morley's companies. The brethren continued ferrying all day; they swam the cattle over. At sundown President Young with President Morley and his counselors Titus Billings and Wm. W. Major and Thomas Bullock as clerk, went up to Zerah Pulsipher's hundred and organized it, by voting in Zerah Pulsipher to be the captain of the hundred, John Benbow captain of fifty and Daniel Wood captain of fifty" (Journal History22, 31 May 1848).

Kimball records: "About 9 o'clock a.m. Heber C. Kimball's company broke up their encampment on the Elkhorn and started for the West. The day was cool and pleasant, but the road soft in places caused by the late storm. On arriving at the Liberty Pole on the main Platte River, they found Isaac Higbee's company encamped" (Journal History25, June 7, 1848).

"Brother H.C. Kimball's Company started from the Horn on the 7th and on the

9th they elected the following officers, viz. Henry Harriman (Herriman), captain of the first hundred, Titus Billings and John Pack, captains of fifties; subsequently, Isaac Higbee was appointed a captain of fifty" (Journal History27; Journal History 28; Smith7, 626; Widtsoe, 626).

Hannah Morley remembered that: "It was quite cold and uncomfortable riding. About 3 o'clock in the afternoon they arrived near the Platte and had a pleasant place to camp with singing and prayers at Brother Morley's wagon. Next day they traveled 13 miles and again camped beside the Platte. Traveled only 10 miles the next day to Shell Creek [Shoal Creek, also known as Locust Creek] and encamped about 2 o'clock. After a heavy shower the men went hunting and Brother Potter killed an antelope. There were plenty of fresh clams in the creek, also fish. Good clear water and plenty of good dry wood, and all well" (Hannah Morley's diary: Esplin, 17).

Also, from Martha Ann Tuttle Gardner's journal: "When [we] camped at night they formed the wagons in a corral shape, and kept the animals in at night and we had to do our cooking outside. We traveled on climbing mountains and crossing rivers, except Sundays as we camped till Monday and meeting was called and they gave us good counsel and urged us not to get tired and weary, as we had a long tiresome journey before us" (Gardner, 3).

The camp, later known as Isaac Higbee's company, was then organized as follows: Titus Billings Captain of First Fifty; William Burgess Captain of First Ten; Joseph G. Hovey Captain of the Second Ten; Newell K. Whitney Captain of the Third Ten; John Cox Captain of the Fourth Ten; Albert P. Griffin Captain of the Fifth Ten. Also, John Pack Captain of the Second Fifty; Joel Ricks Captain of the Sixth Ten; Norton Jacob Captain of the Guard; Wm. Clayton, clerk (Journal History26, June 8 1848).

CHAPTER 77

Winds were high and wagons were lined up double when travel began at 8:30 a.m. Wednesday morning (June 14, 1848). Titus Billings led his group up the north road and Jack Pack's group paralleled them on the south trail. The day was dusty. Eunice and Mary Ann held their bonnet ties over their noses and pulled their brims low in an effort to shield their burning eyes.

"Look!" Eunice shouted. Mary Ann beheld the sight and it saddened her. Pawnee Village, or what was left of it, stretched out charred and desolate. No one was tempted to stop. The place was nearly all burned up. Little was said as they passed by at 2:00 in the afternoon.

The next morning at 9:00 Brother Billings led wagons out single file. Brother Kimball and twenty other wagons lingered behind to search for a cow. The road was anything but smooth. Muddy ground had been dried out by strong, constant winds that left it lumpy-bumpy and difficult to navigate. Not too many hours after they started out, a fast riding horseman raced past Billings' wagon and pulled out in front of him.

"Stop! Stop!" It was Alfred Nelson Billings. "There's been an accident, Pa. Ya gotta stop."

Titus gave signal and halted as quickly as possible.

"What is it?" Diantha asked. Alfred was winded.

"Lucretia Cox," he breathed.

"Little Lucretia?"

"Yes," he nodded his head. "She fell off the wagon tongue. She's been run over!" Diantha stood up in the wagon.

"Take me to her, Alfred. Hurry!"

Obediently the son pulled his mother onto the horse behind him and backtracked with a fast trot. A crowd had already gathered.

"It's Sister Billings," someone called out. "Move back. Let her through."

The sight was more tragic that one could imagine. An innocent, six-year-old child was sprawled on the ground with a front wheel dent across her body and a hind wheel mark embedded into her neck. There was no way to save her. She was already gone. Sadness hovered over the campers as they halted for the night, not far yet from Pawnee. Diantha stayed late at Sister Cox's wagon.

About 8:00 a.m. Alfred walked into camp with his mother's quilt wrapped around him (Friday, June 23, 1848). He had been out herding cattle since 3:00 a.m.

"Where are your mitts?" Diantha asked.

"Don't know, but I need to find them if it stays this cold," he said.

Again in the lead, Brother Billings shouted the "Westward Ho" as his company started out at 9:00 am. This time they took the south road and Brother Pack's group took the north. By noon the sun was blistering and a strong, dry wind blew dust everywhere. They continued west until 5:00 p.m.

As usual, John Wells Tuttle and his bell beckoned saints to meeting on the Lord's Sabbath (June 25, 1848). Brother Titus Billings conducted. After singing, Brother Henry Harriman stated that, "Prayer makes a Christian's armor bright," and he offered the prayer. .

"It is important to heed the counsel of those whom the Lord has set to counsel us," Brother Billings said. "We must be submissive to the Lord in all things. Then and only then, will all be well with us."

Bishop Whitney stood in turn. "We are on the greatest mission that ever was preformed." He spoke in depth on the subject.

Brother Billings added, "It is important that we all should come together to learn our duty. We should consider it a privilege to be able to come and learn our duty."

Brother Kimball instructed, "Let us call on the Lord night and day whether we are tired or not. Be careful. Be humble. All will be well."

Brother Pack inserted, "This is the most agreeable camp I ever seen."

Brother Kimball concluded, "Let no man do anything he would not wish to have done unto him. This will ennoble us in the sight of heaven and angels. We will never have any other heaven or kingdom than that which we make ourselves. This earth is our eternal home. We are now in eternity. We have got to subdue."

Walter Gardner drove his rig alongside his mother-in-law's wagon wherever the trail was wide enough. They followed closely behind the Billings family, not only because they wanted to be near their friends, but also because Martha Ann's special time was nearing and Walt wanted convenient access to both Catherine, the grandma, and Diantha, the midwife.

"Mary Ann, how would you like to ride with your sister tomorrow and the next day?" he asked at the supper fire.

"He's asking if you will drive it," Martha Ann added. She was miserable riding these days, but it beat walking. Anyway, fighting the animals and driving the rig was a bit too much for her delicate condition and Walter was leaving for a two-day buffalo hunt.

"I think I could do it," Mary Ann said. Then she had a great idea. "Could Eunice ride with me?"

"Sure, if she wants to." Mary Ann rushed to find her friend at the next fire. Eunice agreed and together they climbed onto Gardner's wagon the next morning.

"This isn't as easy as it looks," Mary Ann said.

"Doesn't look very easy at all to me," Eunice said.

"Well, at least I have you beside me."

"A lot of good I can do."

Both young ladies were relieved when the wagon train broke for evening encampment. In these last few hours of daylight all the cooking, laundering, and other necessary duties had to be completed. Usually a band performance or dance or sing-a-long was scheduled after dark. No matter what was planned for this night, the two sleepy girls would not attend it.

*   *   *

When July temperatures started climbing Alfred Billings certainly noticed them. "This heat saps the energy right out of you," he commented.

George had to agree. "Especially when you have to fight ornery oxen all day," he said.

"On top of that-- try to stay awake for guard duty all night," their father added.

Mary Ann Tuttle and her friend climbed onto the driver's seat of her sister's wagon for the second day. The sun was brutally hot and somewhat blinding as it bounced off the flat, elongated plain. Chit chat was by far the best way to get one's mind off the heat.

"So, who would you want to marry, if you could choose any man in the world?" Eunice asked.

"Oh, I don't know. Martha Ann did well, I guess."

"Yes, Walter is young and handsome enough."

"Talk about handsome. Look at your brother."

"George? You mean George Pierce?"

"You have to admit he is tall and handsome. Just how tall is he, Eunice?"

"Oh he's tall all right; boasts of six feet and four inches. He's way too pesky, though."

"Well, to you. You are his sister and I think he loves to get your goat."

"I wish my goat would get him sometimes."

"Why do you get so upset when anyone suggests that you be sealed to Elder Kimball?"

"It's not what I want, Mary Ann. I want to find a younger man who is masculine and adventurous, who can sweep me off my feet and make my life exciting every single day."

"What about religious?"

"Yes, very. And hard working."

"That's important."

"And I would enjoy a husband who loves music. One who will sing with me, like my Father does with my —"

Something must have spooked the oxen. For being big, slower animals, they took off wild with uncontrollable speed, yanking the guide reins right out of Mary Ann's hands. She lunged to grab them and pulled back with all her might.

"Help me, Eunice!" she shouted.

Struggling to keep balanced, Eunice also grabbed hold of the reins. Both of them pulled and prayed mightily.

"We can't let it roll," Mary Ann cried.

"Keep pulling," Eunice pleaded.

The delinquent team angled away from the others with a force of fury that bounced belongings out of the wagon at every bump. Whatever was it doing to the delicate mother-to-be resting in back?

Blinding dust bellowed everywhere from the pounding of hoofs on the dry untamed ground.

"What can we do?"

"I don't know. I don't know."

"Whoaaaaaaaaaaaaa. Steady there!" Some one was speaking. Where? Who? How? Oh please . . .

"Whoaaaaaaaaaaaaa," again they heard it. "Whoaaaaaaaaaaaaa," and again. An empty horse raced alongside

472

the unruly team as its driver dangled between them.

"It's an angel," Eunice said. "We are slowing, at last."

The wagon came to a stop and the panting creatures were fully controlled by the time Titus Billings caught up with them.

"Help my sister in back," Mary Ann shouted as she jumped down, into his arms. They rushed around the wagon bed calling her name. Titus opened the flap and Mary Ann crawled in to the biggest mess she had ever seen in her life. Everything was spilled and scrambled together. Nothing moved except dripping, oozing honey.

"Martha, Martha, Martha," Mary Ann feared the worst. "She's gone! I've lost her. She's been thrown out of here."

"Are you sure?" Titus asked, trying himself to catch up with the moment.

"I've killed two of them," she grieved, "my sister and her innocent baby."

Henry Tuttle reached them at last. "Where is Martha?" he asked. Mary Ann wept. "Listen!" he said, poking and rearranging things with his crutch. "I hear something back here."
With care, but quickness, Mary Ann started pulling things out of the way.

"Martha Ann?" She heard a groan. "She's alive!"

Eunice Billings sat stunned on the driver's bench. Although her face was more than windblown, dusty, and streaked with tears, her beautiful blue eyes studied the angel who had just saved her life. She expected him to vanish at any moment, but he remained. He was strong and young and spoke kindly to the troubled animals. Then he patted his horse and turned, not away, but toward her.

"Are your hurt?" he asked. Now she not only saw an angel, but also heard the voice of one.

"I'm fine," she said. "Thank you."

"That was quite a ride. You did well to hold it straight like that. Should have rolled, you know."

She stared at him.

"Do you have a name?"

She nodded.

"What is your name?"

"I'm Eunice Billings."

"Hello Eunice. I am John Ely Warner."

"No," she said.

"No?"

"You are an angel."

Horseshoe Creek was the place of evening encampment on that day of miracles, July 8, 1848. Walter Gardner and the other hunters returned with success at a late hour. Ira Gardner was born during the night.

Historical Background

"Wednesday, June 14 This is a fine, cool morning; the wind is high this morning. The camp started at half past 8 o'clock this morning in double file. Brother Billings' 50 took the lead on the north road, Bro. Pack's 50 on the south road. The southwest wind being high it was very dusty on the road. We passed old Pawnee Village today about 2 o'clock. It is nearly all burned up" (Journal History30; Thompson, 4).

"Thursday, June 15 This is a fine morning with a good breeze from the West. The camps started this morning at 9 o'clock, Brother Billings taking the lead. We went this morning in single file. Brother Kimball with some 20 wagons stopped behind the rest of the company to hunt a cow. The road was some broken today with considerable pitches. Coming down a little pitch Brother Jehu Cox [sic] daughter, Lucretia, fell of [sic] the wagon tong [sic] and was run over the body by the forewheel & over the neck by the hind wheel. She gaspt [sic] 1 or 2 and expierd [sic]. We camped for the night by the old Pawnee Village. Cox was 6 years old" (Journal History30; Thompson, 4).

"Sunday, June 25 This is a windy day. There was a meeting of the brethren this day at 12 o'clock. The meeting was opened by singing and prayer by Henry Herriman. Brother Herriman said that prayer makes a Christian's armour bright. Brother Billings said it was important to take heed of the counsel of those whom the Lord has set to counsel us; to be submissive in all things and all will be well. Bishop Whitney said that we are on the greatest mission that ever was performed. Brother Billings said it was important that we all should come together to learn our duty. We should consider it a privilege to be able to come and learn our duty. Brother Kimball said . . . Let us call on the Lord night and day whether we are tired or not. Be careful; be humble, and all will be well. Brother Pack said that this was the agreeablest camp he ever seen [sic], &c. Brother Kimball said let no man do anything they would not wish to have done to them & this will innoble us in the sight of Heaven and angels. We will never have any other heaven or kingdom than we make ourselves. This earth is our eternal home. We are now in eternity. We have got to subdue" (Journal History23, June16, 1848).

"Timber was scarce throughout much of June, and in place of wood, buffalo chips were used for fuel. Although the chips supplied the necessary heat, on wet mornings an odor was produced from the smoldering fuel which made camp life unpleasant" (MorleyRH, 119; Stout, 243-245).

"Thomas Bullock writes: "July 1 The distance from Winter Quarters was said to be 302 ½ miles (from the Junction of the North and South Forks of the Platte River). July 2 Meeting held with President Young's and President Heber C. Kimball's Camps at 3:30. Isaac Morley was one of the speakers" (Journal History23, June16, 1848).

Although John Ely Warner was the love of her life, his heroic steer-stopping, wagon saving introduction into our story is fiction.

Martha Ann Tuttle Gardner writes: "July 8-9 We camped on Horseshoe Creek. My son, Ira, was born. Brigham Young had called a meeting. My husband [Walter Elias Gardner] had just come in from a buffalo hunt. He had been out all night" (Gardner, 3; Journal History30, 31).

Mary Ann and her mother are not shown on the partial roster of the Second Division, but Martha Ann (sister/daughter) is listed as a Gardner and most likely they were there too. (Journal History- Emigration 1848)

CHAPTER 78

John Wells Tuttle ran through the evening camps (about 6:30 p.m. July, 11, 1848) ringing the warning bell to announce an unusual mid-week meeting. Saints gathered quickly.

"As you know," President Heber C. Kimball said, "two brethren left camp Monday to search for a horse." It came up missing after the buffalo hunt Saturday. "They have not returned. We know Indians are watching us. Several dressed in wolf skins have been spotted. Brethren, I believe it is our duty to send help. We must find those men. Are there any volunteers?"

Alfred Nelson Billings was the first to stand. Daniel S. McKay joined him. Then O.W. Hubbard, A. L. Hale, John Calvert, Gilbert Rolfe, Spencer W. Wilbank, P.W. Conover, C.A. Foster, W.C. Matthews, Oliver Best, Jason W. Steel, W. Childs, O.K. Whitney, J. Harper and J.S. Lott took up the call.

"Choose a captain among yourselves," Elder Kimball instructed. "Appoint one to be mouth and call upon the Lord. Go forth with the fear of the Lord. Do nothing that will make bad feelings among you. If you see Indians do not aggress them or tell them to stand back. You back out, rather than have any disturbance. The Indians will not hurt you. It is against their law as our camp is close by." Peter W. Conover was unanimously chosen captain. The rescue party left at dawn.

"Don't worry, Ma. Alfred will be fine." George tried to comfort his mother, but her caring soul was still troubled. "We sighted a whole band of Indians on the other side of the river when we first came through here last year. They were on horses and rode toward us."

"What did you do?" Eunice asked.

"Parked our wagons in a circle while Brother Woodruff and several others went out to meet them. About thirty crossed over." He paused for effect, enjoying his sister's look of alarm.

"What happened, George?"

"Well, I'm here to speak of it." He laughed.

"What did happen?" his mother asked.

"They rode right up to the brethren and shook hands. The chief carried a banner with an eagle and stripes and some fancy, Greek-like words on it. He gave Woodruff a letter."

"A letter?" Titus was intrigued.

"Yes, something written by a French fur trader they had befriended. 'Supposed to prove the tribe was friendly."

"Wow." Eunice was impressed.

"That's not all. Elder Woodruff said that they came out of curiosity and they wanted food. We mustered up all we could spare. Five chiefs toured our camp.'

"Five chiefs?" Eunice asked.

"Yes. I think they liked the cannon and the guns the most."

"I bet they did," Titus said.

"You won't believe what happened next." Certain that all eyes were upon him and every ear tuned in, George continued his tale. "The head chief requested that he and his wife be allowed to spend the night in our camp."

"You're kidding."

"No, that's a fact.

"Did you let them?"

"Well, it wasn't up to me to decide, but yes. We fixed up a special tent for them. I have to admit they were an impressive people."

"How do you mean, son?"

"They were clean and well dressed."

"What did they wear?" Eunice wondered.

"Buckskin with ornaments and long robes. All of them wore nice moccasins. They looked real noble. And left peacefully the next day. So you see, Mother, there's no need to worry."

The rescue took several days. It was successful. Soon Alfred and the others returned unharmed, though tired and hungry.

"There's Chimney Rock," George Pierce announced. "That means we are getting close to the mountains." He was right. The landscape was changing daily. Prairie grass was thinning out to let wild sage and prickly-pears take over the commonality. "It means we are pretty much half way as well," George added. The ancient rock formation looked like the chimney of an old English factory. It could be spotted miles away.

Mary Ann leaned against the wheel of a parked wagon one evening and began to sketch. The only paper available was her small journal, but the corner of one page would do the job. With tiny, tedious strokes she began to outline the impressive landmark she had studied for days.

"Got enough light for that?" Brother Billings asked. Mary Ann looked up as embarrassment painted her face like the sky at pink sunset.

"It's nothing important," she said.

"Oh, but it must be if you choose to capture it in your journal. May I take a look?" With that her sunset shades darkened. Still she held out the book with respect. He took it, studying only the drawing labeled "Chimney Rock."

"Very good," he said. "I didn't know we had an artist in camp."

She smiled. "I will probably never see this place again," she said.

"Won't need to now. You've captured it well."

At a combined Sabbath meeting (July 16, 1848) Elder Isaac Morley made a motion that the Young and Kimball Divisions be divided into eight smaller companies.

"This will help make the arduous chore of pulling the wagons easier for the cattle and more pleasant for the people," he said. "Dust created by several hundred wagons traveling together is most disagreeable." On that point everyone agreed.

George struck up a good friendship with a new fellow named Warner who started showing up after chores every afternoon. When he was there at suppertime, Diantha tried to include him. He was always polite and helpful.

"I'm taken by that young man who hangs around with our son," Diantha said.

"You mean John?" Titus asked.

"Yes, John Warner. Seems to want to be around George all the time."

Titus smiled. "You don't think he is here to see your son do you?" She looked up at him with more than a trace of confusion. Titus pointed with his thumb to the wagon behind him. John stood talking to someone. Diantha took a few steps to adjust her view enough to see the hem of a rusty brown skirt. It was her daughter's favorite.

"You don't think?" she questioned.

"I certainly do," he answered.

The Mormon Trail continued through Nebraska on the north side of the North Platte River as President Young had advised, while the Oregon Trail stretched through the bluffs on the south side.

"Look over there," George Pierce instructed. "How would you like to struggle through all of that?" Eunice and Mary Ann shielded their eyes to better observe the sight.

"Not something I'd like to do," John Ely Warner said. "We have a good view of it from here, but crossing those bluffs would be rugged. Guess it's good we listen to our leaders."

From a distance the striking formation looked like stone castles.

"That's Scott's Bluff. Quite a story about the spot."

"Tell us George," Eunice said. Mary Ann agreed. By now John Wells Tuttle had caught up with them.

"I want to hear it too," he said.

"Well, the way I heard it, Scott was a fur trapper-trader. His partners were upset with him about something so they put him ashore and left him there to die."

"Gosh, they must have been really mad at him," the younger John said.

"Guess so. Anyway, they say he climbed up one of those three massive formations to die in utter loneliness."

"Sad. I don't like that story," Eunice said.

The fellows laughed at her.

"Sorry, Sis, but that's Scott's Bluff for you."

The next day John Wells spotted a whitened buffalo skull near the side of the trail.

"Look, there's another one, George."

Henry Tuttle bent down to read it. The first company, George's company as he put it, penciled messages onto dry skulls whenever they found some.

"Prayer Circle Bluffs – May 30, 1847."

"Yes, this is where we stopped for a special prayer circle. President Young prayed for all of us on that first trek and for all of you waiting at Winter Quarters." The youthful group deemed it appropriate to have their own, quiet prayer.

They found another marker near Fort Laramie recording a distance of 543 ½ miles from Winter Quarters. Night encampment was set up a couple miles below the fort renamed Laramie after the river. It was one of the few places of civilization along the way. Not long afterward the road turned sandy and the hillside grew steep and uneven.

"Lock your wheels or you'll never make it," Titus advised.

By 5:30 the wagon train had inched its way only eight and a quarter miles. That was enough. They circled to park as lightening flashed. Soon thunder clapped and the rains began.

"Further travel on the north bank is impracticable and will soon be impossible," Elder Kimball said. "We will have to cross the Platte tomorrow. Charge for a flatboat ferry will be $15.00 per rig."

Historical Background

"July 11 The camp was called together about half past 6 o'clock. Heber C. Kimball said there was [sic] 2 of the brethren that left the camp on Monday morning to hunt the horse that was lost on Sat. while hunting buflo. W.K. and Alfred Billings went back to Camp Creek after some cows that was left on the bank of the river. They seen several Indians drest in wolf skins. Heber C. Kimball said the Indians were watching us & he felt it was our duty to get men & send back to see about the brethren. The following brethren volunteered: Alfred Billings, Danl S. McKay, O.W. Hubbard, A. L. Hale, John Calvert, Gilbert Rolfe, Spencer W. Wilbank, P.W. Conover, C.A. Foster, W.C. Matthews, Oliver Best, Jas. W. Steel, W. Childs, O.K. Whitney, J. Harper and J.S. Lott. H C K then instructed them to choose a captain among themselves. Peter W. Conover was unanimously chosen Cap. H C K then instructed them to appoint one as mouth & call upon the Lord & go in the fear of the Lord. Do nothing that will make feelings among yourselves. If you see Indians don't agress tell them to stand back. Back out rather than have any disturbance. The Indians will not hurt you as it is against their law as our camp is close by" (Journal History30).

"July 12 In sight of Chimney Rock" (Thomas Bullock Diary: Esplin 10).

Spotting Chimney Rock in the distance indicated "they were approaching the mountains. Prickly-pears and wild sage became the most prominent type of plant life and the grass diminished each day" (MorleyRH, 121: Words of William Clayton).

"July 15 Turned out the cattle as usual at half past 3; the camp started at 8. As the camp was moving out Noah W. Bartholomew's point box of[f] the hind axel broke & injured the point of the axel. When C.P. Lott was informed of the fact he stoped [sic] his 10 & he and William Thompson returned & helped him to mend his waggon up. Again we were detained by this accident 2 hours; we then pursued our journey again; stoped at noon & watered, camped for the night near Chimney Rock one mile and a half of the river. We dug wells & got plenty of water after digging 5 feet; good feed; no wood" (Journal History30, 32).

481

CHAPTER 79

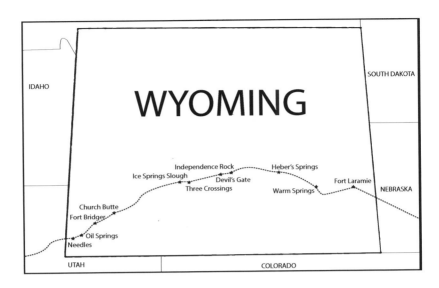

A few days later John Wells [Tuttle] came on the run.
"Where's George?" he asked.

"Hang on Boy. I am right here." George grabbed him by the back of his suspenders. "What's up?"

"Look over there, George. What's that broken down place?"

"Oh, that's Old Fort Platte. 'Was once a fur-trading fort. Lots of rooms, but only one adobe wall still stands. To us it looked like the inside had been burned out."

"Let's go over there, George."

"You know the rules, John. You will have to ask you mother first and then get permission from the captain."

"Will you come with me, if they agree?"

"Sure I will." The eager, long-legged teenager ran off to make his requests.

About seven miles down the river from the fort ruins was a steep cut in the high, rocky bluffs. Heavy winds whipped through the impressive opening where it dropped to the floodplain floor. (Now called Mexican Hill.)

"We've certainly seen some interesting sights," Diantha said as they passed it by.

"God's handiwork has no limits, does it?" Titus said. They continued on for several hours before reaching the next campsite.

"Hurry, Mary Ann," Eunice said. "I think this is my favorite camping spot so far, don't you?"

Most travelers preferred Warm Springs Canyon where clear springs were seventy degrees warmer than the river water. Thus, with much affection, the place was referred to as the Emigrants' Washtub.

"When we get these clothes out to dry we can wash our hair."

"What if John Ely Warner sees you?" Mary Ann teased. Eunice pretended not to care.

"He went after antelope with George and Alfred," she finally admitted.

"Oh, Henry spotted a herd on the run not too far back." Almost to herself Mary Ann added, "I wish he could go hunting. That leg would never let him."

"I know," Eunice said. "But I am sure they will share the meat." Mary Ann nodded agreement with a soft smile and picked up her bundle of dirty clothes. "Let's hurry before they get back."

The day was warm and clear. Several had gone out for buffalo. Captain Stephen H. Goddard and Joseph S. Allen each returned with a kill. While they cut up the meat, Titus unloaded his wagon to make room for it. He and the boys helped the two brethren deliver their prize. Saints spent the rest of the day cooking and drying out buffalo meat.

The next time wagons stopped, Hannah Morley went searching for her aunt. She found Diantha steaming a broth with a little buffalo meat.

"Theresa is ill," she said. "She has been in the wagon for several days." Theresa Morley was now a plural wife of Elder Heber C. Kimball. Diantha took a cup of the thin broth and left with Hannah for Elder Kimball's wagon. Her visit seemed to help more than the broth did.

"We've seen currants and cherries all along the road," Diantha said. "In fact, Eunice is out picking right now. I'll send her with some as soon as we wash them."

"Oh thank you Auntie. And thank you for coming to see me."

"Give your thanks to Hannah. She's the one who informed me." Diantha hugged them both. "Some of those cherries will be for you too, Hannah" she added. Diantha stepped from the wagon and started off. Pausing after a few strides, she returned.

"Theresa, do realize where we are?" she asked.

"No, not really. Is it significant?"

"To you it should be. We are stopped at Heber Springs."

"We are?" Theresa looked interested and so did her sister.

"George says they named this place after your husband because he found water here last year.

"Heber Springs." Theresa smiled. "Thank you for that information, Aunt Diantha. I will have to mention it to Heber when I see him."

Eunice soon appeared with an apron full of wonderful fruit. Her cousins were delighted and Theresa was well again, in no time.

Because the North Platte River had been a valuable travel companion for many miles, its sudden swing southward was a disappointment. Now it ran the wrong direction.

"We must cross over again, one last time" Elder Kimball said. "Here we will leave the Platte and begin to follow the Sweetwater further west." The Mormon wagon train was a welcome sight to a small group of brethren left behind to run the Mormon Ferry.

"It took us five days to cross over last year," George said. "We stopped to build strong rafts because the river was really swollen with spring runoff. Then, when other travelers offered to pay us to help them cross, well Elder Woodruff swapped our services for cash and supplies we needed."

"Looks like a good business now," Titus said. "Let's go down and give them our Howdy."

From the North Platte River their wagons passed through a gap in the hills called Emigration Gap, and started across a long stretch of land that distantly paralleled the Sweetwater, though they could not see it. The travelers noticed a definite rise in the ground as they climbed.

"This is the beginning of the Rocky Mountains," Titus told his wife. Soon they passed through Rock Avenue, a passageway extending a quarter of a mile between high rocks. The July sun was hot and everything was dry. It had been many days since they left the North Platte and the Sweetwater was still far out of sight. Needless to say, water supplies were precious.

"I know there is water around here some place," George said. He was one of three men President Young was sending out to again scout the area. "We'll find it," he promised.

They found Willow Springs, the first clear water-spot since the Platte and marked it well for future travelers.

Wagons wheels rutted a four hundred foot climb to the top of Prospect Hill. When the going got rough Eunice Billings began to sing. Her music seemed to lift spirits and proved to be contagious. Soon an angel was singing beside her. John Ely Warner had a wonderful singing voice, like her father!

"Hey, climb up here," George shouted. "The view is worth it."

John Ely jumped up and reached out a hand to Eunice and one to Mary Ann. Powerfully he pulled them upward. From the top of Prospect Hill one could see the Sweetwater River wind gently through a peaceful valley. Indeed there was hope of better prospects.

"Down there we will have easy access to good water," George said. "The trail is much easier too." He jumped down.

"Where are you going?" John asked.

"To find Pa," he said. "And Ma. They can't miss this."

In central Wyoming, on the north side of the Sweetwater River rests a huge mound known as Independence Rock.

"I can't get over the way that gigantic bump of granite pops out of the flat plain," Diantha said. "This will be an interesting campground."

"Just watch out for rattlers if you go up there," Titus cautioned his family. "They like rocky places, you know." He parked his company in a circle a short distance from the landmark and prepared for the weekend.

Mary Ann was always busy helping her sister with little Ira. He was an adorable baby with an Auntie who seemed to think he was her own.

"Come with us," Eunice invited. "It's a perfect day for a walk."

"We walk every day," Mary Ann laughed, "perfect or not." She was teasing because she believed her best friend wanted to take a more romantic stroll on this fine Sabbath afternoon. Not often was such an opportunity possible. No way did she want to hinder that moment for Eunice and John.

"Little Ira needs me, I think," she said propping the infant over her shoulder. "You go and have a nice time."

"We'll bring you some gooseberries," Eunice promised, "if we find any. George says it's a miracle how they grow out of the top of granite like that."

"I hope you find some," Mary Ann said as Eunice and John

started off hand in hand for Independence Rock. Somehow she didn't think those gooseberries really mattered all that much.

Mary Ann had some secret feelings of her own. A well-respected gentleman, formerly a Major in the Nauvoo Legion and now Captain of the Mississippi Company traveling next in line, had a way of tipping his hat to her every time he passed. He was older than she and had two wives already, but if Major Howard Egan was ever called to take another wife, and if by chance he chose to consider her, well, she could be open-minded about it. *Oh dream on*, she thought to herself. George Pierce Billings was impressive too, but he seemed to have a new interest these days. Her name was Edith Patten.

Monday morning the Titus Billings wagon pulled out, again in the lead. George walked beside it a distance, then started shouting.

"There it is. Oh yes. Do you see it?" His parents strained their eyes peering in the direction that he pointed.

"Look, over there. That's Devil's Gate."

Standing about six miles west of Independence Rock was another granite spectacle. This one, a craggy gorge three hundred and eighty feet deep, had a passageway fifty feet wide through which the Sweetwater River roared. Titus followed a trail south of the rugged canyon. He brought the line to a halt and allowed would-be-sightseers time to take a side trip.

Days later their wagons crossed the Sweetwater three times in a rather short distance.

"We named this place Three Crossings," George said.

They spotted the next marker at Ice Springs Slough.

"That's an unusual name," Diantha said.

"We dug under this thick marshy turf and found ice, last year." George explained. "Want me to dig you some?"

"Sounds refreshing," Diantha said.

Wagon wheels rolled on to a point where the Sweetwater River began to turn northward.

"Got to cross the river again," Titus announced.

"Again? Seems like that is all we do." Diantha was right. They had crossed over that river eight times already.

"Final time," her husband said. We will be leaving the Sweetwater now."

The spot, Burnt Ranch, would become an important Mormon mail station. Ten miles west was South Pass, a place so named by early trappers and located south of the Wind River Mountains. South Pass was the only place to cross the Continental Divide, which separates waters flowing to the Atlantic Ocean from those flowing to the Pacific Ocean. To the pioneers it was the location where they left the Sweetwater Valley, crossed over the top through about fifteen or twenty acres of dry basin and entered into the Green River Valley. Here the sagebrush disappeared. Huge gray bushes of sagebrush had been everywhere, sometimes reaching ten feet high with branches six inches thick. Now, suddenly, all of them were gone. Alfred rode up to his father's wagon.

"There's good grass up ahead," he said pointing to the north. "Want to stop there for the night?" Titus agreed and followed him. They found a good supply of water as well.

Enormous white alkali fields had to be crossed. Often these were six inches deep. Daytime temperatures were hot and miserable. Water would freeze every night the sky was clear. Many animals died. Fast decay from the heat of the day made it necessary to bury them.

Another Mormon Ferry was in place for crossing the Green River and George had a story for it when his father's group arrived.

"Some Missourians built rafts for crossing, but sent them up the river so we 'Mormons' could not use them." No one acted surprised. "So we started another Mormon Ferry," he added.

"Such planning was inspired," Titus said. They were grateful to use it.

A large, sandy, flat-topped butte stood at Black's Fork River crossing.

"Look at that," Eunice said. "It looks like Solomon's Temple."

"How do you know what Solomon's Temple looks like?" George teased.

"I read the Bible. Don't you?"

The large structure did resemble a temple. Others must have agreed because they named the site Church Butte. John Ely Warner agreed with Eunice. That was all that really mattered.

At length Fort Bridger came into sight. An eight-foot log fence surrounded four adjacent, sod-roof cabins that housed about fifty people.

"Jim Bridger did well when he selected this spot" Isaac Morley told his brother-in-law. He had come back to assist with some wagon troubles. Titus had to agree. Aspen and cottonwood trees grew around the fort. Fresh water streams crossed through green meadows.

"Good fishing in there," Heber C. Kimball said in passing. "Better make camp and go after some of that trout."

"Don't mind if I do," Titus said. Diantha was thrilled with his catch.

Fort Bridger was a pleasant stopping place, but not long after leaving it, the trail turned its toughest. Perhaps the anticipation of nearing the journey's end caused premature excitement that weakened stamina and incited impatience. At any rate, great elevation changes presented increased challenges.

"Do you think a little oil will help that wagon?" George asked his father.

"Wouldn't hurt, if we had some," Titus answered.

"There's a natural spring of it up ahead."

Sure enough, a place called Oil Springs had an oily substance that bubbled out of the ground. Titus filled his tar bucket with it for the wagon. Alfred and John Ely used some to oil their gunstocks. Some folks even oiled their shoes.

Wyoming's Needles or Pudding Rocks loomed in the distance. They would have to be crossed.

"This is where President Young got ill last year," George said.

"Rocky Mountain Tick Fever, wasn't it?" Diantha asked.

"Yes, bad stuff. Made him two days late to the valley."

"Watch out for wood ticks," Diantha said. "Pass the word."

By campfire light Eunice and Mary Ann took turns examining each other's long hair and scalp for tiny intruders. This caution they repeated night after night.

George sat on a rock with a sizeable gathering of young men congregated at his feet.

"What is going on over there?" Eunice asked her mother.

"Your brother is organizing a tour to Cache Cave."

"What is that?"

"Supposed to be a well-known, well-used meeting place for trappers."

Eunice had been looking for someone and spotted him in the group.

"So, can ladies go too?"

"Would ladies want to go?"

"Of course. I would."

"Go ask your father, then. I think I'd take a female friend or two." Diantha added. She was more keenly aware of her daughter's interests these days and smiled as Eunice rushed off.

The cave was thirty feet deep and anywhere from four to six feet high.

"We believe trappers 'cached in' or stored their supplies in here," George said.

Henry Tuttle poked his crutch into a corner as if trying to find a treasure of some sort. Eunice, in deep conversation with John Ely, looked radiant and seemed unaware that others were leaving. Mary Ann turned to her brother.

"Take me back to the wagon."

Henry gave her a taunting look, but said nothing. They walked back to the wagon in silence.

Historical Background

"July 16 The camp laid still all day [Sunday]; the cattle were turned loose four times to herd during the day; the sisters who had wood washed. Thomas Bullock was busy preparing the mail for the Valley, and instructed William Thompson, who had been appointed clerk of Kimball's camp, how to make out the returns to send to the Valley. President Young came to my wagon about 2 p.m. and gave me instructions to write an epistle to the Saints in the Valley; he told me that I had been a copyist long enough and that henceforth I must write all the epistles and letters and that I must dive right straight into the spirit of it. Accordingly I commenced with the epistle to the Valley and at 4 p.m. I read to him what I had written. At the hour a meeting was commenced on the open prairie between Brigham Young's and Heber C. Kimball's corrals. After some preaching and teaching, Isaac Morley moved that we break up both companies into four companies each. The motion was seconded and carried. Wm W. Phelps moved that Brother Brigham and Heber draw out those companies, [the motion] carried. President Young then appointed Isaac Morley and his counselors Daniel Garn and Chauncy G. Webb and Brigham Young to draw out a company each. Heber C. Kimball appointed Titus Billings, Isaac Higbee, John Peck and Henry Harriman (Herriman) to draw out a company each. It was agreed to send the mail to the Valley. President Young to send John Y. Greene with horse and mule and Heber C. Kimball to send Benjamin W. Rolfe and horse. Serinus Taylor volunteered to go as the third man with his horse" (Journal History24, 16 July 1848; Journal History30, 33; William Thompson Journal).

"In the evening President Young went down his row of wagons and counted off sixty-seven for Isaac Morley's company and seventy-five for his corral. We then met at his wagon and had a singing meeting.

After I had retired to rest I was called up by Reynolds Cahoon, his son Andrew and others to receive some instructions. We partook of cake and port wine and tarried until mid-night. The evening was clear and cold" (Journal History24, 16 July 1848; Journal History30, 33; William Thompson Journal).

While pioneers were assembled in a Sabbath Day Meeting, Elder Morley made a motion that President Brigham Young's and Elder Heber C. Kimball's companies be divided into eight smaller companies. He explained how smaller companies would help make the arduous chore of pulling the wagons easier for the cattle and more pleasant for the people. The dust created by several hundred wagons traveling together was disagreeable. When whitened buffalo skulls were found near the road, messages were scribbled on them with pencils and left for the later companies to read (Jensen, 904; MorleyRH, 122).

"Thursday, September 14 Cool morning. About half past 6 it commenced snowing & snowed about 2 hours. Camps moved off at half past 8. As we were starting several of the brethren from the Valley came up with 4 horse wagons going to the States on business, among the rest Brother & Sister Louis. Coming to the forks of the road Brother Billings' camp took the south fork & H.C.K. took the north fork. Campt about 5 miles from the fork on the top of the ridge. Plenty of wood & feed. Had to carry our water one mile & half from springs in the side of the bluff" (Journal History30, Thompson).

"Sunday, September 17 Frosty morning. Brethren gathered up the cattle at 7 & Brother Pack & Billings camp moved off at half past 8; leaving Brother Egan & Kimballs camps coreld. We campt on the banks of Echo Creek coming in a little before sundown. Near the cold spring we met Brother James Lawson from the Valley with a span of horses to help Sister Smith. We built a good fire in the corell & the camps met together. The meeting was opened by singing & prayer by Joseph Fielding. The meeting was open for the brethren to do as they felt. Brother Lott spoke for some time concerning the unity of the Saints. He said that H.C.K. instructed Father Billings & him to move on and have a meeting of thanksgiving & dedicate and consecrate ourselves to the Lord afresh. Whereupon C.P.Lott called a vote to see if it was the minds of the meeting to do as H.C.K. instructed us. Unanimous. Brother Thompson, Ryle, Billings, Lawson & other followed with remarks concerning the work we are engaged in, etc. The meeting was good. The Spirit of the Lord was with us. All felt well. Unity of the Spirit prevailed" (Journal History30, Thompson).

On Sunday, September 17, 1848, Thomas Bullock wrote: "The past night was frosty, the morning clear and calm. Ellsworth and my teams did not travel today. I doctored my sick cow and boiled out tar, that I obtained at the spring; the stuff produced about 75 per cent oil or grease, which is very good for wagon wheels, sores on cattle, bruises or cracks on the skin, etc. In the evening the Illinois camp, John Pack's and Titus Billings' companies passed us. President Young is about 16 miles ahead and President Kimball about three miles in our rear" (Journal History29, September 17, 1848).

"Tuesday, September 19: Cool morning. William Thompson & N.W. Bartholomew went back after an ax of Brother Joseph Fieldings that was left at Echo Creek &

found it close to the east side of the willows. Got back previous to camp starting. Camp met for prayer Titus Billings mouth. Moved off at 9. Campt on the east
bank of the Weber near the ford. The sisters commenced to wash as there was
plenty of wood & water close by. Camp met for prayer Brother Myers as mouth.
Several of the brethren & sisters spoke their feelings" (Journal History29, September 17, 1848).

"Entering the Great Salt Lake Valley"
By C.C.A. Christensen (1831-1912)

UTAH: A TIME OF REFINING

Echo Canyon, Big Mountain, Little Mountain, Emigration Canyon, Great Salt Lake Valley.

September 24, 1848: Salt Lake Valley/Sessions Settlement

November 1849: San Pete County/Manti, Utah

1860: Provo, Utah (Billings only)

CHAPTER 80

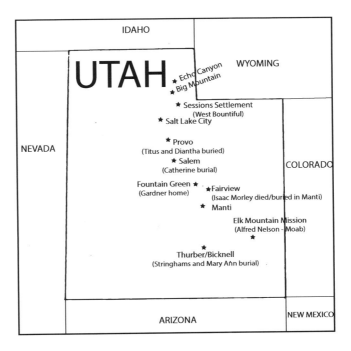

When Heber C. Kimball's Second Division crossed over Big Mountain on September 22, 1848, gathering clouds crossed over with them.

"Here it comes," George shouted. "Any moment now we will lineup with the mountain pass and you will get your first glimpse of the Salt Lake Valley."

"One would think he owned it," Titus said to his wife.

"Seems to own enough excitement for it," she agreed.

They pressed forward to the summit where cheers of exhilaration rippled back to them.

George and John on horseback pulled up to the wagon. "Do you see it, Pa?"

John pulled Eunice onto his horse sidesaddle, and started off for a better view.

"There it is," Titus said. "Over there. Look, right through here." He was excited himself. "Do you see it, dear?"

Diantha stood up in the wagon and strained her eyes. "Oh, I do. I do!"

"The Salt Lake Valley at last," Titus said with softness. "We've found the promised land, Diantha." Behind him teams halted and the sacred Hosannah Shout was repeated three times by grateful, humble, rejoicing saints, even stalwart servants of the Lord.

Descending the western slope of Big Mountain was a monumental job, even in good weather. Just as the Billings wagon started downward a sudden cloudburst complicated matters. In some places huge tree stumps were tied onto wagons and used as drags to slow and control the pace. In other places it was necessary to rough-lock hind wagon wheels. The dark rain only made it worse.

"Alfred, help me unharness the forward cattle on all these wagons. Then get John Wells to help you herd them all down to camp," Titus instructed.

President Kimball rode up on his horse and asked, "Captain Billings, when do you want to stop for the day?"

"Not yet. Do you?" he replied.

"Don't think anyone's ready yet, rain or no rain."

"I suggest we go as far as we can, leaving less distance to cover tomorrow," Billings said.

"Sounds good to me. Pass the word."

Driven as long and as late and as far as possible, the Mormon trekkers finally stopped to make camp on Little Mountain. Their joyful spirits made the darkness seem bright as day.

"Do you suppose anyone will be able to sleep tonight?" George asked.

"Surely not you," his father suggested, "but we should allow the animals some good sense."

Eunice and Mary Ann shared a fat log and huddled under a quilt giggling like little schoolgirls.

"Oh Eunice, can you believe it?"

"We are almost there, at last."

"Only one more day to go!"

"We really should go to bed, but . . ."

"I know. I feel like talking. Do you?"

"I do. Wish the storm would clear so we could see the stars. Bet they look close when you sit on a tall mountain like this."

"I think you still have stars in your eyes, don't you?"

They both chuckled. Between a finger and the thumb of her right hand, Eunice wiggled the ring that rested on her left. It was really a blacksmith nail John had bent for her, but she loved it. A blacksmith diamond, he called it. No money in the world could buy a gem more precious to her.

"Eunice, are you nervous about the wedding?"

"Yes. I am excited and nervous at the same time."

"I can imagine. It's wonderful to be in love, isn't it?"

"It is." For a moment she was caught away in an amazing realization of how her deepest dreams were coming true. John Ely Warner, the love of her life, wanted to take her as his wife in the Rocky Mountains just as soon as a settlement could be established. Who could hope for more? "Father promised to help John build us a cabin first thing, as a wedding present."

"It will be well-built if your father has anything to do with it," Mary Ann said. "I will miss you," she added.

"Miss me? I'm not going anywhere now. We're in the promised land, you know."

"Yes but . . . well, married women can't carry on like we do. Our lives are changing, Eunice."

"Don't know about you, but I am excited about changing. Especially . . ." Eunice stopped herself feeling a sudden burst of shame for her selfish, self-centered behavior.

"But, what about you? Are you ready for change too?"

Mary Ann dropped her head with a shy smile peaking her friend's interest as never before.

"Let me see your hand," she demanded. No ring! "Mary Ann, you know more than you are telling, don't you?" Mary Ann nodded in the affirmative. "You have plans too, don't you?" Mary Ann nodded again. "Tell me, tell me. Can't believe I didn't see this coming."

"You've been a little preoccupied," Mary Ann defended her friend.

"Indeed so, but I am paying attention now. Who is he?"

"You may not approve. I mean, he is older . . . 15 years older than I." She watched for a reaction. "I will be his third wife." Eunice waited in great anticipation. Mary Ann ventured a big question: "Why were you so against Elder Kimball's proposal?"

"Oh, he never proposed to me. It was just something Father wanted to arrange. I'm sure there are many women who would be honored to be sealed to him. Is that who . . ."

"No, no. But, I think you know him. He was captain of the company traveling behind ours."

"You don't mean Egan?"

"Yes!" Mary Ann was radiant.

"Howard Egan? He's a great leader. George said he kept the best journal of their first, exploratory trek out West and President Young refers to it all the time. Wasn't he a body guard to Joseph Smith?"

"Yes, he is a good man." Mary Ann was pleased with her friend's excitement.

"Do you love him?"

"Yes, I think so."

"You think so? What else do you know about him?"

"He was born in Canada. He married Tamson, his first wife, thirteen years ago and they were baptized by Elder Snow [Erastus] in Massachusetts. I come from Massachusetts too, you know."

"Yes, I do know, and my parents as well, but tell me more, Mary Ann."

"Mr. Egan," Mary Ann blushed, "Howard operated a successful rope-making business when they came to Nauvoo. He learned rope-making when he was a sailor in New England, after coming to America."

"Interesting."

"He was serving a mission to New Hampshire when the Prophet Joseph and Hyrum were martyred. He helped with the "Battle of Nauvoo."

"Isn't that the battle your father and brother --"

"Yes, and he brought the cannon they used. Calls it 'Old Sow' and my brother is intrigued with it."

"Oh, he would be. You said you would be his third wife?"

"Yes, he married Nancy Redding three years ago."

"Have you met her?"

"Yes, she is lovely. He was commanded to take another wife and all three of them agreed it should be me!"

"I am so happy for you." Eunice was still stunned. Perhaps she felt obligated to be as open and forthright as her friend had been. "By the way Mary Ann, John was married once before too."

"He was?"

"Yes, his first wife left him. It was before he joined the Church."

"Oh," was all Mary Ann could mutter.

"That's not all, he is sixteen years older than I."

"Really? But you two blend so well together."

"That's because we love each other. We really do, and that's all that matters."

"I couldn't agree more!"

"So, when do you plan to marry?"

"As soon as we settle."

"Well, let's get settled then."

Eunice stood and bundled the wet quilt.

"There you are," Titus said. Diantha and John Warner were with him.

"We've been looking all over for you two," she said.

"Sorry to trouble you," Mary Ann apologized.

"We were pretending we could see the stars up here," Eunice said. John stepped up behind her and wrapped his arms around her waist. "I find my stars in your eyes," he whispered. Then, with a soft voice no one else could hear he added, "I'm the one who found an angel."

Historical Background

"The three-month journey took Titus and the rest of the family into the Great Salt Lake Valley" (Hale, 8).

"From Fort Bridger the teamsters drove their animals, with whip and holla, until they reached Bear River's 7, 700 foot elevation. From there, a short but very steep descent was made to Echo Creek with huge tree stumps tied to the wagons for drags to help hold them back. The journey across the plains took one-hundred and thirty days" (MorleyRH, 125).

"Friday, September 22: The company crossed over 'Big Mountain,' when they had the first glimpse of Salt Lake Valley. Every heart rejoiced, and with lingering fondness they gazed upon the goal of their wearisome journey. The descent of the western side of Big Mountain was precipitous and abrupt, and they were obliged to rough-lock the hind wheels of the wagons, and, as they were not needed, the forward cattle were turned loose to be driven to camp, the 'wheelers' only being retained on the wagons. Desirous of shortening the next day's journey as much as possible, they drove on till a late hour in the night, and finally camped near the eastern foot of the Little Mountain" (Journal History29, September 17, 1848).

"At an earlier hour than usual the captain gave orders for the company to start . . . accordingly the company rolled out. But as the company were [sic] nearing the summit of the mountain a cloud burst over their heads, sending down the rain in torrents, and throwing them into utter confusion. The cattle refused to pull, and to save the wagons from crashing down the mountain side, they were obliged to unhitch, and block the wheels. While the teamsters sought shelter, the storm drove the cattle in every direction, so that when it subsided it was a day's work to find them and get them together" (Tullidge, 348,349).

"Saturday, September 23 Cool morning. Camps commenced moving off at 7. It commenced raining about 8 & got very cold & continued about 2 hours which detained the camps at the foot of the last ridge. When the rain was over we commenced ascending the last ridge. Here we had to put from 4 to 7 yoke of cattle to a wagon as the hill was some wet and slippy. Quite a number of wagons had to camp at the foot of the hill as the creek was so difficult to cross" (Journal History29, September 17, 1848).

"But oh! the joy and pleasure I shall never forget when we reached a hill, from the smmit of which we caught our first view of the Salt Lake valley, the promised land. When we reached the valley, the teams were halted, and the people all took up the shout of hasannah, which was repeated three times" (Snow,EB).

"Egan's personal diary, detailing the long trek across the plains, is full of humorous anecdotes and insights" (OgdenKD). "Following their marriage on December 1, 1819, in Salem Massachusetts, Howard and wife Tamson Ransom were baptized by Elder Erastus Snow into the LDS Church in 1842" (Baker).

"John Ely Warner was 16 years Eunice's senior and single. His first wife had left him. Heber C. Kimball was 29 years her senior and already had several wives" (Hale, 18).

CHAPTER 81

Captain Billings drove his team past the fort to the west side where wagons gathered; his company following close behind.

"I'm so glad the rain stopped," Diantha said.

"Yes, but look." Fresh snow covered the path they had taken only hours before. Titus stood in the wagon to make an announcement.

"This is the Sabbath Day," he said. "Settle yourselves now and meet for prayer at the bowery, 5 o'clock sharp."

Isaac Morley drove one of the first wagons into the valley when Brigham Young's Company had arrived the day before. He located his sister in no time.

"Where's your husband? I've got a property offer for him."

"I'm here," Titus answered before she could.

"Remember Perregrine Sessions? Last year he settled a spot near the mount of North Canyon. It's eight miles north of the Temple Lot," Isaac said.

Titus was listening.

"He's invited a few families to join him. What do you think?"

"Have you checked it out?"

"Took a quick look. Want you to see it."

Titus unloaded the cooking chest and started a fire for his wife.

"Are you good with me going right now?" he asked. Diantha smiled. It pleased her that he always put her needs first, even still, after all the years.

"Of course," she replied. "Make sure it's a pretty place," she added. *At last a home in the Rocky Mountains where no one will make us move again!* She rejoiced at the thought.

Titus was back and at the bowery well before prayer meeting.

"President Young praises the industrious saints who remained in this valley last year," Captain Billings announced. "I too thank them for the preparations they have made, even this bowery where we meet. As saints of God we all need to be a people of industry and build up His kingdom here on earth. Let us praise the Almighty now in song and offer up our united prayer of thanksgiving for safe arrival at His hand." Heartfelt singing filled the air and a more fervent prayer of gratitude was never heard.

Monday morning the new arrivals started staking out places where they could build homes. Morley and Billings were pleased with acreage in what would soon be called "Sessions Settlement" (present day Bountiful).

"Too late and too cold for planting," Titus said. He and Alfred set to work on a cabin. George came back from visiting with disturbing news: "Food is very scarce," he said.

"I guess that is not surprising out here," his mother said.

George had bragged about turning over the first spade of dirt in the Salt Lake Valley, but he was not the first to plant.

"They did plant a good crop," he said, "but crickets devoured much of it."

"Crickets?" Eunice stared with alarm at her brother.

"Yes, the little demons came out of nowhere and were in an instant everywhere!"

"Crickets! Glad I wasn't here," Eunice said.

"'Told me they battled bugs with brooms, and bags, and sticks and hands. Crickets, crickets everywhere!" George waved his arms as he acted out his tale. He was such a story teller, especially if it was a subject that annoyed his sister. Now that a gathering surrounded the wagon, he continued with a more spiritual account.

"It was a miracle," he said. His sister's confusion pleased him. Leaning against the wagon he continued. "After fighting bugs with all their might, well the people looked up and saw a massive flock of seagulls targeting their fields."

Oh no!" was heard from several female voices.

"I can't take it," Eunice said. "Get me out of here!"

"No, no Eunice, listen to this. The seagulls didn't come to eat the crops. They were eating the crickets."

Eunice looked like she was going to be ill.

"It's true! The birds filled themselves with bugs and flew to the lake to regurgitate them so they could go back for more."

"George, are you speaking truth?" Mary Ann asked him.

"Gospel truth," George said. "It was a real miracle!"

Early that evening John Ely invited Eunice to go sego root hunting up the mountainside. He knew George had alarmed her with worry about bugs and food shortages. "We can find wild berries and greens to supplement our diet," he promised.

What a blessing I am marrying John and not George, Eunice

thought to herself, though she almost vocalized it.

By December the food shortage was a serious matter. Hungry beasts and birds started depleting livestock and grain supplies. President Brigham Young proposed a war against the wild wasters and destroyers, appointing John D. Lee and John Pack to captain the effort. Many men met at Heber C. Kimball's home on December 23rd to plan a "Hunt of the Wild." Wolves, wildcats, cougar, mink, bear, eagle, hawk, owl, crow, and magpie were proven varmints they needed to exterminate if the valley saints were to survive the winter.

Each captain selected ninety-three men to be bound by five written articles. First: All men (from both teams) and their ladies were to participate in a dinner social at the expense of the team earning the smallest number of points. Second: Each hunter earned points for his team by producing evidence of the kill (the right wing of each crow = 1 point, each magpie, hawk or owl = 2 points, eagle = 3 points, each skin of pole cat or mink = 5 points, the skin of a wolf, fox, cougar, or wild cat = 10 points, and the skin of a bear or panther = 50 points). Third: The hunt would begin December 25th and end March 1st when all wings and skins were to be produced for counting at 10 o'clock am. Fourth: Isaac Morley and Reynolds Cahoon were appointed judges and would determine the winning team. Fifth: The most successful hunter would receive public recognition at the feast.

On Christmas morning the Billings invited John Ely Warner to breakfast. Eunice wanted a springtime wedding and John wanted to build her a cabin before they wed. The frozen ground was much too hard for building or planting. John would be ready at the first thaw. Today, however, his focus was same as every other able man in the valley: the Hunt! After Eunice and her mother served a rather hearty breakfast, well as hearty as circumstances could allow, John, George, and Alfred grabbed their guns and were off. Titus stood and started for his gun.

"You too?" Diantha asked.

"Might as well," he answered, kissing her for good luck.

Shots, one after another, were heard all around.

"Hundreds of crow met their demise today," Titus reported when he returned.

"Think I've figured out a way to obtain good beef," George announced at the dinner table the next day as his mother served up a watery stew. Everyone looked at him with curious amazement.

"How's that?" asked his father.

"Going to California," George announced. His mother gasped. His father started shaking his head.

"You mean the gold rush," his sister blurted out.

"That's right." George turned to his future brother-in-law, "You should come with me, John. We could find a fortune."

"You know what President Young said about falling into that trap!" Eunice scolded. She reached for John's hand, "This man has better things to do."

"Yeah. Well, I'm not committed to anyone as yet and I believe I could be a good gold digger," replied George.

"You could be a good anything you want to be, son, but please don't leave us now," Diantha said.

"My mind's made up, Ma. I want to go."

George Pierce turned to Alfred Nelson with a hopeful glance.

"Don't look at me, brother. I'm not interested in golden dreams," Alfred said.

"I was left behind when the Battalion marched to California. Now's my chance," George explained as though he was trying to convince himself. Three days later the twenty-two year old adventurer left for the "Golden Coast."

Since John's marriage engagement to Eunice, he was welcomed at the Billings table for supper almost every night.

"What did you think of that strip of land," Titus asked.

"I think it is perfect, if Eunice agrees," John answered.

"Oh, I agree!" Eunice plunged in, leaving no room for doubt. "When can we begin building?"

"We could start fetching lumber tomorrow, if you like," said Titus.

"Oh, John likes! Don't you John?" Eunice said, before he had a chance to respond.

"I do indeed," he said with care and a smile.

Historical Background

"This division left the Elkhorn River June 7, 1848 and arrived in Great Salt Lake Valley on September 24, 1848" (Journal History: Emigration 1848 Rooster).

"Sunday, September 24 This morning was pleasant. We arrived at the Great Salt Lake City and were joyfully received. Heber C. Kimball's company was almost all together" (Journal History30: William Thompson Journal, 54; Journal History31 William Burton Journal, 16).

"Father Morley's wagon was among the first to enter the valley that season" (MorleyRH, 125). "The three-month journey took Titus and the rest of the family into the Great Salt Lake Valley" (Hale, 8). They settled, "put up a log house" (Hale, 8) the first winter, 1848, in a canyon eight miles north of the Salt Lake temple block in Sessions Settlement or Bountiful.

". . . arrangements were made for him [Isaac Morley] to move his family to Session Settlement, a location a few miles north of the temple block, where the present city of Bountiful now stands" (MorleyRH,126).

"Isaac Morley, one of the first pioneers, staked a claim in West Bountiful on 800 West, but was sent to colonize San Pete Valley" (Hugoe/Deppe 14). "He settled first in Session's Settlement, a few miles north of Salt Lake City, but soon established his own community, 'Morley's Settlement,' which was later named Manti a name derived from the Book of Mormon" (BorenKR, 7).

"Bountiful has the distinction of being the second oldest Mormon settlement in Utah. It is the immediate outgrowth of the immigration which followed the original pioneers under Pres. Brigham Young in July 1847. Perregrine Sessions, captain of the 1st fifty of Capt. Daniel Spencer's hundred, arrived in Great Salt Lake Valley late in September 26, 1847, and three days later (September 29) he encamped on a spot of ground later embraced in the town of Bountiful, where he made his permanent home. He was accompanied by Samuel Brown and the two men built a shanty and herded about 300 cattle on the range. In the spring of 1848, Perregrine Sessions built a better cabin for his family and more settlers came to join him, among whom were Aaron B. Cherry, Jezerel Shomaker, Orville S. Cox, John Perry and William Duell. Later the same year Anson Call, Eric G. M. Hogan, Albert Connelly, Cara Clark, James Stevenson, Robinson C. Merkley, Titus Billings, Wm. Empey, Charles Chapman and others also came to the Sessions Settlement, as it was called. About 25 families spent the winter of 1848-49 near the mount of North Canyon, where the pioneers had located. In 1849 more families arrived and Apostle Lorenzo Snow built a house and brought part of his family to the location" (LDS Authors, 80).

"Twenty-five families spent the winter of 1848-49 near the mouth of North Kanyon living in their wagons. In this influx were the families of Anson Call, Orin Hatch, Eric G. M. Hogan, John Moss, John Pack, William Smith Muir, Edwin Pace, Israel Barlow Sr., William Brown, Clarence Loveland, John Barton, Ezra T. Benson, John Ellis, and William Henrie. Another source adds the names of Albert Connelly, Ezra Clark, James Stevenson, Titus Billings, William Emery, and Charles Chapman" (DUP2, V7).

"That first winter they suffered from hunger and cold. The year's crops having been partially destroyed by the crickets made food very scarce. They gathered sego roots, greens and wild berries to supplement their meager rations. But they rejoiced in having reached this promised land in which, though a wilderness, they could rest their weary feet and swell in peace from their enemies" (Esplin, 12).

"Pests such as the wolf, wildcat, cougar, mink, bear, eagle, hawk, owl, crow, and magpie were responsible for killing Mormon livestock and eating their valuable crops during the first year in the valley" (MorleyRH, 127).

CHAPTER 82

"Sister Billings, I'm happy for your husband's new appointment," Catherine called out to her friend.

"Why thank you, Catherine. Titus is honored to serve on the new stake high council. Do you realize nineteen wards have already been organized here in Zion?"

"Oh my, that's wonderful. And your brother was sustained as president of the council, right?"

"Yes, Titus said the elderly and discreet men were called to the city high council and arranged by age. Isaac is the oldest and the president."

"These good men are called because of their faith and good works."

"Thank you, Catherine. Titus also said the younger men were called as a traveling high council to help bishops in the territory."

"Sounds like an orderly plan."

"Yes, the Lord does things in an orderly way." They exchanged smiles. "Catherine, are you coming to the social dinner tonight?"

Catherine was unaware. Diantha cringed. *What have I done?* "It is for the men of the Wild Hunt," she admitted in a sheepish voice.

"Oh that. Henry could not participate with his lame leg and all."

And your Edward is buried at Winter Quarters, Diantha reasoned with herself, a little too late. "I'm sorry," she said.

"No worry. Have a good time."

"We must get together for a better chat."

Catherine agreed and went on her way. *She is such a sweet thing. I must pay more attention to her.* Diantha made a serious mental note and intended to remember it.

The social was fun and well attended. Lee's team, having removed 2,110 varmints, served a fine dinner to Pack's team because they did away with 5,332 varmints. The success of both teams saved a lot of grain. They turned in a great supply of quail in to Church clerks as well.

"Oh John, there's Mary Ann. I must talk to her," Eunice said. She took John's arm and he escorted her across the room to where a dear friend stood beside the heroic, Mr. Egan, and his two other wives.

"Mary Ann! How are you?"

"Eunice! I've wondered about you. Are you married yet?"

"Next month, April 4th! What about you?"

"Last week. It was just a private ceremony." She held out her hand to show the gold band around her finger.

"I'm happy for you!"

"And I for you." Both giggled. "Can you believe it?"

*　　　*　　　*

"Are you ready to go, Titus?"

"I think so. Di, are the cartridges ready?

"Yes, they're right here. I do wish George was here to help you."

"I wish so too, but I can do it."

"Oh, I know you can. I just . . ."

"We better leave - 'posed to be there at 10:00 sharp. Are you sure you want to come?"

"Of course, I'm sure. I will carry the cartridges for you."

"Rightly so," Titus said with a wink to his wife, "After all, you made them."

Titus rolled the cannon into place pointing away from the Old Fort Bowery, where Mormon citizens were gathering.

"We meet to organize the provisional State of Deseret," President Young was saying. "A subcommittee of the Council of Fifty have selected names for nomination. Elder Thomas Bullock will now read the list of candidates."

He read the list. Afterwards President Young dismissed the men saying, "You may now go to Phelps's schoolroom and cast your votes." Diantha stayed beside the cannon. She knew how she would vote if women were allowed the privilege, although expecting to do so never crossed her mind. Six-hundred-fifty-six men voted, and by 4:00 p.m. everyone re-gathered to hear the results. No one was surprised to learn that a strong majority vote had elected Brigham Young as governor. Willard Richards was declared secretary with "assorted legal and public works officials as well as magistrates" selected from the bishops of various wards. A ringing

508

bell was Titus' signal. He fired the cannon and the band began to play. The State of Deseret was now official.

"Too bad George is not here to witness your marriage," Diantha said as she arranged Grandma Morley's lace in soft folds across her daughter's shoulders.

"At least John is here. That's what matters."

Diantha smiled and hugged her daughter. "And Grandma's lace is here too." The significance of her own words pushed past problems to the front of her mind. *We have come so far for this gospel.* No, heart-felt appreciation flooded her rejoicing soul as she edited her thinking: *It is because of the gospel of Jesus Christ, even the Savior himself, that we have been able to endure all and come this far. Praised be the Lord.*

A strong wind blew in from the south and over the bowery, but Eunice didn't notice it. Nothing could mar the day she became Mrs. Warner!

Again at the bowery for Sunday fast-day services, after hearing messages from President Isaac Morley, Apostle John Taylor, and Patriarch John Smith, the Nauvoo Legion was reorganized with Major General Daniel H. Wells in full command. The Silver Grey Company would be led by Lieutenant Isaac Morley.

"I'm still the Keeper of the Cannon," Titus told his wife.

"I guess that means I am still a maker of cartridges."

"Yes please, can't do without you! May have to do it without your married daughter's help though."

"I bet she'll come back and help once she learns that you are still active in the Silver Grey Company."

"Did you notice the age change?"

"Only men 55 years and older can be in the Silver Grey Outfit, right?" questioned Diantha.

"Yes, but it was 45 in Nauvoo."

"Sounds like the rules are aging same as we are," she teased. "Let's see, you are only 56. You barely made it!"

"Oh, you make me sound so young!"

"Well, compared to Isaac you are a young one."

"Now if you can just convince my body of that." They both laughed.

Titus Billings opened the Holy Bible and read Isaiah 2:2

to his family: 'And it shall come to pass in the last days, that the mountain of the Lord's house shall be established in the top of the mountains, and shall be exalted above the hills; and all nations shall flow unto it.' Today is this prophecy fulfilled."

"Wonderful!" Diantha cheered. "You and Alfred look so handsome in your uniforms."

Her husband beamed and her tall son stood a mite taller.

"Let's be off," Titus said.

"To the parade," Alfred said.

It was a glorious parade commemorating the first pioneers to enter the Great Salt Lake Valley. The bright 24th of July sunshine gleamed on the instruments of the Nauvoo Brass Band as they marched with pride behind the Grand Marshall. Two groups of bishops (twenty-four total) followed, each bearing a banner. Seventy-four young men dressed in white and wearing gold crowns, carried copies of the Constitution and Declaration of Independence. Also dressed in white and wearing wreaths trimmed in white roses upon their heads, twenty-four young ladies carried copies of the Bible and the Book of Mormon. President Brigham Young and other Church Leaders followed. Titus and twenty-three of his Silver-Grey Company marched behind their leader, Patriarch Isaac Morley, carrying staffs painted red at the top and trimmed with white ribbons. What a blessing to dwell in the mountain tops of the Lord's promised land!

Historical Background

"Isaac Morley, Phinehas Richards, William W. Major, Edwin D. Woolley, Henry G. Sherwood, Titus Billings, Elisha H. Groves, Shadrach Roundy, John Vance, Ira Eldridge and Levi Jackman were set apart as High Counselors for this stake of Zion. I stated that we should arrange the High Council according to age, with Isaac Morley for President" (Journal History33, February 19, 1849).

"I [Brigham Young] . . . recommended the appointment of elderly and discreet high councilors. I wanted old men in the High Council and young men in the Traveling High Council" (Young, 12, 22). "The traveling high council was organized to assist the bishops of the territory, for the stake high council acted in a spiritual capacity to the Salt Lake wards alone" (Arrington, 237).

"Men are called as high priests because of their exceeding faith and good works" (BofM: Alma, 13).

A total of 6,440 "wasters and destroyers" were removed by the wild hunt. "Because of the success of both teams, the loss of grain was noticeably less in 1849. Enough quill [sic] were furnished to the Church clerks to last for several years" (MorleyRH, 129).

"Eunice was married in the Bountiful area to John Ely Warner" (Bennett, 558; Hale, 8) [Note: They are listed on the wagon train roster as being husband and wife when they crossed the plains. Perhaps the list was recorded at a later date and its writer remembered them as a couple.] A family history search shows that they were married 4 April 1849 in Sessions Settlement, near Salt Lake City, Utah.

"I was married eight miles north of Salt Lake City to John Ely Warner, at the small settlement called Sessions Settlement (now known as Bountiful)" (Gappmayer, 16).

"Twenty-four Silver Greys led by Isaac Morley, patriarch, each having a staff painted red at the upper part and a bunch of white ribbon fastened at the top" (MorleyRH, 135).

"Elected without contest were Brigham Young, governor; Willard Richards, secretary; and assorted legal and public works officials as well as the magistrates, who were the bishops of the wards . . . the bell was rung, cannon fired [by Titus Billings], and band played" (Arrington, 237).

CHAPTER 83

Titus and John cut logs with an upright saw and framed a good-sized cabin. They were shaping shingles with drawing knives when their wives stepped into the roofless structure.

"This is nice," Diantha said.

"Oh mother, I am so excited. I can hardly wait to move in."

Diantha smiled, "Those curtains you're stitching will look adorable in here, Mrs. Warner."

A healthy gust of wind propelled autumn leaves and plummeted many through the open roof and onto the cabin floor.

"You better borrow my broom," Diantha said stepping back outside.

"Yes." Eunice stopped in the doorway and called to the men. "You better get that roof on fast before the snow replaces these leaves."

"Should I fetch your jacket?" Diantha asked her husband. "The wind is really starting to blow out here."

Titus looked up, but his gaze passed by her.

"Well, well, well. Leaves aren't all the wind is blowing our way today."

Diantha turned around to see –

"George! George Pierce Billings! You're home!"

Wind or no wind shingle making halted. Everyone wanted to hear George report his find and tell his gold rush story.

"I found gold," he said. "Then I took it to Old Mexico."

"Why would you do that?" Eunice asked.

"Heard it was a great place to buy cattle and good horses. Thought I'd get some and bring them back.

"Was it? Did you get some?"

"I bought a good herd of cattle and some really fine horses.'

"Where are they?"

"Well, that's the problem."

Worried looks bounced off everyone.

"Was headed back when they got diseased. Spread through the whole bunch. All I got left is the horse I ride."

No one spoke. No one knew quite what to say. George turned a sheepish look toward his father.

"I know you told me not to go, Pa. Guess I should have listened. I am poorer now than I was before I left!"

"Sounds like you're wiser," Titus said embracing his son.

"And you're home! You are alive and well and safe . . ." Diantha hugged him.

"Glad you're back, George," Eunice said.

"Yeh, we need your help gettin' shingles on the house before snows fly," John added with a grin. Everyone laughed.

"You men get to work now. Eunice and I need to start a welcome home dinner," Diantha said.

Chief Walker (a Ute Indian leader often referred to as "Wakara") was well known for the good horses his warriors rode. Walker too found his animals in California. Unlike George he didn't pay for his. Every year he or Sanpete, his general, would steal 800 to 1,000 from Mexicans.

The Chief visited President Young time and again offering a nice southern piece of land for the Mormons to settle if in exchange they would teach his people "how to build houses and till the soil."

President Young sent a party to explore the offer. Parley P. Pratt, leader of the group, made a favorable report. "The land has potential for becoming an asset in the Great Basin Empire," he said. Church leaders accepted his recommendation. The Chief was pleased.

"We smoke the pipe of peace," he said. Walker filled the pipe and first offered it to the Lord by pointing it upward and stepping toward the sun. Once he acknowledged his sun god, he passed the pipe to Brigham Young and sent it around the circle to Mormon leaders.

"I have seen you before," he announced with excitement when the pipe came to Isaac Morley. "I have seen you in vision. You will come and live among my people. We will be brothers."

No one was more surprised than the humble patriarch.

Eunice heard her husband calling and rushed outside.

"What is it, John?" she panicked.

He raised his arm to dangle a beautiful, wild, very dead turkey by its feet.

"Oh John, how wonderful. Just in time for Sunday dinner,"

she said. "What if we invite my parents and George to come over after General Conference? It will be our thanks for their help in finishing our home before snowfall."

"Sounds good to me," John said with ease because his part of the dinner would be done once hr plucked the feathers.

Trees on the mountain side were dressed in blazing colors as the saints gathered for October Conference. Diantha spotted Catherine and waved her down.

"Come sit by us," she said.

"Thank you, Diantha. You look radiant today."

"Oh." Diantha blushed. "It's the season. Don't you just love those colorful mountains?"

"I do." Catherine shaded her eyes for a better view.

"It's a sacred privilege to live in this valley."

Yes, I see why it's the Lord's promised land."

"And we will be free to live in this land as long as we are a righteous people."

"I can tell you read the Book of Mormon," Catherine laughed. In her heart she knew it was not a laughing matter. The saints were here by obedience to God; and only by continued commitment to righteousness would they be permitted to remain in peace. Singing started. Catherine loved to sit beside Diantha and hear her angelic voice.

As was customary at General Conference, President Young stood to make announcements and assign callings. From time to time various saints were chosen to relocate and settle new regions. If your name was called you were to stand. Diantha gasped at the first name.

"Isaac Morley and family."

The list continued. Several other families were called. Titus struggled with his feelings. He would miss Isaac, but worried more about Diantha. As he reached for her hand to offer silent comfort he heard it.

"Titus, Diantha, Alfred, and George Billings."

"Oh no!" Eunice didn't mean for anyone to hear – it just popped out. Her parents were moving! She just got settled beside them and now . . . But where? He hadn't announced where they were going. Eunice strained to hear. Still the list went on.

"Catherine Tuttle and her sons: Henry and John."

"I'm so glad you're coming too," Diantha whispered. Catherine was speechless.

"John and Eunice Warner."

What? We just moved into our first home. How ... Where ... oh dear!

"These faithful saints will colonize the Sanpitch Valley of the Great Basin."

The new Sister Warner had difficulty breathing. John wrapped his arm around her. She grabbed his fingers with one hand and reached out with the other, creating a human circuit for much needed strength.

"We'll build you another house," he whispered.

She smiled and sighed as the Holy Spirit engulfed her.

"Because it is so late in the season these good people need to organize quickly and set out at once. Isaac Morley, Seth Taft and Charles Shumway are called to lead this company."

Eunice was not the only one who found it difficult to concentrate on sermons that followed. After meeting she announced to her family that the first and last dinner served in her new log home would be ready as scheduled.

"Sister Tuttle, I hope you and the boys can come too."

"Thank you dear. I baked a pie yesterday. May I bring it?"

"Oh yes, please!" Catherine Tuttle was known for her pies.

"I feel like a rug has been pulled out from under me," Eunice added. "But, Monday morning we will roll up that rug and take it south."

Everyone smiled at her courage. Titus reached for Diantha's hand. "She's a trooper, like her mother," he said.

Historical Background

"There he [Titus Billings] put up a log house and in July built another log house, sawing the logs with an upright saw and making the shingles with a drawing knife" (Hale, 8).

[When George was twenty-two years old he went to California for the gold rush of 1849.] "It is said that he did find gold; then went to Old Mexico and bought cattle which he intended to drive back to Utah, but on the way the cattle and horses contracted a disease, prevalent at the time, and all of them died. Thus he returned to Farmington, where his folks now resided, much poorer and wiser than when he had left them" (Carter 2:576).

"Walker kept his warriors supplied with good horses ..." (MorleyRH, 140). "[Chief Walker] asked the Mormon leader to send white men among his people to teach them how to build houses and till the soil" (MorleyRH, 140). "I have seen you in vision. You will come and live among my people. We will be brothers" (BorenKR, 5).

"A delegation of Ute Indians, under Chief Walker (pronounced Yawkeraw), [also known as Walkara, Wakara, Wahler, Napoleon of the Desert, Hawk of the Mountain, greatest of all horse thieves, and more (Bailey, preface)] appeared in Salt Lake City, June 14, 1849. He and his six brothers: Arapeen, Grocepeen, Sanpitch, Ammon, Tabinaw, and Yankawalkets" (DUP 32), "requested colonists for Sanpitch Valley, to teach the natives how to build homes and till the soil" (Lever, 12). "224 settlers accepted Ute Chief Walkara's invitation to settle in Sanpete Valley at a location named Manti" (Allen/Leonard, 249).

"At the General Church Conference held October 6, 1849, Titus was again sustained as a member of the Great Salt Lake High Council" (Journal History35, October 6, 1849). "Titus and his wife Diantha were called to colonize a new settlement in southern Utah; Sanpete County" (Cook, 102; Gappmayer, 16; Jensen5). "President Young immediately called for volunteers to colonize Sanpitch Valley, and sometime later 50 families from Salt Lake City and Centerville responded" (Sidwell/ Bramwell/Freschknecht, 20).

[Note: Tuttles were not called, but because we do not know where Catherine and her sons settled at this point in time, we choose to include them in this migration. Her daughters were married.]

"Then, after completing the house, we [Eunice (Billings) and John Ely Warner] ate only one meal when we were called to go to Manti and settle the country where the Indians were the first settlers [At October Conference 1949]" (Hale, 8).

CHAPTER 84

The sun was near setting when he knocked on her new door.

"Uncle Isaac, come in. Welcome to our new home," Eunice said.

"You just missed a delicious dinner," Diantha said boasting of her daughter's cooking.

"Yeah, John's bride is as talented as she is charming," Titus bragged.

Eunice blushed. "Well, you got here in time for some of Sister Tuttle's pie," she announced. "And I'll fix you a plate. Think some of John's bird is left."

"Are you just getting home from Church?" Diantha asked.

"Yes, we have been organizing our move to the Sanpete. President Young has a great vision for the wilderness we are going to tame." John pulled up a chair for the aging gentleman. Isaac turned to George. "We've been authorized to take one of the Legion's cannons with us. We will tow it behind the last wagon. I'd like you to be Keeper of the Cannon, George. Will you do it?"

"Of course, Uncle Isaac." The news brought with it the largest smile George had mustered since returning empty handed from his gold rush trip. In a way it was validation that the Lord still loved him and needed his service.

"Brother Nelson Higgins is going with us to represent the military. You'll report to him."

"Yes Sir."

"Brother Seth Taft and Brother Charles Shumway will represent us to civil and ecclesiastical authorities. He paused to look around. "I love this charming home," he said. "What a blessing the Lord wants you to duplicate it in the newest part of his Zion."

No one spoke. He continued.

"We will depart October 28th." Sighs of relief were heard.

"That gives us three weeks to pack," John told his wife, and everyone present, for that matter.

Catherine Tuttle served Father Morley a huge slice of her wild berry pie. He ate as he talked.

"Chief Joseph Walker will escort us to our new home."

"Chief Joseph Walker?" Titus asked. "Are you talking about

519

the Lamanite leader, Wakara?"

"Yes, we just held a meeting with him. He wanted a Mormon name and really likes being called after the prophet of the restoration."

"I hope the name will give him similar qualities" Titus said, causing several chuckles, including a hearty one from Isaac who really hoped it would be true.

After a delightful evening with guests in their new little home on Onion Street, John started a fire, the first in his new fireplace. He sat with Eunice who warmed her toes and talked.

"We have been so blessed, John. We live at a marvelous time in the history of man. We have the true gospel of Jesus Christ which teaches us how to live. Not to mention the Lord's atoning sacrifice whereby we can be forgiven and made holy. And now we find ourselves safe in the Rocky Mountains. We live in such a beautiful place." She stopped and fell deep into thought.

"We'll find another beautiful place," John said reaching for her hand. "After all, the Lord picked it out."

"And you will build another home for us just like this one?" she teased knowing carpenter work was not his thing, though he had come through with flying colors.

"Sure I will, with your father's help."

Eunice sighed and spoke softly. "I don't care where I live as long as I live with you."

"I feel the same," he said with tenderness. Then, he spoke again with an abrupt change of voice, "Don't you think it is getting too hot in here?"

"At least we know your fireplace works before we have to leave it behind," she laughed.

John spread the coals and yawned.

"Looks like we better turn in," she said. He nodded.

"After all, we need to start packing in the morning." He said nothing. "Too bad we can't pack up your fireplace and take it with us."

"Too bad," he said half asleep.

*   *   *

"Are you boys packed up and ready to go?" George asked his buddies. Henry's face radiated with excitement ever since George dubbed him "Assistant Keeper of the Cannon."

"Sure. We're good and ready. Why, John and I could pack everything we own in our back pockets!"

George laughed, but it was almost too true to be funny. Tuttles weren't the only ones with little means. No one took much because no one had much to take. Wagons were filled with basic needs: a few tools, farm implements, some crude furniture, and whatever personal supplies would fit. Nonetheless, these saints were eager, willing, and even honored to have been chosen to help s-t-r-e-t-c-h the Lord's Zion. They had followed him clear across the continent, some even starting from other continents. And they would continue to follow wherever, whenever He required. Perhaps they were short on the side of possessions, but they were mighty rich on the more important side of faith.

"Come on boys, let's get this wagon there before it is too late," George said when at last they had the heavy cannon loaded.

"Did your mother find a ride?" he asked.

"Yes, she is helping a family with young children so she will ride with them," Henry said.

"That means both of us get to ride with you," John said with obvious satisfaction.

George parked the cannon rig behind thirty family wagons. Drivers and passengers had paused for a farewell blessing from President Young. The October sun was at high noon when they started out. With Chief Joseph Walker on horseback at his side Father Morley led the would-be Sanpete settlers to Utah Valley. They stopped at Fort Utah [Provo].

"Why did we stop?" Henry asked.

"More families are joining us here," George said. "Let's hope they have some cute girls among them."

"Yeah," Henry agreed.

"Who needs girls anyway," Johnny said with disgust.

"Your turn will come," George amused.

"In due time," Henry added.

"In due time," George agreed with a laugh. "Hey, you guys keep guard of the cannon and I'll go check things out."

Already John felt exhausted. With sore feet he climbed onto the driver's bench, stretched out as much as was possible, and shielded his face with his tattered hat. The lad was in deep sleep when George returned.

"We're stopping for a few days to recuperate," he told

Henry. "Enjoy it because this is the last settlement we'll see this trip."

A few days later Morley's company headed out with a caravan twenty families longer. George lingered until every other wagon fell in line. His job was to keep the cannon in the back.

Anything south of Fort Utah was new territory to Father Morley.

"Chief Joseph, you take the lead now. We will follow you in faith."

Driving emigrant cattle (as they were called) kept John Ely Warner and his horse on the lurch. Seems the cattle wanted to stray or maybe just stop and be satisfied on the spot. At any rate, they were necessary for survival and needed constant prodding. John was herding strays not too far from Fort Utah, when he spotted a camp of Indians. Hoping not to be noticed he returned to camp to report.

"They Utes," Chief Walker said to everyone's relief. "Chief Tabby, he friendly."

After traveling several days along the base of the Wasatch Mountains the rugged trail elevated to a mountain peak covered with snow. Father Morley pulled out his instructions from President Young. "It says to turn left at this point," he told Chief Joseph who agreed.

"We go into tall canyon now." Walker said.

"Salt Creek Canyon?"

"Yes, tall canyon cut out of stone by creek."

Devoted pioneers followed Chief Walker into the narrow passage.

"This place worries me," Henry said.

"The canyon walls are mighty steep here, aren't they?"

"Every time you turn the wagon it looks like we are going down a dead end."

The wagon train came to a complete stop in a rather narrow pass.

"Guard the cannon, boys. I'll go check things out."

George walked all the way to his father's wagon. "What's happening?" he asked.

"Gotta clear the road. Come give us a hand, son." Alfred was already on duty.

Before long Isaac made his way to the action. "Sure glad

you hard workers are on our team," he said. "Looks like we're going to have to build a bridge up ahead."

"A bridge?"

"Titus, we choose you to lead the project."

Brother Billings kept working, but did not reply.

"Will you do it?" Isaac asked.

"If that's what you want."

"Yes, and it is what the Lord wants, I'm certain."

George rolled the last boulder out of the way.

"I appreciate the fact that my brother-in-law has so many skills and talents," Isaac remarked.

Titus turned away. He didn't like attention or praise. He just had a habit of doing what needed to be done.

". . . and I'm thankful that he never lets me down." Isaac continued.

"Alfred, George, come with me. Let's see what we are getting ourselves into" Brother Billings said.

Historical Background

"President Brigham Young sent a band of staunch pioneers into the Sanpitch Valley to establish a new settlement. In charge of the company were Isaac Morley, Seth Taft and Charles Shumway, all men of courage and determination" (Peterson, 3).

"The commanders were Isaac Morley, Seth Taft and Charles Shumway, who represented the civil and ecclesiastical authorities and Nelson Higgins the military. Among the original pioneers were the following men, some being accompanied by their families: D.B. Huntington, Barney Ward, John Lowry, Sr., Titus Billings, G.W. Bradley, Albert Petty, O.S. Cox, Albert Smith, Jezreel Shomaker, Cyrenus H. Taylor, Azariah Smith, Abram Washburn, John D. Chase, Isaac Case, Sylvester Hulet, William Potter, Gardner Potter, James Brown, Joseph Allen, M.D. Hamilton, William Richey, Harrison Fugate, Sylvester Wilcox, Gad Yale, John Carter, Isaac Behunnin, William Mendenhall, Edwin Whiting, William Tubbs, John Hart, John Baker, John Elmer, John Butterfield, Amos Gustin, John Cable, and W.K. Smith" (Lever, 13; Sentinel).

"They left Salt Lake Valley on October 28. Other than a little crude furniture, some tools and some farming implements, personal belongings could not have added up to much more than men could put in their pockets. Nothing was plentiful. What they weren't short on they didn't have at all. Nothing was plentiful, that is, except what they called their 'faith.' Their wagons had to be bursting at the seams with that, and maybe that was one reason they didn't miss a lot of other things that just wouldn't fit into their boxes and wagon bed" (Antrei, 28).

"... we reached Provo ... our cattle being what was termed emigrant cattle, foot sore, jaded and nearly exhausted we tarried at this place a few days to recuperate" (Bradley, 1). "Where Payson now stands we found a camp of Indians of the Ute Tribe. Tabby, their chief appeared to be friendly" (Bradley, 2).

"The Nauvoo legion loaned the company a cannon which was towed behind the last wagon" (MorleyRH, 139).

"When the handsome Lamanite Chief led Morley's company into the Sanpete Valley, he was called Joseph Walker" (MorleyRH, 139; Roberts).

"William S. Muir acquired the property in West Bountiful owned by Isaac Morley when Isaac was called to help colonize Sanpete Valley" (Hugoe/Deppe, 15).

"About noon, the thirty volunteer families began the trek to Sanpete and while proceeding through Fort Utah, added twenty more families to the company. The Nauvoo Legion loaned the company a cannon which was towed behind the last wagon" (Deseret, 1/31/35; MorleyRH, 145).

"President Morley secured the service of Chief Joseph Walker, leader of both the Utah and Sanpitch tribes, to guide the Mormon families to their new home in Sanpete Valley. During the twenty-six day journey, the Chief became better acquainted with the company's leader and began to develop an abiding faith in his pale-faced friend" (Cox, 14-15; MorleyRH, 145).

"After about two weeks traveling along the base of the Wasatch Mountains, they got to that snowy peak they were to name "Mount Nebo." Here they turned left, following Brother Brigham's instructions, up the steep, narrow canyon cut by Salt Creek. They dug, filled, chopped, and shoveled a road up that canyon hand-over-hand, foot-by-foot, and mile after weary mile" (Antrei, 28).

CHAPTER 85

Only half a spoonful of drippings were left in the pot. Diantha positioned them into a tin cup and added hot water. Leaving the spoon in the cup after stirring, she carried it to the wagon and climbed inside.

"Here is some broth for you, Eunice. Let me help you lift your head to sip it."

Eunice turned. She was so miserable she wanted nothing at all.

"You must try a swallow or two," her mother coaxed. "Come on now, let's taste it while it's still warm."

Diantha's only daughter was with child. The rugged daily routine and intense cold at night worsened her situation. Diantha dipped up a spoonful. "Take this for the baby," she instructed. Eunice downed the first and another and another.

"Thank you, Mother."

"I only wish I could take your place so you didn't have to suffer."

Eunice gave a weak smile. "Oh mother, do you remember Nauvoo?"

Nauvoo, seems so long ago now. "Yes dear, I remember."

"You were so sick and I was so young." She found it difficult to say more.

"And Sister Vilate brought me dainties to keep me alive." Diantha finished the thought for her. "I wish we had some of Sister Kimball's dainties now, for you."

Eunice closed her eyes. Her mother kissed each of them. "If I could get through that, you can get through this," she promised.

Titus and the boys, all of the men for that matter, were preoccupied with bridge building and road making. With picks they chipped out stone. With shovels they replaced dirt, sometimes filling gaps and sometimes emptying them. They put in hard labor for long hours, but they were not alone. Sisters were called upon to do more than their share as well; juggling the little ones while driving the team, mending flesh wounds and finding nourishment. Before leaving the pass Father Morley assigned a group to harvest a supply of salt.

Diantha drove the Billings wagon. Because Eunice was too ill to drive George asked Henry to drive the Warner wagon and left John to drive the cannon. He rode his horse again to the end of the line.

"Prepare to cross the creek," he said.

"Again?" John asked with surprise, concern and amazement. "How many times do we have to cross it?"

"Well, this makes number six. Let's hope it is the last."

"You gonna help me again?"

"Hey, you're getting pretty good at it." George recognized terror in Johnny's blue eyes.

"Sure, I'll be back to help," he said before riding off.

*   *   *

"We'll have to take this pass one wagon at a time," Titus said. Restraining ropes were tied everywhere possible. Still the excessive man power required for the job put a great strain on backs, shoulders, arms and legs. The jubilation of reaching bottom was in an instant extinguished by the realization that it must be done again and again and again.

John and Titus approached the Warner wagon about midday. Both felt as though they had put in a full day already. Diantha heard their voices and opened the wagon flap.

"This one is next," Titus said.

"She's not well enough," Diantha said. "Hasn't been able to sit up for days now."

"That's why we waited, but we must do it today," he said, helping Di to the ground.

John climbed into the wagon bed to fetch his wife. Her face was so pale it frightened him.

"Eunice, it's me dear. I've come to take you down the gully."

"Oh John, I'm sorry. I just can't do it."

"I know," he said. "But it is too dangerous in the wagon." He removed the quilt and reached down for her. "I'll have to carry you down."

"Oh John, I'm so sorry," she kept saying.

Titus reached up to catch his daughter while her husband climbed out of the wagon. "Are you sure you can get her down?" he asked.

"If you can get the wagon I will get the lady."

526

"It's a deal," Titus agreed.

Diantha despised the day she drove her wagon down. Even with ropes and manpower all around it the ordeal was terrifying. She detested the idea of her ailing daughter being carried down the treacherous slope. *I can't watch*, she thought. Then her courage mustered: I must do this so I can be there to help." Another long battle with the mountainside began.

Camping on level ground for the night was a welcome luxury for most, though Diantha slept not a wink. All night she nursed her daughter's fever. By morning the men gathered to evaluate their position. A large group volunteered to search for a better trail. *Maybe I'll have time to get something done,* Diantha reasoned, hoping to work in a short nap as well. Perhaps just the thought of it was restful enough. At any rate, she found no time for sleep. The day passed quickly. All too soon night darkness fell in around them.

"The boys aren't back yet," Titus said. Diantha was worried by the alarm she saw in his face. *Our sons and son-in-law! What could have happened? Why aren't they back? Half our manpower is gone. We will never make it without them – but more important: are they suffering?* Horrible scenarios flashed before her. *No, I refuse to go there,* she told her mind.

"Titus, will you say a special prayer for us?" He held her in his arms and prayed aloud.

Diantha kept dabbing her daughter with cool cloths. The fever was more intense and Eunice seemed more frenzied. "Where is John? I need my John!"

"He left with your brothers . . ."

"Why," she interrupted.

"They're trying to find a better route."

"I need John. Please go get him." She grew more panic-stricken, almost hysterical.

Titus lifted the flap and called in, "How is she doing now?"

"I can't reason with her any more. She wants John and she wants him now!"

"Keep trying," was all he could think to say.

Titus turned toward the fire where Henry Tuttle warmed his lame leg while holding his sleeping brother's head in his lap. Titus bent down to stir the fire.

"Wish I were with them," Henry said softly. Brother Billings was an aging man and his hearing was less, but he heard more than the comment. He heard the pain of a young man who felt left out and a bit useless, probably because of his lame leg. Resting his weary bones on a log nearby, a quiet, caring servant of the Lord petitioned in silence for inspiration. Worry was not helpful so he chose to put it aside and seize the moment. The two talked heart to heart until Diantha called from the wagon.

"The fever broke!"

"At last," Titus said, rushing to help her down. "Is she still calling for John?"

"She is sleeping right now."

"Maybe you should try to sleep too."

"Yes," the idea sounded divine. "Do you men need a drink?"

"I'll fetch you one," Titus said. He started for the water barrel on far side of his wagon. No sooner had he dipped a cup when he heard a loud, hearty laugh. "They're back!" he shouted.

Diantha looked confused. "How do you know?"

"I just heard Shoemaker's laugh."

"Are you sure?" Diantha had good hearing, but she heard nothing.

"I would know that laugh anywhere," Titus declared.

He was right. The men were back!

Historical Background

Chief Walker "led the company through the Salt Creek Canyon, which opens up to form the Sanpete Valley. Since the canyon walls are steep, every abrupt turn gave the appearance of a dead end" (Morley, 146). They cleared roads, built bridges and successfully passed through Salt Creek Canyon. [Note: August 21, 1849 "Chief Wah-kar and his subchiefs had paid a visit to President Brigham Young in Salt Lake City, and had requested that he send colonists to Sanpitch" (Sidwell/Bramwell/Freschknecht, 20).]

"All through the Salt Creek Canyon the men did all of the shovel-and-shoulder work, and while they did, their women picked up the reins or the bullwhip" (Antrei, 29).

"Some of the company built a road up the canyon while others obtained a supply of salt" (Bradley, 3).

"With a pick and shovel in hand, filling a gully here, smoothing a projection there, with the men often walking all day while the women drove the teams, these hardy pioneers made their way through Salt Creek Canyon" (Morley,

145RH; Sidwell, 1).

"Wagons were let down gullies one at a time, restrained by ropes and the arms, legs, shoulders of the men. Up the other side, their beasts of burden had to be helped often in the same way. Their cattle and sheep were headed by boys on horseback, probably in front of the train, for they could go faster" (Antrei, 29).

"One day a number of brethren left the company to locate a better trail and were not back when night camp was made. Until the hearty laugh of 'Thop' Shoemaker was heard coming nearer the camp through the darkness, those in camp were almost hysterical not knowing what danger might have befallen them" (MorleyRH, 146).

CHAPTER 86

Diantha awoke in misery. *The nurse is not supposed to get sick,* she said to herself. But, nurse or no nurse Diantha Morley Billings was deathly ill. Her man was already up and out for the day. She tried more than once. No use, I just can't get up. She was by herself so she let it out. All the stress and worry and pain began to trickle out of her in the shape of teardrops. She cried until her pillow was wet. *Now, now, that's quite enough.* Rotating her pillow to its dry side she demanded self composure! Her timing was good because moments later the wagon flap lifted.

"Mother, are you well?"

An answer would be difficult. Might make me start crying again. Sister Billings tried to stay in control – of her feelings and her words.

"Mother, oh no!"

"Don't come in, Eunice, you may get sick again."

"Oh Mother. I didn't mean to give it to you. You said you would rather be sick yourself, but I didn't mean for it to happen."

"It's no one's fault, dear. It's just life."

"Don't worry. I'll take care of you. I know what to do now." She left to make warm broth and fetch cold watered cloths."

*   *   *

"Eunice, where's mother?" George asked.

"She's ill, George, really ill. Please don't disturb her."

"Guess you'll have to help me then."

"Of course. What do you need, my brother?"

"I'm on a life saving mission."

"Whose life are you trying to save?" Eunice was confused.

"Yours!"

"What?"

"Yours and mine and everybody in camp."

"What's going on, George?"

"The Indians want food. President Young told Uncle Isaac to 'feed them, not fight them,' and that is what he is trying to do.

"I see. Come with me. I'll make a contribution from the stock in my wagon."

George followed. Now Eunice had a proposition for him.

"Mother is too ill to drive her wagon. If you can let Henry keep driving ours I will be able to drive for her."

"Are you sure you are up to it?"

What? That was not George, but John's voice. Eunice turned around with surprise.

"John, I didn't know you were here."

"Well, I am and I am concerned about you. Do you really think you can do it?"

"Oh yes, John. Thanks to mother's help I'm all better."

"Good, and I'm grateful" said John. "But remember, you are seven months with child."

"How could I forget," she laughed. It was decided. Eunice would do what Eunice believed she should do, like Eunice always did. She drove her mother's wagon over the Great Divide, through another canyon pass and at last into open valley, even the Grand Valley of the Sanpitch!

"Mother, Mother, we've reached the valley at last! It's so spacious out there. The gaze is delightful."

Diantha appreciated the news, but her mind was on fire. "Eunice, tell your father I need a blessing," she said.

*   *   *

The journey had been too busy, too long and too rough for proper journaling, but Catherine Tuttle, who wrote as though she were reporting to her deceased husband, determined to record her feelings of the day. "November 21, 1849: Today, after three exhausting weeks of blazing our own trail, we entered Sanpete Valley for the first time and found it cold and bleak with sagebrush everywhere. Somehow, somewhere out there in all that alkali desolation we are supposed to build a new settlement unto the Lord. My heart longs for beautiful Nauvoo and how life could have been . . . Then I recall the horror that came upon us there and refuse now to murmur. Many of us are sick. All of us are weary, but this is where the Lord wants us to be and here we will build His Zion."

Again at evening, with light from the fire she added a postscript to the day's entry: "Our first night in the Sanpete! Brother Charles Shumway discovered a spring and we are camping beside it tonight, He is naming the place "Shumway Springs," of course. Many think we will make our home in this spot, though I heard

Father Morley state that no decision would be made until daylight tomorrow. Also, I am pleased with the new outlook on life that our Henry has acquired this trip. I am unaware of a cause for the change, but I welcome it with all my heart."

At the dawning of day weary Sanpete travelers were ready to conclude their journey and start settling down in this new place to be called "Shumway Springs." Father Morley, however, received a strong impression during the night that they had not yet stopped in the right place. Wanting to be better seen and heard, Isaac stood in his wagon to address his followers.

"Over there," he said pointing southward "is the termination of our journey. We shall settle in close proximity of that hill (where the Manti Temple now stands). God be willing, we will build our city in that spot."

Many were unhappy with the decision and not afraid to voice opposition.

"This is only a long, narrow canyon, and not even jack rabbits could exist on its desert soil!" said Brother Seth Taft. Others wanted to leave the valley as well.

Weakened by illness Diantha's soul suffered for her brother. Even though she was confined to her bed in the wagon she was aware of alarming whisperings and contentions buzzing through the camp. Titus returned from a long Council Meeting. He rested his weary bones on a bedside box and held a warm drink out to his precious wife for sipping.

"Is Isaac doing all right?" she asked.

"Oh sure. He's strong. He'll be fine." Titus believed every word, but still he ached. *The Book of Mormon is full of warning about murmuring,* he thought in silence. *Saints of the Lord should be united in spirit and purpose.* "How can we build Zion if we are not of one heart?"

"I thought Elder Pratt predetermined the site for out settling," Diantha said.

"He did."

"Where is it?"

"Where Isaac has chosen."

"Then why all the arguing?"

"It's only a handful who oppose. I think the majority are in agreement."

"It's a test. Another test and my brother sits smack dab in the middle of it."

"You don't have to worry about your brother. He's a leader through and through."

A slight smile crossed Diantha's dry lips. "He learned how to lead men during the War," she said.

Her words brought a smile to his face too as he remembered how proud Isaac was of serving in the War of 1812.

"He's always been on the front lines for the Church too," he added.

Di knew what he meant. Isaac, her only other family member to join the restored church, had been there from its beginning. No matter the hardship or persecution, he never faltered.

"My brother is sixty-three years old -- that's forty-four years older than the Church. He has always been stalwart and obedient, learning about sacrifice through trials along the way. This is just another. Still, we need to pray for him," she said.

"Always."

Another thought crossed her mind. "What does Chief Walker have to say about the matter?"

"He sat beside Isaac during the entire meeting, but never voiced an opinion. However, he once told President Young how he liked the Mormons and the way they treat their families."

"Oh great, and now he has to watch all this bickering? What kind of an example is that?"

Titus agreed with a shake of the head. "You feeling better?"

"Yes, I'm improving" she reached for his hand. "I will be better soon. And Isaac will be fine too."

The next morning her humble brother stood with courage and spoke with boldness.

"This is our God-appointed abiding place; and stay I will, though but ten men remain with me. If we labor harmoniously together and give the soil a chance to be productive, it will! Soon we will no longer see sand, but waving grain, cool streams, tall trees, at last: the promised land!"

Historical Background

"Train Captain Nelson Higgins and Patriarch Isaac Morley handed out food instead of resistance" (Antrei, 29).

"Resumed our journey crossing creek six times before reaching the Forks of the Canyon where we camped for three days" (Bradley, 3). "We passed over the divide. Charles Shumway not only discovered "Shumway Springs" near this camp but also suggested to President Morley that this location be made the company's permanent settlement. No decision was made that night, however" (MorleyRH, 149). "The trip occupied three weeks of continuous journey" (Snow, 1).

"There is the termination of our journey in close proximity of that hill. God be willing, we will build our city [there]" (Manti Centennial Committee, 20; Sidwell, 3; Young, 11/22/18).

"The majority of the company readily chose to remain with Father Morley at the site actually chosen by Elder Parley P. Pratt, while a few argued against the location" (Morley,RH, 148).

Other men in the company felt the location was a poor choice. Seth Taft gave vent to his feelings by exclaiming, "This is only a long, narrow canyon, and not even Jack rabbit could exist on its desert soil!" Father Morley opposed the idea of leaving the valley by saying in a manner indicative of self conviction, "This is our God appointed abiding place; and stay I will, though but ten men remain with me." He also declared if the brethren would labor harmoniously together and give the soil a chance to be productive, they would "see no longer sand, but waving grain, cool streams, tall trees, at last: the Promised Land!" (MorleyRH, 147).

"The hill spoken of is the same prominent hill on which the Manti Temple now stands" (MorleyRH, 149).

CHAPTER 87

Once snow began falling it did not stop. A three-foot blanket covered everything before the two-hundred-and-twenty-four souls had time to build shelter.

John maneuvered his wagon down the snowy mountainside with his father-in-law on the seat beside him. Their load of logs grew smaller because the ground was getting harder, not to mention that their fingers and toes were frozen to the bone. Titus took a start when he saw his wife climbing out of the wagon as they pulled up. She had been bedridden for days.

"Goodness sake, Di, where are you going?"

"Mary Lowery fell. They think her leg is broken.

"But Di, you've been so ill!"

"Captain Higgins' baby is not doing well either. I have to go help."

"You have to take care of yourself first."

"Titus, I am the only doctor person in this company."

"You're a mid-wife."

"Well, I'm the best they've got. I have to try."

"Do you need me to go with you?"

"No. Mary Lowery's brother will be back any minute to escort me. Don't worry. I know you have a lot of work to do before dark."

"Wait. Take the snowshoes. They really help you walk on this stuff." He helped her fasten his home-made pair onto her shoes.

"I feel so awkward with these."

"You'll get it. Just need a little practice."

"Well, I guess Isaac would be proud of me."

"Chief Walker would be proud of you too!"

At Father Morley's request last week's meeting was turned into a snowshoe making class taught by Chief Joseph Walker. Titus really liked wearing them. With her long skirt tangling it appeared that his wife did not. To her rescue Mary Lowery's oldest brother appeared with a comfortable horse.

"You ride, Sister Billings, and I will guide the horse." She needed no persuasion. Kicking off the snow shoes she let Titus help her onto the horse and they were off, young Brother Lowery wearing the snowshoes.

When Titus reached his wagon, John had it nearly unloaded.

"Let's get these split like the others," he said.

"Hope we got enough now," John said.

"If we saw all of these in half tonight I think we can start building tomorrow."

"Eunice will like that. She wants to be moved in before the baby comes."

"Think I'll like it too." Titus smiled as he patted John on the back. "What do you say we hurry this job along and go see what your wife has in the cooking pot."

"Anything warm will make me happy."

The stew was watery, but some of it was still on the hot coals when Sister Billings returned hours later. Diantha did not taste it. Her discomfort and sickness seemed like nothing when compared to the heartbreak Sister Higgins and Sister Shoemaker were suffering. Two tender graves would need digging at dawn, if the frozen ground would permit it.

George returned to his father's wagon after a weary day of digging. Not only did he help dig a grave for his friend, Theophilus Shoemaker, but he helped the Tuttle boys finish their dugout as well. Last week he helped Arapeen, Chief Walker's brother, bury a wife and horse and a dog.

"Would you like a hot biscuit, George?" his mother asked.

"Sure. I ate with Tuttles already, but I would like one anyway."

She smiled and handed one over.

"Did you get the Tuttles situated yet?"

"Yes, Henry and I finished their dugout today."

"Thanks, Son."

"Of course, John helped with it too," he added.

"Are you and Alfred sleeping warm enough in your dugout?"

"Sure, Mom. Our dugout is great. You ought to try it."

"You know how dead set your father is on helping John replace Eunice's house as soon as possible."

"He wouldn't mind building the first house in the settlement either."

"I don't know about that, but the wagon sure gets cold at night."

"Even since we stacked sagebrush all over it?"

"That helps, but . . . You boys were smart to dig your dugout before the blizzard came."

"And before the ground froze up. It's more difficult now because we have to chisel it out."

"You've been mighty busy helping Uncle Isaac get dugouts for all his wives and now Sister Tuttle. I'm proud of you and your brother."

"Thanks Ma." George tipped his head with an embarrassed look.

"You're so much like your pa." He appreciated the compliment, because his pa was the best worker he knew, but to his mother the compliment was two-fold. Although her son was confident and out-going, he had a bashful streak when it came to praise -- just like his father.

Snow or no snow Brother Warner and Brother Billings labored on the cabin at every chance. They made sheeting for the roof and another for the floor. Their half-log boards were secured all around for the walls of the house. They mudded small pieces or chips of the wood into the cracks between the logs. After three weeks of constant snowfall the skies cleared. It was plenty cold, but nice to work without snowflakes in the eyes. By the week's end the entire structure had been mudded, inside and out. That's when Alfred and George showed up to help.

"Better hurry if you're going to beat Brother Bradley," George said.

"I didn't know we were racing," his father said.

"Too late," Alfred chirped in, "Jezeral Shoemaker finished his cabin last week."

Eunice looked at her husband with disappointment. She knew he wanted to build the first house in the new settlement for her. John didn't flinch. He knew all about the matter.

"Shoemaker built the first house with a dirt floor," he announced. "And with a little luck we'll have the finishing work done so we can move into the first house built with a wooden floor!"

Historical Background

"The first camp was made on City Creek on the evening of November 22, 1849, and temporary houses made of wagon boxes, comprised the town. In a few days snow began falling and continued almost incessantly until the ground was covered to a depth of three feet or more, and the colony changed quarters to the south side of temple hill, where some families had dugouts, while others occupied their improvised wagons and tents" (Lever, 13).

Isaac Morley, "with a company of 224 people" (McCormick, 63), "arrived at the present site of Manti in Sanpete Valley on November 22, 1849. The establishment of this community was an outgrowth of a request Chief Walker had made of Brigham Young to send colonists to his region for the purpose of teaching the Indians to live as white men lived" (Hale, 16; Sidwell/Bramwell/Freschknecht, 20).

"The Roll-Call of families and individuals who arrived on November 19 to 22, 1849 at the site of Manti, Provincial State of Deseret" includes: Titus, Diantha, Alfred, George Billings; John and Eunice Warner; Isaac, Philena, Editha Ann, Calista, Arathusa, Cordelia, Theresa, and Isaac Jr. Morley. (Antrei, 353-355).

"For six weeks [we] lived out of wagons with only brush covering for protection from the storms" (Snow1, 1). "Titus fixed a sagebrush bowery to cover his family from the snow and it snowed every day for six weeks" (Pyne 5). "The majority of the colonists, including Morley, made dugouts in the south side of Temple Hill and were fairly comfortable" (MorleyRH, 150). "Isaac Morley's cabin was the first one up, whether [Seth] Taft started first or not . . . the main competition was between George Bradley and Titus Billings" (Antrei, 34).

"The settlement of Sanpete Valley was the beginning of the most unusual friendship between Isaac Morley, president of the Mormon colony, and Walker, chief of the Sanpete Utes" (Boren, 7). "The official date of Thomas Rhoades mining ventures, [The Lost Rhoades Mines] was bound with an oath between Chief Walker, Brigham Young, and Isaac Morley at the Endowment House in July 1852. Chief Walker . . . stated that he had seen Isaac Morley in a vision and it was he that the gold was to belong to . . . "(Boren/Rhoades, 1-2).

"In the meanwhile my husband [John Ely Warner] went to the mountains and there sawed logs with an upright saw to construct our dwellings" (Snow, 1).

"Chief Walker taught [us] to make snow shoes" (Bradley, 3).

"Captain Higgins infant daughter became very ill at the Salt Creek Canyon encampment . . . Mary Lowery fractured her ankle at the same camp . . . and Theophilus (Thop) Shoemaker died shortly after the company arrived at City Creek," (MorleyRH, 148; Sidwell, 4). "Nelson Higgins' baby got sick and Mary Lowry, who must have been about thirteen years old, broke an ankle" (Antrei, 31).

"Arapeen, whose proper name is Senior-roach" (MorleyRH, 139) "buried [his] squaw and horse and dog" (Bradley, 3).

Titus built the first home with a wooden floor in Manti, Sanpete, Utah. "It was built of rock from the rock quarry, now Temple Hill" (Larsen, 1) where Titus worked. [OR] "Titus Billings and Jezrell Shomaker built the first houses, which were followed by others before winter" (Esplin, 13; Judd, 11; Lever, 17).

[Author's Note: Several accounts in Manti history mention that Shomaker built the first home in Manti; many others credit Billings with the first. This was bothersome until the discovery that Jezrell Shomaker built the first Manti home with a dirt floor and Titus built the first Manti home with a wooden floor.]

CHAPTER 88

"I thought your father was biting off more than he could chew when he insisted we bring the little stove with us," Diantha said with grateful heart as she bent down to wrap her daughter's cold feet. After spending six miserable weeks of winter in a wagon bed, then moving into a cabin with a wooden floor, a welcome fireplace warming one end and a tiny stove pumping more heat from the other, it mattered not that there was only one room with no rug or carpet.

Eunice Billings Warner was heavy with child. Winter exposure had taken its toll. Her face was bleached out. She felt weak and weary all over her body. "I'm thankful for that little stove in our little cabin," she said. "And I'm thankful you are here, Mother" she added.

Diantha Morley Billings was the only mid-wife in Sanpete. Already she had delivered two babies: little Almeda Washburn, the first white child born in the valley and little Almon Taylor, the first male child. When the Higgin's baby got sick on the trail and wouldn't get better, it seemed nothing could heal her. Diantha tried everything she could think of doing. True, her specialty was birthing. She had never lost a mother or a baby, even on the shores of the Mississippi when they had to evacuate Nauvoo. Since their arrival she had already helped set young Mary Lowry's ankle and it healed well. Thop Shoemaker's accident was so sudden no one had a chance to help him. Nonetheless, it tortured her that she could not help Sister Higgins save her child.

Titus looked like a snow-man when he opened the cabin door.

"It's started up again," he announced. "Had to stop work on the fort. It's a blizzard out there!"

"Oh dear!" Eunice gasped holding her middle. "I don't feel right mother."

Diantha rushed to her. "Titus, don't take off your coat. We are going to need a lot of firewood. You better fetch John too."

Smoke puffed out of the little chimney as fast as new snow fell. Diantha appreciated the cabin shelter more than ever. She was experienced at delivering babies out under the stars, even under rain clouds or snow clouds, but what joy to assist her daughter with the birth of a grandchild under the roof of a warm shelter. With utmost care she helped Eunice to the bed. Her slim fingers checked pulse and forehead. Sudden concern engulfed her, though she was too experienced to speak of it. This mother-to-be was on fire and her heart was racing. Fever, a very high fever, was nature's way of warning. Something was wrong. She pulled up leggings to find swollen ankles.

"Oh Mother, my head is throbbing!"

Without a word Diantha flew into action. Reaching outside she broke icicles from the roof, wrapped them and positioned them under the back of the neck. She dabbed cold cloths and rubbed limbs for circulation. Hour after hour she labored in a constant state of prayer, trying every skill she had ever learned. At great length, with energy spent and wits frazzled, Diantha witnessed delivery at last: the delivery of a beautiful baby girl. Diantha's dignified composure failed the moment her eyes beheld the tiny infant. During the painful hours she had spoken positive and encouraging words, refusing to address a terrible concern that harbored within her. All was not right. And now it lay before her. The beautiful baby girl, her very own granddaughter, was stillborn. Too well she knew the agony of such loss. Her own babies: Little Thomas and twin daughters who would have been older than Eunice.

"No, no. God please . . . no!" The heart wrenching cry bellowed out of her. She could not contain it. She was no longer in control. Not of her voice, not of her body which dropped to her knees, and not of the situation. The innocent baby was dead!

Both father and grandfather entered at once.

"I've assisted birth in the back of wagon, on the ground, under the stars, in rainstorms and in blizzards, even during mob evacuation – God has given answers and miracles time and again, but now when it is my own granddaughter, He sends no miracle!"

Titus stood helpless, agonizing with his sobbing wife.

"He could have saved her," Diantha tortured herself.

"If it was right He would have saved her. Remember when Joseph told us about his brother?"

"You mean the vision of --"

"Some spirits are not required to walk this life."

Diantha turned to console the first time mother. Only then did she realize Eunice was delirious. She handed the stiff bundle to its father with instruction for Titus to help wrap it and flung her all into the work of trying to save her daughter, her beautiful, precious, only living daughter.

"Live Eunice! Live! You must live!" she commanded. She had no time for tears, only time for prayers, lots of prayers, fervent prayers. She would do all in her power and expected the Lord to do the rest. He was the Savior. She pleaded that it would be right for Him to save!

John and Titus laid hands upon their beloved calling upon the powers of heaven to save. Then with tenderness they repeated the process pronouncing a blessing upon the head of the dedicated and distraught midwife of Sanpete Valley.

*   *   *

"Chief Walker is back," Titus said.

"Did he bring his people like he said he would?" Diantha asked.

"Yes, several hundred. They're settling about a mile north of us.

"Makes me nervous," Eunice said. She was bed ridden, but still alive.

"You know that was Walker's plan from the beginning. He offered this land to President Young so we would settle here and teach his people our ways," John said.

"They still scare me," Eunice said.

"Walker says this is the coldest winter the valley has ever known." Her father was trying to change the subject.

"I believe that – everything is cold or frozen," his wife agreed. "Never have I seen so much snow. I think the Lord is dumping all of it on top of us. Did he forget about the rest of the world?"

Titus laughed. "He just wants us to have adequate water for our crops next summer."

"Did Jerome Bradley's company ever return from Salt Lake with supplies?" Diantha was concerned.

"Not to my knowledge," Titus said looking at John who shook his head.

"No, the canyon is blocked with snow."

"Not good," Eunice said.

The new Sanpete settlers, their Indian neighbors, even wild animals were all desperate for food. Titus and Diantha were strict about apportioning every morsel they had, in hopes it would see them through until the next harvest. Cattle that survived the horrendous journey to Sanpete were now dropping one or two a day because snow covered all the feed grass. Frigid temperatures preserved them for meat. President Morley's willingness to share the frozen beef with neighboring Indians probably prevented problems between them.

John, Titus and every other available male set out with shovels to uncover pasture for their starving livestock. Because Indians burned grasses before they knew the White Mormons were coming, it was even more difficult to find feed. The men agreed on a spot two miles south of the encampment where some warm springs had been located.

"If we are going to leave them unguarded we need to sharpen their horns so they have a chance to protect themselves from coyotes and wolves," Titus said. The cows were readied, then driven to the spot and left for the night with only a few fire tenders. His home-made snow shoes proved a blessing, but the bright glare of sunlight reflected from the never-ending spread of white snow caused Titus and many other workmen to suffer with snow-blindness. Every morning he took bran to the cows and milked them, but John had to be his eyes and lead the way. As they were returning one day John saw an Indian approaching.

"I think I see Tabinan," he said.

"You mean Chief Walker's brother?

"Yes. Looks like death warmed over. Think he's headed for Uncle Isaac's place."

"Will you take me there?"

"Sure."

Men were gathering when they arrived. Word was the weary travelers led by Jerome Bradley had been delayed at Fort Utah because of a Ute Indian uprising. Tabinan was able to lead them out, but now they were trapped in Salt Creek by snowy blizzards.

"Bishop Bradley is leading a search party to find his son and the rest of the company that went for supplies. Get your snow-shoes and join them," Isaac said.

John took his father-in-law home and left at once with the rescue party. They found Salt Creek Canyon plastered with snow, some drifts even 20 feet high. Miraculously the rescue party found the stranded travelers. Some chose to remain and guard the supply wagons until spring thaw. Others, several men and one woman (Daniel Henrie took his wife, Amanda), were ready to leave the canyon. They loaded hand sleds with all the supplies they could carry and hauled them back to aid the suffering saints.

Snow shoes proved to be the best means of travel. John's group stopped at the summit to spend a night. They built a fire on the snow in a clump of trees and lay down beside it hoping to keep warm. When they awoke the fire had melted down a good fifteen feet and was still dropping. Four more days were required to make it home. The others did not follow until March.

Would Sanpete winters always be so unforgettable?

Historical Background

"Titus fixed a sagebrush bowery to cover his family from the snow and it snowed every day for six weeks" (Pyne 5). "For six weeks we lived in our wagons with a brush covering to protect us from the storms" (Snow1,1).

""On one piercing January night, two beautiful babies were born and wrapped in a single cow hide to keep them from freezing to death" (MorleyRH, 154).

Almeda daughter of Abram and Clarinda Washburn being the first white child born in the valley, November 22; and Almon, son of Cyrenus and Emily Taylor, was the first male" (Sidwell, 7).

"On December 13, 1849, Chief Walker . . . returned with several hundred Indians to establish a camp about one mile north form where the Mormons were located" (MorleyRH, 150). The Indians said this winter was the worst they could remember," (MorleyRH, 150; Sidwell/Bramwell/Freschknecht, 21).

"These were Sanpitch Indians. The tribe showed "no signs of hostility" and lived around the new settlement all winter and spring" (Peterson, 6).

"The establishment of this community was an outgrowth of a request Chief Walker had made of Brigham Young to send colonists to his region for the purpose of teaching the Indians to live as white men lived" (Hale, 16; Sidwell/Bramwell/Freschknecht, 20).

In a letter to President Young dated February 20, 1850, Father Morley reported four deaths in the new settlement: "John Warner's child which died at birth as well as Nelson Higgins' youngest child, Mr. Shoemaker's seventeen-year-old son, 'Thope,' and Brother Cable's one-year-old daughter" (Jensen5; Manti Centennial Committee; MorleyRH, 154; Snow1, 1; Young, 2/20/1859).

[Two weeks later, Eunice gave birth to her first child. Diantha was the only doctor, nurse or midwife in the new settlement and this was the third Sanpete delivery.] "Dr. Richards, a physician sent out by President Brigham Young, to aid the saints of Manti" (Sidwell/Bramwell, 20) came later.

The baby girl was stillborn, but named Diantha, after her grandmother. Eunice nearly lost her own life and was ill a long while.

"The following year their first baby was born--a little girl who died at birth, also a second one the following year who also died" (Bunnell, 1).

Note: The above was quoted from Eunice's own story. In "Valiant in the Faith" Eunice (Billings) and John E. Warner are listed as parents of a stillborn daughter called Eunice who was born and died on 14 January 1850. Also, it shows a daughter, Diantha, born in Manti, Utah on 11 May 1851 who died in 1854. Eunice only mentions the two living sons: "John Adelbert born 24 October 1852 and Samuel Dwight born 26 March 1854" (Bennett, 562).

"John Ely Warner and Eunice Billings had four children, all born in Manti, Sanpete Utah. Diantha (about December 1849) stillborn. Eunice Warner (born about 1851), died young, no date given. John Adelbert Warner (born 24 October 1852) married Emily Maranda Porter (16 Feb 1874) and died 15 Nov 1934. Samuel Dwight Warner (born 26 Mar 1854), married Lucinda Pearce (born 26 Mar 1884). Date of his death is uncertain" (Hale, 16).

Snow-blocked canyons prevented travel that winter so Titus and Diantha "were very particular in apportioning our foods every day, so that they would last until the next seed time and harvest, and by that means we did not suffer during the first long, cold winter" (Hale, 8, 9; Pyne 5). "It was difficult to get supplies from other settlements or from Salt Lake City on account of the means of transportation through the canyons being blocked with snow" (Snow1, 1).

"My parents were very particular in apportioning our foods every day" (Snow1, 2).

"Many cattle died that first winter. Carcasses were used for food. The Indians considered the white people princes of generosity in giving them all the beef. . . Out of 240 head of cattle brought to the valley, there were only 100 survivors in June" (Billings/Shaw/Hale, 31; Sidwell, 5). "Morley permitted the starving Indians to retrieve the frozen carcasses of cattle that were dying daily; of the **250** cattle brought into Sanpete Valley in November, only 100 remained alive when the snow melted" (BorenKR, 9).

[Titus and John drove their cattle to Warm Springs that first winter. Each morning they fed bran to the cattle and milked them.] "That gave us fresh milk once a day and in that way we felt we had some of the luxuries of life" (Gappmayer, 17; Hale, 8).

"The first winter (1849-1850) was extreme in its fury. By the middle of December there were three feet of snow on the valley floor and some drifts ranged from eight to 20 feet deep. Indians claimed it was the most severe winter in their memory" (Sidwell/Bramwell/Freschknecht, 21). "Even the horns of cows and oxen were sharpened by filing, to give them better means of defense in fighting wild animals, and enable them to break through the crust of the frozen snow in search of the dry grass" (Lever, 14).

Shortly after the new camp was prepared for Sanpete's first winter, Jerome

Bradley led a company of twelve men back to Salt Lake for supplies. "Indian hostilities" detained the group and record snowfall blocked the canyon. One day in January Tabinan, Chief Wakara's brother, rode into Manti with news that "a white man was lying across the Sanpitch River, almost dead" (Lever, 14). Immediately Bishop George W. Bradley led a search party on snowshoes. They found one member of the supply company wading through deep, deep snow, trying to reach them. His companions were "snowed in." "Sleds were drawn by hand over the snow, ranging in depth from 8 to 20 feet" to carry people including Daniel Henrie and his wife into camp. It was March before supplies could be retrieved (Lever, 14). ". . . as soon as the crust on the snow would bear the weight of a hand sled; this was not until March, when loading one sled with bedding and provisions and placing Sister Amanda Henrie on the other, they commenced their hazardous journey" Sidwell, 5). "The supply wagons remained snowbound until March 1, 1850, but in the meantime supplies were hauled on hand sleds back to the settlement in sufficient quantities to sustain the colonists" (MorleyRH, 154).

". . .they became snow bound in Salt Creek Canyon. Tabian, one of Chief Walker's brothers led one of them to the Sanpete settlement" (MorleyRH, 153).

[Note: We have no proof that John Ely Warner went with the rescue party, but the events described really happened.]

CHAPTER 89

"Measles! Snow blizzards! Indians! Is this really a promised land?"

"Don't get yourself worked up, Eunice. Perhaps the Lord is just testing His people." If anyone had a "right" to question, it would probably be Diantha, but she would not allow herself to go there. "We are really blessed and we have a lot to share with those not so blessed."

Eunice thought of their meager rationed meals. She was tired of all the snow. She was afraid of measles and terrified of Indians. Her mother sensed her upset and endeavored to comfort, inspire and teach correct principles of love and faith.

"The Lamanite people are suffering more than we." Diantha's brother Isaac preferred to call the Indians by their Book of Mormon name. "Measles is a 'civilized' disease they've never been exposed to before and many of their number are dying from it."

"I know but--"

"I think it was kind of Chief Walker to send for your uncle and meet him outside of town rather than bring all those sick people in to us."

Patriarch Morley met him eight miles out and gave medicine to twenty-four victims. Both leaders knew they would need more.

Eunice had watched her mother coming and going, reaching out to help so many. *Mother has a caring heart*, she thought to herself. *What's wrong with me? I had the same calling pronounced upon my head by the same prophet that I too would be a midwife and healer.*

"Don't be too hard on yourself, my dear." It was as though her mother read her thoughts. "Remember, you have been very ill. It will be easier when you are stronger."

"I hope so."

"In His kindness the Lord has spared you. I'm sure He has good reason."

"Why didn't he spare my child?" Her mind was aching as much as her heart. She wasn't alone. All the babies Diantha had saved and yet she could not save this one, who to them meant the most. A tortured grandmother threw her arms around the agonizing mother and together they sobbed.

* * *

By late February the snowfall ceased and temperatures began to climb, a little. Arapeen, Chief Walker's brother, carried his spotted, dying child to Father Morley who, with his sister's help, tried to save him. He was too far gone and died the next morning. Many Lamanites died, but he was the only one to die inside the Mormon settlement.

A large log building erected near the stone quarry was soon ready for public meetings and regular worship services. John Warner, who not only owned a gifted singing voice, but also a very valuable twenty-four silver mounted flute -- the only musical instrument in the valley, was performing constantly. He was called to take a turn leading the choir and at the same time to serve as ward clerk to Bishop John Lowry, the first bishop of the new settle-ment. When the district court was in session, he acted as clerk for Judge Peacock and his well educated Massachusetts upbringing assisted him as clerk at all public meetings as well.

Sister Warner was proud of her talented husband. She loved singing in his choir. Her parents and Aunt Hannah Morley were loyal members too. Isaac enjoyed the choir and was generous with his praises of its singers. He entertained one-year-old Simon Thomas, the pride and joy of his later years, while his mother Han-nah sang. After meeting he took Hannah (his second wife) by the arm and the threesome started for home. Diantha was speaking with Catherine Tuttle when she saw them pass.

"Isaac," Diantha called to him. "When are you going to give our town a name?" She knew the settlers had selected him to choose the name and she knew he was excited about doing so. Her question made his smile broaden.

"We're working on it," he teased.

"Going to spell Isaac backwards?" Titus inserted into the conversation. Isaac laughed.

"I don't think so." By now he had a pleasing audience listen-ing in and he knew it. "I'm considering a name from the Book of Mormon."

"Really?"

"From the Book of Mormon?"

552

"Plan to announce it as soon as President Young's letter of approval arrives. Due any day now."

Diantha knew she would get nothing out of him while the setting was so public. She would have to try later when they were more alone.

By now Brother Billings' vision had improved to the point he could work on building the school house. John and other younger men drove four or five miles across the snow to fetch the pine. Billings helped split and plane it. He was heavy into his work when Diantha walked up. Marched up? No she stomped up to him. The woman was displeased.

"What's the huff, my dear?"

"You think I'm upset! You should talk to my brother."

"Maybe I should."

"No, I'll tell you."

"Please do, if you like."

"What I don't like is that uncivilized monster who calls himself a chief."

"You must mean Walker."

"I certainly do. Isaac found his mother hiding in the bulrushes. She had been beaten and was starving to death when he found her."

"That's a shame, but why do you blame her son?"

"Because he did it. He beat his own mother and left her to die of starvation."

"Oh, I believe that's Indian custom."

"What is?"

"For the old to go out and die off to make way for the new."

"Well, Tishum Igh is wrinkled and small, but she is strong and she escaped."

"Where is she now?"

"Isaac tried to take her home, but she would not go. He gave her some food and I am going to give her more, if I can find her."

Food was scarce for everyone, Lamanites and Mormons alike. Isaac too had tried to change the situation by going straight to Walker.

"Yes, I try to kill mother so she not suffer long time old age."

"You said you wanted to be like Mormons and adopt our way of life."

"Yes."

"Mormons don't kill their mothers or leave them to starve."

"You know nothing of the customs of my people."

"You've read the Book of Mormon and said you believe it."

"I do."

"The Book of Mormon teaches mercy for the poor and honor for fathers and mothers. You must let her back into the village."

"Do you think only Mormons know best?" He stormed off. Nonetheless, a few days later Tishum Igh was allowed back among the wickiups.

"Any news from Walker these days?" Titus asked Isaac.

"No, nothing. Haven't seen a single Indian since we talked, but I want you to meet someone," Isaac answered. "This is Mr. Barney Ward."

"Glad to meet you, sir." They shook hands.

"He brought an express from General Wells about a recent battle with Utes in Utah Valley. We are calling a council. Walker is coming. Want you to come too."

The men gathered. Chief Joseph Walker, a very handsome man formerly known as Walkara, had six brothers: Arapeen, Groceepeen, Sanpitch, Ammon, Tibbinaw (or Tabinan), and Yankawalkits. Their father was chief of the Utah Nation until he was murdered –shot in the back by one of the Timpanogos Tribe. At his father's burial Walkara assumed command of the Utah Nation.

Morley knew of a dream or vision Walkara claimed. Years before while trading with white trappers in the Uintah Valley he became very ill. His spirit left his body for twenty-four hours during which time he remembered visiting heaven, but was told it was not his time to stay. He envisioned many white settlers moving into the land of his people. He was commanded to befriend them as they would bring education and happiness to his tribe. Thus he was eager to lead colonizers to the valley and had become good friends with their leader, Isaac Morley, excepting for a disagreement on the matter of old age customs.

The chief was unaware of a Ute scrimmage until Mr. Ward announced it. Everyone turned to Walker for advice. He was not a man of many words, but spoke without hesitation about the concern.

"Let them fight it out; all is right if your big captain does not

554

interfere. I will not. All is right. The Utes are bad. They will not take my counsel. They have killed my son, Battee. I feel bad. I want you Mormons to make me some presents of guns, blankets, and such and then I will be satisfied. I want the Mormons to stay here and plant and sow and do us good and we will be friends. If the Utes fight and be killed it is alright."

The meeting ended with good feelings among them and all parted in friendship. Morley vowed a "No Interference Policy." Walker commanded his brothers and his people to refrain from fighting the Mormons. There were, however, a band of warriors who refused his leadership and desired Mormon scalps. Walker warned Isaac to arm his people and have them travel in groups of at least ten. He offered to trade oxen, ponies and valuable furs for Mormon bread. Father Morley counseled with President Young and they determined it best for only an occasional exchange of goods. Food should be shared without requirement.

And then it happened. March 1, 1850 Chief Walker rode his white horse to Morley's dugout and called out to its owner. His squaw, among others, rode beside him. Never before had he threatened the colonists. He wanted them here, on his land. They were friends. Isaac Morley was not prepared for the senseless demand.

"Exchange papoose for colony!"

Stunned, Isaac could not comprehend the request, or rather, the command. His bright-eyed baby boy? The love of his life? Sacrificed for the safety of the entire settlement? No, no. He was willing to give up anything else . . . but not his innocent eighteen-month-old son!

"Take bread or beef . . . all you want, but not my son!"

Walker sat tall on his saddle-less steed. His eyes were stern. His face was stiff. His spirit was wild and relentless. *Do I even know this man?* Isaac questioned.

"No attack people. No harm child."

"Take me! Take my life! Please, please don't take my son!"

"You give Walker papoose or Walker kill all Mormonee in Sanpete Valley!"

He would settle for no other prize and pulled the child from his father's arms onto his horse with a wicked, conquering grin. Hannah fainted. Isaac bent to help her as Walker and his tribesmen rode off with the precious child.

No one slept that night. They prayed. Father Morley tried to be strong.

"Hold onto your faith, Hannah."

"How can I have faith in a devious, cunning demon like Walkara?

"Don't have faith in him. Have faith in the Lord. The Savior can save him . . . if it be His will." Aloud they prayed and wept the entire night. By dawn of day they were well exhausted and heart-broken.

"Listen! I hear horses again."

"What will they take from us now?"

"It mattereth not." Isaac opened the door and stepped out of his dugout. His former friend sat again on his white horse. Only one other horse and rider accompanied him this time, his Squaw. She who had coveted the white child held him in her arms. He was dirty, but seemed unharmed yet eager to see his mother. Hannah rushed to the horse and reached for her son. Walkara's squaw spoke to her: "He sleep tight in my arms all night." With a reverent gentleness she lowered the child into his mother's arm.

"Thank you. Thank you," Hannah sobbed. Her gratitude was for the Lord. Nonetheless, it made the squaw smile. Isaac too was grateful and very confused.

"Why?" was all he could say.

Walkara answered: "Your squaw feel bad. We bring him back."

Isaac processed the event over and again in his mind. Perhaps it was an Abrahamic test. Hannah did not acknowledge his philosophy. Her son was wrongly taken. Now he was back. To her, that was all that mattered.

But there was much more that mattered very much. Sacred, important seeds had been planted. In the Lord's due time they would sprout and be harvested.

Historical Background

"The measles have made a general sweep through this part of the country and many of the natives have died . . . Arapeen's child lived until the next day" (Jensen, 5; MorleyRH, 155).

"As soon as possible the brethren erected a large log building . . . where we held meetings. My husband, Brother Warner, conducted the singing and led the first choir in Manti" Snow1, 2). [Seems Warner and Billings were both accredited for

556

leading the first choir in Manti.] "Titus Billings was the first band leader and the first choir director at Manti. The Billings family awakened a great desire for the development of music in the community" (Billings LB, 2).

"We are erecting a school house 20 by 26 feet of beautiful pine logs" (MorleyRH, 155).

"Walker was one of seven sons. [His] father was murdered in 1843. [He] became ill and claimed that he beheld a vision. He asked the Mormon Leader to send white men among his people to teach them how to build houses and till the soil" (MorleyRH, 138-141). [Walker's words in this chapter are a direct quote.] He "warned the colonists about a band of nonconformist warriors in his tribe who desired to kill Mormons" (MorleyRH, 156).

March 1, 1850, Chief Walker rode his white horse to Morley's dugout and demanded that Isaac trade his papoose for the safety of the colony. "A promise was given that no attack should be made and that the baby would not be harmed if the request was granted" (Manti Centennial Committee, 47). "Walker's squaw coveted the infant. Walker might have employed this cunning method to test Morley's courage, as God had tested Abraham of old by asking him to sacrifice his beloved son Isaac, to see if he could be trusted" (MorleyRH, 158-60). "Chief Walker, therefore, very much pleased, carried President and Sister Morley's baby to his wigwam" (Sidwell, 19).

When asked why, Walker explained, "Your squaw feel bad. We bring him back." Quickly his wife added, "He laid in my arms all night and sleep tight." "Ever after a deep friendship seemed to bond the two leaders" (RobertsV1, 464).

Another account records that Walker's kidnapping ordeal lasted two weeks! "Two weeks passed and not a single Indian was seen in the area. Then, at daybreak on 13 March 1850, Walker and his band rode into the settlement and went directly to Morley's dugout. Little Simeon, dressed in buckskins, his face painted white with red stripes, and wearing a headband with a single feather in it, was tied onto the back of a small pony. Walker, in contrast to his attitude of a fortnight earlier when he had taken the boy, now wore a broad smile on his handsome, high-cheek boned face. "Walker bring your papoose home," he said. "All is right" (BorenKR, 11).

CHAPTER 90

With treacherous weather behind them the Sanpitch saints were eager to build a city unto their God. President Morley, having studied, prayed and pondered all winter on a name that would be worthy of all he wished the place to become, had submitted his recommendation to Church headquarters in Salt Lake City. Approval from the Prophet arrived at last. Isaac addressed the waiting congregation.

"I stand to testify to you, my beloved friends, that the Book of Mormon is the word of God. I believe a sincere heart will find answers to all of life's questions if he or she will search this book in earnest and pray in faith. Our Lord and Savior Jesus Christ knows all things. He inspired this volume." Morley held his treasured copy high for all to see.

"Scribes of old recorded truth on plates of precious metal as moved upon by the Holy Spirit. This sacred record was preserved and protected, even guarded by an angel of God until according to the Lord's due time it was brought forth by the young Prophet of the Restoration. These words were prepared for our generation." He waved the book for emphasis.

"I repeat myself, a sincere heart will find answers of truth in this volume because it testifies of Jesus Christ, His birth, His work, His glory, His atoning sacrifice to save us all, and His expectation of us. Through Him, and only through him, can we attain eternal life." Father Morley pulled the well-read scripture to his heart. "I love the Book of Mormon. Why? Because the Book of Mormon teaches me about the Son of God."

Morley set the book on the pine pulpit before him and began strumming its pages. "Many weeks ago you invited me to select a name for our fair city." Some snickered. There was no fair city as yet, but they, like him, knew it soon would be so. All listened with great interest.

"My search led me to the Book of Mormon. The name I have selected is mentioned therein twenty-six times. Let me share just two of them with you now."

It seemed the entire congregation sat forward. Diantha did. She had no idea what name her brother-leader had chosen and like the rest, she was impatient to know.

"Let's consider Alma 58:39: (quote) 'And those sons of the people of Ammon, of whom I have so highly spoken, are with me in the city of Manti; and the Lord has supported them, yea, and kept them from falling by the sword, insomuch that even one soul has not been slain.' (unquote) I like the feeling of a place like that. Here is another. In Alma 1:15 we learn what happened to a wicked man who killed the righteous Nephite hero Giddeon: (quote) 'And it came to pass that they took him; and his name was Nehor; and they carried him upon the top of the hill Manti, and there he was caused, or rather did acknowledge, between the heavens and the earth, that what he had taught to the people was contrary to the word of God; and there he suffered an ignominious death' (unquote).

"Brothers and Sisters, we who have come here at our own peril and sacrifice to establish a piece of Zion in this part of the Lord's vineyard: Let us raise up a city the Lord will support and protect (quote) 'insomuch that even one soul [shall] not been slain' (unquote). Let us call this place Manti and build it close to the God of Heaven that His approval and blessing may rain down upon us daily."

A vote was called. No one opposed. Thus the City of Manti in the valley of Sanpete in the territory of Deseret was official and ready to "blossom like a rose."

*   *   *

Food was scarce. When her wheat was gone Catherine Tuttle, like all of the others, resorted to using corn flour, less nutritious, but filling. The amazing thing was that every time Henry hobbled to the foot of Temple Hill, as Father Morley called it, he came back with fresh greens to eat. The life saving gift was a miracle from God and she knew it. Tuttles were not alone. Many saints harvested the miraculous "manna."

Both her boys had gone to the hill early one morning and seemed to be later than usual coming home. *Probably found someone to talk to*, she mused to herself as she opened the lower cupboard door.

"A snake! A rattlesnake!" She screamed kicking the door shut and ran from the dugout. Outside her sons approached with such great excitement she couldn't get out a warning.

"Look at this, Ma." Henry held up a long rattler dangling

560

from a stick.

"Henry killed it with his cane, Ma" John reported with pride for his brother.

"Are you sure it's dead?"

"It's dead alright. Won't be messing with me again."

"Henry, there is another one in the cupboard! It's very much alive!"

Warm weather brought hundreds of the slimy reptiles out of hibernation. Every rock on Temple Hill seemed to be occupied by an unwanted guest. Dugout owners were bombarded with the visitors. Women were afraid to sleep at night. Eunice wouldn't open her door. The critters were everywhere. Horses and cattle were snake bitten. People watched the ground for fear of stepping on one of the dangerous devils.

"Be really careful," George Billings told his friends. "Snakes are temporarily blind when they first wake up so they strike out at anything that moves!"

Hissing and rattling abounded everywhere from snakes of all sizes.

"The smaller ones are the most dangerous." George sounded like an expert, but he had been trained at an emergency priesthood meeting and wanted everyone to know. "They are too young to control their venom so it all comes out at once. Get bitten by a baby and you get it all."

Knowing that rattlesnakes travel during the early evening hours the brethren armed themselves with pine knot torches and warfare began. Five hundred demons were exterminated the first night!

"Ma, Ma, you should have seen all of them!" Such a sight was the last things Sister Tuttle wanted to view.

"It was unbelievable, Mother. George Billings killed thirty snakes all by himself! We go to battle again tomorrow night."

Even though John's mother was glad he was not as terrified of the deadly twisting creatures as was she, her mother heart could not help but worry about his safety. Talk was that the serpents should be skinned and cooked as meat. Many were being sent to the Indian camp just south of town. Starving as she was, Catherine did not think she could bring herself to taste one. Most likely her boys would relish the idea. *Source of protein, I guess. They will have to prepare their own!*

Night after night the snake fighting soldiers marched. A full week passed before authorities dismissed the emergency status. For Catherine and many other Sanpete sisters the alarm was not ended. Nonetheless, their praises ascended to God above. Multitudes had slithered in and out of every dwelling. Every person had seen them. Some stepped on them. Some discovered them at the foot of the bed when they awoke in the morning. Snakes outnumbered the Saints by far and yet, not one man, woman, or child was ever bitten! Again Father Morley stood to speak.

"The Lord guided us here, just like he led the children of Israel to their promised land. He has provided "manna" for our needs, as He provided for them. And now we have been through a plague, if you will, like unto the days of Egypt in Pharaoh's court. Here let me quote Helaman, the son of Alma, when he speaks of the City of Manti in the Book of Mormon: (quote) '. . . and the Lord has supported them . . . insomuch that even one soul has not been slain.' (unquote). Brothers and Sisters I say unto you, we have our own Manti Miracle. To paraphrase: '[Here] the Lord has supported [us] insomuch that even one soul has not been [bitten]!' Let me continue with verse 40: (quote) '. . . nevertheless they stand fast in that liberty wherewith God has made them free; and they are strict to remember the Lord their God from day to day; yea, they do observe to keep his statutes, and his judgments, and his commandments continually; and their faith is strong in the prophecies concerning that which is to come' (unquote). May we continue forth as did they." Morley bore his testimony and received a strong "Amen" from the grateful congregation.

Thick blankets of snow began to melt fast. As they cultivated the virgin soil and dug irrigation ditches, it soon became evident that the heavy burden of snow blizzards was yet another blessing in disguise. Ditch diggers discovered water saturation reached three feet into the ground! They positioned five acre fields and ten square rod gardens were positioned around the Manti City Plot consisting of one-hundred and ten blocks (twenty-six rods square). Each family received a one-acre lot. The industrious community wasted no time sowing seeds and building homes.

Diantha placed chairs in a circle. Again her home had been selected as the meeting spot and as always, she had it ready when the brethren began to gather. Both President Morley and Bishop Lowry arrived with their counselors.

"Have a good meeting," she said, kissing her husband

562

"good bye" and leaving him to host the distinguished guests in their important assignment to plan for a new council house. Diantha, Manti's first Relief Society President, was off with food and newly knit socks for neighboring Indians who were in even greater need than the struggling saints and their families.

Historical Background

"Being an ardent student of the Book of Mormon, President Morley decided on a name mentioned in that work – Manti" (MorleyRH, 157).

Before the first successful harvest, food was very scarce. When wheat was not available the pioneers substituted an inferior corn flour. The colonists supplemented their diet with greens which sprang up in a miraculous manner at the foot of Temple Hill. "These plants grew so rapidly that they could be gathered every day without diminishing the supply and were to a large extent responsible for the good health of the colonists" (MorleyRH, 166).

"A general warfare [against rattle snakes] was inaugurated by the aid of pine-knot torches, and many hundreds of the reptiles were killed, nearly five hundred being slaughtered in one night. The strangest thing connected with the raid of these deadly serpents was that not one person was bitten, though the coiled enemies were everywhere present, in threatening attitudes" (Lever, 15).

"For several nights the unusual encounter continued, until the hordes of reptiles were exterminated and marvelous as it may be, not a man woman nor child was bitten" (Peterson, 6).

"Rattlesnakes are extremely dangerous upon waking from a comatose sleep because they are temporarily blind and will strike at anything that moves. The men in camp immediately armed themselves with pine knot torches and began the battle of extermination, with one settler killing thirty" (MorleyRH, 164).

When President Young read that Manti Settlers "notwithstanding their limited supply of provisions, could not refrain from administering to the Indians who would sometimes cry with hunger [he] proposed that assistance in the form of cattle, wagons, and every other necessity be gathered and forwarded at once" (MorleyRH, 161-2).

Many moved into dugouts by the stone quarry where numerous rattlesnakes visited, but never harmed them. (Snow1, 1).

"The blankets of snow melted fast" (MorleyRH, 162).

"On March 6, 1850, President Morley and his counselors with Bishop Lowry and his counselors met at the home of Titus Billings to adopt the best plan to lay the walls of a Council House. At this meeting it was moved that the stone masons have $944.00 for building the walls of this house. They decided to build it near the stone quarry near the hill that had been their home the first winter. This building was struck by lightening before it was finished, and in favor of a sentiment toward moving the settlement up near the Tabernacle block it was never finished. In the fall of 1854, the same year the fort was built, the council house was torn down and rebuilt on the northeast corner of the Tabernacle Block. In the summer of 1850 they built a large bowery on this block where they held their meetings" (Antrei, 339: by Elizabeth Crawford Munk; DUP, 23-24; Esplin 13). "A Bowery was built south of the Council House, about where the Manti High School now stands" (Judd, 15).

"Diantha Morley Billings was called to be the first Relief Society President in Manti" [John Lowry was bishop with her son-in-law, John E. Warner acting as ward clerk.] (Snow1, 2; Worsley, 6). The work of Relief Society continued as it had been started back in Nauvoo and "although all the Saints were comparatively poor, yet they helped those in greater need and fed and clothed the wandering Indians" (Carter, Vol. 14:70).

Manti Sesquicentennial Monument 1849-1999

Isaac Morley and many other Manti settlers spent their
first winter in hillside dugouts.

(Courtesy S.B. Mitchell, 2013.)

CHAPTER 91

Few things pleased Brother Billings more than leading a good band or directing a fine choir. Music was a serious thing to Manti residents and Captain Billings looked for opportunities to promote his band.

"This will be the first time our nation's birthday is celebrated in these mountains. We need to make it glorious," he told his wife.

"I love your idea, Titus. Think the Lord will like it too. What does Isaac think about it?"

"Guess I'll have to go find out."

Isaac accepted his proposal enthusiastically. Captain Billings wanted it perfect. He marched his men in single file up the stone quarry hill (now Temple Hill) and drilled them again and again until at last he felt it was appropriate.

"Tomorrow we won't have time to warm up. Come with your voices strong on the first try. We want to inspire the saints, impress General Morley, honor our country, and most of all we want God to hear our praises," the captain instructed.

Sure enough, the next morning Billings' men on the hilltop shouted "Hosanna" three times like it had never been proclaimed before. And that's not all. Come early afternoon the band presented a concert at the bowery. For a people once persecuted for religious reasons and expelled from her boarders, these Manti, Utah saints honored their country's birth in style and with sincere devotion.

"The Book of Mormon teaches us that this is the promised land and we as a people will be blessed to remain in this land of freedom only as long and we remain righteous and obedient to the commands of the God of this land!" Morley made the message clear. His people embraced it whole-heartedly with gratitude. This 4th of July celebration was one to be long remembered.

Three days later the obedient saints gathered for their regular Sabbath Day worship at the bowery. President Morley stood to teach about relationships. He was in the process of counseling the congregation about future interactions with the Lamanites when Chief Joseph Walker and his tribesmen -- more than five-hundred of them – crashed the meeting!

"We come in peace. We want to learn your ways."

"Welcome my brother. Bring your people close so they can hear my words."

Morley laid out Heavenly Father's Plan of Happiness, the full Plan of Salvation, in pure, simple words. He taught by the Spirit and all present felt of that same sweet Spirit, even the Holy Ghost. Feelings of warmth, peace and hope filled every heart. As prompted Father Morley called all to baptism by immersion as the Lord Jesus Christ had exemplified and commanded.

Chief Walker, known for his moodiness -- sometimes friendly and sometimes frightful -- stood to accept the invitation.

"Baptize me like Jesus!"

He and one-hundred-twenty others were baptized in City Creek and confirmed at the water's edge. Three months later Walker was the first member of his tribe to be ordained to the high priesthood of God.

*   *   *

"Catherine, Titus is leaving first thing in the morning if you still want to catch a ride to Salt Lake City."

"Yes, Diantha. Please thank him. I can hardly wait."

"Congratulations again on being a grandma. Mary Ann will be so happy to see you."

"And I to see her and the new baby boy."

"Bet you would rather have been up there when the snakes were swarming down here."

"Oh my, yes. Thought they'd be my demise, though I have to admit it is easier for me to leave the boys behind now that things have settled down a bit."

"We'll invite them to dinner while you're gone and have George keep an eye on them, if you like."

"That would be wonderful. Thank you."

Word from Chief Walker was that more warriors were dissenting. He reminded President Morley to have Mormons travel in groups. Billings' wagon would be one of several heading north with home-made shingles for the Salt Lake council house. The shingles were a volunteer payment for supplies furnished months earlier when Manti settlers were suffering. Billings could see fresh tracks on the trail.

"Those are oxen tracks. Must be from the four freight teams

that started out yesterday," he said.

"I heard Chief Walker warned us not to go anywhere in small groups," Catherine said.

"More important the brethren have counseled us against it," Titus replied.

"Oh, I do hope they're safe."

"We'll probably find them at Canal Creek. They were advised to wait for us there and travel across the divide and through the canyon with us."

Canal Creek was not far from Manti. The horse teams arrived there in no time, but the place was deserted. "They must have decided to go on ahead. Maybe we will catch up with them."

Catherine sat tall on the seat taking deep breaths and keeping her bonnet straight forward so her searching eyes would be less noticeable. Perhaps she could have better managed the insecurity swelling in her heart if she had not sensed a stiff and troubled vibration coming from her driver. About noon the company neared Duck Springs (now Fountain Green) where the wagons slowed to an eerie stillness in the air.

"Stop your wagon!" someone shouted. "You don't want to see this."

"Wait here," Titus instructed as he climbed down.

Catherine could see wagon parts strung out like puzzle pieces, a wheel here and another way over there. None were left on the frame. Little did she know a man's body parts were likewise scattered.

"It's Brother Reed," Titus said upon returning.

"Is he dead?"

"He's more than dead."

Billings maneuvered his wagon away from the scene and toward other stilled wagons where every bag of grain had been slashed and wasted. Two more bodies baked in the sun. Titus recognized one of them.

"That's William Luke!"

"Oh no! Not Brother Luke." Catherine knew him rather well. The dear man told a touching story. He embraced the gospel in England. His wife was the daughter of a prominent minister who very much opposed William's affiliation with the new church. William migrated to Zion and established himself. When he returned with funds to fetch his family, he found his wife had become bitter. She refused to accompany him. Heartbroken he journeyed back alone. Now everyone in Manti knew the Luke boys were coming from England and their father was overjoyed and eager to meet up with them in Salt Lake City.

"Guess he was too excited to wait for us."

The mourners loaded three dead bodies into a wagon. There should have been four.

Who is missing? Titus wondered. Just then Judge Peacock approached him.

"Any sign of Thomas?" *Oh, Thomas Clark, Peacocks half-brother.*

"No, but I'll help you look."

"He's a splendid runner and long winded. I hope he got away."

Titus looked out and about at the wide-open, barren land-scape and saw no place to hide. *How could anyone out run savages on horseback.*

"Sure hope he did," he said anyway.

The saddened party had not wherewith to build caskets nor blankets to wrap the bodies.

"Here," Sister Tuttle insisted. "Take my apron to cover Brother Luke's face."

She made no effort to hide her searching eyes on the journey to Salt Creek. Not only was she searching for Indians, but now she was hoped to spot a single runner. The more they rode the less she expected success. At Salt Creek the three were laid to rest. Sister Tuttle turned away as the grave was filled. Pains of her husband's burial resurfaced and squeezed her tender heart. Though hers was the only female voice, she offered it freely when they sang a hymn. Brother Billings prayed over the new grave before the company moved on. Not until they returned again to Manti did the mourn-ers learn that Brother Clark's body was buried under the spilled grain.

Mary Ann Tuttle Egan was thrilled to see her mother, de-lighted with her precious bundle from God and ecstatic to be a wife and mother.

"You look radiant, my dear."

"Oh Mother, I could not be happier."

"You don't mind being wife number three?" Catherine tested.

"The others are so kind to me, especially Nancy. And Howard treats me with such respect."

"Respect?"

"Oh yes, mother. He is a first-class gentleman." She laughed. "He's as strong and masculine as a man could be and yet, he treats his wives with gentleness."

"Respect, gentleness? Is there any room for love?

"Yes. You can't help but love him."

"Good," Catherine was satisfied. "May I hold Little Hyrum," she asked.

Time passed with a rude swiftness. All too soon the wagon train was ready to leave.

"Mother, Howard has offered to take you back if you would like to stay on a few more days." Catherine was tempted until she remembered Brother Luke.

"No, we've been counseled to travel in large groups."

Mary Ann looked disappointed.

"I know your man is a hero and I greatly appreciate his kind offer, but I cannot take such risk or ask him to do so. He would be coming home alone and we've been counseled to travel in large groups only. These are perilous times. We must be wise and obedient. You understand, don't you?"

"Of course, Mother. Thank you for coming."

Catherine kissed Hyrum William Egan on the head and hugged her daughter. Brother Billings jumped down to assist her climb onto the wagon. He paused to greet the new baby boy.

"Looks healthy and handsome" he said. "You are looking fine too. Nothing makes a woman more radiant that motherhood."

Mary Ann blushed. "Thank you," she said.

*   *   *

Isaac was at the cabin when Titus' wagon pulled up.

"Glad you're back. We need your help."

An instant flash of troubles filled Billings' mind: Indians, snakes, damage of some kind?

"The President is coming from Salt Lake."

"Brigham Young?"

"Yes. We need to prepare to receive him."

"He's coming to see how we are. Let's just show him."

"Of course, but I wanted a special program with you leading the band and George firing the cannon. Diantha has agreed to manage a banquet."

"Good enough. When does he come?"

"Letter says his party will leave Salt Lake City July 31st. How long does it take?"

"About four or five days. We'll be ready."

George, often referred to as the "Giant of the Cannon" carried the heavy weapon (on loan from Salt Lake) to the top of the hill. Titus and John were coming behind him when a loud explosion startled them.

"George! George!" No answer. John rushed ahead. Titus scrambled as fast as his feet would let him. They found the younger man seated on the ground with his legs sprawled out in front of him.

"What happened?" John asked.

"Are you hurt?" Titus asked.

George looked up with a sheepish grin.

"That cannon has a mind of its own," he said. "I set it down and it went off."

"You are a lucky man!"

"Yeah. Good I was beside it and not in front of it." Such was an understatement. The blast carved a trench in the mountain side. "Good I listened to you, Pa."

George wanted to fire the weapon in town. His father insisted he take it to the top of the hill. *Whatever would have happened if it exploded in town*, Titus wondered. "You need to anchor it down somehow," he said.

"How 'bout chaining it to that huge cedar tree?

"That should work. I'll stand guard while you fetch a chain."

The First Presidency arrived right on schedule and their entrance to Sanpitch Settlement was announced and celebrated with an impressive cannon blast from the hilltop. The next day they enjoyed trout fishing before meetings began. President Young renamed the valley from Sanpitch (name of an Indian chief) to Sanpete (name of the tribe). Many thought it sounded better. He also "christened" the settlement with the official name of "Manti" and blessed all who lived therein.

Later, while President Morley drove him around the development President Young commented upon the peaceful spirit he felt in the air of this place between the mountains. He was impressed with their crops, stating he had seen none better in all of the places he had visited. Morley drove him up the hill where he shook hands with George, the cannon giant, and designated a future temple site nearby.

Diantha and all the Relief Society Sisters supplied a special picnic at the Fort at 2 p.m. After much mingling and celebration everyone gathered at the "multi-purpose school-chapel-city hall" for more meetings. Before the session ended the Prophet offered an enticing invitation to the brethren of Sanpete.

"I will give you $200 to build a good road through that difficult Salt Creek Canyon."

Everyone cheered.

All too soon it was time to bid the beloved leader farewell. The president's traveling party pulled out with a renewed respect for the saints who struggled in Sanpete. They camped a night at Uintah Springs so they would have new energy and a new day with which to tackle the difficult canyon.

"What's this?" the President asked with great surprise as they entered the Salt Creek canyon.

"Someone we love and admire put up $200 for us to repair this road, so we are on top of it, Sir," Brother Billings reported.

"Indeed you are." The hard working crew was impressive and it pleased Brigham that they were so quick to obey his wishes. Picks and mallets were pounding all around. "How many workers are on duty?" he asked.

"Ten men, Sir. We'll have a better road next time you visit."

"I trust you will and it pleases me very much, but even more important it pleases the Lord to have such worthy saints building his Zion."

Titus smiled with pure delight and raised his hat. "Praise the Lord!" he said.

"Praise the Lord," his crew echoed.

Historical Background

"To honor the Nations Natal Day, how or what to do puzzled us, to celebrate this day. Brother Morley and Titus Billings proposed we ascend the Stone quarry hill in Indian file. This we did and somewhere on the spot where the temple now stands, Brother Billings called a halt. Our Captain Billings referred to our General Morley for further orders. He replied let us shout Hozanah [sic] three times. It was feared it could not be done appropriately, so our captain drilled us till at last we gave three such shouts as were never heard there before nor since, only on its repetition at the dedication of the Manti Temple" (Bradley).

"On that day President Isaac Morley presided and gave special instructions regarding future dealings with the Indians" (DUP, 23). "Inasmuch as [ye] shall keep my commandments [ye] shall prosper in the land of promise" (1 Nephi 2:20, 1 Nephi 4:14, 1 Nephi 14:2, 1 Nephi 17:13, Mosiah 1:7, Mosiah 2:22, Ether 2:7, Ether 2:8, Ether 2:9, Ether 6:12, 2 Nephi 1:5, 2 Nephi 1:9, Alma 48:25, D&C 57:2).

"On March 13, 1850, Chief Walker came at President Morley's invitation and offered himself to be baptized for the remission of his sins" (MorleyRH, 160).

"On 13 March 1850, Chief Walker and his brother Arapeen waded into the ice-choked waters of City Creek and submitted to immersion under the trusted hand of Isaac Morley" (BorenKR, 11). "They were challenged to baptism and accepted. After the meeting, one-hundred-twenty were baptized" (Judd1, 10-11; MorleyRH, 166).

[The kidnapping incident was] "a test, and when the Mormon leader sent no militia to recover the child, it was concluded that Morley was a man of honor who could be trusted, and who lived the precepts he taught. Now Walker had another surprise in store for Morley: he announced that he was ready to be baptized for the remission of sins, and had convinced his brother Arapeen to do likewise" (BorenKR, 11).

"Two weeks later, March 13, 1850, Chief Walker was baptized (Antri, 63) in City Creek by Isaac Morley. Three months later, June 9, 1850, he was ordained an Elder, the first of his tribe to be so honored" (RobertsV1, 464).

"Hyrum W. Egan was a son of Mary, the third wife" (Egan, 282).

"Throughout that first summer many wagon loads of wooden shingles and other lumber supplies were sent to Salt Lake. Grain was returned in payment" (MorleyRH, 167).

[I first learned of William Luke's story when my Visiting Teacher, Debbie Luke, shared it, December 2012 in Springville, Utah. His place of burial is unknown. Funeral dialog here is fictitious.] "The bodies of Nelson and Luke were found near the wagons. Brother Luke was on his way to Salt Lake to meet his three sons who had just arrived with the European immigration. Thomas Clark could not be found, and strong hopes were entertained that he had made his escape to Salt Creek" [now Nephi] (Sidwell, 17). "His body was afterward discovered where it had been buried beneath the grain . . ." (Sidwell, 18).

"With its only cannon, the city of Manti welcomed President Brigham Young on his first visit to the new community on July 31, 1850" (Judd, 9; Morley, 168). [Or] "On the 5th of August 1850 President Young visited Sanpitch for the first time and gave our valley a more euphonious name of Sanpete and the settlement itself was christened Manti" (DUP, 23; Manti Centennial Committee; Sidwell, 9). When Titus' son, George Pierce Billings, carried the cannon "up the hill east of the stone quarry" it went off as he set it down, digging a trench in the side-hill. "George was lucky to be to one side of it" (Anteri, 52).

"The cannon was shouldered by our young giant, George P. Billings, of whose Herculean strength we loved to boast, and carried up, on the summit of the hill, just east of where the Temple now stands and chained to a large cedar tree, where the firing was successfully continued without further damage to either life or property" (Manti Centennial Committee; Sidwell, 9).

"The county was called Sanpete after the Indian Tribe of Chief Sanpitch" (Lever, 16).

"The scribe of the visiting party writes that he never visited a branch of the Church where a better feeling was manifested than in the Sanpete settlement. All were willing to hearken to counsel" (Manti Centennial Committee).

"Some of the settlers claim that during this visit President Young designated the Manti Temple site"(MorleyRH, 168).

"Diantha Morley Billings was called to be the first Relief Society President in Manti" (Snow1, 2; Worsley, 6). "She was the only mid-wife or doctor there for many years" (Bennett 559; Bennion, 2; Gappmayer, 17; Pyne 5). "Rigorous pioneering days saw courageous Relief Society women comforting and helping those in greater need than themselves . . . From the beginning, one meeting a month has been devoted to the sewing of bedding, rugs, and clothing for those in need, and the remaining meetings featured educational work" (Manti, 69; words of Leona F. Wintch).

"Friday, August 9, 1850, President Brigham Young and party, after breaking up their camp at the Uintah Springs, passed through Salt Creek Canyon where they found about ten men at work repairing the road which was under the direction of Brother Titus Billings. President Young having offered the brethren of Sanpete $200 to make a good road through the canyon, they had taken hold with energy and spirit to make one" (Journal History36, August 9, 1850; Manti Centennial Committee).

CHAPTER 92

"Hurry up, Johnny. We have to be at the school house by nine-o-clock!" Henry Tuttle was excited. "We're voting in officers of the infantry today," he told his mother.

"Then we get to help George fire the cannon!" John added.

"Wear your coats," Catherine advised. "It's a beautiful day out there, but it is December."

"You coming, Mother?"

"I may walk down to the foothills when this bread gets out of the oven."

"Listen for the cannon."

"Oh, I'm sure to hear the cannon, no matter where I am," she laughed.

A good crowd congregated to organize the infantry. After conducting the election of officers Captain Higgins marched a handful of soldiers to the Temple block were they erected a Liberty Pole. Their ascent from Temple Hill was the signal. Captain Titus Billings gave the command and artillery fire began. Catherine Tuttle and everyone else heard the thunderous roar followed by "hurrahs" from the mountain top answered with "Amen and Amen" from the Valley.

*   *   *

"I'm really proud of you, George." He said nothing, but kept working. "John tells me it is amazing that you could chisel out such a magnificent millstone for the mill without the tools to do it!" George smiled at his sister's words. Still he did not look up. "Sure will be nice to have a real mill and not have to pass around that old grinder anymore."

"Ya think so, do you?" George knew the stone was crude and very rough, but it would work. He relished his sister's admiration. All the tough labor had made him very strong and he was well aware of the fact. Eunice positioned herself on a nearby stump. She was again in a motherly way and felt a sudden burst of weakness. George didn't notice.

"John is pretty proud of his new mill, isn't he?" he said.

"It's only one-third his," Eunice corrected, "but yes, he is very excited about it . . . and grateful to you for all your help."

After his recent visit President Young invested in a mill for Manti. Uncle Morley matched his funds and John Warner put up the rest. When William Black was sent by President Young to deliver grist mill irons and leather for the elevators, he longed to reside in Manti, but had no relatives or place to stay. Father Morley took him in and treated him as a son. William claimed "Morley" as his middle name ever afterward. Soon President Young sent Phineas W. Cook to Manti to oversee construction of the mill.

"Brother Cook is coming for supper tonight," Eunice said. "Would you like to come too, George? I'm sure John would be pleased to have you there."

"Sure. Thanks. I'll be hauling this load up to them any minute now."

"Could I go along? I'd love to see how it's coming."

"Sure."

Eunice stood to start for the wagon.

"Oh no!" she gasped and doubled over. George could not help, but notice this time.

"What's the matter?"

"Oh George, could you help me to the cabin?"

"Of course."

She cringed again when he reached for her arm.

"This will never do," he said picking her up. Manti's giant carried his sister to her cabin and rushed to find their mother.

*   *   *

Again Chief Walker rode to President Morley's door and shouted for him to come out.

"What is it, Chief Joseph? You sound troubled."

"I am troubled!"

"What can I do to help you?"

"You Mormons must execute three chiefs."

"What?" Isaac was confused and alarmed.

"Pat-sow-e-ett. Un-ker-wen-det. Tis-u-nah. Must kill so I sleep in peace."

"Why? What are you saying?"

"They kill your horses, your mules, six cattle!"

"We knew someone was taking from us."

576

"They kill my cattle too."

"That is wrong, but we need to teach them. We can't just kill people."

"They call me 'woman' because I baptized in White Man's Church. They must die!"

Diantha, who happened to be visiting her brother's house, saw it all and listened as Isaac tried to teach the Gospel to his new convert. That is she listened until her son came on the run.

"Hurry Mother! Eunice needs you!" He grabbed his mother's hand and pulled her faster than she could have advanced on her own. *God help me! She has buried two babies already. Please let her keep this one . . . if it be Thy will!*

After George delivered his mother to Eunice's side, he jumped into the wagon and started for the mill. His approaching speed was a bit alarming to men already on duty.

"That man takes his work mighty serious," Brother Cook said.

"Yes he does, but this seems a bit more serious than usual." John was suspicious.

"It's Eunice. Think you better come."

"I'll unhitch my horse. You take your father and Brother Cook back after you unload?"

George agreed. John was off.

By the time George finished unloading and headed back to town with his father and Brother Cook, they found John Ely Warner strutting as proud as a peacock. George, who feared the worst for his sister, was relieved at first sight of the new father. Diantha must have heard them coming. She appeared in the doorway.

"Welcome back, Grandpa." She turned to George. "A little girl wants to meet her uncle." George leaped to the porch where his mother hugged him. "Thanks for your help, Son."

They entered the room and gazed at the tiny baby.

"Does this little girl have a name?" the Grandpa asked.

Eunice smiled at her father. "You will like the name. Come meet Little Diantha."

Historical Background

"A liberty pole is a tall wooden pole, often used as a type of flagstaff, planted in the ground, surmounted by a Phrygian cap - a cap historically worn by Ancient

Rome's freed slaves. Liberty poles were often erected in town squares in the years before and during the American Revolution [e.g. Concord, Massachusetts; Newport, Rhode Island; Caughnawaga, New York; Savannah, Georgia and Englewood, New Jersey]" (Wikipedia).

"December 7, 1850: The weather was pleasant. The people assembled at the school house at 9 a.m., and Captain Higgins preceded to organize a company of infantry, which was done by electing its officers. Captain Higgins proceeded to Temple block and raised a liberty pole, then returned to the foot of Temple Hill, amid the deafening roar of artillery which was commanded by Captain Titus Billings; also, the hurrahs were re-echoed back from the mountains and deep defiles, answering 'Amen and Amen'" (Manti Centennial Committee).

"Soon after the visit of President Young a small grist mill was erected in the canyon east of the city" (Lever, 16). "Until then residents had shared a huge coffee grinder, passing it from house to house for milling. Phineas W. Cook was sent to Manti, by Bingham Young for the purpose of directing the building of this first mill" (DUP, 25). "President Young sent William Black on an errand to Manti with a load of grist mill irons and leather for elevators" (MorleyRH, 179).

President Young and President Morley invested the capital needed. John Ely Warner claimed ownership of one-third of the mill. His brother-in-law, George Pierce Billings, was the strongman who chiseled out the millstone. It was rough and crude, but with what they had to work with it was amazingly crafted.

[Another account claims that Phineas T. Cook came to Manti in 1850 and "put up a solid mill and Isaac Morley, who paid a third of the cost to build it to Brigham Young's two-thirds, labored in it at that time" (Antrei, 62). "The timbers required in its construction were 'whip-sawed' by O.S. Cox and George P. Billings" (Manti Centennial Committee; Sidwell, 11). "Manti's first grist mill was completed in January 1851; stones were hauled from a canyon twelve miles away. When completed the grist mill proved a great boon to the community" (MorleyRH, 174).

"Chief Walker told Morley he wished the Mormons would execute Pat-sow-e-ett, Un-ker-wen-det and Tis-u-nah so he could sleep in peace" (MorleyRH, 163).

"On January 14, 1850 the first child of John and Eunice was born, a girl named Eunice. She died at birth. Also, that same year a boy, Gideon, was born on July 14, 1850 and he also died. On May 11, 1851 a girl was born, Diantha. She died in 1854" (Nelson, 1). "The following year their first baby was born--a little girl who died at birth, also a second one the following year who also died" (Bunnell, 1).

CHAPTER 93

Nervous excitement hovered over President Isaac Morley as he packed and readied himself for a trip to Salt Lake City. He, an invited guest speaker, would address the Semi-Annual Conference of the Church in Salt Lake City. In no time the eager servant was ready to go.

"Aren't you heading out a bit early?" Titus asked him.

"President Young wants Orson Hyde to attend before he returns to Winter Quarters so we are meeting a month earlier than usual."

"That explains it."

"Wish you were going with me, but as my new first counselor you need to remain here to preside over our beloved stake of Manti while I am away."

Titus agreed.

"If you have any troubles use that new high councilor who resides in your household."

Titus agreed again. George was excited about his new calling and a good person to have around.

"You could always call on the other counselor too, ya know."

Titus shook his head, again in agreement. Brother Edwin Whiting was capable and willing as well.

"We'll be fine. Hope there's enough money here for Diantha's gift."

Isaac smiled at the bag of coins knowing what an effort it must have been to save so many without his clever on-top-of-everything sister noticing them. "I'm pretty sure you did. Hope I can pick out what you want."

"You're a musician. I trust your judgment."

"Thanks. I trust you too."

"You be careful! Have the wagon train watch out for the disgruntled Indians out there."

"Sure thing," Isaac said.

The trip was long and provided good time for study and pondering. Father Morley was prepared when he arrived. Good thing, because he was the first speaker of the opening session of the General Conference.

"It is a privilege to meet again with you the main body of the Saints. My heart is full of blessings for the people . . . I want a company of good men and women to go to Sanpete, and I do say that no man shall dwell in the valley who is in the habit of taking the name of God in vain." He continued with an inspiring address. After which President Brigham Young stood to speak.

"I have it in my heart to ask the congregation if Father Morley shall have the right and privilege to select such men as he wishes to go with him to Manti?"

A motion was carried and moved that Morley could select one-hundred families. Before the choosing began President Young added: "It is as good a valley as you ever saw; the goodness of the soil cannot be beat. There is only one practicable road into it, and that is up Salt Creek. The inhabitants there are number one; and when I was in that valley I prayed to God that he never would suffer an unrighteous man to live there."

Morley was inspired by the conference and overjoyed by the willing spirit of the newly called Manti settlers. Days that followed were filled with important happenings. Families were preparing to follow President Morley back to Sanpete, and a letter of good news was delivered to President Young from John Bernhisel, Mormon delegate to Congress.

"President Morley, this letter from Washington D. C. states that the existing mail route from Salt Lake City shall now be extended to your Manti."

Isaac was elated.

"By the first of next year your little town will be sufficiently well established to be recognized by the nation's capital. This means the township of Manti will be included on the map."

Things were falling into place one after another. Isaac relished in it all, but he had been a Mormon long enough to know about opposition in all things. Among all that was good and positive on this trip one dark worrisome event saddened his heart and alarmed his soul. Because he was in town, had time available and like everyone else was very curious about the outcome, Isaac entered the courtroom to witness Utah's first murder trial. The Honorable Zerubbabel Snow, Judge of the First Judicial District Court of the United States for the Territory of Utah, called the session to order.

A new lawyer, George A. Smith, stood to speak. "I am not prepared to refer to authorities on legal points, as I would have been had not the trial been so hasty; but as it is, I shall present my arguments upon a plain, simple principle of reasoning. … All I want is simple truth and justice. This defendant asks not his life, if he deserves to die; but if he has done nothing but an act of justice, he wishes that justice be awarded to him.

"I am happy to behold an intelligent jury, who are looking for justice … It was admitted on the part of the prosecution, that James Monroe, who is alleged in this indictment to have been killed by Howard Egan, had seduced Egan's wife; that he had come into this place in the absence of her husband, and had seduced his family, in consequence of which, an illegitimate child had been brought into the world; and the disgrace which must arise from such a transition in his family, had fallen on the head of the defendant. This was admitted by the prosecution. Now, gentlemen of the jury, according to plain mountain English, a reasonable creature will not commit such an outrage upon his fellow man; that is the plain positive truth, as we understand things.

"The principle, the only one that beats and throbs through the heart of the entire inhabitants of this Territory, is simply this: The man who seduces his neighbor's wife must die, and her nearest relative must kill him!

"Call upon the testimony of the witness, Mr. Horner, and what does he say? After Mr. Egan had killed Monroe, he was the first one to meet him. Egan said, "Do you know the cause?" Mr. Horner had been made acquainted with it; he said he advised Monroe, and told him for God's sake to leave the train, for he did not wish to see him killed in his train. Mr. Horner knew that common law of this Territory: he was acquainted with the genius and spirit of this people; he knew that Monroe's life was forfeited, and the executor was after him, or he (the executor) was damned in the eyes of this people for ever. "Do leave the train," says Horner; "I would not have you travel in it for a thousand dollars."

"I make this appeal to you, that you may give unto us a righteous verdict, which will acquit Mr. Egan, that it may be known that the man who shall … seduce his neighbor's wife, … may expect to find no more protection than the wolf would find, or the dog that the shepherd finds killing the sheep: that he may be made aware that he cannot escape for a moment.

"Enough has been said to show you that this defendant has a right, upon just and pure principles, to be acquitted."

Isaac left when the jury was dismissed. He was eager to hear the outcome, but had pressing matters to attend to and knew the news would come to him. Indeed it did.

"They deliberated for a mighty long time," someone said.

"Too much was at stake to rush it," another remarked.

"I like Egan. I wanted him acquitted."

"Did you know Monroe?"

"No, not at all."

"Well, he was a good man too. From New York, but he joined the church."

"A lot of good men do bad things."

"I'm glad he didn't come after my wife. Not sure what I'd do."

"Guess you'd better defend her. Isn't that what the NOT GUILTY verdict means?"

Father Morley stepped out of the mercantile with a package wrapped in brown paper and tied with a tight string. The contents pleased him. What a gift of love. His sister would be elated. Ole Titus Billings had proved himself a capable husband just as Isaac had predicted so long ago.

Before leaving town he had one more errand to fulfill. Catherine Tuttle would need details of her daughter's situation. *How much easier it would be if I take Mary Ann home to Manti,* he thought. *Then she could explain everything and enjoy her mother's comfort.*

"We have room for you and the little one," he said.

"Thank you kindly, but I need to honor my cleaning contract."

Isaac, knowing how meager the sum of her employment must be, worried about the young woman and her baby.

"Thank you for your kind offer, but I have decided to stay where I hope more job opportunities will come available to me."

Isaac started to protest her decision.

"We'll be fine," she insisted. "Please, will you deliver this letter to my mother?"

"Of course I will, dear child. Don't forget, our invitation still stands. I believe you will find peace and joy again in the beloved land of Manti."

Historical Background

In the spring of 1851 the first high council in Manti was organized. Titus' son, George Pierce, was called to be a member. "Titus and Edwin Whiting were called as counselors to the stake president, Isaac Morley" (Antrei, 57; Billings/Shaw/Hale, 32). "While on his second visit to Manti, President Young organized Sanpete into the first stake of Zion in the Great Basin Kingdom. Isaac Morley was called to be the first stake president over the Sanpete Stake. By 1851 many Saints who lived at Morley's Settlement in Illinois had moved to Manti. Both of President Morley's new counselors had been residents of Yelrome" (MorleyRH, 175).

The General Conference quotes by Morley and by President Young are exact (MorleyRH, 170; B.Y.J.H. September 6, 1850).

Brigham Young did receive a letter October 2 from Delegate John Bernhisel that the mail route would be extended from SLC to Manti (MorleyRH, 171).

"At the October Term of District Court occurred the trial of Howard Egan for killing James Monroe, the seducer of his wife. This was the first murder in Utah" (Gardner, insert; WhitneyOF, 480).

The Lawyer statements in this chapter are direct quotes from the Honorable George A. Smith. The full account follows:

"I am not prepared to refer to authorities on legal points, as I would have been had not the trial been so hasty; but as it is, I shall present my arguments upon a plain, simple principle of reasoning. Not being acquainted with the dead languages, I shall simply talk the common mountain English, without reference to anything that may be technical. All I want is simple truth and justice. This defendant asks not his life, if he deserves to die; but if he has done nothing but an act of justice, he wishes that justice be awarded to him.

"I am happy to behold an intelligent jury, who are looking for justice ... It was admitted on the part of the prosecution, that James Monroe, who is alleged in this indictment to have been killed by Howard Egan, had seduced Egan's wife; that he had come into this place in the absence of her husband, and had seduced his family, in consequence of which, an illegitimate child had been brought into the world; and the disgrace which must arise from such a transition in his family, had fallen on the head of the defendant. This was admitted by the prosecution. Now, gentlemen of the jury, according to plain mountain English, a reasonable creature will not commit such an outrage upon his fellow man; that is the plain positive truth, as we understand things.

"The principle, the only one that beats and throbs through the heart of the entire inhabitants of this Territory, is simply this: The man who seduces his neighbor's wife must die, and her nearest relative must kill him!

"Call upon the testimony of the witness, Mr. Horner, and what does he say? After Mr. Egan had killed Monroe, he was the first one to meet him. Egan said, "Do you know the cause?" Mr. Horner had been made acquainted with it; he said he advised Monroe, and told him for God's sake to leave the train, for he did not wish to see him killed in his train. Mr. Horner knew that common law of this Territory: he was acquainted with the genius and spirit of this people; he knew that Monroe's life was forfeited, and the executor was after him, or he (the executor) was damned in the eyes of this people for ever. "Do leave the train," says Horner; "I would not have you travel in it for a thousand dollars."

"Not Mr. Horner only, who has testified that he knew the cause of the deed, but a number of others. When the news reached Iron County, that Egan's wife had been seduced by Monroe, the universal conclusion was, "there has to be another execution" and if Howard Egan had not killed the man, he would have been damned by the community forever, and could not have lived peaceable, without the frown of every man."

"There is no doubt but this case may be questioned, but there is an American common law, as well as an English common law. Had I the books before me, which are at hand in the public library, I might show you parallel instances in the United States, where persons standing in a like position to this defendant have been cleared. I will refer to the case of "New Jersey v. Mercer," for killing Hibberton, the seducer of his sister. The circumstance took place upon a public ferryboat, where Hibberton was shot in a closed carriage in the most public manner. After repeated jury sittings upon his case, the decision was NOT GUILTY. We will allow this to be set down as a precedent, and, if you please, call it American common law. I will refer to another case: that of "Louisiana v. Horton," for the killing of the seducer of his sister. The jury in this case also found the prisoner NOT GUILTY. This is the common practice in the United States that a man who kills the seducer of his relative is set free.

"The jury will please excuse my manner of treating this matter: I am but a young lawyer—this is my first case, and the first time I ever undertook to talk to a jury in a court of justice. I say, in my own manner of talking upon the point before you, a fellow citizen, known among us for years, is tried for his life . . . If Howard Egan did kill James Monroe, it was in accordance with the established principles of justice known in these mountains. That the people of this Territory would have regarded him as accessory to the crimes of that creature, had he not done it, is also a plain case. Every man knew the style of old Israel, that the nearest relation would be at his heels to fulfill the requirements of justice.

"Now I wish you, gentlemen of the jury, to consider that the United States have not got the jurisdiction to hang that man for this offense . . . The act of killing has been committed within the Territory of Utah, and is not therefore under the exclusive jurisdiction of the United States.

"I make this appeal to you, that you may give unto us a righteous verdict, which will acquit Mr. Egan, that it may be known that the man who shall insinuate himself into the community, and seduce his neighbor's wife, or seduce or prostitute any female, may expect to find no more protection than the wolf would find, or the dog that the shepherd finds killing the sheep: that he may be made aware that he cannot escape for a moment.

"God said to Cain, I will put a mark upon you, that no man may kill you. I want the crocodile, the hyena, that would destroy the reputation of our females to feel that the mark is upon him; and the avenger upon his path, ready to pounce upon him at any moment to take vengeance; and this, that the chastity of our women, our wives and daughters, may be preserved; that the community

584

may rest in peace, and no more be annoyed by such vile depredations.

"I feel very thankful to the honorable court, and to the jury, as also to the spectators, for the audience given me; and, as I said, in the commencement, my health not being good, I was unable to take hold of this business so as to treat it in a manner to satisfy myself, and do justice to the case of my client; and I would say further, what I have said has been in my own mountain English; what the learned prosecutor may be able to show I cannot tell; enough has been said to show you that this defendant has a right, upon just and pure principles, to be acquitted" (WhitneyOF, 481-482; YoungB, Journal of Discourses vol. 1 – various authors).

"While he was away on a mission for the church one of his wives [Tamson Parshley married to Egan December 11, 1836; Nancy A. Redding married to Egan January 23, 1846; and Mary Ann Tuttle married to Egan in 1849] became pregnant. "Upon his return Egan killed the other man. Because of this the other two wives were released from their marriages to him" (Billings/Brady1).

On September 21, 1851, Hosea Stout recorded:

"I learned today that Howard Egan, who has returned from the gold mines lately, and upon learning that his wife had been seduced or in other words had had a child willingly by James M. Monroe during his absence. Said Monroe had also gone to the States for goods for Reese and was now on his return here, whereupon Egan went and met him near Cache Cave and after talking the matter over sometime Egan drew a pistol and shot him dead which makes the second man who has been deliberately shot dead for the same offence in less than one year in the Territory (Brooks, 404). A footnote adds: The Egan-Monroe killing was mentioned by many diarists. Monroe, the schoolteacher at Nauvoo, whose record has been mentioned, was evidently a close friend of the Egan family, living at least part of the time in their home. Egan had married two other wives and was away a great deal on official assignments. It was the child of Monroe and Mrs. Egan who preserved and copied the records of James M. Monroe and who also prepared the diaries of Egan for publication" (Brooks, 404).

"Later that year, on October 17, the famous Howard Egan Case came up for trial. He was defended by George A. Smith and W.W. Phelps. Seth M. Blair, Attorney General, served as prosecuting attorney. Judge Snow presided over the trial. When Egan returned from the California mines, where he had gone to seek employment, he found that his wife had been seduced by James Monroe. This sin had resulted in the birth of an illegitimate child. After appraising the situation, Egan killed Monroe, who was a Jack-Mormon, then made a full confession to the proper authorities. State Attorney Blair stated the case for the prosecution. W. Phelps began the arguments for the defense. He used Bible History, Homer, Virgil, and the last authorities on seduction as precedents to prove that Egan was justified in his act. George A. Smith then took the stand and used stronger arguments: 'no man can seduce the wife of another without endangering his own life . . . The man who seduced his neighbor's wife must die, and her nearest relative must kill him.' Judge Snow instructed the jury to bring in a verdict of not guilty. After retiring for 15 minutes, they did, so Egan was discharged. 'This,' says Hosea, 'is likely to be a precedent for any who has his own wife, sister or daughter seduced to take the law into his own hands and slap the seducer" (Stout1, 151).

"Court was held before the Honorable Z. Snow, Judge of the First Judicial District of the United States in the Territory of Utah, October Term 1851. In the case of the murder of James Monroe, who had seduced Howard Egan's wife while he was away and she had a illegitimate child, George A. Smith gave the plea in defense of the defendant. He [Egan] was acquitted, but was excommunicated from the Church" (Young,95).

"[Her] first husband was Howard Egan in 1849 . . . he had three wives. While he was away from home one of his wives got into trouble with a school teacher who had come there to board, and she had child . . . he called the school teacher out and shot him . . . he was charged for murder and all his wives were released from him. He was acquitted. He took her son away and she never saw him again" (Williams, 1).

"September 1851, tragedy struck the Egan family. Howard Egan had been on a freighting trip to California. Upon his return home he received a penitent confession from one of his wives. James Monroe, a freighter had violated the sanctity of his home. Egan resolved to kill the perpetrator. He met Monroe on the trail returning from the east with a wagon train of freight, accosted him and shot him! Egan turned himself into the law" (Archibald, 7). "At the October 1852 court term, the Egan-Monroe homicide trial, the first murder trial tried by Judge and jury in Territorial Utah, was presided over by Judge Zerubbel Snow" (Archibald, 7).

"Brigham Young dissolved the marriage sealing of Mary Ann to Egan" (Archibald, 8). "Because of this all of the wives were released from their marriage to Mr. Egan" (BillingsEML2).

CHAPTER 94

Catherine recognized her daughter's handwriting and sat down to read the letter the moment it was delivered to her.

Dear Mother,
My heart is broken. By now you have heard of my husband's trial for murder. He was acquitted, but President Young has dissolved my marriage sealing to Mr. Egan. Nancy's was dissolved as well. Tamson has remained with him. I so wish this had not happened. Mr. Monroe was really a freighter, but he took on the job of schooling Tamson's children and was thus invited to lodging in the home. I know this is a usual course of events, but Nancy and I grew alarmed and when we tried to share our concerns our efforts were dismissed and ignored. Howard was worried too. We could tell by his letters. He was always reminding us to watch our conduct and be strong in our prayers and gospel study. I am not finding fault. Tamson has suffered extreme grief. I would that I could stay to console her, but believe I must follow counsel given to me. I am now unmarried with a one-year-old son to care for and for the time being have decided to remain in the Great Salt Lake City, where I hope for more abundant opportunity to find good employment. I will start interviewing at some of the mansion houses tomorrow. You taught me to be a good housekeeper and I am not afraid of work. I will close this now as I wish to send it along with Father Morley. Please don't worry. We will be fine.
    I love you.
    Mary Ann

She signed it just Mary Ann. I know how proud she was to be Sister Egan. And now, at no fault of her own the honor has been dissolved. "Don't worry" she says. How can my mother heart do anything else?

Catherine knelt by her bed and sobbed a prayer. After drying her eyes and even wiping her nose on her apron she slipped the letter under her pillow until she could read it again.

Manti's stake president received an important letter too. In fact, his quick obedience to all correspondence from Salt Lake earned Morley a unique title. President Young referred to him as being "Firm as a Mountain." This firm mountain acted at once on a letter about horse thieves. Forty head had been stolen from Utah Valley and would be passing through Sanpete on the way to California. The letter included a "brand sheet" to identify the animals Salt Lake wanted returned.

"We know you Manti Mormons are supplying the Indians with as much food as you can spare and we know that arresting these thieves will cause a need to feed them as well. Thus we instruct you to return our stolen horses and send the dishonest men on to California with only the horses for which they can prove ownership."

Another letter advised Morley to create a plan for eliminating as many wolves, foxes, and bears as possible to preserve crops and livestock. They completed a Church census through the mail. Because tithing was paid by donating labor, President Young suggested that Manti officials use Manti tithing efforts to build a bridge over Salt Creek River and widen a good road all the way through the canyon so it would be ready for a stage coach run by springtime. The season was inconvenient for outdoor building, but the faithful residents of Manti pulled it off as directed.

Communication with Church leaders by letter was effective, but soon it became apparent that verbal communication with locals was not as clear as it should have been. The stake's first counselor spoke with concern about the problem in church meetings.

"We must learn to communicate with each other! Some of our members are going away as a consequence of miscommunication. It is of utmost import that we have more correct translation between us, the English speakers, and our Danish neighbors."

Heads nodded in concurrence. Brother Billings continued: "As we seek to overcome our linguistic challenges, let us also go out of our way to cherish each other's cultural differences. Let our diversities enhance our community rather than divide us. Let us merge together as one fold faithful in following the Good Shepherd. Only when we are united in heart and in purpose can we be called the children of God and avow ourselves as builders of Zion."

Sister Billings was grinning from ear to ear after the meeting. "I loved your talk!" she said. Her embarrassed husband gave only a grunt. "I know how to bridge the gap," she added. Those words got his attention, like she knew they would.

"How do you mean?" he mumbled.

"Christmas!"

"Christmas?"

"Yes, Christmas. Let's go out of our way to celebrate Christmas like they do in Denmark." The idea was brilliant. Manti's first Relief Society President lost no time. She and a team of loving sisters interviewed their Danish counterparts with sincere interest.

"*Juleaften* we call it. You call it Christmas Eve. It's the biggest occasion of the year."

"Ya, ya, we party all night!" laughed another sister.

"What do you eat? Anything special?"

"Ya, ya, we eat traditional prune-stuffed roast goose with red cabbage, fried potatoes and cinnamon-laced rice pudding."

"Sounds really good. You must teach us how to roast a prune-stuffed goose."

Big smiles spread throughout Manti. Children learned about *Nisse*, a mischievous elf known for hiding himself in the loft.

"We feed him grod," one boy told another.

"What is that?"

"Rice porridge, you would call it pudding."

"Is it good tasting?"

"Oh ya, good enough to make Nisse happy. Leave out a bowlful on Christmas Eve so he will play kind jokes on your family. Sometimes he even helps on the farm."

"If you are well behaved Julenisse will hide surprises in your clogs!"

Children searched fields and barns for a little man wearing a red bonnet, red stockings and gray woolen clothes. Mothers learned how to cook grod. The sisters ordered a bag of almonds from Salt Lake and shared, one per family for hiding in the rice pudding. "Whoever finds the "magic almond" in their grod at Christmas Eve dinner gets a special prize!"

Fathers cut down Christmas trees. Mothers met in groups to craft decorations from bright paper and bits of wood and straw. They prepared Danish pastries and cakes with love. They placed dishes of seeds outdoors for wild birds. Manti was a magical place at Christmas time and no one was more delighted than Father Morley. He knocked on Billings' door.

"Merry Christmas, Isaac!" Diantha hugged her brother and invited him in. The fireplace glowed. Candles glimmered from turnip holders on the wall and on the table. Eunice was lighting mores candles on the tree. Catherine Tuttle was slicing sweet cake.

"Come join us, Isaac. We were just getting ready to gather

589

around the tree and sing carols and hymns like Danish families do."

Morley smiled. "I need to get back to my family so we can do the same." He handed a package and a money pouch to Titus. A few coins were left inside the pouch proving there had been enough change. Diantha sent her brother home with a plate of stacked pastries explaining how wealthy Danes gave plates of biscuits and fruit as gifts to their servants at Christmas time.

"What's in your mystery package?" Diantha asked.

"Your Christmas present."

"Oh, good. Let's open it."

"Tonight?"

"Yes, yes. It's Christmas!"

"Well, I really think you could use it tonight."

"Oh good. Then you approve?"

"I didn't even get it under the tree." He handed the bundle to his wife who kissed him as she took it.

"Oh Titus, I am so excited. Whatever could it be?"

"Something I've wanted to get for you for a long time."

"Hmm, it's mighty big for a music box." A private communication flashed between them.

Everyone sat down; Eunice on her husband's knee.

"Oh Titus! How did you ever . . ."

No need to ask if she liked it. The brown paper spread open on her lap, and Sister Morley started strumming the beautiful dulcimer on top of it. Tears filled her eyes as memories filled her heart. So many years ago the dulcimer she treasured from childhood and carried from Massachusetts to Ohio to Missouri . . . it with everything else had burned in Jackson County. But now, here in Manti – her fingers were tired and worn, but they remembered. How well they remembered. She strummed and everyone sang grateful praises to God who gave His all, even His Only Begotten Son!

Father Billings read the Christmas story from the Bible and then testified to his family of the miracle of Christmas. Christ was the gift; the most important of all. He gave us a perfect example to follow. He gave us scriptures to learn from. And He gave himself as an atoning sacrifice to make Heavenly Father's Plan work in our lives.

"He didn't have to do it," Titus said. "He was part God – His father was Divine. Yet, He was part mortal – as was his mother. Do you understand what that means?" No one moved a muscle. A silent teardrop fell on Diantha's cheek.

590

"Jesus had the power to destroy those soldiers! No one could take His life from Him. He alone chose to lay it down – so He could pick it up again. So He would have power over death that He might resurrect us as well."

Sister Tuttle sighed with longing, knowing without doubt that because of this gift of the Christ Child her Edward would be resurrected in due time and she would be with him again!

They sang another hymn. Then Diantha spoke.

"Do we understand the implication of the three gifts engendered by the wise men?" A reverent stillness permeated the room. "Their gifts were most significant: Gold because He was a King, even the King of kings; Frankincense because He was a God, even our mediator with God; and Myrrh because His mortal body would be sacrificed and buried for us. The Atonement of Jesus Christ is a gift of HOPE."

*   *   *

If only communication with their Indian neighbors could progress as well as it had done between the English and the Danes, Manti residents could have fused friendships free of foe. Chief Joseph Walker's hot or cold disposition not only made it difficult to predict his mood, but also made it impossible to know when he was for or when he was against the Mormons. He started spending more time up north and word came back that his presence was not always peaceful.

In an effort to upgrade the Indian standard of living, Governor Brigham Young asked Father Morley to have Manti saints build a home for Walker's brother, Arapeen. He too was a chief and it was hoped that his example would motivate his tribesmen. The saints completed his and many other dwellings and began construction on a huge fort. At length Arapeen moved into the wooden house, but his people were very slow to build likewise.

Morley's congregation had adopted President Young's "feed not fight" approach from the beginning and continued faithful in administering it. Diantha's relief work often took her and other Society sisters into the nearby camp where Indian women welcomed their gifts and seemed to be responsive. Some were even baptized. One day an Indian mother walked her young daughter to Diantha's home and proposed a trade.

"You trade food and clothes for daughter."

Diantha was aghast. How could any mother . . . But what was she to do? The humble Relief Society President loaded the squaw with a generous supply of food and clothing, and then took the child inside for a hot bath.

"If you keep her you must make it legal," Titus insisted. They took the steps to adopt the child who became known as Rose Billings.

Time and again the Mormons believed they had bonded with a local band of Indians only to witness major disappointments. When a group of Spaniards came to Sanpete, the Mormons were shocked to learn that their gentle, peace-pipe smoking Chief Arapeen was selling Indian children as slaves to Mexico!

An Indian sub-agent, Major Stephen B. Rose, led an armed company from Salt Lake to arrest the slave traders and place the captive children in custody. The Governor dispatched special instructions to Morley who accompanied Rose back to Salt Lake for a trial. Arapeen testified in his own defense favoring slave trade. Such had been his means of revenue for years. Little Piute boys earned him $100 each and the girls were sold to rich Mexican aristocrats for $200 each because they could be trained as excellent house servants.

Judge Snow's ruling forbade further slave trade. Arapeen, however, refused to comply. He persisted in stealing children from the Piute tribe. Buyers became harder to find. Arapeen took a load of slave children to the Provo River where some Mormons were camped and argued with them that they should purchase the children because Mormon Law had ruined his trade. They could not convince the chief of his wrong-doing. He became so provoked that he grabbed a child by the heels, spun it around his head, dashed its brains on the ground, and then tossed the corpse at the disbelieving Mormons. "You have no heart or you would have bought and saved life!" he shouted.

President Morley was called to Salt Lake for Arapeen's second trial at the same time he was elected to the state legislature. He lingered there for six weeks attending prayer meetings with General Authorities, filling in for Patriarch Smith as "Acting Church Patriarch," and sitting in on the legislative assembly. His aggressive efforts promoted the passing of a law prohibiting slave-trade in the Territory of Utah.

Before leaving the city he searched out a little mother and her now two-year-old son.

592

"Do you think there could be any teaching positions open-ing in Manti?" Mary Ann asked.

"I'm certain you will find something there, my dear."

"I thought perhaps little Hyrum could entertain my mother while I teach or work whatever job is available."

"Sounds like a good plan. No doubt your mother will ap-prove it."

"Thank you for your kind offer, Father Morley. Hyrum and I will be ready to leave with you tomorrow morning."

"You've made a wise decision. Manti will be as good for you as you will be for Manti." The old gentleman tipped his hat and smiled at Manti's newest resident.

Historical Background

"Brigham Young dissolved the marriage of Mary Ann to Egan. She resorted to household duties for those more fortunate than [sic] her" (Archibald,8).

"A letter dated December 23, 1850, informed Morley that horse thieves had sto-len around forty head of horses in Utah Valley and were taking them to Califor-nia by way of Manti" (MorleyRH, 173).

"An important early social conflict at Manti" resulted from linguistic and cultural differences. The Manti Ward minutes for January 31, 1852, record: [Titus Billings] "remarked that he had heard that some of the English brethren were going away in consequence" (Antrei/Scow, 117).

"Titus Billings of Manti spoke in church of the importance of having instruc-tions and information correctly interpreted for the Danish as a first step to fuller understanding between the peoples" (Antrei/Scow, 82).

"After the snow of the second winter melted, Brigham Young asked Isaac Morley to have a house built for Arapeen" (MorleyRH, 177).

"About this time my mother adopted a little Indian child" (Snow, 6). An Indian mother brought her young daughter to Diantha as a trade for food and clothing. She was adopted, christened Rose Billings, taught the gospel of Jesus Christ, and was baptized. "When she was grown, she moved to Salt Lake City and joined the Vern Halliday family" (Bennion,2; Pyne,5).

"Arapeen brought some slaves to the Provo River where Daniel W. Jones and some other men were camped. Since Mormons were responsible for outlawing slave trade to the Spaniards, Arapeen argued that Jones and others who were Mormon should buy the children from him" (MorleyRH, 182).

"Initially the native tribes of the area were friendly towards the settlers while still at war with one another. When one tribe had a victory over another, often the women and children of the opposing tribe were taken as slaves. Upon seeing the cruel treatment of the newly enslaved children, the pioneers would sometimes purchase the children from their captors to liberate them. Titus Billings purchased a young Indian girl and gave her to Diantha to raise as a daughter. Diantha named the girl Rose Billings. After a few years the pioneers were able to convince the tribes that the Great Spirit was displeased with them for their cruelty to prisoners and the practice gradually died out" (Kimball, Solomon F. "Improvement era, Volume 11" 1908 pg. 738).

CHAPTER 95

"Hello Mother."

Catherine looked up with delighted surprise.

"Mary Ann! Is it really you?"

Henry Tuttle followed his sister inside carrying her carpet bag in his cane-less hand. John arrived with little Hyrum William Egan on his shoulders.

"I take it you did not receive my letter."

Sister Tuttle shook her head.

"I wrote you that we were coming."

"We have an undependable letter keeper," Henry said.

"Yeah, he tips the bottle too much," John added.

"He is a problem, but I expect he will be replaced very soon now. President Morley was just deemed postmaster of Manti."

"Oh yes, that should take care of it," Mary Ann laughed. "Anyway, sorry we just dropped in – hope it works for us to stay a spell."

"Of course! "I am so happy! This is an answer to my prayers."

*   *   *

The settlers made great effort to complete the Manti Fort in time for the Fourth of July celebration. Eunice, though heavy with child and carrying little Diantha on one arm with a basket of sliced bread on the other, headed out for the construction site. She found her husband and the other men laboring with great diligence.

"I knew you wouldn't stop for lunch so I brought you a bite."

"Thanks, you're an angel." John kissed his wife and his daughter.

"Looking good out here. Do you think you will have it complete in time to celebrate the country's birthday?"

"That's the plan."

Eunice served a morsel to her father and her brothers as well.

"I'm sorry you have to spend all this time building a fort, but

595

it does make me feel better."

"How's that?" George teased. He was well aware of his sister's fear of Indians. When Chief Walker and his seven hundred tribesmen pitched their wickiups near the Mormon settlement it made everyone uneasy.

"Oh, I just think it is a good idea to be prepared at all times for all things."

Titus smiled at the interaction.

"Well, I'm off to visit Mary Ann Tuttle. She's back in town you know."

George knew. Seems everyone wanted to help him get hitched. His brother, Alfred Nelson Billings, married Deborah Patton only six months ago. George kind of liked her sister, Edith, though he was careful not to let it be known. He would do his own finding and his own choosing in a time frame of his own making.

"Don't let me keep you from your work," Eunice said. "Mary Ann and I are on the committee to decorate this fort so you have to finish it in plenty of time."

"We will," George promised.

True to his word the men completed the new fort in record time, and it was well decorated by the Fourth of July celebration. Father Morley's face beamed as he passed out his little American flags. Manti citizens gathered at the fort by 9 o'clock a.m. where Elder Titus Billings offered a prayer to dedicate the new structure to the Lord. *The Declaration of Independence* was read out loud. Orations were given. Toasts were made. Singers sang original songs. A procession marched around the temple lot and a huge, satisfying dinner was served to all.

"George, how is our newest high councilor?" Uncle Isaac asked.

"Oh, I'm fine, sir."

"Good. I have an important assignment for you." An apprehensive excitement exuded from the younger man's face. "This is more a community than a church assignment . . . well, I guess the two go hand in hand." By now George was really confused, yet curious nonetheless.

"Governor Young has requested that a block stone be quarried from our Manti limestone and delivered to Salt Lake. Brother Chapman is coming to select the stone and transport it by horse team. I want you to receive him and assist in any appropriate way.

Will you do it?"

"Of course. Whatever you wish."

"Would you like to know its purpose?"

"Sure, if you would like me to know."

Isaac smiled at the young man's suspense.

"William Ward, a Salt Lake architect and sculptor will be carving the stone for our nation's Washington Monument."

"You mean it is going to Washington D. C.?"

"It is. And you may help it get there, if you like."

"Oh yes, sir. Of course, sir. I will be happy to, sir."

Isaac chuckled to himself as George bounded off like he was going to tell the world. Yet it pleased him even more when the excited young man stopped, turned around and shouted back.

"Thank you, Uncle Isaac!"

*   *   *

"Sister Billings, the baby is coming! Eunice needs you now!"

Diantha grabbed her bag and with Mary Ann rushed to the Warner cabin. There was no time to spare. John was at the mill. Titus was in Salt Lake helping Isaac with a special assignment to bring Chief Joseph Walker in for negotiations with the Shoshone Chief Antlers.

"Mary Ann, can you help me?"

"Of course. Anything."

"Good." The two set to work as though they had rehearsed it or worked together before. In no time they heard a cry; the strong cry of a healthy baby boy! Eunice was elated and exhausted.

"Tell my husband his little name sake is here," she said.

John Adelbert Warner was several weeks old when at last his grandfather met him. Titus cuddled the infant in his arms. *He is healthy! His mother is well! Praise the Lord!*

"Well, did it work?" Diantha asked her husband.

"Did what work?"

"President Young's peace effort between the Ute and the Shoshone?"

"Yes, I think so, for now at least. Walker and Antlers agreed that both tribes should smoke a peace pipe on the matter."

"Good. If the Indians will stay at peace with each other maybe they will stay at peace with us." Such was the plan. Such was the hope. Such was short lived. In a few months Chief Walker was riled again, not with Chief Antler's tribe, but this time with Governor Young who had labored to help make peace. One of Young's pale faces, a so-called Mr. Ivy, tried to stop an Indian from beating his squaw and killed the brave in the process. Indian custom allowed squaw beating and slave trade. Young's people were changing everything. The enraged chief, resenting change and growing bitter toward the Mormons, waged war upon the Salt Lake and Utah counties.

For some reason the Walker War did not travel to Sanpete. However, one-hundred and fifty Scandinavian Saints did. These skilled, hard working newcomers added great strength to the community in Manti.

Historical Background

"While Morley, who was postmaster of Manti, was away with Governor Young visiting the southern settlements, a local mailman exemplified neither dignity nor dependability in the execution of his duty" (MorleyRH, 185-6).

Early in July Chief Wakara led 700 of his Ute Tribe into the valley and "Pitched their wickiups in a large semicircle, east and south of the settlement" (Peterson, 7).

Manti's patriotic settlement was ready again to celebrate the nation's birthday. On July 4, 1852, "at 9 o'clock, the citizens having assembled in the Fort, a dedication prayer was offered by Elder Titus Billings" (Journal History38, August 17, 1852). The "Declaration of Independence" was read aloud. Orations and toasts were given. Original songs were sung. A procession marched around the temple block and a "sumptuous" dinner was served.

"During this period, Governor Young instructed Isaac Morley to have a stone from Manti limestone quarried and sent to Salt Lake City . . . William Ward . . . . carved the block of stone for the Washington Monument in the year 1852" (MorleyRH, 187).

"On October 24, 1852 a baby boy was born to them [John Ely and Eunice (Billings) Warner]. He was named John Adelbert Warner" (NelsonSW, 2).

"The Governor elected himself mediator between Chief Walker and Chief Antlers, giving Morley a special assignment to bring Walker in for peaceful negotiations" MorleyRH, 186).

On 17 July 1853, Walker was incited to war when James Ivie, who lived on Spring Creek in Utah Valley, struck a belligerent brave over the head with a broken gun barrel, killing him. Angered because the Mormons refused to turn Ivie over to him for justice, Walker declared war on the settlers. Outbreaks occurred all over the Territory. At Manti, Father Morley ordered the settlers into the newly constructed fort.

"Walker, the Utah Chief, declared war again – not on the Shoshone, but on the peacemaker himself, Brigham Young" (MorleyRH, 186). "The incident which climaxed Walker's anger occurred when a Mr. Ivy struck and killed an Indian who had beaten his squaw according to Indian custom" (MorleyRH, 187).

"Later that year, 150 Scandinavian Saints moved to Manti" (MorleyRH, 188).

CHAPTER 96

Effects of the Walker War spread to Nephi and Payson. Soon Indian incidents popped up in Manti too. Mormon men started carrying guns with them. Women and children were more cautious and stayed closer to home. Eunice worried about her husband. His gristmill was a mile out of town on the edge of Manti Canyon. Men started taking turns guarding the mill while John was grinding.

"Are you worried?" Sister Warner asked when she saw John take down his rifle and start for the wagon.

"No more than usual," he said.

By afternoon gunshots echoed. All Manti's residents were alarmed. Eunice was beside herself, when at last she heard John's wagon and ran out to meet him.

"We heard gun shots!'

"You did?"

"Yes, several of them. John, what happened?"

With proud smugness her husband pulled two dead rabbits from the wagon bed.

"I thought you might enjoy cooking these for dinner tomorrow, but if little gun shots are going to scare you I guess I'd best give up hunting for my family."

"Oh John!" Relief, gratitude and exquisite joy wrapped around the happy couple as they embraced.

"Shall I cook them both and have the folks come too?"

"Might as well." John smiled. He, like every other good man, enjoyed pleasing his wife. "Maybe you should invite your little friend as well."

"Mary Ann?"

"And her family."

J. E. Warner had a tender heart. He was sensitive to this wife's sorrowing for a life-long friend who was trying to raise a son on her own because of a dissolved relationship. His part ownership of the gristmill was a great blessing to his family.

"When we have, we want to share," he added.

The gunshots were only for meat yet they seemed to scare off many families. John had difficulty getting anyone to accompany him to the mill the next day for grinding.

"You can't go alone!" Eunice insisted.

"I'll take my gun. I'll be okay."

Just then a stranger pulled up.

"You Warner?"

"Yes, I am."

"The one who owns the mill?"

"The same."

"My name is Mills."

How ironic, Mr. Mills wants to go to the mill, Eunice thought as she stood holding Little John in her arms and exposing her motherly condition.

"They tell me you are looking for a partner today."

"That's right, I am. You willing?"

"Yeah. I need to gather wood."

"You're new around here aren't you?"

"Yes, arrived last week, but we like the place and want to build a cabin."

"Well, you help me get the hopper grinding and I'll help you gather wood."

"Sounds like a deal." The men shook hands.

Eunice busied herself all day preparing a banquet. My cup runneth over, she thought while skinning rabbits, racing after two toddlers, and setting a pretty table. All things were ready when guests started to arrive. Her mother came first with a basket of greens for a salad; her father toting a pot of buttered squash. Sister Tuttle brought two hot loaves of bread and some of Henry's honey. Mary Ann carried some of her mother's choke cherry jam. Soon all was in readiness, except for John.

"I wonder what is keeping him," Eunice said.

"He didn't go alone, did he?" her father asked.

"No." She told about Mr. Mills. No one had heard of him. "He's not a member, but he wants to build here. Offered companionship to John and John offered to help him find wood."

Titus played his mouth organ to stall a bit.

"The food is getting cold. Guess we better eat." Eunice had her father offer a blessing on the food.

"Go ahead and eat. I'll start up the canyon and hurry them along. Probably wanted a full load; maybe I can help them."

Brother Billings started for the wagon.

"Please, can I come too?" asked Henry.

Billings turned to Henry's mother who nodded agreement. "I guess so, if you want to go."

They had not gone very far when they ran into the formation of a new posse. The bulk of riders were already on their way.

"What's happening?"

'Something is wrong at the mill."

"What!?"

"Someone said he went to pick up flour and found the stones grinding at top speed with no wheat in the hopper!"

"I don't understand."

"He didn't either. That's why he came for help."

Horrifying pain perforated his soul and seemed to paralyze Billings in mind and body.

"Brother Billings! Are you well? Your face is white as snow."

"I must get up there to John!"

"Let me help you. I'll drive," Henry said.

They started up. Loud grinding sounds that haunted the evening air ceased of a sudden as they neared the mill.

"Someone's turned it off."

Titus could see the mill. George spotted him.

"Don't come up, Father!"

Too late, he was there with haste.

"The stones are ground to powder! Must have been in operation since early this morning."

"Where's John?"

"They found both bodies over there, next to the mill."

"No!"

George reached his father in time to break a faint.

"You don't want to see him."

Too late again. John's handsome face was maimed beyond recognition. *How could anyone do this to another human being? Flashes of Gideon Carter's mutilation at the Battle of Crooked River revisited his memory. A friend! Now a son-in-law! Oh dear Lord, how much is required?*

Sister Warner never saw her husband's face again. In his wisdom her father insisted John be delivered in a nailed coffin to prevent her the torment of his disfigurement. Even with that she agonized with such twisting and wrenching and grieving that her pregnant body threatened loss.

Diantha, fearing the worst, confined her daughter to complete bed rest at the Billings cabin so she could impart around the clock care.

"Brother Billings!" It was Henry Tuttle. Johnny was with him. Titus Billings opened his cabin door.

"What is it my boy?"

"Could you step out here for a minute?"

"Of course." The aging man left the cabin, closing its door behind him.

"Did you see all the smoke?"

"Where?" His voice was full of dread. Henry pointed toward the canyon.

"It's the mill," he said. "The Indians are burning it to ashes."

Sadness covered his already sad face. No use trying to save anything.

"Thanks boys," was all he said. Before he could re-enter his house two Indians on horseback crossed into the yard. One was waving John's rifle in the air. He shouted loud exclamation in his native tongue and both rode off.

The next night Eunice felt like sitting up at the dinner table at last. Diantha was lifting the cooking pot from the fire when the door ripped open. Two large, raw red men strutted in and dumped a pile of paraphernalia onto the table. John's possessions! The pocket rule he carried everywhere! Parts from his treasured pen-knief: a corkscrew, a blade, a screwdriver, and an ear spoon. The animals were proud of their cache. Eunice looked up to see her husband's favorite necktie around one fat, dirty neck! Reacting to the rage brewing inside her the weak, pregnant, grief stricken woman grabbed a butcher knife and lunged to her feet. Titus seized his daughter and carried her out of the room.

Before midnight Samuel Dwight Warner was born. He was early, but well. His mother cuddled his swaddled body beside her and wept. Her head throbbed, her heart pounded, her breathing was pained. This baby was her last link to John, the love of her life.

Dear God, how can I go on without him? Before finishing the prayer she felt loving arms around her. Was it John? Was it the Holy Ghost? She wasn't sure, but nonetheless, she felt comforted.

Historical Background

"John owned one third of the gristmill built on the edge of Manti Canyon, about one mile from town. He and other owners took turns grinding wheat for Manti residents. Men usually accompanied him as guards, but on October 4, 1853 no one was willing to go with him. He always carried a gun up there and the day before gun shots had alarmed the community, but John brought two rabbits home to eat. Eunice had them cooking when word came that John was dead. She didn't believe it at first. Mr. Mills, a nonmember who needed wood had agreed to go along, but John would not let him gather alone. After filling the hopper with wheat the two of them set out to gather the wood" (Snow6, 1).

"That evening a young man went up to the mill to get some flour. No one was there, but the mill was running at top speed with no wheat in the hopper. He rushed back for help and a posse headed out again. Both bodies were found near the mill. Cattle had also been killed with poisoned arrows" (Snow6, 1).

"The mill was "still running, grinding its own stones to powder. It was concluded by the condition of the stones, that the men had been killed in the morning (afterward verified by the Indians) and not discovered by the people until evening" (Sidwell, 16). "John's face was so badly disfigured that his wife was not allowed to see it" (DUP, 26; Snow6, 1).

"One of them had John's necktie around his neck. They were showing these things to Titus and Diantha when their grief stricken, pregnant daughter grabbed a butcher knife and started for them" (Bennett, 560).

"John Warner and William Mills were killed at the mouth of Manti Canyon within sight of Phineas Cook's grist mill" (Antrei, 72). "The Indians converted the saw mill to charcoal and ashes" (DUP, 26).

CHAPTER 97

Diantha was strumming her dulcimer when Titus returned. She was so beautiful to him. Yes, they had aged together. They did everything together and he wanted nothing in the world to change that, but now he wore a worry on his shoulder that had not been his before he left.

How could Isaac think I could ever . . . No, it isn't from Isaac, I know that. Many good men who have – But I never wanted to . . .

"You seem preoccupied in thought, my dear. Was it a difficult meeting?"

"Oh Di, I can't begin to tell you."

"Titus! What is wrong? You act as if –"

He knelt down in front of her as if he were going to propose again.

"My heart is ripped open wide!"

"Whatever?" She set the instrument beside the chair and took his hands. They were trembling. "My dear, dear man. What has happened? How can I help you?"

He dropped his face into her apron. He was crying. She stroked his head and prayed for understanding. In future weeks she would find herself praying again and again for the understanding or at least for trusting faith to accept and carry on. Elder Titus Billings had been called by God to take a second wife.

He had no prospects and asked Diantha to make the selection for him. Now she was the victim of emotional turbulence. Her mind required a couple days to process, accept and then consider options. At length the answer came. To her it seemed obvious.

"Mary Ann Tuttle," she announced. "No one is more deserving." Titus had to agree.

Mary Ann agreed as well. Grateful, humbled, and overjoyed, she was married and sealed to Titus in the Salt Lake Endowment House on January 20, 1854. Always she had respected Brother Billings, admired his Diantha, and adored Eunice, his daughter – her best friend. Now she was part of the family!

"Well, he's old enough to be your father," Eunice teased. Yes, you should know all about that."

"I am happy for you, really. Kinda happy for me too. After all, you will be my new step-mother!"

*   *   *

Brother Billings, though always on time, arrived much earlier than expected for the stake presidency meeting and found President Morley most distraught.

"Isaac, what is it. You seem upset."

"I am upset," the usually calm and gentle man admitted. "Have you heard the accusations against me?"

"Oh, I've heard some little rumors about you getting old, I guess." An honest man could not lie. "I don't pay much mind to them though. We're all getting old."

"Word is that President Young thinks I am too old to serve another term."

"You've done a great work for the Territory legislative council."

"I've tried my best, but maybe that isn't . . ."

"Have you talked to Governor Young about the matter in person?"

"No, but I am sixty-seven years old. Maybe that is too old to be a good delegate."

"I don't buy it. A prophet of God would discuss problems with you firsthand, not just toss them into the air as hearsay."

"Thank you, Titus. I will write him a letter of inquiry tonight."

Next morning the "new" Sister Billings was hanging wash when a visitor rode up on horseback. He nodded at her with a grunt and headed for the cabin door. Mary Ann watched as Titus and Diantha both stepped outside closing the door behind them. She stood motionless, hearing every shocking word.

"Chief Walker, like we told you before, our daughter has no intention of marrying you."

What? How dare he? First he wanted Mary Lowry to be his white squaw. In desperation Mary had claimed to be married to Judge Peacock and a fast marriage was arranged to protect her from the lie. They had moved to Salt Lake, but her father, Bishop John Lowry never forgave Uncle Isaac for not reprimanding the Chief. *Now that Eunice's husband is gone –murdered by his people-- Walker expects to take her as his wife? Poor Eunice!*

The arrogant chief persisted. He would give her a little more

608

time to get up and going again. He returned to his horse and rode off. Diantha returned to the cabin. Titus walked to the clothesline.

"Guess you heard all of that?"

Mary Ann nodded.

"We don't want to trouble Eunice about it until she's a little stronger."

"Of course not."

"She won't like it."

"No she won't." No question about that.

Titus retrieved the remaining wet items from the basket and handed them to Mary Ann for hanging.

"He's been here several times. Don't think he'll give up. I fear Eunice will have to go into hiding."

"If there is anything I can do –"

"Thank you."

He walked her back to the house, but before entering he spotted Isaac and started out to meet him.

"You're looking cheerful and at peace today."

"I feel more at peace, thanks to you."

"How so?"

"Well, I wrote a letter asking President Young in which duties I had failed and this is his reply." He held out two letters.

"Do you want me to read them?"

"Yes. They will affect you too."

Titus read out loud: "Permit me to say that I was somewhat surprised that one of your years, judgment and experience should allow himself to be affected and weighed down by mere reports …."

"Think that's a bit of a rebuke," Isaac interrupted.

The letter went on to assure President Morley that the Governor would notify him in person "as he always did before on matters of consequence" or if he felt a need to replace him in the legislature.

Titus opened the second letter and read: "I do not wish you to even dream of resigning, but rather, bring your certificate of election and take your seat in the assembly. I have reflected upon your age, circumstances, and probable feelings and feel today that it would please me much if you would arrange your affairs with the view of returning and living with us here in this city at the earliest reasonable date."

"You're moving up north?"

"Yes, we'll arrange for some of my family to move up there right away."

"Sure be different without you."

"I'll miss this fair and righteous city." Visions flooded his mind: the wide streets lined with sidewalks, rows of shade trees edging streams, the beautiful gardens, and orchards and farms. "Some of my family will remain. I'll be back."

"We're family too, remember. You better step in and tell Diantha."

Isaac agreed.

Shortly thereafter Isaac moved to Salt Lake City, where he addressed the saints Sunday morning on the subject of "Indian Activities in Sanpete." During President Young's talk, "Be Ye as Perfect as Ye Can Be" in the afternoon session he used Elder Morley as his example: "[This principle of perfection] will apply to every man . . . including Brother Morley who spoke to you this morning. If he has done the best he could in the late Indian difficulties in the district where he lives, and acted according to the spirit of revelation in him, he is as justified as an angel of God!"

Eunice went into hiding. Indian affairs grew more troublesome and frightening with each new day. Eunice and her little ones remained in hiding week after week.

Mary Ann, very much pregnant, and her little four-year-old tag along, Hyrum, went to visit and deliver fresh supplies.

"We're all moving into the fort soon," Mary Ann told her friend/step daughter. "Surely we can hide you there."

"Sounds good to me."

Before they had a chance to sit down, they heard scream-ing from the irrigation ditch. Eunice handed baby Sam to Mary Ann and started running. Johnny was wet and crying. Hyrum held onto him and pointed screaming: "Diantha!"

Eunice saw her three-year-old daughter in the water. She lunged, but the child was out of reach. The water and her long skirt slowed her ability to walk. Stretching and straining she caught the wet dress and pulled the limp child into her arms. Mary Ann laid the blanketed baby on the ground and reached to pull Eunice from the ditch.

"She's not breathing!" The horrified mother rolled the child to her tummy and tried patting her back. Mary Ann grabbed her head, turned it sidewise holding the tiny face in her hands. No response. Not a breath. Eunice clutched the child to her heart and sitting on the ground in wet clothes began to rock her back and forth.

"No, no God, please!"

Mary Ann gathered the baby and two boys and started them toward the cabin.

"Oh John! Please help me John! I know she was the apple of your eye, but I need her too. Please, please, do you have to take her now?"

Historical Background

"While living in Manti, Titus was called to take on a second wife and was married to Mary Ann Tuttle January 20, 1854" (Black; family group sheet). "Previously Mary Ann had been the third wife of Howard Egan" (Egan,282; Ogden, 225). "Conditions arose between them of a disagreeable nature; she was released from this marriage by President Brigham Young; she had one son by this marriage, Hyrum W. Egan" (Coombs2, 1; Egan 291; Farnes).

Mary Ann brought one son, Hyrum William Egan, born July 24, 1850, to the marriage when she was sealed to Titus. [Born in Salt Lake City, Utah, (Egan Family Group Sheet).] A daughter, Emily was born to them November 12, 1854 and another, Theresa, February 28, 1859 (or January as per Larsen, 1). Their son, Alonzo, was born February 25, 1862. "All were born in Manti" (Black 86; BillingsCD1; Billings Family Group Sheets; BillingsEM, 1). Lewis Gardner was born in Fountain Green (Gardner Family Group Sheet).

"[Chief Walker] would marry a white squaw and this would further cement the peaceful relations of the two peoples. [President Young agreed] If you can find one that will give her consent you may marry her." (DUP, 27). "Walker had his eye on Bishop Lowry's daughter, Mary. He entered without knocking . . . expressed his intentions . . . describing his wealth . . . afraid . . . she refused . . . blurted out that she was already married to a white man . . . her sister's husband, Judge Peacock. Walker angrily plunged his knife into the kitchen table and left" (BorenKR, 13).

"President Young sent a message of good will to Walker with a beef to assuage the lacerated heart of the disappointed chief" (DUP, 28). [Bishop Lowry demanded Morley reprimand Walker.] "Morley insisted that Walker had been entirely within his rights to propose and had done nothing wrong; moreover, Morley pointed out that Mary Lowry's lie, when found out, could incite another Indian war. Lowry left in a huff, accusing Morley of caring more about the Indians than he did his own people" (BorenKR, 13).

"Upon receipt of this news [rumors] the sixty-seven-year-old delegate [Isaac Morley] immediately wrote Governor Young asking, "In what duties have I failed?"" (MorleyRH, 191). Letter excerpts are actual quotes from President Young's letters. The perfection statement is quoted from President Young's talk (BYJH,vol 2, pg 130; MorleyRH, 192).

"Lowry's faction pressured Brigham Young and Heber C. Kimball to effect Morley's replacement. A special Ward meeting was convened on Wednesday 23 November 1853, and the resultant confrontation between the two factions resulted in Isaac Morley's resignation. Brigham Young called for Morley to return to Salt Lake City immediately" (BorenKR, 14).

"March 6, 1850 Isaac Morley, President of the Stake and his councillors [sic] with Bishop Lowry and his councillors [sic], met at the home of Titus Billings to adopt the best plan to lay up the walls of a council house" (Antrei/Scow, 339; Carter5, 58). One account infers discord between President Isaac Morley and Bishop John Lowry, Sr. over the construction of a council house in Manti. In 1853 Elijah Averett and Titus Billings sought counsel about the matter and Morley's replacement from Brigham Young and Heber C. Kimball in Salt Lake City. "Upon their return, a special ward meeting was convened on Wednesday, November 23, 1853, and a tense showdown between the two factions resulted in Isaac Morley's resignation" (Other 49ers, 30).

"Soon after my son was born, Indian Walker, one of their chiefs, came to our house one day, and said he intended to take me [Eunice Billings Warner] for his wife as soon as I got around again. He told my father and mother his intentions, but they did not tell me till I was up and around, and he had come several times to see me" (Snow6,2)

[Warner family records show that John and Eunice had a daughter named Diantha born 11 May 1851 who died in 1854. No cause of death is given. In an effort to include her in our story we have used an actual Manti report of an anonymous child "falling into an irrigation ditch and drowning" (MorleyRH, 185).]

"The children of Eunice Billings and John Ely Warner: Eunice, died; Diantha, died; John Adelbert (married Emily M. Potter); and Samuel Dwight (married Lucinda Pierce).

The Warner Family resided in Manti, Sanpete, Utah" (BillingsEMB3).

CHAPTER 98

"The "Big Fort" is ready!"

Acting President Titus Billings labored to move Manti residents into its safety and keep his daughter in hiding safe from Chief Walker. Living together at the fort, it was hoped, would protect families from the rampant threat of Indians.

In spite of the dangers Manti farmers had filled the ground with seeds at spring planting and now rejoiced as their fields began to sprout healthy grain. Life depended upon it. Soon an unexpected multitude of grasshopper eggs started hatching all at once and began devouring all the new shoots.

"The grasshoppers are more dangerous to us than the Indians!" Titus said.

Diantha, still abiding the loss of her little name sake and worrying about food and safety, mustered strength to fulfill her midwife responsibilities. Her first delivery at the new fort was a baby girl. Catherine Tuttle was present to assist.

"Titus, come meet your new daughter," Diantha said.

Mary Ann looked young and radiant for one in her condition. She examined her husband's eyes. He was aging from the burdens of life and heavy leadership responsibilities, but he was the father of her child. Titus lifted the infant with gentleness and smiled with welcoming love. *He's such a good man*, Mary Ann thought in her happy heart.

"Do you have a wish for her name?" he asked.

"I would choose Emily, if you agree," she said. Of course, he did.

On his way to settle business dealings in Manti Father Morley took time to stop at Meadow Creek in Millard County where Chief Walker was camped. The powerful Indian leader was struggling for breath as pneumonia tried to squeeze life out of him. He smiled and tears filled his eyes at the sight of his Mormon friend.

"I feared we would never meet again," he said.

"We're brothers," Isaac said. "The Great Spirit Towats will not part brothers. Even when we die we will meet again in the Lord's heaven."

"When Walker die my brother Morley will speak to Towats

613

when I am buried?"

"I promise," Isaac said. He bent down to embrace his weak friend and was startled to receive a heartfelt hug in return. Such was not customary. It would never be forgotten.

Eunice had been in hiding for six weeks when word came: "Walker, Chief of the Utah Indians, died at Meadow Creek in Millard County. Arapeen, his half-brother, will succeed him as Tribal Chief. The Walker War is ended!"

Four large, heavily painted, and well armed warriors rode their horses to the fort and demanded audience with Captain Billings, as they called him. Two of them dismounted.

"You good man. Morley gone. You come now. Escort Chief Wakara to the Happy Hunting Ground." One of them grabbed Billings and tied his hands behind his back.

"You be companion to Chief in death."

"Great honor!"

They laid Billings across one of their horses.

"Sit him up like hero" shouted one of the riders.

"Just kill him now," said another. They started contending in their native tongue. Before white men could gather, the new Chief Arapeen charged his horse to the spot and shouted.

"Touch this man and I will have every one of you killed!"

They argued. Although Billings could not understand the words he felt heat from the tone of them. Arapeen waved his arms with supremacy, shouted commands, and spun his horse around to make eye contact with each misdirected brave. With reluctance one warrior freed Billings' hands and dropped him to the ground. The four left, never to return.

To prove his love and friendship to the Mormons, Chief Arapeen/Seignerouoch deeded the entire county of Sanpete with its land and timbers, ten horses, four cows, one bull and farming tools, all totaling $155,765.00 to the Church Trustee, President Brigham Young.

Elder Morley returned to visit the part of his family still living in Manti. He looked worry worn and troubled to Diantha. She insisted he come for dinner before heading out.

"Thanks for taking my place, Titus. I'm sure glad they didn't

614

send you to the Happy Hunting Grounds with Walker."

"Me too,"

"I had a terrible experience on my way down here," Isaac said. "Can't get it out of my mind no matter what I do."

Diantha knew something was wrong. She seated herself with the others to listen.

"I had promised Walker on his death bed that I would consecrate his grave and send his soul to heaven. Well, I stopped at Meadow Creek. His body was already buried on the mountain top in a deep crevice. As Chief Arapeen took me up to it I kept hearing crying screams coming from the tomb." Isaac held his head with both hands and spoke without looking up. "They buried two Piute children with him."

No one moved. No one spoke, just listened to a grieving man tell his story.

"They were buried alive! A small boy and a little girl, so their crying would frighten evil spirits away from stealing the chief's soul. I would rather they had taken me. There was nothing I could do to rescue them. Any attempt would have started another war and exterminated all white settlers in this land."

Titus put a strong hand on his brother-in-law's back and squatted down beside him.

"You're right, Isaac, there is nothing you could have done."

"The poor things were left to starve or freeze to death. What sacrifice! I trust it will secure them eternal salvation." He shook his handkerchief, already in use, and dabbed his eyes. "So I left them there, in the hands of the Lord, and the company of my dead Ute brother, Chief Walker of the Sanpete."

Titus stood placing both hands on the weary man's shoulders and squeezed.

"I've instructed Isaac Junior to return my body to Manti when I die," Elder Morley announced.

"I was thinking that now Walker is gone and Arapeen has proven to be a dependable friend to Mormons we might begin to spread out again in the valley," Titus said.

"Oh yes, I hope so," Isaac agreed. Then he announced his own focus. "President Young wants me to travel throughout the territory administrating patriarchal blessings to the saints."

"Oh, Isaac, that's wonderful," Diantha said. "You've been a patriarch for a long time, but you've always had so many other duties as well."

"Since Far West when the Prophet Joseph Smith himself ordained me, November 7, 1837."

"You remember the date?" Titus smiled at the dear soul with affection.

"Indeed. And I'm excited to serve as such full-time now."

Not long after Elder Morley returned to Salt Lake, an assignment came from Church Headquarters. Alfred Nelson Billings was called to lead a company of forty men from Sanpete to establish a new settlement in the Elk Mountain country and make friends with the Indians. To his mother the mission was worrisome. To his father it was a great honor.

"I'm proud of you, son. Go forth with faith in the living God and love the people you lead," he counseled. Alfred embraced his father and kissed his mother goodbye. The Elk Mountain mission leader led fifteen wagons, thirteen horses, sixty-five oxen, sixteen cows, two bulls, one calf, two pigs, twelve chickens, and four dogs across the Grand River and on to erect a Mormon fort at a place that would come to be known as Moab.

"I'm ready, Ma," George said.

"Ready for what, George?" She looked up at the intriguing grin accenting his face and the almost mischievous gleam in his eyes. *What is he up to now?* He jumped in before she could speak again.

"Look, Ma."

"It's a ring. George, it's a wedding ring!"

"Sure enough."

"I wondered how long you were going to make her wait."

"Just until tonight. What do you think of that?"

"Oh George, I think it's beautiful. You know we adore Edith Patton. This is proof that you do too!"

"Enough to give her a ring . . . not to mention enough to give her my name."

"That's such good news, George." She tipped to her toes to kiss him and with barely a moment to savor the joy she heard the door bang open.

"Bad news," Eunice exclaimed as she entered her mother's fort lodging. "Pa is talking with some colonists who just returned from Elk Mountain. Indians attacked the fort. Several have been killed!"

"No!" Diantha's emotions dropped in an instant as low as they had soared only moments before. "Alfred! Not Alfred!"

"I'll go check it out," George volunteered. He was relieved to learn his brother had survived a gun shot. Three others had not: Wiseman Hunt, William Behunin, and Edward Edwards were dead. The rest were on their way back to Manti.

"Oh, Alfred!" Her son's mutilated fore-finger was a pathetic sight, but he was alive. She labored to clean it and dressed it with care. "You've got to keep infection out of this," she said. Then in grateful reflection she added: "It's a miracle one finger could capture the brunt of an angry bullet like that!"

Alfred's mind had rehearsed that fact over and over. *I should have been one of the dead ones! Why was I spared? Why did they have to die?*

"We built a nice stone fort," he told his father. "Our crops were growing well and we even baptized a number of the Indians. Then, out of the blue they started attacking us. They torched our outbuilding and haystacks. Burnt 'em to the ground. We retreated to the fort, but they encircled it and started shouting their intention to massacre all of us."

Eunice was beside herself. She had no tolerance for savages who killed without reason. Alfred continued. "Some of their chiefs intervened in our behalf and allowed us to leave as long as we agreed to abandon the settlement and leave the entire Grand Valley to the Utes."

Alfred looked at his father with keen disappointment. "It could have been a grand settlement, Pa."

"You did the right thing, son; the only thing you could do."

"The Lord spared your life," Diantha added. "He has more work for you to do."

Of course she was right. Before the year was out Brother Ezra Taft Benson nominated Alfred Nelson Billings to the office of Sanpete sergeant-at-arms. He won the election and built a home across the road from his father.

Manti Temple in Construction Post Card

Photograph by G.E. Anderson 1886. Alfred Nelson's home is pictured in the bottom right-hand corner. (Notice the three eyebrow windows.) The Titus Billings home is directly across the street. Post Card published by Basin Plateau Press. Early Western Images. P.O. Box 155 Eureka, Utah 84682.

George Pierce Billings married his Edith on the sixth day of May, 1856. After all of their waiting to be sure timing was right for them to start a family, the summer they picked proved to be one of the most difficult for survival in Manti. Another grasshopper plague devoured the new shoots of their wheat crop.

"The ground was beyond hard this spring, planting excruciating and now after all that effort there will be no harvest."

Edith sympathized with her groom. She had worked beside him planting for their future. Now is seemed all for naught.

"We'll survive this," she told her new husband. "The Lord doesn't raise us up to fail."

George held her in his arms. She continued, "And even if we do meet our demise we will meet it together. We were sealed for eternity in the Endowment House. That's what really matters." George squeezed her tighter. He had married right.

"We'll make it," he reassured. "With you and the Lord on my side, nothing can stop me!"

Historical Background

"The 'Big Fort' was built in the summer of 1854" (DUP, 28). Manti citizens moved into "a log fort at Manti, a protection only recently built on the town site" (Antrei, 72).

"A census of Sanpete taken in 1853, the year of the Walker War, showed the population consisted of 765 people . . . 647 located in Manti" (DUP, 29). "At the time of the evacuation from Spring City all men, women and children of the county, moved into the fort at Manti and remained there until the spring of 1854" (Lever, 20). "Many more emigrated from the British Isles and Scandinavia that year" (DUP, 29).

"In the fall of 1854, the grasshoppers came in clouds so thick as to darken the air. This danger was more to be dreaded than the Indians. The colonists had succeeded in getting plenty of seed for the spring planting and the grain came up in rank, healthy growth. But the eggs of the grasshoppers hatched profusely and this 'crop' of hoppers ate all the new green shoots" (DUP, 28).

Emily Billings was born to Titus and Mary Ann Tuttle Billings 12 November 1854 (Family Group Sheet).

[Isaac Morley] "visited for the last time with his old friend, Chief Walker, who was camped on Meadow Creek. Morley wrote in his journal: There were tears in Walker's eyes. He was ill, and thought we might never see one another again. I told him that Towats would never allow brothers to be parted, and that should either of us die, or both, we would meet again in the Lord's Heaven. He seemed pleased and comforted at that. 'When Walker die,' he said, 'my brother Morley will speak to Towats when I am buried?' I told him I would. We parted with an embrace, which thing is not customary with Walker. He is the most unforgettable man I have ever known" (BorenKR, 14).

". . . I [Eunice (Billings) Warner] was obliged to hide for about six weeks, until the news came one morning that Walker was dead. He had died very suddenly, to me it was the best news ever to come. I was in terror all the time" (Snow6, 2).

"January 29, 1855, Walker, Chief of the Utah Indians, died at Meadow Creek, Millard County. His brother Arapeen succeeded him as chief" (Sidwell 19). "On January 20, 1855, Walker died at Meadow Creek, in Millard county, and the war ended" (Lever, 21).

"Four large, painted Indians came to the house to kill my father [Titus Billings] or get him to go with Walker" (Bennett, 561; Hale 7). "This would have been Ute Indian Chief Wakara" (Hale, 15). "Arapeen rushed in. He had heard of these four Indians coming down to our fort. He knew they were mad and he told the Indians if they touched my father [Titus] he would have every one of them killed. He preached to them quite a little time before he could get them quiet, but they went off when they got ready" (Bennett 561; Hale, 7).

"Succeeding his brother as Chief, Arapeen (Seignerouoch) demonstrated his love and friendship for the Mormon people by deeding the entire county of Sanpete to the Church Trustee, President Brigham Young. His gift included that great portion of land and all timber on it as well as ten horses, four cows, one bull and farming tools valued at a total of $155,765.00" (Book B, County Recorder's Office; DUP, 28).

"Two Piede children, a boy and a girl, had been entombed alive, condemned to slowly starve to death, their crying calculated to scare away evil spirts which might try to steal Walker['s] soul on its three-day journey to the great beyond" (BorenKR, 15).

"Brother Morley made a request of his son Isaac, Jr. that he return his father's body to "lovely Manti" for interment after his death" (MorleyRH, 193).

"Isaac Morley's activities were turning more and more toward his patriarchal calling . . . ordained . . . by Joseph Smith in Far West" (MorleyRH, 194).

After Chief Walker died "Manti began to spread herself, and extend her boarders beyond the limited bounds of 'Stone Quarries,' 'Stone Forts,' 'Log Forts,' and 'Little Forts' " (Sidewell, 19).

"Alfred N. Billings led a company of forty-one men with fifteen wagons over the Old Spanish Trail to the Crossing of the Colorado. Here at present Moab, the Elk Mountain Mission planted crops and built a fort during the summer. Early relations with the natives were friendly, and a number of them were baptized into the Mormon fold. But fall brought Indian troubles resulting in attacks on the fort and death to three of the colonists. Their isolated situation being considered untenable, the party abandoned the mission" (Larson, 71).

"On May 21, 1855, A. N. Billings and a company of forty men were sent from Sanpete to settle the Elk Mountain country and make peace with the Indians. They crossed the Grand River and erected the Mormon fort, where Moab is now located. In August some of the colonists returned to Manti, and on September 3rd the Indians made an attack, killing Wiseman Hunt, Edward Edwards and William Behunnin and wounding Capt. A. N. Billings. The colonists entered the fort, which the Indians immediately surrounded and gave notice of their intentions to massacre all the inmates. The next day some of the chiefs interceded in behalf of the white men and the imprisoned colonists were permitted to return to their homes unmolested, with the understanding that the settlement should be abandoned and Grand Valley left in undisputed possession of the Utes" (Lever, 25).

"News arrived that the Indians attacked [sic] the brethren at the Elk mountain Mission and killed three to wit [sic] Wiseman Hunt, William Behunin and Edward Edwards. President A.N. Billings was wounded in the fore-finger. They abandoned the fort and took the Horses & left for Manti where they arrived on the 30th Sept. The affair took place on the 22nd Sept" (Stout1, 561).

Alfred Nelson Billings returned to Manti and built a home on the corner lot across the road from his father's corner lot. [Note: In 1996 my sister Nancy Billings Allen, dad's cousin Beatrice Gappmayer Pyne, and I were checking out the Titus Billings property in Manti. I was standing in the road taking a picture of the house on his property when a kind gentleman came out of the house across the street. "If you are interested in 1800 houses," Larry Garmus said, "come look at the one I just restored." He gave us a grand tour; his work was exquisite. A stairway wall of rough hand-hewn lumber was still exposed from the remodeling. He let me touch it as we both wondered who had planed the wood with hand tools. A picture hanging in the City Building identifies the structure as Alfred's home. The next time I visited Larry and Gail had sold the home to John and Karen Russell who let us take another photo. See in Appendix A - Billings Family.]

During the 1850's son George P. built a house in Manti that is still standing today (1996). "He was sheriff of Sanpete County for several years, and a good stone mason" like his father. His Manti home was "visited in past years by Porter Rockwell on matters of business connected with observance of the law" (Antrei, 223).

CHAPTER 99

The Manti famine took its toll on Titus Billings. Perhaps age was part of it. His tired body had crossed the Great Plains at fifty-five years and now it was starving a decade later. Mary Ann was young and determined. Her children were hungry. Emily was only two years. Hyrum [Egan] was six years and beginning a rebellious streak. His "real father" was a Pony Express hero and he knew it. Living with an elderly grandpa figure was not as glorious as he glamorized Captain Egan to be.

"You will respect your elders," Mary Ann taught her son. "Father Billings is a good man and I love him."

But the good man she loved was thin and starving. She feared he would soon melt away.

"Dear God, we have tried to live thy gospel and are thankful for it. But our bodies cannot function without nourishment. Thou who hast created us with such need must now be relied upon to supply that need. I beseech thee in respectful soberness. Please provide food for my children and my mother and my husband and his other wife. If it be thy will please grant me strength and means to provide for these I love. I know all things are possible to thee. I trust thee to guide me to the food thou wilt have us eat. And, should it not be thy will for us to come off conquers of this trial please help us endure it well and take us in thy keeping according to thy great plan." Mary Ann ended her prayer in the Savior's holy name. Then she washed her face, picked up a basket and started out. *If the Lord wants my family to eat today He will provide.*

Mary Ann had not gone far when she met up with George and Edith.

"Sister Billings, look what we've found!" Edith was beside herself with excitement. She held up a basket full of . . .

"Whatever is it?" Mary Ann wondered.

"Pigweed! You'll find it on the south side of Quarry Hill" George said.

"I've never heard of such a thing."

"Neither had we, but its there and it's eatable. Praise the Lord!"

"Praise the Lord indeed." *I thank thee, dear Lord.*

"You have to cut it down," George added. "Here, let me go

with you."

"I'll take this home and start boiling it," Edith said.

In no time George filled Mary Ann's basket with a good supply of pigweed. She carried it home with excitement. Already her step felt lighter. The Lord was with them in this. By a miracle He would feed them today.

Mary Ann cleaned, cooked, and served pigweed to her family who relished it. Each day she returned to the hill for a fresh supply.

"I have never seen such a food before," Titus said. No one had. Nonetheless, it sprouted in the same place all season feeding the blessed families of Manti. [Pigweed kept everyone alive in 1856, but afterwards it was never seen again.]

Mary Ann was taught by the best. She shadowed Diantha's mid-wife duties until she learned enough to go solo. There was a great need in the valley, and when distance was a factor one of them would travel and wait it out with the expectant mother while the other looked after the house and children left behind. Mary Ann found herself going more often than not, when traveling started to impose a hardship upon Diantha.

"Shall I fetch your dulcimer, Diantha?"

"Yes, dear. I would like that."

The first wife was very weak from a recent illness. The second wife cared for her every need. Diantha's health was on the mend now. Mary Ann felt her spirit could use a boost.

"There's nothing like music."

Diantha sat up and strummed a few strokes.

"You play it now."

"Are you sure?"

Diantha had schooled Mary Ann in music, both singing and playing the instrument. Now she just wanted to listen.

"I'm happy to play for you. Even willing to sing, but you will get better, you know!"

"If you say so," Diantha said smiling.

"Oh, I say so." Mary Ann began to play. Diantha closed her eyes and started humming. Their husband entered the room.

"You sound like angels," he said.

Each night Mary Ann serenaded her counterpart before going to bed. Soon Diantha seemed stronger and more cheerful.

"I want you to keep the dulcimer," she said one night.

Mary Ann was stunned by the offer.

"This was your gift from Titus. You treasure it . . . and you play it so well."

Diantha smiled. "Yes, I treasure it. And I treasure you too. I want you to have it."

Mary Ann clutched the wooden stringed music maker to her heart. She had never owned such a possession.

"I will take good care of it. Thank you, Di." Mary Ann caught herself. She had never called Diantha by the nickname Titus used. Perhaps that was inappropriate.

Diantha smiled. *We've come a long way together for her to be able to call me that.*

"Just let me play it again from time to time. Will you?"

"Of course. Would you like to play it now." With renewed tenderness she laid the dulcimer onto Diantha's lap where the gifted musician began to strum the strings. The song was beautiful and played with perfection. Then, of a sudden she stopped in the middle of it.

"Diantha?"

"I'm finished. You take it now." *Finished!* The thought was alarming. *Not now, not yet.*

"Perhaps you just need to rest." Mary Ann tucked her in and blew out the candle.

The night Theresa was born Diantha was well enough to sit up and give birthing instructions to Catherine. She was well and on duty with Catherine again when Alonzo Billings entered this world. Mary Ann was the mother of two daughters and two sons. Like all good mothers, her children meant the world to her.

Between giving speeches and giving blessings Elder Morley kept busy. He traveled up and down the state inspiring saints everywhere he went. Much of his focus was in the area of St. George and Santa Clara. He always spoke in General Conference.

"If we, as individuals, are right before God, all will go well with us and the Lord will prosper us . . . If we can prepare our hearts and our lives, we need not fear anything about our enemies. The greatest fear is that I shall not sustain and carry out correct principle[s] in my bosom. I believe that our grand objective is to have all things right within. If we do this, we shall do well."

Diantha loved to hear her brother speak. Well, everyone did, for that matter.

"We should reflect upon the covenants and obligations that we have made unto God and before our brethren. There are many keys in those holy covenants whereby we can derive comfort. Obedience is the grand key whereby this people [will be] exalted.

"It is the mind that makes the man. If that mind is centered upon correct objects – if it cultivates and cherishes them, that mind is improving. I learn this daily. And there are no hours that pass but there are opportunities for our advancement in the principles of exaltation."

At length Father Morley retired to the home of his daughter Lucy Diantha in North Bend [Fairview, Utah]. By now Rose Billings had grown to adulthood and been invited to join the Vern Halliday family in Salt Lake. Titus prepared the wagon and Rose loaded her belongings into it.

Hyrum Egan walked up to the wagon with a load over his shoulder.

"What are you up to?" Titus asked him.

"I'm going with you to Salt Lake City."

"You're welcome to ride along, son. What's in the bag?"

"I won't be coming back."

"Your mother won't like that."

"I'm fourteen now. I can make my own decisions."

"And what decisions have you made?"

"I'm going to live with my real father."

"You know that will break your real mother's heart."

"You can take care of her. She belongs with you. I belong with him."

By now Diantha stood beside the wagon with worry written all over her face.

"Hyrum, at least talk to your mother before you go."

"When's she coming back?"

"You know she's gone to help your Aunt Martha. No one knows when the baby will come. She'll be back as soon as she can."

"I'm going now."

Diantha gave Titus a look of panic and wonderment. *What do we do?* She didn't say a word, but deliberated it.

"What can I say to change your mind?" Titus asked.

"Noth'in. I've decided and that's final."

"Should I make some more sandwiches for you?"

"No, you always send plenty. We will be fine."

"Hurry back. I don't relish the job of telling Mary Ann of her son's desertion."

Hyrum climbed in the wagon bed. Rose, already seated beside the driver, was silent through it all. Diantha had tears in her eyes for both of them.

"Best wishes, Hyrum."

"Thanks, Ma'am."

"God bless you Rose." She reached to her step-daughter for another farewell embrace, and then ran around the wagon. "Be careful, Titus." He kissed her and started off.

Rheumatism took its toll on Isaac Morley. He battled it with courage for many days. On June 24, 1865 his battle ended. Isaac Junior, came to take the body back to Manti as he had promised.

"The funeral will be in two days," he said.

"We'll leave tomorrow," Joseph Allen promised. Lucy Diantha made preparations and they started out right on schedule. They were half way across a stream when the team stopped. Joseph stood in the carriage and tried every trick he knew to urge the horses forward. It was as though they sensed a danger on the other side. They would not budge. No amount of coaxing made a difference.

"It's no use, Lucy. Something is wrong. We have to turn back."

Sorrowing disappointment pained them. They missed the funeral of a great man, even a beloved father.

"Your father knows, Lucy" Joseph comforted after they learned about Indians lying in wait to kill them on the other side of the river.

"I know. Father was protecting us. He sent us back to safety," Lucy said.

"Your father lived to save souls," Joseph added with greatest respect.

"And he is still looking out for us – only now mother is again at his side."

Historical Background

"Provisions were very scarce in the summer of 1856 but to the amazement of all, pigweed sprang up in abundance on the south side of the quarry hill" (Lever,23). "It was cut each morning, cleaned, boiled, and served with a little meat and potatoes. Quote from Hans Denison, 'This weed had never grown there before nor has it ever grown since, and no man has ever been enabled to solve the problem

627

of how the seeds came to be there'" (Manti Centennial Committee).

Quotes from Isaac's speeches are exact excerpts (MorleyRH, 197-199). He traveled extensively pronouncing patriarchal blessings on the heads of hundreds. "In traveling as he did, he took a severe cold and rheumatics set in [making him] almost helpless for ten months" (Cox1, 3). "Isaac Morley developed rheumatism and shortly thereafter, on June 24, 1865, died" (MorleyRH, 200).

Emily Billings was born 12 November 1854 in Manti, San Pete, Utah. [She died February 1889.]

Theresa Billings was born 28 Feb 1859 in Manti, San Pete, Utah. [She died 2 March 1931.]

Alonzo Billings was born 25 February 1862 in Manti, San Pete, Utah. [He died 28 November 1944.] (Family Group Sheet)

A membership record shows a Titus Billings listed as a son to Titus and Mary Ann Billings. "Children of spouse #2: Emily, Titus, Theresa, Alonzo Billings" (Black1, 371). Family records do not support this claim and the family believes there were only three children born to that union.

An Indian mother brought her young daughter to Diantha as a trade for food and clothing. She was adopted, christened Rose Billings, taught the Gospel of Jesus Christ, and was baptized. "When she was grown, she moved to Salt Lake City and joined the Vern Halliday family" (Bennion,2; Pyne,5).

CHAPTER 100

To say Mary Ann was upset would be a gross understatement. When she returned home and found out that Titus Billings had taken her son to Salt Lake City and left him there to live with his father; she was irate! Without hesitation she began to pack.

"Hyrum has wanted to go for a long time. Maybe this will get it out of his system."

No comment.

"You should at least wait to hear what happened, what Titus has to say about it."

No comment.

"I'm so sorry, Mary Ann, but I know this can be worked out."

Nothing Diantha said seemed to help. Mary Ann, her children and every evidence of them would be gone when "that man" gets back!

"It would seem to me that you are doing the same thing . . . I mean you are taking his children away . . . I mean . . ." It was no use. "At least sleep on it and start out after the children have breakfast in the morning."

To that she did agree.

Neither adult slept well. Mary Ann was hurt to the core and she felt betrayed. Diantha felt helpless. She didn't know what to say, what to do. Titus would be devastated. She worried how it would affect his diminishing health. If only Mary Ann would wait and give him a chance.

Diantha was up early and made a hearty breakfast. The children were too young to realize what was happening. Emily was ten, Theresa five, and Little Alonzo was only two years old. *I love these children. Can't stand to see them go.*

"Mary Ann, please reconsider. I don't know what we will do without you!"

"I can't Diantha. I have to leave. I have to leave now."

"Where will you go?"

"It's best you don't know. Then you can honestly say that you don't."

"Please take the dulcimer with you."

"Don't know how I can carry it."

"Titus has the wagon. You could take the buggy."

"No. I wouldn't be able to return it."

"How are you going to carry your bags? What about the children."

"We're in no hurry. We can walk."

"At least take the little vegetable cart to put your stuff in. Maybe Alonzo can sit on top."

Diantha ran to the shed and returned with a one-wheel contraption Titus had built for garden use. She watched Mary Ann slap the bags into it.

"Please take the dulcimer. I want the children to have it. You play it so well. Maybe it will comfort you."

Mary Ann returned to her room for a last look. The lonesome dulcimer was all that remained. She touched its case with her finger. *I hate to leave you behind. After all, you are rightfully mine now.* She snatched it up as if to load it into the cart before she could change her mind.

Diantha noticed, of course, but she said nothing about it. She kissed the children as if they were going on a big trip.

"Take care of your mother," she instructed. Tears filled her eyes. What could she do? It was final. Mary Ann and her wee ones were on their way. Diantha watched until they could be seen no more.

Things were never the same in the Billings household. The innocent questions, happy hugs, and blessed laughter of little voices were gone. Singing at night to a dulcimer happened no more. Titus watched and waited, but Mary Ann never came back.

George built his Edith a nice brick home in Manti where he was elected Sheriff.

"Porter Rockwell is coming to town, Pa. He will be a guest in our home." George was honored and excited. His increasing interest and dedicated work in law enforcement connected him with many important leaders. Rockwell, a neighbor back in Nauvoo, had always been one of his heroes.

"You and Ma will have to come over for dinner and see him."

"Thanks, son. We'd like that."

Alfred Nelson bought property in Provo where he built a home and planted an orchard. Titus and Diantha sold their home and Manti property to Robert and Elizabeth Johnson. Their wagon was loaded. They were ready to take off.

"I'm going to miss you being right here, Ma," Eunice said.

"I'll miss you too, dear, but I think it's for the best."

"Alfred's lucky to have you and father move in with him."

"We are lucky he offered to have us."

"I would offer if I could, you know."

"Of course, dear. I appreciate that, but you have a new husband now. Your place is here in Manti with George Washington Snow."

"I know."

"After all, Provo isn't the end of the world. We can visit each other."

All exchanged farewell hugs to everyone. Titus and Diantha took their belongings to Provo and settled into Alfred's home.

*   *   *

Many months passed before Sheriff Billings discovered the whereabouts of Mary Ann and the children. The distraught mother, having sought out her sister Martha Ann Gardner, had been living in Richfield.

"Word is they moved back to Fountain Green," George said.

"I need to visit them," Titus told his wife.

"But you just sold your team and wagon. How will you go?"

"On foot --"

"Titus, it will take you a whole week to walk that far."

"And another week to walk back, I know, but I need to do it."

She knew he was right. He needed to see Mary Ann and try to work things out.

"Diantha, if you agree I'd like to take some of the money from selling the wagon and buy a cow for Mary Ann and the children."

"Will you make the cow walk to Fountain Green too?"

He grinned. "Yes, unless you want to do it."

She shook her head. This was between him and his second wife. She was pleased that he cared so much and wanted to help them. He purchased a good cow. Alfred's first crop of apples was ready too. Titus placed red beauties into a bag for the trip.

"Here's food for the road," Diantha said as she handed him another well-filled bag. Titus tied the two bags together with a piece of rope, straddled them over the animal's back, kissed his wife and started off.

The trip was the last significant thing Titus Billings would ever do. His children were delighted with the apples.

"Oh Father, these are divine," Theresa said. "I've never seen or tasted anything so wonderful in my whole life!"

Mary Ann accepted the cow with gracious gratitude. Nonetheless, she refused to come back. Rather, she asked for a divorce. Her plan was to become second wife to her sister's husband, Walter Elias Gardner.

Brother Billings returned to Provo a broken man. His stalwart heart was anguished and he died nine months before Mary Ann remarried.

Historical Background

Once while Mary Ann was on overnight midwife duty, Titus made a trip to Salt Lake and delivered Hyrum Egan to his father, Major Howard Egan. This upset Mary Ann. She took her three Billings children and left Titus and Manti (BillingsEM2, 1). The next year, "1863, Titus and Diantha moved to Provo, Utah" (Cook,102).

"The Billingses are all gone. I remember George P. Billings very well. He was sheriff of Sanpete County for several years, and a good stone mason. The house he built is standing today [1983]. It was visited in past years by Porter Rockwell on matters of business connected with observance of the law" (Antrei/Scow, 223).

When Manti Mayor Shoemaker was "shaken by disunity" in the City Council he "indicated a desire to consult with the stake presidency, in the person of first counselor Titus Billings" (Antrei, 154).

"Members of the Thomas Cordner family were the first to spend an entire winter in the Provo Bench . . . Soon other full-time settlers arrived, including the families of Thomas J. Patten, Andrew G. Johnson, John S. Park, M.J. Knight, Alfred N. Billings, Samuel Hadfield, J. W. King, James Loveless, Samuel Skinner, Joseph Evans, David S. Park, Peter M. Wentz, James Stratton, Amasa Mecham, Thomas Barrett, Sam Baxter, Newell Knight, August Johnson, Charles Johnson, and Elliott A. Newell" (DUP2, V7).

"At one time I [Theresa Billings (Coombs)]well remember him returning from Provo. He gave me a large apple, for which I was much pleased. To this day I can fancy the taste in my mouth. I believe it to be the first apple I ever ate, and no doubt was amongst the first produced in Provo, or the first season of production of apples" (CoombsT1, 1).

Titus Billings had given them the cow. "This cow was the only piece of property that I knew of coming from my father," Theresa recalled. "One day, on a trip to "The Springs" Theresa found the cow was dead. "[Believing]it had eaten poison herbs, possibly poison barley that grew around the Springs. This made me feel very bad. It not only deprived us of milk, but gave us a small calf to look after" (CoombsT1,2).

"She [Mary Ann] obtained a divorce from her husband [Titus] and so she had her children to support. This proved to be a bad move, because greater hardships and hard times followed" (Larsen, 1).

"Mary Ann became the second wife of her brother-in-law, Walter E. Gardner, on November 28, 1866 in the Salt Lake Endowment House" (BillingsEM2, 1).

Things did not work out very well for Mary Ann with Mr. Gardner "because he was always drunk" (BillingsEM2, 1). As Theresa put it: "Uncle Walter, always she called him that, was sometimes accustomed to getting boozy which made it very disagreeable" (CoombsT1,3). Mary Ann moved out with her children and supported them by teaching school.

"Difficulties arose and a separation came between my father and mother followed by a divorce"(CoombsT,2).

"In 1864 Alfred Billings built a new home in Provo, Utah and there on February 6, 1866, Titus died and was buried in the Provo City Cemetery" (BillingsMD/Snow8, 7; Deseret News Obituary).

CHAPTER 101

"What's that you say? I have a visitor? Of course let her come in. No, don't sit me up. I'll just visit from my pillow," Diantha inhaled a long, deep breath to aid her weariness. "I feel so weak these days."

Mary Ann entered the room with a quiet reverence. She noticed Diantha's deep breathing and how her snowy hair blended in with the white pillowcase. As Mary Ann neared the bedside Diantha recognized and acknowledged her.

"You've come to see me at last," she said, extending a hand toward her guest. With bony fingers Mary Ann grasped the soft, well-aged hand in both of hers.

"Diantha," Mary Ann began. "I've made a big decision and I need your blessing."

"Now why would you need my blessing, child?"

"Because I've asked my son, to take me back to Salt Lake." She paused.

"You mean Alonzo? I wouldn't mind going to Salt Lake again myself."

Mary Ann knelt beside the bed, still clutching Diantha's hand. With anxiety she blurted out her news. "We're going to the Endowment House. I want to be re-sealed to Titus."

Diantha closed her eyes. A slight smile seemed to cross her serious face.

"I hope you approve, Diantha." Mary Ann held her breath.

Diantha's eyes did not open, but her lips parted. "More important," she said, "I believe Titus will approve."

Mary Ann sighed as Diantha's smile expanded. Her eyes never opened, but her heart seemed to do so.

"Yes, Titus will be pleased with that," she said.

"I hoped you would be pleased too," Mary Ann said.

"Certainly, my dear. I have no reason to be otherwise."

"Thank you, Diantha." Mary Ann blinked through tears that dropped onto the bed sheet as she kissed Diantha' hand and repeated her gratitude. "Thank you."

"Thanks be to you, my dear."

Mary Ann hoisted herself from her knees to her feet so she could bend down close to this woman she had admired for so many years.

"I suppose we shall be sharing eternity then," she whispered.

Diantha opened both eyes and looked into the sad, longing
eyes of sweet Mary Ann. She knew not the details of the poverty,
heart-ache, abuse from a drunken spouse, gleaning of wheat and
thrashing it with a broom so her children could eat, making a lamp
out of an ink bottle until they could afford a real lamp and oil,
shoeless children using two wooden shingles to step on in order to
walk over the snow, suffering the loss of milk when the cow died,
teaching school for parents who wouldn't pay, taking in laundry,
sewing for others, and midwife duty all hours of the night. No, she
could not know all things. She didn't need to know any of them.
She felt the goodness of a sister who, like herself, had endured the
refiner's fire.

"I suppose we shall," Diantha said. She mustered the
strength to open both arms and Mary Ann allowed herself to fall
with tenderness into them.

Outside Alonzo waited with a wagon carrying everything
his mother owned. She was moving to Thurber.

Mary Ann left the house with a burning in her soul. *I buried my mother last May and now Diantha . . . I'll miss both of them
so much.* She sighed and caught her bearings. *How blessed am I
to have been taught by the best!* Mary Ann dried her eyes and Al
helped her onto the wagon seat.

"I'm ready now, son. Thank you for waiting."

"Are you sure, Ma. Do you really want to do this?"

"I'm very sure, Alonzo. Emily needs me now."

"Emily won't last long, Mother. She is dying. You know that
don't you?"

"Yes, I know that, and her husband knows it all too well.
George and the children will need my help more than ever and I
am ready to give it to them."

She paused and gave her son a stern look of expectation.

"At least I will be ready, after you take me to the Endowment House and re-seal me to your father."

"That will be an honor, Mother," Alonzo said with his broad-
est smile.

Mary Ann reached behind her and pulled the beloved dulcimer to her lap.

"I'll have to teach the children how to play this wonderful instrument," she said.

"I reckon you will teach many things when you move in with all the little Stringhams."

"Sing with me Al."

Beautiful strains filled the air as talented fingers strummed the strings. Alonzo sang like his father. His pleasing voice deepened Mary Ann's longing.

Oh Titus, I want to be with you again. I will wear out my life in service trying to become worthy. Please take me back.

The precious mother began to sing with her son. She sang like an angel. She was an angel . . . on her way to engage in a most angelic work.

Historical Background

Catherine Vanever Geyer died in Salem, Utah on 24 May 1878. Her dear friend, Diantha Morley Billings died in Provo, Utah, 14 May 1879.

"She [Mary Ann Tuttle] was re-sealed to him [Titus Billings], while she was still living, on 22 September 1905, her son, Alonzo, standing proxy" (Billings CD; Hansen).

"Mary Ann moved in with the George Stringham Family when Emily Billings Stringham (Mary Ann's oldest daughter) died of pneumonia in Thurber (now Bicknell) Utah in February of 1889" (Gardner, 20).

"In February 1899 Emily Stringham was stricken with pneumonia. In her sickness she experienced a visit to the Spirit World where she saw some of her family members and acquaintances. She was privileged to return and tell of her experience and bear her testimony to her family, which was recorded" (Gardner, 20).

The Dying Testimony of Mrs. Emily [Billings] Stringham to her Children:

"Awake ye saints of God, awake. Call on the Lord in mighty prayer. I have prayed earnestly to know why our May was taken away in her purity, and I have been in this heavy grief ever since she died. Now I know what the Holy Spirit is. I never could stand upon my feet and bear my testimony. I have prayed for a testimony that I might reveal it to my children. I never could tell why the Lord should tear our hearts asunder, but now I know. The Lord took her to Himself to try our faith. This is what life is to all. This solemn testimony I bear to you tonight. I cannot tell why I was carried away in this vision. [On Wednesday, February 8, 1899] Something will come in the future to let you know why I was carried away in this vision. Father in Heaven, help me that I may deliver this message alright.

We never could know of the tender feelings of love and affection, if we had not been permitted to come to earth and take bodies for a short season. And wilt Thou look in mercy upon Thy children that they may understand the plan of salvation. The Lord told me in his infinite wisdom that we must be united and built up, and that we must be humble and prayerful. This has been given to me through inspiration.

Now, Father in Heaven, in thy infinite mercy, remember the awakening that comes upon thy people when they know why they are placed upon the earth. Sickness and death were placed upon us to scourge us and bring us to salvation. We must humble ourselves that we may inherit crowns, principalities and power, worlds without end. The world is asleep and does not know what awaits it. Great things shall transpire to awaken them from their slumber. I never was proud nor haughty, no never. The Lord does not love those that are lifted up in pride of their hearts. Our children cannot live in the pride of the world without we let them, and they cannot be saved without we save them. Joseph Smith told us we must live pure lives to gain a glorious exaltation. "The sealed book was opened unto me to judge me." The sun, the moon, and stars the Lord made and placed them in the heavens for the benefit of mankind.

I see my children and Pate Keele standing there, but I cannot go to them until I have returned to earth to bear this powerful testimony to my children. The unknown realities of life are ages and ages, eternities and eternities of the world to come. It was given unto me in vision to know that my children in the Spirit World are all right. The kingdom of God has been set upon the earth never more to be thrown down or given to another people. You must humble yourselves or you will never know why these things are.

My children: be comforted. The Lord knows the prayer of your hearts. Love the Lord our Savior and honor the Priesthood. This is a great testimony to you, my children, to know that I have been in the Spirit World to learn the power of the Priesthood. I have deep sympathies for you, my children. I know the Lord loves you. Be obedient that he may not chastise you. The mysteries of God's Kingdom are deep and never to be known upon this earth. Father, in His infinite wisdom saw fit to choose me for his instrument to bear this testimony to you.

The Law of Tithing is all right, so is prayer and fast offerings if you could only under- stand it. We are not perfect upon this earth; everybody is imperfect. The world awa- keth, the world awaketh. Help me, Father to save my children. I know what death is. It is that we may be resurrected. I know that the resurrection will come. Nothing ever came by chance. Every[one]was placed on earth by the Lord and he calls them home in His own due time. I did not know that I had to soar into endless worlds to find out these things, but now I understand thoroughly. The Lord does not like His children to slander one another, for He loves them all. No bond of sympathy is stronger than the bond of brotherhood. We love the holy Priesthood. We do not want to be away from it. We love it with our whole heart and soul. Children, love and obey. Heavenly Father, guide and direct us alright, that we may understand the principles of life and salvation, and know how to live and be saved in His Celestial Kingdom."

In her upstairs bedroom [at the Stringham home] Mary Ann "spent her spare hours in her sanctuary – reading scriptures, ripping rags for loomed rugs, and making pieced quilts. She was self-supporting with her pin-money from her milk, cream, butter, and egg projects. One time, while doing her chores, she was charged by a wild cow, which resulted in a broken collar bone" (Gardner, 21).

Mary Ann "was Primary President in Thurber for many years, and her programs were the most entertaining programs ever witnessed" (Gardner, 22).

"On the 10th of December 1910 the serenity of the Stringham home was dealt another blow when Grandmother Mary Ann Tuttle Egan Billings Gardner Billings passed away after a brief illness" (Gardner, 21).

Tributes to Mary Ann: "Grandma Gardner was very superior to me, she was kind, gentle and very exacting. She had a way of controlling one. She had snappy black eyes, white hair, and always wore the conventional hair cap on her head. She did a wonderful job of helping in the Stringham home." ~Sarah Lovina Stringham (Gardner, 23).

"To coin a phrase: After spending poverty stricken years wandering through the wilderness and tasting the refiner's fire, Mary Ann emerged a woman who endured to the end!" (Author unknown, (Gardner, 22).

My Testimony to the World - written by Eunice Billings Warner Snow, April 29, 1913:

"To Whom It May Concern, I was born on January 3, 1830, at Kirtland, Ohio, Geauga County; the year the Church of Jesus Christ of Latter-Day Saints was organized.

The first I remember seeing the Prophet Joseph Smith was in Far West, at the time the mob took him. I knew him as intimately as a child knows a grown person; my parents being closely associated with him and his family. My mother did a great deal of work for them of different kinds. I attended the school at Nauvoo which Eliza R. Snow taught, in company with his children. I was at their home almost every day, having as my associate their adopted daughter, Julia Murdock. I have received numerous blessings under the hands of the Prophet. He frequently asked me to sing for him

I was in attendance at the laying of the corner stone of the Nauvoo Temple, also at the dedication, and sang in the choir on that occasion, the first song being:

"Ho, Ho, for the Temple's Complete - The Lord hath a place for His Head." I received my endowments in that Temple on my sixteenth birthday and officiated there two weeks.

I was at the meeting when the Prophet told the Saints he was going like a lamb to the slaughter, and remember it distinctly. He and his brother, Hyrum, passed our home on the morning they wre taken to Carthage. Joseph raised his hat to us, but his brother, knowing keenly the coming evil, never looked up. The next news was their cold blooded murder. My mother and I went to the Mansion House and saw them both after they were laid out.

I DO KNOW THAT HE WAS AN INSPIRED PROPHET OF THE LIVING GOD.

I am leaving this testimony to my children and to the world and expect to meet it in the great beyond. [signed] Eunice Billings Snow

Allen. Charles W. Allen. "The Crooked River Battle Site." 1979. [Note: This is labeled page 12, but we have not been able to identify where it came from. It is a map in possession of my father, Evan A. Billings, in Independence, Missouri. Wish we could give proper credit.]

Allen2. Charles W. Allen. Caption on photo of road from Far West to Crooked River.

Allen/Leonard. James B. Allen and Glen M. Leonard. The Story of the Latter-Day Saints. Salt Lake City: Deseret, 1976.

AndersonKR. Karl Ricks Anderson. Joseph Smith's Kirtland: Eyewitness Accounts. Salt Lake City: Deseret, 1989.

AndersonLF. Lavina Fielding Anderson. "Kirtland's Resolute Saints." The Ensign, January 1979: pg. 49-55, Salt Lake City: 1979.

AndersonLF1. Lavina Fielding Anderson. "Like Gold Seven Times Purified: Early Saints in Missouri." The Ensign, April 1979: pg. 52, Salt Lake City: 1979.

Andrus. Hyrum L. Andrus. "The Second American Revolution: Era of Preparation." BYU Studies: Winter 1960. Volume 2, Number 1. (Personal sketch by Lyman Wight of his life, written to Wilford Woodruff, enclosed with a letter from Texas, August 24, 1857).

Antrei. Albert C. Antrei. High, Dry and Offside. Manti City Council Centennial, Manti: 1996.

Antrei/Scow. Albert C. T. Antrei and Ruth D. Scow. The Other 49ers: A Topical History of Sanpete County, Utah 1840-1983. Western Epics Pub Co., Salt Lake City, Utah; First Edition (June 1983).

Archibald. May Snow Archibald. "My Maternal Great Grandmother: Mary Ann Tuttle Egan Billings Gardner Billings." Personal history, Glenwood, Alberta, Canada.

Arrington. Leonard J. Arrington. Charles C. Rich: Mormon General and Western Frontiers man (Studies in Mormon History). Brigham Young University Press, 1974.

Arrington1. Leonard J. Arrington. From Quaker to Latter-Day Saint: Bishop Edwin D. Woolley. Salt Lake City: Deseret, 1976.

Arrington/Bitton. Leonard J. Arrington and Davis Bitton. The Mormon Experience: A History of the Latter-day Saints. University of Illinois Press; 2 Sub edition. March 1, 1992.

Arrington/Fox/May. Leonard J. Arrington, Feramorz Y. Fox, Dean L. May. Building the City of God. Salt Lake City: Deseret, 1992.

Backman. Milton V. Backman Jr. The Heavens Resound. Salt Lake City: Bookcraft, 1983.

Backman1. Milton V. Backman Jr. (with assistance from Keith Perkins and Susan Easton Black). "A Profile of Latter-Day Saints of Kirtland, Ohio and Members of Zion's Camp 1830-1839 Vital Statistics and Sources." Provo: BYU Department of Church History and Doctrine, 1982.

Backman/Cowan. Milton V. Backman and Richard O. Cowan. Joseph Smith and the Doctrine and Covenants. Salt Lake City: Deseret Book Company, 1992.

Bagley/Slaughter. Pat Bagley and William W. Slaughter. Church History Time Line. Salt Lake City: Deseret, 1996.

Baker, Doran. "Howard Egan: Utah Pioneer with the Pony Express." SUP (Sons of the Utah Pioneers) Pioneer Magazine, Volume 57, No. 2, page 14. 2010.

Barrett, Ivan J. "Joseph Smith and the Restoration." Provo: Brigham Young University Press, Provo, Utah 1967/1973.

Baugh. Alexander L Baugh. "150 Years Ago Today: Added protection for Horses, Cattle Z1." Church News, February 8, 1997, Salt Lake City: 1997.

Bennett. Archibald F Bennett. (with Ella M. Bennett, Barbara Roach, Ann S. Bell and Deanne C. Jackson). "Valiant in the Faith." Roylance Publishing, 1989.

Bennett1. Archibald F. "Life of Gardner Snow." Family History.

Bennion. Elva Billings Bennion. "A Brief History of Titus Billings Family." Family History.

Bennion1. Elva Billings Bennion. "Titus Billings Family Group Sheet."

BerrettWE. William E. Berrett. The Restored Church. Salt Lake City: Deseret Book, 1961.

Berrett/Burton. William E. Berrett and Alma P. Burton. Readings in LDS Church History (from Original Manuscripts). Salt Lake City: Deseret Book, 1953.

BillingsCD. Claude D. & Lydia Billings. "Personal Letter from Genealogical Society of LDS Church." Salt Lake City, Utah: 1968.

BillingsCD1. Claude D. & Lydia Billings. "Titus and Mary Ann (Tuttle) Billings Family Group Sheet. Salt Lake City, Utah.

BillingsEA. Evan A. Billings. "Billings Family Pedigree Chart." Provo, Utah, 4 Apr 1980.

BillingsEA1. Evan A. Billings. "Church History Trip and Personal Interview with Evan A. Billings, Great-Grandson of Titus Billings." 2000.

BillingsEA2. Evan A. Billings. "Notes from Delta and Yuba Dam tour with Evan A. Billings, Great-Grandson of Titus Billings." 2001.

BillingsEA3. Evan A. Billings. "Wayne City Landing and Milford Dam for Delta, Utah Interview with Evan A. Billings, Great-Grandson of Titus Billings." 2000.

BillingsEM. Elda MaeLewis Billings. "Billings Picture Pedigree Chart." 1996.

Billings EML1. Elda Mae Lewis Billings. "Personal Conversation with Ronald E. Romig, RLDS Church Library/Archives." 1996.

BillingsEML2. Elda Mae Lewis Billings. "Interview with Lillian Billings Brady-Granddaughter of Titus Billings." 1980.

BillingsEML3. Elda Mae Lewis Billings. "Children of Eunice Billings Warner." Email letter 1996.

BillingsGO. George O. Billings. "History of my father, Alonzo Billings." Delta, Utah: 30 June 1979.

BillingsLB. Leonard B. Billings. "History of George Pierce Billings." No date, Family History.

Billings/Shaw/Hale. Melvin D. Billings, Randy Shaw, and Marba Peck Hale. Titus Billings or "Titus Billings Early Mormon Pioneer." Provo, Utah, 1990.

BillingsT. Titus Billings. "Missouri Claims Letter." 24 May 1839.

BillingsT&D. Titus and Diantha Morley Billings. "1845 Nauvoo Letter." Personal Letter to William and Ester Pynchon in Springfield, Massachusetts, handwritten: 1 1/2 pages by Titus, 1/2 page by Diantha, Nauvoo, 1845. [See Appendix].

BillingsV. Virginia Billings. "Samuel Billings History by his daughter." On file in Lake County Historical Library, Kirtland, Ohio.

BillingsV1. Virginia Billings. "Ebenezer Billings - Billings/Crary Genealogy." Includes Samuel Billings History by granddaughter V.A.B. and Mary Russell Billings History. Located in the Lake County Historical Society at Mentor, Ohio. (Discovered by Larry Coombs while on mission 2002).

BillingsV2. Virginia Billings. "Samuel Billings-Brother of Titus." Unpublished history. On file at Lake County Historical Society at Mentor, Ohio.

BillingsV3. Virginia Billings. "Mary Russell Billings" unpublished history.

Bitton. Davis Bitton. "Guide to Mormon Diaries & Autobiographies: David W. Patten."

Black/Hartley. Susan Easton Black and William G. Harley. The Iowa Mormon Trail. Heliz Publishing, Orem, Utah. 1997.

Black. Susan Easton Black. Membership of Church of Jesus Christ of Latter-day

Saints 1830-1848. Volume 2. BYU HBLL Family History Department.

Black1. Susan Easton Black. Who's Who in the Doctrine and Covenants. West Valley City: Bookcraft, 1997.

Black2. Susan Easton Black. "I am Not Any Longer to be Alone." *The Ensign*, Jan. 1989.

Black3. Susan Easton Black. "A Legacy of Faith" Lecture at BYU Devotional, 22 November 1994. (pg.3 of print out).

Boggs. L.W. Boggs. "Order of Extermination." Ordered by Governor Lilburn W. Boggs. Head quarters of the Militia, City of Jefferson, October 27, 1838.

BorenKR. Kerry Ross Boren. "The Saint and the Savage." Online.

BorenKR&LL. Kerry Ross and Lisa Lee Boren. The Gold of Carre-Shinob. Bonneville Books; distrib. By Cedar Fort, 1998.

Bradley. Bishop George Bradley. "Sketch of life of ex-bishop Bradley" Moroni, Utah. BYU Special Collections Ref. # 434577.

Brady. Lillian Billings Brady. "Letter - Questionnaire." Fairview: 1995.

Brewster. Hoyt W. Brewster, Jr. Doctrine and Covenants Encyclopedia. Salt Lake City, Utah: Bookcraft/Deseret Book Company. 1988.

Brooks. Juanita Brooks. On the Mormon Frontier: The Diary of Hosea Stout 1844-1861. Salt Lake City: University of Utah Press, 1964.

Bunnell. Marie Warner. "Brief Life History of John Ely Warner" [Author unknown, given to author by Marie Warner Bunnell].

Cannon/Cook. Donald Q. Cannon and Lyndon W. Cook. Far West Record. (Minutes of the Church of Jesus Christ of Latter-day Saints 1830-44). Salt Lake City: Deseret, 1983.

Carter. Kate B. Carter. Our Pioneer Heritage. Vol. 2. Salt Lake City: Utah Printing, 1959.

Carter1. Kate B. Carter. Our Pioneer Heritage. Vol. 9. Salt Lake City: Utah Printing, 1959.

Carter2. Kate B. Carter. Our Pioneer Heritage. Vol. 14. Salt Lake City: Utah Printing, 1959.

Carter3. Kate B. Carter. Our Pioneer Heritage. Vol. 20. Salt Lake City: Utah Printing, 1959.

Carter4. Kate B. Heart Throbs of the West. Compilation, Daughters of Utah Pioneers, volume 3, Salt Lake City, Utah, 1941 and 1948.

BIBLIOGRAPHY

CES. Church Educational System. Religion 341-343 <u>Church History in the Fullness of Times</u> <u>Student Manual.</u> Salt Lake City: LDS Church, 1989.

Clark. James R. Clark. <u>Messages of the First Presidency</u>. Vol.1, page 11. Salt Lake City: Bookcraft, 1965-1975.

Clayton. William Clayton. "Personal Journal of William Clayton. Beginning in Nauvoo, February 8, 1846 to October 21, 1847."

Cook. Lyndon W. Cook. <u>Revelation of Joseph Smith</u>. Provo: Seventy's Mission Bookstore, 1981.

Cook1. Lyndon W. Cook. <u>Nauvoo Deaths & Marriages</u>. Orem: Grandin Book, 1994.

CoombsLS. Larry Snow Coombs. "Titus Billings Story." Written by Larry Snow Coombs while serving as a missionary for the Church of Jesus Christ of Latter-day Saints in Kirtland, Ohio 2002.

CoombsT. Theresa Billings Coombs. "Mother's Genealogy: Life History of Mary Ann Tuttle Billings." Logan: 1919.

CoombsT1. Theresa Billings Coombs. "Life Story of Theresa Billings Coombs."

CoombsT2. Theresa Billings Coombs. Family Group Sheet.

Cottam/Malouf. Naomi M. Cottam and Beatrice B. Malouf "Landmarks and Events Along the Historic Mormon Trail." Salt Lake City, Utah Printing Company, 1990.

Cowan. Richard O. Cowan. <u>Temples to Dot the Earth.</u> ("The House of the Lord in Kirtland: A 'Preliminary' Temple.") Bookcraft, SLC, Utah. 1989.

Cox. Cordelia Morley Cox. "Personal Journal of Cordelia Morley Cox." Harold B. Lee Library Special Collections, Provo: Brigham Young University.

Cox1. Cordelia Morley Cox. "A Sketch of the Life of my Father Isaac Morley, Sr. –One of the Pioneers to Salt Lake Valley in 1848." Biography of Isaac Morley, holograph, BYU. Provo, Utah.

Crary. Christopher G. "<u>Pioneer and Personal Reminiscences.</u>" Pages 6, 7, 20. Marshall Printing Company, Marshalltown, IA, 1893.

Curtis/Romig. William J. Curtis and Ron Romig. "Independence Tourism Markers." Missouri Mormon Frontier Foundation Newsletter. Number 20, Winter 1999, page 10.

Curtis. William J. Curtis "Colesville School Monument." Missouri Mormon Frontier Foundation Newsletter Aug 2000- Jan 2001, Jackson County, Missouri, Number 25, page 16.

D&C. Doctrine and Covenants. Original chapter heading to Section 63.

D&C1. Doctrine and Covenants. Revised chapter heading to Section 63.

D&C2. Doctrine and Covenants. Section 20, verse 1.

D&C3. Doctrine and Covenants. Section 25.

D&C4. Doctrine and Covenants. Section 41, verse 7.

D&C5. Doctrine and Covenants. Section 42.

D&C6. Doctrine and Covenants. Section 63, verse 38-40.

D&C7. Doctrine and Covenants. Section 110, verses 5,6, 7, 9-12, 16.

D&C8. Doctrine and Covenants. Section 123, verses 1-6.

Davidson. Karen Lynn Davidson. Our Latter-Day Hymns. Salt Lake City, Utah, Bookcraft of Deseret Book, 1988.

DavisH. Harriet Coombs Davis. "Family Group Sheet for Edward Tuttle Family." Spanish Fork, Utah.

DavisI. Inez Smith Davis. The Story of the Church. Independence. Herald, 1938.

DavisI1. Inez Smith Davis. The Story of the Church. Revised Edition, Independence: Herald, 1981.

Deseret News. "Obituary for Titus Billings." Salt Lake City, Utah. August 30, 1866: page 309.

Deseret News1. "Sanpete Trek Story." Salt Lake City, Utah. January 31, 1935.

Duncan. Chapman Duncan. "Autobiography of Chapman Duncan." Typescript, BYU-S, 1812-1846.

Duncan1. Chapman Duncan. "Autobiography of Chapman Duncan Sr." 2nd Ed. Typescript, BYU-S, 1812-1846.

DUP. Daughters of the Utah Pioneers of Sanpete County, Utah. "These . . . Our Fathers." Springville: Art City,1947.

DUP2. "Pioneer Pathways" volumen 7, complied by International Society of Daughters of Utah Pioneers Lesson Committee, Salt Lake City, Utah, 2004.

Egan. William M. Egan. Pioneering the West. Special Collections, Harold B. Lee Library, Provo: Brigham Young University.

Elders. "Elders' Journal." November 1837.

Elders1. "Elders' Journal." July 1838.

Esplin. Hattie Esplin. "History of Isaac Morley." Salt Lake City: 1950.

Esplin1. Hattie Esplin. "Titus Billings and Diantha Morley Family Group Sheet." Salt Lake City, Utah.

Esshom. Frank Esshom. Pioneers and Prominent Men in Utah. page 1044 Isaac Morley; 1282 Titus Billings.

Evans. John Henry Evans. An American Prophet. New York: Macmillian, 1936.

Farnes. Margie Egan Farnes. "Howard Egan and Mary Ann Tuttle Family Group Sheet." Idaho Falls, Idaho.

Faust. James E. Faust. Heroes of the Restoration. Salt Lake City: Bookcraft 1997.

Flake. Lawrence Flake. Mighty Men of Zion: General Authorities of the Last Dispensation. Salt Lake City: Karl D. Butler, 1974.

Foester. Bernd Foester. Independence, Missouri. Independence: Independence Press 1978.

Gappmayer. Louis B. Gappmayer. "Titus Billings and Diantha Morley Billings: Early Members of the Church of Jesus Christ of Latter Day Saints." St. George: 1999.

Gardner. Martha Ann Tuttle Gardner. "A Sketch of Martha Ann Tuttle Gardner from her Personal Journal."

Geddes. Joseph A. Geddes. The United Order Among the Mormons. Out of print, no longer available.

Genosky. Rev. Landry Genosky. People's History of Quincy and Adams County, Illinois: A Sesquicentennial History. Jost & Kiefer Printing Company. Quincy, Illinois.

Gibbons. Ted Gibbons. I Witnessed the Carthage Massacre: A Testimony of Willard Richards. W.R. Enterprises, Orem, Utah; 1988.

Godfrey/Derr/Mulvay. Kenneth W. and Audrey M. Godfrey, and Derr, Jill Mulvay. Women's Voices: an Untold History of the Latter-Day Saints. 1830-1900." SLC, UT: Deseret Book Company, May 1982.

Gregg. T.H. Gregg. History of Hancock County. Chas. C. Chapman & Co., Chicago, Illinois, 1880.

Hale. Marba Peck Hale. "Eunice Billings Warner Snow Tells Her Own Story with End Notes."

Hancock. Levi Hancock. "Personal Journal of Levi Hancock." Manuscript, Special Collections, Harold B. Lee Library, Provo: Brigham Young University.

HancockCo. Hancock County Historical Society. "Lest We Forget: Morley Town AKA Yelrome." Newsletter volume XIX, Number II, July 2002.

Hansen. Sarah M. Hansen. "Notes" on Martha Ann Tuttle Journal Excerpt.

Hansen1. Sarah M. Hansen. "Letter to Special Services Temple Department." 25 June 1981 Salt Lake City, Utah, from Joseph City, Arizona.

Harter. Mary Harter. 1830 Federal Population Census of Ohio. Columbus: Ohio Library Foundation, 1964.

Hartly. William J. Hartly. "Priesthood in Action/Deacon Power." The New Era. May 1975: p.6., Salt Lake City: 1975.

Hawley. David C. Hawley. The Treasures of the Steamboat Arabia. Self Published for the Arabia Steamboat Museum, Kansas City, Missouri, 1995.

Heslop. J. Malan Heslop. " Thumbnail Sketches of People in the Doctrine and Covenants." Deseret News, December 9, 1984, Salt Lake City.

Holzapfel/Cottle. Richard N. Holzapfel and T. Jeffery Cottle. Old Mormon Kirtland and Missouri. Fieldbrook Productions, Inc. Santa Ana, California 1991.

Holzapfel/Cottle/Stoddard. Richard Neitzel Holzapfel, T. Jeffery Cottle, Ted D. Stoddard. Church History in Black and White: George Edward Anderson's Photographic Mission to Latter- day Saint Historical Sites 1907-1908". Brigham Young University Religious Studies Center, Salt Lake City: Distributed by Bookcraft, 1995.

Howard. Richard P. Howard. Restoration Scriptures. Independence: Herald.Huff, Kent W. Joseph Smith's United Order, A Non-Communalistic Interpretation. Orem: 1988 (Self Published).

Huff. Kent W. Huff. Joseph Smith's United Order: A Non-Communalistic Interpretation. Self Published. Orem, Utah, 1988.

Hugoe/Deppe. LaRue Hugoe & Edith Deppe. West Bountiful, a Pictorial History. Horizon Publishers, Bountiful, Utah 1989.

Jenson. Andrew Jensen. Church Chronology: A Record of Important Events Pertaining to the History of The Church of Jesus Christ of Latter-day Saints. Salt Lake City: Deseret News, 1914.

Jenson1. Andrew Jenson. Latter-day Saint Biographical Encyclopedia. Vol. 1, 2, 3, 4. Andrew Jensen History Company 1901; Reprinted: Western Epics, 1971, Salt Lake City, Utah .

Jenson2. Andrew Jenson. "Manuscript History of the Church in Missouri." Independence: Jackson County Courthouse, 1981.

Jenson3. Andrew Jenson. Encyclopedic History of the Church. Deseret News Publishing Company; 1ST edition (1941).

Jenson4. Andrew Jenson. Day By Day With the Utah Pioneers. Provo, Utah, 1997, Griffin Associates- Community Press, with permission from Salt Lake Tribune, June 14, 1934.

Jenson5. Andrew Jenson. "The Building of Utah and her Neighbors." The Deseret News, January 31, 1935.

Jenson6. Andrew Jenson. Historical Records: Volume Nine. Deseret News Press, Salt Lake City, 1889. Pg. 509.

JohnsonCV. Clark V. Johnson. "An Index to Early Caldwell County Land Records." Edited by Clark V. Johnson.

JohnsonCV1. Clark V. Johnson. Mormon Redress Petitions Documents of the 1833-1838 Missouri Conflict. Salt Lake City: Bookcraft, 1992.

JohnsonS. Sherrie Johnson. "A Gathering of Saints" The Friend, March 1993.

JonesD. Captain Dan Jones. History of the Latter-Day Saints. Published in Welch in 1847, trans-lated by Professor Ronald D. Dennis, printed by J. Jones, RHYDY-BONT, date unknown.

JonesG. Gracia N. Jones. Emma and Joseph: Their Divine Mission. American Fork: Covenant Communications, Inc., 1999.

Journal History. "Emigration of 1848: Second Division Roster." Heber C. Kimball-Company: 29 May 1848 – 24 September 1848.

Journal History1. 25 October 1831. LDS Historical Department, Salt Lake City, Utah.

Journal History2. 31 December 1831. LDS Historical Department, Salt Lake City, Utah.

Journal History3. 4 April 1832. LDS Historical Department, Salt Lake City, Utah.

Journal History4. 26 May 1832. LDS Historical Department, Salt Lake City, Utah.

Journal History5. 3 July 1832. LDS Historical Department, Salt Lake City, Utah.

Journal History6. 25 June 1833. LDS Historical Department, Salt Lake City, Utah.

Journal History7. 1 July 1836. LDS Historical Department, Salt Lake City, Utah.

Journal History8. 1 August 1837. LDS Historical Department, Salt Lake City, Utah.

Journal History9. 7 November 1837. LDS Historical Department, Salt Lake City, Utah.

Journal History10. 5 February 1838. LDS Historical Department, Salt Lake City, Utah.

Journal History11. 6 March 1838. LDS Historical Department, Salt Lake City, Utah.

Journal History12. 29 November 1838 LDS Historical Department, Salt Lake City, Utah.

Journal History13. 25 March 1847. LDS Historical Department, Salt Lake City,

Utah.

Journal History14. 28 March & 1 April 1843 . LDS Historical Department, Salt Lake City, Utah.

Journal History15. 2 February 1841. LDS Historical Department, Salt Lake City, Utah.

Journal History16. 1 May 1841. LDS Historical Department, Salt Lake City, Utah.

Journal History17. 4 September 1841. LDS Historical Department, Salt Lake City, Utah.

Journal History18. 21 July 1842. LDS Historical Department, Salt Lake City, Utah.

Journal History19. 8 October 1844. LDS Historical Department, Salt Lake City, Utah.

Journal History20. 8 February 1847. LDS Historical Department, Salt Lake City, Utah.

Journal History21. 4 August 1846. LDS Historical Department, Salt Lake City, Utah.

Journal History22. 31 May 1848. LDS Historical Department, Salt Lake City, Utah.

Journal History23. 16 June 1848. LDS Historical Department, Salt Lake City, Utah.

Journal History24. 16 July 1848. LDS Historical Department, Salt Lake City, Utah.

Journal History25. 7 June 1848. LDS Historical Department, Salt Lake City, Utah.

Journal History26. 8 June 1848. LDS Historical Department, Salt Lake City, Utah.

Journal History27. 21 July 1848. LDS Historical Department, Salt Lake City, Utah.

Journal History28. 21 August 1848. LDS Historical Department, Salt Lake City, Utah.

Journal History29. 17 September 1848. LDS Historical Department, Salt Lake City, Utah.

Journal History30. 24 September 1848. LDS Historical Department, Salt Lake City, Utah.

Journal History31. 24 September 1848 (con.). LDS Historical Department, Salt Lake City, Utah.

Journal History32. 16 February 1848. LDS Historical Department, Salt Lake City, Utah.

Journal History33. 10 February 1849. LDS Historical Department, Salt Lake City, Utah.

Journal History34. 3 April 1849. LDS Historical Department, Salt Lake City, Utah.

Journal History35. 6 October 1849. LDS Historical Department, Salt Lake City, Utah.

Journal History36. 9 August 1850. LDS Historical Department, Salt Lake City, Utah.

Journal History37. 3 July 1852. LDS Historical Department, Salt Lake City, Utah.

Journal History38. 17 August 1852. LDS Historical Department, Salt Lake City, Utah.

Journal History39. 8 February 1847. LDS Historical Department, Salt Lake City, Utah.

Journal History40. 16 June 1854. LDS Historical Department, Salt Lake City, Utah.

Judd/Andersen. Andrew Jackson Judd and Fannie Kenner Andersen. "A History of Manti." Manti: 1958.

Kimball. Heber C. Kimball. "Writings of Early Latter-Day Saint: Letter to Daughter Helen Whitney." WE:39:1.

Kinsley. Alvin Kinsley. Biographical Dictionary of the Latter-Day Saint Ministry. RLDS Special Collections.

Knight. Newel Knight. "Personal Journal of Newel Knight." October, 1845.

Knight/Kimball. Hal Knight and Dr. Standley B. Kimball. 111 Days to Zion. Deseret News Press. Deseret News 1978.

Knowles. Knowles, Sister. "Isaac Morley Farm." Kirtland Visitor's Center Script, January 1998.

LakeCo. Lake County Historical Society. Here is Lake County, Ohio. Mentor, Ohio, 1964.

LakeCo.1. Lake County Historical Society. South Kirtland Cemetery Book.

Lambert. George. Early Scenes from Church History. Salt Lake City: Bookcraft, 1968, pg. 78.

Larsen. Rachel C. "History of Theresa Billings." Manti, Utah.

LDS. Authors. Encyclopedic History of the Church. Volume B.

LDSAF. Ancestral File of the Church of Jesus Christ of Latter-Day Saints.

LDS Historic Site. "Kanesville Tabernacle Visitor Center" (pamphlet) Council Bluffs, Iowa, no date given.

LDS Historic Site. "1846-1848 Mormon Burial Plot at Winter Quarters." (map)

Lee. John D. Lee. "Nauvoo Neighbor." December 1844 [Note: John was clerk for the dedication of the Seventy's Hall and reported it in this edition].

LeSueur. Stephen C. LeSueur. The 1838 Mormon War in Missouri. University of Missouri Press, Columbia, Missouri.

Lever. W.H. Lever. History of Sanpete and Emery Counties of Utah. Ogden, 1898.

Lightner. Lightner, Mary Elizabeth Rollins Lightner. "Autobiography of Mary E. Lighner." (1818-1913).

Lisonbee. Janet. "A Street By Any Other Name . . . Is Just a Street: Billings Road." The Kirtland Gazette. pages 7-8, Date unknown.

Lloyd. R. Scott Lloyd. "Finding History in Modern Jackson County." Church News:May 9, 1998.

Ludlow. Daniel H. Ludlow. A Companion to Your Study of the Doctrine and Covenants. Vol. 1 Salt Lake City: Deseret Book,1978.

Ludlow1. Daniel H. Ludlow. Encyclopedia of Mormonism. New York: Macmillian, 1992.

Lund. Gerald A. Lund. The Work And The Glory. Volume 7: pg 179. Salt Lake City: Bookcraft, 1996.

MadsenC. Carol Cornwall Madsen. In Their Own Words: Women and the Story of Nauvoo. Salt Lake City: Deseret Book, 1994.

MadsenTG. Truman G. Madsen. "Joseph Smith the Prophet." Deseret Book, Salt Lake City, Utah. January, 1993.

Manti. Manti Centennial Committee: Ellis E. Johnson, Helen Dyreng, R. Clair Anderson, Marie Anderson, Lila Keller. Song of a Century 1849-1949. Manti: 1949.

McCormick. Mark L. McCormick. The Father of the Prophet: Stories and Insights from the Life of Joseph Smith, Sr." Bookcraft. Salt Lake City, Utah. 1993.

McCune. George M. McCune. Personalities in the Doctrine and Covenants and Joseph Smith History. Salt Lake City: Hawks.

McNeil. Marjann McNeil. "Making Fabrics" - Notes from telephone call to Rapid City, South Dakota, 2001.

Millennial Star. Millennial Star. Volume 17: page 435.

Millennial Star. Millennial Star. Volume 21: page 506.

MitchellSB. Susan Billings Mitchell. "Word of Honor in Nauvoo." Friend, April 2001, page 22. Salt Lake City, Utah., 2001.

Moody. Thurman Dean Moody. "Nauvoo's Whistling and Whittling Brigade."

Provo: BYU Studies, 15:4, 1974-75.

MorleyRH. Morley, Richard Henrie. "The Life and Contributions of Isaac Morley." Master's Thesis, Brigham Young University, Provo: 1965.

MorleyRH. Morley, Richard Henrie. Appendix B of "The Life and Contributions of Isaac Morley." Master's Thesis, Brigham Young University, Provo: 1965.

Mortimer. Wm. James Mortimer. (President and Publisher). Deseret News 1995-96 Church Almanac. 1995.

Nauvoo. "Nauvoo Deaths & Burials" April 23, 1890, page 3.

Nauvoo1. Nauvoo Restoration Committee. "Old Nauvoo Burial Grounds 1840 - 1846." October 7, 1989.

Nelson. Susanne Warner Nelson. "John Ely Warner" Provo, Utah, 2012.

Nibley. Preston Nibley. Joseph Smith, The Prophet. SLC, Utah, Deseret News Press, 1944.

Ogden. D. Kelly Ogden. "Two from Judah Ministering to Joseph." Regional Studies in Latter-day Saint Church History.

Packard. Noah Packard. "Writings of Early Latter-Day Saints: Noah Packard Auto." BYU-S:7:2 Provo: Brigham Young University.

Perkins. Keith Perkins. "The Way It Looks Today." The Ensign. January 1979, page 31-48, Salt Lake City: 1979.

Perkins1. Keith W. Perkins. "Land Owndership in Kirkland."

Peterson. Wm. H. Peterson. "The Miracle of the Mountains."

Pratt. Parley P. Pratt. Autobiography of Parley P. Pratt. Salt Lake City: Deseret Book (1938 1st pub.) 1968.

Prusha. Anne B. Prusha. A History of Kirtland, Ohio. (Unknown binding) 198. 1982.

Pyne. Beatrice Gappmeyer Pyne. "Diantha Morley Billings."

Pyper. George D. Pyper. The Story of our Hymns. Kessinger Publishing, LLC. September 10, 2010.

Rich. Russell Rich. Ensign to the Nation. Provo: Brigham Young University, 1972.

Ricks. Kellene Ricks. "Heroes and Heroines: Caroline and Mary Elizabeth Rollins" Friend, January 1989.

RobertsV1. B.H. Roberts. A Comprehensive History. Vol. 1. Provo: Brigham Young University Press, 1965.

RobertsV3. B.H. Roberts. A Comprehensive History. Vol. 3. Provo: Brigham Young University Press, 1965.

RobertsV4. B.H. Roberts. A Comprehensive History. Vol. 4. Provo: Brigham Young University Press, 1965.

RobertsV6. B.H. Roberts. A Comprehensive History. Vol. 6. Provo: Brigham Young University Press, 1965.

Robinson. Mary Elizabeth Grover Simmons Robinson. "History of Mary Elizabeth Grover Simmons Robinson."

Romig. Ronald E. Romig. "Law of Consecration: Antecedents and Practice at Kirtland, Ohio." Restoration Studies VI. RLDS Church Library-Archives, Independence, Missouri.

Romig1. Ronald E. Romig. "Faithful Men who were assigned property in Independence upon their return there." Comments to Elda Mae Lewis Billings, about Kirtland, Ohio. May 26, 1835.

Romig2. Ronald E. Romig. "Research Notes." (Annotated Jenson List - 1864). RLDS Church Library-Archives. Received April 26, 1999.

Romig3. Ronald E. Romig. Q & A Comments to Susan Billings Mitchell. April 26, 1999. RLDS Church Llibrary-Archieve, Independence, Missouri.

Romig4. Ronald E. Romig. Regional Studies in Latter-day Saint Church History. RLDS Church Library-Archives, Independence, Missouri.

Romig5. Ronald E. Romig. "Map of Church and Member Lands Jackson County Missouri 1831-1833." RLDS Church Library-Archives, Independence, Missouri.

Romig/Siebert. Ronald E. Romig & John H.Siebert. Restoration Studies III: A Collection of Essays About the History, Beliefs, and Practices of the RLDS Church. RLDS Church Library-Archives, Independence, Missouri.

Romig/Siebert1. Ronald E. Romig & John H. Siebert. Restoration Studies IV: A Collection of Essays About the History, Beliefs, and Practices of the RLDS Church. RLDS Church Library-Archives, Independence, Missouri.

Rowley. Dennis Rowley. "The Ezra Booth Letters." Dialogue: A Journal of Mormon Thought 16. (Autumn 1983): 136, 53. ira Ames Autobiography, LDS Archives.

Russell. Mary Russell. Personal letter (sent by email) to author from Mary Russell of Canada. 14 Nov 2002. Includes the "Dying Testimony of Mrs. Emily [Billings] Stringham to her Children."

Sentinel. The Sentinel, Newpaper of Sanpete. "Sketch of the Life of Ex-Bishop Bradley." Prize Articles No. 7 by D.C. reporting the life of Bishop George Washington Bradley. (photo copy in public domain) 1890.

Shurtliff. Luman Shurtliff. "Writings of Early Latter-Day Saints: Luman Shurtliff Autobiography." Typescript, BYU-S: 53:1.

Sidwell. Adelia B. Sidwell. Early Manti. "Reminiscences of Early Days in Manti" Written about 1889 Includes: "Tales of Early Manti" by Viola Bramwell and "Novel Indian Move Gave Sanpete County Impetus" by Mrs. W.G. Freschknecht, Deseret News Correspondent.

Sjodahl. Janne M. Doctrine and Covenants Commentary. Salt Lake City: Deseret, 1965.

Smith. Joseph Smith Jr. History of the Church. Index. Salt Lake City: Deseret Book, 1974.

Smith1. Joseph Smith Jr. History of the Church. Vol. 1. Salt Lake City: Deseret Book, 1974.Smith2. Joseph Smith Jr. History of the Church. Vol. 2. Salt Lake City: Deseret Book, 1976.

Smith3. Joseph Smith Jr. History of the Church. Vol. 3. Salt Lake City: Deseret Book, 1976.

Smith4. Joseph Smith Jr. History of the Church. Vol. 4. Salt Lake City: Deseret Book, 1976.

Smith5. Joseph Smith Jr. History of the Church. Vol. 5. Salt Lake City: Deseret Book, 1976.

Smith6. Joseph Smith Jr. History of the Church. Vol. 6. Salt Lake City: Deseret Book, 1976.

Smith7. Joseph Smith Jr. History of the Church. Vol. 7. Salt Lake City: Deseret Book, 1974.

Smith8. Joseph Smith Jr. Messages of the First Presidency. Vol. 1, page 11.

Smith9. Joseph Smith Jr. The Journal of Joseph: The Personal Diary of a Modern Prophet. Council Press, Provo, Ut.; Second edition (1980).

SmithJSHC. Joseph Smith Historic Center. "Joseph Smith's Red Brick Store." Nauvoo Pamphlet. Nauvoo, Illinois.

SmithJF. Joseph Fielding Smith. Church History and Modern Revelation. Vol. 2,3. Deseret Book.   August 14, 2009.

SmithLM. Lucy Mack Smith. History of Joseph Smith by His Mother. Salt Lake City: Bookcraft 1901.

Sorber. Phyllis. "Ebenezer and Ester (Joyce) Billings Family Group Sheet." Prepared in San Pedro, California.

Snow. Eunice Billings Warner. "A Sketch of the Life of Eunice Billings Snow" Woman's Exponent. Vol. 39, Sept. 1910 and November 22, 1911. Also, (Revised)

April 18, 1910, Provo, Utah.

Snow1. Eunice Billings Warner. "My Trip to Manti."

Snow2. Eunice Billings Warner. "Personal Testimony to the World." 1913.

Snow3. Eunice Billings Warner. "Titus Billings." 1911.

Snow4. Eunice Billings Warner. "Nauvoo Legion Sword." (text to slides). Presidents of the Church Slide Set G # G-60.

Snow5. Eunice Billings Warner. "Death Masks of the Prophet Joseph and Hyrum Smith with Historical Commentary." (text to slides). Presidents of the Church Slide Set G # G-71.

Snow6. Eunice Billings Warner. "Troubles with the Indians." Provo, Utah. August 1903.

Snow7. Eunice Billings Warner. "Mini Sketch of Life."

Snow8. Eunice Billings Warner. "History of Titus Billings" complied by his daughter.

Snow9. Eunice Billings Warner. "A Brief History of the Titus Billings Family" by Eunice Billings Warner Snow. (Obtained from Laird Billings).

Snow 10. Eunice Billings Warner Snow "Mormon Pioneer Overland Travel 1847 – 1868" as per Eunice, Women's Exponent 1912, pg 47-48.

Sperry. Sidney Branton Sperry. Doctrine and Covenants Compendium. Salt Lake City: Bookcraft, 1960.

Stout. Hosea Stout. "Writings of Early Latter-Day Saints: Hosea Stout." Vol. 2. BYU:41:1, 2:42. Provo: Brigham Young University.

StoutW. Wayne Stout. Hosea Stout: Utah's Pioneer Statesman. Salt Lake City: 1953.

Stringham. Emily Stringham. "The Dying Testimony of Mrs. Emily Billings Stringham to Her Children" typed by Elaine and Benj B. Strigham for Bryant Stringham (according to letter).

Tanner. Susan W. Tanner (with research by Lucile C. Tate and Elaine R. Harris). "Daughters in My Kingdom: The History and Work of Relief Society." Published by The Church of Jesus Christ of Latter-day Saints, Salt Lake City, Utah.

Tibbitts. Joy Tibbitts. A Tribute to the Ponca Tribe: Poncas and Mormons, 1846-2008. Self published, Sioux Falls, South Dakota, 2008.

Tibbitts2. Joy Tibbitts. Poncas and Mormons, A Friendship Renewed. Online book, 2013.

Times and SeasonsV1. Vol. 1. "Nauvoo, Illinois." Marriages performed by Titus Billings. October, 1840: pg. 19.

Times and SeasonsV2. Vol. 2 page 287 "Councilors." (Nine to be elected).

Times and SeasonsV3. Vol. 3. "Choir of the Stake of Zion in the City of Nauvoo." 1 January 1842, Whole No. 41.

Times and SeasonsV4. Vol. 4. "A Short Sketch of the Rise of the Young Gentlemen and Ladies Relief Society of Nauvoo." 1843.

Times and SeasonsV5. Vol. 5. "History of Joseph Smith." April, 1832.

Times and SeasonsV6. Vol. 6. "History of Joseph Smith." June 25, 1833: pg. 362-363, November 13,1833: pg. 898, October 10, 1833: pg. 864.

Tullidge. Edward W. Tullidge. The Women of Mormondome. New York City: Tullidge & Crandall, 1877.

WhitneyEA. Elizabeth Ann. 'Writings of Early Latter-day Saints: Elizabeth Ann Smith Whitney." Auto in Woman's Exponent 7. 1878.

WhitneyNK. Newell K. "Personal Collection." Film box 4/Mss. Film #14,pg.3, Special Collections, Provo: Brigham Young University.

WhitneyOF. Orson F. Whitney. History of Utah. Vol. 1 page 480-482. Salt Lake City, Utah: George Q. Cannon & Sons Co., Publishers, March 1892.

WhitneyOF1. Orson F. The Life of Heber C. Kimball. Salt Lake City: Bookcraft, 1945.

Widtsoe. John A. Widtsoe. Joseph Smith: Seeker After Truth, Prophet of God. Salt Lake City: Bookcraft, 1951.

Wilcox. David F. Wilcox. "Quincy and Adams County." The Lewis Publishing Company, Chicago and New York, 1919.

Worsley. Diantha Billings Worsley. "Grandfather, Titus Billings." 1914.

YoungB. Brigham Young. Journal of Discourses. Volume 1 and Volume 9. Los Angeles: Lithographed Printing and Litho,1956.

YoungB1. Brigham. "Brigham Young Journal History." May 16, 1831. Salt Lake City: LDS Church Historian's Office.

YoungB2. Brigham. "Brigham Young Journal History." September 6, 1850. Salt Lake City: LDS Church Historian's Office.

YoungLD. Lorenzo Dow. "Personal Biography."

Appendix A

Billings Family Photos and Historical Documents

Titus Billings 1793-1866

(Courtesy Billings Family.)

Titus and Diantha (Morley) Billings
(Courtesy Billings Family.)

Titus and Diantha (Morley) Billings
(Courtesy Provo DUP Pioneer Museum.)

Mary Ann (Tuttle) Billings

(Courtesy Billings Family.)

Original Sandstone Markers
(Courtesy S.B. Mitchell. 1999.)

Titus Billings' original sandstone marker (left), located in the Provo Utah Cemetery, was broken in half. When it and Diantha's marker (center) were replaced with a marble headstone the old markers were donated to the Manti Heritage Museum to be displayed indoors along with Isaac Morley's sandstone marker (right). Note: Isaac Morley is buried in the Manti Utah Cemetery.

Original Sandstone Marker, Titus

(Courtesy Karen Russell 2007.)   (Courtesy Central Utah Pioneer
                                    Heritage Association, 2008.)

Original Sandstone Marker, Diantha

(Courtesy Karen Russell 2007.)   (Courtesy Central Utah Pioneer Heritage Association, 2008.)

Diantha Morley and Titus Billings
New marker in Provo Utah City Cemetery.
(Courtesy S.B. Mitchell. 1999.)

Mary Ann's Grave

(Courtesy S.B. Mitchell. 2002.)

Mary Ann Tuttle-Egan-Billings-Gardner-Billings is buried beside a large pine tree in the quiet cemetery of Bicknell, Utah. (Formerly Thurber.)

Her tall, beautiful tombstone stands at the end of Stringham family markers. (Emily Billings Stringham is her oldest daughter.)

Row of Stingham Graves

Evan A. Billings returning to car.

The day we found Grandma's grave

Later in her life Mary Ann chose to be re-sealed to Titus Billings and descendants wondered if her remains should be moved to the Provo Cemetery so she could be buried beside him in a plot already purchased. When her great grandson, Evan A. Billings, set out to locate her grave and plan the move he was pleasantly surprised to find her final resting place already in a peaceful spot, beside a large tree with an impressive marker.

Mary Ann, called "Grandma Gardner" back then, moved into the George Stringham home to help raise the children when Emily died. Now she is buried beside Emily, George, and their infant children. "I believe she is where she wants to be," Evan said. *Susan Billings Mitchell - 2013*

Alfred Nelson Billings
(Courtesy Billings Family.)

Alfred's gravesite in Provo, UT
(Courtesy S.B. Mitchell, 2013.)

George Pierce Billings

(Courtesy Billings Family.)

Edith   George   Jerusha

Gravesites as situated in Manti, UT

(Courtesy S.B. Mitchell, 2013.)

Eunice (Billings) Warner Snow
(Courtesy Billings Family.)

Gravesite in Provo, UT
(Courtesy S.B. Mitchell, 2014.)

1914 "Testifiers of the Prophet Joseph Smith"

(Courtesy Provo DUP Pioneer Museum Artifact Collection.)

Names: Margaret Allen Harris, Marinda M. K. Glazier, Martha Ann S. Harris, Marilla J. M. Daniels, Eunice Billings Snow, Joanna H. Patten, Alice M. B. Wilkins, Sarah L. F. Turner, Percia Grover Bunnell, Hannah C. Robbins, and Sarah Topham Clark.

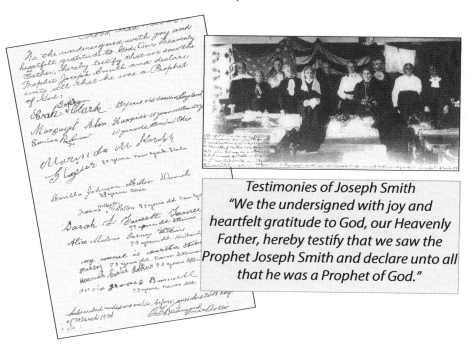

Testimonies of Joseph Smith
"We the undersigned with joy and heartfelt gratitude to God, our Heavenly Father, hereby testify that we saw the Prophet Joseph Smith and declare unto all that he was a Prophet of God."

Provo, Utah Mar. 24 1914.

We the undersigned with joy and heartfelt gratitude to God, Our Heavenly Father, hereby testify that we saw the Prophet Joseph Smith and declare unto all that he was a Prophet of God:

Sarah Tophan Clark. 83 years old born in England

Margaret Alen Harrice 86 years old Born in N.Y.

Eunice Pulnow 84 years old Born in Ohio

Marinda M Knobs G Lasier 84 years New York State

Marilla Johnson Miller Daniels 83 years Conn.

Frannie Hollyster Patton, 80 years old New York.

Sarah L Fawsett Tanner 79 years old Illinois.

Alice Malena Barney Wilkins 79 years old. Kirtland Ohio.

My name is Martha Eton Tuets Harris 73 years old. Navoo Illinois.

Hannah Carter Robbins 73 years. Illinois

Percia Groves Bunnell 73 years Navoo Ill.

Subscribed and sworn to before me this 24th day of March 1914

Fred Richmond Notary Public

Testimony signed on the back of the photo of "testifiers."

John Ely Warner

Pioneer Drum

Played by John Adelbert Warner and Samuel Warner, sons of John Ely Warner.

(Courtesy Susanne Warner Nelson and Cathy Warner Habing, 2012)

Front

Back

Gravesite in Manti, UT

This sandstone marker rests in the Manti Cemetery at Plat A-Block 12-Lot 17, the location given for John Ely Warner's grave. Age has removed all writing, but we believe this to be his grave site.

(Courtesy S.B. Mitchell, 2014)

In Memory of John Ely Warner and William Mills

Monument marks the mountain side spot of the first gristmill in Manti, Utah honoring the first two white men "killed by Indians" in Utah while working at the mill October 4, 1853.

(Courtesy S.B. Mitchell, 1999.)

Before   After

Marker Repaired by Boy Scouts.

(Courtesy S.B. Mitchell.)

David and Theresa Billings Coombs
(Courtesy Larry Coombs.)

Gravesite in Logan, Utah
(Courtesy Shawna Merrill Jacobson, 2013.)

Alonzo and Parna Ann (Keele) Billings

(Courtesy Billings Family.)

Gravesite in Delta, Utah

(Courtesy S.B. Mitchell, 2013.)

Ebenezer and Ester Billings Graves

Gravesites in Greenfield, Massachusetts
Green River Cemetery
(Courtesy Gregg and Lauralee McDermott, 2013.)

Finding Graves

Matthew Sean McDermott (fifth great-grandson of Ebenezer Billings) stands beside Ebenezer's grave; his wife, Nataly, stands beside Ester's grave to show the distance between them. Green River Cemetery, 256 Wisdom Way Greenfield, Massachusetts.

(Courtesy Gregg and Lauralee Mcdermott, 2013.)

Grave of John Wells and Billings Wives
(Sisters to Titus Billings)

After Salome Billings Wells died her husband, John, married her sister, Emily Billings Wells. A remaining piece of Salome's sandstone marker is pictured in front. Later, a nice marker was erected in honor of all three of them.

Gravesite in Kirtland, Ohio
(Courtesy Larry and Carol Coombs, 1994.)

Grave of Samuel Billings
(Brother to Titus Billings)
Samuel Billings 1791-1869 and Mary R [Russell] 1799-1889.

Gravesite in Kirtland, Ohio
(Courtesy Larry and Carol Coombs, 1994.)

Billings Road Sign in Kirtland, Ohio

Larry Coombs, descendant of Titus and Mary Ann's daughter, Theresa Billings Coombs, stands beside Billings Road, named after Samuel Billings (brother of Titus Billings).

(Courtesy Larry and Carol Coombs, 1994.)

Another Sam Billings at Sam Billings Road in Kirtland, Ohio
A descendant of Titus and Mary Ann (Tuttle) Billings' son, Alonzo.

(Courtesy L. K. Billings.)

Billings Homes in Manti

(Courtesy S.B. Mitchell, 2013.)

Titus Billings built the first home on this property 1849 to 1860.
Sold to Robert Johnson in 1860.

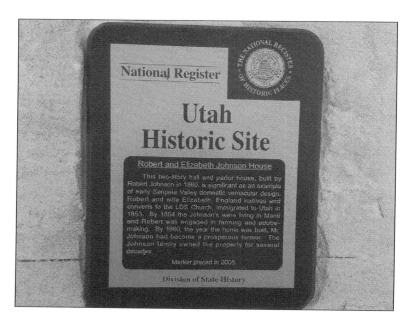

Alfred Nelson Billings built this home
(Courtesy S.B. Mitchell, 2013.)

George Pierce Billings built this home
(Courtesy S.B. Mitchell, 2013.)

No 1.

Titus Billings

BE IT KNOWN, THAT I,

Of Jackson county, and state of Missouri, having become a member of the church of Christ, organized according to law, and established by the revelations of the Lord, on the 6th day of April, 1830, do, of my own free will and accord, having first paid my just debts, grant and hereby give unto *Edward Partridge* of Jackson county, and state of Missouri, bishop of said church, the following described property, viz:— *Sundry articles of furniture valued fifty five dollars twenty seven cents, — also two beds, bedding and extra clothing valued seventy three dollars twenty five cents, — also farming utensils valued forty one dollars, — also one horse, two waggons two cows and two calves valued one hundred forty seven dollars*

in Jackson county Mo

For the purpose of purchasing lands, and building up the New Jerusalem, even Zion, and for relieving the wants of the poor and needy. For which I the said *Titus Billings* do covenant and bind myself and my heirs forever, to release all my right and interest to the above described property, unto him the said *Edward Partridge* bishop of said church. And I the said *Edward Partridge* bishop of said church, having received the above described property, of the said *Titus Billings* do bind myself, that I will cause the same to be expended for the above-mentioned purposes of the said *Titus Billings* to the satisfaction of said church; and in case I should be removed from the office of bishop of said church, by death or otherwise, I hereby bind myself and my heirs forever, to make over to my successor in office, for the benefit of said church, all of the above described property, which may then be in my possession.

In testimony whereof, WE have hereunto set our hands and seals this _____ day of _____ in the year of our Lord, one thousand eight hundred and thirty _____.

IN PRESENCE OF _____

[SEAL]

[SEAL]

[Seal]

Independence Stewardship Deed-Partridge Signature

(Courtesy Intellectual Property From Church History Library.)

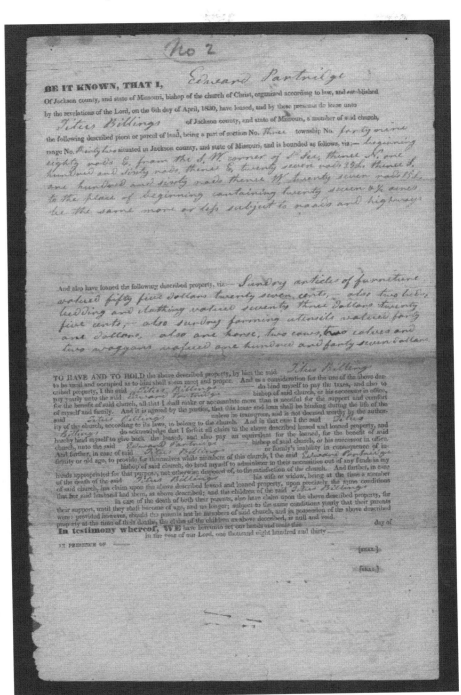

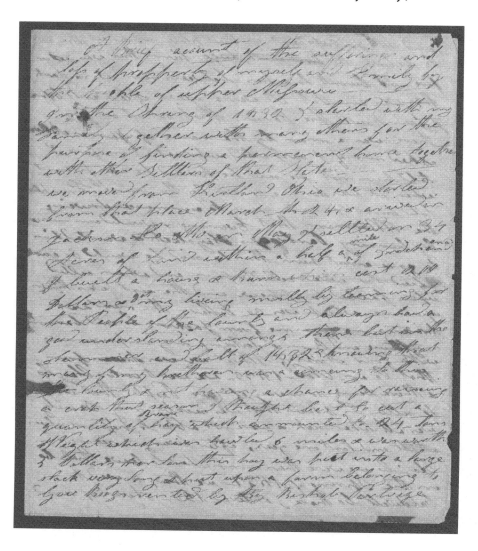

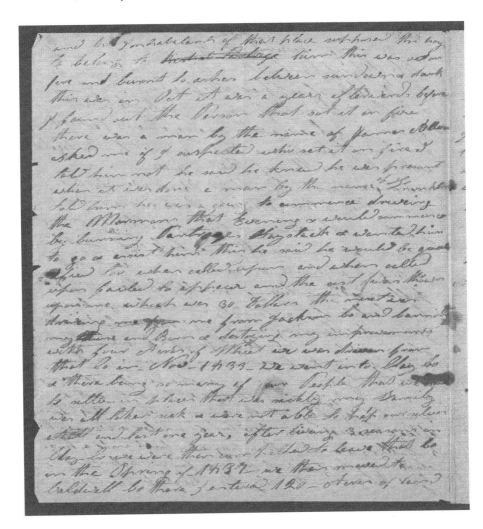

and the inhabitants of that place supposed this bay
to belong to him this was set on
fire and burnt to ashes between sundown a dark
this was in Oct it was a year of time and before
I found out the Person that set it on fire
there was a man by the name of James Allen
asked me if I suspected who set it on fire I
told him not he said he knew he was present
when it was done a man by the name of Franklin
told him he was a going to commence driving
the Mormons that Evening or would commence
by burning Cartages they stacked a went to him
to go a against him then he said he would be good
a[fire?] the other cellar upon and when called
upon failed to appear and the next was their
experience which was 30 Dollars the next a
driving me from Jackson to and burning
my [house?] and Barn a destroying my improvements
with four stands of wheat we was driven from
that Co in Nov 1833 we went into Clay Co
a there being so many of our people that would
to settle in Clay that all sickly my family
was all other sick a were not able to help our selves
e still and last one year after living 3 a [more?]
they were than our fathers to leave that Co
in the Spring of 1837 we then moved to
Caldwell Co there I entered 120 a [acres?] of land

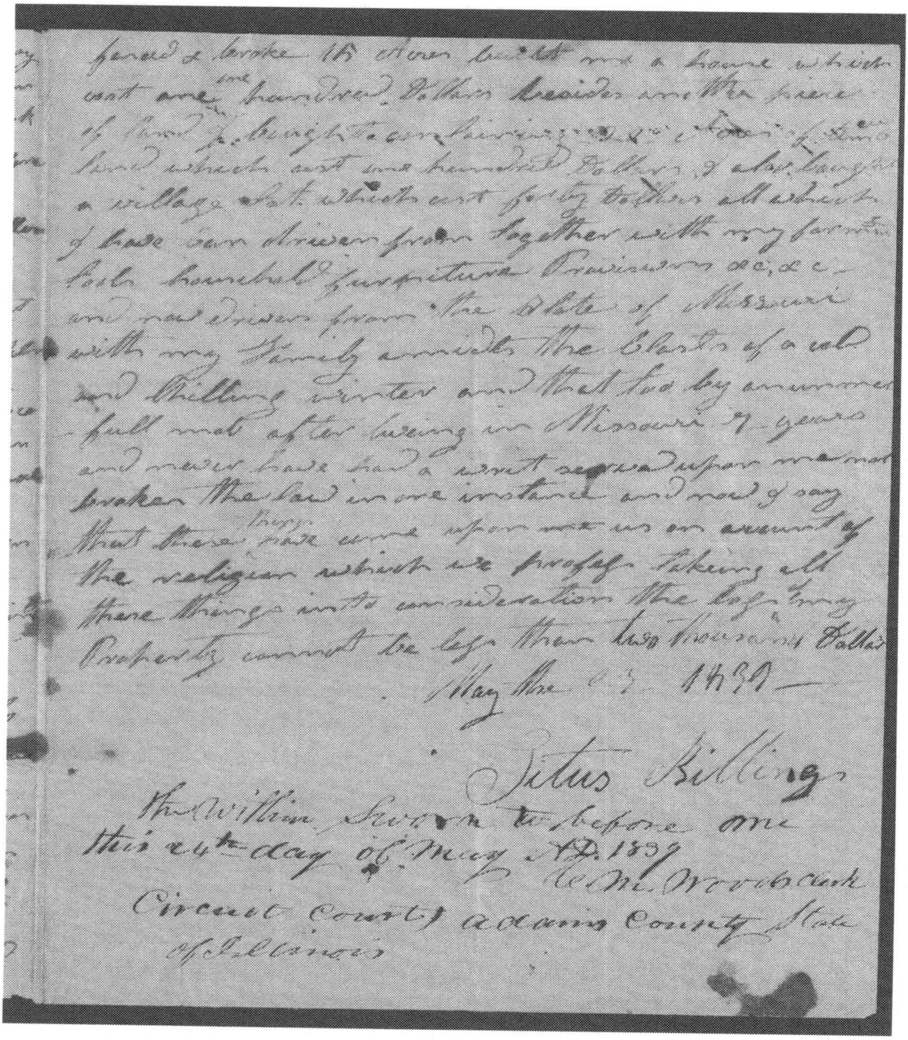

Signers of People on Missouri Persecutions

"Memorial of inhabitants of Nauvoo in Illinois, praying redress for injuries to their persons and property by the lawless proceedings of citizens of Missouri" (excerpt of page 35).

Used by permission given to Elda Mae Billings 1996.

LDS Church Historical Department.

Titus Billings Nauvoo Property Deed Cover

(Courtesy L. Tom Perry Special Collections, Harold B. Lee Library, Brigham Young University, Provo, Utah.)

Titus Billings Nauvoo Property Deed

(Courtesy L. Tom Perry Special Collections, Harold B. Lee Library, Brigham Young University, Provo, Utah.)

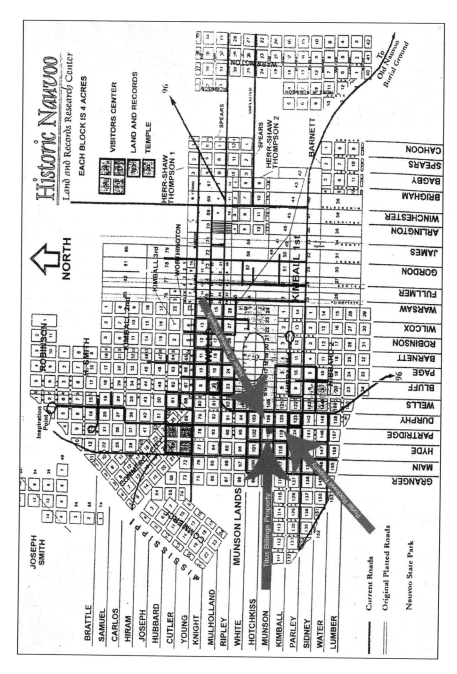

Titus Billings Property in Nauvoo

Titus Billings purchased a lot on the corner of Munson and Partridge Streets
Heber C. Kimball lived straight east across the street. Orrin Porter Rockwell lived
across the road directly south.

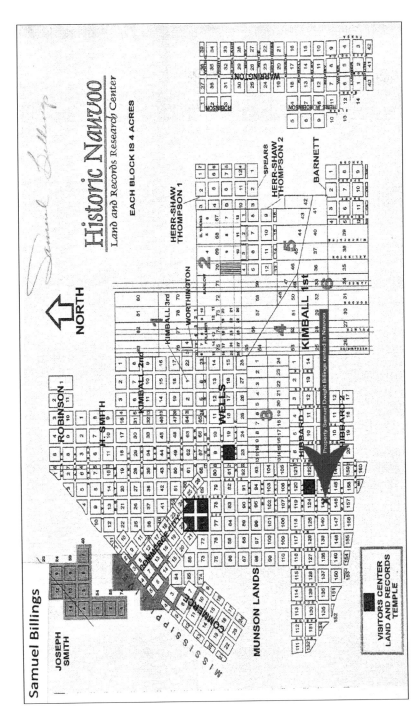

Samuel Dwight Billings Property in Nauvoo

Samuel Billings rented property on Partridge and Sidney Street.

Nauvoo Legion List for Field Artillery: Titus Billings, Capt.

(Courtesy L. Tom Perry Special Collections, Harold B. Lee Library, Brigham Young University, Provo, Utah.)

Nauvoo Legion Returns of Field Artillery: Capt. Billings

(Courtesy L. Tom Perry Special Collections, Harold B. Lee Library, Brigham Young University, Provo, Utah.)

Return of Field Artillery

Titus Billings — Capt

P. S. Wilber, 1st Lieut
Stephen Winchester Jr. } Lieutenants
John C. Annis, 3d }

Sergeants
David Dort 1st }
Isaac Higbee 2nd }
Stephen Godard 3 }
Aaron Johnson 4th }

Corporals
Nathan Cheney 1st }
John Lytle 2d }
David Garnet 3d }
Stephen Dort 4th }

Within the age of 18 & 45
J. W. Phippin
Wm Field
Amos Barlow
John M. Tippits
Jesse Hunter
Isaac Allred
Thomas Spears
Josep W. Pierce
Lyman Stevens
Wm Huett
Allen Weeks
Joseph Young
Lindsey Brady
Elisha Edwards
David Clough
P. H. Bird

Daniel S. Thompson
Benj. T. Clapp
Goswell Stevens
Benj. S. Boydston
George Wilber
David S. Dort
John M. King
Stephen Winchester Jr
H. H. Wilber
George Grant
Horace Randall
Lorenzo Brown
Wm H. Edwards
Abram Jones
Bradley L. Wilber
Samuel T. Williams
Truman Gillet
Joseph W. Coolidge
W. S. Wilber
Nathaniel Leavett
John M. Chidister
Willard Baldwin
James Moses
Mc Intire

The Company above consists of 53 rank and file liable to do duty

Nauvoo Legion Election Poll: Titus Billings Voting

(Courtesy L. Tom Perry Special Collections, Harold B. Lee Library, Brigham Young University, Provo, Utah.)

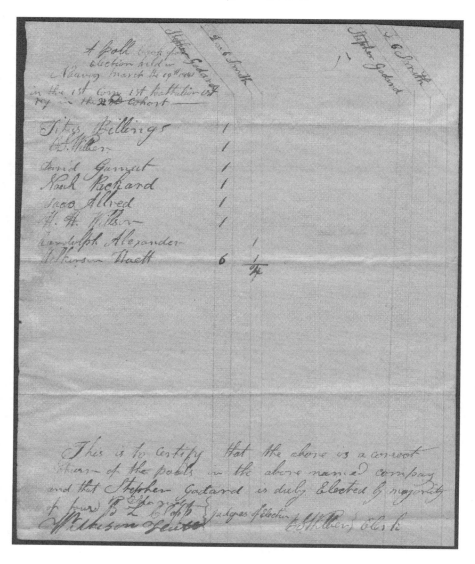

Nauvoo Legion: Titus Billings, Brevet Major

(Courtesy L. Tom Perry Special Collections, Harold B. Lee Library, Brigham Young University, Provo, Utah.)

Nauvoo Legion Band: Samuel Billings, Flute

(Courtesy L. Tom Perry Special Collections, Harold B. Lee Library, Brigham Young University, Provo, Utah.)

Nauvoo Legion Company Roll: Ebenezer Billings

(Courtesy L. Tom Perry Special Collections, Harold B. Lee Library, Brigham Young University, Provo, Utah.)

Death Records of Titus Billings Jr.

Died March 14, 1844 at 10 years of age from Inflammation of the Brain.

(Source unknown.)

NAME	DIED		AGE		CAUSE	PAGE
Beeman, Sarah	Aug 29	1840	65 yr	2 mo 12 da		TS
Bidwell, Gazelem C	Bf Sept 24	1842	11 mo		Inflam of brain	Wasp
Bell, Jonah R.	April 5	1845				A
Bell, Robert	March 18	1844	1 yr		Inflam in head	16
Bell, Samuel	Sept 14	1844	5 yr	10 mo 12 da	Whooping Cough	21
Bell, Theresa	Jan 8	1844		8 mo 4 da	Inflam of brain	New
Benjamin, Hannah E.	Jan 11	1845	13 yr 1 mo 14 da		Consumption	25
Benjamin, Julina	Oct 3	1844	15 yrs		Remitting Fever	22
Bennett, Hannah	March 20	1843	87 yr 1 mo 12 da		Old age	4
Bennet, Lydia	Bt June 15-July31	1842	26 ys		Blank	2
Bennett, Mary	Bf Oct 8	1842	1 yr	1 mo	Fever	
Bennett, Mary C.	July 28 1844		11 mo		Inflamation	18
Benson, Oliver	Bf Sept 29,	1845	43 yr		Typhus Fever	
Bentley, Patience	Blank		65 yr	1mo 8 da	blank	1
Bentley, Phoebe Ann	Jan 5 1841		34 yr	7 mo	Consumption	24
Bernard, Elizabeth	Af Oct 16	1843	38 yrs		chill & fever	new
Berry, Jesse	Aug 6 1844		52 yr	6 mo	Fever	19
Bigby, Elizabeth	Bf Sept 25	1843	15 da			
Bigelow, Herbert S.	Jan 28	1844	2 yr	5 da	Measles	15
Bigler, Mary Ann	Bf Nov 5	1841	20 yr		Typhus Fever	NN
Bigley , Elizabeth	Bt Sept 25-Oct 2 1843		15 da		Convulsion/fits	10
Bickmore, Wm N	Aug 18 1845		7 yr		Typhus Fever	
Bidwell, Gazelam G	Sept	1842	11 mo		Inflam of brain	Wasp
Billings, Titus	Mar 14	1844	10 yr		Inflam of brain	16

Death Records (Source Unknown)

[Note: Titus Billings listed is son of Titus and Diantha Morley Billings]

```
            OLD NAUVOO BURIAL GROUND
       780 EAST 2300 NORTH SONORA TOWNSHIP
       INVENTORY OF MARKERS AND GRAVES ETC.

A.   NAME  BILLINGS, Titus               NAUVOO RIN #  22717
     FATHER BILLNGS, Titus
     MOTHER MORLEY, Diantha
     HUSBAND
     WIFE
B.   DEATH DATE 14 Mar 1844(1843)(NN)& Cen AGE   10 yr
     BIRTHDATE      abt 1834
C.   LOCATION;(*) EAST      FEET.   NORTH           FEET.
         BLOCK       LOT       GRAVE     STONE NUMBER
D.   INFORMATION SOURCE CODE  A, E-1,I     (SEE T BELOW)
E.   MARKER TYPE:       &        &
         0.   NONE;   1.  HEADSTONE;  2. FOOTSTONE;  3. SUPPORT
       STONE;  4. UNMARKED STONE;  5. LIMESTONE NATIVE;
       6. MARBLE;  7.  GRANITE;  8. SANDSTONE; 9 OTHER.
F.   INSCRIPTION & EPITAPH (BEST COMBINED INFORMATION)
```

1845 Nauvoo Letter Written by Titus and Diantha Billings

Photo of original letter with both signatures enlarged.

(Courtesy L. K. Billings and B. F. Ashworth)

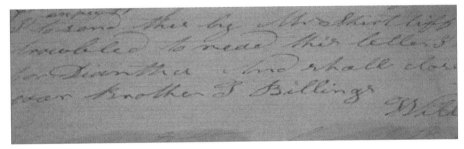

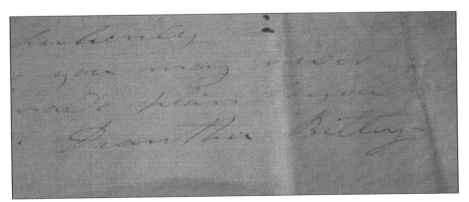

1845 Nauvoo Letter Written by Titus and Diantha Billings

(Courtesy Intellectual Property From Church History Library.)

Nauvoo Oct the 27th 1845

Dear brother & sister and all enquireing friends
I seat myself at my table at this time to write a few
lines that you may know that we are alive and that
we are enjoying tolerable health at present we have ben
called to part with our youngest Child since I saw you
Titus he was Ten years old when he died I do not know what
will interest you the most for news although I will
venture to write something of the news of the day
and the scenes that are transacted in Illenoise although
my heart sickens at the thought and if I should attempt
to give you a history of the persecution of the Latter day Saints
in this place it would take more than a quire of paper
to do it justice, suffice it to say, many have sealed their testimony
with their blood Joseph Smith and Hyrum Smith &
others Joseph Smith has been a man of affliction ever since he was
called of god to go and take the Plates from the earth he has ben taken
with writs 30 times and all on account of his religion for there never
was an action sustaind against him for I have ben acquainted with him
since the fall of 1830 his life & time has ben for the good of mankind
and so has his Bro Hyrum that while they gave themselves up
and the Governor and the people had promised to protect them
they rushed into jail and murdered the two Smiths and left
for dead John Taylor on the floor but that once recovered
and many of the latter day Saints have ben persecuted unto death
they have ben driven from their homes in Misoure and their bones
are bleeching in the Prairies for nothing but their religion
But I know it is very natural for you to ask why all this fuss
why all this persecution why dont the other sects of the day
have the trouble that the latter day Sts do I can
answer the question just for a moment go back and look at the
Apostolic church at jerusalem and see what they had to pass through

700

1845 Nauvoo Letter Written by Titus and Diantha Billings

(Courtesy Intellectual Property From Church History Library.)

We have a beautiful City here the Census was taken this fall their is eleven ~~thousand~~ thousand Inhabitants in this City 15,100 in this County in other Countys & in this about 30,100 are expecting to remove in the spring in a body for California Oregon or some other good place I often think of my Relations in Mass with gratitude for they were kind to me there and I know that many of them would have been glad to had me any thing but a Mormon although that is a nickname given here And I sincerely believe that we shall be the means of saving many of our friends when the judgements of God are spread abroad over the earth The times here are good Crops of all kinds are first rate Wheat 40 cents Corn 12½ cts I to send thee by Mr Shirtliffs of Russell I expect you will be troubled to read this letter I write so seldom I shall leave a space for Diantha And shall close by bidding you adieu their from your Brother T Billings

        William and Esther Dynchion

as ____ has left a space for me I will ____
____ although he has written the most yet I ____
testify to the truth to what he has written ____
it may appear like an idle story but it is the
~~____~~ ____ and you will sooner or later have
to acknowledge it and you cannot say in a
coming day as we have not warn you of these things
we have got to leave our homes to a distant ____
____ ____ we have just got ____ ____
we have a frame house and a good well of water
other conveniances so as to make life ____ but
it is no more than the ____ ____ to suffer ____
and I hope we shall bear it patiently ____
I must draw to a close hoping you may never
reject truth whenever it is made ____ to you
from your ____ and Sister Diantha Billings

Heads of Families in the Township of Mentor
Titus Billings on bottom row.

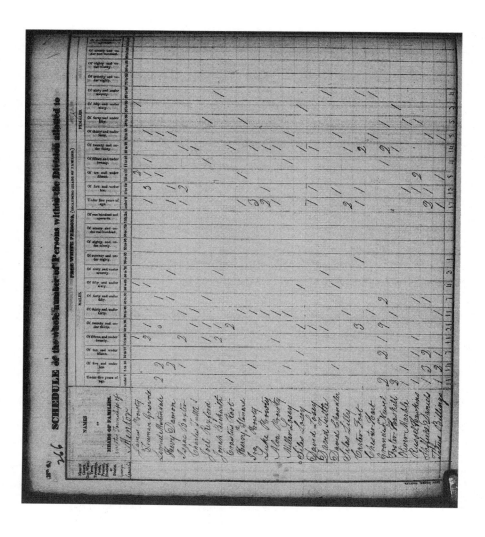

Titus Billings Book of Mormon

(Courtesy Provo DUP Museum, 2013.)

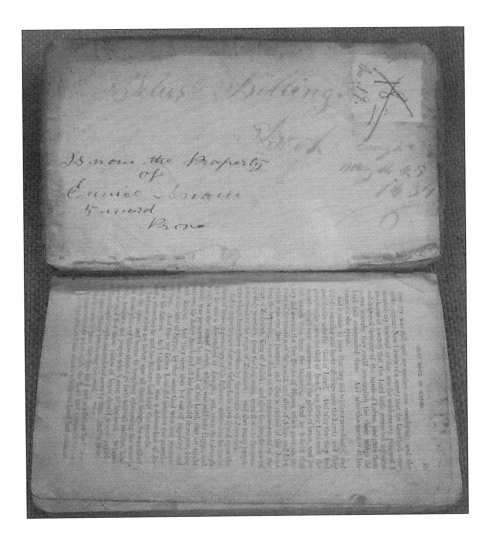

Family Group Sheet
Titus Billings and Diantha Morley Billings
(Courtesy Billings Family.)

HUSBAND BILLINGS, Titus
Born: 24 Mar 1793 — Place: Greenfield, Franklin, Mass.
Marr: 16 Feb 1817 — Place: Kirtland, Geauga, Ohio (of Mentor, Ohio)
Died: 5 Feb 1866 — Place: Provo, Utah, Utah
Bur: 6 Feb 1866 — Place: Provo City Cem, Provo, Utah, Utah
Husband's Father: BILLINGS, Ebenezer (1750)
Husband's Mother: JOYCE, Esther
Other Wife: (2) 20 Jan 1854 EH, TUTTLE, Mary Ann

WIFE (1) MORLEY, Diantha
Born: 23 Aug 1796/5 — Place: Montague, Franklin, Mass
Died: 14 May 1879 — Place: Provo, Utah, Utah
Bur: Provo City Cem, Provo, Utah, Utah
Wife's Father: MORLEY, Thomas (1758)
Wife's Mother: MARSH, Editha (2 Oct 1762)

Name of husband or wife submitting record: Mrs Elva B. Benion, 855 East 1400 South, Orem, Utah
Ward: Sharon Stake
Family Representative: BENION, (Mrs) Elva Billings
Relation of F.R. to wife: 2 g g dau

TEMPLE ORDINANCE DATA

Wife: Baptized "Kirtland" 15 Nov 1830 — Endowed "Kirtland" 11 Dec 1845 — Sealed to husband 30 Jan 1846 M

Sex	Children (given names)	When born	Where born	Date of first marriage / To whom	When died	Baptized	Endowed	Sealed to parents
M	BILLINGS, Samuel Dwight	1818	Ohio		In St. Louis, leaving 3 children		11 Dec 1845	17 July 1889 M
M	BILLINGS, Thomas	1819	Ohio		infant in Ohio		9 July 1889 MT 10 July 1889	17 July 1889 M
F	BILLINGS, Emily (twin)	1819			at birth 1819		child	17 July 1889 M
F	BILLINGS, Martha (twin)	1819			at birth 1819		child	17 July 1889 M
M	BILLINGS, Ebenezer	1820		on Mass River, 9 Dec 1851	abt 1847, left Nauvoo & not heard from again, 9 July	child		17 July 1889 M
M	BILLINGS, Alfred Nelson	23 Aug 1825	Mentor or Kirtland	PATTEN, Deborah	14 Mar 1882	Nov 1833	17 July 1889	17 July 1889 M
M	BILLINGS, George Pierce	25 July 1827	Mentor	(1d & May 1856 EH) PATTEN, Edith	2 Dec 1896	12 July 1851	21 June 1846	17 July 1889 M
F	BILLINGS, Eunice	3 Jan 1830	Mentor	abt 1848 (1) WARNER, John ELy	25 Nov 1914	25 July 1834 in church	3 June 1846	17 July 1889 M
M	BILLINGS, Titus Jr.	1834	Clay Misr	March 1871 1844 Nauvoo		child		17 July 1889 M

Other Marriages: #7 George Pierce md (2) SHOEMAKER, Jerusha; #8 Eunice husb John E. Warner was killed by the Indians, while working on grist mill; #8 Eunice md (2) SNOW, George W.

Necessary Explanations: Titus was called to be 2nd coun. to Bishop Edward Partridge (the 1st Bishop of the Church) and Isaac Morley was 1st coun. Then a member of High Council in Far West, Mosr.; Was Capt. of Hundred on Pioneer Plains; Was in G.C. Kimball's Co. while 2nd City Capt. Father;...

Sources of Information: husb Titus death rec., Des. News 15-309 Obit film F Utah 52, #42088, pt 3; #7 Geo.P. sld to Edith PATTEN #25165, pt 15, pt 14, No.60, EH sealings; children sld to parents film #23052, pt 2, p 334; #7 Geo.P. death date; #7 Geo.P. death Obit F Provo City Cem. Rec. for husb Titus death date; Utah 52, pt 3, Des. News 5 Dec 1896, film #4 1896; Titus & Diantha md in Geauga Co. Ohio mar rec. #41094, pt #1094, pt 87; Also mar rec. Geauga Co. #5013, pt 1 #21922, pt 6, p 1054. This indicates that all ch. were born in Geauga Co., except the youngest. (Crossing plains... #1 Samuel bapt & end in MT tmpl rec. age 16-17... Indexed & copied by D.A.R., p L2;

Family Group Sheet

Titus Billings and Mary Ann Tuttle Billings

(Courtesy Billings Family.)

Where was information shown on this family record obtained?
Family Record of
Gladys O. Billings
O. Sta. 3-23-149 Utah

Name and address of person submitting this sheet:

HUSBAND Titus Billings
Birth 25 Mar 1793 Place Greenfield, Franklin Co., Mass.
Chr. Place
Death 6 Feb 1866 Place Provo, Utah Co., Utah
Burial Place
Father Ebenezer Billings Mother (Maiden Name) Esther
Mar. 20 Jan 1854 Place Endowment Thomas S.L.C., Utah
Other Wives (if any) Diantha Morley

WIFE Mary Ann Tuttle (Egan)
Birth June 1830 Place Johnstown, Mass
Chr. Place
Death 10 Dec 1910 Place (Thurber) Bicknell, Wayne Co, Utah
Burial Place
Father Edward Tuttle Mother Catharine Vannum Green State
Other Hus. (if any) Jame. W.D.N. Gardner Ward

Sex	CHILDREN (Give names in full in order of birth)	WHEN BORN Day Mo. Yr.	WHERE BORN Town County	State or Country	DIED Day Mo. Yr.	MARRIED
M.	1 Hyrum Egan					Date To
F.	2 Emily Billings	27 Nov 1857	Manti, Sanpete	Utah	Feb 26 1889	Date To Geo W Stringham 1875
F.	3 Theresa "	28 Feb 1859	"	"	6 Mar 1931	Date 4 Jan To
M.	4 Alonzo "	25 Feb 1862	"	"	28 Nov 1944	Date 25 Dec 1884 To Anna Ann Keele
	5		Fountain Green	"		Date To
M.	6 Lewis Gardner		"			Date To
	7					Date To

logical and Historical Data on Reverse Side

705

Family Group Sheet
Titus Billings and Mary Ann Tuttle Billings, General Authority Copy
(Courtesy Billings Family.)

Family Group Sheet (handwritten genealogical record)

HUSBAND (2) Titus Billings
Born 24 March 1793, Place Greenfield, Franklin, Massachusetts
Husband: Titus Billings
Wife: Mary Ann Tuttle (1793)

WIFE (2) Mary Ann Tuttle
Born 5 June 1830

CHILDREN:
1. Emily Billings — 12 Nov 1854 — Manti
2. Helaman — 23 Jan 1859 — Manti
3. Alonzo — 25 Feb 1862 — Manti

This is a General Authority copy — you will require your own authentic file.

© 1972 The Genealogical Society of The Church of Jesus Christ of Latter-day Saints, Inc.

FAMILY GROUP SHEET WORK COPY ONLY. "Do not send to the Genealogical Society."

Family Group Sheet

Howard Egan and Mary Ann Tuttle Egan

(Courtesy Billings Family.)

HUSBAND'S Name (in full) Howard Egan — 181
Wife Mary Ann Tuttle

TEMPLE ORDINANCE DATA

HUSBAND
Baptized 3 NOV 1964
Endowed 16 Dec. 1845
&. dan

(Relationship of Family Representative to Husband)

WIFE
Baptized 2 Sep 1843
Endowed 6 Feb 1846
Sealed to Husband —9 NOV '60 1F
step & dau

(Relationship of Family Representative to Wife)

Where was information shown on this
family record obtained? SIS
From the Book Pioneering
the West

p 289, 290; adjusted for
Claude D. Billings (G-son to
wife) 375 Logan Ave, SLC, Ut
(14 Aug 1968)1 fam rec1

Family Representative:
Ora Egan Simmons
Name and address of person submit-
ting this sheet.
Markie Egan Barnes
720 N. Wabash
Idaho Falls, Idaho

	BAPTIZED (Date)	ENDOWED (Date)	SEALED To Parents Date & Temple
HUSBAND	14 Oct.1902	16 Oct.1902	-9 NOV '60 1F

HUSBAND (1) (No.1) HOWARD EGAN *
Birth 15 June or July 1815 Place Tullimore,Kings, Ireland
Chr. Place
Death 16 Mar 1878 Place
Burial Place
Father Howard Egan * Mother Ann Meade
1809
Married 11 Dec. 1836 Tomson Parshley, 12/ 1846 Nancy A., Redding
/23 Jan

WIFE 3) MARY ANN TUTTLE *
Birth 5 June 1830 Place Boston, Sflk, Mass
Chr. Place
Death 10 Dec 1910 Place Thurber, Wayne, Utah
Burial 12 Dec 1910 Place Thurber, Wayne, Utah
Father Edward Tuttle Mother Catherine Vanever Geyer
(2) 20 Jan 1854 Titus Billings * (3) 28 Nov 1866 Walter Elias Gardner

Sex	CHILDREN List each child (whether living or dead) in order of birth	WHEN BORN Day Mo. Yr.	WHERE BORN Town	County	State or Country	DIED Day Mo. Yr.	MARRIED List Additional Marriages with Dates on Reverse Side of Sheet
M	1	Hyrum William Egan *	24 July 1850	Salt Lake City.	Salt Lake,	Utah	24 Mar.1888	Date. 30 Jan.1872 To Mary Selome Prestor
	2							
	3							
	4							
	5							
	6							
	7							
	8							
	9							
	10							
	11	NOTE: Mary Ann Tuttle was seald to Howard Egan before it was known she had been sealed in life to Titus Billings.						
	12		Endowment reconfirmed for above				
	13		Hus, on 3 Nov 1964 in the Salt Lake Temple.				
	14						
	15						

Family Group Sheet
Walter Elias Gardner and Mary Ann Tuttle Gardner
(Courtesy Billings Family.)

Family Group Sheet for Walter Elias Gardner and Mary Ann Tuttle Gardner

HUSBAND (3) GARDNER, Walter Elias *

Born	5 July1828	Place Stockbridge, Brkshr, Mass
Chr.		Place
Marr.	28 Nov 18__	Place Endowment House, Salt Lake City, S-Lk, Utah
	23 June1886	Place Salem, Utah, Utah
Died	26 June1886	Place " "
Husband's Father	GARDNER, Elias	
Husband's Mother	SNOW, Harriet Smith	
Other Wives	(1) 28 Apr 1847 TUTTLE, Martha Ann *	

WIFE (2) TUTTLE, Mary Ann

Born	5 June1830	Place Boston, Sflk, Mass
Chr.		Place
Died	10 Dec 1910	Place Thurber, Wayne, Utah
	12 Dec 1910	Place " "
Wife's Father	TUTTLE, Edward *	
Wife's Mother	GEYER, Catherine Vanever	
Other Husbands	(1) 1869 MOAN, Howard * (2) 20 Jan 1854 BILLINGS, Titus *	

GARDNER, Walter Elias 18__

Name & Address of person submitting this record: Theresa B. Coombs / 126 So. 3rd E, / Logan, Utah

Family Representative: GARDNER, Lewis Wells (d)
Relation of F.R. to Husband: son
Relation of F.R. to Wife: non

TEMPLE ORDINANCE DATA

	BAPTIZED (date)	ENDOWED (date)	SEALED (dau. & years) WIFE TO HUSBAND	SEALED (son & years) CHILDREN TO PARENTS
HUSBAND	26 May 1964	6 Feb 1846		
WIFE	2 Sep 1843	6 Feb 1846	28 Nov 1846	EH
	10 Oct 1962	14 Oct 1891		BIC

CHILDREN

Sex	SURNAME (capitalized) GIVEN NAMES	WHEN BORN (Day Month Year)	WHERE BORN (Town County State or Country)	DATE OF FIRST MARRIAGE TO WHOM	WHEN DIED (Day Month Year)
1 M	GARDNER, Lewis Wells	11 Apr 1868	Fountain Greens, Snpt, Utah	CROWTHER, Annie Elizabeth	5 May 1950
2					
3					
4					
5	Endowment reconfirmed for above husb on 26 May 1964 in the Salt Lake Temple.				
6					
7	Endowment reconfirmed and all former sealings ratified for above wife on 13 Nov 1967.				
8					
9	Endowment reconfirmed and all former sealings ratified for				
10	above child #1 on 10 Oct 1967.				
11					

SOURCES OF INFORMATION: FAM REC:

NOTE: It is assumed that the sealing of Mary Ann Tuttle to Walter Elias Gardner was cancelled as she was sealed while living to Titus Billings on 27 Sep 190_

ARCHIVE RECORD

708

Appendix B

Morley Family Photos and Historical Documents

Isaac Morley 1786-1865

(Courtesy Morley Family.)

Painting of Isaac Morley's Original Sandstone Tombstone
by Carl Purcell.
(Photograph courtesy Karen Russell, 2007.)

Isaac Morley's Grave in Manti, Utah

Original Sandstone Marker

Isaac's original marker donated
to Manti Heritage Museum.
(Courtesy S.B. Mitchell. 1999.)

(Courtesy Central Utah Pioneer
Heritage Association, 2008.)

Verse on Marker

"My flesh shall slumber in the
ground Until the angel's horn shall
sound Then burst my chains with
sweet surprise And in my Savior's
image rise."

New Granite Marker

(Courtesy Jeanine Cardon Teeples, 2014.)

[Note: Plat A, Block 14, Lot 25.]

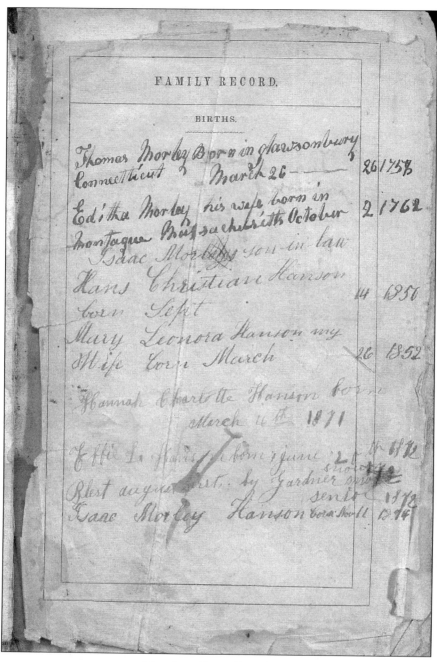

Morley Family Bible

(Courtesy Intellectual Property. From Church Historical Library,
Salt Lake City, Utah.)

1835 Letter of Recommendation

Signed by Joseph Smith Jr. and The First Presidency acknowledges Edward Partridge and Isaac Morley as Church Leaders.

(Courtesy Intellectual Property. From Church History Library.)

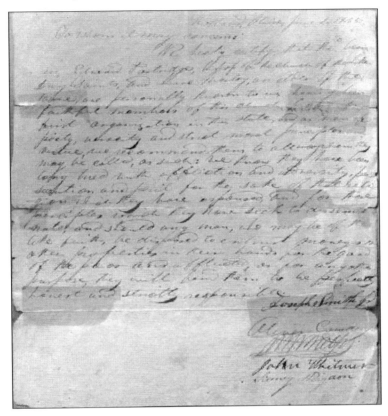

Content of Letter: Kirtland, Ohio, June 1, 1835. To Whom it may concern: We hereby certify, that the bearers, Edward Partridge, bishop of the church of the Latter-Day Saints, and Isaac Morley, an elder in the same, are personally known to us, having been faithful members of this church from its first organization in this state, and as men of piety, veracity and strict moral principles and virtue, we recommend them to all to [among] whom they may be called, as such: we know they have been long tried with affliction and adversity, persecution and peril for the sake of that religion which they have espoused, and for those principles which they now seek to disseminate, and should any man who may be of the like faith, be disposed to entrust moneys of other properties in their hands for the good of the poor and afflicted, or for any other purpose, they will find them to be perfectly honest and strictly responsible. [Signed] Joseph Smith Jr, Oliver Cowdery, W[illian] W. Phelps, John Whitmer, Sidney Rigdon.

Mission Report

Written by Isaac Morley. Calvin Beebe companion.

(Courtesy Intellectual Property. From Church History Library.)

Journal of Isaac Morley & Calvin Beebe 1835

In company with Calvin Beeby on the 17th February 1835 we left Missourie for Kirtland on a mission to preach by the way with aut [about] [...] and in makeing out our returns to the Bishop in Kirtland we are happy to say that in trusting in the promises of the Lord we have been amply rewarded we have proclaimed the Gospel to the people forty times to the people in our travels to this place — he [&c] we have had many private interviews with the people in regard to the new and everlasting covenants — we have held eight meetings with our Brethren while on our way to this place we spent seventy one [...] days in our journey we have baptized two — and found friends in all of our travels Elder Beeby and my self have credencials to present to the Bishop of — requested from the high Counsel in Missourie likewise from the Bishop of that place we have traveled according to our records eight hundred and seventy five miles we traveled through the State of Missourie — Illinois Indeana and Ohio from Dark Co to this place, we have names of all the counties and principal towns that we have passed in our travels to Kirtland and we he [believe] that we can point out to the traveling saints as good a rout to travel in as there is to Clay Co Missourie we arrived in Kirtland Aprial 29th 1835

Elders — Isaac Morley

Calvin Beebe

Isaac Morley Grievance Letter

(Courtesy LDS Historical Department.)

Illinois Quincy May 28 1839

A Bill of Damage against the State of
Missouri in consequence of the Governors
Exterminating order

first for moving into the State $ 100 . 00
for Damage in Jackson county
Being Driven from the same
and for loss of property 1833 $ 615 00 . 00
for being Driven from Clay co
to Caldwell Loss, property and time
being thrown out of business $ 2 000 00
for Loss of property in Caldwell
Co. and being Driven from the
State time and expenses $ 2 000 . 00

                                              2,866 . 0 .

I was allso imprisoned in
Jackson county falsly both hours and shot
at by a mob in 1863
imprisoned in Richmond Ray county 20 Days
and have never had an accusation found against
me in the State this war in 1838 —

I certify the above account to be just and
true according to the best of my knowledge

                                        Isaac Morley

Sworn to before me this 28th
day of May AD 1839
                    Chs. M. Woods Clerk.
                         Circuit Court
                              Adams County Ill.

Nauvoo Legion Rank Roll: Isaac Morley

(Courtesy L. Tom Perry Special Collections, Harold B. Lee Library,
Brigham Young University, Provo, Utah.)

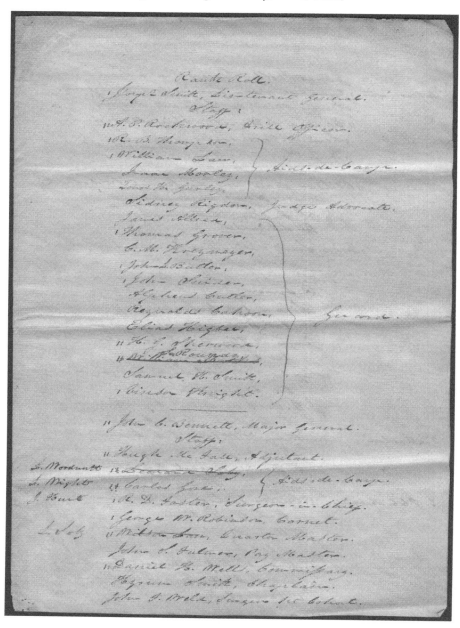

Thomas and Editha Morley Gravesite

Parents of Isaac and Diantha. Kirtland, Ohio.

(Courtesy Larry and Carol Coombs, 1994.)

Children of Thomas and Editha Morley

Arthusa (6 Mar 1784)
Isaac (6 Mar 1786)
Horace (29 Jan 1788)
Tirzah (1 Jan 1790)
Editha (14 Feb 1792)
Thomas (15 July 1794)
Diantha 23 (Aug 1796)
Louisa (11 Nov 1798)
Alfred (20 Aug 1805)

Cutler's Park and Winter Quarters' Burials (page 1)

(Courtesy Caryle B. Jensen and Gail Geo. Holmes, "A Grave Experience at the Mormon Pioneer Winter Quarters Cemetery" October 1999.)

Cutler's Park and Winter Quarters' Burials
Alphabetical Listing
Grave # inverted in black box ■ = Cutler's Park, Regular Type = Winter Quarters, All CAPS = ON PLAQUE BUT NOT ON SEXTON'S RECORD.

Name	Grave #	Name	Grave #	Name	Grave #	Name	Grave #	Name	Grave #
Adams, Henry	54	Brinkerhoff, James	1	CHAMBERLIN, HOPE H.		Cummings, James	120	FIELDING, JOHN	
Aiken, Samuel	91	Brinton, Elizabeth	10	CLARK, DANIEL WEDEN		Cummings, James W. Jr.	13	Flake, Frederick	47
Akley, John	35	Brinton, Robert H	10	Clark, David W.	57	Cummings, Susannah	92	Flake, Samuel B.	114
Alexander, Nancy	66	Browett, Moroni	11	Clark, Felina	17	Cummins. Geo. A.	56	Foster, Thomas	236
Allen, Joseph D.	201	BROWN, (FEMALE)		Clark, Gardner	129	Dalton, Martha J.	150	Gardner, Emma	10
ALLEY, SARAH		Brown, Emily Jane	160	Clark, Mary	159	Daniels. Francis A.	20	Gardner, Genet	2
Alsworth, Orson H.	60	Bruce, Mary Ann	41	Clayton, James	271	Daniels. Francis G.		Garner, Silva	226
Anderson, Adney A. C.	151	Bullock, Isabella	136	CLEMENT, NANCY		DAS, M.		Gates, Caroline E.	40
Angel, Martha Ann	23	Bullock, Janet	82	Clements, Alpheus G.	90	Davidson, Joseph S.	300	Gates, Mary E.	40
Angel, Truman C	240	Bullock, Willard Richards	104	Clynes, Ann E.	301	Davis, Isaac	155	Glasgow, Josinnah	164
Angell, Almira	44	Burdick, Ephraim	195	Colburt, Sarah	293	Davis, Lydia	115	Glines, James E.	255
Angus, William	38	Burnham, Mary C.	117	Collins, Charles H.	260	Dayton. Moses M.	110	Goddard,	142
Armstrong, Nancy	207	Burnham, Mary Lowery	184	Colvert, Alma	233	Dewey, Ashebell	19	Godfrey, Eliza Jane	169
Arnold, Caroline	239	BUTTER(FIELD), ABEL		Commins, John	2	DODDER, NORGA		Grant, Heber C.	37
AROWSMITH, HANNAH		Butterfield, Percis	213	Conklin, Benjamin F	279	Dowdie, Robert	223	Grant, Loisa M.	48
Babcock, Amos	61	Butterworth, Sarah	36	Conover, Evelin	260	Duncan, Dolly H.	12	Grant, Mary Ann	60
Babcock, Benjamin A.	105	Buzenbark, William I.	292	Cook,	236	Duncan, William	59	Grover, Sarah Jane	2
Babcock, Cirvilla Jane	74	Calbert, Nancy	247	Cook, Charlotte Aurelia	297	Dykes, Cynthia	50	Guley, Henrietta	215
Babcock, George	193	Caleyhem, Lyman	39	Cook, Eliza H.	152	Dykes, Rachel	50	Haight, Isaac	26
Baker, Susannah E.	305	Calkins, Luman Israel	175	Cook, Joseph Y.	44	Earl, Caroline	281	Hakes, Patty C.	20
Barton, Mary	256	CALL, HYRUM		Cook, Loisa		Earl, Rhodanna	280	HALE, JONATHAN M.	
Beakly, Mary	33	Callister, Thomas	149	Corbit, Mary	216	Earl, Wilber	261	HALLEY, SARAH	
BELLINGTON, T.		Calvet, David	78	Corlass, Ellen	65	Eddims, George	143	HALLINS, P. J.	
Benbow, Jane	15	Cambell, Charity	63	Corry, George	6	Edwards, Maria E.	166	Hammond, Mary	295
Bigler, Susannah	100	Cambell, Charity A.	70	Coventon, Sarah A.	25	Eggleston, Samuel	208	Harmon, Annie	57
Billington, Sarah	230	CAMPBELL, JOAN		Covey, Delia Ann	172	Eldredge, Helen L.	216	Harmon, Appleton	231
Blackhurst, Margaret	51	Canfield, Myron	209	Covey, Dianah	172	Empey, Brigham	222	HARMON, ISAAC	
Boggs, Francis	84	Carpenter, Abigal	9	Cox, Mariah	211	Ensign, Horace	15	Harper, Ellen	212
BOSLEY, BRO. & SIS.		Carpenter, Sam'l E.	12	Cox, Phelina	14	Fairbanks, Joseph	89	Harris, Priscilla	67
Bostwick, Leach	112	Carrington, Albert Jr.	72	Cox, Phelina L.	46	Fausett, William	243	Harris, Robert	183
Bralley, Elijah	186	Carter, Sally S.	84	Croaslow, James	47	FEIVE, A. F.		Harrison, Sabrina Ann	86
Brigham, Jenne	273	Cavet, Julia	297	Cuiter, Sophronia	249	Felshaw, Anna M.	289	Hart, Harriet A.	52
Bringhurst, Charles H.	43	Chamberlin, Hooper	53	Cummings, Harriet	140	Fielding, Hyrum T.	190	Harvey, (son)	299

Cutler's Park and Winter Quarters' Burials (page 2)
Lucy Gunn Morley buried in Lot 285.

(Courtesy Caryle B. Jensen and Gail Geo. Holmes, "A Grave Experience at the Mormon Pioneer Winter Quarters Cemetery" October 1999.)

Name	Grave #	Name	Grave #	Name	Grave #	Name	Grave #	Name	Grave #
Harvey, Adelia	299	Littleton, Mary Ann	305	Packer, Sarah Elizabeth	32	Richards, Elizabeth	121	STARKE, ELIZA BLAKER	
HARVEY, (wife of Joseph)		Lott, Harriet A.	246	Parckel, Charles		Richards, Welby L.		Steavenson, Catherine	134
Hatch, Abigail	83	Lott, Joseph D.	280	Patten, John	131	Richardson, Loly Ann	202	Stillman, Dexter	178
Hatch, Elizabeth	278	Lott, Lyman C.	277	Patten, Rachel	227	Richie,	217	Stirut, Elizabeth	291
Heath, Barbary		Lovett, William	88	Pearce, Mary H.	103	Roberts, Charles D.	303	Stool, Marinda	15
Hess, Amanda A.	210	Luce, Thomas Benton	252	Pearson, Ephrim	8	Robinson, Wm.	17	Stout, Louisa	192
Hickenson, Joseph	263	Lutz, Nathan K.	28	Pearson, Henry	245	Robinson, Mary E.		Stow, Ether	257
Hill, Charles	146	Lyman, Don Carlos	30	PEHRSON, ELIZA A.		Robinson, Susan A.	101	Swap, Agnes	44
Hill, Isabella	109	Lyman, Richard	188	Pendleton, Emmeline	115	Rolf, David L.	50	Sweet, Mary Ann	264
Hill, Sally	87	Lyman, Ruth Adelia	296	Pendleton, Parmelia M.	196	Rollins, Ephraim E.	205	Synder, Olive	162
Holmes, Joshua S.	44	Lytle, Sarah	188	Pendleton, Silvy	228	Rordy, Edman	41	Tanner, Cintha Marie	200
Holmes, Lucy Elvira	161	Mangem, Rebecca	86	PETERSON, MICHAEL		ROSS, EDMUND		Tanner, Louisa	
Horlick, Julia	219	Mangum, Braily Franklin	246	Petty, John B.	76	Ross, Elizabeth S.	19	Tanner, Mason A.	16
Houston, Mary	115	Mann, Ann E.	54	Phippen, Isaac F.	263	Roundy, Joannah	75	Taylor, Mary R.	274
Hovey, (Daughter)	268	Martin, Edward H.	220	Pierce, Dorothy	4	Rushton, Isabella H.	24	Tenney, George A.	304
Hovey, Jane	5	Martin, Edward John	220	Pierce, Mary H.	14	Sanders, Eliza Jane	123	Terry, Brigham A.	294
Hovey, Martha A.		Maybury, Rebecca	163	Pierson, Mary M.	262	Serrine, M. A.	307	Thane, Jane	232
Huls, Lewis	111	McCard, Hirum		Pitt, Cornelia M.	137	Sheets, Margaret	68	Thatcher, Hezakiah Jr.	96
Hunter, Caroline R.	32	McCoulough, Clarinda	171	Pixton, Robert Hasman	6	Sheets, Margaret	68	Thomas, Daniel	290
Jacob	126	McCoulough, Emilly J.	187	Pond, Abigail A.	30	Shumway, Harriet	132	Thomas, Morgan M.	77
Jones, Hannah	22	McDonald, Washington	165	Pond, Almira	154	Shumway, Julia A.	63	Tibbets, Alva	254
Jones, Jane	133	McFate, Lucy B.	106	Pond, Harriet M.	25	Shlen, Joseph H.	206	Tibbets, Alvah	180
Jones, Mary	31	Melvil, Elizabeth	62	Pond, Laura Jane	21	Smith, Caroline	194	Trane, Phebe P.	107
Kay, John	173	Mitchel, Eliza	49	Pool, Lyman	56	Smith, David Gould	9	Turley, Francis	20
Kelly, Brigham	214	Mitchell, Persis	7	Porter, Amy	126	Smith, David Kimball	147	Turley, Hyrum S.	95
Kelly, Wm. Thadius		Morley, Lucy	285	Porter, Benjamin (twin)	38	Smith, Don Carlos	174	TURLEY, JONATHAN	
Kelsey, Melissa	42	Morse, Wm A.	96	Porter, Joseph (twin)	38	Smith, Hannah	45	Turley, Joseph Smith	95
Kelsey, Mineva N.	269	Mumford, Walter B.	157	Potter, Gardner G.	266	Smith, John	124	Turley, Princetta	148
Kimball, Rachel	147	N. R.		Pratt, Vanson	182	Smith, Nancy A.	138	Turley, Sarah E.	148
Kimball, Sophronia	55	Neeley, Elizabeth	73	Proctor, John	103	Smith, NancyClemmond	118	Turner, Hyrum	119
King, Elizabeth	224	Neeley, William	73	Proctor, John	103	Smith, William	71	Tuttle, Edward	200
Knight, Orpha	251	Neff, Cyrus	94	Pulischer, Henry	275	Smoot, AO's sik child	144	Tuttle, Luther	197
Knowles, John	129	Neibour, (stillborn)	276	Pulney, Jerry	135	Snow, Mary Minerva	178	Utley, Henry	242
Lamb, Robert P.	9	Noah, Pleasant D.	22	Ralston, Augustus P.	29	Spear, George	59	Utley, Jacob J.	281
Lance, Wm. J.	130	Noblee, Hyrum B	51	Ranck, Mary C.	11	Spear, Samatha Ellen	2	Ubey, James W. S.	259
Lawrence, Angelina E.	34	Nobles, Sarah	45	Rench, William	11	Williams, Ellen Aurelia	167	Utley, Maria	246
Lawrence, John	39	Gokey, Eliza	141	Randall, Henry	13	Spears, Mary		Ubey, Sarah E.	262
Lawrence, John	99	Olmstead, Alonzo	266	Reading, Martha M.	102	Spears, Wm.	97	VAN WAGONER, H. J.	
Lawrence, Rhoda A.	36	Olmstead, Mary Jane	257	Reeves, Martha	86	Spicer, Abney	158	VAN WAGONER, MARY	
LEDINGHAM, (male child)		Orton, James	238	Reding, Joseph C.	203	Sprague, Abagail	56	Vance, Lehi M.	
Lemon, Francis	253	Ott, Frederick J.	87	Reeves, James Colia	198	Sprague, Elizabeth	46	Vanvelzor, Henry G.	153
Leonard, Ezra	48	Owen, Lydia		Remington, Sally	177	Sprague, Mary Eliza A.	302	Wadsworth, Ann	18

Lucy Gunn Morley
(Courtesy Morley Family.)

Mormon Pioneer Cemetery at Winter Quarter
(Courtesy S.B. Mitchell, 1994.)

Wait, Rebecca	272	West, Julia Ann	199	Wiley, Elizabeth	42	Woodward, William S.	3	Young, Jane
Walker, Joseph E.	122	West, Sally	79	Williams, John H.	127	Wright, Enoch	27	Young, Moroni
Weaks, Arvin	139	Whitney, Don Carlos	14	Williams, Peter	30	YOUNG, DAVID I.		Zabriskie, Mary A. M.
Welch, Nicholas	229	Whitney, Enoch K.	181	Woodruff, Ezra	34	Young, Delinea Adalia	16	
West, Alvy	5	Whitney, Helen R. A.	147	Woodruff, Joseph	58	Young, Elizabeth	61	

1846 - 1848 Mormon Burial Plot Map

Numbers on this map correspond to grave numbers listed on the Winter Quarter's Cemetery sexton's records which are listed in the book *A "Grave" Experience at the Mormon Pioneer Winter Quarters Cemetery* by Carlye B. Jensen and Gail Geo. Holmes October 1999

Book can be found in the Pioneer Trail Center Research Library Code numbers MPC 4 and 4a

* 1 William and Mary are not buried at Winter Quarters, but were listed at the end of the burial records.

* 2 Samantha was not buried at Winter Quarters, but burial is listed at the end of the burial records indicating that she was buried 2 1/2 miles north of Warsaw, Illinois.

* 3 Henry was not buried at Winter Quarters, but burial is listed at the end of the burial records indicating that he was buried in Davis Camp, Pottawatomie Co., Iowa.

Cutler's Park and Winter Quarters' Burials (page 3)
(Courtesy Caryle B. Jensen and Gail Geo. Holmes, "A Grave Experience at the Mormon Pioneer Winter Quarters Cemetery" October 1999.)

Isaac Morley's cabin at Morley Settlement
"Yelrome" in Hancock County, Illinois
(Courtesy Lovell Killpack)

Marker of Morley's Settlement at Tioga, Illinios
(Courtesy S.B. Mitchell, 2002.)

Isaac Morley Early Home in Manti

Framed photo hangs in upper hallway of Manti City Building.
(Courtesy S.B. Mitchell, 2013.)

MORLEY, Isaac wives:

20 Jun 1812 - MORLEY, Isaac married to **Lucy Gunn in Montague**, in Franklin, Massachusetts.

14 Jan 1846 - MORLEY, Isaac married to **Hannah Blakeslee Finch** in Nauvoo, Hancock, Illinois.

14 Jan 1846 - MORLEY, Isaac married to **Abigail Leonora Snow** in Nauvoo, Hancock, Illinois.

22 Jan 1846 - MORLEY, Isaac sealed to **Harriet Lucinda Cox** in Nauvoo, Hancock, Illinois.

22 Jan 1846 - MORLEY, Isaac sealed to **Hanna Sibley (Hannah Libby)** in Nauvoo, Hancock, Illinois.

22 Jan 1846 - MORLEY, Isaac sealed to **Nancy Black (Nancy Anne Bache, Nancy Ann Bach)** Nauvoo.

22 Jan 1846 - MORLEY, Isaac sealed to **Eleanor Mills** in Nauvoo, Hancock, Illinois.

22 Jan 1846 - MORLEY, Isaac sealed to **Betsy B. Pinkham** in Nauvoo, Hancock, Illinois.

11 Mar 1856 - MORLEY, Isaac sealed to **Ann Dayer** in Salt Lake City, Utah.

23 Aug 1862 - MORLEY, Isaac sealed to **Sarah Scott** in Salt Lake City, Utah.

725

Manti City - Sanpete Monument
Isaac Morley Dug Out Replica
(Courtesy S.B. Mitchell, 2013.)

Manti Monument Dug Out Interior

(Courtesy S.B. Mitchell, 2013.)

Manti City - Sanpete Monument

Isaac Morley Dug Out Replica

(Courtesy S.B. Mitchell, 2013.)

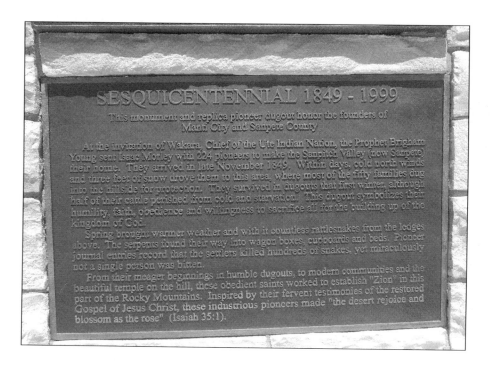

SESQUICENTENNIAL 1849 - 1999

This monument and replica pioneer dugout honor the founders of
Manti City and Sanpete County

At the invitation of Wakara, Chief of the Ute Indian Nation, the Prophet Brigham Young sent Isaac Morley with 224 pioneers to make the Sanpitch Valley (now Sanpete) their home. They arrived in late November 1849. Within days, cold north winds and three feet of snow drove them to this area, where most of the fifty families dug into the hillside for protection. They survived in dugouts that first winter, although half of their cattle perished from cold and starvation. This dugout symbolizes their humility, faith, obedience and willingness to sacrifice all for the building up of the kingdom of God.

Spring brought warmer weather and with it countless rattlesnakes from the ledges above. The serpents found their way into wagon boxes, cupboards and beds. Pioneer journal entries record that the settlers killed hundreds of snakes, yet miraculously not a single person was bitten.

From their meager beginnings in humble dugouts, to modern communities and the beautiful temple on the hill, these obedient saints worked to establish "Zion" in this part of the Rocky Mountains. Inspired by their fervent testimonies of the restored Gospel of Jesus Christ, these industrious pioneers made "the desert rejoice and blossom as the rose" (Isaiah 35:1).

Nauvoo Temple Endowment Register 1845

NAUVOO TEMPLE ENDOWMENT REGISTER
(Chronological Listing)

December 11 1845.
First Company.

Name	Priesthood or sex	Birth Date				Temple Ordination Dates		Complaints and Additional Information
		Date	Town	County	State	Washing and Anointing	Endowment	
1. Cutler, Alpheus	m	29 Feb 1784	Plainfield	Cheshire	N.H.	11 Dec 1845	11 Dec 1845	Alpheus Cutler in sig r
2. Cutler, Lois	f	24 Sep 1788	Lebanon	Grafton	N. H.	11 Dec 1845	11 Dec 1845	Lois Lathrop in sig rec
3. Cahoon, Reynolds	m	30 Apr 1790	Cumberland	Washington	New York	11 Dec 1845	11 Dec 1845	
4. Cahoon, Tirzah	f	18 Oct 1789	Brandon		Connecticut	11 Dec 1845	11 Dec 1845	Theresa Stiles in sig r
5. Morley, Isaac	m	11 Mar 1786	Montague	Franklin	Massachusetts	11 Dec 1845	11 Dec 1845	
6. Morley, Lucy	f	24 Jan 1786	Montague	Franklin	Massachusetts	11 Dec 1845	11 Dec 1845	Lucy Gun in sig recopt
7. Spencer, Orson	h.p.	14 Mar 1802	West Stockbridge	Berkshire	Massachusetts	11 Dec 1845	11 Dec 1845	
8. Spencer, Catherine C.	f	21 Mar 1811	Canaan	Columbia	New York	11 Dec 1845	11 Dec 1845	Catherine Curtis in sig
9. Clayton, William	m	17 Jul 1814	Penworthham	Lancashire	England	11 Dec 1845	11 Dec 1845	
10. Clayton, Ruth	f	13 Jun 1817	Eccleston	Lancashire	England	11 Dec 1845	11 Dec 1845	Ruth Moon in sig record
11. Lott, Cornelius P.	m	27 Sep 1798	New York	New York	New York	10 Dec 1845	11 Dec 1845	Cornelius Peter Lott in
12. Lott, Permelia	f	15 Dec 1804	Otago	Otsego	New York	11 Dec 1845	11 Dec 1845	Pamelia Darrow in sig r
13. Smith, Lucy	f	8 Jul 1776	Gilsum	Cheshire	N. H.	10 Dec 1845	11 Dec 1845	Lucy Mack
14. Thompson, Mercy R.	f	15 Jun 1807	Honidon	Bedfordshire	England	11 Dec 1845	11 Dec 1845	Mercy Rachel Fielding in sig record

Source: L. D. S. Biographical Encyclopedia, Andrew Jenson, Salt Lake City, Utah, 1901, Vol. 2, p. 690.

The Prosperity of the Saints Dependent Upon Their Being Right Before God—Prayer and Watchfulness, Etc.

(Remarks by Patriarch Isaac Morley, delivered in the Tabernacle, Great Salt Lake City, Sunday Morning, November 8, 1857. Reported by J.V. Long. -- Journal of Discourses.)

I am in hopes that what I do say will be dictated by the right guide, as brother Heber says. I do not wish for any other. It is difficult for me to communicate my ideas, though I do not make this statement because I wish to apologize or to excuse myself from any duty.

I think I realize with you, brethren, the situation that we are in and the circumstances that surround us. Every reflecting mind will rest his thoughts and attention upon our present situation; and if we have in us the light of the Holy Ghost, we shall believe it is all right. This is my conclusion, and I presume it is the conclusion of most of you.

If we, as individuals, are right before God, all will go well with us and the Lord will prosper us. I do not think that the reform that we have undertaken and that is undertaken with this community is done with. I find that it becomes me to concentrate my mind daily and hourly upon the grand things that lie before me.

As to the enemy that is come up to destroy or curtail us in any of our blessings, I care but little about them. It makes me think of the past, when my mother used to have a rod over the mantelpiece for me to look at. I think we have got one that we can look at, and it is where it can be used; and probably if it is used, it will be used to our advantage.

If we can prepare our hearts and our lives, we need not fear anything about our enemies. The greatest fear is that I shall not sustain and carry out correct principles in my own bosom. I believe that our grand object is to have all things right within. If we do this, we shall do well.

We are taught in one place to "pray without ceasing," and watching is as necessary as prayer. I am of the opinion that we can correct our thoughts so far as to know and understand what our motives are and what our affections are placed upon. If our minds are wandering to the nations of the earth, what will it benefit us? The grand place for our operations to begin is in our bosoms, and to see that our minds and bodies are influenced by those principles that pertain to light, life, and immortality.

There are great attainments in reserve for the faithful of this people. I believe that we may enjoy even more peace and satisfaction than we do now, which may be obtained by prayer and watchfulness.

We should reflect upon the covenants and obligations that we have made unto God and before our brethren. There are many keys in those holy covenants whereby we can derive comfort.

Obedience is the grand key whereby this people are to be exalted; and I sincerely believe that the Presidency are [sic] comforted by the obedience that is rendered to their requirements.

It is the mind that makes the man; and if that mind is centered upon correct objects—if it cultivates and cherishes them, that mind is improving. There is no time nor circumstances through which we may be passing but there is opportunity for improvement. I learn this daily. And there are no hours that pass but there are opportunities for our advancement in the principles of exaltation.

I believe that reformation and union can be carried to a greater extent than they have been. If there is a love for the truth in the people, it will be manifest in true plainness and true honesty: our yea will be yea, and our nay will be nay. The Scriptures say, "Whatsoever cometh more than this is evil;" but true plainness and true honesty is what we want.

If we are not advancing in light, we are either standing still or going backward. The great principles that we are to be governed by dwell in simplicity; they are easy to be understood by any and all who will apply themselves.

The condescension of Heaven is great: there can be no greater condescension than is manifested to us. We have attained our heir ship. We know there is such a principle as well as we know there is a God.

Baptism for remission of sins and the laying on of hands for the gift of the Holy Ghost are as simple as anything can be. All the great fundamental principles of salvation are simple. We can comprehend and understand them—we can increase and grow by the power of them.

In adding to our faith, it is necessary that we should add virtue first, then knowledge; and these we should cultivate daily and hourly.

Brethren, I intend, as far as I have power, to instruct by example. Without it, I would give very little for all the precepts that are or can be set forth in a family or abroad among the people. May God bless you, is my prayer, in the name of the Lord Jesus. Amen.

Appendix C

Tuttle Family Photos and Historical Documents

Sister Billings, Grandma Gardner, Mary Ann [Tuttle]
(Courtesy Billings Family Collection.)

Gravesite in Bicknell, Utah

(Courtesy S.B. Mitchell, 2002.)

Edward Wells Tuttle

Oldest son of Edward and Catherine V. Tuttle -- remained in Massachusetts with his brothers when the family moved to Nauvoo. Records show that he died in Massachusetts. His parents were baptized in Nauvoo. We do not have proof that he ever joined the church, but his work was done in Manti.

(Courtesy Tuttle Family.)

Edward Wells Tuttle
Oldest son of Edward and Catherine Tuttle.

Tuttle's Bakery

Edward and Catherine operated a bakery on Main Street in Nauvoo (Munson and Main). They leased a home down the street a block (corner of Main and Kimball Street.)

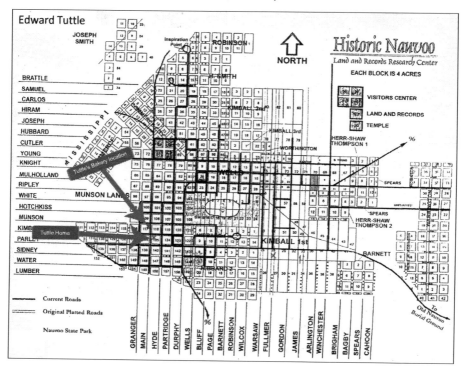

Edward Tuttle's Grave

Beside a tree (below) and just right of angel's name plaque (left) is grave # 200 where Edward was lovingly laid to rest on 17 Aug 1847. Notice how the sun's ray marks the spot.

(Courtesy S.B. Mitchell, 1994.)

The Pioneer Monument

Mormon Pioneer Cemetery at Winter Quarters

(Courtesy S.B. Mitchell, 1994.)

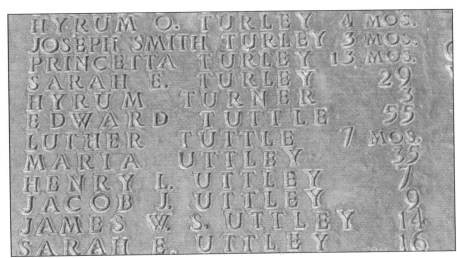

HYRUM O. TURLEY	4 MOS.
JOSEPH SMITH TURLEY	3 MOS.
PRINCETTA TURLEY	13 MOS.
SARAH E. TURLEY	29
HYRUM TURNER	3
EDWARD TUTTLE	55
LUTHER TUTTLE	7 MOS.
MARIA UTTLEY	35
HENRY L. UTTLEY	7
JACOB J. UTTLEY	9
JAMES W. S. UTTLEY	14
SARAH E. UTTLEY	16

Winter Quarters Plaque

Edward Tuttle's name and age appear on a monument honoring Mormon Pioneers.

(Courtesy S.B. Mitchell, 1994.)

Cutler's Park and Winter Quarters' Burials
Alphabetical Listing
Grave # inverted in black box ■ = Cutler's Park, Regular Type = Winter Quarters, All CAPS = ON PLAQUE BUT NOT ON SEXTON'S RECORD.

Name	Grave #	Name	Grave #	Name	Grave #	Name	Grave #	Name	Grave #
Adams, Henry	54	Brinkerhoff, James	1	CHAMBERLIN, HOPE H.		Cummings, James	120	FIELDING, JOHN	
Aiken, Samuel	91	Brinton, Elizabeth	10	CLARK, DANIEL WEDEN		Cummings, JamesW Jr.	13	Flake, Frederick	47
Akley, John	35	Brinton, Robert H	10	Clark, David W.	57	Cummings, Susannah	92	Flake, Samuel B.	114
Alexander, Nancy	66	Browett, Moroni	11	Clark, Felina	17	Cummings, Geo. A.	56	Foster, Thomas	236
Allen, Joseph D.	201	BROWN, (FEMALE)		Clark, Gardner	129	Dalton, Martha J.	150	Gardner, Emma	10
ALLEY, SARAH		Brown, Emily Jane	160	Clark, Mary	159	Daniels, Francis A.	20	Gardner, Genet	2
Alsworth, Orson H.	60	Bruce, Mary Ann	41	Clayton, James	271	Daniels, Francis G.		Garner, Silva	226
Anderson, Adney A. C.	151	Bullock, Isabella	136	CLEMENT, NANCY		DAS, M.		Gates, Caroline E.	40
Angel, Martha Ann	23	Bullock, Janet	82	Clements, Alpheus G.	90	Davidson, Joseph S.	300	Gates, Mary E.	40
Angel, Truman C.	240	Bullock, Willard Richards	104	Clynes, Ann E.	301	Davis, Isaac	155	Glasgow, Josinnah	154
Angell, Almira	44	Burdick, Ephraim	185	Colburt, Sarah	293	Davis, Lydia	115	Glines, James E.	255
Angus, William	38	Burnham, Mary C.	117	Collins, Charles H.	269	Dayton, Moses M.	110	Goddart,	142
Armstrong, Nancy	207	Burnham, Mary Lowery	184	Colvert, Alma	233	Dewey, Ashebell	19	Godfrey, Eliza Jane	169
Arnold, Caroline	239	BUTTER(FIELD), ABEL		Commins, John	2	DODDER, NORGA		Grant, Heber C.	37
AROWSMITH, HANNAH		Butterfield, Percis	213	Conklin, Benjamin F	279	Dowdie, Robert	223	Grant, Loisa M.	48
Babcock, Amos	61	Butterworth, Sarah	35	Connover, Evelin	260	Duncan, Dolly H.	12	Grant, Mary Ann	69
Babcock, Benjamin A.	105	Buzenbark, William I.	292	Cook	236	Duncan, William	59	Grover, Sarah Jane	2
Babcock, Cirvilla Jane	74	Calbert, Nancy	247	Cook, Charlotte Aurelia	267	Dykes, Cynthia	50	Guley, Henrietta	215
Babcock, George	103	Caleyham, Lyman	39	Cook, Eliza H.	152	Dykes, Rachel	50	Haight, Isaac	26
Baker, Susannah E.	305	Calkins, Luman Israel	175	Cook, Joseph Y.	44	Earl, Caroline	281	Hakes, Patty C.	20
Barton, Mary	256	CALL, HYRUM		Cook, Loisa		Earl, Rhodanna	280	HALE, JONATHAN M.	
Beakly, Mary	33	Callister, Thomas	149	Corbil, Mary	218	Earl, Wilber	281	HALLEY, SARAH	
BELLINGTON, T		Calvet, David	78	Corless, Ellen	55	Eddins, George	143	HALLINS, P. J.	
Benbow, Jane	15	Cambell, Charity	63	Corry, George	6	Edwards, Maria E.	166	Hammond, Mary	295
Bigler, Susannah	100	Cambell, Charity A	70	Coventin, Sarah A.	25	Eggleston, Samuel	208	Harmon, Annie	57
Billington, Sarah	230	CAMPBELL, JOAN		Covey, Delia Ann	172	Eldredge, Helen L.	216	Harmon, Appleton	231
Blackhurst, Margaret	51	Canfield, Myron	209	Covey, Dianah	172	Empey, Brigham	222	HARMON, ISAAC	
Boggs, Francis	64	Carpenter, Abigail	9	Cox, Mariah	211	Ensign, Horace	15	Harper, Ellen	212
BOSLEY, BRO. & SIS.		Carpenter, Sam'l E.	12	Cox, Phelina	14	Fairbanks, Joseph	89	Harris, Priscilla	87
Bostwick, Leach	112	Carrington, Albert Jr.	72	Cox, Phelina L.	45	Fauset, William	243	Harris, Robert	183
Brailey, Elijah	186	Carter, Sally S.	84	Crosstow, James	47	FEIVE, A. F.		Harrison, Sabrina Ann	86
Brigham, Jenne	273	Caves, Julia	297	Cutler, Sophronia	249	Felshaw, Anna M.	289	Hart, Harriet A.	52
Bringhurst, Charles H.	43	Chamberlin, Hooper	53	Cummings, Harriet	140	Fielding, Hyrum T.	190	Harvey, (son)	299

Cutler's Park and Winter Quarters' Burials (page 1)

(Courtesy Caryle B. Jensen and Gail Geo. Holmes, "A Grave Experience at the Mormon Pioneer Winter Quarters Cemetery" October 1999.)

Name	Grave #	Name	Grave #	Name	Grave #	Name	Grave #	Name	Grave #
Hatch, Elizabeth	278	Lott, Lyman C.	277	Putten, Rachel	227	Riche,	217	Stout, Elizabeth	291
Heath, Barbary		Lovell, William	93	Pearce, Mary H.	103	Roberts, Charles D.	303	Stout, Marinda	15
Hess, Amanda A.	210	Luce, Thomas Benton	252	Pearson, Ephrim	8	Robinson Wm.	17	Stout, Louisa	192
Hickerson, Joseph	263	Lutz, Nathan K.	28	Pearson, Henry	149	Robinson, Mary E.	49	Stow, Ether	237
Hill, Charles	146	Lyman, Don Carlos	36	PEHRSON, ELIZA A.		Robinson, Susan A.	101	Swap, Agnes	4
Hill, Isabella	109	Lyman, Richard	188	Pendleton, Emmeline	113	Rulf, David L.	59	Sweet, Mary Ann	264
Hill, Sally	81	Lyman, Ruth Adelia	296	Pendleton, Parmelia M.	196	Rollins, Ephraim E.	205	Synder, Olive	162
Holman, Joshua S	44	Lytle, Sarah	168	Pendleton, Silvy	228	Rosly, Ednah	41	Tanner, Cintha Maria	266
Holmes, Lucy Elvira	161	Mangum, Rebecca	168	PETERSON, MICHAEL		ROSS, EDMUND		Tanner, Lousia	16
Horlick, Julia	219	Mangum, Boely Franklin	246	Petty, John B.	76	Ross, Elizabeth S.	19	Tanner, Mason H.	18
Houston, Mary	116	Mann, Ann E.	54	Phippen, Isaac F.	283	Roundy, Joannah	75	Taylor, Mary R.	274
Hovey, (Daughter)	288	Martin, Edward H.	220	Pierce, Dorothy	4	Rushton, Isabella H.	24	Tenney, George A.	304
Hovey, Jane	5	Martin, Edward John	220	Pierce, Mary H.	14	Sanders, Eliza Jane	123	Terry, Brigham A.	294
Hovey, Martha A.	1	Maybury, Rebecca	183	Pierson, Mary M.	262	Serrine, M. A.	307	Thane, Jane	232
Huls, Lewis	111	McCard, Hirum	37	Pitt, Cornelia M.	137	Sheets, Margaret	68	Thatcher, Hezekiah Jr.	98
Hunter, Caroline R.	32	McCollough, Clarinda	171	Picton, Robert Hasman	6	Sheets, Daniel	68	Thomas, Daniel	290
Jacob	126	McCollough, Emily J.	187	Pond, Abigail A.	30	Shumway, Harriet	132	Thomas, Morgan M.	77
Jones, Hannah	22	McDonald, Washington	165	Pond, Almira	154	Shumway, Julia A.	43	Tibbets, Alva	254
Jones, Jane	133	McFate, Lucy G.	106	Pond, Harriet M.	25	Skien, Joseph H.	206	Tibbets, Alvah	180
Jones, Mary	31	Melvil, Elizabeth	62	Pond, Laura Jane	21	Smith, Caroline	194	Trane, Phebe P.	107
Kay, John	173	Mitchel, Eliza	49	Pond, Lyman	56	Smith, David Gould	7	Turley, Francis	20
Kelly, Brigham	214	Mitchell, Percis	7	Porter, Amy	125	Smith, David Kimball	147	Turley, Hyrum S.	95
Kelly, Wm. Thadius	1	Morley, Lucy	285	Porter, Benjamin (twin)	38	Smith, Don Carlos	174	TURLEY, JONATHAN	
Kelsey, Melissa	42	Morse, Wm. A.	96	Porter, Joseph (twin)	38	Smith, Hannah	45	Turley, Joseph Smith	95
Kelsey, Mineva N.	268	Mumford, Walter B.	157	Potter, Gardner G.	298	Smith, John	124	Turley, Princetta	148
Kimball, Rachel	147	N. R.,	26	Pratt, Vanson	162	Smith, Nancy A.	*138	Turley, Sarah E	146
Kimball, Sophronia	65	Neeley, Elizabeth	73	Proctor, John		Smith, NancyClemmond	118	Turner, Hyrum	119
King, Elizabeth	224	Neeley, Elizabeth	73	Proctor, John	108	Smith, William	71	Tuttle, Edward	200
Knight, Orpha	251	Neff, Cyrus	94	Pulispher, Henry	275	Smoot, AO's sis child	144	Tuttle, Luther	197
Knowles, John	128	Neibour, (stillborn)	276	Putney, Jerry	135	Snow, Mary Minerva	178	Utley, Henry	242
Lamb, Robert P.	9	Noah, Pleasant D.	22	Ralston, Augustus P.	29	Spear, George	59	Utley, Jacob J.	281
Lance, Wm. J.	130	Nobles, Hyrum B.		Ranck, Mary C.	*1	Wiley, Samatha Ellen	*1	Ubey, James W. S.	259
Lawrence, Angelina E	34	Nobles, Sarah	46	Ranck, William	*1	Williams, Ellen Aurelia	167		248
Lawrence, John	30	Oakey, Eliza	141	Randall, Henry	*3	Spears, Mary	52	Utley, Sarah E	262
Lawrence, Joseph	99	Olmstead, Alonzo	296	Reading, Martha M.	102	Spears, Mary	97	VAN WAGONER, H. J	
Lawrence, Rhoda A	36	Olmstead, Mary Jane	257	Reaves, Martha	88	Spicar, Abney	158	VAN WAGONER,MARY	

Cutler's Park and Winter Quarters' Burials (page 2)

Edward Tuttle is buried in Lot 200.

(Courtesy Caryle B. Jensen and Gail Geo. Holmes, "A Grave Experience at the Mormon Pioneer Winter Quarters Cemetery" October 1999.)

46 - 1848
mon Burial
Plot Map

ers on this map
d to grave numbers
he Winter Quarter's
y sexton's records
e listed in the book
" Experience at the
oneer Winter Quarters
Cemetery
le B. Jensen and
Geo. Holmes
ctober 1999

n be found in the
er Trail Center
earch Library
de numbers
PC 4 and 4a

illam and Mary are not
at Winter Quarters, but
listed at the end of the
burial records.

anths was not buried at
r Quarters, but burial is
at the end of the burial
rds indicating that she
uried 2 1/2 miles north of
Warsaw, Illinois.

nry was not buried at
r Quarters, but burial is
at the end of the burial
ds indicating that he was
uried in Davis Camp,

State Street

Monument

Trail Center

Temple

Cutler's Park and Winter Quarters' Burials (page 3)

(Courtesy Caryle B. Jensen and Gail Geo. Holmes, "A Grave Experience at the Mormon Pioneer Winter Quarters Cemetery" October 1999.)

Mormon Pioneer Cemetery at Winter Quarters

(Courtesy S.B. Mitchell, 1994.)

Tuttle Sisters

Martha Ann Tuttle Gardner

(Courtesy Billings Family.)

Mary Ann Tuttle Billings

(Courtesy Billings Family.)

Brigham Young University Lee Library L. Tom Perry Special Collections; MSS P 1

Tuttle Sisters (Martha Ann and Mary Ann)

(Courtesy L. Tom Perry Special Collections, Harold B. Lee Library,

BYU, Provo, Utah.)

NAUVOO TEMPLE ENDOWMENT REGISTER
(Chronological Listing)

January 3, 1846

First Company (continued)

Name	Priest-hood or sex	Birth Data Date	Town	County	State	Washing and Anointing	Endowment	Comments and Additional Information
1. Bailey, Sarah	f	15 Aug 1806	Alemsbury		Massachusetts	3 Jan 1846	3 Jan 1846	Sarah Kindrick Currier in slg rec
2. Baldwin, Nathan P.	sev	27 Jan 1812	Augusta	Grenville	Canada	3 Jan 1846	3 Jan 1846	Nathan Bennet Baldwin in slg rec.
3. Allen, Lucinda	f	2 Jun 1824	Dresden	Washington	New York	3 Jan 1846	3 Jan 1846	
4. Baldwin, Sarah Ann	f	4 Jul 1819	Tenmouth	Rutland	Vermont	3 Jan 1846	3 Jan 1846	Sarah Ann Pine in slg record
5. Chase, Eli	sev	9 Nov 1808	Ellisburg	Jefferson	New York	3 Jan 1846	3 Jan 1846	
6. Chase, Olive	f	12 Aug 1815	Brookfield	Madison	New York	3 Jan 1846	3 Jan 1846	Olive Hills in slg record
7. Randall, Almena	f	28 Nov 1814	Madrid	St. Lawrence	New York	3 Jan 1846	3 Jan 1846	
8. Alley, George	sev	30 Dec 1792	Lynn	Essex	Massachusetts	3 Jan 1846	3 Jan 1846	
9. Alley, Mary	f	7 Aug 1795	Salem	Essex	Massachusetts	3 Jan 1846	3 Jan 1846	Mary Symonds in slg record
10. Tuttle, Edward	sev	1 Jul 1792	Chelsea	Middlesex	Massachusetts	3 Jan 1846	3 Jan 1846	
11. Tuttle, Catharine B	f	3 Aug 1797¹	Boston	Middlesex	Massachusetts	3 Jan 1846	3 Jan 1846	Catherine Vanever Geyer in slg rec
12. Tidwell, John	sev	14 Jan 1807		Shelby	Kentucky	3 Jan 1846	3 Jan 1846	
13. Tidwell, Jane	f	5 Jun 1812			Virginia	3 Jan 1846	3 Jan 1846	Jane Smith in slg record
14. Callister, Thomas	sev	17 Jul 1821			Isle of Man	3 Jan 1846	3 Jan 1846	Tomas Callister in slg record
15. Callister, Caroline	f	6 Jun 1820	Potsdam	St. Lawrence	New York	3 Jan 1846	3 Jan 1846	Caroline Smith in slg record
16. Smith, John L.	sev	17 Nov 1828	Potsdam	St. Lawrence	New York	3 Jan 1846	3 Jan 1846	John Lyman Smith in slg record
17. Smith, Augusta B.	f	7 Dec 1828	Cincinnatti	Hamilton	Ohio	3 Jan 1846	3 Jan 1846	Augusta Bowen Smith in slg record

w.a: washing and anointing; pig: sealing; apex: apostle, h.h.: high priest, sev: seventy; eld: elder; f: female; m: male   1: 3 Aug 1796 - slg record.

TUTTLE, Edward KIN #24643

Nauvoo Temple Endowment Register 1846

Edward and Catherine

TUTTLE, Mary Ann   RIN #24664

NAUVOO TEMPLE ENDOWMENT REGISTER
(Chronological Listing)

292

Februa 6, 1846
Second Company (continued)

	Priest-hood or sex	Birth Data				Temple Ordinance Dates		Comments and Additional Information
Name		Date	Town	County	State	Washing and Anointing	Endowment	
1. Higgins, Alvira	f	25 Apr 1826¹				6 Feb 1846	6 Feb 1846	
2. Conyers, John	sev	25 Apr 1814¹				6 Feb 1846	6 Feb 1846	
3. Conyers, Priscilla	f	11 Dec 1825¹				6 Feb 1846	6 Feb 1846	Prescilla Conyers in w-a record
4. Hills, James W.	sev	19 Jan 1809¹				6 Feb 1846	6 Feb 1846	
5. Moseley, Mary	f	6 Sep 1812	Kingsley	Stafford	England	6 Feb 1846	6 Feb 1846	Mary Beardmore in sig record
6. Groesbeck, Garret	eld	1 Feb 1795	Stillwater	Washington	New York³	6 Feb 1846	6 Feb 1846	Garrett Lewis Groesbeck in TIB record
7. Crosby, Mercy	f	13 Mar 1802²	Verona	Oneida	New York³	6 Feb 1846	6 Feb 1846	Mercy Bosworth in TIB record
8. Manhart, Fanny	f	11 Mar 1823²	Tuft	Cheshire	England	6 Feb 1846	6 Feb 1846	Fanny Richardson in sig record
9. Worthen, Samuel	sev	21 Dec 1825	Northwich	Cheshire	England	6 Feb 1846	6 Feb 1846	
10. Worthen, Sarah	f	14 Sep 1823⁴	Stockport	Cheshire	England	6 Feb 1846	6 Feb 1846	Sarah Mallais in sig record
11. Dudley, Joseph	eld	8 Jul 1817	Elizabethtown	Hardin	Kentucky	6 Feb 1846	6 Feb 1846	
12. Dudley, Sarah	f	14 Mar 1816	Chippewa	Ontario	Canada	6 Feb 1846	6 Feb 1846	Sarah Stevens in sig record
13. Read, William	eld	29 Jun 1825		Randolph	Missouri	5 Feb 1846	6 Feb 1846	
14. Atchison, Elizabeth	f	1830¹				6 Feb 1846	6 Feb 1846	
15. Harmon, Sarah L.	f	17 May 1830¹				6 Feb 1846	6 Feb 1846	
16. Adkns, Samuel R., Jr	eld	7 Jan 1827¹	New Salem	Franklin	Massachusetts³	6 Feb 1846	6 Feb 1846	
17. Tuttle, Mary Ann	f	5 Jun 1830	Boston		Massachusetts	6 Feb 1846	6 Feb 1846	

w-a: washing and anointing; sp: spouse; h.p.: high priest; sev: seventy; eld: elder; f: female; m: male   1: w-a record only.   2: 1 Mar 1823 - sig record   3: TIB (unverified).
4: 14 Dec 1823 - sig record.

Nauvoo Temple Endowment Register 1846

Mary Ann

Catherine Vanever Geyer Tuttle

To our knowledge, this is the only
photo ever taken of Catherine.
(Courtesy Tuttle Family.)

Salem City Cemetery

Catherine is buried beside her son, John Wells Tuttle and his eight children who
all died in childhood. Mary E., his wife, is really buried in SLC.

(Courtesy S.B. Mitchell, 2013)

743

Walter and Martha Ann Tuttle Gardner
(Courtesy Tuttle/Gardner Family.)

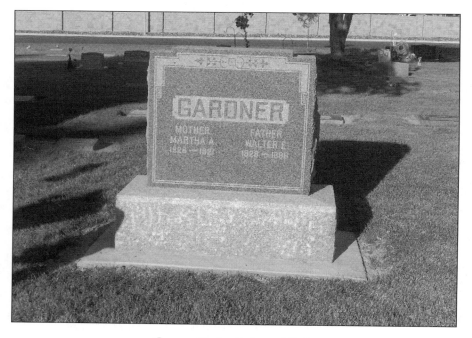

Gravesite in Salem, Utah
(Courtesy S.B. Mitchell, 2013.)

Family Group Sheet
Edward Tuttle and Catherine Van Geyer Tuttle
(Courtesy Tuttle Family.)

HUSBAND (1) TUTTLE, Edward — 1792

	Date	Place
Born	1 July 1792	Chelsea, Sffk, Mass
Chr.	20 Aug 1792	Chelsea, Sffk, Mass
Marr.	12 Nov 1816	Boston, Sffk, Mass
Died	17 Aug 1847	Winter Quarters, Dgls, Nbrs

Husband's Father: TUTTLE, Joseph
Husband's Mother: PRATT, Elizabeth (Eliza)

WIFE GEYER, Catherine Vanever — 4th

	Date	Place
Born	3 Aug 1798-97	Boston, Sffk, Mass
Chr.		
Died	24 May 1878	Salem, Utah, Utah
Bur.	May 1878	Salem, Utah, Utah

Wife's Father: GEYER, George (2) James Davenport
Wife's Mother: LOCKLAND, Mary

Stake or Mission: Spanish Fork Stake

FAMILY REPRESENTATIVE
DAVIS, (Mrs) Harriet (Coombs) — K K dau / K K dau
Mrs. Harriet G. Davis, 355 East 1st South, Spanish Fork, Utah, 84660
from Mary Russell

TEMPLE ORDINANCE DATA

	Baptized (date)	Endowed (date)	Sealed to Husband / Sealed (date)	Children
Husband	2 Sep 1843	3 Jan 1846	NV / 3 Jan 184_	
Wife	2 Sep 1843	3 Jun 1846	NV	

CHILDREN

Sex	Name	When Born (Day Mo Yr)	Where Born (Town)	County	State	Date of First Marriage	To Whom	When Died	Baptized	Endowed	Sealed
M	TUTTLE, Edward Wells	Chr. 23 Feb 1817	Boston	Sffk	Mass		TAYLOR, Almira		15 Oct 1889	16 Oct 1889	18 Oct 1
M	TUTTLE, Joseph Wells	Chr. 23 July 1818	Boston	Sffk	Mass				15 Oct 1889	17 Oct 1889	18 Oct 1
M	TUTTLE, Thomas Wells	Chr. 19 Apr 1820	Boston	Sffk	Mass			22 Sep 1801	16 Dec 1902	17 Dec 1902	18 Dec
F	TUTTLE, Caroline Elizabeth	Chr. 17 Nov 1822	Boston	Sffk	Mass		KEEN, Lewis	2 Feb 1903	15 Oct 1889	17 Oct 1889	18 Oct 1
M	TUTTLE, Henry Withington	Chr. 12 Nov 1825	Boston	Sffk	Mass	28 Apr 1847		2 Mar 1921	2 Sep 1843	22 Jan 1908	28 Jun
F	TUTTLE, Martha Ann	Chr. 27 July 1828	Boston	Sffk	Mass		GARDNER, Walter Elias	10 Dec 1910	2 Sep 1843	6 Feb 1846	18 Oct 1
F	TUTTLE, Mary Ann	Chr. 25 July 1830	Boston	Sffk	Mass	20 Jan 1854		14 Apr 1897	2 Sep 1843	27 June 1/17	18 Oct 1
M	TUTTLE, John Wells	Chr. 1 July 1832	Boston	Sffk	Mass	1877	GARDNER, Louisa Jane (1)		child	child	28 Jun
M	TUTTLE, Samuel Wells	Chr. 17 Aug 1834	Boston	Sffk	Mass		(Died as a child)		child		18 Oct 1

SOURCES OF INFORMATION
1- Index File, Temple & Family rec in poss of Mr.& Mrs Claude D.Billings.
2- Ira W.Gardner Record Book np 1,2,35.
3- Manti Temple Record Book B pp 192, 418 (6690)

OTHER MARRIAGES
* John Wells Tuttle Md(2)11 Feb 1886 GARDNER, Mary Elizabeth.
#7 Mary Ann md (3) Walter Ehis Gardner
#7 " " (1) HOWARD EGAN

NECESSARY EXPLANATIONS
Only Henry, Martha, Mary & John came Utah.
Henry was a cripple and never married.

Grandma Tuttle's Monument Project 2014
After 136 years Grandma Catherine V. Geyer Tuttle finally has a marker on her grave.

Catherine's descendants, even the young ones, helped earn the money for the project, then celebrated its placement in the Salem City Cemetery, Salem, Utah, on Memorial Day 2014.

Because Catherine and her husband, Edward Tuttle, were endowed and sealed in the Nauvoo Temple its image has been engraved onto her headstone. Edward died at Winter Quarters and is buried there. Catherine was laid to rest in Salem beside her son John and his ten babies.

42043836R00425

Made in the USA
San Bernardino, CA
26 November 2016